THE
FEMINIST ENCYCLOPEDIA
OF SPANISH LITERATURE

Dr. Charles Caulfield

THE
FEMINIST ENCYCLOPEDIA
OF SPANISH LITERATURE

N–Z

Edited by
Janet Pérez and Maureen Ihrie

GREENWOOD PRESS
Westport, Connecticut • London

Library of Congress Cataloging-in-Publication Data

The feminist encyclopedia of Spanish literature / edited by Janet Pérez and Maureen Ihrie.
    p.   cm.
    Includes bibliographical references and index.
    ISBN 0–313–29346–5 (alk. paper: set)—ISBN 0–313–32444–1 (alk. paper: A-M)—ISBN 0–313–32445–X (alk. paper: N-Z)

    1. Spanish literature—Women authors—Encyclopedias. 2. Spanish literature—Encyclopedias. 3. Women authors, Spanish—Biography—Encyclopedias. 4. Feminism and literature—Encyclopedias. 5. Women in literature—Encyclopedias. I. Pérez, Janet. II. Ihrie, Maureen.
PQ6055.F46   2002
860.9'9287—dc21   2002019922

British Library Cataloguing in Publication Data is available.

Library of Congress Catalog Card Number: 2002019922
ISBN: 0–313–29346–5 (set)
ISBN: 0–313–32444–1 (A-M)
ISBN: 0–313–32445–X (N-Z)

First published in 2002

Greenwood Press, 88 Post Road West, Westport, CT 06881
An imprint of Greenwood Publishing Group, Inc.
www.greenwood.com

Printed in the United States of America

The paper used in this book complies with the Permanent Paper Standard issued by the National Information Standards Organization (Z39.48–1984).

10 9 8 7 6 5 4 3 2 1

Every reasonable effort has been made to trace the owners of copyright materials in this book, but in some instances this has proven impossible. The author and publisher will be glad to receive information leading to more complete acknowledgments in subsequent printings of the book, an in the meantime extend their apologies for any omissions.

Contents

Preface

Like *The Feminist Encyclopedia of German Literature* (Greenwood, 1997), *The Feminist Encyclopedia of Italian Literature* (Greenwood, 1997), and *The Feminist Encyclopedia of French Literature* (Greenwood, 1999), this reference approaches a particular national literature from a women's studies perspective, with entries arranged alphabetically and written by expert contributors. Spanish literature, even when limited to that of the Peninsula, and to literature in Castilian (excluding other Peninsular languages), is nonetheless a far larger subject than can be covered in a single volume. Thus this encyclopedia does not pretend to be exhaustive. Further limitation results from our focus on selected aspects of that literary corpus, as suggested by the adjective *feminist*, which likewise requires some clarification. This encyclopedia is feminist insofar as the criteria of inclusion are narrowed to those aspects most likely to interest readers seeking information in areas including women's studies, gender studies, gynocritics, and feminist criticism: Spanish women writers and their works; Spanish women important as historical and cultural figures; important Spanish feminists and defenders of women's rights; the treatment of women by significant male writers in Spain; overviews of Spanish women's history and of Spanish women's production in certain genres; assessment of

women's condition in significant moments of the last several centuries in Spain; and finally, certain terms peculiar to feminine gender in Spain. As an initial consequence, many important male writers do not appear or may be represented by a single work that stands out because of its female protagonist (or conversely, its negative treatment of women). A secondary consequence, therefore, is that some major literary works (including titles in the "masterpiece" category) do not appear, either because they have few significant female characters or because they are essentially neutral in their portrayals of women, neither especially misogynist nor noteworthy for the creation of autonomous women characters or espousal of women's rights.

The editors lament the necessity of excluding the many excellent and important women writers past and present in other languages of Spain, especially in Catalan and Galician. We have included survey articles on the present state of women's literature in those languages and also in Basque (*euskera, vascuence*) in the hope of giving some notion of the richness of current production by women in the vernacular languages and providing readers with guidance on sources of additional relevant information; we have opted not to try to represent the less-used vernacular languages, due to their limited histories and the absence of recognized canons and experts. The inclusion of individual entries on the many significant women writers in Catalan, Galician, and Basque would have necessitated at least a three-volume format, which was not an option. Similarly excluded are other women writers in the Spanish language (in Latin America, on which the publishers contemplate a separate volume). The target area of the present work thus covers works by and about women written in Spanish and limited to Spain.

Within this area, readers may still notice the presence of lacunae, as a number of authors and titles listed in the original prospectus for the project could not be included for several reasons: the lack of qualified experts interested in providing entries on certain topics, the relative inaccessibility of certain materials, the "defection" of would-be contributors who made the commitment to write on various subjects but failed to produce. This scenario will seem familiar to those who have prior experience in editing reference works; it qualifies as an occupational hazard of the genre and merits mention here largely because neither of the coeditors set out to figure among the most assiduous collaborators, but both found themselves forced to fill in resulting gaps where possible. Eventually, it became necessary to delete the remaining desiderata and conclude the project because those materials received early in the course of compilation (some seven years before) risked becoming dated. For this reason also, some early entries may not show death dates for recently deceased subjects (and even when not very recent, these are extremely difficult to secure at times). The varying lengths and degrees of thoroughness of different entries may reflect individual resources available to collaborators and do not necessarily reflect editorial judgments of a subject's importance. Similarly, individual bibliographies are not exhaustive, and what is listed often reflects collaborators' assessments of importance; one constant, however, has been accessibility, for which reason we have privileged books and works in English in the bibliographies.

Anything that dares to call itself encyclopedic is necessarily a perennial work in progress. The explosion of Spain's population of women writers in the second half of the twentieth century and the corresponding increase in research on them and on women's issues in Spain continue unabated, with numerous important new works appearing each year. Spain today has far more artistically important, highly visible, and successful women writers than at any time in its history. Some who have achieved significance at the beginning of the third millennium were only emerging when this project began (and thus did not figure in the original prospectus). As a result, many women who began publishing in the 1980s and 1990s do not appear but would be candidates for inclusion in a future edition. If this work serves its readers well, perhaps it can be expanded at a future date.

A further word concerning the "feminist" orientation: feminist criticism as a discipline is in some respects still emerging from primeval chaos, divided into various national and ideological camps and not taken too seriously in Spain where a majority of women writers—including some of the most important exponents of feminist issues and writers on women's topics—reject the feminist label for varied and complex cultural and political reasons. Many women included here would dispute their inclusion; hence we record the caveat that feminism, political, literary, or otherwise, is not an essential criterion (as evinced by the presence of entries on notorious misogynists and a series of both male and occasionally female writers in the patriarchal tradition who qualify as indifferent or negative in the area of women's rights and condition). Our intention is to present the cultural background against which Spanish women writers have produced their works, the climate in which they were formed, and in many cases, against which they react in their writings, not simply to select those relatively few Spanish women writers who would accept the feminist label.

Similarly, collaborators have not been restricted to "feminist critics" but draw upon many Hispanists both male and female from a variety of methodological and theoretical backgrounds who share an interest in women's writing, gender studies, women's history, and specific writers or works. There is no single or dominant critical methodology represented, as indeed would be well-nigh impossible in any work of collective authorship with hundreds of entries and scores of contributors. The mixture results in a tone much closer to the objective discourse generally associated with reference works than the occasionally trenchant language of the stereotype (or caricature) of feminist criticism, but such moderation of discourse is not the result of editorial intervention; we have generally made only minimal corrections (of obvious errors, misspellings, problems with English style, and the like). Individual contributors' judgments and opinions have been respected, as well as their discourse, where possible.

General Format of Entries and a Word on the Index and the Appendix

Entry titles may be related to biographical names (or, in a very few cases, well-recognized pseudonyms), literary titles or characters, genres, general and specific topics, and specific terms. Authors and titles have been cross-referenced to facilitate locating entries. As much as possible, dates (biographical, composition, publication, time frame) and/or specific focus are also included in titles to clarify the scope of the entry. Because of the time elapsed since original submission of some entries, significant recent events (death of an author, recent major awards, or latest publications) may not appear. Punctuation is consistent with the following examples: Benavente, Jacinto (1866–1954): His Portrayal of Women in *La noche del sábado* and *La malquerida*; *Don Quijote de la Mancha* (Part I, 1605; Part II, 1615): Its Representation of Women.

Within the main text of each entry, the first time a published title authored by the entry subject is mentioned, it is followed by a literal translation to English (unless the title is the name of a character), placed in parentheses. The English translation is generally preceded by the publication date of the original unless the date has already been mentioned. If a published English translation of a work has been found, that title is given, underlined, and followed by its publication date. Only readily available published translations to English are given. Titles of journals, newspapers, and so forth, in an entry are not generally translated unless they are pertinent to the subject. The entry of a work with a published translation appears as follows: *El color de agosto* (1988; *The Color of August*, 1994). A work where a published translation has not been included is listed according to the following example: *La niña lunática y otros cuentos* (1996; The Lunatic Girl and Other Stories). Quotes and other terms in Spanish are also generally translated to English.

Most entries conclude with a two-part bibliography. Part one lists work by the author and part two provides work about the author, work, or entry topic, providing some secondary bibliography. Each part is generally arranged alphabetically, although a few of the longest survey entries may be subdivided further. An attempt has been made to include recent sources, but neither section is exhaustive, and the criteria followed were left in large part to the discretion of individual authors. The intent is to provide a starting point for readers who wish to explore further.

English alphabetical order has been followed; thus *ch*, *ll*, and *ñ* are not treated as separate letters but are interfiled. Just as in English, where *an*, *a*, and *the* are ignored when alphabetizing titles, when arranging Spanish-language titles *el*, *la*, *los*, *las*, *un*, *una*, *unos*, and *unas* have been disregarded when alphabetizing bibliographies. Entry titles begin after any definite or indefinite article. Thus, *El corbacho* is listed as *Corbacho, El* (1438), and the "el" is disregarded when alphabetizing the bibliography.

Queens and canonized saints are indexed under their first names, but surnames (or surnames of pseudonyms) are used for all other biographical figures, including noncanonized religious figures.

Cross-referencing has been indicated with asterisks (*). If a person, topic, title, or term that appears as a main entry elsewhere in the *Encyclopedia* is mentioned in an article, the first mention of the item carries an asterisk that is placed immediately before the part of the name or title under which it is entered. If there are other complementary subjects or titles not indicated through asterisks, they will be listed at the end of the main text of an entry. In a very few cases, plural forms of an entry have been asterisked, although the entry appears in its singular form. Eponymous titles and characters are treated as equal, as are the Spanish terms *honor/honra* and the English equivalent *honor*.

Entry authorship is indicated at the conclusion of each article, following the bibliography.

In addition to a comprehensive general index, an Appendix with a rough chronological listing of entries by century has been provided, arranged according to birthdates, beginnings of movements, and so on. The volume closes with a selected, general bibliography of major studies.

The coeditors offer sincere thanks to all those who helped make this project possible, including those whose names appear in the list of Contributors and those agencies that provided support in the respective academic institutions, especially the Graduate School of Texas Tech University, for assistance to Janet Pérez with early stages of the project, and Kansas State University, which provided a one-semester sabbatical leave for Maureen Ihrie, furthering progress on formatting, indexing, and editorial preparation of the final manuscript. To both, our gratitude.

Nacimiento, Cecilia del

See Sobrino, Cecilia (late sixteenth century–1646), a.k.a. Cecilia del Nacimiento

Navales, Ana María (1945–)

The works of Ana María Navales reflect a longing for the past and a search for redemption that move the characters of her novels, short stories, and even her own poetry toward a world of imagination and self-discovery. Born in Zaragoza, she first became known as a poet, publishing several poetry collections. Most of her poems reflect an interest in philosophical ideas, especially the passing of time. In general, her poetry tends to distance itself from the poet in order to concentrate on that other self that is hidden within.

Navales's first published work of fiction, *Dos muchachos metidos en un sobre azul* (1976; Two Boys Put in a Blue Envelope), is a collection of 12 short stories with varied themes and styles. Her first novel, *El regreso de Julieta Always* (1981; The Return of Julieta Always), presents as its protagonist an older, psychotic painter who uses the pseudonym Julieta Always to sign her paintings. Through flashbacks of her childhood and younger years, Navales presents various perspectives on the development of the character and the events that shaped her protagonist's person-

ality. At the end of the novel, Julieta is confined to an asylum, alone and totally unaware of the exposition of her paintings and the success she had yearned for, for so many years. This sense of failure is also present in another novel of the same year, *La tarde de las gaviotas* (The Afternoon of the Seagulls). In this case, the protagonist Mila searches aimlessly to find herself and her inner truth. As with Julieta, her journey ends in failure. Both Mila and Julieta are left with a deep sense of defeat that only leads them to find emptiness in their lives. *See also* Short Fiction by Women Writers: 1975–1998, Post-Franco

Work by

Cuentos de Bloomsbury. Barcelona: Edhasa, 1991.
Del fuego secreto. Zaragoza: Institución Fernando el Católico, 1978.
Los espías de Sísifo. Madrid: Hiperión, 1981.
Hallarás otro mar. Madrid: Libertarias, 1993.
Los labios de la luna. Madrid: Torremozas, 1989.
Mester de amor. Madrid: Rialp, 1979.
La tarde de las gaviotas. Zaragoza: Unali, 1981.
Tres mujeres. Madrid: Huerga & Fierro, 1995.

Work about

Ferrer Solá, Jesús. "La poesía de Ana María Navales." *Los espejos de la palabra (Antología personal).* Zaragoza: Universidad de Zaragoza, 1991. n.p.
Miró, Emilio. "Francisca Aguirre y Ana María Navales." *Insula* 35 (1980): 404–405.
Pérez Gallego, Cándido. "Ana María Navales y el arte de novelar." *Insula* 38 (1983): 442.

Delmarie Martínez

Nebrija (or Lebrija), Francisca de (sixteenth century)

The daughter of scholar Antonio de Nebrija and Doña Isabel Montesinos de Solís, Francisca de Nebrija is reputed to have successfully substituted as instructor in rhetoric for her father in the lecture hall at the University of Alcalá de Henares. She probably assisted him in his research and writing as well, although no work of her own survives. *See also* Nuns Who Wrote in Sixteenth- and Seventeenth-Century Spain

Work about

Parada, D. Diego Ignacio. *Escritoras y eruditas españolas*. Vol. 1. Madrid: 1881.

Elizabeth T. Howe

Nelken, Carmen Eva, Pseudonym Magda Donato (1900–1966)

The younger sister of the famous feminist Margarita *Nelken y Mausberger (1896–1968), Carmen Eva Nelken wrote under the pen name Magda Donato. Born and raised in Madrid, she was a woman of remarkable education and talent, very well known and widely acclaimed as a journalist, short story writer, and playwright for children during the 1920s and 1930s. Nelken and her companion, the popular illustrator and writer Salvador Bartolozzi, worked together creating the *Aventuras de Pipo y Pipa* (Adventures of Pipo and Pipa), a series of high-quality theater pieces for children that met enormous success. In 1939, at the end of the war, Nelken and Bartolozzi moved to Paris, and after the German takeover in 1941 they sought exile in Mexico, where they continued their theatrical career. While Bartolozzi directed the children's theater in Bellas Artes, Nelken became a well-known actress for theater and cinema; she died six years after being named best Mexican actress in 1960.

In her book *Novelas breves de escritoras españolas (1900–1936)* (1989) Angela Ena Bordonada provides most of the known data about Nelken, among them an interview of Nelken by Artemio Precioso, editor of the collection "La Novela de Hoy." The interview (Madrid, 1924) offers some insight into Nelken's position vis-à-vis feminism. For her, feminism should stand for *feminidad cultivada, elevada y consciente* (cultivated, elevated and conscious femininity); it should never be confused with "masculinity." Nelken favored women's franchise and opposed marriage, being an ardent defender of free unions on the basis of honesty and true commitment, a position frequently maintained at the time in certain feminist organizations. In all she appears as a widely traveled intellectual and independent thinker. She began to write for newspapers when she was 17 and continued to do so all her life. During the 1920s and 1930s she wrote for *El Imparcial*, *El Liberal*, and *La Estampa*, where she published a series of noted articles about women prison-inmates, after having posed as an intern for a month in Madrid's Cárcel Modelo. Pilar Nieva de la Paz lists her publications on children's theater from 1924 (*El cuento de la buena pipa. Comedia infantil en tres actos* ["The Story of the Good Pipe. Children's Play in Three Acts]), published in the children's magazine *Pinocho*, to *Pipo, Pipa y el lobo Tragalotodo* (Pipo, Pipa and the All-Eating Wolf), coauthored with Bartolozzi and staged in 1935 with enormous success. This play culminated the series of *Pipo y Pipa* comedies, which were regularly presented in the María Isabel Theater from 1933 on. Nelken also adapted French plays for the Spanish stage, such as ¡*Maldita sea mi cara!* (1929; Damn My Face!) by Kolb and Belieres, in collaboration with the well-known playwright Antonio Paso, and in Mexico she continued to translate from French, among other pieces, Ionesco's *The Chairs* (1960). While she clearly enriched the Mexican cultural scenario in the 1940s and 1950s, the history of Spanish women was truncated and depleted by Nelken's absence and that of many other Spanish women who found exile in Mexico, including her sister Margarita, Maruja Mallo,

Remedios Varo, and María *Zambrano (1904–1991). This transatlantic migration of Republican women to Mexico, Argentina, and many other countries embodies an underresearched connecting line between Latin America and Spain in the field of gender studies.

Work by

El cuento de la buena pipa. Comedia infantil en tres cuadros. Pinocho (March–April 1925): 6–7.

¡Maldita sea mi cara! Farsa cómica en tres actos. Adapted from Kolb and Belieres' *Le père Lampion.* Madrid: La Farsa, 1929.

Pipo, Pipa y el lobo Tragalotodo. Comedia infantil en dos actos y doce cuadros. With Salvador Bartolozzi. Madrid: La Farsa, 1936.

Pipo, Pipa y el lobo Tragalotodo; Pinocho en el País de los Cuentos. Ed., study, notes César Vicente Hernando. Madrid: Publicaciones de la Asociación de Directores de Escena de España, 2000.

Work about

Bordonada, Angela Ena. ed. *Novelas breves de escritoras españolas (1900–1936).* Madrid: Castalia. 1990. 313–320.

Nieva de la Paz, Pilar. "Las escritoras españolas y el teatro infantil de preguerra: Magda Donato, Elena Fortún y Concha Méndez." *Revista de Literatura* 55.109 (1993): 112–128.

María Elena Bravo

Nelken y Mausberger, Margarita (1896–1968)

A writer, art historian, and political activist, Margarita Nelken y Mausberger played a prominent role as a feminist and legislator in Spain during the 1920s and 1930s and as an art critic in Mexico after 1939. She wrote pioneering works on the social conditions of Spanish women and on their contributions to Spanish culture. Nelken's parents were of German-Jewish origin, owners of a jewelry store in Madrid. Nelken received the rigorous formal training of a classical French baccalaureate and studied music, painting, and languages as well. Historical events divided her life into three relatively distinct periods: her youth as a writer, critic, and feminist be-

fore the advent of the Second Spanish Republic (1931–1939); a period of intense political activism on behalf of socialist revolution in the 1930s; and her return to art criticism as a Republican exile in Mexico after 1939.

Nelken was 15 when she published her first article, a piece on the Goya frescos at the hermitage of San Antonio de la Florida, in a British periodical. While still a very young woman she contributed to art journals in France, Germany, Italy, England, and Spain and gave lectures on art at the Prado and the Museum of Modern Art in Madrid, at Spanish schools, universities, and clubs, and at the Louvre in Paris. Her book *Tres tipos de vírgenes: Fra Angelico, Rafael, Morales* (1929; Three Types of Virgins: Fra Angelico, Raphael, Morales) developed an extended argument about cultural attitudes in the representation of a feminine figure (*Marianism). Nelken published prolifically during this early period of her life: She wrote several short novels, a book on Goethe, and many translations from French and German into Spanish and from Spanish into French. She was the author of the first translation of Franz Kafka (1883–1924) into Spanish.

As a young woman, Nelken was deeply concerned with the situation of women in Spanish society. In 1919 her polemical study *La condición social de la mujer* (Women's Social Condition) contributed to the swelling debate on the "woman question" in Spain. She was active on behalf of women at Madrid's Casa del Pueblo and founded a daycare center for working women's children in Ventas, a suburb of Madrid. Later, at the beginning of the Second Republic, she helped to organize a strike by women workers in the cigar factories (*cigarrera). She also discussed women's concerns—albeit in a light and witty tone—in her monthly column for the popular illustrated magazine *Blanco y Negro.* Nelken accepted contemporary medical and scientific views in considering the maternal instinct a fundamental aspect of women's biological and sexual makeup, but on the very grounds of women's reproductive responsibility she argued for greater freedom, better education, and improved working conditions for women. In both *La condición social de la mujer* and the later book *La mujer ante las cortes constituyentes* (1931; Woman before the Constitutional Congress [convened to reform the Constitution of the Second Republic]), she vigorously advocated legal reforms and government policies aimed at salary equity, health and safety provisions for women workers, protection for domestic workers, and the right to divorce. She maintained that ending the economic dependence of middle-class Spanish women would liberate the nation's "bravest and most energetic" force. In *Las escritoras españolas* (1930; Spanish Women Writers)—the first rigorous and scholarly history of Spanish women's writing—Nelken showed that women had made important contributions to Spanish culture from the Middle Ages on.

Her short novels, *La trampa de arenal* (1923; The Sand Trap) and *La aventura de Roma* (1923; The Roman Adventure), presented fictional models of a liberated woman and the obstacles facing her. In her own life Nelken bravely refused to conform to the traditional feminine norm. Her first child, Magdalena (1917–1956), was born out of wedlock. Her marriage to Martín de Paul y de Martín Barbadillo produced a son, Santiago, but Nelken and her husband lived separate lives from the late 1920s on.

Despite her concern with women's problems, Nelken opposed giving Spanish women the vote because she believed it would require years of education and social change to attenuate the powerful influence of the Catholic clergy over the majority of Spanish women. One of only three women elected to the Spanish legislature in 1931, she opposed the new constitution's woman *suffrage provision because she thought women would vote with the conservatives and jeopardize the reforms needed to realize a liberating feminist and social project. Nelken's distance from standard feminist positions grew pro-

nounced after her election to the Cortes and her increasingly close association with the Socialist agenda. Her writing on women and the Soviet Union revealed that by 1937, when she joined the Spanish Communist Party, she had come to believe that socialist revolution would solve all the inequities experienced by women.

During the embattled years of the Second Republic and the Spanish Civil War, Nelken's energies were absorbed by the struggle for social justice. Her strong support for the workers' rebellion in 1934 was expressed in *Por qué hicimos la revolución* (1935; Why We Made the Revolution). After the Civil War broke out, Nelken was very active in the defense of Madrid and undertook diplomatic missions on behalf of the Spanish Republic in Denmark, Holland, Switzerland, and Mexico. She was also a key Spanish figure at the Second International Congress of Writers for the Defense of Culture (Madrid and Valencia) in July 1937.

One of the last Republican intellectuals to leave Spain before the triumph of Nationalist forces, Nelken accepted asylum in Mexico, taking her mother, daughter, and granddaughter with her. In Mexico City Nelken participated in the work of various organizations dedicated to helping Republican exiles, supporting the clandestine struggle against the Franco dictatorship in Spain, and aiding Spanish political prisoners. As a result of an internal struggle over the post–Civil War strategy of the Spanish Communist Party, she was expelled from the party in 1942. She remained loyal, however, to the ideals she believed were exemplified in the Soviet Union, about which she still wrote glowingly in books like *Las torres del Kremlin* (1943; The Kremlin Towers). And she continued to use her pen and her many connections to support antifascist and anti-Franco causes as long as she lived.

Nelken turned again to art criticism as a means of supporting herself and her family in Mexico. An omnipresent figure at gallery openings and expositions, Nelken helped consolidate the Mexican avant-garde canon with her book on Mexican expressionism (1964; *El expresionismo en la plástica mexicana de hoy* [Expressionism in Today's Mexican Plastic Arts]) and books and articles on such artists as Ignacio Asúnsolo, Carlos Mérida, and José Agustín Cuevas. Nelken died in Mexico City. *See also* Feminism in Spain: 1900–2000; Women's Situation in Spain: 1786–1931: The Awakening of Female Consciousness

Work by

La aventura de Roma. In *Novelas breves de escritoras españolas (1900–1936)*. Ed., intro., notes Angela Ena Bordonada. Madrid: Castalia, 1989.

La condición social de la mujer. Madrid: CVS, 1975.

Las escritoras españolas. Barcelona and Buenos Aires: Labor, 1930.

El expresionismo en la plástica mexicana de hoy. Mexico City: Instituto Nacional de Bellas Artes, 1964.

La trampa del arenal. Ed., notes Angela Ena Bordonada. Madrid: Castalia, 2000.

Work about

Borrachero, Aranzazu. "Una mujer sonada y un nuevo orden social: La narrativa y el ensayo de Margarita Nelken (1896–1968)." *Confluencia* 13.2 (Spring 1998): 20–29.

Bretz, Mary Lee. "Margarita Nelken's *La condición social de la mujer en España*: Between the Pedagogic and the Performative." *Spanish Women Writers and the Essay: Gender, Politics and the Self*. Ed. and intro. Kathleen Glenn and Mercedes Mazquiarán de Rodríguez. Columbia: U of Missouri P, 1998. 100–126.

Kern, Robert. "Margarita Neiken: Women and the Crisis of Spanish Politics." *European Women Writers on the Left*. Ed. Jane Slaughter and Robert Kern. Westport, CT: Greenwood P, 1981. 147–162.

Susan Kirkpatrick

Niña de los embustes, Teresa de Manzanares, La (1632)

The third Spanish picaresque novel with a female protagonist was written by the most prolific prose author of the day, Alonso del Castillo Solórzano (1584–1648). Like other picaresque novels, it presents the reader with the life account of a rogue, from her modest origins to the present moment in which she writes. And as with the previous two picaresque novels protagonized by women, there are fissures in the autobiographical frame of Teresa's story. In this case her life account is preceded by an authorial statement that reminds the reader of the fictitious nature of the protagonist. Teresa, says the author, is not a real woman; her life has been constructed by piecing together the lives of many poor Spanish women. Thus, the most striking feature of the novels of *picaras*, the alienation of their voices, continues in this novel. Unlike their male counterparts, the *picaras* do not enjoy narrative autonomy to write their life stories. Their narration is constantly and openly controlled by the voice of male moral authority.

The story of Teresa de Manzanares is one of the most interesting accounts written about the life of a poor woman in Golden Age Spain. Teresa is born poor in Galicia. Following the death of her father she becomes a maid. Later, accompanied by her mother, Teresa moves to Madrid, where she works at an inn. After the death of her mother Teresa works as a maid for two women. At this job she learns to read, write, and be a hairdresser for women of high society. A few years later, having saved a sum of money, Teresa decides that it is time to quit being a simple maid. The only option available to her is marriage, so Teresa weds a rich old man. She does not love him and is continually unfaithful. Finally the old man dies, but he leaves no inheritance to the *picara*. Poor again, Teresa resumes work as a maid, but her new job does not last long. She is expelled due to her lies and intrigues. Fleeing the police, Teresa moves to Cordoba and sets up shop as a hairdresser. Once again she runs into trouble with the police and escapes to Malaga. There she unsuccessfully attempts to pass for a lady. With no job and nowhere to go, the *picara* happens to run into an ex-lover, an actor and addicted gambler. She marries him, and until his death, Teresa works with him as an actress. Like any poor widow she is desperate for money and protection. To obtain both she marries a rich, miserly man, whom she implicates in a murder. Pursued by the police, Teresa escapes to Toledo and proceeds to deceive several men. She then takes off for Madrid. When her third husband dies, the *pícara* marries yet again, this time a brutal man for whom she works as a prostitute.

The life of the third Spanish *pícara* revolves around the survival mechanisms available to poor women of Imperial Spain: delinquency, manual labor, prostitution, and the use of marriage. Among the other stories of *pícaras*, that of Teresa is the most compelling, in part because Castillo Solórzano makes evident the social awareness of this *pícara*. Teresa's only ambitions are to guarantee her economic stability and protect her autonomy. To obtain these she uses any means available to a woman of her condition. After all, throughout the narrative Teresa repeatedly states that all persons should be granted access to the privileges that only the nobility enjoys.

Yet although the ideological profile of this *pícara* is more clearly drawn than those of the other female rogues, the final result of her adventures is not very different. Teresa, like the others, fails in her attempts to be an autonomous woman. Castillo's fictional solution to the *pícara*'s desire of autonomy seems to coincide with the historic alternatives. Further, the cynical conclusion of Teresa's story points to the virtual impossibility of breaking the social barriers imposed on poor women in Golden Age Spain. Thus, it can be said that a common thread connects the three novels of *pícaras*. Whenever the female rogues manage to secure a modest fortune, they must face the inevitable need for protection. In other words, although they can improve their own economic status, they can never achieve autonomy. Ultimately the *pícaras* are forced to seek protection through marriage, which only means their subjugation to the authority of their husbands, who in turn desecrate the *pícaras*' fortunes and then prostitute them.

Work by

Castillo Solórzano, Alonso del. *La niña de los embustes, Teresa de Manzanares*. Ed. Emilio Cotarelo y Mori. Madrid: Librería de la Viuda de Rico, 1906.

Work about

Dunn, Peter. *Castillo Solórzano and the Decline of the Spanish Novel*. Oxford: Blackwell, 1952.

Hanrahan, Thomas. *La mujer en la novela picaresca española*. Madrid: Porrúa, 1967.

Lourdes de Heriz, Ana. "Castillo Solórzano: El oficio de escribir entre *La niña de los embustes, Teresa de Manzanares* y *La garduña de Sevilla, anzuelo de las bolsas*." *Quaderni del Dipartimento di Lingue e Letterature Straniere Moderne* (Italy) 8 (1996): 59–96.

Manny, Karoline. "The Function of Multiple Layers of Fiction in the Works of Castillo Solórzano." *Torre de Papel* 4.1 (Spring 1994): 53–61.

Rey Hazas, Antonio. *Picaresca femenina*. Barcelona: Plaza & Janés, 1986.

Ronquillo, Pablo. *Retrato de la pícara. La protagonista de la picaresca española del siglo XVII*. Madrid: Playor, 1980.

Soons, A. *Alonso de Castillo Solórzano*. TWAS 457. Boston: Twayne, 1977.

Reyes Coll-Tellechea

Noche del sábado, La

See Benavente, Jacinto (1866–1954): His Portrayal of Women in *La noche del sábado* and *La malquerida*

Novela negra

See Detective Fiction by Spanish Women Writers

Nuns Who Wrote in Sixteenth- and Seventeenth-Century Spain

When discussing "writing nuns" in Spain, three important facts must be kept in mind. First, until the late seventeenth century, this term was practically synonymous with that of women writers, as the only educational opportunities available to women were those offered privately in the home or in the convent. Second, there is very little recorded female literary activity (religious or otherwise) until the seventeenth century: Fewer than 300 learned women are known to have existed in all of western Europe prior to 1700. Lastly, most of the texts written by religious women residing in convents remain unpublished to this day and so have been virtually unknown by those outside convent walls, with the exception of a handful of researchers.

Spanish religious women have written in many genres: poetry, drama, fictional narrative, letters, autobiography, convent history, prayer manuals, translations, and interpretations of Scripture. The motivations that sparked such writing are also varied, including poetry contests, ceremonies of profession or religious holidays, or vision-inspired writing, the recording of which was often ordered by a confessor. There is also writing by religious women who never formally professed vows in a convent, such as works of Luisa de *Carvajal y Mendoza (1566–1614) or those of the *beatas* (holy women). Many of the *beatas*, because of illiteracy or illness, were unable to write themselves and so dictated their experiences or observations to other nuns who acted as scribes.

Many of the works of writers such as Santa *Teresa de Jesús (1515–1582) and Sor Juana Inés de la Cruz (1651–1695) are considered to form the beginnings of feminist thought in Hispanic letters. Though the literary style of each woman is entirely different, they both addressed problems faced by women of their time. Santa Teresa was very concerned with the poor health of many women religious, and Sor Juana with their lack of educational opportunities. The Catholic Church has always acknowledged the spiritual equality of men and women (especially in New Testament teachings), but this equality has not been extended to the social or political realms. Before 1700, women were not allowed to read the Bible or attend university and were discouraged from any type of literary endeavor. Therefore, the mere act of

writing from within convent walls could be considered a challenge to the patriarchal hierarchy of the Church.

Even in the best of circumstances (Germany during and after the Protestant Reformation, for example), it was not seen as proper to have educated women circulating freely in society. Women have traditionally been expected to choose either a religious profession or that of wife and mother, and until the late nineteenth century, women's education emphasized proficiency in these areas, rather than intellectual pursuits. A religious profession was one of the few ways a woman could gain some degree of authority and autonomy, evidenced in part by the number of female saints in Europe from the eleventh to the fifteenth centuries, which greatly outnumbered that of men. Undoubtedly religious life had a special appeal for women who wished to pursue a respected career or profession.

Some of the issues related to the writings of women religious that have interested literary critics are: (1) the development of voice and authority—how does the writer find her voice within the clear hierarchical structure of the Church that surrounds her writing? (Arenal and Schlau; Lerner; Jordan); (2) the topic of humility and resistance to writing of women religious, due to fear of reprisals of Church authorities and/or scrutiny of their works (Velasco; Weber; El Saffar); (3) the subversion of traditional "women's concerns," such as those of mother and wife, to criticize the institutions that would curtail women's intellectual activity (Weber); and (4) the relation between physical illness and writing, especially in the case of mystic writers (Bell; Velasco; El Saffar).

Recently more attention has been given to the foremothers and followers of Santa Teresa, the major figure of Spanish women religious writers. Santa Teresa was aware of the tradition of *beatas* in her native city of Avila. They served as models for her, just as she served as a model for many who wrote after her. *Beatas* were charismatic holy women who did not necessarily take vows to become nuns but instead maintained active lives as members of larger communities and often had large followings. Because of their woman-centered style of worship, and the emphasis on visions, they were often accused of heterodoxy. Religious women writers also served as models for secular women writers, as in the case of María de *Zayas (1590–after 1647?), who, in her *Desengaños amorosos* (1649; Disillusions in Love), cites several religious women writers as examples of virtuous women. Women religious and the convent as a place of study and sanctuary have a very positive role in her fiction as well.

Most of the *beatas*, like the *alumbradas* (illuminati), were not writers. They were, however, representatives of lower-class women, which could be one of the reasons they suffered greater persecution. The great majority of nuns who wrote were members of the upper echelons of Spanish society but not all. Isabel de Jesús (1586–1648), not to be confused with *Isabel de Jesús (1611–1682), is one of the exceptions. She dictated her *Vida* to be written down during the last three years of her life. Not only was this writer exceptional because of her socioeconomic background (her parents were shepherds); she also had been married and given birth to children before becoming an Augustine nun. Santa Teresa united these two feminine spiritual traditions: that of unlettered *beatas* whose visions caused them to have great followings and those who actually professed and wrote their autobiographies.

Of all the followers of Teresa, two have been written about extensively: Ana de *San Bartolomé (1549–1626) and María de San José (1548–1603). Both were nuns in the Discalced Carmelite convent that Teresa founded in Avila, both were prolific writers, and both were persecuted for their defense of Teresian reforms in the Church. Madre Ana wrote, among other things, *La defensa de la herencia teresiana* (1981; Defense of the Teresan Legacy) and was beatified in 1917. Madre María cofounded a discalced convent in

Seville with Teresa. Most notable of her writings are poems, letters, and the *Libro de recreaciones* (1979; Book of Diversions). In addition, both of them wrote autobiographies.

María de Guevara, the countess of Escalante (?–1683), in her *Desengaños de la corte* (1664; Disillusions of the Court), published the names of 205 women writers, 77 of whom were religious, which indicates that there were many more women religious writers in seventeenth-century Spain than have been written about or whose works have been published. There are also numerous women religious cited in Serrano y Sanz's bibliography of Spanish women writers, very few of whom have been brought to light. Some who have been studied, or at least named in several different sources, are: María de Barahona (?–?), a poet and musician who both wrote music and sang, who wrote a panegyric for Pérez de Montalbán when he died; Eugenia de Contreras (?–?), a poet whose *liras* (metrical verse form) were published in 1631; Estefanía de la Encarnación (1597–1665), who published an autobiography in 1631; Mariana de Jesús (?–?), a discalced nun who also wrote her autobiography, and Sor Cecilia del Nacimiento (1570–1646; Cecilia *Sobrino), who was a playwright.

Another playwright whose history is somewhat ironic is that of Sor Marcela de *San Félix (1605–1687), one of the illegitimate daughters of Lope de *Vega (1562–1635), who had to run away from home to be able to pursue her studies in an environment conducive to study and reflection. Even the most acclaimed of all women religious writers, Sor Juana Inés de la Cruz (1651–1695), had to give up her literary pursuits toward the end of her life due to the tremendous pressures placed on her and her convent by the diocesan authorities.

The last two "writing nuns" to be mentioned stand apart from the rest, one because of her very unusual life, spent mostly in men's clothing, and one because of her extensive correspondence with Philip IV of

Spain. Catalina de *Erauso, known as the *monja alférez* (nun ensign), wrote an autobiography (*Vida i sucesos de la Monja Alférez* [Life and Events of the Nun Ensign]), the theater adaptation of which was made famous by Pérez Montalbán. Unlike all the other autobiographies mentioned above, Erauso's was written years after having left the convent, and the veracity of several accounts has been challenged. What makes her case particularly interesting is that she was reportedly a lesbian (*lesbianism) who dressed as a man, joined the army, and traveled to America. In her *Vida*, she claims that she obtained permission from the pope later in life to "live as a man." Clearly this manuscript holds fascination for anyone interested in the roots of feminism in Spain. The convent plays an important, yet brief, role in her life, as it represents a refuge from the inevitable arranged marriage she would have been subject to, had she remained in her parents' house.

Sor María de *Agreda corresponded with Philip IV and was in many ways an adviser to him. Clark Colahan speaks of their "30-year friendship" and claims that both Sor María and Philip thought of her as morally superior and intellectually equal to him. She wrote a history of the Virgin (*The Mystical City of God*), which her confessor ordered her to burn but which she rewrote 12 years later, in 1655. Sor María rewrote it only to have it censured by the Sorbonne. This book was part of the controversy over the Immaculate Conception (*Marianism) in which Spain was involved. Sor María was also instrumental in convincing the king to restrict the power of the Inquisition in Aragón so that it would only deal with questions of faith, an idea the king had originally resisted. In addition to a history of the Virgin Mary, Agreda wrote a geography of the world and is credited with having caused Indians in New Mexico to convert to Catholicism. She had visions in which she "traveled" to America and, being quite moved by the situation of the Indians there, urged them to become

Christian. This phenomenon of "bilocation," as it is called, was one of the arguments used in the petition for her canonization. Her knowledge of the geography of the area was surprisingly accurate, according to a Fray Damián, member of the León-Massanet expedition. Sor María de Agreda is a perfect example of how a narrowly prescribed social role could be subverted to become a source of power and influence. The convent provided an atmosphere in which she could develop her administrative talents as well as stimulate her visions. Although women's religious communities fell under the control of the greater Church hierarchy, they did provide a space for women free from the family definitions of wife and mother, yet symbolically the women who entered them became wives of Jesus and both sisters and mothers to the other nuns.

The convent also served as a place of retirement for women when their husbands died and from which they wrote letters, memoirs, and convent histories that have provided insight into the social reality of the time. One of the best known was Catalina de la Cerda y Sandoval, the seventh countess of Lemos, who founded the convent of the "Franciscanas Descalzas de Santa Clara" in Monforte de Lemos in 1622. *See also* Autobiographical Self-Representation of Women in the Early Modern Period.

Work by

Agreda, Sor María de Jesús. *La mística ciudad de Dios.* Ed. Augustine Esposito. Potomac: Scripta Humanistica, 1990.

Erauso, Catalina de. *Vida y sucesos de la monja alférez.* Ed. Rima de Vallbona. Tempe: Center for Latin American Studies, Arizona State U, 1992.

Jesús, Sor Isabel de. *Vida (Vida de la Venerable madre Isabel de Jesús, recoleta Augustina en el convento de San Juan Bautista de la villa de Arenas. Dictada por ella misma y añadido lo que faltó de su dichosa muerte.* Madrid: Viuda de Francisco Nieto, 1675.

San Félix, Marcela de. *Marcela de San Félix: Obra completa.* Ed. Georgina Sabat de Rivers. Barcelona: n.p., 1988.

Zayas y Sotomayor, María. *Desengaños amorosos.* Ed. Alicia Yllera. Madrid: Cátedra, 1983.

Work about

Abad, Camilo María. *Una misionera española en la Inglaterra del siglo XVII: Doña Luisa de Carvajal y Mendoza*. Comillas: Universidad Pontífica, 1966.

Arenal, Electa. "The Convent as Catalyst for Autonomy: Two Hispanic Nuns of the 17th Century." *Women in Hispanic Literature: Icons and Fallen Idols*. Ed. Beth Miller. Berkeley and Los Angeles: U of California P, 1983. 147–183.

———. "Leyendo Yo y Escribiendo Ella" [The Convent as Intellectual Community]. *Journal of Hispanic Philology* 13. 3 (Spring 1989): 214–229.

Arenal, Electa, and Stacey Schlau. *Untold Sisters: Hispanic Nuns in Their Own Words*. Trans. Amanda Powell. Albuquerque: U of New Mexico P, 1989.

Bell, Rudolph. *Holy Anorexia*. Chicago: U of Chicago P, 1995.

Berruezo, José. *Catalina de Erauso: La monja alférez*. San Sebastián: "Grupo Dr. Camino de Historia Donostiarra" de la Real Sociedad Vascongada de los Amigos del País (C.S.I.C), 1975.

Bilinkoff, Jodi. "The Holy Women and the Urban Community in Sixteenth Century Avila." *Women and the Structure of Society: Research from the Fifth Berkshire Conference in History*. Ed. Barbara J. Harris and Jo Ann McNamara. Durham, NC: Duke UP, 1984. 74–80.

Colahan, Clark. *The Visions of Sor María de Agreda: Writing Knowledge and Power*. Tucson: U of Arizona P, 1994.

Deleito y Piñuela, José. *La vida religiosa española bajo el cuarto Felipe*. Madrid: Espasa-Calpe, 1952.

El Saffar, Ruth. *Rapture Encaged: The Suppression of the Feminine in Western Culture*. London: Routledge, 1994.

Jordan, Constance. *Renaissance Feminism*. Ithaca, NY: Cornell UP, 1990.

Lerner, Gerda. *The Creation of Feminist Consciousness*. New York: Oxford UP, 1993.

Perry, Mary Elizabeth. "*Beatas* and the Inquisition in Early Modern Seville." *Inquisition and Society in Early Modern Europe*. Ed. and trans. Stephen Haliczer. London: Croom Helm, 1986. 147–168.

Sánchez, Magdalena. "Confession and Complicity: Margarita de Austria, Richard Haller, S.J., and the Court of Philip III." *Cuadernos de Historia Moderna* 14 (1993): 133–149.

Serrano y Sanz, Manuel. *Apuntes para una biblioteca de escritoras españolas desde el año 1401 al 1833*. 2 vols. Madrid: Rivadeneyra, 1903.

Simón Palmer, María del Carmen. *Spanish Women Writers*. Madrid: Chadwyck-Healey, 1992.

Surtz, Ronald E. *The Guitar of God: Gender, Power and Authority in the Visionary World of Mother Juana de la Cruz*. Philadelphia: U of Pennsylvania P, 1990.

Swietlicki, Catherine. "Writing 'Femystic' Space: In the Margins of St. Teresa's Castillo Interior." *Journal of Hispanic Philology* 13.3 (Spring 1989): 274–290.

Weber, Alison. *Teresa of Avila and the Rhetoric of Femininity*. Princeton, NJ: Princeton UP, 1990.

Weinstein, Douglas, and Rudolph M. Bell. *Saints and Society*. Chicago: Chicago UP, 1982.

Nancy Cushing-Daniels

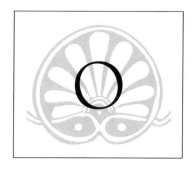

Ojeda, Pino (1916–   )

Best known as a poet, Pino Ojeda has written several plays and a novel, and she is also a painter. Her poetic work shows affinities to postwar Spanish social poetry. Like other so-called social poets, her writing is much imbued with personal experience, expressed dramatically from a female perspective. The Spanish Civil War strongly affected Ojeda; her husband died in the war shortly after they married, and this tragic event seems to have been a main trigger for her career as a poet. Her work that deals with this loss represents an attempt to escape loneliness through poetry. By this process she tries to defeat time and pursue knowledge. The highly emotive and intuitive energy of her first books evolves to a more mature and restrained expression in later works.

Her first poems were published in the magazine *Mensaje*, where she was a regular contributor. *Mensaje* also published her first book, *Niebla de sueño* (1947; Mist of Sleep). This work focuses almost exclusively on love as a personal experience. The absence of her husband becomes a central issue, as the book displays memories of lost love. These poems are very classical in their structure, with the sonnet widely preferred throughout. Around 1954, Ojeda started publishing some poetry broadsheets called *Alisios* (Tradewinds). In *Como el fruto en el árbol* (1954; Like Fruit on the Tree), winner of the second Adonais poetry prize in 1953, Ojeda's perspective shifts from the personal to the more universal and general. Here, the poet opens up a dialogue with herself and the world outside that continues in her next book, *La piedra sobre la colina* (1964; The Rock on the Hill). This dialogue between poet and the world is highly symbolic and reflects on passion and existential anguish. *El salmo del rocío* (1993; Psalm of the Dew). After *El alba en la espalda* (1987; Dawn at One's Back), Ojeda's last published work is *El salmo del rocío* (1993; Psalm of the Dew).

Work by

El alba en la espalda. Madrid: Torremozas, 1987.
Como el fruto en el árbol. Madrid: Rialp, 1954.
La piedra sobre la colina. Madrid: Rialp, 1954.
El salmo del rocío. Madrid: Fernando Rielo, 1993.

Work about

Nuez Caballero, Sebastián de. *Antología de la poesía Canaria del siglo XX. Contemporary Poetry from the Canary Islands.* Trans. Louis Bourne. London: Forest Books, 1986.

Violeta Padrón

Olmo, Lauro (1921–1994): *La soltera* (Spinster) and Other Female Characters in His Drama

One of the first male playwrights of post–Civil War Spain to project a feminist viewpoint, Lauro Olmo showed the sociological and psychological factors that made freedom impossible for Spanish women. In *La camisa* (1962; The Shirt) Olmo created one of his strongest female characters: Lola, a woman of the *arrabales* (city slums), who defies her husband Juan and emigrates to earn money to feed her family when he is unable to find work but refuses to leave Spain.

More psychological than *La camisa*, *La pechuga de la sardina* (1963; The Breast of the Sardine) shows the lives of women in a working-class rooming house. Its stark dramatization of their oppression represented a new phenomenon for the Madrid stage. Concha, a young girl jobless, pregnant, and abandoned by the cowardly father who is afraid to assume any responsibility and wants her to abort, feels only the sense of worthlessness instilled in her by her mother and by Doña Elena, the elderly single woman in the rooming house. The latter, with her spyglass and the notebook in which she records the other roomers' goings and comings, represents the sexual repression and hypocrisy the play condemns. Paloma, a young student who represents Olmo's hopes for a new Spain in which women are free, tries to convince Concha that she is stronger than the forces destroying her. Soledad, another boarder, who turned to prostitution after her fiancé left her, attempts to escape loneliness in a series of affairs that she leaves unfinished as they become coarse and vulgar. Falling into profound depressions, she feels her very sanity to be threatened. However, it is Doña Elena who is the greatest victim of all: "The old maid! A Product 'Made in Spain.'" In a poignant scene, Paloma surprises the elderly woman in Soledad's room, when the latter is absent, holding one of Soledad's intimate garments up to her body in front of the mirror.

The play's humorous title comes from Juana the landlady's warning as she sees Concha leave for mass following the footsteps of two *beatas: A certain cousin wore a girdle that looked like it was made of tin, with *la sardina enclaustrá!* (the sardine packed inside). She finally died of grief. If Concha continues to deny her own youth and vitality, her fate could be the same. The play ends as Soledad is brought home beaten by some man she was with, as church bells toll a dirge. However, the final words are those of an old woman in the street who calls for her cat, adding that if she doesn't find it, her sardine breast will rot. The television version of the play was well received in the 1980s.

La señorita Elvira (1963), a television play often presented on stage, is an intimate glimpse into the empty existence of a lonely single woman near death. Elvira answers questions posed by a nameless official interested only in recording her name in his book of blank pages. However, Elvira, feeling the need to review and validate her life, to prove that she is more than a name, insists upon reconstructing key moments of her existence—which are reenacted with the aid of masks—as an hourglass indicates that her life is inexorably coming to its end. Her parents, whose stern faces are projected on a screen, represent the repressive and hypocritical sexual attitudes that have conditioned Elvira's existence. Two scenes in which she recalls her experiences with young men make clear the fears and obsessions inspired by her parents as she became aware of her sexuality. The parallels with *La pechuga de la sardina* are marked: Elvira has lived as paralyzed with fear as Concha and as obsessed with being abandoned and ending up alone as Soledad. The emptiness Elvira feels is underscored at the end when she sees a chihuahua, asks it if it, too, is alone, and embraces it just before Death reads aloud the one-line epitaph he writes in his book.

Olmo's condemnation—and ridicule—of *machismo* (male exaltation) is seen above all in *El cuerpo* (1966; The Body), a tragicomedy of two women: Doña Ceño, the long-suffering wife of Don Víctor, a "supermacho" who constantly works out with a punching bag, and Cuquina, the former's young niece. Doña Ceño is aware of her own victimization since she suspects that Victor, who lives off of her money and does not work, would not have married her were it not for the lands she inherited. Although she genuinely loves her husband—whom she first met at a parade in which he appeared in full military regalia and was applauded by all the women of the neighborhood, who called him *el cuerpo* (the body)—she is capable of defending herself and of even attacking him where he is most vulnerable. When he berates her for accusing him of trying to impress Cuquina and her young friends and boasts of his musculature, she counters that though his body is hard, it increasingly resembles rigor mortis. Olmo contrasts the fears of the middle-aged Doña Ceño to the joy and spontaneity of Cuquina. This contrast is seen in their ideas about marriage. When the aunt warns her niece not to take Quique, the medical student who loves her, for granted, Cuquina, like Paloma of *La pechuga de la sardina*, although she does not reject marriage, responds that there are alternatives. When Doña Ceño insists that the only solution is still a husband, Cuquina replies that her aunt has come into the world tied up hand and foot, like a parcel, marked "Fragile: Husband Needed." Nevertheless, Doña Ceño realizes that the attitudes of Cuquina and her young friends are healthier than those of her own generation. The inevitable defeat of power based on force is suggested when Don Víctor ascends a podium to lift a huge weight suggesting a globe of the world and cannot continue. Olmo stated that *El cuerpo* was a subtle story about a pair of biceps, a criticism of *machismo* on a domestic scale. However, the play constitutes a strong denunciation of political oppression as well as a strong defense of women's rights.

English Spoken (1968) portrays one of Olmo's strongest female characters: Luisa, a young language student just returned from working in London. She could be another Lola of *La camisa*, younger and better educated, who returns from emigration with new experiences and abilities that prepare her for the future. Like Paloma of *La pechuga de la sardina*, Luisa has an immense love for Spain and a strong faith in herself. The other female students are portrayed as weak, even allowing themselves to be attracted to El Míster, an emigrant who has returned and is involved in prostitution on an international scale. Luisa, who perfects her English to obtain a secretarial position, together with Lola of *La camisa* and Paloma of *La pechuga de la sardina*, is among Olmo's strongest female characters.

Work by

English Spoken. Madrid: Escelicer, 1969.
La pechuga de la sardina. Madrid: Escelicer, 1967.
La señorita Elvira. In *Teatro realista de hoy*. Ed. Eduardo Galán Font. Zaragoza: Luis Vives, 1993.
Teatro (La camisa. El cuerpo. El cuarto poder). Madrid: Taurus, 1970.

Work about

Halsey, Martha. "Olmo's *La pechuga de la sardina* and the Oppression of Women in Contemporary Spain." *Revista de Estudios Hispánicos* 13.1 (1979): 3–20.
Lauzière, Carol. "El heroísmo femenino en *La camisa* de Lauro Olmo." *De lo particular a lo universal. El teatro español del siglo XX y su contexto*. Ed. John P. Gabriele. Frankfurt: Vervuert, 1994. 119–136.
Nicholas, Robert. "Texto dramático y contexto social: El dilema de Lauro Olmo." *Estreno* 22.1 (1996): 41–46.

Martha T. Halsey

Ortiz, Lourdes (1943–   )

Now emerging as one of Spain's recognized post-Franco literary forces, Lourdes Ortiz—a consistently productive and versatile author—has written more than half a dozen novels, seven or more plays, and numerous short stories as well as published essays on literary criticism (including books on Rimbaud and Larra), communication theory, children's books, translations, and a variety of articles for newspapers. In addition, Ortiz taught communication theory at the Complutense University of Madrid and is currently professor of art history at the university's Royal School of Dramatic Art.

Born in Madrid, Ortiz demonstrated at an early age a proclivity for writing. This interest was relegated to a place of secondary importance during her turbulent university years (1962–1968), as she became heavily involved in the political struggle as a onetime member of the Spanish Communist Party and the growing feminist movement. After abandoning these activities, Ortiz wrote her first, and as yet unpublished, novel that deals with the themes of political struggle, ideological disenchantment, repression, and homosexuality.

A number of these themes reappear in Ortiz's first published novel, *Luz de la memoria* (1976; Light of Memory), which traces the life of protagonist Enrique García from childhood to his final ambiguous demise. Rejected by his parents as a child, abandoned by his wife, and a failure both as writer and political conspirator, the protagonist's emotional crisis lands him in a psychiatric hospital where his confused mental and emotional states are portrayed at the level of story and that of discourse. Representation of this confusion is achieved discursively through experimental techniques such as shifting narrative voices, among them the second-person narrator that starts the novel, multiple viewing perspectives, a fragmented and nonlinear story line, and a deliberate blurring of the line between discourse and story.

Technical experimentation is eschewed in Ortiz's next novel, *Picadura mortal* (1979; Fatal Bite), which employs the highly formulaic *detective fiction genre that was attaining popularity and limited critical acceptance in Spain during the period. While the novel is quite innovative in its use of a female detective, the first in Spanish literary history, Ortiz's narrator-detective Bárbara Arenas is only superficially feminist and in many areas (notably her attitude toward violence and casual sex) emulates her male models while at the same time she reinforces, perhaps par-

odically as suggested by some critics, negative female stereotypes.

Ortiz's third novel, *En días como éstos* (1981; On Days Like These), revisits the thematic terrain of opposition to the government, this time in the form of terrorism. The protagonist Toni is a member of an unnamed, militant terrorist organization who, while on the run from the law and later in prison, tries to come to terms with the reasons behind his own political militancy, the question of confidence among fellow comrades, the use of violence, and ultimately the utility of revolutionary action.

In her most widely acclaimed novel, *Urraca* (1982), Ortiz once again employs a popular genre of the period, the historical novel, to portray the life of Queen *Urraca of Castile and Leon (1109–1126). Ortiz painstakingly researched the subject for two years. However, the lack and partiality of information concerning the life of the queen in turn provided the author the artistic liberty to reconstruct this elusive figure and reinscribe Queen Urraca into Spanish history. Written from the prison cell in which she is held captive by order of her son, Urraca chronicles her reign not as a public confession, as the abbot demands, but rather in the attempt to give voice to her truth and justify her actions. As a result, the chronicle challenges and demythifies a number of issues including popular and official versions of history, medieval male heroes and religious figures, patriarchal stereotypes of womanhood, and the relationship of women to power, specifically Urraca's conflicting roles as woman and sovereign. In addition, *Urraca* foregrounds the empowerment produced from the process of writing from a female perspective.

Ortiz's following novel, *Arcángeles* (1986; Archangels), further explores the metafictional vein by centering the story on the process of creation, the female author's struggle to write the novel. The first part of the text is occupied by discussions between the author and the angel Gabriel regarding the content of the novel and the procedures for initiating it. The fruit of these discussions takes form in the second part, which narrates the story of Manolo and his desperate quest for economic and moral survival in chaotic, contemporary Spain. As in *Urraca*, in the third section the frontiers between process and product appear to merge as Ortiz foregrounds their dialectical relationship.

Antes de la batalla (1992; Before the Battle) leaves behind the metafictional mode of *Arcángeles* but does continue and amplify the thematic focus on life in contemporary Spain. Caught in a midlife crisis, the protagonist Ernesto struggles to find meaning beyond his dead-end bureaucratic job and unsuccessful relationships by means of a documentary on Faust. Just as he believes to have realized his aspirations, Ernesto discovers that the man who will make them possible murdered the son of longtime friends. The novel ends with Ernesto desperately trying not to confront his "Faustian" bargain.

La fuente de la vida (1995; The Fountain of Life) interweaves the stories of two very different men, from vastly diverging circumstances, who coincide in their pursuit of two fascinating, desirable, unobtainable women, forever beyond their grasp. Inadvertent witnesses to events in which they are later implicated, their lives are endangered, as the plot involves the kidnapping of children for illegal adoption as well as trafficking in human organs in settings as diverse as Third World countries and a nation of the former Communist bloc.

The collection of short stories *Los motivos de Circe* (1988; Circe's Motives) is recollective of *Urraca* in its intent to give a voice to female figures of ancient and modern history, among them Eve, Salome, and the Mona Lisa. Customarily denied the power of self-portrayal, here the women inscribe their version of their story from a perspective that revalues their roles and, in several cases, explains and/or annuls the culpability traditionally associated with the figures. In 1998, Ortiz published *Fátima de los naufragios* (Fa-

tima [Patron] of Shipwrecks), a collection of half a dozen stories, three featuring female protagonists. Subtitled "Tales of Land and Sea," the collection treats absence, the anonymity of death, unfulfilled desires, epic passions, and unsuspected sentiments.

This interest in the demythification of female figures is also apparent in several of Ortiz's staged but as yet unpublished plays, *Electra Rey*, *Fedra*, and *Penteo* (which is constructed around the latent presence of Agave), and in *Cenicienta* (Cinderella), a parable in two acts published in *Los motivos de Circe*. Other plays include *Yudita*, *Pentesilea*, and *El local de Bernadeta A* (Bernadete A's Premises). As is evident, however, Ortiz's writing is not restricted to a single sphere thematically or formally. Her proven success in exploring varied thematic terrain and experimental techniques augurs an interesting literary future. *See also* Short Fiction by Women Writers: 1975–1998, Post-Franco

Work by

Antes de la batalla. Madrid: Planeta, 1992.

Arcángeles. Barcelona: Plaza & Janés, 1986.

En días como éstos. Madrid: Akal, 1981.

Fátima de los naufragios. Barcelona: Planeta, 1998.

La fuente de la vida. Barcelona: Planeta, 1995.

Luz de la memoria. Madrid: Akal, 1976.

Los motivos de Circe; Yudita. Ed., intro., notes Felicidad González Santamera. Madrid: Castalia, 1991.

Picadura mortal. Madrid: Sedmay, 1979.

Urraca. Madrid: Puntual, 1982.

Work about

Ciplijauskaité, Biruté. "Historical Novel from a Feminine Perspective: *Urraca*." *Feminine Concerns in Contemporary Spanish Fiction by Women*. Ed. Roberto Manteiga, Carolyn Galerstein, and Kathleen McNerney. Potomac: Scripta Humanistica, 1988. 29–42.

Hart, Patricia. "The Picadura and Picardía of Lourdes Ortiz." *The Spanish Sleuth*. Rutherford: Fairleigh Dickinson UP, 1987. 172–181.

Ordóñez, Elizabeth. "Rewriting Myth and History: Three Recent Novels by Women." *Feminine Concerns in Contemporary Spanish Fiction by Women*. Ed. Roberto Manteiga, Carolyn Galerstein, and

Kathleen McNerney. Potomac: Scripta Humanistica, 1988. 6–28.

Pérez, Janet. "Lourdes Ortiz." *Contemporary Women Writers of Spain*. Boston: Twayne, 1988. 165–167.

Spires, Robert C. "Lourdes Ortiz: Mapping the Course of Postfrancoist Fiction." *Women Writers of Contemporary Spain*. Newark. U of Delaware P, 1991. 198–216.

Kathleen Thompson-Casado

Orto y ocaso del feminismo

See Colmeiro Laforet, Carlos (1906–1986)

Ozores, Ana

See Regenta, La (1885): Protagonist Ana Ozores.

Padilla Manrique y Acuña, Luisa María de, Condesa de Aranda (1590–1646)

The author of four books on history, archaeology, and standards of proper behavior, it is believed she was born in Burgos, where she spent her childhood. Her father, Don Martín de Padilla y Manrique, was commander in chief of Castile, secretary of state and war, admiral, and participant in various military campaigns, including the Battle of Lepanto (1588). He died when she was quite young. Her mother, Doña Luisa de Padilla y Acuña, gave 1,800 ducats to the Jesuits to support their preaching and grammar instruction in the mountains of Burgos, then joined the Discalced Carmelite order, becoming prioress of the Carmen monastery in 1612. Luisa María de Padilla was one of seven children; one brother became commander in chief of Castile, and another sibling married into the family of the duke of Lerma. Padilla herself married Don Antonio Ximénez de Urrea, count of Aranda, in 1605, subsequently living in Epila. An avid reader even as a child, letters she wrote to historian Andrés de Uztarroz reveal that as an adult she pursued historical and archeological research. In her will, Padilla left funds to a hospital, a *colegio* (school) in Zaragoza, and "20 impoverished maidens."

Regarding her writings, some critics believe that she wrote them as models of conduct for her children, while others maintain that she apparently had no direct heirs. She did not publish her works, but they were printed, some without recognizing her as author. *Nobleza virtuosa* (Virtuous Nobility) was printed by Juan de Lanaja y Quartanet in Zaragoza under direction of Pedro Henrique Pastor, provincial of the order of St. Augustine in Zaragoza. Divided into four parts, part one states at one point that it is the work of a gentleman and at another that it is by "a great lady." It treats matters of the Catholic faith. The second part, "Noble perfecto y segunda parte de la Nobleza virtuosa" (1639; [The] Perfect Noble and Second Part of Virtuous Nobility), gives counsel on how to conduct one's life. "Lágrimas de la Nobleza" (Tears of Nobility), part three, explains how to prepare for death. Part four, "Idea de nobles y sus desempeños en aforismos, parte cuarta de la nobleza virtuosa" ([The] Idea of Nobles and Their Duties in Aphorisms, Part Four of Virtuous Nobility), is in turn divided into four sections that discuss, respectively, the religious, moral, political, and military virtues of the nobility.

Padilla's *Elogios de la verdad e invectiva contra la mentira* (1640; Praises of Truth and Invective against the Lie) was also printed by Pedro Lanaja in Zaragoza, under the direction of Pedro Henrique Pastor. *Excelencias de la castidad* (1642; Excellence of Chastity) was dedicated to the sisters of the Discalced Convent of the Immaculate Conception in Epila. It treats ideas found in another work composed by Fray José de Jesús María de la Orden de los Descalzos de la Virgen María del Monte Carmelo. Padilla also composed an unpublished work titled "Cartilla para instruir niños nobles" (Primer for Teaching Noble Children).

Work by

Elogios de la verdad e invectiva contra la mentira. Zaragoza: M. Pedro Lanaja y Lamarca, 1640.

Excelencias de la castidad. Zaragoza: M. Pedro Lanaja y Lamarca, 1642.

Nobleza virtuosa. 6 vols. Zaragoza: Juan de Lanaja y Quartanet, 1637–1642.

Work about

Serrano y Sanz, Manuel. *Apuntes para una biblioteca de escritoras españolas desde el año 1401 al 1833.* Madrid: RABM, 1905. 2: 95–120.

Elena Cámara

Palacio Valdés, Armando (1853–1938): Women in His Works

Women occupy various positions of narrative authority in Armando Palacio Valdés's works, which span several decades and various literary movements present at the end of the nineteenth and beginning of the twentieth century. Feminine characters generally occupy roles of secondary importance in his novels, even when they represent title characters. Thus, literary criticism both past and present has tended to focus on the male protagonists.

Laura, the servant who captures the attention of Octavio Rodríguez in Palacio Valdés's first novel, *El señorito Octavio* (1881; Master Octavio), also occupies the role of unhappy wife to the count of Trevia. In the end, after the count is informed of Laura's adulterous relationship with Pedro, he murders her and Octavio after the latter warns the lovers of the count's threats. The abuse Laura suffers from her husband establishes her vulnerability in a marital relationship plagued by violence. The fact that she endured a harsh childhood points to deterministic forces, characteristic of naturalist thought of the period, which necessarily foreshadow her demise. Dendle argues that character development in this novel places the subjectivity of Laura and Pedro opposite the objectivity of Octavio. However, Palacio Valdés accomplishes this unconvincingly since, upon examining her situation, Laura selects a role submissive to Pedro.

The next novel published by Palacio Valdés, *Marta y María* (1883), evolves from a Carlist crisis in the fictitious Asturian town of Nieva. The dualism embodied in the title characters' spirituality versus practicality is complemented by comparisons of Carlists versus Liberals, romantic versus realist fervor, and women's role in the historical period, especially in the case of Marta's conspiracies to assist Carlist supporters. Although protagonist Ricardo initially pursues the older sister, Marta, he marries María after circumstances related to Marta's involvement with the Carlist movement lead her to enter a convent. Via the distinct personality traits of the two women, the obvious opposition of the religious and the secular creates the primary conflict of the novel. María's devotion to that which leads to a saintly existence is exposed as an exercise of immodesty, indulgence, false praise, and an inclination toward sexual perversion, as described in the scene of Maria's flagellation by a servant. Her self-serving actions regarding spiritual life represent the emptiness with which the clergy performs its duties. Although her challenge to the traditional patriarchal values of society abound, in the end María succumbs to the expectations of feminine inferiority. By contrast, Marta demonstrates traits that place her on an equal platform with the women of her time. As the character who fusses over work done in the traditional feminine space of the kitchen, the motivating forces behind Marta emphasize the modest femininity found in her air of ordinariness and practicality. As suggested by Dendle, the treatment of sexuality with regard to Marta deals more with her transformation in terms of nature into adulthood than with the peculiar practices associated with her sister.

The importance of nature is perceived in *El idilio de un enfermo* (1884; Idyl of a Sick Man), set primarily in the fictitious Asturian town of Riofrío. Palacio Valdés's incorporation of naturalist thought explains the emphasis placed on environment, as seen in the ironic title. As the love interest of Andrés Heredia, Rosa's distinction as a member of the peasant class fuels her initial rejection of Heredia's advances. She also, and rightly so, rejects her Uncle Jaime's marriage proposal despite the encouragement of her father Tomás. In Rosa's name the immediate association with nature suggests a beautiful, delicate creation that contrasts markedly with the reality of the female. As a powerless adolescent, Rosa suffers beatings at the hands of her father in an attempt to convince her to accept the marital arrangement. Rosa refuses to succumb to physical violence and in her escape to her aunt's care, accompanied by Heredia, defies the abuse that surrounds her. Although she continues in the role of servant, she is distanced from her family in the end, and Heredia, after having returned to Madrid, dies soon after. The futility of the relationship between Rosa and Heredia arises from the naturalist tenets of determinism as a statement that, as creatures of nature, human beings who form part of the oppressed classes are destined to remain in their state of oppression, without hope of overcoming the obstacles they face. The importance of the outdoors as an archetypal universe of Nature, as established by Dendle, also serves to support the naturalist tendency in the novel, which contributes to the underlying tone of pessimism. Palacio Valdés does stray somewhat from this tendency, however; he allows for a hint of sarcasm and for the interpretation of the protagonists' actions, against the traditional naturalist voice of unadulterated objectivity.

Also in the naturalist vein, Palacio Valdés creates in *José* (1885) a group of women who together comprise the lowest dregs of society. In addition to resorting to physical violence against one another, they exhibit undesirable traits and crude behavior involving greed and self-interest, as in the case of Isabel's attempts to thwart her daughter Elisa's plans of marriage to the title character. Isabel's overpowering demeanor shadows the frailty of Elisa. A marked contrast exists in the mother-daughter relationship as the author develops the two as a portrayal of the dichotomy between the female figure as "monster" or "angel" (**angel del hogar*).

Continuing with the line of opposition typical in Palacio Valdés's narrative, characters in *Riverita* (1886) present another conflict between strong and weak. The display of power of Angela Guevara, Petra, and Anita over Julia and Maximina demonstrates the author's inability to deviate from the good versus evil, angel versus monster characterization of women. The plot of this novel continues in its sequel, *Maximina* (1887), in which the title character is positioned within the traditional patriarchal society, playing the role of dedicated, religious wife and mother.

Palacio Valdés explores the importance of religion in society in *El cuarto poder* (1888; The Fourth Estate), again employing the good versus evil dichotomy. Venturita, daughter of Doña Paula, represents those straying from the traditional spiritual life. Gonzalo breaks his plans for marriage to Venturita's sister Cecilia in order marry Venturita; the resulting union underscores a predominance of immorality over morality.

In the novel considered his most popular, *La hermana San Sulpicio* (1889; Sister San Sulpicio), Palacio Valdés explores numerous contrasts between Galicia and Seville as perceived by the Galician Ceferino Sanjurjo in his encounters with Sister San Sulpicio, or Gloria Bermúdez, the novice nun who at the opening of the novel has not taken her permanent vows. In following her to Sevilla, where she relinquishes her religious aspirations, Sanjurjo as narrator expresses his interpretations of Andalusian life that oppose his experience as a northerner. *La hermana San Sulpicio* portrays the female as exotic, as part of an almost foreign culture. She is viewed as "other" in terms of Sanjurjo's history and serves as a model of woman as foreigner in a male-dominated society.

The novels of Palacio Valdés published in the 1890s include few significant female characters. An illegitimate daughter, Clementina of *La espuma* (1892; Froth), the seductress Obdulia of *La fe* (1892; Faith), the sensual Amalia of *El maestrante* (1893; The Grandee), and the apparently perfect Cristina of *La alegría del capitán Ribot* (1899; The Joy of Captain Ribot) serve primarily to complement the male protagonists. The lack of importance placed on feminine contribution in these works does not surprise modern critics, given that the legitimacy of examining society from the feminine point of view was barely recognized. Palacio Valdés utilizes elements from both tendencies, leading to the injection of subjectivity and partiality, taboo for the naturalists who must follow the rules of objectivity and distancing within the narrative. In accord with literary tendencies of his time, women in Palacio Valdés's works were generally given a position of inferiority to male protagonists.

Work by

La espuma. Madrid: Castalia, 1990.
La fe. Oviedo: Grupo Editorial Asturiano, 1992.
La hermana San Sulpicio. Barcelona: Orbis, 1984.
Obras completas. Madrid: Aguilar, 1968.
Las tres novelas andaluzas: La Hermana San Sulpicio; Los Majos de Cádiz; Los Carmenes de Granada. Ed. José Luis Campal. Oviedo: Grupo Editorial Asturiano, 1995.

Work about

Dendle, Brian J. "Armando Palacio Valdés y el romanticismo." *Siglo Diecinueve* 4 (1998): 189–200.
———. "Erotismo y anticlericalismo en la primera edición de *Marta y María*." *Boletín de la Biblioteca Menéndez Pelayo* 65 (1989): 305–316.
———. *Spain's Forgotten Novelist: Armando Palacio Valdés* (1853–1938). Lewisburg, PA: Bucknell UP, 1995.
Glascock, Clyde. *Two Modern Spanish Novelists*. Austin: U of Texas P, 1926.
Pageaux, Daniel Henri. "Elements por une lecture de *La hermana San Sulpicio* de Armando Palacio Valdés." *Iberoromania* 16 (1982): 95–109.
Yáñez, María Paz. "Por una estética de la integración: *La hermana San Sulpicio* de Armando Palacio Valdés." *Siglo Diecinueve* 3 (1997): 69–87.

Lisa Nalbone

Palencia, Isabel de (1878–1974)

Born to the Oyarzábal family of Málaga, social activist and writer Isabel de Palencia was the daughter of a Scottish mother and a Spanish father. Her education in convent schools was typical of a young woman of her time, focusing on music, languages, and homemaking skills. She spent time visiting her mother's family in Great Britain, thereby becoming familiar with two cultures and two languages, although the Spanish culture predominated in most ways, to the extent that her Protestant mother converted to Catholicism. Her parents, however, especially her mother, held relatively liberal social views, so that she was granted much more freedom than other Spanish women of her generation. During her visits to Britain, Palencia was greatly influenced by the growing women's rights movement there. After her father's death, her mother accompanied her to Madrid, where she aspired to become an actress, in spite of the negative reaction of most of her mother's friends. Her acting career was of short duration, but she began to write and in collaboration with a friend established a magazine for women. This publication filled a great need for Spanish women, who had virtually no reading material since most people assumed that women had no interest in reading. As her career flourished, Palencia became the Spanish correspondent for the Laffan News Bureau in London. After a great deal of reflection about how such a serious step would change her life, she married Ceferino Palencia, the artist son of a playwright and actress. Abetted by her mother, before they married, she refused Ceferino's request that she give up her career, and he agreed to let her continue writing.

By 1915 Palencia had two small children, but at this point she was profoundly affected by the discovery that her husband was involved with another woman. She contemplated leaving him but instead threw herself with great fervor into the women's movement, speaking frequently at the Trade Union Headquarters and the Casa del Pueblo. Her commitment to women's rights and her growing political involvement on behalf of the workers resulted in her being chosen as the Spanish representative to the Congress of the International Suffrage Alliance in Geneva in 1921 and in Rome in 1923. Since they opposed the dictatorship of Primo de Rivera, the Palencias joyfully greeted the Republic in 1931. They both had active roles in the new government; she represented it at several conferences, including the League of Nations. In 1936 she was appointed ambassador to Sweden, the first Spanish woman ever to be so honored. Later she served simultaneously as the Spanish emissary to Finland. During the years of the Civil War, she frequently made trips to Spain and also spoke on behalf of the Spanish government in the United States, Canada, and the British House of Commons. The end of the war found the entire Palencia family, including their grandson, in Stockholm, whence they all immigrated to Mexico to build a new life there, still with the hope of returning to a free Spain. Their dream was never realized, of course, and the family remained in Mexico, where, along with other Spanish refugees, they had a remarkable impact on that country as they became incorporated into Mexican society and culture.

As might be expected, Palencia's social and political views were often reflected in her writing. Her autobiography, *I Must Have Liberty* (1940), was written and published in the United States in order to arouse support for the Republic in exile. Likewise, *Smouldering Freedom: The Story of the Spanish Republicans in Exile* (1945) was published in New York, presumably for the same purpose. She also published novels, short plays, essays, children's literature, and a book on Spanish regional costumes. See also Feminism in Spain: 1900–2000; Women's Situation in Spain: 1786–1931: The Awakening of Female Consciousness

Work by

The Agony of Spain. London: Labour Party, 1936.

En mi hambre mando yo. Mexico: Libro Mexicano, 1959.

I Must Have Liberty. New York: Longmans, Green and Company, 1940.

Juan, Son of the Fisherman. New York: Longmans, Green and Company, 1941.

The Regional Costumes of Spain. London: Batsford, 1926.

El sembrador sembró su semilla. Madrid: Librería Rivadeneyra, 1922/1923.

Smouldering Freedom: The Story of the Spanish Republicans in Exile. New York: Longmans, Green and Company, 1945.

Spain, Sweden, and Mexico. Mexico: Society of American Friends of the Mexican People, 1939.

Jean S. Chittenden

Palou, Inés (1923–1975)

Both chronologically and aesthetically, Inés Palou belongs to the so-called mid-century generation, post–Civil War cultivators of the neorealistic "social novel" whose primary focus was upon socioeconomic inequities and problems, tacitly assumed to result from policies of the Franco regime. Most such writers focus on the problems of workers and the poor; Palou differs in portraying a different social problem: the situation of women accused of crimes and imprisoned. Although she is not well known and completed only two novels, her explorations of life in women's prisons and the consequences of female incarceration will interest feminists and others studying women's problems.

Clearly evident autobiographical substrata undergird Palou's two novels, *Carne apaleada*

(Beaten Flesh) and *Operación dulce* (Sweet Operation), both published in 1975, the same year that the novelist committed suicide. Palou grew up in a solid middle-class family and was well educated for the period; she obtained a job whereby she achieved a moderate degree of autonomy and financial independence but then was accused of altering books of the firm employing her, convicted, and sentenced to prison. Little in Palou's works suggests that she was guilty; indeed, the attitudes expressed toward crime in her works combine apprehension and incomprehension, with crime viewed as some kind of infernal, Kafkaesque pit into which one might fall unawares but could never escape. It is believed that the desperation engendered by her inability to put the experience behind her provoked Palou's suicide.

Although there were a good many women imprisoned under the Franco regime as political prisoners, Palou's interest was specifically in the civil (as distinct from political) prisoner, those convicted of criminal behavior. Berta, the protagonist of *Carne apaleada*, a probable alter ego of the author, is forever changed by her imprisonment and several significant experiences during her incarceration. Several of the women she meets in prison exercise profound, mind-altering influences, and Berta is slowly transformed, changing from naive, timid, and passive to a woman who is stronger, braver, and more nurturing. Prison experiences also prompt her realization that she is a lesbian. The protagonist of *Operación dulce*, Caridad, appears as one of the secondary characters in Berta's story; in Caridad's own story, the reader learns much more about her, from the time an immature, inexperienced adolescent was drawn into crime in search of adventure and excitement, through her years behind prison walls, and the final futile struggle to escape her past and live a normal existence following her release. Like Berta, Caridad (whose possibly ironic name means "Charity") is a dynamic character who changes significantly in the course of the narrative, maturing and learning to make positive decisions and later struggling to break free from her former life of crime. This, unfortunately, proves to be beyond her control, and at novel's end she appears hopelessly trapped.

Palou's work is significant for various reasons: She was a skillful and talented narrator who mastered her craft quickly, producing skillfully wrought, well-structured, absorbing works; she dealt with subjects that few members of her generation (of either gender) cared to tackle; and she produced chronicles of lives and situations that are still valid today as records of the experiences, thoughts, and feelings of a much-silenced and marginalized group. Women as a whole were an oppressed group under the Franco regime, even when they had not run afoul of the law and the criminal "justice" system; perpetual minors under the law, they had few civil rights at best. Palou becomes the voice of what may have been Spain's most oppressed minority during the Franco years, women prisoners. Those especially interested in the topic may want to read the prison memoir by Dolores *Medio, *Atrapados en la ratonera: Memorias de una novelista* (1980; Caught in the Rat-Trap: Memoirs of a Novelist), chronicling her wartime imprisonment (of which a fictional version appears in *Diario de una maestra* [1961; A School-Teacher's Diary]), and psychiatrist Eva *Forest's *Onintze en el país de la democracia* (1985; Onintze in the Land of Democracy), a ferocious account of her horrendous experience as a political prisoner in the twilight months of the Franco regime when accused of complicity in the assassination of a ranking government minister, Admiral Carrero Blanco. All these women write from personal experience about women's prisons and women prisoners, as do Tomasa Cuevas and Teresa Pàmies concerning the years of the Civil War and its early aftermath. Palou's accounts are among the most carefully wrought, together with those of Medio.

Work by

Carne apaleada. Barcelona: Planeta, 1975.
Operación dulce. Barcelona: Planeta, 1975.

Work About

Cárdenas, Karen Hardy. "Female Morality in the Novels of Inés Palou." *Continental, Latin American and Francophone Women Writers, Vol. II.* Ed. Ginette Adamson and Eunice Myers. Lanham, MD: UP of America, 1990. 15–22.

Janet Pérez

Pardo Bazán, Emilia (1852–1921): Reception of Her by Male Colleagues, 1870–1921

In the strictest sense of the word she was an anomaly in literary Spain during the more than four decades of her own writing and publishing. Emilia Pardo Bazán was not simply a *poetisa* (woman poet) who occasionally published some sentimental verse that could warm bland hearts and pass beneath the notice of serious men of letters. Endowed with unflagging energy and a strong sense of self and vocation, she shunned the example of Fernán Caballero (1796–1877), George Sand (1803–1876), and George Eliot (1819–1880) by refusing to adopt a masculine pseudonym. Although her early life as the daughter of wealthy and socially prominent parents was conventional enough, her upbringing fostered real intellectual curiosity and provided her besides with the solid knowledge of the French language and culture that would prove important in her literary career. Also important was that her marriage on July 10, 1868, to José Quiroga y Pérez Deza was for love to a man only three years older than she and that she did not have children until 1876, 1879, and 1881. Hence, unlike many women of her class, she was not ruled over by a man who was her father or grandfather's age, and she had the time to read, study, and develop habits of intellectual work.

Through family contacts Pardo Bazán met in 1870 the prestigious Krausist philosopher Francisco Giner de los Ríos and undertook the program of reading and study he created for her. The first notice within the literary establishment of Pardo Bazán's arrival seems to be in a June 19, 1875, letter from the Krausist Gumersindo Laverde y Ruiz (1840–1890) to Marcelino Menéndez Pelayo (1856–1912), who was well on his way to being recognized as the leading Spanish academic of his time. The former notes that Galician periodicals are showing that Pardo Bazán and one Enriqueta González de Rubín (using, note well, the pseudonym "La Gallina Vieja" [The Old Hen]) may be added to "the list of woman writers." In 1876 Pardo Bazán wins a significant literary prize with her "Ensayo crítico de las obras del padre Feijóo" (Critical Essay on the Works of Father *Feijóo). By 1879 she publishes her first novel, *Pascual López*, and is corresponding on literary matters directly with Menéndez Pelayo, who already holds a chair of Spanish literature at the University of Madrid.

Despite the favorable notice *Pascual López* received from influential critic Manuel de la Revilla, and other successful literary projects, it was the great reaction to her study of Zola and French naturalism, titled *La cuestión palpitante* (The Burning Question), that changed her life. Published first between November 1882 and April 1883 as a series of 20 articles in the Madrid newspaper *La Epoca*, and then later in 1883 in book form, *La cuestión palpitante* seems today an innocuous work. Moreover, as Pardo Bazán admits in a letter to Menéndez Pelayo, *La cuestión palpitante* clearly suffers from its origins as a hardly revised version of hastily written newspaper pieces. Nonetheless, the articles and then the book, with a prologue by Leopoldo Alas (1852–1901), the leading critic of contemporary literature after the death of Revilla, placed their author at the center of then-contemporary literary debate over the aims and techniques of the novel. While extremely orthodox writers and the public, which normally were not readers of Zola, denounced the scandal for them of a Spanish woman of the upper classes writing about— but criticizing, it should be added—the fatalism and determinism associated with French naturalism, the Spanish literary establishment recognized and took seriously the social, cultural, and literary issues addressed by Pardo Bazán.

Hence, by the end of 1883, even though the *Los pazos de Ulloa* (1886; *The House of Ulloa*, 1992), her fifth novel and the one considered by many to be her masterpiece, is still in the future, Pardo Bazán is a part of the Spanish literary establishment, albeit as a woman whose high profile produces in 1883 the lifelong separation from a husband no longer able to accept her as she is and wishes to be. The 1886 translation, and prologue, by Albert Savine into French of *La cuestión palpitante* augments and extends beyond Spain the reputation of Pardo Bazán. A reading of different epistolary collections of literary figures in this period provides necessary context for the rest of our discussion: that it was always remembered that Pardo Bazán was a woman but that until the late 1880s she was judged by the establishment mainly on the merits of her critical and creative work.

The unique treatment she receives during this period for being a woman is revealed in the stated but not intentionally prejudicial way typical of the period. A letter from Leopoldo Alas to Benito Pérez Galdós (1843–1920), the dominant Spanish novelist of his period, is illustrative. Writing on July 3, 1885, Alas's note mentions his favorable review and opinion of Pardo Bazán's fourth novel, *El cisne de Vilamorta* (1884; *The Swan of Vilamorta*, 1891). Then, reacting to comments in a letter from Galdós to him, Alas states that he is happy that Galdós shares his high opinion of her, citing her talent, penetrating vision, and exceptional character for a Spanish woman. Now whatever this last ambiguous characterization may mean exactly, it is important to note that Pardo Bazán, no matter what the level of her achievement until then, is not "one of the boys." There is a noteworthy condescension toward her because she is a woman.

The public critical success of *Los pazos de Ulloa* gives no public evidence from the literary establishment of the kind of sexist res-

ervation regarding Pardo Bazán that Alas's above-cited comment hints at. While virtually all members of that establishment consider it a fine novel in its own right and the best of the author's five novels, fault is found with the prologue titled "Apuntes autobiográficos" (Autobiographical Notes). The important novelist José María *Pereda (1833–1906), for instance, praises the novel in a letter dated February 15, 1887, to Galdós but finds "intolerable and indigestible" the "Apuntes" because of their tone: that of a "semi-stupid, pretentious poor taste that knocks one down." Read today that characterization of the "Apuntes," which satisfied the editors' request for "notes on the author's life and works," seems out of place and incorrect. Instead the reader agrees with Pardo Bazán's laments about how infrequently Spanish authors write about themselves and wishes furthermore that Pereda, Galdós, Alas, and the rest would have followed her example.

Another aspect of the growing rejection of Pardo Bazán as a person is found in the senior Spanish novelist of the time: Juan *Valera (1824–1905). While his *Apuntes sobre el nuevo arte de escribir novelas* (1887) should be read as a perfectly professional response to *La cuestión palpitante*, containing points of agreement and disagreement with its author, his 1887 correspondence with Menéndez Pelayo is filled with a mixture of respect for much of Pardo Bazán's written work but a total disdain for her as an individual. She strikes him as a publicity- and fame-hungry person who engages in shameless networking in Spain and France and thereby is successful in advancing her career. For his part, Menéndez Pelayo admits in a June 29, 1887, letter to Valera that Pardo Bazán possesses "vast culture and ready intelligence and stylistic talent," but despite her fine treatment of him, he is fed up with her and that hers "is the most depraved taste in the world."

The next stage in Pardo Bazán's career intermingles the private and the public in the complex way of flesh-and-blood people. From

June or so in 1888 Pardo Bazán has two lovers. The more important because more greatly felt and of much longer duration seems to be Pérez Galdós. The other is more of an adventure, the magazine owner and editor José Lázaro Galdiano. In a letter to Galdós, which probably dates from November 1889, Pardo Bazán states the need to "emancipate herself" financially from her parents, upon whom she and her children have depended greatly since the separation from her husband. It concerns her that such aspects of her life as her intimate relations with Galdós—or with Lázaro Galdiano—are inconsistent with that dependence. She wants to support herself through her writing because that will justify her freedom of action in other regards. She characterizes the process through which she is passing as "a kind of transposition from the condition of woman to that of man." While acknowledging the contradictory aspects of this situation, she is firm in wanting to acquire and exercise those male virtues that foster independence but at the same time is very happy in her intimate relationship with Galdós. Unfortunately we know of Galdós's views on this matter only indirectly, but it seems that, as years later with Concha Ruth Morell and Teodosia Gandarias, Galdós found it stimulating to combine his professional and sentimental life with an intelligent woman. The contradictions and complexities of this relationship and of the situation of a late-nineteenth-century woman and man as they try to negotiate them find significant elaboration in three 1889 novels: Galdós's *La incógnita* and *Realidad* and Pardo Bazán's *Insolación (Midsummer Madness*, 1907), dedicated to Lázaro Galdiano "as a token of friendship." When read in conjunction with the Pardo Bazán–Galdós correspondence, the three novels give fictive reflections of how the writer/lovers dealt with such issues as: what Pardo Bazán referred to as her "material infidelity" to Galdós with Lázaro Galdiano; the distinct sets of rules of sexual morality for men and

women; and the discovery by a woman of her own right to independence and freedom.

The years 1889–1892 mark not only the increasing creative and critical productivity and public acknowledgment of Pardo Bazán in Spanish society—including the inheritance from her father of the royally acknowledged papal title countess of Pardo Bazán but also the more or less public rejection of her by the literary establishment. The same years are also characterized by Pardo Bazán's militant feminist period; her discourse/essay "La educación del hombre y la de la mujer: Sus diferencias" (The Education of Man and That of Woman: Their Differences) and her founding of the book collection "The Woman's Library" are typical of her activities, with the discourse/essay developing fully ideas already outlined in the 1886 "Apuntes autobiográficos." This is the context in which letters between Menéndez Pelayo and Pereda show both to be fierce opponents of her pretensions to become a member of the Spanish Royal Academy of the Language for the same nonprofessional, blatantly sexist reasons that Valera expresses in the essay, published under pseudonym, titled "Las mujeres y las academias. Cuestión social inocente" (1891; Women and Academies. An Innocent Social Question). Part of Pereda's hostility and soon that of Leopoldo Alas is produced by the editorial policies of Lázaro Galdiano for his journal *La España Moderna*. Along with Alas, Menéndez Pelayo, Valera, Galdós, *Campoamor, Echegaray, *Palacio Valdés, and other leading cultural figures, Pardo Bazán is listed on the first of December 1889 editorial board of *La España Moderna*. But soon Alas and Pereda, apparently without being privy to the intimate relations of Pardo Bazán with Galdós and Lázaro Galdiano, become convinced that Lázaro in fact gives precedence to her articles over theirs. For reasons of pride and finances this situation leads to a complete break of Pardo Bazán with Alas and Pereda. Each new review or reply by Alas, Pereda, or Pardo Bazán to a new book of the other side becomes more negative and personal. Pardo Bazán's "Los resquemores de Pereda" (Pereda's Itches), a criticism of Pereda's view of the critical establishment expressed in *Nubes de estío* (1891), is answered by his February 1891 newspaper article "Las comezones de la señora Pardo Bazán" (Ms. Pardo Bazán's Tinglings). A little later in the year, in his letter of June 17 to Galdós, Alas mocks Pardo Bazán's favorable 1891 review of Father Coloma's *Pequeñeces* (1891; *Currita, Countess of Albornoz*, 1900); then, in a way that perhaps reflects more directly than any other the feelings of much of the male literary establishment toward her, the truly great Leopoldo Alas descends to the ultimate *ad mulierem* attack by affirming: *Es una puta, hombre* (Man, she's a whore). This of a woman who by then has published 11 volumes of fiction and many others of literary and cultural study and whose firm place in the living literary history of Spain cannot be in doubt!

The culmination of Pardo Bazán's deteriorating relations with the male literary establishment comes in the last decade of her life when some of her chief opponents—Alas, Valera, Pereda—are already dead. Even though she continued to write tomes of short stories, some very important novels, and scholarly studies, for example, the novel *La quimera* (1905; The Chimera) and *La literatura francesa moderna* (3 vols., 1910, 1912, 1914; Modern French Literature), two of her goals were not realized: She was never elected to the Spanish Academy, and the professors at the University of Madrid—who added Menéndez Pelayo to their number at his 22 years of age—never allowed her to be one of them. When the minister of national education Julio Burell tried in 1916 to frustrate this totally prejudicial situation by naming Pardo Bazán to the chair of Neo-Latin Languages and Literatures, the male establishment and students found it easy to circumvent Burell's action: Since the course she gave was not an obligatory part of the curriculum, it was simply boycotted, and within a short time Pardo Bazán desisted in giving classes to an empty room. The reader can speculate upon the ironies associated with the University of Madrid suspending classes for a day upon Pardo Bazán's death in 1921 and consider besides the lessons to be garnered from the fate Pardo Bazán's many merits suffered in the Spain of her day. *See also* Poetry by Spanish Women Writers: 1800–1900; Short Fiction by Women Writers: 1800–1900

Work by

"Apuntes autobiográficos." *Obras completas.* Vol. 3. Madrid: Aguilar, 1973. 698–732.
Cartas a Galdós. Madrid: Turner, 1975.

Work about

Bieder, Maryellen. "Women, Literature, and Society: The Essays of Emilia Pardo Bazán." *Spanish Women Writers and the Essay: Gender, Politics and the Self.* Ed. and intro. Kathleen Glenn and Mercedes Mazquiarán de Rodríguez. Columbia: U of Missouri P, 1998. 25–54.
Bravo Villasante, Carmen. *Vida y obra de Emilia Pardo Bazán.* Madrid: E.M.E.S.A., 1973.
Clemessy, Nelly. *Emilia Pardo Bazán como novelista.* 2 vols. Madrid: Fundación Universitaria Española, 1981.
Hoffman, Joan. " 'Torn Lace' and Other Transformations: Rewriting the Bride's Script in Selected Stories by Emilia Pardo Bazán." *Hispania* 82.2 (May 1999): 238–245.
Ortega, Soledad, ed. *Cartas a Galdós.* Madrid: Revista de Occidente, 1964.
Pattison, Walter T. *Emilia Pardo Bazán.* New York: Twayne, 1971.
Revuelta Sañudo, Manuel, ed. *Marcelino Menéndez Pelayo. Epistolario.* 23 vols. Madrid: Fundación Universitaria Española, 1982–1991.
Rodríguez, Adna Rosa. *La cuestión feminista en los ensayos de Emilia Pardo Bazán.* Sada: Edicións do Castro, 1991.

Stephen Miller

Pasamar, Pilar Paz (1933–)

Poet Pilar Paz Pasamar was born in Jerez de la Frontera (Andalusia) where she received her primary and secondary education. During her university years, she was strongly attracted to the theater, although she had already begun writing poetry, publishing her first collection, *Mara* (1951), when barely 18. Her fledgling effort was highly praised by the dean of Spanish poets, Juan Ramón *Jiménez, then living in exile and one of the century's most exigent critics. The collection, primarily metaphysical in orientation, completely disconnected from contemporary literary currents of social realism, independent of other poets of the day, and unrelated to cultural context or immediate surroundings, presents a search for God, a poetic universe of pantheistic quietism, solitude, and existential doubt. Pasamar dialogues both with the deity and with poetry per se.

In 1954, Pasamar's second book, *Los buenos días* (The Good Days), was runner-up to poet Claudio Rodríguez for the 1953 Adonais Poetry Prize (both books coincidentally express metaphysical quests, a search for ultrasensorial essence). Critics have detected in Pasamar's two initial books echoes of the mature Juan Ramón Jiménez, especially in his most hermetic work, *Dios deseado y deseante* (God Desired and Desiring). Similar poetic inspiration and themes are repeated in *Ablativo amor* (1956; Ablative Love) and *Del abreviado mar* (1957; Concerning the Abbreviated Sea), both of which employ much the same intrinsic conception of poetic language, although styles diverge. Sonnets predominate in *Ablativo amor* with much freer forms used in *Del abreviado mar* where something resembling free verse evokes the interior monologue. The thematic nucleus of *Ablativo amor* consists of existential concerns, an urgent quest in search of an increasingly silent God. The poet's struggle with loneliness takes place against the backdrop of her love for nature and humanity. In *Del abreviado mar*, meditations upon God are cast in maritime language well known to Pasamar, a resident of the port of Cádiz since the time of her marriage (while still a university student). *La soledad, contigo* (1960; Solitude, With You) continues seeking God in the minutiae and trivia of quotidian existence, in daily happenings of the poet's domestic

world, searching for the Holy Spirit in herbs and spices of her kitchen. Retaining something of the earlier pantheistic spirit, this book is more human and concrete, less abstract in its language, and unmistakably feminine. Filled with maternal duties and domestic tasks, it is a book that could only have been written by a woman; the author's pleasures and frustrations are likewise strongly gendered female. In 1964, Pasamar published a lengthy essay, *Poesía femenina de lo cotidiano* (Feminine Poetry of Every-Day Things).

Violencia de lo inmóvil (1967; Motionless Violence), the most disquieting collection to date by Pasamar, treats life's mysteries, and especially Mystery, life's ultimate meaning, contrasting quotidian perceptions of the world with abstract, intellectualized vision. The text shuttles between clarity and indefiniteness, concreteness and ambiguity, with images no longer drawn from the domestic world and maternal experience but from more literary contexts, including contemporary intertexts. Rather than a compilation of individual poems, this book comprises a single, uninterrupted lyric discourse.

Both by reason of her Andalusian origins and residence as well as chronologically, Pasamar belongs to the poetic group known as "Platero" (a southern branch of the "mid-century generation" or Generation of the 1950s, including poets José M. Caballero Bonald, Julio Mariscal, Fernando Quiñones, José Luis Tejada, and others, with whom Pasamar participated in literary *tertulias* and collaborated in publishing a literary magazine—contacts that set her apart from many women poets). Her poetic concerns were always very personal, however, differing from the predominantly "social" poetry of the "Platero" group. Following her 1957 marriage and numerous children, Pasamar renounced her writing during a 15-year hiatus between *Violencia inmóvil* and *La torre de Babel y otros asuntos* (1982; The Tower of Babel and Other Matters). Rather than a thematically integrated whole, this is a compilation of mostly unrelated, previously unpublished works. *La alacena* (1985; The Kitchen Cabinet), an interesting anthology, contains excerpts from all of Pasamar's earlier collections, as well as from *Orario* (then a work in progress whose title—a play on homophones—alludes both to timetable and prayer schedule).

Pasamar, while not feminist, is distinctly feminine in both discourse and in her thematics, a poet of intelligence, taste, humor, and refined sensibility. With clearly defined major preoccupations that range from the maternal and domestic to the metaphysical and transcendental, Pasamar offers both depth and breadth. Her metrics are as varied as her themes, her lyrics finely crafted, and some metaphors exquisitely wrought. She becomes the voice of another long-silenced and usually silent cohort, women involved in domestic tasks, expressing varied facets of this aspect of women's condition, at the same time that she continues her metaphysical and existential quest. Definitely her own person, Pasamar is a delightful read.

Work by

Los buenos días. Madrid: Rialp, 1954.
Del abreviado mar. Madrid: Agora, 1957.
Mara. Madrid: Altamira, 1951.
Retraso de la primavera y otras obras de teatro infantil. Santiago: Andrés Bello, 1985. Contains work of Pasamar and others.
La soledad, contigo. Arcos de la Frontera: Alcaraván, 1960.

Janet Pérez

Pastoral Literature

See Diana, La (1559)

Pedrero, Paloma (1957–   )

She first participated in stage productions during her high school years and then studied sociology and theater arts at the University of Madrid. In the early 1980s she acted and coauthored texts for the independent theater group Cachivache, whose creative efforts encompassed children's theater and experimental works. As a professional actor, Pedrero's search for plays that addressed social problems of the day and portrayed the personal conflicts of individuals led her to begin writing her own full-length works. Her dramatic production has spoken especially to the problems of the troubled youth of democratic Spain and has been well received by younger spectators. In 1984 she won a prestigious award for *La llamada de Lauren . . .* (1987; The Call of Lauren), which led to its professional staging in 1985 with Pedrero herself acting in the role of Rosa. Since this time, her plays have been successfully produced both in Spain and abroad. Her works have inspired much enthusiasm among Hispanists and especially feminist critics in recent years. She currently resides in Madrid where she continues to perform on stage and writes poetry as well as scripts for theater, television, and film. She also contributes frequently to the theater journal *Primer Acto*.

Pedrero's theatrical production to date portrays present-day situations and psychological conflicts with a realistic style that is direct and accessible to her audiences. At the same time, however, her plays have a poetic and dramatic force that is due in part to her adept use of symbols and visual images that come to dominate the action. Well constructed and succinct, her works create a dramatic tension that holds the spectator's attention until the final curtain. They often touch sensitive nerves, inspiring heated debates among theatergoers and critics. By means of metatheatrical techniques that include play-acting and disguises as well as altered states of consciousness induced by alcohol or other methods, Pedrero reveals the innermost struggles of her characters in their search for personal truth, freedom, and identity. Common themes include loneliness, frustration, and love as a positive or destructive force. Personal relationships are at the core of Pedrero's works, which often focus on the effects of the changing roles of men and women in contemporary society. Frequently dealing with emotionally charged issues and portraying characters from society's fringes, her plays both fascinate and disturb her public.

Several of Pedrero's works are written for two characters, and their action consists of an intense process of self-examination and discovery that takes place in a few hours. These plays examine interpersonal relationships that include marriage, dating, friendship, casual acquaintance, and the bond between parent and child. In *La llamada de Lauren*, her most controversial work to date, a young married couple prepares to celebrate carnival by donning disguises, he as Lauren Bacall and she as Humphrey Bogart. The lighthearted game of cross-dressing suddenly turns serious when the husband Pedro reveals his deep-seated resentment of his traditional masculine role, imposed upon him from childhood. The audience, like the young wife Rosa, reacts with surprise and then horror as Pedro bares his soul and confesses his true feelings that have homosexual overtones. The play's conclusion is ambiguous. Rosa accepts the truth her husband has revealed and helps him prepare to go out alone dressed as Lauren, but once alone she gives way to tears. Spectators are left questioning the way in which gender roles dictate attitudes and limit personal identity and freedom.

Resguardo personal (1988; Personal Protection) is a one-act play that portrays the breakdown of a marriage and all communication between husband and wife. Determined to hurt each other, a couple fights over custody of their dog, and their argument reveals the husband's controlling behavior that has objectified his wife. In the short time of their separation, she has become aware of her desperate need to discover her identity apart from her husband. In a surprise ending, typical of Pedrero's dramaturgy, the audience learns that the wife has been "acting" in order to trick her husband into believing that the dog has been put to sleep. The dog's appearance at the play's conclusion marks the woman's personal triumph and an important step toward independence.

The problematic friendship between two women artists is the subject of *El color de agosto* (1989; *The Color of August*, 1994), first staged in 1988. Laura and María are reunited after eight years of separation in which María has enjoyed success in both her career and her personal life. Laura, the more talented painter of the two, has been forced to work as a model to make ends meet. By means of a series of metatheatrical games that vacillate between violence and tenderness, the two characters uncover the conflicting demands of creativity and relationships for the woman artist. Due in part to the alcohol they have consumed, they are able to take off their masks and express with the passion indicated by the play's title their most intimate needs and desires. Through their self-examination it becomes clear that as women they are subject to mental paradigms that lead them to depend on others, rendering difficult their creative vocation. By the play's end both characters have come to the realization that they must free themselves from dependence on others in both their personal and professional lives.

Three one-act plays presented together with the title *Noches de amor efímero* (1991; Nights of Ephemeral Love) scrutinize nights of intimacy between strangers from a feminine perspective. The night is the time in the three works for the blurring of reality and fiction, and it makes possible, for a fleeting moment, the illogical. In *Esta noche en el parque* (Tonight in the Park) a young woman seeks revenge for having been seduced and then abandoned by an older man in a previous encounter. Humiliated, she attempts to usurp the role of aggressor, demanding at knifepoint that the man give her the orgasm she feels he owes her. She is unsuccessful, however, in her "masculine" role, and at the play's conclusion she herself is the victim of the knife. The final image on stage is that of the woman's lifeless body on a swing. *La noche dividida* (A Night Divided, 1994) is a more lighthearted look at a chance meeting between a man and woman. An actress who awaits a call from her French lover, who has controlled her life, invites in a door-to-door Bible salesman. The two discover, with the help of alcohol, that they have much in common and are able to comfort each other. In the play's final scene the French lover arrives to find the couple asleep in a hammock. The third play of the trilogy, *Solos esta noche* (Alone Tonight), takes place in a Madrid subway station. This work begins as an extremely frightening experience for a middle-class woman who finds herself alone with an unemployed, homeless man, waiting for a train that never arrives. By the play's conclusion, however, the woman has come to understand how many beliefs and values the two share and how alike they are as human beings. She is content to spend the night in the arms she is offered by her companion, no longer a stranger.

Although *Una estrella* (1995; A Star) includes four characters, it resembles Pedrero's two-character works in that the action centers on the intense examination of a relationship and takes place in a short period of time. Estrella, the female protagonist, is a 30-year-old writer who drinks coffee in a bar and takes notes on the atmosphere and the men gambling in the adjoining room. After the bartender tries unsuccessfully to force her to leave, a man who has already had too much to drink enters the bar. He strikes up a conversation with Estrella, claiming to have been a friend of her father. The play focuses on the problematic relationship between a daughter and her absent father who over the years spent his time drinking and gambling. As frequently occurs in Pedrero's theater, metatheatrical role-playing makes it possible for underlying motives and personal truths to be revealed. Gender and generational conflicts are confronted, and the work concludes with reconciliation between father and daughter. The two have gained a new understanding and are able to view the events of the past from the perspective of the other.

Pedrero has written to date three plays that include several characters and take place over a longer span of time. In two of her earlier works, *Besos de lobo* (1987; Wolf Kisses) and *Invierno de luna alegre* (1987; Winter of Happy Moon), a female character is the pivotal point of the action, around which four male characters revolve. *El pasamanos* (1995; The Handrail) portrays an elderly couple's struggle with the injustice and lack of true compassion in today's society.

Besos de lobo takes place in a small Castilian town and covers 10 years in the life of Ana, the young protagonist. The play centers on her relationships with her father, her homosexual friend, her suitor, and her absent lover. A strange and reclusive woman, Ana's life is a mystery for the spectator as she remains silent about events of her past. In her silence, however, her actions reveal her inner world and her fear of society's judgment. Only with Luciano, her homosexual friend, does she feel safe to be herself, engaging in play-acting and storytelling. As the years pass, Ana is reputed among the townspeople to be a madwoman and a witch. She herself doubts her sanity and attempts to take her life upon the death of her father, only to change her mind at the last moment. Without explanation, the play's last scene shows Ana waiting for a train, ready to leave the small town. She explains that a telegram from her absent lover has opened her eyes to the way in which she has lost precious time waiting and not living. Her lover arrives in the same train she will take to leave. The two never see each other, and upon reading the note she left for him, Raúl realizes that he has arrived too late. Pedrero's surprise ending subverts the work's intertextual allusions to *García Lorca's (1898–1936) Doña Rosita la soltera*. Unlike Rosita, Ana has found her voice at the play's conclusion, and she expresses her desire to live and to grow, looking for her own identity, apart from dependence on any man.

Invierno de luna alegre presents on stage the lives of vagabonds and street performers who live on the fringes of society in contemporary Madrid. In contrast to Pedrero's other plays, this work does not delve so much into the inner conflicts of its characters. It is like her other works, however, in that it focuses on the individual's search for love and personal freedom. Reyes, the only female character, is a young woman who has never known the comforts of home and family and began stealing at an early age. She meets Olegario, an aging former bullfighter, on the street where he presents his show for passersby. The two become friends as she contributes her musical abilities to his performance and shares his room in a rundown boardinghouse. The other three male characters are friends or neighbors of Olegario, also on the down and out, who all find themselves attracted to his vivacious roommate. Much to Olegario's consternation, Estrella becomes romantically involved with Víctor, his young and athletic neighbor who is studying computer science. In spite of her obvious feelings for Olegario, Reyes abandons him at the play's end, having been offered a chance to work in a chorus line.

Generational conflicts and the materialism of today's world are the subject of one of Pedrero's most recent work, *El pasamanos*. This play presents on stage the problems of society's weakest and most vulnerable members, the very old. An elderly couple's demand for a handrail that will make it possible for them to lead normal lives is portrayed on television by pseudojournalists only interested in the story's commercial potential. The televised version of the couple's plight humiliates the two and does not result in the justice they seek. It is revealed in the play's second scene that instead of convincing their landlady to provide the needed handrail, the program's producers have themselves had one installed. They plan to show viewers the couple's reaction, hoping for an emotional scene. The play's conclusion is ambiguous as the furious handicapped man falls on the stairs and then is undecided whether to try to leave his home or not. Like so many of Pedrero's characters, he finds himself alienated in a depersonalized society. Unwilling

to give in, however, he will attempt through whatever means possible to gain control of his life in a chaotic world. *See also* Drama by Spanish Women Writers: 1970–2000; Feminist Theory and the Contemporary Spanish Stage

Work by

Besos de lobo; Invierno de luna alegre. Madrid: Fundamentos, 1987.

Juego de noche. Nueve obras en un acto. Ed. Virtudes Serrano. Madrid: Cátedra, 1999.

Parting Gestures: Three Plays. Trans. Phyllis Zatlin. University Park, PA: Estreno, 1994. Contains *The Color of August, A Night Divided, The Voucher*.

Work about

Hodge, Polly J. "Poetic Drama, Images, and Windows: *Aliento de equilibrista* by Paloma Pedrero and Isabel Ordaz." *Estreno* 23.2 (Fall 1997): 30–37.

Leonard, Candyce. "Body, Sex, Women: The Struggle for Autonomy in Paloma Pedrero's Theater." *La Chispa '97: Selected Proceedings*. Ed and prol. Claire J. Paolini. New Orleans: Tulane, 1997. 245–254.

Rodríguez, Alfredo López Vázquez. "La mujer en el teatro español del siglo XX: De María Martínez Sierra a Paloma Pedrero." *Estudios sobre mujer, lengua y literatura*. Ed. Aurora Marco. Santiago de Compostela, Spain: ULPGC—USCompostela, 1996. 121–136.

Carolyn Harris

Pensadora Gaditana, La (1763–1764)

This eighteenth-century periodical, whose title translates as The [Female] Cádiz Thinker, is the first one written in Spain for a female audience. Its author was a Cádiz-born writer who used the pen name Beatriz de *Cienfuegos. She wrote her *Pensamientos* (Thoughts) as an answer to the male views expressed by José Clavijo y Fajardo (1726–1806), who also used a pseudonym (José Alvarez Valladares) to write *El Pensador* (1762–1767), a weekly with "Thoughts" commenting on the moral and cultural concerns of the Spanish Enlightenment. Clavijo denounced manners of contemporary society such as the *petimetre* (dandy), marriage, bullfights, false prudery, and *cortejos* (courtship). In her first *pensamiento*, Cienfuegos explains that she writes because it is time to have articles written by a woman capable of thinking after reflection, offering prudent correction, chastising with maturity, and criticizing with humor.

The *Pensadora*'s true identity became an issue in her own day. Today the lack of historical records has moved some critics to assert that a man is hidden under her pseudonym, possibly a priest, who used a woman's name to more credibly address women's concerns. In her articles, Cienfuegos herself refers several times to this controversy, insisting on her need as a woman to use a pseudonym. She asserts that no one will ever know her identity.

Fifty-two issues of her paper, dealing with all sorts of contemporary concerns of the Spanish Enlightenment, were published between 1763 and 1764. Her *pensamientos* discussed social issues, mostly of a moral and cultural nature, for example, men's effeminacy, the evils of excessive luxury, dress styles, parents' lack of concern in choosing the right husbands for their daughters, love, life in the country, death, *maridos-cortejos* (husbands-wooing). In 1786, the 52 issues were collected into a four-volume set. *See also* Women's Situation in Spain: 1700–1800

Work by

La Pensadora Gaditana. Cádiz: Manuel Ximénez Carreño, 1786.

Work about

Clavijo y Fajardo, José. El Pensador Matritense. Barcelona: D. Pedro Angel de Torazona, 1774.

Ferreras, Daniel F. "Fictional Strategies in El pensador matritense by José Clavijo y Fajardo." Hispania 78 (December 1995): 780–787.

Serrano y Sanz, Manuel. Apuntes para una biblioteca de escritoras españolas desde el año 1401 al 1833. 2 vols. Madrid: Rivadeneyra, 1903–1905.

Sullivan, Constance. "Gender, Text, and Cross-Dressing: The Case of 'Beatriz Cienfuegos' and La Pensadora Gaditana." Dieciocho 18.1 (Spring 1995): 27–47.

María A. Salgado

Pereda, José María de (1833–1906): His Portrayal of Women

A seasoned intellectual of the realist movement and member of the Generation of 1868, José María de Pereda is one of the great regionalist writers. Novels set in his *patria chica* (hometown) area of Santander have proven his most convincing realist fiction. Most criticism, much of which is either in the form of monographic studies or biographical in nature, has neglected to closely examine the female characters playing secondary roles in his works.

El buey suelto (1878; The Bachelor), Pereda's first *novela de tesis* (thesis novel), depicts the life of Gedeón, a bachelor determined to live in defiance of religious traditions; he lives and dies alone in spite of being the father of two children. Secondary characters of the work are used to construct the thesis against bachelorhood that at the same time attacks nineteenth-century bourgeois society. The poor servant Solita plays the role of submissive female who depends on the male character for her own personality. She falls in love with Gedeón and bears two children before he rejects her. Another female character, Regla, represents the unsuccessful attempts to change Gedeón's opinion of marriage. The text's rejection of marriage can also be perceived as a rejection of the feminine in that female characters create a sense of frustration in Gedeón, and they make no contributions to his life nor, by extension, to the life of nineteenth-century man in general. Another negative portrayal of the female is found in Osmunda, wife of the title character in *Don Gonzalo González de la Gonzalera* (1879). As a nagging wife whose actions serve as public humiliation of Don Gonzalo, Osmunda plays only a secondary role in plot development.

In *De tal palo, tal astilla* (1880; A Chip off the Old Block), following the death of Doña Marta, her daughters Agueda and Pilar become charges of Sotero Barredera, Doña Marta's majordomo. Sotero is in love with

Agueda and competes with the rival suitor Fernando, a liberal, freethinking atheist. The sisters' need for protection underscores their circumstances as weak creatures unable to survive on their own. Sotero, Fernando, and later Sotero's nephew each pursue marriage to Agueda, positioning the male character as caretaker responsible for the well-being of the feminine condition. The failure of each to do so reflects the breakdown of religious acumen more than a sense of power in Agueda. After her rejection, Fernando commits suicide. The implications of Agueda as a good wife, *pura, recta y enamorada* (pure, honest and in love) according to the author, are never realized, leading to the futility of characterizing a role that would never be. González Herrán considers Agueda as protagonist in this novel, citing commentaries of Menéndez Pelayo, Montesinos, Antonio Valbuena, and F.B. Navarro. Agueda's outspokenness and her strong personality invite the conflict with Fernando that ends in his suicide.

Although considered the best of Pereda's first-series novels, *El sabor de la tierruca* (1882; The Feel of the Good Earth) deals primarily with contemporary political issues and excludes the role of women except as companions to the politicians' children. As a biographical note, Madariaga del Campo confirms that the figure of Ana coincides with that of Pereda's own daughter María, suggesting that the daughter as secondary to the male figure of the novel imitated reality.

Pereda's two opposing female characters who serve as Pedro Sánchez's love interest in the 1883 novel of the same name again play only a secondary role in plot development. Pedro Sánchez expresses his preference for Clara, a superficial woman who sees a relationship with Pedro as one of social convenience. Montesinos noted that Pereda avoids profound character development in feminine figures, and *Pedro Sánchez* is no exception. Klibbe points to Pereda's general failure to portray women in compelling fashion, with the exception of the title character of *Sotiliza*

(1885), who is a believable, independent figure.

Klibbe finds physical and moral strength in Pereda's portrayal of Silda, known also as Sotileza. Three male characters, Cleto, Muergo, and Andrés, vie for Sotileza's attention; the actions of brutal Muergo manage to gain her interest. Montes Huidobro finds this a logical development, considering that Sotileza grew up in an environment of cruelty and was likely to prefer the brutal appeal of Muergo. However, it is Andrés who then asks for her hand in marriage after an innocent conversation between the two is misconstrued as an amorous liaison. Sotileza questions authority and refutes the necessity of marriage based solely on the restoration of her *honor that was not tainted in the first place. The character Sotileza is unprecedented in Pereda's narrative and has inspired criticism, both in support of and against the will of Silda. The role of female in pursuit of the male has been reversed here, for it is Cleto, Muergo, and Andrés who seek the attentions of Silda. While Menéndez Pelayo and Laureano Bonet agree that Pereda fails to paint a strong feminine protagonist, Navarro, Leopoldo Alas, and Gumersindo Laverde judge Pereda's creation of Sotileza to be masterful, as stated by González Herrán.

Montes Huidobro alludes to erotic elements in *Sotileza* such as the key used by Carpia to lock Silda and Andrés in a room together with the intentions of dishonoring the couple, which the critic associates with its Jungian interpretation as a reference to sexual intimacy. The concept of combining pleasure with pain is evident in the scene in which Silda sews a button on Cleto's pants, even though the day before he had kicked her out of his way instead of asking her to step aside. Despite Sotileza's independence and mental fortitude, she offers justification for accepting his behavior, since he is not evil but *bruto* (ignorant). In all, the characterization of Silda depends on the naturalist movement for its definition. Pereda focuses on the dismal, harsh environment surrounding Sotileza and treats her, according to Montesinos, as the bright star in a sky of darkness.

The role of women returns to secondary sphere in *Peñas arriba* (1895; The Peaks Above) in which Facia, a noteworthy female character, breaks the mold of traditional, subservient maiden and attempts to blackmail protagonist Celso. She meets her demise in a freezing snowstorm. Facia's role as the *mujer gris* (equivocal lady) contrasts directly with that of Lita, future bride of Marcelo, Celso's nephew and successor. However, since little conflict surrounds the sentiments of Lita and Marcelo, their relationship is basically free of obstacles, making Lita a conventional female prototype whose worth is measured by that of her husband. According to Medina, she represents the typical devout Catholic woman with maternal instinct and domestic aspirations. Montesinos considers her one of the most unsatisfactory of the Peredian gallery of feminine types. Nevertheless, Lita stands out in the Peredian narrative as the feminine character that comes closest to the female figure in her demeanor and description.

In the novel that most closely approximates the naturalist tendency, *La Montálvez* (1888), both Verónica and her daughter Luz demonstrate qualities that classify them as powerful protagonists. Bonet studies the *deserotización* (de-eroticizing) utilized by Pereda in his description of Luz, which combines the forces of nature with the expected fatalistic plot development of the novel. Verónica's efforts to secure a more comfortable life for herself and her daughter fail amidst the limitations of naturalistic determinism, based on Verónica's experience of familial breakdown. Her character contrasts markedly with Pereda's own strong religious faith in that Verónica's life contains details that separate her from the Catholic ideal. Pereda offers insights into her psyche via the narrator and through Verónica's autobiographical notes; this double view suggests that Verónica is partly responsible for her destiny within the

deterministic framework of this naturalist novel. And finally, only minimal character development of the female figure can be found in *La puchera* (1889; The Stew) and Pereda's last two novels, *Nubes de estío* (Summer Clouds) and *Al primer vuelo* (On the First Flight), both published in 1891. Inés, Irene, and Nieves each conform to the model of the feminine as the powerless figure.

Pereda's convincing reality is conservative and suspicious of the democratic liberalism of his day. He created the literary prototype of the late-nineteenth-century bourgeois Cantabrian man and woman: man as the central figure of importance and woman as a secondary figure. In his fiction, Pereda mirrored his own condition in society and transmitted his own religious convictions through his protagonists.

Work by

El buey suelto. Bocetos al temple. Santander: Tanin, 1990.

Don Gonzalo González de la Gonzalera. Santander: Tanin, 1991.

Obras completas de José María de Pereda. Santander: Tanin, 1989.

Peñas arriba. Barcelona: Planeta, 1992.

Work about

Bonet, Laureano. "Asexuación e ideología en las figuras femeninas de Pereda." *Insula* 342 (1975): 3.

González Herrán, José M. *La obra de Pereda ante la crítica literaria de su tiempo.* Santander: Colección Pronillo, 1983.

Klibbe, Laurence H. *José María de Pereda.* Boston: Twayne, 1975.

Madariaga del Campo, Benito. *Pereda: Biografía de un novelista.* Santander: Librería Estudio, 1991.

Medina, Jeremy T. *Spanish Realism: The Theory and Practice of a Concept in the Nineteenth Century.* Potomac: Studia Humanitatis, 1979.

Montes Huidobro, Matías. "Un retrato femenino: Erótica de *Sotileza*." *Hispanófila* 25 (1982): 17–31.

Montesinos, José F. *Pereda o la novela de idilio.* Madrid: Castalia, 1969.

Serven, Carmen. "La mujer a la moda en la obra novelística de José María Pereda y Juan Valera: Dos opiniones divergentes." *Actas del XI Simposio de la Sociedad Española de Literatura General y Comparada.* Ed. Tua Blesa, María Teresa Cacho, et al. Zaragoza: Universidad de Zaragoza, 1994. 1: 371–375.

Lisa Nalbone

Pérez de Ayala, Ramón (1880–1962): His Portrayal of Women

In some of his later novels, Ramón Pérez de Ayala attacks a series of myths (the word *myth* is used following the definition presented by Roland Barthes in *Mythologies* where myth is a type of discourse) that have been established as social truths. These myths deal primarily with the themes of sexuality and the role of women in society. By presenting them, Pérez de Ayala attempts to also show the negative repercussions suffered by the patriarchal society that supports them.

A novelist, critic, poet, and essayist, Pérez de Ayala was born in Oviedo Asturias. He studied law in Oviedo, and there met Clarín (Alas). After traveling in Europe and the United States, in 1916 he became a war correspondent for *La Prensa* of Buenos Aires. He served as ambassador to England during the Second Republic but moved to Paris in 1936 due to political disturbances in Spain. In 1940 he went to Argentina to continue his journalistic writing and remained there until 1954 when he decided to return to Spain, residing in Madrid until his death in 1962.

Although the foundation of his inspiration is the intellectual essay, the novel constitutes Pérez de Ayala's most valuable artistic contribution. According to the author himself, his novels belong to two main phases. The first one includes primarily novels of an autobiographical nature, such as *Tinieblas en las cumbres* (1907; Darkness on the Heights), *A.M.D.G.* (1910; To the Greater Glory of God), *La pata de la raposa* (1912; The Fox's Paw), and *Troteras y danzaderas* (1913; Mummers and Dancers). This phase is followed by a transitional period with the publication of three "poematic novels," titled *Prometeo* (Prometheus), *Luz de domingo* (Sunday Sunlight) and *La caída de los limones* (The Fall of the House of Lemons), all from 1916. The

second phase that follows is characterized by "great theme" works and includes what some consider to be among the best novels in Spanish literature: *Belarmino y Apolonio* (1921), *Las novelas de Urbano y Simona* (1923; The Novels of Urbano and Simona), *Tigre Juan* (1926; Tiger Juan), and its second part, *El curandero de su honra* (1926; The Healer of His Honor).

Of the "great theme" works, *Las novelas de Urbano y Simona* stands apart for its treatment of sexuality and women. In this novel, which is composed of two volumes (*Luna de miel, luna de hiel* [Honeymoon, Bitter Moon, 1990] and *Los trabajos de Urbano y Simona* [The Labors of Urbano y Simona, 1990]), Pérez de Ayala presents a series of myths regarding the nature of sexual relations. By demythifying or illustrating the negative consequences of the established myth, Pérez de Ayala illustrates how the lack of sexual education gives rise to a series of problems that result in the failure/frustration of the marriage. *Las novelas de Urbano y Simona* attempts to present the Spanish ideology behind sexuality and the manner in which it leads to unhappiness. The main idea revolves around the fact that virginity is a fundamental aspect in marriage (for men as well as for women). The four parts of the text, which correspond to the waning and waxing of the moon, present the story of the arranged marriage between Urbano and Simona, two youngsters who are totally unaware of the sexual intimacy involved in marriage. In their absolute innocence they spend their honeymoon chasing butterflies and playing like children. The attraction that grows between them leaves both confused and dazed about what is expected of one of other in their married role. Upon finding out the truth, Urbano fears he will never be able to perform as a husband, because the sheltered life he has led makes him view any type of sexual relations as a monstrous act. He decides that in order to be a man he first must become one and take control of his life. Equally ignorant of her duties as a wife, Simona is absolutely devoted to fulfilling whatever role she must and does not question any of Urbano's decisions. She patiently waits for him to take control of their marriage, willing to follow him to the end, as a faithful wife should. On the way to their honeymoon Simona becomes convinced that an angel of the Annunciation told her that she is expecting a baby. Upon confiding in her grandmother about her pregnancy, the older lady confuses Simona even more by presenting a very traditional view of the female position as one of demure subjugation, where every natural instinct must be oppressed and overcome. She instructs her granddaughter to avoid embarrassing discussions with her husband. If a pregnancy occurs, she should only whisper it to him, preferably in a dark setting to avoid seeing his face when such indelicacies are being mentioned.

Micaela, Urbano's mother, is the antithesis of Simona. When she was her daughter-in-law's age Micaela was sexually experienced and well versed in every dark, secret aspect of life. Having lost her innocence at a very early age, she opted to save her son from the same fate and so kept Urbano unaware of what she considered "the dirty sides of human nature," supervising every aspect of his life to ensure that he remain as innocent as a newborn. Micaela is a very strong presence throughout the novel, dominating all men that come into her life. Following a Freudian interpretation, Micaela longs to have been a man, and it is also hinted that her gender has limited her from living up to her potential.

The figure of the mother plays a central role in these novels. The woman as a mother becomes a creature of veneration and sanctity. For Don Leoncio, Micaela is the adored woman, mother of his child, a woman to be respected, venerated, and to some extent, feared, from a distance. Micaela has helped reinforce this idea since she willingly subjugates her role as a wife to her duties as a mother. After her son's birth, she absolutely

rejects a second maternity and lives only to tend and protect Urbano, ignoring the husband completely. Once Urbano is fully grown and newly enlightened about the facts of life, Micaela longs for a second child to raise. However, for Don Leoncio the thought of intimate contact with his wife now repulses him. Motherhood has become a sacred condition that changes the image of a woman and totally deprives her of any sensuality. Once a woman becomes a mother, she is no longer seen as a sexual being. In order to satisfy his desires, a man such as Don Leoncio must resort to a woman of the streets who lacks the virtues of the decent mother and wife.

The common distinction between Eve and Mary (*Marlanism) is ever present in this novel. Where on one hand there is the wife, the good woman, opposite which appears the figure of the lover and the prostitute, the sensual sinner who exists to satisfy the male figure's sexual appetite. The ideal woman that Don Leoncio envisions would be a fusion between the soul of Micaela and the tempting body of Maria Egipciaca, his lover—a woman that would be both good and evil, sensuality and sensibility. Such confusion regarding a woman's image creates frustration and unhappiness both for the men and the women who must go against their natural instincts to conform to rules stipulated by society. The characters of the seven sisters, denied their right to self-realization, present a grotesque image of what spinsterhood and beatitude can cause in a woman. A state of celibacy can turn a woman into a monster, and this, paired up with beatitude, can create the most horrific form of monstrosity.

The older male characters (Don Leoncio, Don Cástulo) with their attained life experience have come to realize that sexual relations are a part of life meant for the enjoyment of human beings and not limited to the purpose of procreation. Don Leoncio reflects on how Church and society have stigmatized sex to be a dark and hidden aspect of human nature that is only acceptable after the sacrament of marriage. The same behavior that is repulsive and embarrassing before marriage becomes an act of love once it receives the blessing of the Church. He defends love as a separate entity from Church and society where love has meaning in itself and by itself, regardless of whether it is sexually expressed before or after the blessing of the Church. Even though events in these *Novelas* are taken to an extreme in order to illustrate the ideology behind the myth, the use of ridicule serves to show an exaggerated version of reality where ignorance is passed on as innocence. By showing the extreme form of the myth, the reader is moved to think and reflect about it. The hyperbolic nature of these novels distances the reader from the story and allows him/her to understand the magnitude of the problem and the extent of society's repression of the female.

With *Belarmino y Apolonio* Pérez de Ayala's novels become more intellectual and full of symbolism but maintain very believable and human characters. Love is also a prevailing theme, but it is treated as a force that aids communication and understanding other beings. Problems of sexuality are not a central aspect. *Belarmino and Apolonio* tells the story of the two shoemakers in the title and their children, shifting from the present to the past and then back to the present. A series of love episodes are interwoven with other events in the novel. The delicate Angustias, a prostitute who resembles a *virgen de Rafael* (virgin by Raphael), is abandoned by her family and the man she was supposed to marry, forced to sell her body to survive. When Guillén, the man who left her (now a priest) finds Angustias he assumes responsibility for the outcome of her life and apologizes to her. On the other hand, the behavior of Beatriz, the duchess of Somovia, departs drastically from any conventionalities. She smokes cigars, swears at whim, and administers all the affairs of Apolonio's shoe-

maker shop. She is strong and exuberant without being as tyrannical as Xuantipa, Berlarmino's wife. Finally, there is Felicita, a confirmed spinster who loves Novillo and finds this love reciprocated but is unable to secure happiness. She fears male desires and is doomed to live alone because of her own prejudices. Determined to prevent others from suffering, she aids the young lovers Guillén and Angustias with their plans to elope. *Belarmino y Apolonio* presents in a philosophical manner the many possibilities of love ranging from the frustration of Felicita to the unselfish and charitable acts of Don Guillén. Society is no longer ridiculed or attacked, despite the inclusion of some humorous irony, but rather is viewed in the scope of people's relation to the world that surrounds them.

Work by

A.M.D.G. Ed. Andrés Amorós. Madrid: Gredos, 1983.

Honeymoon, Bitter Moon and *The Labors of Urbano and Simona.* Trans. Barry Eisenberg. Intro. Andrés Amorós. London: Quartet, 1990.

Obras completas. Ed. José García Mercadal. 4 vols. Madrid: Aguilar, 1963–1969.

Poesías completas. 3rd ed. Buenos Aires: Espasa-Calpe, 1944.

Work about

Amorós, Andrés. *La novela intelectual de Ramón Pérez de Ayala.* Madrid: Gredos, 1972.

Best, Marigold. *Ramón Pérez de Ayala: An Annotated Bibliography of Criticism.* London: Grant and Cutler, 1980.

Bobes Naves, María del Carmen, et al. *Homenaje a Ramón Pérez de Ayala.* Oviedo: Servicio de Publicaciones, 1980.

Fernández, Pelayo H. *Simposio Internacional Ramón Pérez de Ayala.* Gijón: Flores, 1981.

Macklin, John. *The Window and the Garden: The Modernist Fictions of Ramón Pérez de Ayala.* Boulder, CO: Society of Spanish and Spanish-American Studies, 1988.

Rand, Marguerite C. *Ramón Pérez de Ayala.* New York: Twayne, 1971.

Vinuela, Miguel. *Desmitificación y esperanza en la*

novela de Pérez de Ayala. Oviedo: Instituto de Estudios Asturianos, 1991.

Delmarie Martínez

Pérez Galdós, Benito
See Doña Perfecta (1876); Pardo Bazán, Emilia (1852–1921): Reception of Her by Male Colleagues, 1870–1921; *Tormento* (1884); *Tristana* (1892)

Perfecta casada, La
See León, Fray Luis de (1527–1591); León, Fray Luis de (1527–1591): Admiration and Misogyny in *La perfecta casada*; León, Fray Luis de (1527–1591): Women in His Poetry

Pícara Justina, La (1605)
López de Ubeda's *El libro de entretenimiento de la pícara Justina* (1605; *The Life of Justina, the Country Jilt,* 1707) is the first picaresque novel with a female protagonist (**pícara*). It is also one of the first novels in the Spanish picaresque tradition, preceded by the anonymous *Vida de Lazarillo de Tormes* (1554) and *Guzmán de Alfarache* (1599 and 1604) by Mateo Alemán (1547–1616?). As in the cases of the fictional lives of her predecessors Lázaro and Guzmán, Justina's life story is presented to the reader as an autobiographical account. The protagonist and narrator is a humbly born Spanish woman of Jewish descent named Justina. Yet certain elements distinguish Justina's account from those of her male counterparts, namely the *pícara*'s lack of moral transformation and her non-apologetic tone. Contrary to the moral pretentiousness of Guzmán, a repentant *pícaro*, Justina offers no advice to the reader, and from beginning to end she maintains her status as a marginal, antisocial figure. As opposed to Lazarillo, a thoroughly hypocritical narrator, Justina hides nothing from the reader.

The issue of Justina's authorial intent is ambiguous. Her predecessors claimed to tell their life stories in an attempt to clarify the reasons for their past behavior, to clear their names, or to warn others about the dangers of amoral conduct. Justina does not proclaim to have redeemed herself socially, and she has no desire to teach a moral lesson. It is, in fact, quite unclear why she decides to make public her life story, for it is never revealed why Justina writes at all. Justina sets a different path for the two subsequent novels of *pícaras, La *Hija de Celestina, La Ingeniosa Elena* (1612–1614) by Alonso Jerónimo Salas Barbadillo (1581–1635) and *La *Niña de los embustes, Teresa de Manzanares* (1632) by Alonso del Castillo Solórzano (1584–1648).

The men who wrote the novels of male rogues carefully distinguished between narrator and actor. The *pícaro* as narrator is different from the *pícaro* as protagonist. Thus, the difference between the *pícaros*' past behavior and their self-proclaimed present moral conscience makes their confessions credible and, above all, autonomous. The *pícaros* confess voluntarily because they have an agenda; at the moment in which they are writing their tales, Lázaro and Guzmán claim to have become good citizens. In *La pícara Justina,* however, an external force replaces the lack of moral conscience in the female rogue and provides the novel with an alternate moral voice, that of the male author.

This intricate novel consists of three prologues and four books, each subdivided into several chapters, parts, and numbers. Each episode is preceded by a set of stanzas, then Justina recounts some adventures, and finally the voice of the male author offers moral advice. Displaying an overwhelmingly baroque literary style, Justina trots from her childhood to her present time in which she writes and openly declares herself to be a syphilitic prostitute of Jewish descent. In equally unflattering terms she describes the gruesome deaths of her parents and the battle she wages against her siblings in order to recover her inheritance. Justina also narrates her numerous wanderings through villages and towns, how she is kidnapped and raped by a group of students, how she deceives them, and finally how she takes her revenge against them. During other trips she encounters lawyers, innkeepers, Moorish women, textile workers, and vagrants. In each case the *pícara* misleads, scorns, robs, and cheats everyone. Ultimately Justina manages to acquire a modest fortune, then turns to the only option available to protect herself and her money: marriage. After careful consideration of several potential candidates, she marries, three times. Her account ends on her wedding night to, ironically, Guzmán de Alfarache, the most famous of the Spanish *pícaros*. To write her story Justina uses an obscure language. Her numerous puns, colloquialisms, and cryptic allusions are only partially understandable by modern readers, and to make matters worse, she constantly deviates from her main topic to describe buildings, streets, and clothing. Justina thus accompanies her life wanderings with a wandering narrative. Indeed, at times she seems to lose control of her own life story.

It has been said that the book was a *roman à clef*, meant to be read by a small group of courtiers for whom the constant puns, jokes, and hieroglyphs would have made perfect sense. However, *La pícara Justina* was printed twice in 1605 (Medina del Campo and Barcelona) and later in Brussels (1608), Barcelona (1640), Madrid (1735 and 1912), and Paris (1847). It was translated into Italian (1624), French (1635), and English (1707) and was followed in Spain by two other novels of *pícaras*, all of which demonstrates that the book was of interest beyond a particular reading circle. Traditional scholarship, however, has relegated this novel to the category of works with a mere linguistic interest.

From a feminist perspective, *La pícara Justina* stands as the first attempt within the Spanish picaresque tradition to portray the life of a poor woman as if she had written it herself. As such, the differences observed between Justina and her male counterparts need not constitute obstacles but tools for the interpretation of the picaresque novel. If picaresque novels are to be analyzed in terms of the historical conditions in which they were produced, as has been done in the case of the *pícaros*, then the social conditions of the time for men and for women must be taken into account. Spain of the picaresque was the Spain of the Counterreformation, a period with a penchant for strict control, especially by power groups such as the nobility and the Church. The methods for controlling women are well documented in manuals of social behavior, in written confessions and interrogations, as well as in sermons, legislation, scientific and moral discourses, and the picaresque novel. According to these social narratives women were to be confined primarily by physical boundaries (**Encierro*): the home, convent, or brothel, all places that facilitated their control. Free women were considered to be a menace to the social order; thus it is not coincidental that Justina is repeatedly defined by López de Ubeda as a "free woman."

When examined within this historical frame the *pícara* reveals herself as a woman who not only converts her sexuality into a way of life, but one who does not renounce her freedom and who never shows remorse for her actions. Hers is not a story of repentance and the acceptance of social rules but one of defiance; because she represents a threat to the system, she is not given complete autonomy to recount her life but instead must be accompanied by a qualifying voice that exposes her in all her indecency and reveals her lack of self-control. The construction of a female rogue in the Spanish picaresque novel forced López de Ubeda to apply new methods of discourse control in order to warn his readers against the dangers represented by free women like Justina. And thus appeared the most striking feature of the novels of *pícaras*, the alienation of their voices. *See also* Sex in Spanish Golden Age Literature (1500–1700); Syphilis as Sickness and Metaphor in Early Modern Spain: 1492–1650

Work by

The Life of Justina, the Country Jilt. Trans. John Stevens. London: Samuel Bunchley, 1707.

La pícara Justina. Ed. Bruno Damiani. Madrid: Porrúa, 1982.

Work about

Bataillon, Marcel. *Pícaros y picaresca. La pícara Justina.* Madrid: Taurus, 1969.

Damiani, Bruno. *Francisco López de Ubeda.* TWAS 431. New York: Twayne, 1974.

Davis, Nina Cox. "Breaking the Barriers: The Birth of López de Ubeda's *Pícara Justina.*" *The Picaresque: Tradition and Displacement.* Ed. G. Maiorino. Minneapolis: U of Minnesota P, 1996. 137–158.

Dunn, Peter. *Spanish Picaresque Fiction. A New Literary History.* Ithaca: Cornell UP, 1993.

Friedman, Edward. *The Antiheroine's Voice: Narrative Discourse and Transformations of the Picaresque.* Columbia: U of Missouri P, 1987.

Hanrahan, Thomas. *La mujer en la novela picaresca española.* Madrid: Porrúa, 1967.

Rey Hazas, Antonio, ed. *Las pícaras.* Barcelona: Plaza & Janés, 1986.

Ronquillo, Pablo. *Retrato de la pícara. La protagonista de la picaresca española del siglo XVII.* Madrid: Playor, 1980.

Reyes Coll-Tellechea

Pícaras and Pícaros: Female and Male Rogues in the Spanish Picaresque Canon

Picaresque novels, which originated in sixteenth-century Spain, may be defined as the fictional life stories of female and male rogues, *pícaras* and *pícaros*. Usually the rogue narrates the story of her/his life from its very humble beginnings to the present moment in which she/he writes. This is the rogue's tale: Orphaned or abandoned, an innocent child must leave her/his home at a very early age. She/he struggles to survive, going from master to master (or from husband to husband) and from town to town in search of work, food, shelter, and a better life. Very quickly she/he learns that for an individual of her/his modest origins survival cannot be achieved by honest means. She/he then becomes a rogue, deceiving, stealing, and hoaxing others. Generally, rogues do not succeed in their attempts to improve their social and economical situation. Frustrated and wishing to take revenge on society, rogues write their life stories and blame others for their misfortunes and crimes. Picaresque novels were produced and avidly consumed in seventeenth-century Spain. When compared to traditional literary characters such as knights, noblemen, ladies, idealized shepherds, and princesses who inhabited the fictional worlds of the chivalric, pastoral, Moorish, and Greek novels, *pícaras* and *pícaros* were a novelty. Speaking with the voice of the underworld, these newcomers were vagrants, prostitutes, and thieves who dared to write about their marginal lives. Casting their voices on center stage the rogues satirized everything and everyone in their life accounts.

The first picaresque novel, the anonymous *Vida de Lazarillo de Tormes* (Life of Lazarillo de Tormes), was published in 1554. One year later a sequel to this text appeared in Flanders. The second picaresque novel, part one of *Guzmán de Alfarache* by Mateo Alemán (1547–1616?), was published in 1599, followed by a sequel by Juan Martí (1570?–1604?) in 1602. Alemán's part two of *Guzmán de Alfarache* was printed in 1604, followed by *El Guitón de Honofre* (1604) by Gregorio González, *Libro de Entretenimiento de la *Pícara Justina* (1605; *The Life of Justina, the Country Jilt*, 1707) by Francisco López de Ubeda, *La *hija de Celestina* (1612 to 1614); and its revision *La ingeniosa Elena* (1614; *The Daughter of Celestina*, 1912) by Alonso Jerónimo Salas Barbadillo, *Vida del Escudero Marcos de Obregón* (1618; *The History of the Life of the Squire Marcos de Obregón*, 1816) by Vicente Espinel, *La desordenada codicia de los bienes ajenos* (1619; *The Sonne of the Rogue*, 1638) by Carlos García, *Lazarillo de Manzanares* (1620) by Juan Cortés de Tolosa, *Segunda parte de Lazarillo de Tormes* (1620) by Juan de Luna, *El donado hablador* (1624; *The Chattering Laybrother*, 1844–1845) by Jerónimo de Alcalá Yáñez, *El Buscón* (1626; *The Life and Adventures of Don Pablos, the Sharper*, 1957) by Francisco de *Quevedo, *La *Niña de los embustes, Teresa de Manzanares* (1632; The Child of Hoaxes, Teresa de Manzanares) by Alonso Castillo Solórzano, and *Vida y hechos de Estebanillo González, hombre de buen humor, compuesto por él mismo* (1646; *The Life of Estebanillo González . . .* , 1707).

Traditionally the Spanish picaresque novel has been described as a group of narratives that pays close attention to ethnic and socioeconomic determinants: The rogues are portrayed as low-life individuals (poor) and members of ethnic minorities (of Moorish or Jewish descent). Little attention has been paid to the fact that the rogues are constructed as male or female by their authors. Because issues of gender have not been addressed in traditional approaches to the picaresque novel, picaresque studies have not fully considered important features present in the life accounts of female and male rogues.

The life stories of rogues, male and female, who populated the Spanish novel at the turn of the seventeenth century forced their readers to confront, in fiction, the potential disintegration of the established social order. The *pícaro* and the *pícara* appeared not as an accident of nature in a well-ordered Christian society but rather as a product of the friction caused by the clashing socioeconomic forces of a medieval hierarchy and an incipient modern capitalism. The intense fascination exerted by picaresque rogues attests to growing interest in the arbitrary nature of the boundaries separating feudal from modern, societal from individual, and female from male. In particular, the rogue served as a means to discuss social problems regarding women, men, and systems of control in early modern Spain.

Picaresque life stories are not autobiographical texts, because they were not written by the rogues themselves. However, the first specimens of the picaresque novel demonstrate an autobiographical disposition. That is, they are presented to the reader as first-person life accounts in which the roles of narrator and protagonist coincide. This led traditional scholarship to define the picaresque novel as a fictional autobiography of a humbly born individual. This, in turn, had the effect of excluding from the picaresque canon many novels written in this literary tradition that were not presented as autobiographical, including some with female protagonists.

The picaresque rogue has been repeatedly described as a male antihero, a man without *honor who believes that others are not better than him. His life account is full of resentment and censure against the society that marginalized him. In his tale, the rogue offers the reader moral advice but, at the same time, shows no respect for moral or civil laws. The rogue is a selfish man whose aspirations are freedom and social advancement. His adventures always have an economic base. He has no time for love or friendship. At the time that he tells his story the rogue has undergone some type of transformation: repentance, imprisonment, a trip overseas, and so on. These new circumstances provide him with a new point of reference to recall his past life and satirize everything and everyone in his narration.

Using this portrait as the main criterion for classification, most critics have reduced the picaresque canon to three titles, all of which happen to have male rogues as protagonists: *La vida de Lazarillo de Tormes*, *Guzmán de Alfarache*, and *El Buscón*. As a result, the rest of the novels written and read in the picaresque tradition have scarcely been mentioned, studied, edited, or taught.

Although classified as a literary genre by nineteenth-century historiographers and developed by twentieth-century scholars, the "picaresque" label is hardly a modern term. References to "picaresque tales" or "tales of picaresque style" can be found as early as the seventeenth century. Intertextual references are also found in several seventeenth-century texts, such as *La pícara Justina* and *Don Quijote* (1605) by Miguel de Cervantes Saavedra.

These suggest some type of generic consciousness in writers, editors, and readers about what we now call the Spanish picaresque novel. In the twentieth century, disagreement about the picaresque novel surfaced. Modern scholars are divided on the issue of the very existence of a separate picaresque genre. Traditionalists restrict the picaresque to two or three titles, others deny the possibility of a separate category, and still others expand the picaresque canon to include not only seventeenth-century Spanish narratives but also later and foreign ones, such as *Simplicius Simplicissimus* (1669) by Hans Jakob Christoffel Grimmelshausen or *Moll Flanders* (1722) by Daniel Defoe.

Yet canon formation is not a matter of mere mechanical classification. Certain aspects of this debate demonstrate the importance of ideological criteria in picaresque canon formation. For instance, although the three privileged picaresque novels show acute differences among themselves, the terms in which they presented certain social issues served as a basis for the discussion of all other novels of rogues. That is, the rogues' critique of certain religious practices (Christian charity), moral values (honesty), and social structures (the code of honor, purity of blood) became, for traditional critics, the core of the picaresque. In order for a novel to qualify as a "true picaresque" story, it had to conform to the rigid mold established by the three privileged narrations. A special category of "minor picaresque" (*picaresca menor*) was established for those novels that did not comply with the so-called picaresque generic rules, either because of their limited or divergent involvement with the topics chosen by critics as the core of the picaresque novel or due to a perceived lack of literary quality by their authors. It is in this second group, the "minor picaresque," that all picaresque novels with female protagonists fall. Critics and historiographers cited poor quality, the authors' lack of understanding of generic rules, and even the implausibility of female rogues as reasons to discard novels protagon-

ized by *pícaras*. These are: *La pícara Justina*, *La hija de Celestina/La Ingeniosa Elena*, and *Teresa de Manzanares*. However, the main obstacle to their canonical inclusion lies in the constraints embedded in the traditional definition of the Spanish picaresque: The rogue is male, and the issues of marginality present in the picaresque novel could not be applied to a female character without breaking the generic rules. A woman could not be a *pícaro*.

Over the past decades a series of major transformations in literary scholarship have occurred that have radically questioned traditional understanding of the Spanish picaresque novel as an object of study. There are questions of what constitutes a literary genre in general, and the Spanish picaresque in particular, as well as the question of what criteria should be used to expand the picaresque canon. And moving beyond problems of literary classification, modern researchers view literary texts as cultural artifacts, as sources for the research of social practices of control, dissidence, and marginality within a given culture. Therefore, along with moral, philosophical, religious, pedagogical, medical, and legal documents of the period, all Spanish picaresque novels constitute a privileged site for study of such social practices in early modern Spain.

The consideration of gender construction and gender control in the picaresque novel brings a new, crucial element to the discussion of modes of social control in Golden Age Spain. The fact that some picaresque novels have women as protagonists profoundly affected their content and their form, making them different in many ways from those novels focused on male rogues. It is important to note that there is no sign of repentance in any of the novels of *pícaras*, no moral transformation of the characters. Contrary to their male counterparts, female rogues go from one job to another and avoid service in favor of more lucrative activities such as prostitution, fraudulent marriages, or modest commercial activities. Moreover, the criticism distilled by the novels of *pícaras* is not directed against society as a whole but against the women themselves. Next to the *pícara's* voice, the reader perceives a male voice (that of the male author) who condemns the "female nature" of the protagonist, her hypocrisy, ambition, moral degeneration, inclination to criminal behavior, and desire for freedom. Thus the gender factor, and not the inexperience of "mediocre" authors dealing with new generic literary rules, may explain the abundant differences founded in the novels of *pícaras*. It may not after all be a lack of understanding of literary rules but of the very different real-life conditions that men and women of early modern Spain had to endure.

Picaresque fictions reveal Spain's growing concern with issues of gender and social deviance. These narratives served to rearticulate, discuss, and reinforce prevalent moral values and contemporary social, scientific, and religious thought. The issue of female deviance (prostitution, access to economic means of survival, and manipulation of the institution of marriage), although thoroughly explored in the novels of *pícaras*, has not been fully addressed by critics. The same could be said about the novels of *pícaros*. From a feminist point of view, all picaresque novels offer a window to the mentalities and ideologies of early modern Spaniards regarding women, men, and certain aspects of deviation and marginality that have seldom been approached in traditional scholarship: the control of the sexuality of individuals, and the gender politics of the modern state. *See also* Sex in Spanish Golden Age Literature (1500–1700); Syphilis as Sickness and Metaphor in Early Modern Spain: 1492–1650.

Work about

Chandler, F. *Romances of Roguery*. New York: B. Franklin, 1961.

Cruz, Anne J. *Discourses of Poverty: Social Reform and the Picaresque Novel in Early Modern Spain*. Toronto: U of Toronto P, 1999.

De Haan, F. *An Outline of the History of the Novela Picaresca in Spain*. The Hague: M. Nijhoff, 1903.

Dunn, Peter. *Spanish Picaresque Fiction. A New Literary History*. Ithaca, NY: Cornell UP, 1993.

Fiore, Robert. *Lazarillo de Tormes*. Boston: Twayne, 1984.

Hanrahan, Thomas. *La mujer en la novela picaresca española*. Madrid: Porrúa, 1967.

Maravall, José A. *La literatura picaresca desde la historia social*. Madrid: Taurus, 1986.

Parker, A. *Literature and the Delinquent: The Picaresque Novel in Spain and Europe, 1599–1753*. Edinburgh: U of Edinburgh P, 1967.

Rey Hazas, A., ed. *Picaresca femenina*. Barcelona: Plaza & Janés, 1986.

Ricapito, J. *Bibliografía razonada y anotada de las obras maestras de la picaresca española*. Madrid: Castalia, 1980.

Rico, Francisco. *The Spanish Picaresque Novel and the Point of View*. Trans. Charles Davis. Cambridge: Cambridge UP, 1984.

Ronquillo, Pablo. *Retrato de la pícara. La protagonista de la picaresca española en el siglo XVII*. Madrid: Playor, 1980.

Reyes Coll-Tellechea

Pinar, Florencia (late fifteenth century?)

One of a handful of medieval Spanish women writers whose work has survived, although very little is known about the life of this *cancionero* (late-medieval songbook) poet, Florencia Pinar with her poetry provides a rare and compelling example of a late-medieval feminine voice. In the absence of historical documents, speculation on Pinar's literary career and intellectual formation must derive from information gleaned from her poetic production. The fact that Pinar's poems are included in the *Cancionero general* (1511), a songbook compiled by Hernando del Castillo (late fifteenth–early sixteenth century), sheds light on her literary reputation. Castillo published his songbook in part to provide his public with a collection of exemplary works from some of the most renowned poets of the period, and the inclusion of Pinar's poems attests to the prestige she enjoyed. Moreover, Pinar's knowledge of contemporary poetic tendencies, illustrated by her use of strophic patterns and themes common to works composed by poets who participated in the active literary and intellectual circles that often formed part of royal and noble retinues in fifteenth-century Spain, is a likely indication that she received some type of education and that she came from an affluent family. The poetic muse appears to have touched another member of her family, known most often as Pinar (but also referred to as Gerónimo de Pinar [late fifteenth century?]), whose works are included in several *cancioneros* and who is thought to have been Florencia's brother.

At the same time, and in contrast to other women *cancionero* poets, one is able to speak with more certainty about the characteristics of Pinar's poetry. Pinar is the only female *cancionero* poet to whom an appreciable amount of verse may be attributed, even though questions concerning the number of works that are actually hers continue to intrigue scholars. The rubrics to four poems included in the *Cancionero general* clearly indicate that they were written by a woman, that is to say, by Florencia Pinar: "Canción de una dama que se dice Florencia Pinar" (Song by a Lady Called Florencia Pinar), "Otra canción de la misma señora a unas perdices que le enviaron vivas" (Another Song by the Same Lady on Some Live Partridges Sent to Her), "Glosa de Florencia" (Gloss of Florencia), and "Canción de Florencia Pinar" (Song of Florencia Pinar). While the first three poems are found exclusively in the *Cancionero general*, which was reprinted and augmented on several occasions during the sixteenth century, the "Canción de Florencia Pinar" also forms part of another manuscript that originally dates from around 1500, 11 years before the *Cancionero general* was first published.

Three of Pinar's poems, with the exception of the "Glosa de Florencia," are *canciones*, a poetic genre popular during the fifteenth century that tended to treat lighter themes and that consisted of at least two stanzas of octosyllabic verses, the most popular type of medieval Spanish lyric poetry, with the first stanza usually shorter than the ones that follow. In keeping with this tradition, Pinar's three *canciones* consist entirely of octosyllabic verses, arranged in stanzas of five and nine lines, with the "Canción de Florencia Pinar" possessing stanzas of four and eight lines, varying slightly. One, the "Canción de una dama que se dice Florencia Pinar," treats the theme of love in a manner commonly found in *cancionero* poetry. As such, the poem is permeated by the typical language of conceit, that is, contrasting terminology such as "Ay plazeres ay pesares / ay glorias ay mil dolores" (vv. 6–7; Oh pleasures, oh sorrows / oh joys, oh pains), in order to present the theme ambiguously and abstractly by depicting both the pleasure and the pain caused by love.

Perhaps the most intriguing question concerning Pinar's poetry is whether or not the modern reader can detect any features identifying a female voice. Indeed, a case may be established for the presence of this voice in the three remaining poems that can be attributed to her with certainty. In "Otra canción de la misma señora a unas perdices que le enviaron vivas," Pinar equates her feelings of frustration with the concrete image of the caged partridge and concludes that, just as the songs of the partridges turn to cries after they have been trapped by hunters, she is disillusioned because of her own capture. Moreover, Pinar writes that both she and the partridges feel similarly deceived after being caught. Understood against the backdrop of Pinar's situation as a woman in fifteenth-century Spain, the cries of the partridges would represent Pinar's own dismay at her limited possibilities in a male-dominated society.

While the "Canción de Florencia Pinar," like the "Canción de una dama que se dice Florencia Pinar," deals with love, the theme here is presented from what may also be interpreted as a female perspective. In the poem Pinar writes of the cunning of love and again evokes a concrete image—in this instance, a phallic symbol (*gusano* [worm])—seemingly to denigrate the male role in the loss of a female's virginity. The poem may also be read in a larger context as an expression of Pinar's dissatisfaction with the contemporary status of women. In this sense, Pinar's assertion that the treachery of love is enduring, "que si entra en las entrañas / no puede salir sin ellas" (vv. 11–12; because once it enters one's heart / it leaves accompanied by that heart), would symbolize concern with a women's inability to improve her social standing.

The "Glosa de Florencia," although performing a different literary function than the *canciones*, is similar in form to the other compositions with 12 octosyllabic verses divided into two stanzas of 4 and 8 verses, respectively. Beginning in the fifteenth century, the *glosa* became a common way for poets to comment on another poem or popular saying. If the poet were commenting on an entire poem, the *glosa* would frequently follow the same strophic pattern as the poem being glossed. However, in the case of a popular saying, or *mote*, the text to be glossed often consisted of only one line, which the *glosa* would attempt to elaborate. Pinar's "Glosa de Florencia" endeavors to expound on the *mote* "Mi dicha lo desconcierta" (My fortune disrupts it) by applying it to her personal situation. In the poem Pinar appears to express her frustration at not being able to obtain the lover she desires. Pinar's affection for this person, expressed in terms of the typical *cancionero* image of the encumbered and servile lover, has not been reciprocated because of an impediment that has prevented the union. Once again, close scrutiny of the imagery enables a female voice to surface: Pinar's attempts in the poem to serve, presumably in courtly society, meet with frustration, because her fortune, which may be understood here to be that of being born a woman, belies her success.

A number of additional poems, many with rubrics that list the poet as "Pinar" or "dicho Pinar" (said Pinar) have been traditionally attributed to Florencia's brother. Some may be Florencia's, although the masculine ending of the adjective "dicho" in the rubrics to several poems suggests a male author. Notwithstanding the uncertainty concerning the number of poems Pinar actually wrote, the corpus of work known to be hers enlists Pinar as the most prolific female *cancionero* poet and provides the modern reader with a rare vision of a female perspective on the limited social possibilities for women during the waning decades of the Spanish Middle Ages.

Work by

Cancionero general. Comp. Hernando del Castillo. Facs. edition and intro. Antonio Rodríguez-Moñino. Madrid: Real Academia Española, 1958. Folios 125v–126r, 144r, and 185v.

Work about

Deyermond, Alan. "Spain's First Women Writers." *Women in Hispanic Literature: Icons and Fallen Idols*. Ed. Beth Miller. Berkeley and Los Angeles: U of California P, 1983. 27–52.

Fulks, Barbara. "The Poet Named Florencia Pinar." *La Corónica* 18.1 (1989–1990): 33–44.

Recio, Roxana. "Otra dama que desaparece: La abstracción retórica en tres modelos de canción de Florencia Pinar." *Revista Canadiense de Estudios Hispánicos* 16.2 (1992): 329–339.

Snow, Joseph. "The Spanish Love Poet Florencia Pinar." *Medieval Women Writers*. Ed. Katharina M. Wilson. Athens: U of Georgia P, 1984. 320–332.

Gregory B. Kaplan

Poema de Mio Cid (twelfth–thirteenth centuries): Its Portrayal of Women Characters

As the epic genre constructs and exalts an essentially male universe of military feats and struggle, it is not surprising that female characters in the *Poema de Mio Cid* (c. 1207; *Poem of the Cid*, 1998) are few and largely invisible. Women in this epic occupy a paradoxical role. Their participation in the plot is limited, but their presence is crucial to the structure of the narrative. Ubiquitous in the background of the Reconquest landscape are

Christian and Moorish women referred to collectively (l. 16b, 465, 1179). Relatively foregrounded are *Jimena and Doña Elvira and Doña Sol who, cast in the domestic roles of wife and daughters of the hero, owe their significance to their ties to the male protagonist. These women serve as measures of the hero's growing economic status and as instruments for extending his political scope.

The marriage of the Cid and Jimena is a symbolic representation of the feudal order whereby Rodrigo Díaz, as lord, is responsible for providing protection, shelter, and economic security in exchange for the loyalty and obedience of his wife and daughters. An image of the ideal wife, Jimena's fate is linked to that of Rodrigo. With Rodrigo forced into exile by King Alfonso VI, Jimena and her daughters are given refuge in the monastery of San Pedro de Cardeña. Her meeting there with the hero as he departs from Castile puts into relief their respective roles. While Jimena kneels reverently before her lord and begs for advice for herself, her daughters and her ladies-in-waiting, Rodrigo's concerns center on the economic—on endowing the Church sufficiently to ensure the welfare of his female kin during his absence and on eventually achieving advantageous marriages for his daughters (lines 240–284). Though Jimena features more prominently in this encounter than at any other point in the plot, her posture remains one of passivity and self-effacement. In her lengthy prayer (lines 325–365), she pleads only for reunion with the hero, an event that will reinforce her subordinate domestic position. Her marginality is confirmed after she is summoned to the Cid's newly conquered domain of Valencia (lines 1570–1609); despite courtly gestures to his lady, the hero will exclude Jimena from all decisions, including those regarding the marriage of her daughters, which, as Lacarra comments, are her right by law.

Female figures are essential organizing elements in the deep and surface structure of the plot of the Poema de Mio Cid, for they serve as external symbols of the hero's increasing *honor, power, and favor with the king and as catalysts in development of the action. As Rodrigo triumphs in battle and conquers new territories, he gradually wins the king's approval by remitting to Castile part of his booty as a gift (lines 810–884, 1270–1281, 1789–1814, 2111–2120), and the themes of women and marriage are embedded in each gift transaction after the first. Along with the second gift, the Cid requests the king's permission to reunite with his wife and daughters, and with the third gift are delivered the marriage banns of his vassals to Jimena's ladies-in-waiting. The gift-giving/wife-exchange pattern culminates in the king's invitation of Rodrigo back to Castile to arrange the wedding of Doña Elvira and Doña Sol to the lofty counts of Carrión. This marriage provides the foundation for the second move in the narrative, in which the daughters' circumstances reflect and finally increase the hero's dignity on a wider scale. Their dishonor by their first husbands in the forest at Corpes brings about events that lead to the greater honor of their later marriage to royalty—to the princes of Navarra and Aragón. As virtual objects of exchange in the gift-giving transactions, female characters operate as both barometers and instruments of enhancement in the economic and social status of the hero and his men.

The sisters command our attention in the savage episode at the Corpes Forest. Motivated by a desire for revenge against the Cid and his men for perceived slights, the counts of Carrión sexually brutalize and abandon their wives en route to their ancestral estates in León. Lacarra regards the sisters' response as analogous to the dignity and passive courage that characterize Jimena's conduct and in consonance with the feudal values instilled in their upbringing. Treated as whores by the counts, the women remain inconspicuous after the incident. Far from taking matters into their own hands and asserting their rights, they rely on their male kin in the Cid's army to initiate the legalistic proceedings of the

Courts at Toledo that will restore their honor. They are also absent from view when their virtue is vindicated as their royal nuptials are announced—marriages approved, this time, by their father. These alliances, therefore, serve more to emphasize the hero's influence through his lineage for generations to come than to reinstate the honor of his daughters.

The passive and silent consent with which Doña Elvira and Doña Sol enter both sets of marriages is representative of the marginal roles assigned to women, yet, as Lacarra observes, it is a less accurate reflection of the actual latitude permitted women under Spanish medieval legislation—an observation that Arias feels may lead to the conclusion that the poem reflects customs of an earlier period parallel to when the story took place rather than when the text was set down. Of questionable accuracy too are details surrounding the daughters' two sets of marriages. Ultimately, however, the function of women and all the marriages represented in the *Poema de Mio Cid* is to assure the prestige of the hero's efforts and the future of his line.

Work by

Poema de Mio Cid. 2nd ed. Madrid: Castalia, 1978.
The Poem of the Cid. Trans. Rita Hamilton and Janet Perry. Intro. and notes Ian Michael. New York: Viking Penguin, 1984.
Poem of the Cid. Trans. Paul Blackburn. Ed. George Economou. Intro. Luis Cortest. Norman: U of Oklahoma P, 1998.

Work about

Arias, Consuelo. "El espacio femenino en tres obras del medioevo español. De la reclusión a la transgresión." *La Torre* (1987): 365–388.
Bluestine, Carolyn. "The Role of Women in the *Poema de Mio Cid*." *Romance Notes* 19 (1978): 404–409.
Clarke, Dorothy Clotelle. "The Cid and His Daughters." *La Corónica* 5 (1976): 16–21.
De Chasca, Edmund. *The Poem of the Cid*. Boston: G.K. Hall, 1976.
Duggan, Joseph. *The "Cantar de Mio Cid." Poetic*

Creation in Its Economic and Social Contexts. Cambridge: Cambridge UP, 1989.
Lacarra, María Eugenia. "La mujer ejemplar en tres textos épicos castellanos." *Cuadernos de Investigación Filológica* 14 (1988): 5–20.
Pavlovic, Milija, and Roger Walker. "Money, Marriage and the Law in the *Poema de Mio Cid*." *Medium Aevum* 51 (1982): 197–212.
———. "Roman Forensic Procedure in the Court Scene in the *Poema de Mio Cid*." *Bulletin of Hispanic Studies* 60 (1983): 95–107.

Alicia Ramos

Poetry by Spanish Women Writers: 1800–1900

In her introduction to *Las Románticas*, Susan Kirkpatrick identifies 1841 as the date when Spanish women "began to make themselves heard," initiating a continuing tradition of women's writing in Spain. While this is the time when a group of women writers emerges, Vicenta *Maturana de Gutiérrez (1793–1859) began publishing some two decades before, novels in 1825 and 1829, then the poetry collections *Ensayos poéticos* (1828; Essays in Poetry) and *Himno a la luna: Poema en cuatro cantos* (1838; Hymn to the Moon: Poem in Four Cantos). While her initial lyrics consisted of pastoral odes, sonnets, and other traditional forms, the latter is a long prose poem, much more innovative in that it marks one of the earliest appearances of that genre in Spain and clearly romantic in its emphasis on emotions and impressions. The most nearly complete edition of Maturana's poetry, *Poesías de la señora Doña Vicenta Maturana de Gutiérrez* (1841; Poems of Madam Vicenta Maturana de Gutiennez) was published in France, as was *Himno*, where she chose to live in voluntary exile following the death of Fernando VII. Maturana exemplifies women's struggle to write, more than anything resembling feminist themes, but serves as a precedent and encouragement for younger writers.

Carolina *Coronado published her first poems in Madrid in 1839, her first lyric collection in 1843 (the 1840s were a time of flowering of Spanish romantic poetry, a time when Spanish women began writing for the press and reading French and Spanish romantic writers). The *Poesías* of Gertrudis *Gómez de Avellaneda appeared in 1841, and several minor poets emerged in this decade and the mid-century era: Robustiana Armiño (1821–1890), Vicenta García Miranda (1816–?), Rosa Butler y Mendieta (1821–?), Dolores Cabrera y Heredia (1826–?), Amalia Fenollosa (1825–1869), Rogelia León (1828–1870), Enriqueta Lozano de Vilchez (1829–1895), María Verdejo y Durán (1830–1854), and Vicenta Bridoux (1835–1862). Angela *Grassi (1826–1883) and Pilar *Sinués de Marco (1835–1893)—neither primarily a poet, although both published poetry—actively echoed traditional, patriarchal norms, promoting conservative gender models. Grassi's *Poesías de la señorita doña Angela Grassi* (1851; Poems by Miss Angela Grassi) treat religious themes—odes to the Virgin, hymns, and elegies, in traditional meters and inspirational tones; her *Poesías* (1871) reprints previously published poetry, adding new compositions with some on new themes, including unrequited love, national history, and memories of autobiographical episodes. Sinués wrote especially legends in verse: *Mis vigilias* (1854; My Vigils) and *Luz de luna* (1855; Moonlight). Among her other verse collections are *Cantos de mi lira* (1856; Songs from My Lyre) and *Amor y llanto* (1857; Love and Weeping). *Flores del alma* (1860; Flowers of the Soul), a personal anthology of lyric poems, was followed by *Mis poesías* (1855; My Poems). Nearly all the poetry of Sinués employs traditional forms and espouses traditional values. Another poet who does not quite belong with the romantics is Micaela de Silva y Collás (1809–1884), who wrote under the pseudonym "Camila Avilés." She studied languages and worked as a translator never publishing her "creative" works in volume form in her lifetime. *Emanaciones del alma* (1885; Emanations from the Soul) was compiled from her poems published in the periodical press and released as a single-

volume collection following her death. *Un novio a pedir de boca* (1963; A Sweetheart Made to Order), a posthumously published satire in *octavas reales* (stanzas of eight hendecasyllables), describes the ideal suitor, listing such virtues as honesty, decency, and fidelity and painting the kinds of men to avoid: womanizer, gambler, wife-abuser, narcissist, wastrel, and glutton (perhaps sufficiently explanatory of her decision not to publish the poem in her lifetime).

María del Carmen Simón Palmer's bibliography of nineteenth-century Spanish women writers listing nearly 5,000 publications proves that the traditional silence imposed upon women was definitively broken in the romantic period and documents a dramatic increment of writing by women in the postromantic era. Faustina *Sáez de Melgar (1834?–1895), likewise not primarily a poet but a fiction writer and editor-director of children's magazines, turned to poetry after her children's deaths, publishing *La lira del Tajo* (1859; Lyre of the Tagus) and patriotic poetry, *Africa y España* (1859).

The most significant women lyricists of the romantic or mid-century period were Coronado and Avellaneda, followed by Rosalía de *Castro in the postromantic era. Coronado first achieved fame for her poetry, although she later wrote novels, unsuccessful theater, and essays. Standard sources give her dates as 1823–1911, although later critics have produced a baptismal certificate dated 1820. She was primarily home educated and lamented familial restrictions on reading and her lack of familiarity with Spanish versification. She began publishing in an oppressive environment, when only a fraction of potential readers were women (Noël Valis indicates in the introduction to her edition of Coronado's *Poesías* that 81 percent of Spanish women were illiterate). Coronado evidently wrote with the intent to include male readers and published her best-known work in newspapers, most of it appearing in the 1840s (she wrote only sporadically after her marriage in 1852). Although often treated simply as a transitional figure from romanticism to realism, or a civic poet, her intimate, often Arcadian thematics anticipate postromantics Gustavo Adolfo *Bécquer and Rosalía de Castro. Most critics emphasize her poetry of nature and flowers, conventional "feminine" motifs in the neoclassic pastoral tradition. While often dismissed as bland and girlish, she was also socially active and collaborated in decidedly feminist-leaning periodicals. Some of her more progressive poems express a feminine pacifism, protest women's reification and marginalization, and call for the abolition of slavery in Cuba. Her best, mature pieces add nostalgia and historical themes, as well as feminist, satiric, political, and social concerns. Love poetry and philosophical meditations were also significantly represented.

Gertrudis Gómez de Avellaneda (1814–1873) is often omitted by Spanish literary historians; she was born and died in Cuba, although she lived most of her adult life in Spain, writing and publishing nearly all of her work there, including two poetry collections, six novels, and some 15 full-length dramas as well as several shorter plays. She wrote essays and short stories and published an extensive correspondence and collections of legends. Her love life was considered scandalous; she was characterized as a "Spanish Georges Sand," suffering from social marginalization, as well as rejection and jealousy from male writers of the period. Avellaneda allegedly began writing poetry following her mother's remarriage; *Poesías* (1841) contained 45 poems, including seven translations; a second volume, also entitled *Poesías*, appeared in 1850. Her archetypal romantic interests included medieval history and legends, and she was attracted by the period of conquest and discovery, writing repeatedly on patriotic themes. Also noteworthy is her incorporation of the romantics' exaltation of art as divinely inspired, although she emphasizes feminine attributes such as peace, love, and harmony, thereby identifying women poets with the spirit of poetry. Her theme par

excellence, however, is love in all its varied manifestations: passion, exultation, ecstasy, the depths of disillusionment and pain, mysterious sentiments, eroticism, divine and mystic love; later, she also treated nature, religion, poetics, and other poets, travel, daily life, and autobiographical topics. Her metrics and rhyme schemes were varied; Harter observes that she employs a compendium of styles in Hispanic poetry from late neoclassicism through romanticism. Avellaneda epitomizes romanticism, and her feminism is exemplified even more in her life and her novels than in her poetry.

Rosalía de Castro (1837–1885) suffered not only from the marginalization affecting most women of her time but also from the circumstances of her illegitimate birth as the unwanted daughter of a seminarian (also identified as presbyter or priest) and a well-born spinster. Given the secrecy attending noble "scandals," she was hidden away until adolescence, essentially rejected by and separated from her mother and never acknowledged by her father, receiving a low-cost education, but beginning to express her sentiments in writing at an early age. Having commenced versifying almost as soon as she learned to write, she published six rather extensive romantic poems as *La Flor* (1857; The Flower); approximately a year later, she married the young critic who praised this first lyric collection of brief, intensely emotional poems replete with such romantic motifs as fate, doomed love, despair, lost innocence, hostile destiny, disillusionment, grief, treachery, and deception. Her second lyric collection, *A mi madre* (1863; To My Mother), was inspired by her mother's death and published shortly before her first major success, *Cantares gallegos* (1863; Galician Songs), composed in the rural Galician dialect while Castro was suffering intense homesickness. Castro's life clearly shapes her lyrics; her fiction is more imaginative. *Cantares gallegos* is credited with reviving popular Galician literature via glosses and imitation and sings of Galicia's lakes, mountains, fields, fjord-like *rías*, flora, fauna, myths, folklore, customs, and ancient traditions. Other themes include twilight and solitude, as well as epic, celebratory visions of Galician archetypes (lusty country lads, robust farmgirls, aged beggar women, itinerant bagpipe players), revered religious icons, pilgrimages, and dances. Some poems anticipate social themes, protesting hardships suffered by Galician harvesters and migrant farmworkers, while others reflect contemporary realism with descriptions of customs, samplings of village humor, rustic jokes, and tricks. Her second collection of poems in Galician, *Follas novas* (1880; New Leaves), turns more somber; more intimate and subjective, it projects the poet's disillusioned vision of human existence. Love, too, shows a more somber face, and accompanying it are themes of solitude, anguish, being toward death, suffering, misfortune, and pain. Social themes are better represented, also, especially compositions dealing with the problem of emigration, the women abandoned by their husbands, and their strength in aloneness, hardships, and suffering. The poet's best-known collection, and the only one composed in Castilian, *En las orillas del Sar* (1884; *Beside the River Sar*, 1937), was for many years the basis of her reputation. Published only a few months before her death, it contains poems written over a period of many years, intimate portrayals of the poet's sense of solitude, nostalgia, hopelessness, frustration, loss, and sorrow. Some dealing with religious themes express faith in God, while others express doubt or existential despair and question God's existence (these have been seen as precursors of poems of Antonio Machado and Miguel de *Unamuno, while her cultivation of folklore and social themes has been considered as a forerunner of the postwar "social poets"). Although she wrote some half-dozen novels, she is best remembered for her poetry, and her fame has grown continually since her death. In the post-Franco era of local autonomy of the regions distinguished by vernacular languages and cultures, of which Galicia is one of the most

important, Rosalía de Castro has become a Galician cultural icon.

Excluding poets writing in Catalan (which, like Galician, enjoyed a postromantic renaissance), there were few women of note between the death of Castro and turn-of-the-century poets. Rosario de *Acuña (1851–1923), primarily a dramatist, also wrote short stories, essays, and poetry, including *Ecos del alma* (1876; Echoes of the Soul), *Morirse a tiempo* (1880; To Die on Time), and the comic *Sentir y pensar* (1884; Feeling and Thinking). Blanca de los *Ríos de Lampérez (1862–1956) began writing in adolescence. *Esperanzas y recuerdos* (1881; Hopes and Memories) appeared three years after her first novel (she was also a literary critic, short story writer, and editor). Josefa Ugarte Barrientos (1854–1891), playwright and folklorist, collected traditional legends, retelling them in verse in *Recuerdos de Andalucía* (1874; Memories of Andalusia) and *Páginas en verso* (1882; Pages in Verse). Her best achievements were republished posthumously as *Poesías selectas* (1904; Selected Poems).

Unquestionably the most significant poet of this period, and one of Spain's most remarkable women, was Sofía Pérez Casanova de Lutoslawski (1861–1958)—poet, journalist, and brilliant foreign correspondent during World War I and the Russian Revolution, as well as a pioneering feminist, social worker, prolific novelist, translator, and author of children's books, short stories, essays, plays, and political commentary. After marrying a Polish nobleman in 1887, she lived most of her 95 years outside Spain. Well acquainted with the works of Coronado and Avellaneda, she "idolized" Rosalía de Castro, and her first collection, *Poesías* (1885), likewise reflects Galicia, although it is background, not leitmotiv. In prototypical romantic fashion, Casanova uses Gothic settings: ruined castles, Romanesque chapels, cemeteries, ancient cities. Yet she also celebrates progress, paints fishermen and miners, and exalts the dignity of work—themes closer to realism and naturalism. *Fugaces* (1898; Fleeting Things) reprints 14 poems from her first collection, plus 60 new compositions. Some convey travel impressions, especially her reactions to the frozen gloom of arctic winters and snow-covered steppes— silence, darkness, pale shapes, clouds, ice, and Siberian winds. She also expresses fear for the future of her infant daughters, while other poems are dedicated to friends, family, and other writers (mostly women). Poems on art and beauty reveal modernist influences, while others treat her daughter's death and her suffering of conjugal disaster (after bearing four daughters, her husband abandoned her for not giving him a son and married a young disciple). From 1904 to 1915, once more in Spain, she received the distinction (rare for a woman) of election to the Royal Galician Academy (1906) and the modernist Academia de Poesía Española (1911). *El cancionero de la dicha* (1911; Songbook of Happiness), prefaced by eight sonnets from modernist poets, contains selections from earlier collections plus 33 new compositions, 14 grouped under the title rubric and 19 subtitled "Los días de hoy" (Present Days). Less confessional and autobiographical, these modernist poems emphasize metric and formal experimentation but avoid decadence in favor of spiritual and moral concerns, light, music, beauty, unrealized ideals, death, fin-de-siècle tedium, disillusionment, and boredom (the latter being themes that recall Manuel Machado). Several poems describe paintings or evoke national heroes, while more specifically modernist motifs—roses, lilies, pagan gods, nymphs, and pale princesses—might be mistaken for Rubén Darío's. Casanova was much admired by writers of the first two decades of the twentieth century and later celebrated for her chronicles of war and revolution, returning triumphantly to Spain in 1919 to receive the country's highest medal for service to humanity, La Gran Cruz de Beneficencia. She was nominated in 1925 for a Nobel Prize and figured among very few women mentioned

in the Espasa-Calpe Encyclopedia (1913), where she received equal space with *Pardo Bazán. The only Spanish reporter covering World War I, the Russian Revolution, and World War II and its aftermath, she was confined behind the Iron Curtain for her last 20 years and essentially forgotten by her death. Although her modernist poetry has long since passed from fashion, male modernist poets have remained in the canon, while Casanova and her more personal, heartfelt pieces have been consigned to oblivion.

Work by

Casanova de Lutoslawski, Sofia. *El cancionero de la dicha*. Madrid: Regino Velasco, 1911.
———. *Fugaces*. La Coruña: A. Martínez, 1898.
———. *Poesías*. Madrid: A. J. Alaria, 1885.
Castro, Rosalia. *Obra poética*. Ed. Benito Varela Jácome. Barcelona: n.p., 1972.
———. *Obras completas*. 6th ed. Madrid: Aguilar, 1966.
Coronado, Carolina. *Poesías*. Edición, intro., and notes Noël Valis. Madrid: Castalia/Biblioteca de Escritoras, 1991.

Work about

Alayeto, Ofelia. "Sofía Casanova: A Bibliography." *Bulletin of Bibliography* 44.1 (1987): 46–61.
———. *Sofía Pérez Casanova (1861–1958): Spanish Poet, Journalist and Author*. Potomac, MD: Scripta Humanistica, 1992.
Albert Robatto, Matilde. *Rosalía de Castro y la condición femenina*. Madrid: Partenón, 1981.
Harter, Hugh A. *Gertrudis Gómez de Avellaneda*. Boston: G.K. Hall, 1981.
Kirkpatrick, Susan. *Las Románticas: Women Writers and Subjectivity in Spain, 1835–1850*. Berkeley and Los Angeles: U of California P, 1989.
Kulp-Hill, Kathleen. *Rosalía de Castro*. Boston: G.K. Hall, 1977.
Lazo, Raimundo. *Gertrudis Gómez de Avellaneda: La mujer y la poetisa*. Mexico: Porrúa, 1972.
Simón Palmer, María del Carmen. *Escritoras españolas del siglo XIX: Manual bio-bibliográfico*. Madrid: Castalia, 1991.

Janet Pérez

Pompeia, Nuria (1938–)

Born in Barcelona into a cultured and refined upper-class family, the intelligent and well-educated woman who writes under the pseudonym of Nuria Pompeia has not publicly revealed her real name. Reared during the most oppressive period of the postwar regime, she subsequently reacted with humor and decisiveness against the prevailing Victorian morality and conventional, patriarchal mores governing the education of women and girls during the Franco period. Beginning as a journalist, she cultivates the short story and cartoon and achieved unusual success with a series of cartoon books subverting traditional mores and phallocentric values and lampooning macho stereotypes, as well as patriarchal gender models for women. To Pompeia belongs the somewhat unusual distinction of having been the only woman in Spain to achieve fame as a cartoonist. Her character Palmira resembles Lucy of the "Peanuts" strip, an irrepressibly unpleasant brat known to newspaper readers not only in Spain but throughout the Spanish-speaking world. Pompeia's cartoons and comics are not for children, however, but for adolescents and adults; she writes primarily for and about women but without totally excluding the male reader. The style of both her humor and her graphics also recalls Jules Feiffer and his serious spoofs of contemporary neuroses and hang-ups.

As a journalistic cartoonist, Pompeia collaborated regularly with the Barcelona weekly newsmagazine *Triunfo* (comparable to *Time* and *Newsweek*); she later became managing editor of another weekly, *Por favor*. Pompeia writes both in Castilian and Catalan and has created something of a personal hybrid as her trademark genre, books with a blend of cartoons and texts incorporating both literary and graphic aspects. Predominantly if not exclusively feminist in her thematics, her writing in the satiric vein is frequently hilarious but never without an underlying seriousness.

Y fueron felices comiendo perdices (1970; And They Lived Happily Ever After Eating Partridges) alludes to a popular refrain at the same time that it subverts the Cinderella myth whereby all a woman's problems end happily at the altar, at the moment she embarks upon the married state. *Pels segles dels segles* (1971; For Centuries and Centuries) continues in the same vein, puncturing the balloons of stereotypical "happily ever after" romance. Another collection of cartoons featuring Palmira, this one contrasts masculine and feminine views of woman's lot, subtly combatting the traditional patriarchal view of marriage as the logical and proper goal of woman's existence. *La educación de Palmira* (1972; Educating Palmira) employs similar tactics, taking on Spain's educational establishment and particularly those in charge of educating girls and young women. Pompeia exposes the underlying premises of Spanish education as simplistic, erroneous but systematic deformations of woman's natural intelligence and creativity, a process that lays the groundwork for future existential alienation and frustration. Both completely serious and screamingly funny, Pompeia's graphics plus texts on the subjects of women's [mis]-education are masterpieces of their kind.

Mujercitas (1975; Little Women) presents a compendium of themes found in her earlier collections, combining incisive satire and side-splitting humor to indict socialization that transforms the active, creative, energetic, spontaneous girl-child into a passive, inhibited, bored, and boring adult. The clichés of sexist role-typing, traditional gender stereotyping, idealization of marriage and motherhood, as well as biblical justifications for male domination and double standards are juxtaposed to varied visions of contemporary feminine reality and frequently exploded in the process. Still more incisive, if possible, is *Maternasis* (1967; The Disease of Maternity), the collection most clearly linked with *Mujercitas* (neither of these features Palmira). Tremendously ironic, *Maternasis* relies heavily on visual effects to communicate the changes in a woman's body and woman's lifestyle that come with impending motherhood, subverting myths that idealize maternity as an idyllically happy state. Pompeia, herself the mother of several children, clearly writes from experience; although the medium depersonalizes her message, she manages to show the comical side of discomfort and pain, even as the pedestal is pulled from beneath the pregnancy myth.

Cinc centims (1981; Five Cents), a dozen short stories with predominantly feminist themes, is Pompeia's first exclusively verbal collection, composed in precise, vivid, colloquial Catalan. Incisive critiques of bourgeois lifestyle and values comprise a secondary thematic nucleus, appearing in scenes of a drunken dinner party, ritual weekend outings, varied pseudointellectual pursuits, and pseudoart collections. Sexist education, matrimony as patriarchal despotism, sexual politics, and the frustrations of women's aspirations toward liberation by one regime after another are among subjects treated.

Pompeia is clearly feminist, albeit somewhat unconventionally so, even if she does not belong to the Spanish Feminist Party. Because of the medium selected—journalistic cartoons and comics—and its wide diffusion, she had an enormous impact, not on literary critics (who as a whole took little or no notice) but on the reading public of all ages, especially girls, adolescents, and young women during the twilight years of the dictatorship who became the feminists of democratic Spain. *See also* Feminism in Spain: 1900–2000.

Work by

Cambios y recambios. Barcelona: Anagrama, 1993.
La educación de Palmira. N.p.: Andorra, 1972.
Maternasis. Barcelona: Kairós, 1967.
Mujercitas. Barcelona: Kairós, 1975.
Pels segles dels segles. Barcelona: Edicions 62, 1971.
Y fueron felices comiendo perdices. Barcelona: Kairós, 1970.

Janet Pérez

Portal, Marta (1930–)

Born in Nava, Asturias, writer, journalist, and literary critic, Marta Portal holds a Ph.D. in journalism from the Universidad Complutense of Madrid and teaches contemporary world literature at the same university. As a journalist she has written opinion columns and articles on current events and literary criticism for newspapers such as *ABC*, *PYRESA*, *Pueblo*, and *El Alcázar*. Her literary criticism has focused on Mexican literature (her doctoral dissertation was entitled "Procesos comunicativos en la narrativa de Juan Rulfo" [Communication Processes in the Narrative of Juan Rulfo]), but she has also written about other Latin American and Spanish authors. Particular fields of interest include indigenous Mexican literature, the literature of the Revolution, and contemporary Mexican literature. As a novelist she became known in 1966 with *A tientas y a ciegas* (Blindly and Gropingly), which won the Premio Planeta. Her work also merited the Adelaide Ristori prize for her fiction in 1983, the Horizonte 92 journalism award for her essay "El descubrimiento de América: Largo viaje hacia el futuro" (The Discovery of America: Long Journey toward the Future), and a Rotary Club prize in 1990 for her article "Europa es nuestro argumento" (Europe Is Our Theme/Argument). She has held positions on magazine editorial boards and in associations dealing with Hispano-American issues (especially Hispano-Mexican) and has served as juror for prestigious literary prizes such as the Premio Nacional de las Letras Españolas.

Portal's novels deal with problems that affect contemporary women, particularly in marital relationships. Her protagonists very often want to break free from a situation of unhappiness and pain brought about by selfish husbands who act in an insensitive, indifferent, nonunderstanding or even tyrannical way. These women are conscious of oppression and humiliation, but whereas some try to act to establish a sense of themselves and of their worth as human beings, others choose passivity. Portal offers readers a profound analysis of the psychological and emotional forces that move her protagonists. Her contribution to Spanish literature resides precisely in her ability to create complex characters who do not stand for prescribed, simplistic images of women. Her women struggle, suffer, doubt, and they wish to find solutions for themselves and their problems, but sometimes without success.

Another important aspect of her work is its profound philosophical and ethical content, which gives her writing a universal and abstract dimension. Her protagonists consider the implications of their behavior, and this leads them to question the necessity and validity of a set of mores and values that guide human conduct. The main metaphysical issues of her concern are the limits of freedom for the individual, the consequences of injustice and oppression, the loss of values in contemporary society, language as a concealment of reality, skepticism and boredom versus an attitude of engagement with life, passivity versus vitality, the capacity of humans to survive, and the possibility of self-knowledge. Adultery is a recurrent topic explored in Portal's narrative. Several of her protagonists face problems of conscience brought about by their relationships with another man. The affair, however, is usually lived as an authentic experience that fulfills them. Portal situates the problem outside the relationship (e.g., the idea of an "illegitimate" baby) in order to explore the moral implications of their conduct.

In *A tientas y a ciegas* (1966) a 30-year-old woman, Sara, considers the emptiness of her routine activities, her selfishness, and her condition as a parasite of the husband who sustains her. She decides to break with the tedium and take something from life. She then returns to study at the university, falls in love with her professor of French literature, Don José Vidal, and has an affair with him. This does not affect her married life as she and her husband were already sleeping in separate beds, and he was having affairs with several other women. Sara feels happy with José because he fulfills both her intellectual and emotional needs. Nevertheless, when she learns that she can become fertile after a medical intervention, she decides to have a

legitimate child with her husband Antonio and goes back to him.

Un espacio erótico (1982; An Erotic Space), a novel of introspection, narrates the confrontation of the protagonist with herself. Elvira returns to her country, Spain, in an attempt to regain a sense of herself after having lived a nightmare in Mexico with a ruthless husband who has sexually degraded her and expressed resentment toward her because he thinks of Elvira as a representative of the "invader" culture from the time of the Spanish colonies. He blackmails her with incriminating pictures, forcing her to abandon her only son. Back in Spain, Elvira works as a journalist and lives in an apartment her cousin has lent her. The narration of her present life story (her love relationships with Montoro and her cousin Elena) is combined with her remembrance of past dejection and the impotence she experienced in the absurd life with her husband. To exorcise her anguish, Elvira must confront her life and innermost self with great honesty, to accept herself as she was in those past moments of complete weakness and reconcile them with her new life. From this process of self-analysis she learns that despite her earlier self-defeating attitude, comfortable masochism, and loss of dignity, she can break with her pain and misery. She is then able to understand her weaknesses, her strengths, and her capacity to act and stand for life; she now has the wisdom of the survivor, which makes her even stronger.

Pago de traición (1983; Payment of Betrayal) constitutes one of Portal's most elaborate novels both in narrative technique and metaphysical insight. In this work, the protagonist's goal is to get to know herself entirely. The sentence that opens the first part of the novel ("I know more than my conscience") points to the need to use other capacities, apart from reason, to achieve self-knowledge. Instinct, intuition, memory, feelings, and spirituality, therefore, are sources from which to draw in order to understand one's personal story. However, the protagonist's search becomes more difficult as she arrives in Madrid and routine begins once again to dominate her life until, in the end, she lets herself be carried away by circumstances. Other important subjects of philosophical investigation are time, love, the existence of the world separated from conscience, the afterlife as stipulated by religion, infancy as a stage of innocence that has been lost, the struggle between thoughts and feelings, and human relationships.

Her recent novel *El ángel caído* (1994; The Fallen Angel) concerns the life of Eugenio Reverte, a successful lawyer and businessman. The conflict arises because the protagonist is not able to distribute his time between his job and the people close to him (his wife, daughter, and lover). His professional triumph implies a failure of the man and the family. Alicia, his wife, is an unhappy woman who remains with her husband only for the sake of the children. When they grow up, she seeks a divorce, since the function imposed upon her by society has ended. The daughter, Cecilia, is a spoiled "daddy's-girl" who marries, quickly separates, and then commits suicide when she learns about her father's lover. Pilar, Eugenio's secretary, represents the resented lover who despises her situation but nevertheless stays with her man. This novel explores different images of women that have become literary archetypes.

Portal's novels illustrate the search for what Elvira, in *Un espacio erótico*, terms "a certain kind of erudition of life," wherein knowledge and the capacity for vitality complement one another harmoniously. This "erudition of life" that comes both from intelligence and from experience bestows wisdom on human creatures about life and survival. The ideal result of this knowledge is to reconcile the reality of experience with one's reflections upon that experience. Portal's novels present the rupture of this balance and the protagonists' endeavors to set it straight. *See also* Eroticism in Contemporary Spanish Women Writers' Narrative

Work by

El ángel caído. Barcelona: Planeta, 1994.
A ras de las sombras. Barcelona: Planeta, 1968.
A tientas y a ciegas. Barcelona: Planeta, 1966.
El buen camino. Barcelona: Planeta, 1975.
"La enmatada." *Relatos de novelistas españolas, 1939–1969*. Madrid: Castalia, 1994. 379–449.
Un espacio erótico. Madrid: Ibérico Europea, 1982.
Ladridos a la luna. Barcelona: Plaza y Janés, 1970.
El malmuerto. Barcelona: Planeta, 1968.
Pago de traición. Barcelona: Planeta, 1983.
La veintena. Madrid: Magisterio Español, 1973.

Work about

Bobes, María del Carmen. "La novela y la poética femenina." *Signa*. Madrid: UNED e Instituto de semiótica literaria y teatral, 1994. n.p.
García Viño, M. "Marta Portal: De la estética al conocimiento." *Arbor* 117 (January 1984): 127–131.
González, Carlos. *El periodismo de Marta Portal*. No city: n.p., 1994.

Eva Legido-Quigley

Puértolas Villanueva, Soledad (1947–)

Born in Zaragoza, this prolific writer moved at age 14 to Madrid, in whose outskirts she has lived since, except for time spent in Norway and Santa Barbara, California, places that sometimes appear in her fictions. Soledad Puértolas studied journalism in the Centro Juan XXIII in Madrid. Her thesis, "El Madrid de *La lucha por la vida*" (Madrid as seen in [Baroja's] *Struggle for Life*), published in 1969, contrasts Pío *Baroja's descriptions of the city with those in the press of the time. She subsequently obtained a master of arts degree in Spanish and Portuguese Language and Literature at the University of California in Santa Barbara. Puértolas has worked in the Ministry of Culture in Madrid as an adviser, at Editorial Destino publishing house, and as a journalist.

In addition to a steady stream of novels— *El bandido doblemente armado* (1979; The Doubly Armed Bandit), *Burdeos* (1986; *Bordeaux*, 1998), *Todos mienten* (1988; They're All Liars), *Queda la noche* (1989; The Night

Remains), *Días del Arenal* (1992; Quicksand Days), *Si al atardecer llegara el mensajero* (1995; If the Messenger Should Arrive at Dusk), *Una vida inesperada* (1997; An Unexpected Life), *La rosa de plata* (1999; Silver Rose), and *La señora Berg* (1999; Mrs. Berg)— Puértolas has published two long narratives for young readers—*El recorrido de los animales* (1975; Travels/Route/Inspection of the Animals) and *La sombra de una noche* (1987; The Shade of One Night)—and several collections of short stories—*Una enfermedad moral* (1987; A Moral Illness), *La corriente del Golfo* (1993; The Gulf Current), *Gente que vino a mi boda* (1998; People Who Came to My Wedding), and *Adiós a las novias* (2000; Good-Bye to the Brides). She published a book of essays, *La vida oculta* (Anagram Prize for Essay, 1993; The Hidden Life), where, in discussing the relation of life with literature, she makes it clear that she wishes to be known as a good writer, not as a good *woman* writer. *Recuerdos de otra persona* (1996; Somebody Else's Memories) is an autobiographical text. Her works have been translated to French, Portuguese, English, German, Italian, and Greek.

Puértolas's first novel, *El bandido doblemente armado* (Sésamo Prize, 1979), is narrated by a budding young writer who is fascinated with his friend Terry's family, dominated by the presence and influence of the mother, Mrs. Lennox. Events are hinted at more than real. The adventures never quite happen. The title, a metaphor for different options in life, refers to the strategies in flipping a coin: staying always with heads or tails, or waiting for the first failure to change sides. The outstanding accomplishment of the novel is that despite the fact that it maintains the readers' expectations and interest and is recounted in the intimate first person, the narrator really tells us very little. He is a master of ambiguity, subtlety, evasion, and omission. The clandestine business in which Terry Lennox is involved and the reasons for the suicide of the narrator's office

mate, husband of Eileen, are just two of the mysteries we are left to unravel.

Burdeos (1986) consists of three loosely related stories. Published in the year of Spain's entrance into the European Common Market, it is a "European" book because of its setting and principal character. For example, the indeterminate narrator of "Las capitales del mundo" (World Capitals) relates the experiences of a female American traveler— Lillian Skalnick, whose father had immigrated to America from an unnamed European country. She undertakes a trip of discovery from America to Europe, looking for adventure in Paris, Bordeaux, Rome, and Venice, but finds little more than trivial and transient love affairs.

Puértolas's protagonists, both male and female, tend to experience—or rather react to—the possibility, reality, or perception of adventure. For Pauline in *Burdeos*, the "adventures" are those of others around her (including a classic case of battered-wife syndrome). Several stories in *Una enfermedad moral* feature protagonists who lead singularly unexciting lives into which an unexpected incident intrudes. These are of a physical nature in "Un país extranjero" (A Foreign Land), "Contra Fortinelli" (Against Fortinelli), and "La llamada nocturna" (The Nocturnal Summons). In "Contra Fortinelli," a slap of male aggression is eventually returned in just retribution with a female kick, sending the would-be Don Juan into a "womanly faint." Place—and sometimes description of place—is important in some works, as an impulse in itself to possible adventure, underscored in titles: *Burdeos* and two of its three subtitles, "Entre dos mares" (Between Two Seas) and "Las capitales del mundo," and other story titles, such as "Un país extranjero," "La orilla del Danubio" (The Bank of the Danube), and "En el límite de la ciudad" (At City Limits). There is a tendency in this book, as in others by Puértolas, toward unusual, exotic-sounding names and places like "Koothar," "Hirvink," "Lathi."

Puértolas's 1988 novel, a *bildungsroman* titled *Todos mienten*, which begins with the phrase "My house was full of women," is as much about women's lives as about the life of its passive male narrator-protagonist and the influence of women in his life, especially the mother and grandmother, two key figures that reappear in Puértolas's writing ("El origen del deseo" [The Origin of Desire] in *Una enfermedad moral* and *Queda la noche*).

Until *Queda la noche*, Puértolas avoids women narrators, which she later has explained as a deliberate attempt to distance herself from autobiographical involvement. Thus readers see the inscrutable Eva in a story of *Una enfermedad moral* through the eyes of the male novelist whom she has come to interview. The narrators of other stories in the volume assume an asexual, impersonal identity and maintain a respectful distance between themselves and the female protagonists: The narrator of "Un país extranjero" refers to "la señora Ebelmayer" only by her married name, while the narrator of "Contra Fortinelli" alternates between "la señora Empson," "Rosalyn," and "Rosalyn Walls," according to the situation in which others view the woman, as wife, ex-actress, stepmother. "El origen del deseo" is narrated by an asexual voice that eventually and almost imperceptibly reveals a female identity.

Honored by the Planeta Prize three years after Spain entered the Common Market and as the country was preparing for the Quincentennial celebration, Puértolas's bestseller *Queda la noche* (1989) reflects the history and reality of its time. It opens new avenues, as a novel of adventure, discovery, travel, and new Spanish realities in an era of openness that is both economical and cultural. *Queda la noche* represents a change in direction from the Spanish novel of the previous decade, dominated by metaliterary introspection on the processes of writing and reading and by fragmented, complicated stylistic structures. The novel is straightforward, with a strongly narrative first person and external occurrences in a concrete contemporary world. It is a novel of adventure, suspense, mystery,

and intrigue that breaks with the post-Franco tendency to examine the past and focuses instead on the present lived by a liberated contemporary woman free to travel in an international environment. Like the new Spain that was entering the adventure of new economic and international relations, Aurora, the protagonist of *Queda la noche*, travels to India and "discovers" Europe. Travel is no longer exile but adventure, *female* adventure. Women are no longer subject to masculine domination like their foremothers. The traditional female destiny of boredom here is an impulse toward adventure, fueled by a hyperactive imagination. As Carmen *Laforet's *Nada* did back in 1944, *Queda la noche* captures the spirit and atmosphere of a decisive moment of Spain, a country now open to new currents, like Aurora, holding on to its past but no longer enclosed in it. In *Queda la noche*, discovering other places leads to self-discovery.

In her next novel, *Días del Arenal* (1992), Puértolas revisits settings (El Saúco, El Arenal), characters (Carolina Arranz, Ramiro, Araceli), and the idea of a chain of coincidences from *Queda la noche* to narrate the "secret" lives of several characters linked by somewhat ephemeral or accidental circumstances. Three of the four stories present some extramarital relation that figures as a momentary liberation or as the realization of fantasies, as much for women as for men. The love adventures are rather trivial, except for those who live them, and appear inspired by the conviction (developed in Puértolas's next novel) that "having only one life is very little" and by the characters' desire to live a life different from their own. The only fantasy motivated by reasons other than passion is that of a female character whose aspiration is to publish her poetry. For the others, their wishes to live the impossible dream do not go beyond efforts to free themselves a little from their routine lives. Echoes of *Don Quijote* abound, especially in the influence of books (here romantic novels and movies). Places and symbolic spaces, especially interior spaces ("women's" space) are featured, as well as topics of women's issues, such as the situation of abandoned women with children, personal freedom, and the right to adventure.

La corriente del Golfo (1993) shows Puértolás's mature mastery in a variety of short story types: the mystery story ("El anuncio" [The Advertisement]), the surprise ending ("A la hora en que cierran los bares" [The Hour When The Bars Close]), the metaliterary narrative ("El reconocimiento" [The Recognition]), and the story in which nothing seems to happen amid expectation, strangeness, and ambiguity.

Si al atardecer llegara el mensajero (1995) is as innovative with regard to genre as was *Queda la noche*. It is at the same time mythology, fable, science fiction, and allegory. Its characters, some human and others semidivine, have exotic names reminiscent of *El bandido doblemente armado* and *Una enfermedad moral*. The main characters are not women, which is surprising in an era of *feminism. In fact, if the author's name were not on the cover, it would be difficult to identify the novel as having been penned by a woman. Puértolás indulges in philosophical speculation about the "great questions" of life, death, time, and the afterlife that have been largely absent from "women's literature." The novel is based on the suggestive premise that mortals know the date of their death. The protagonist, Tobías Kaluga, whose abode is heaven and who has over the centuries assumed diverse human identities, suggests to God the experiment of testing whether it would be better for mortals to be ignorant of their day of death. God gives him the chance to try his theory, and Tobías does so with Arturo Nizranín Nirkaunsiri, who assures him that knowing how much time he has left is the greatest torture and accepts the terms of the proposal. The rest of the novel follows the consequences of the experiment, though other concerns rise to the fore as Tobías identifies with Arturo, who strangely is almost his double. The novel is largely a lei-

surely colloquium or Socratic dialogue between the two men from different worlds, and occasionally other participants, with descriptions of Eternity and the Afterlife. The characters discuss solitude, friendship, war, women, the institution of the family, the marvel of dreams, liberty, human emotions, communication, the existence of evil, and above all, the value of human love above even divine love. Along with the conversation, mystery, strange coincidences, and happenings maintain reader interest in a sort of philosophical magical realism. A good deal of the conversation is about literature itself, which is understandable in this writer in whose novels and short stories "adventure" is as much a creation of the mind as of reality.

Puértolás's most recent fictions continue to explore worlds of both imagination and reality. In *La rosa de plata*, it is the fabled Arthurian world of chivalry, with overtones of the *Quijote*; in *La vida inesperada*, it is subjective reality through which the anonymous woman protagonist-writer defines and constructs her identity, much in the same way that Puértolás has in all her works.

Work by

Adiós a las novias. Barcelona: Anagrama, 2000.

El bandido doblemente armado. Madrid: Anagrama, 1979.

Bordeaux. Trans. Francisca González Arias. Lincoln: U of Nebraska P, 1998.

Burdeos. Barcelona: Anagrama, 1986.

La corriente del Golfo. Barcelona: Anagrama, 1993.

Días del Arenal. Barcelona: Planeta, 1992.

Una enfermedad moral. Madrid: Trieste, 1982; 3rd ed. Barcelona: Anagrama, 1988.

Gente que vino a mi boda. Barcelona: Anagrama, 1998.

El Madrid de "La lucha por la vida." Madrid: Helios, 1969.

Queda la noche. Barcelona: Planeta, 1989.

El recorrido de los animales. Madrid: Júcar, 1975.

Recuerdos de otra persona. Barcelona: Anagrama, 1996.

La rosa de plata. Madrid: Espasa, 1999.

La señora Berg. Barcelona: Anagrama, 1999.

Si al atardecer llegara el mensajero. Barcelona: Anagrama, 1995.

La sombra de una noche. Madrid: Anaya, 1987.

Todos mienten. Barcelona: Anagrama, 1988.

La vida oculta. Barcelona: Anagrama, 1993.

La vida se mueve: A pesar de las convenciones, los prejuicios y la desigualdad. Madrid: País-Aguilar, 1996.

Work about

Bellver, Catherine G. "Two New Women Writers from Spain." *Letras Femeninas* 8 (1982): 3–7.

Camarero Arribas, Tomás. "Lógica de una narrativa en *Una enfermedad moral* de Soledad Puértolas." *Ventanal* 14 (1988): 133–157.

Fajardo, José Manuel. "Escribo lo que puedo, no lo que quiero" (interview). *Cambio 16*, November 6, 1989: 38–39.

Fernández Cubas, Cristina, and Soledad Puértolas. "Feminismo y literatura no tienen nada que ver." *Mester* 20 (1991): 157–165.

———. "Soledad Puértolas: La ciudad de las almas." *Historia y crítica de la literatura española.* Ed. Francisco Rico. Barcelona: Grijalbo, 1992. 9: 371–375.

Intemann, Marguerite DiNonno. *El tema de la soledad en la narrativa de Soledad Puértolas.* Lewiston: Mellen UP, 1994.

Irizarry, Estelle. "Aventura y apertura en la nueva novela española: *Queda la noche* de Soledad Puértolas." *Homenaje a Donald Bleznick.* Ed. Delia Galván, Anita Stoll, and Philippa Yin. Cleveland, OH: Cleveland UP, 1995. 59–74.

Mattalia, Sonia. "Entre miradas: Las novelas de Soledad Puértolas." *Ventanal: Revista de Creación y Crítica* 14 (1988): 171–192.

Pritchett, Kay. "Soledad Puértolas. *Queda la noche.*" *World Literature Today* 65 (1991): 275–276.

Riera, Miguel. "Los vacíos del tiempo: Entrevista con Soledad Puértolas." *Quimera* 72 (1987): 42–48.

Talbot, Lynn K. "Entrevista con Soledad Puértolas." *Hispania* 71 (1988): 882–883.

Treacy, Mary Jane. "Soledad Puértolas." *Spanish Women Writers: A Bio-Bibliographical Source Book.* Ed. Linda Gould Levine, Ellen Engelson Marson, and Gloria Feiman Waldman. March 5, 1998. Interview. Westport, CT: Greenwood, P 1993. 397–403.

Tsuchiya, Akiko. "Language, Desire, and the Feminine Riddle in Soledad Puertolas's *La indiferencia de Eva.*" *Revista de Estudios Hispánicos* 35 (1991): 69–79.

Urbanc, Katica. Entrevista. Soledad Puértolas: "He vuelto a la realidad de otra manera . . ." http://www.ucm.es/info/especulo/numero8/k_urbanc.htm

Estelle Irizarry

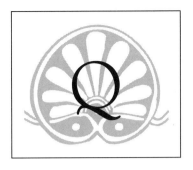

Quevedo y Villegas, Francisco de (1580–1645): His Portrayal of Women

Born September 17 in Madrid to an aristocratic family—both of his parents held positions at Court—Francisco de Quevedo y Villegas studied first with the Jesuits and later at the Universities of Alcalá and Valladolid, obtaining an excellent humanistic education. One of the first writers to partake in the modern "culture of celebrity," he made a character out of his persona and eventually became a folkloric figure. In 1617 Philip III named him knight of the Order of Santiago. Rising to become counselor to Pedro Téllez Girón, duke of Osuna, and viceroy of Sicily and Naples, he was arrested several times for political and literary reasons. In 1634 he wed Doña Esperanza de Mendoza in a brief, unfortunate marriage. He is the master satirist in the history of Spanish literature, well regarded by contemporaries such as Miguel de Cervantes and Lope de *Vega and bitter lifelong enemy of poet Luis de Góngora. His excellence as a writer derives in part from his ability to weave the discourse of high culture with marginalized discourses such as underworld slang and the obscene.

Quevedo is not a systematic thinker, but he is very challenging as a social and political writer. The sum of his contradictions, assertions, and doubts provides one of the better literary documents concerning the representation of women during the baroque period. Quevedo supports the status quo, but he discusses it so much and returns so many times to the same issues that on occasion he ends up challenging his own views and those of the aristocratic order. Nonetheless, in his wide-ranging opus, the dominant portrayal of woman is negative and misogynist.

Quevedo's love poetry is heir to the classics, the *courtly love tradition, cancionero (songbook) poetry, and Renaissance literature. He follows the topics of these traditions closely, showing originality in his striking use of language as he strives to surpass the clichés of Petrarchism. As a modern poet, he rejects the medieval concept of service to the beloved. The role of vassal holds no interest; instead, Quevedo uses love poetry to explore his personality as a lover. The lady, typically distant, inaccessible, and lacking personality, is sketched via standard literary topics; whether addressed as Laura, Beatriz, Elisa, Filis, Flori, Floris, or Lisis, she is the same woman, and her role is that of a foil to enhance the suitor's worth.

Women who deviate from this idealized role of beautiful young foil are criticized or attacked. Thus Quevedo rejects intellect in a woman, for a *mujer discreta* (intelligent woman) does not function as a foil. Crosby observes that Quevedo criticizes men who pursue ugly or intelligent women because, for him, such behavior violates the natural order. For Quevedo women are objects of physical desire, made to be touched (*palpar*), valued for a beauty that is meant to be exploited by men. Many poems capture woman's beauty in a still life, as in "A Flori, que tenía unos claveles entre el cabello rubio" (To Flori with Carnations in Her Blonde Hair), or "A un bostezo de Floris" (To Floris's Yawn). Communication between the lovers occurs through the eyes, following the tradition of Renaissance animism.

Despite Quevedo's definition of the ideal woman as beautiful object to be consumed, his love poetry also betrays an implicit rejection of woman beneath the surface adoration. One important group of poems explores the link between love and death, of which the most famous is "Polvo enamorado" (Loving Ash). Considered by Dámaso Alonso to be the finest love poem in the history of Spanish poetry, it tells of a lover who continues loving after death. At the same time, the topic of "loving ash" symbolizes the impossibility of love: This lover may wish to demonstrate his love through eternity, but he reaches the height of passion only when the woman is absent. The closest that the poetic voice comes to expressing a sexual encounter in the love poetry is found in the poem "¡Ay Floralba! Soñé que te . . . ¡Direlo?" (Oh, Floralba, I dreamed that I . . . Shall I Say It?), and it happens in a dream.

As observed above, women who deviate in any way from the role of idealized object of physical desire, as defined in the love poems, are denigrated by Quevedo throughout his writings. A favorite target is the old woman. With this topic Quevedo attacks not only senescence but also arrogance. The old woman represents death and also delivers death to those close to her. The *Celestina* character is another of Quevedo's favorite targets, as seen in Pablos's mother in his picaresque narrative *El buscón* (written before 1610; The Life of a Scoundrel). He also scorns old women who attempt to remarry,

portraying them as lascivious, returning in this case to the medieval characterization of women as physical creatures unable to control such appetite. In the unbound poems, those that remained unpublished for decades because of censorship fear, the attacks are extremely bitter. His *Sueños* (Dreams), a collection of apocalyptic satiric essays, also contains much invective directed at women. In the *Alguacil endemoniado* (Bedeviled Bailiff), he likens men who pursue old women to homosexuals. The *Alguacil endemoniado* also inveighs harshly against men who fall in love with nuns, because one cannot make love to them. Ugly women end up in hell because they always want to sin; beautiful women also sin, but they have time to repent. The *diablas*, the female devils, are extremely ugly, but none of them is from Spain. Any relationship with a *dueña, another stock type routinely criticized and ridiculed by many writers of the day, is for Quevedo a worse punishment than death by hanging or galleys. The attack on *dueñas* is especially bitter in the essay *El sueño de la muerte* (Dream of Death).

Another theme that inspired much satiric verse is modern women's ungoverned appetite for money. Critics agree that Quevedo is one of the strongest defender of values of the *ancien régime* and the sacralized society of the seventeenth century, a moment when the divorce between aristocracy and estate was becoming apparent. Failing to understand that modern marriage is an interchange of patrimony instead of lineage, Quevedo was sincerely bewildered by women who seek money instead of nobility from the male aristocracy. Maravall, among others, has noted that while the Middle Ages scorned women primarily for being lecherous, in the baroque period the problem is greed. In Quevedo's *Sueños*, husbands walk about naked, having been forced to give their wives everything they had. Ladies of the court are seen to behave as prostitutes when they marry for money, a motivation that Quevedo accepts in lower-class women but finds abhorrent among the nobility. In other satiric poems, he attacks cuckoldry when husbands are "kept" by the lovers of their wives' lovers. He also mercilessly attacks women lovers of priests, false virgins, prostitutes who ply their trade in carriages, and the new "female consumer" who disappears in an assemblage of clothes, cardboard, leather, wigs, *cosmetics, cork, wool, dyes, silk, wood, bones, and jewels.

Female characters from mythology can also become targets of Quevedo's satire. Orpheus is congratulated for having lost his wife twice. In a burlesque version of Heroe and Leander's myth, Heroe is sturdy and horny. When Quevedo rewrites the myth of Apollo and Daphne, he does not condone Apollo's violence and his attempt to rape the nymph; but in the case of Diana and Actaeon, after seeing her taking a bath naked, his dogs kill him. The moral of the poem is that the uncontrolled desire for women will kill men. At the other end of the spectrum, his picaresque poems, called *jácaras*, feature both male and female ruffians, the so-called *valentonas*. Other *jácaras* satirize old women who get married, *dueñas*, female social climbers, prostitutes with *syphilis, and male and female black slaves.

In his religious poetry Quevedo has poems to the Virgin Mary like "Mujer llama a su Madre cuando expira" (He Calls His Mother Woman When He Expires). These are conventional poems, in this one the Mother of God restores the order lost in nature after Eve's sin.

In Quevedo's essential *misogyny, all women are the same—made for their physical use by men. Distinctions of class are ultimately irrelevant, and in this, he expresses prevailing views among many contemporary writers, in Spain as well as other parts of Europe. There are times when his attitude is more lenient and less patriarchal. In "Genealogía de los modorros" (Genealogy of the Dull), he established that women are neither worse nor better than men. In the *Sueño La hora de todos* (Everybody's Time), Maravall has identified an episode dedicated to fair

vindication of women. For a short period of time, women acquire rights as free and able human beings equal to men. During the uprising, women present their statements of vindication, and the narrator inserts no negative comments. Women label men as tyrants because even if women comprise half of humankind, men made the laws to subdue them. Men do not let women study because they (justly) fear women will excel therein. Men forbid women to bear arms out of fear. Men declare wars and women suffer the consequences. There is a double standard in adultery, death penalty for women, entertainment for men. Women cannot control their gaze or how they are ogled by men. And as Sor Juana subsequently observes in "Hombres necios que acusáis," Quevedo says that bad women are ultimately the result of evil men.

Work by

La hora de todos. Ed. Luisa López-Grigera. Madrid: Castalia, 1975.

Obras completas. Ed. José Manuel Blecua. Barcelona: Planeta, 1971.

Poesía varia. Ed. James O. Crosby. Madrid: Cátedra, 1989.

Sueños y discursos. Ed. James O. Crosby. Madrid: Castalia, 1993.

Work about

Baum, Doris L. *Traditionalism in the Works of Francisco de Quevedo*. Chapel Hill: U of North Carolina P, 1970.

Iffland, James. *Quevedo and the Grotesque*. 2 vols. London: Tamesis, 1978, 1982.

Kercher, Dora M. "The Economy of Misogyny in Quevedo's *Mundo por de dentro*." *Women in the Literature of Medieval and Golden Age Spain*. Ed. Sandra M. Foa. Syracuse: Onondaga Community College, 1978. 64–73.

Maravall, José Antonio. "Sobre el pensamiento social y político de Quevedo (una revisión)." *Homenaje a Quevedo: Actas de la II Academia Literaria Renacentista*. Ed. Víctor García de la Concha. Salamanca: U de Salamanca, 1982. 69–131.

Mas, Amédée. *La caricature de la femme du mariage et de l'amour dans l'œuvre de Quevedo*. Paris: Ediciones Hispano-Americanas, 1957.

Maurer, Christopher. " 'Soñé que te . . . ¡dírelo?' El

soneto erótico en los siglos XVI y XVII." *Edad de Oro* 9 (1990): 149–167.

Morreale, Margherita. "Un poema mariano de Quevedo (son. 176), leído con criterios tradicionales." *Serta philologica. F. Lázaro Carreter: Natalem diem sexagesimun.* Madrid: Cátedra, 1983. 355–364.

Pozuelo-Yvancos, José María. *El lenguaje poético de la lírica amorosa de Quevedo.* Murcia: Universidad de Murcia, 1979.

Salvador A. Oropesa

Quiroga, Elena (1921–1995)

Primarily a writer of fiction, Elena Quiroga was born in the province of Santander, the sixteenth of 17 children of a minor Galician nobleman. Her mother died when she was not yet two years old, and she spent her childhood with her father and numerous siblings in a small Galician village, variously identified as Villoria and El Barco de Valdeorras (Orense). She received a traditional Catholic upbringing, spent six years in a convent school in Bilbao, and finished her high school in Rome just before the outbreak of the Spanish Civil War in 1936, subsequently spending some time in southern France. In 1938, she returned to Spain, living for the remainder of the war in Galicia. From early in life, she had read extensively in her father's and grandfather's libraries and continued to do so; after moving to La Coruña with her father in 1942, she began to take a more active interest in literature and published her first novel, *La soledad sonora* (1949; Sonorous Solitude), a somewhat melodramatic love story set against the background of war and featuring the Spanish volunteers (largely Falangists) of the "Blue Division" who fought with the Nazis on the Russian front. This work was not included in the author's complete works, and she essentially repudiated it later in life.

Viento del norte (1951; North Wind), reminiscent with its air of naturalism of some rural Galician novels of *Pardo Bazán, presents a study of the orphaned or abandoned peasant girl, Marcela, and the wealthy landowner, Alvaro, in whose home she was raised. Marcela later accepts marriage with him, believing she must obey the master's wishes, and bears a son, although the relationship is distant and becomes more so when her husband is confined to a wheelchair. Marcela begins to spend time with her husband's aunt and cousin on a neighboring estate but is followed by one of her husband's associates who attempts to seduce her. When she belatedly realizes her love and gratitude for her protector and rushes home, she finds that he has died, alone. Despite the somewhat melodramatic ending, the novel was well received in Galicia; critics elsewhere found it anachronistic, and Quiroga, embarrassed by her early efforts, began to investigate literary theory and structure. Afterward, she told interviewers that each of her subsequent novels was in some sense different, a new experiment. In 1950, Quiroga married Dálmiro de la Válgoma, a specialist in heraldry, moving to Madrid, where she lived for the rest of her life.

La sangre (1952; Blood) utilizes an experimental perspective: The novel is narrated from the viewpoint of an ancient chestnut tree that has grown for several generations beside the ancestral mansion of a family of rural Galician nobility, witnessing the incidents of a dynastic chronicle narrated from the tree's limited perspective (when characters move beyond the tree's radius of observation, they disappear from the narrative). Culminating events include both the felling of the tree and extinction of the dynasty, on the eve of the Civil War. The novelettes, *La otra ciudad* (The Other City) and *Trayecto uno* (Bus #1), both published in 1953, still fairly conservative, are noteworthy mainly because the author's focus shifts to the city, continuing in *Algo pasa en la calle* (1954; Something's Happening in the Street). This novel, one of Quiroga's best, and unquestionably her most sophisticated work of the 1950s, is more experimental, utilizing a dead protagonist, Ventura, who lies awaiting burial. Readers must reconstruct Ventura's personality from the partial perspectives of other characters and eventually decide whether his death was suicide or an accident. Most of the novel is told via interior monologues of those who knew Ventura, a university professor: his legal wife Esperanza and daughter Agata, her husband Froilán (the most objective "witness"), his common-law wife Presencia and their son Asís, the priest who administered the last rites, and a few marginal characters who serve largely to characterize the wives or expand the vision of Ventura. Set in contemporary Madrid, the novel daringly treated a taboo subject: the impossibility of divorce and its impact upon those involved in incompatible marriages, as well as upon families not recognized by society or the Church. The two wives seem calculated as opposites, with the legal wife being vain, selfish, coquettish, hypocritical, the "other woman" a compendium of Christian morality and virtues. Quiroga creates a situation wherein the officially sanctioned marriage appears to have been more immoral than the unrecognized one, implicitly defending those women victimized by the Franco regime's abolition of divorce (which had been legal under the Republic); subsequent marriages were held invalid. Although the novelist avoids the word "divorce," it appears that Ventura and Esperanza were legally separated, implicitly divorced during the time of the Republic.

Quiroga repeats the technique of interior monologues by a series of characters who serve to characterize a mute protagonist in *La enferma* (1955; The Sick Woman); although not dead, she is immobilized and has refused to speak since her fiancé abandoned her years before. Again, readers must combine and compare contrasting and sometimes contradictory perspectives to determine the relative rightness or wrongness of Liberata (the sick woman) and Telmo (her boyfriend), as the Galician fishing village is divided in pro-Liberata and pro-Telmo factions. A second story line concerns a woman from Madrid who is visiting in the village while settling an estate (she, like the reader, must try to determine the somewhat nebu-

lous facts and motivations). On one level, the novel might be seen as an implied commentary on Spanish society in the early part of the twentieth century, when it was usually socially disastrous for a woman to be jilted (as portrayed in *García Lorca's *Doña Rosita la soltera o el lenguaje de las flores*); on another level, Quiroga combats stereotypical reader expectations, because there are strong hints that Liberata was spoiled, possessive, and domineering and that her attempts at total control drove Telmo away.

The stream-of-consciousness technique reappears in *La careta* (1955; The Mask), a psychological analysis of Moisés who, as a child during the Civil War, witnessed the brutal assassination of his parents and has since lived in a state of alienation, coddled by relatives who believe he is a martyr and hero. In actuality, he is revealed as amoral and egotistical, hiding a dreadful secret slowly revealed in the course of the narrative: His mother was wounded but had not died when shot by the terrorists who killed his father; she was allowed to bleed to death and perhaps asphyxiated by Moisés in his efforts to keep her from summoning help and thereby putting him also at risk. Beneath his mask of innocence is a sadist who enjoys subtle psychological tortures of his relatives; he eventually kills one cousin in "self-defense" after obliging him to share his lover. Imbued with existentialism, the novel emphasizes the concept of inauthenticity—hence, the ironic significance of the title. Several women appear in the novel, but all are filtered through the consciousness of Moisés, an unreliable narrator.

Plácida, la joven, y otras narraciones (1956; Young Plácida and Other Tales) brings together three novelettes, two of them previously published separately: *La otra ciudad* concentrates on the development of four characters who are connected with the cemetery just outside the Madrid city limits and lacks plot in the traditional sense. *Trayecto uno* (in the vein of *El pez sigue flotando* by Dolores *Medio) presents a heterogeneous group of characters, unrelated except for their being in the same place for a certain period of time—in this case, on the bus that follows a route passing the author's home, precisely on the afternoon of January 15, 1953. For the first time, Quiroga employs objectivist techniques. In *Plácida, la joven*, the novelist returns to rural Galicia to focus on an orphaned peasant who dies in childbirth at age 20, leaving an orphaned infant to begin again the same cycle of poverty, hardships, hunger, and suffering. Quiroga dedicates the novel to Plácida, the young fishwife who was a real-life model, as well as to all Galician women and their enduring patience in difficult lives. Four different characters in this novel, including the narrator, have lost their mothers at birth, and Plácida's biography is typical: Raised by neighbors, working from childhood, never having anything of her own, she married when already pregnant and, because her husband went to sea to support his family, was alone when the baby came. She did not summon help until after being in labor for some time, and by the time a doctor arrived, she had bled almost to death. The doctor, a spokesperson for Quiroga, indirectly reveals via his diatribe both the stoicism and self-sufficiency of peasant women who seek help only in matters of life and death. This novelette is one of the most feminist of Quiroga's narratives.

Her most fictional or imaginative novel (i.e., with no connection to her own experience) is *La última corrida* (1958; The Last Bullfight). Set beyond her familiar regions of Galicia, Santander and Madrid, it has as its protagonist an aged, unglamorous, mutilated bullfighter, at the end of a mediocre career (actually, three bullfighters appear, at different career stages). Most of the novel employs objectivist techniques (third-person, external, cinematographic narrative), with the remainder relying mostly on dialogue. Presumably Quiroga wished to demonstrate that she could handle topics beyond "women's themes"; women's roles in this novel are minor, limited to the protagonist's relationships

with Prado, a prostitute, and his marriage to Clemencia, both given relatively short shrift.

Quiroga's best novels form a cycle of interconnected narratives that together relate the life of the protagonist. *Tristura* (1960; Sadness), which won the prestigious Critics' Prize, has been considered Quiroga's most significant contribution. It narrates the childhood of Tadea, the protagonist, who may be in some respects a mask of the author: They are the same age, raised partly by a widowed father in rural Galicia and partly by a repressive grandmother in Santander, attending Catholic boarding schools. The autobiographical substrata permit Quiroga to evoke with special accuracy and intensity the oppressive atmosphere of conservative, patriarchal education of upper-class Spanish girls during the 1920s and 1930s, imbued with religiosity, conformity, and hypocrisy. The problems of growing up female are developed in conjunction with themes of absence and silence, interwoven into a larger *bildungsroman* constituted by this novel and its continuations. In the sequel, *Escribo tu nombre* (1965; [Liberty] I Write Your Name), Tadea—no longer a little girl but now in boarding school—is placed in an atmosphere constituting a microcosm of Spain prior to the Civil War. The title is taken from a longer epigraph that reads in full: "On the convent school notebooks, Liberty, I write your name." This is Quiroga's longest novel, daring in its expression of muted cries for freedom (as Spain was still under the Franco dictatorship); even more significantly, it offers an unprecedented depiction of adolescent female sexuality, and its importance was recognized by selection as Spain's entry in the first international Rómulo Gallegos contest for novels in Spanish. These two novels are part of a longer cycle, also comprising *Se acabó todo, muchacha triste* (It's All Over Now, Baby Blue), set during the Civil War; Quiroga was said to be still working on this latter title at the time of her death in October of 1995. Her overall plan for the Tadea cycle reportedly was to follow the protagonist through her marriage in a fourth volume, until her death, in a fifth part of the series.

Meanwhile, Quiroga published *Presente profundo* (1973; Profound Present), one of her most significant and successful novels and, although relatively short, having perhaps the most complex structure, as it recreates the lives and deaths of two very different women, joined only by association in the mind of a young Galician doctor who investigates their suicides and contrasts their lives. Offering a probing analysis of the feminine condition, the two women involved are sufficiently different to constitute a compound symbol or metaphor of all women. Daría, an older Galician woman, is a baker's wife, neglected emotionally and physically and eventually cast aside for a younger female. When her children also forget her, she simply walks into the sea. Blanca, a cosmopolitan young divorcée, the daughter of an international millionaire, is separated from a beloved child, drifting into drugs and eventually dying from an overdose while staying in a hippie compound. The young doctor, who accidentally has contact with both, offers a kind of existential meditation upon time, death, and the spirit. *Presente profundo* includes many more of Quiroga's enduring concerns: moral issues, the positive and negative manifestations of religion, female psychology and feminist problems, freedom and solitude, and the condition of women in Spain. At the time of her death, Quiroga was said to be working on yet another novel to be titled *Grandes soledades* (Great Solitudes), reportedly autobiographical in nature. The significance of her work was implicitly recognized when Quiroga became the second woman ever elected to the Royal Spanish Academy of the Language (1983). *See also* Galician Women Writers: A Brief History.

Work by

Algo pasa en la calle. In *Las mejores novelas contemporáneas*. Ed. Joaquín de Entrambasaguas. Barcelona: Planeta, 1971.
Escribo tu nombre. Barcelona-Madrid: Noguer, 1965.
Presente profundo. Barcelona: Destino, 1973.
Tristura. Barcelona-Madrid: Noguer, 1960. Reissued, Barcelona: Plaza y Jané, 1984.

Work about

Barney, Kristen R. "The Quiet Revolution of Elena Quiroga." *Revista Hispánica Moderna* 46.1 (June 1993): 103–116.
Bousoño, Carlos. "Elena Quiroga Privado." *Biblioteca de la Real Academia Española* 80 (January–April 2000): 7–25.
Olazagasti Segovia, Elena. "Resonancias bíblicas en *La enferma*, de Elena Quiroga: Un caso de intertextualidad." *Explicación de Textos Literarios* 19.1 (1990–1991): 1–9.
Riddel, María del Carmen. "El suicidio como incidente estructurante en la narrativa femenina contemporánea: *Presente profundo* de Elena Quiroga y *The Anna Papers* de Ellen Gilchrist." *Literatura femenina contemporánea de España*. Ed. Juana Arancibia, Adrienne Mandel, and Yolanda Rosas. Westminster, CA: Inst. Literario y Cultural Hispánico, 1991. 139–148.
Torres-Bitter, Blanca. "*Tristura*, de Elena Quiroga: De los signos temporales a la organización antitética del relato." *Analecta Malacitana* (Málaga, Spain) 10.2 (1987): 405–421.
Zatlin, Phyllis. "Writing against the Current: The Novels of Elena Quiroga." *Women Writers of Contemporary Spain: Exiles in the Homeland*. Ed. Joan L. Brown. Newark: U of Delaware P, 1991. 42–58.
Zatlin Boring, Phyllis. *Elena Quiroga*. Boston: Twayne, 1977.

Janet Pérez

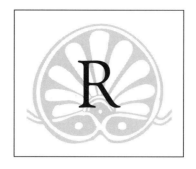

Rafael Marés de Kurz, Carmen

See Kurtz, Carmen, Pseud. of Carmen de Rafael Marés de Kurz (1911–).

Rameras

See Women's Professions in Early Spanish Literature: *Santas, Rameras, Casadas, Amas,* and *Criadas* (Saints, Whores, Wives, Governesses, and Servants)

Ramírez de Guzmán, Catalina Clara (1618–1684)

Born in Llerena (Badajoz) to Francisco Ramírez Guerrero, a career soldier and officer in the Inquisition, and Isabel de Guzmán, two prominent local families, Catalina Clara Ramírez grew up in a loving, large family that she depicted in many of her poems—thereby providing virtually the only source of information for her life and poetic accomplishments. Her contemporaries speak of her talent, culture, beauty, and charm. Also an accomplished guitar player, she was regularly invited to play at local festivals. Several men courted her, but Ramírez maintained an ongoing romance with Juan de Almezquita, against both families' wishes.

During her lifetime, Ramírez—whose poetic name was "Clori"—was considered a prolific and inspired poet, one whose poems were solicited and to whom other male and female poets addressed their texts. Although she is best known for her anecdotal poems, she also wrote love poetry and moral and philosophical reflections. Her epigrammatic texts have been compared to Villamediana's, because of the sobriety of her discourse and the precision and sharpness of her attacks; her poem "A unos ojos dormidos" (To Some Sleeping Eyes) has been compared to Lope de *Vega's love poetry, and her sonnet "La esperanza" (Hope) to the best philosophical poems of her day.

With the passage of time, most of her works have been lost, among them a book in prose and verse titled *El extremeño* (The Extremaduran), thought to have been a mixture of pastoral and chivalric modes. Today, only the imprint of the poems preserved in manuscript form at Madrid's Biblioteca Nacional remains. Analysis of these poems reveals a writer who preferred a classical, more measured tone over the excesses of the gongoristic style then in vogue. She also wrote a number of poems to be sung and was equally at ease writing popular *romances* (ballads) and love *letrillas* (rondels) as with composing philosophical sonnets. Most of her poems, however, depict popular types and customs, portray family and friends, including herself, and comment on the happenings of the day. Many are *poemas de ocasión* (poems for an occasion) requested by others, while others are inspired lyrical reflections of her own subjective experiences.

Work by

Poesías. Ed. and notes Joaquín de Entrambasaguas y Peña. Badajoz: Antonio Arqueros, 1929.

Work about

Borrachero, Aranzazu. "Voces femeninas del barroco español: La poesía lírica de Catalina Clara Ramírez de Guzmán (1618–1684). *Cincinnati Romance Review* 16 (1997): 60–66.

Carrasco García, Antonio. "La poetisa Catalina Clara Ramírez de Guzmán (1618–1684)." *La plaza mayor de Llerena y otros estudios.* Valdemoro: Tuero, 1985. 97–135.

Serrano y Sanz, Manuel. *Apuntes para una biblioteca de escritoras españolas desde el año 1401 al 1833.* 2 vols. Madrid: Rivadeneyra, 1903.

María A. Salgado

Regenta, La (1885): Female Enemies in the Novel

Physically and mentally vulnerable and inexperienced in the intrigues of the upper-class citizens of Vetusta, Ana Ozores, protagonist of Clarín's *La Regenta*, falls prey to the ruthless drive toward self-gratification of both men and women. While there is no doubt that Ana was neglected and abused by men, a more in-depth look at the personalities and roles of some of Ana's female antagonists reveals that the downfall of Vetusta's official beauty from her pedestal to a bottomless pit of collective scorn would never have happened without the scheming and plotting of women who were supposed to give her love, friendship, and loyalty.

Among Ana's governess, aunts, servant, and close friends, it is difficult to decide who did her the most harm. And should one or several stand out because of this achievement, it would only be due to a lesser degree of shrewdness on the part of the others and certainly not to less envy or fewer evil intentions. Rather than competing with each other, these female antagonists built the trap

of Ana's misfortune together, through an unwitting cooperative effort.

Leaving aside the inadvertent role that Ana's mother played in her daughter's unhappiness by marrying a man from a higher social class and then dying during childbirth, the first woman to systematically ruin the little girl's life was Doña Camila, her governess. She did so to avenge her own failure to seduce Ana's father, Don Carlos Ozores. Every night Camila sent Ana to bed too early, turning off the light and letting her cry herself to sleep. For punishment, she would lock Ana in a closet without food. Her greatest moment for revenge arrived after Ana's innocent adventure with her childhood friend Germán. Camila took full advantage of the incident, blowing it out of proportion with her lascivious, vengeful mind, thereby damaging Ana's psyche and reputation forever.

Chronologically, Ana's aunts are the next females to contribute to Ana's destructive upbringing. Proclaiming their good deeds on a daily basis to Ana and the rest of the world, the spinsters raise their niece as a prize pig, intending to marry her to the first interested, well-off candidate available, since Ana's "shady" background precludes a match with an aristocrat. When her aunts' announcement that a millionaire wants to marry her evokes no joy in Ana, Doña Agueda (the worse of the two) reacts with fury, losing whatever was left of her thin layer of hypocritical kindness toward Ana. Ana is then forced to accept the second candidate, Don Víctor Quintanar, old enough to be her father but less repulsive than the millionaire.

As *la regenta* (regent's wife), Ana becomes an object of the ambition and desire of clergy and laymen, particularly Don Fermín de Pas and Don Alvaro Mesía. This situation, only exacerbated by her beauty and virtue, in turn triggers the envy of all the other Vetustan women. The most wicked ones, shrewd and driven by their own frustrated ambitions, are Petra, Ana's maid, and Visita, her "close friend." Petra schemes strategies of destruction from the very moment she enters the

Quintanars' service, making Don Víctor discover his wife's infidelity and also ensuring that Don Fermín knows. While Petra takes care of this aspect of Ana's downfall, Visita works diligently to encourage Ana's submission to Don Alvaro's charms. In addition to her desire to bring the most virtuous woman of Vetusta down to her own level, Visita also seeks to satisfy obscure masochistic impulses.

Even though Ana is abandoned, neglected, used, and seduced, respectively, by her father, husband, spiritual director, and lover, the ones who lay the groundwork for this abuse are the women in her life. The men's weaknesses, ambitions, and selfishness become strings in the hands of female puppeteers. Both puppets and puppeteers abandon the scene when their program has been carried out, leaving Ana on the floor of the cathedral, despised and ostracized by all except her faithful friend Frígilis. The slimy kiss of Celedonio the acolyte seals her betrayal by all others. *See also Regenta, La* (1885): Protagonist Ana Ozores

Work

La Regenta. Ed. Gonzalo Sobejano. 2 vols. Madrid: Castalia, 1981.
La Regenta. Trans. John Rutherford. Athens: U of Georgia P; New York: Penguin, 1984.

Work about

Barrera-García, Consuelo. "Ana Ozores retorna al tiempo de su infancia." *Notas y Estudios Filológicos* 7 (1992): 71–105.
Valis, Noël. "On Monstrous Birth: Leopoldo Alas's *La Regenta.*" *Naturalism in the European Novel: New Critical Perspectives.* Ed. B. Nelson. New York: Berg, 1992. 191–209.

Alma Amell

Regenta, La (1885): Protagonist Ana Ozores

La Regenta (1885) is one of the most significant fictional works of nineteenth-century Spain. Protagonist Ana Ozores is a beautiful, sensitive young woman married to a prominent, old, impotent man, Víctor. Besieged by the boredom and alienation of life in the provincial town of Oviedo (Vetusta in the novel), her desire to be loved holds psychological, social, and religious implications. Ozores has a complex personality, a mixture of neurotic pride and vulnerability to an unrestrained need for sensual love. To fight this urge, she attempts to stay with her spiritual ego, where she convinces herself that she will find a solution to her problem. Frustrated sexually and maternally after the wedding, Ana tries to divert the demands of erotic instinct into abstract poetic and mystic channels. She is torn between her sensuous attraction toward Alvaro, a Don Juan figure, and a Platonic, mystical love inculcated by her confessor, Don Fermín de Pas. This priest manipulates Ana and precipitates her fall. Ana's sexual repression and sense of guilt stem from childhood, when she spent the night alone with a boy. Confused by the apparent sinfulness of sex, and by her unanswered mystical longings, she is forever restraining her natural impulses, preferring to believe in a divine and personalized kind of love. The fact that satisfaction of her sexual drive is condemned by the Church is complicated by her inability to feel a direct relationship with God. Don Fermín represents the ecclesiastical and social authority of Vetusta, and his humble, loveless childhood is compensated for by his power and control over souls. Ana is a challenge for the priest who wants to possess her and also prove that he is socially superior.

La Regenta presents a moralistic judgment of society in decline and the degeneration of the Spanish Restoration. Born in this society, Ana's permanent conflict with her environment influences her attraction to Alvaro and Don Fermín de Pas. Initially she finds refuge in nature and books; later the abstract beauty of religion permits sublimation of her erotic drive. When this mystical experience fails, she succumbs to the temptation of sexual pleasure with Alvaro. A jealous and vengeful Don Fermín reveals the love affair to Ana's husband, driving him into a duel and to his death. Ana Ozores is finally condemned by a town that could forgive her adultery but not her lack of tact, nor that she lost control of the situation. *See also Regenta, La* (1885): Female Enemies in the Novel

Work by

La Regenta. Ed. Gonzalo Sobejano. 2 vols. Madrid: Castalia, 1981.

La Regenta. Trans. John Rutherford. Athens: U of Georgia P; New York: Penguin, 1984.

Work about

Blanco de Lalama, María Asunción. "Ana Ozores y 'La regenta': Del personaje romántico a la novela naturalista." *Revista de Filología Hispánica* (Pamplona) 9.2 (1993): 153–169.

Charnon Deutsch, Lou. "*La Regenta* and Theories of the Subject." *Romance Languages Annual* 1 (1989): 395–398.

Sánchez, Elizabeth. "The Missing Mother: Locating the Feminine Other in *La Regenta.*" *Romance Languages Annual* 1 (1989): 597–602.

Valis, Noël M. *The Decadent Vision in Leopoldo Alas.* Baton Rouge: Louisiana State UP, 1981.

———. "Order and Meaning in Clarín's *La Regenta.*" *Novel* 16 (1983): 246–258.

José Ortega

Repetición de amores (c.1495–1497)

This is one of the few fifteenth-century Castilian treatises against women. The antifeminist movement in fifteenth-century Castile is known indirectly through the literature that refutes traditional opinions on the evil of the female nature; works such as *Libro de las virtuosas y claras mujeres* (1446) by Alvaro de Luna, *Grisel y Mirabella* (c. 1480) by Juan de Flores (fl. 1500), and *Cárcel de amor* (1492) by Diego de *San Pedro (fifteenth century), among others, were written in opposition to a medieval tradition based on Ovid (43 B.C.–A.D. 17) and Juvenal (60?–140?) and voiced by the Church Fathers and Boccaccio (1313–1375). Literature against women is strikingly scarce by comparison; along with some *Cancionero* poetry, the treatise *Reprobación del amor mundano* (1438; also

referred to as *El *Corbacho*) by Alfonso Martínez de Toledo, Arcipreste de Talavera (1398?–1468?), clearly indebted to Bocacio's *Corbaccio*, is the best known. However, it was the poem entitled *Maldezir de las mugeres* (c. 1440), written in Castilian by the Catalan poet Pere Torroella, that became the archetype of *misogyny, finally launching in Castilian courts a debate similar to the one that had raged in France and Italy during the thirteenth and fourteenth centuries.

Very little is known about the author of the *Repetición de amores* (Scholany Exercise on Loves); Luis de Lucena (fl. 1497). Most likely he was a converted Jew who attended the University of Salamanca c. 1484–1496 and later served as prothonotary at the court of the Catholic Monarchs *Isabel and Ferdinand.

Repetición de amores follows the form of a scholarly exercise, a *repetición*. This exhaustive study of a given topic, prepared according to strict university standards, was one of the requirements for a degree at Salamanca. Lucena's work appears to be a defense of Torroella's malicious opinions, although it could be a parody of conventional diatribes against women, given the clumsy manner in which Lucena handles his sources.

Lucena conventionally dedicates his work to "his very noble lady" and begins by praising exemplary women in history—Lucretia, Penelope, Minerva, and the Virgin Mary—just to present them as exceptions to the vices described in one of the stanzas of Torroella's *Maldezir*. Building on the accusations of that particular stanza, the *Repetición* narrates the author's unfortunate experience with a woman and musters traditional arguments and examples of infamous women taken from the expected sources of the Bible, classical mythology and history, Plato, Aristotle (filtered through Boccaccio's *Corbaccio*), Seneca, and Church Fathers, along with some verses extracted from contemporary poetry. The virulent portrait that emerges is clearly of medieval lineage: A woman is an imperfect animal, a lascivious monster, a constant source of confusion for men. Lucena chastises women's insatiability, their fondness for amusements, the tricks they play to hide their imperfections; he calls attention to the evanescence of female beauty by stressing its inescapable corruption and its most repulsive characteristics.

Some critics class the *Repetición* in the genre of sentimental romance, since the alleged autobiographical experience of the author—actually, a remaking of the *Historia duobus amantibus* (1444) by the Italian humanist Aeneas Silvio Piccolomini—introduces a reflexive analysis of feelings and a minimum plot soon interrupted by the misogynist treatise.

For the modern reader, the *Repetición* lacks originality and passion but remains a primary source for arguments used in the Castilian debate against love and against woman's evil nature and depraved ways.

Work by

Repetición de amores. Ed. and intro. Jacob Ornstein. Chapel Hill: U of North Carolina P, 1954.

Work about

Gómez Jesús. "Literatura paraescolar y difusión del humanismo en el siglo XV: *La Repetición de Amores* de Lucena." *Actas del III Congreso de la Asociación Hispánica de Literatura Medieval*. Ed. María Isabel Toro Pascua. Salamanca: Biblioteca Española del Siglo XV, Departamento de Literatura Española e Hispanoamericana, 1994. 399–405.

Matulka, Barbara. *An Anti-feminist Treatise of Fifteenth-Century Spain: Lucena's* Repetición de amores. New York: Institute of French Studies, 1931.

Thompson, B. Bussell. "Another Source for Lucena's *Repetición de amores*." *Hispanic Review* 45 (1977): 337–345.

Sol Miguel-Prendes

Reprobacion de amor mundano
See *Corbacho, El* (1438)

Resino, Carmen (1941–)
Her distinguished career as a writer began during her student years at the University of Madrid, where she published poetry in literary journals while pursuing a degree in history. After completing her studies, Carmen Resino lived for a time in Switzerland and there became interested in the theater. Upon returning to Spain in the late 1960s, she began to write diverse plays for independent theater groups. She continued to compose works for the stage throughout the Franco years, but her unconventional plays did not appeal to middle-class tastes and so were not welcomed by commercial theaters. In spite of the difficulties she has faced in seeing her works presented, Resino has written with persistence over the years. She is considered to be the most versatile of Spain's women dramatists today, having composed to date more than 20 plays, many of which have been successfully staged and published. Her works range from plays that incorporate elements of theater of the absurd and black humor to straightforward historical dramas. She has also created gentle comedies that focus on the ironies and frustrations of everyday life. A recipient of prestigious prizes for her theatrical works and for novels, she currently resides in Madrid, writing actively and teaching history at a secondary school.

Critics have emphasized the universality of Resino's dramatic production, pointing out that her works frequently treat such themes as the lack of authentic communication in contemporary society and the resulting frustration and alienation of individuals. Self-centeredness and the lack of solidarity among human beings are recurring motifs. Without detracting from their universality, however, many of her works have clearly feminist overtones, as they portray the obstacles women face as they aspire to develop their full potential as human beings. A sensation of failure at the individual and collective levels permeates Resino's drama. Conflicts between personal desire and societal obligations lead her characters, both male and female, to look within themselves in an attempt to understand inner conflicts. Metatheatrical techniques are frequently employed in order to search a character's psyche and examine the frustrated desires that lie below the surface. Although her works generally depict situations from everyday life or from history with a direct and straightforward style, they also make use of symbolism to present a scathing critique of contemporary society.

Resino has written several one-act plays that explore ageless conflicts in a very limited time frame with characters who are reduced to their most fundamental traits. The reduction of time and space renders a sense of urgency to the characters' oppression and frustration, feelings that are most often caused by their isolation and the unsatisfying roles they must play in society. *La sed* (1981; Thirst), one of Resino's first works to be staged in Madrid, demonstrates the playwright's frequent use of symbolism and black humor in presenting an absurd situation. Although two characters are present on stage, the work is really the granddaughter's monologue that expresses her unfulfilled sexual desire as she examines her reflection in the mirror and reveals the abuse and objectification she has suffered and routinely accepted in a patriarchal society. Her grandmother calls out from time to time, asking for water, but she is ignored by her companion, who finds her dead at the play's conclusion. The complete lack of communication between the two women points to the absence of the feminine voice in society and the need for solidarity among women and human beings.

La actriz (1990; The Actress) and *Ultimar detalles* (1984; Wrapping Up Details) are metatheatrical one-act plays of two characters in which the female protagonists unsuccessfully attempt to change the roles assigned them by society. The Actress begs her Manager for a chance to play roles of substance, wishing to discard the image he has carefully created for her as a sex symbol. By the play's conclusion it has become evident that this change is impossible at this stage in her career. She is unable to walk or speak in any other way than that dictated by her image and must finally resign herself to accepting the scripts that the Manager chooses for her. Lunarcitos, the protagonist of *Ultimar detalles*, plans to give up her job in a chorus line to marry a wealthy widower. The "details" of the title are conditions for their marriage that the future husband wishes to impose. The details, or "corrections" as he also calls them, include changing her name and her way of dressing, moving, and talking. Lunarcitos assents to these conditions, but Mr. Rueda also demands that she give up her current friends and any contact with her grown-up son. This she cannot accept, although she recognizes in her final monologue that her son has severed all connection between the two. Lunarcitos rejects the advantageous marriage and chooses to continue the difficult life of a chorus girl rather than sacrifice her very identity.

In *Ulises no vuelve* (1983; Ulysses Isn't Returning) Resino demythicizes the Homeric character's relationship with his faithful wife, presenting the events from the perspective of a quite modern Penelope. Ulysses does not return in Resino's play because his cowardice caused him to return years earlier. He hides in Penelope's bedroom out of fear of his father, who had threatened to receive him with a bullet if his behavior in the war were anything but exemplary. Pen, as she is called in this play, has hidden her husband for 20 years, being both father and mother to their troubled son while fending off various suitors. Fed up with the situation, she demands that Ulysses confess to his father. When her husband decides to leave rather than face the truth, Pen sees her opportunity to sell the house and begin a new life elsewhere in freedom. At the play's conclusion, however, Ulysses does present himself to the family, only to be informed by his father that a new war has been declared. Destiny imposes itself, and both Ulysses and Pen have no choice but to accept the roles assigned them by history.

The inability to change one's historical

circumstances is a recurring theme in Resino's dramatic production, and many of her characters, like the Actress and Pen, accept the limitations imposed upon their freedom. Those who refuse to do so face tragic consequences. The protagonist of *Nueva historia de la princesa y el dragón* (1989; New Story of the Princess and the Dragon) is a Chinese princess who refuses to accept her assigned role and rebels actively against it. In this revision of the traditional children's story, the princess refuses to wait passively to be rescued by a prince. In the play's first act, Wu-Tso tells her parents clearly that her ambition is to have real political power in their country. Her mother relates her own victimization at the hands of the patriarchy and informs her daughter that her only options are resignation or disgrace. The second act takes place in Japan, where the princess, now married to a weak son of the Japanese emperor, looks for a way to become empress and rule that nation. She refuses to leave the court when war breaks out, and the shame caused by her behavior drives her husband to commit suicide. Wu-Tso kills the other contenders for the throne in battle but is herself mortally wounded at the play's conclusion. In her attempt to obtain power she has sacrificed human values normally associated with femininity and has become the dragon of the play's title. Although she is seen as cause of the tragedy, the princess is also portrayed as victim of an inflexible society that severely restricts a woman's possibilities for action.

Los eróticos sueños de Isabel Tudor (1992; The Erotic Dreams of Isabel [i.e., Elizabeth I] Tudor) examines the inner world of an important historical figure and discovers the conflict that exists between her public persona and her innermost feelings. Isabel's servant and confidante, María, is really her double and represents Isabel's more passionate and spontaneous side that is hidden from her subjects. The two characters' dialogue exposes the queen's divided consciousness that is torn between her political obligations and her personal desires. A solitary woman at age 54, the Queen Elizabeth of Resino's play dreams about her most powerful enemy, Felipe II of Spain, whom she has secretly loved for many years. In her dreams, however, Felipe often turns out to be Sir Francis Drake, a man the queen has disdained. In the second act, Isabel uncharacteristically follows her heart and accepts an invitation to meet with the Spanish king in Dover. This romantic encounter has a dreamlike atmosphere, according to the stage directions, and the queen, along with the spectator, wonders later if this meeting ever took place. As she examines her situation rationally, Isabel comes to realize that her obsession with Felipe is an impossibility and that she must finally accept the triumph of her duties as queen over her dreams of personal fulfillment.

Los mercaderes de la belleza (1992; Merchants of Beauty), published with *Los eróticos sueños de Isabel Tudor*, takes place in contemporary Spain. Although apparently very different in scope, it has in common with the historical work the theme of frustration and the discovery of the protagonist's divided inner world. Alejandro is an art expert who has grown tired of his life of deception and so attempts to free himself of the influence of David, a gallery owner who has become rich deluding clients who know little about art. Alejandro finds distasteful and even obscene the buying and selling of beauty, but it is not easy to break with well-established patterns and the comfort of his lifestyle. The play concludes with the protagonist's recognition of the powerful attraction he feels for David and his inability to free himself from their relationship. As frequently occurs in Resino's theater, the exploration of a character's most intimate thoughts and desires leads to an awareness of the eternal conflict between the individual and society. *See also* Drama by Spanish Women Writers: 1970–2000; Feminist Theory and the Contemporary Spanish Stage

Work by

Bajo sospecha: (tiempo de gracia) / *Carmen Resino.* Intro. and notes R.L. Nichols. Murcia: U of Murcia, 1995.

Los eróticos sueños de Isabel Tudor; Los mercaderes de la belleza. Madrid: Fundamentos, 1992.

No, no pienso lamentarme. Esencia de mujer: Ocho monólogos de mujeres para mujeres. Ed. Charo and Joaquín Solanas. Madrid: La Avispa, 1995. 19–28.

Nueva historia de la princesa y el dragón. Madrid: Lucerna, 1989.

O'Connor, Patricia, ed. *Dramaturgas españolas de hoy: Una introducción.* Madrid: Fundamentos, 1988.

Work about

Gabriele, John. "Entrevista con Carmen Resino." *Estreno* 22.2 (Fall 1996): 32–34.

———. "Estrategias feministas en el teatro breve de Carmen Resino." *Letras Femeninas* 21.1–2 (Spring–Fall 1995): 85–95.

Paco, Mariano de. "El teatro histórico de Carmen Resino." *Anales de la Literatura Española Contemporánea* 20.3 (1995): 303–314.

Carolyn Harris

Ribera, Suero de (c. 1410– c. 1480)

Little is known of Suero de Ribera except that he was active in the courts of Juan II of Castile and of the Aragonese Alfonso V in Naples. Believed to have been of Castilian or Valencian origin, his works appear in numerous Castilian and Aragonese *cancioneros* (songbooks).

A prominent defender of women in response to Pedro Torrellas's "Coplas de las calidades de las donas" (*Maldezir*), Ribera closed the *Cancionero de Estúñiga* (c. 1458) with "Respuesta de Suero de Ribera en defensión de las donas" ([Reply of Suero de Ribera in Defense of Ladies]; "Poema XVI" in Periñán's edition, which is used throughout this entry). Torrellas accuses women of "feminine" vices including hypocrisy, false virtue, coquetry, caprice, and egoism, but he partially excuses them with Aristotle's explanation that Nature failed to give them enough heat to excel. Menéndez y Pelayo, not finding this "natural" explanation of in-

herent feminine inferiority insidious, judges the poem a toothless satire. Salvador Miguel believes it shows keen penetration into female psychology. Periñán points out that Torrellas intended the satire primarily as praise for his lady whom he exempts from female defects: He was no more antifeminist than Ribera was feminist. Indeed Torrellas himself introduced the argument that Ribera, and later Sor Juana Inés de la Cruz, developed: Men induce women to sin so they are responsible for her "lightness."

Ribera does not counter all Torrellas's arguments. Instead he criticizes Torrellas as ungentlemanlike in launching such an attack, which only reveals the impotence of the badmouther. He argues that all gentlemen should come to the defense of ladies who are not to be blamed for the errors of a few.

Failure to follow gentlemanly rules of etiquette is also the criticism Ribera launched on Fernán Pérez de Guzmán, whose poem places his lady above all those of the court, including the queen. In Ribera's response, "Poema XV," which closed the *Cancionero de Baena* (1445), *mesura*, or circumspection, requires proper regard for hierarchy in praise. Ribera moves from praise of the queen to criticism of Guzmán's lady. In a rather ungentlemanly satire Ribera says she is surpassed not only by Christians and Moors but by 40 shepherdesses and that Guzmán is a badmouther.

Periñán identifies Ribera's norms for the lover established in "Poemas XIX and XX" ("Reglas a los galanes" [Rules for Beaux]) as liberality, constancy, devotion to a single lady, enduring flatterers, and discretion. Of Provenzal origin, Ribera's rules foreshadow those of Baldassare Castiglione (1478–1529), especially in the emphasis on grace in riding, hunting, dressing, drinking, eating, speaking, dancing, singing, playing musical instruments, and composing poetry. Ribera approves a truly cavalier treatment of creditors. Two anti-semitic poems (XVII and XXI), probably directed against Juan Poeta, cruelly parody *conversos* (Jewish or Moorish converts to Christianity) for their financial, religious, and dietary practices.

Ribera's famous "Poema XIII," the "Misa de amores" (Mass of Love), parodies the mass, converting it to an amorous context. Deyermond judges this poem to establish Ribera as one of the best younger poets in the *Cancionero de Baena*. Exchanges between religious and secular spheres have been popular since the Song of Songs, if not before. Ribera's *misa* derives from the goliardic poets who composed parodies of religious themes in their Latin love poetry. Although the poem limits its parody to the external elements of religious ritual, it was expurgated from the *Cancionero de Estúñiga*, the *Cancionero de Roma*, and the *Cancionero del Palacio* and excluded from the *Cancionero de Venecia*. Ribera adapted each section of the mass. In the "Confesión," an abandoned lover complains that Love fails to reward him but then realizes that unrequited love improves virtue. The "Gloria in excelsis" implores Love's kindness to the discreet lover. The "Epístola" gives a lesson to Love's martyrs, the unhappy who receive few of Love's whimsically distributed prizes, and the "Credo" repeats this theme of Love's arbitrariness and urges lovers not to despair for their fortune may change. The "Prefacio" declares the justice of loyal hearts suffering great passion. "Et Ydeo" urges those free of love to pity its victims. The "Sanctus" warns lovers not to put faith in their hope of a return. The "Agnus Dei" addresses the Lamb of the God of Venus in whom both the unloved and the loved put faith. Finally, the "Ite, missa est" gives thanks to Love that is good. Both Periñán and Salvador Miguel supply detailed analyses and comparison with similar poems by other authors. "Poema I," among those of doubtful attribution, is more daringly sacrilegious, for it places the lady above God.

In his love poetry Ribera records his unrequited passion for a lady whose name he conceals (V). He supplies a conventional portrait of her beauty (II), which surpasses that of ancient heroines (III, X), and of her cruelty toward himself (I, IV, VII, VIII, IX, XII). Oddly, Ribera never mentions the lady's virtue except in the generic "Poema XIX," where he declares "virtuous" ladies will love the noble gallant, and in the occasional "Poema XIV." Greatest emphasis is placed upon the lover's pain in complaints to Fortune (I, V, VI), Misfortune (VI), Gentility (XII), and Love (X, XIII). He sometimes admits that he has only himself to blame and that love is its own reward (II, XI), and at other times he attacks gossips for turning the lady against him (XII). In "Poema XIV" Ribera identifies by name six Neapolitan ladies and asks the Conde de Oliva to decide which is foremost in beauty, grace, virtue, and high station. Ribera attributes virtue to the countess of Adorno, the woman from Gátula and Lucrecia of Nido.

The *villancico* (eight-syllable verse form) "Por una gentil floresta" (Through a Pleasant Grove), usually attributed to *Santillana (1398–1458), may be the work of Ribera, as may also be the *Refranes* (Proverbs). The *villancico* is similar in mood to "Poema IV," also of doubtful attribution, in which the poet approaches several ladies dancing in French style. When they ask him to identify his lady, he refuses. They pity him for his tribulations and pray that he receive a reward. Both poems are superior to Ribera's known works in the concreteness of situation and character. In these poems the ladies actually speak and interact with the lover, something that never occurs in Ribera's poems of sure authenticity. Usually, as Salvador Miguel points out, the woman is only the object and destined recipient of the poem in which the man is actor and agent. *See also* Courtly Love

Works by and about

Deyermond, A.D. *A Literary History of Spain: The Middle Ages*. London: Ernest Benn Limited; New York: Barnes and Noble, 1971.

Foulché Delbosc, R. *Cancionero castellano del siglo XV*. 2 vols. Madrid: Bailly Balliére, 1915.

Gerli, Michael. *Poesía cancioneril castellana*. Madrid: Akal, 1994.

Le Gentil, Pierre. *La poésie lyrique espagnole et portugaise a la fin du moyen age.* 2 vols. Rennes: Plihon. Editeur, 1952.

López Estrada, Francisco. *Introducción a la literatura medieval española.* 3rd ed. Madrid: Gredos, 1966.

Menéndez y Pelayo, Marcelino. *Historia de la poesía castellana en la edad media.* 2 vols. Madrid: Librería General de Victoriano Suárez, 1914.

Ochoa, Eugenio de. *Rimas inéditas de don Iñigo López de Mendoza, marqués de Santillana, de Fernán Pérez de Guzmán, señor de Batres, y de otros poetas del siglo XV.* Paris: Fain y Thunot, 1844.

Periñán, Blanca. "Las poesías de Suero de Ribera: Estudio y edición crítica anotada de los textos." *Miscellanea di studi ispanici* 16 (1968): 5–138.

Salvador Miguel, Nicasio. *La poesía cancioneril: El Cancionero de Estúñiga.* Madrid: Alhambra, 1977.

Judy B. McInnis

Rico Godoy, Carmen (1939–2001)

Born in Paris, writer Carmen Rico Godoy received a cosmopolitan education as a result of her journalist-correspondent parents and studied political science in Washington. She has worked as a journalist in Madrid since 1970, writing weekly columns for the magazine *Cambio 16*. Her reputation as an author is due to her seemingly autobiographical essay *Cómo ser mujer y no morir en el intento* (How to Be a Woman and Not Die Trying), published in 1990 with huge success and turned into a film directed by Ana Belén in 1991. This first book was closely followed by two others, *Cómo ser infeliz y disfrutarlo* (1991; How to Be Unhappy and Enjoy It) and *Cuernos de mujer* (1992; Female Cuckold), which similarly were adapted for films directed by Enrique Urbizu with Rico's scripts in 1992 and 1994, respectively. Rico Godoy has also written scripts for several other films such as *Miss Caribe* for director Fernando Trueba, and *Los pazos de Ulloa*, for Manuel Gutiérrez Aragón and Fernando Trueba.

Her bestseller *Cómo ser mujer y no morir en el intento* reflects the difficult life of a modern professional woman at the end of the 1980s who has to juggle a demanding career with the traditional roles of wife and mother. The stark contrast between this type of woman and her masculine counterpart, a "traditional but modern" man (the one who allows his wife to work and takes all the advantages of this condescending situation), underlies much of the book's delightful humor. The narrative seems to contain much autobiographical material: The profession, situation, name, and character of the protagonist fit its author perfectly. In fact, the author asserts in the short vita that appeared with the work that "this is her first book and most probably her last." Rico Godoy manages to portray the frustration of women in marriage in a way that seems spontaneous and natural, with a kind of innocence in the rendering of misunderstanding between man and woman. Rather than accusations she presents the statement of a lack of accord due to two different natures born not to reach agreements or subdue one another but to live in different worlds. This bestseller was followed by two other essays written in the same humorous vein that gradually turns into bitter sarcasm in her last, less popular narrative.

In *La costilla asada de Adán* (1996; Adam's Roasted Rib), bitterness, denunciation, and the impossibility of understanding are paramount, as seen in some of the short stories that compose the book. Particularly interesting in this line are the last two: "No quiero" (I Don't Want To), which reflects on the impossibility of equality and harmony in marriage for a professional couple; and "La mujer total" (The Total Woman), which denounces the same situation for a traditional couple, the housewife and working husband, where the wife is strangled by the jealousy-mad husband. Rico Godoy's women talk like men, a coarse language, full of expletives and void of any inhibition. Various gender-related questions loom about the narrative: Are women really so much like men when they arrive at this level of disinhibition? Is the problem between men and women really that underneath they are so similar in their less-than-attractive traits? These attributes appear in the short stories about vacationing female friends, "El paraíso ya no es lo que era" (Paradise Isn't What It Used to Be). Probably these negative, traditionally selfish masculine attributes exhibited by women as a trophy of liberation are what make this book hard and hopeless. The rest of the stories are more in the fantasy line but equally black in humor and negative tone.

Work by

Cómo ser infeliz y disfrutarlo. Madrid: Temas de Hoy, 1991.

Cómo ser mujer y no morir en el intento. Madrid: Temas de Hoy, 1990.

La costilla asada de Adán. Madrid: Temas de Hoy, 1996.

Cuernos de mujer. Madrid: Temas de Hoy, 1992.

La neurona iconoclasta: más vale morir de risa que de asco. Madrid: Temas de Hoy, 2000.

Work about

Valdivieso, L. Teresa. "Para una teoría de la cultura: La narrativa paródica de Carmen Rico Godoy." *Visión de la narrativa hispánica: Ensayos.* Ed. and intro. Juan Cruz Mendizábal and Juan Fernández Jiménez. Indiana, PA: Department of Spanish and Classical Languages, Indiana U of Pennsylvania, 1999. 235–242.

María Elena Bravo

Rincón Gutiérrez, María Eugenia (1926–)

A poet and educator born in San Esteban de Gormaz (Soria), María Eugenia Rincón spent her childhood and adolescence in Barcelona. After earning a doctorate in Romance Philology from Madrid's Complutense University, she taught at the University of Valencia and directed the Aula de Poesía. In 1963 she received the Premio Valencia de Poesía for her book *Corazón en órbita* (Heart in Orbit), later included in the second edition of *Frontera de la sombra* (1973; Border of Shadow). She has been professor of Catalan literature at Madrid's Autonomous University and visiting professor at San Francisco University

(California). Rincón won a Fundación March Fellowship for her work *Ideología literaria de Gregorio Marañón* (Literary Ideology of Gregorio Marañón).

Rincón's poetic work consists of three books: *Tierra secreta* (1962; Secret Land), *Frontera de la sombra* (1968), and *Boca sin tiempo* (1974; Mouth without Time). General characteristics of her poetry include a feeling of sorrow and disillusion exempt from skepticism, intimism, and melancholy, and a consciousness of the flow of time. Within those general characteristics, each volume has its own individuality. *Tierra secreta* deals with love and maternity. In the contemplation of nature the sea echoes her longing for love that dissolves in delusion and nostalgia echoed in dead nature. By contrast, the longed-for child is conveyed by the image of running waters, while the destiny of the poet that is to be born, to grow, to give birth, to bleed, and to die a little every day communicates a fruitless search for love, interior solitude, and emptiness with only God as hope.

In *Frontera de la sombra* the main themes are death and the flowing of time. This is perhaps the most autobiographical of her books, with a eulogy to her dead father and frequent childhood memories, including references to the Civil War. With anguish but devoid of desperation, Rincón expresses the inexorable flow of time, progressing without return, changing people and objects, with only the sea remaining unchanged. *Boca sin tiempo* deals with the theme of love, and although no personal reference is made specifically, the lover, characterized at times as a child, can easily be inferred to be a child, whose portrayal is made by a female poet.

In general Rincón's poetry exhibits sorrow and disillusion that is exempt from skepticism and desperation. There is intimism and melancholy and a consciousness of the flow of time. Rincón belongs to the group of Spanish women who, following a trend already clear in the 1930s and accelerated after the Civil War, became part of the professions, especially writers and educators. Although the themes of her poetry could be considered more in accord with a feminine rather than a feminist stand, that does not imply sentimentality on her part. The themes of filial love, maternity, and the affection for a beloved are expressed with an existential depth, frequently using the sea as a symbol. In addition to her poetry, Rincón has authored several anthologies, providing prologue, notes, and translation from Catalan to Spanish of several writers, among them Eugenio d'Ors.

Work by

Boca sin tiempo. León: Provincia, 1974.
Frontera de la sombra. Madrid: Cultura Hispánica, 1968.
Tierra secreta. Valencia: Vives, 1962.

Work about

Marciano, Carlos. "María Eugenia Rincón. Bibliografía." *La Estafeta Literaria* 575 (1975): 14–16.

Pilar Sáenz

Ríos Nostench de Lampérez, Blanca de los (1862–1956)

Born in Seville in the bosom of a well-to-do family, as a young girl Blanca de los Ríos initiated her writing career with the anagram Carolina del Boss. She moved later to Madrid, where she wrote regularly for magazines and newspapers including *Renacimiento, Revista Contemporánea, La Ilustración Española y Americana,* and *La Elegancia.* She founded and directed the magazine *Raza Española* from 1919 to 1930. Her writings could be categorized in three areas, as follows: creative works—novels, short stories, theater, poems; literary criticism and history; and research on Hispanoamerican issues. Her work *La rondeña* (1902; Native of Ronda) was influenced by Merimée. Highlights of her literary criticism include studies on Tirso de *Molina, Lope de *Vega, *Calderón de la Barca, Santa *Teresa, and Menéndez Pelayo. Ríos was a member of the Hispanic Society of America (1927) and an honorary member of the American Association of Teachers of Spanish (1931).

Work by

Cuentos andaluces: La saeta. El molino de los Gelves. La rondeña. Barcelona: Publicaciones Mundial, n.d.
Del siglo de Oro. Prol. Marcelino Menéndez Pelayo. Madrid: Bernardo Rodríguez, 1910.
Los diablos azules. Madrid: Alrededor del Mundo, 1910.
Don Juan. Madrid: La España moderna, 1889.
Esperanzas y recuerdos. Madrid: Central, 1881.
Las hijas de don Juan. Madrid: José Blass y Cía., 1907.
Madrid goyesco. Madrid: Blass y Cía., 1908.
La niña de Sanabria. Melita Palma. Sangre española. Madrid: Idamor Moreno, 1907.
Romancero de Don Jaime el Conquistador. Madrid: Enrique Rubiños, 1891.
La rondeña. Cuentos populares. El Salvador. Cuentos varios. Madrid: Idamor Moreno, 1902.
El tesoro de Sorbas. Madrid: Bernardo Rodríguez, 1914.

Work about

Catálogo de las obras de Blanca de los Ríos de Lampérez y algunos juicios críticos acerca de ella. Madrid: V.H. Sanz Calleja, 1927.
Ferreras, Juan Ignacio. *Catálogo de novelas y novelistas españoles del siglo XIX.* Madrid: Cátedra, 1979.
Glenn, Kathleen M. "Demythification and Denunciation in Blanca de los Ríos's *Las hijas de Don Juan.*" *Nuevas perspectivas sobre el 98.* Ed. and pref. John P. Gabriele. Madrid: Iberoamericana; Frankfurt: Vervuert, 1999. 223–230.
Simón Palmer, María de Carmen. *Escritoras españolas del siglo XIX. Manual bio-bibliográfico.* Madrid: Castalia, 1991.
Ugalde, Sharon Keefe. "Reconfigurations of the Female Lyric Subject in 'Canto de Ofelia' de Blanca de los Ríos." *Monographic Review Revista Monográfica* 13 (1997): 182–189.

Carmen de Urioste

Rivera Garretas, María-Milagros (1947–   )

A contemporary feminist theorist and professor of women's history and of women's studies at the University of Barcelona, María-Milagros Rivera Garretas holds a Master of Arts from the University of Chicago and a doctorate in history from the University of Barcelona. Her major areas of research interest are the social history of Castile during the Middle Ages and the analysis/interpretation of the lives and works of medieval women. She holds a chair of Medieval History in the Faculty of Geography and History at the University of Barcelona, where she cofounded the Center for Investigation of Women's History (CIHD) in 1982 and serves as its current director. She teaches graduate courses in women's history and in women's studies, as well as contributing to a doctoral program in "Women, Gender and Power." In addition to numerous articles, she is the author of *Textos y espacios de mujeres: Europa siglo IV–XV* (1990; Women's Texts and Spaces: Europe, Fourth-Fifteenth Centuries) and *Nombrar el mundo en femenino* (1994; Naming the World in Feminine [Terms]).

In the latter, Rivera Garretas sets out to combat the traditional misogynist denial or deprecation of women's capacity for abstract or philosophical thought, identifying women from many historical periods who demonstrate the ability for a feminine "creation of symbolic order": Heloise, Marguerite Porete, Teresa de *Cartagena, *Teresa de Jesús, Virginia Woolf, María *Zambrano. She indicates that while such creativity is a vital necessity in dealing with the accumulation of things that make no sense in life, when this activity has been undertaken by women, it has been called hysteria, depression, undetermined anxiety, or—as recently as the 1980s—fear. Rivera Garretas draws upon recent women's writing from Italy as well as contemporary feminist writers from the United States, England, France, Germany, and Spain. *Nombrar el mundo en femenino* offers an impressive compendium of recent writing relevant to women's history and thought from much of Europe (some Spanish titles appear below in lieu of writings "about" Rivera Garretas). Following a historical overview comes a synthetic consideration of contemporary feminist thought, with chapters devoted to "feminist materialism" (or Marxist feminism), lesbian thought, gender theory, the "politics of sexual difference," and critiques of the latter, including especially the accusations of essentialism and elitism, plus a meditation on liberty.

Work by

El cuerpo indispensable: Significados del cuerpo. Madrid: Horas y Horas, 1996.

"Las escritoras de Europa. Cuestiones de análisis textual y de política sexual." *Arabes, judías y cristianas: Mujeres en la Europa medieval.* Ed. Cela del Moral. Granada: Universidad, 1993. 195–207.

El fraude de la igualdad. Barcelona: Planeta, 1997.

"La historia de las mujeres y la conciencia feminista en Europa." *Mujeres y sociedad. Nuevos enfoques teóricos y metodológicos.* Ed. Lola G. Luna. Barcelona: Universitat, 1991. 123–140.

"Las infanzonas de Aragón en la época de Jaime II." *El trabajo de las mujeres en la Edad Media hispana.* Ed. Angela Muñoz Fernández and Cristina Segura Graiño. Madrid: Al-Mudayna, 1988.

Nombrar el mundo en femenino. Barcelona: Icaria, 1994.

"Las prosistas castellanas del Humanismo y del Renacimiento (1400–1550)." *Breve historia feminista de la literatura española, 3.* Ed. Myriam Díaz-Diocaretz and Iris Zavala. Barcelona: Anthropos, 1995.

Textos y espacios de mujeres. Europa siglo IV–XV. Barcelona: Icaria, 1990.

Work about Spanish Women's History and Gender Studies

Amelang, James, and Mary Nash, eds. *Historia y género. Las mujeres en la Europa moderna y contemporánea.* Valencia: Alfons el Magnànim, 1990.

Amorós, Celia, ed. *Feminismo e Ilustración. Actas del Seminario Permanente, 1988–1992.* Madrid: Universidad Complutense y Comunidad Autónoma, 1992.

Arana, María José. *La clausura de las mujeres. Una lectura teológica de un proceso histórico.* Bilbao: Universidad de Deusto, 1992.

Birules, Fina, comp. *Filosofía y género. Identidades femeninas.* Pamplona: Pamiela, 1992.

Díaz-Diocaretz, Myriam, and Iris M. Zavala, coord. *Breve historia feminista de la literatura española (en lengua castellana).* 6 vols. Barcelona: Anthropos, 1993–2000.

Fagoaga, Concha. *La voz y el voto de las mujeres. El*

sufragismo en España, 1877–1931. Barcelona: Icaria, 1985.

Falcón, Lidia. *Mujer y poder político. Fundamentos de la crisis de objetivos e ideología del Movimiento Feminista.* Madrid: Vindicación Feminista, 1992.

———. *La razón feminista. 1. La mujer como clase social y económica. El medio de producción doméstica. 2. La reproducción humana.* Barcelona: Fontanella, 1981–1982.

Graña Cid, María del Mar, ed. *Las sabias mujeres, I: Educación, saber y autoría (siglos III–XVII).* Madrid: Asociación Cultural Al-Mudayna, 1994.

López, Aurora, and M. Angeles Pastor, eds. *Crítica y ficción literaria: Mujeres españolas contemporáneas.* Granada: Universidad de Granada, 1989.

Luna, Lola G. *Género, clase y raza en América Latina. Algunas aportaciones.* Barcelona: Universitat, 1992.

Maquiera, Virginia, and Cristina Sánchez, eds. *Violencia y sociedad patriarcal.* Madrid: Fundación Pablo Iglesias, 1990.

Mujeres, ciencia y política. Madrid: Debate, 1987.

Mujeres en la historia de Andalucía, Las. Actas del II Congreso de Historia de Andalucía. Córdoba: Junta de Andalucía, 1994.

Navarro, Mercedes, ed. *Diez mujeres escriben teología.* Estella: Verbo Divino, 1993.

Osborne, Raquel. *La construcción sexual de la realidad. Un debate en la sociología contemporánea de la mujer.* Madrid: Cátedra, 1993.

Roig, Montserrat. *Digues que m'estimes encara que sigui mentida.* Barcelona: Edicions 62, 1991.

Sabuco de Nantes Barrera, Oliva. *Obras.* Prólogo de Octavio Cuartero. Madrid: Ricardo Fe, 1888.

Sau, Victoria. *Diccionario ideológico feminista.* Barcelona: Icaria, 1989.

Scanlon, Geraldine. *La polémica feminista en la España contemporánea: 1868–1974.* Madrid: Siglo XXI, 1976.

Segura Graíño, Cristina, ed. *La voz del silencio, I: Fuentes directas para la historia de las mujeres (siglos VII–XVIII).* Madrid: Al-Mudayna, 1992.

———. *La voz del silencio, II: Historia de las mujeres: Compromiso y método.* Madrid: Al-Mudayna, 1993.

Sendón, Victoria, María Sánchez, Montserrat Guntín, and Elvira Aparici. *Feminismo holístico. De la realidad a lo real.* Spain: Cuadernos de Agora, 1994.

Tristán, Flora. *Peregrinaciones de una paria.* Madrid: Istmo, 1986.

———. *La unión obrera.* Barcelona: Fontamara, 1977.

Zambrano, María. *Filosofía y poesía. (1939 y 1987).* Madrid: Fondo de Cultura Económica y Universidad de Alcalá, 1993.

Janet Pérez

Rodríguez del Padrón (de la Cámara), Juan (1399?–1450)

Credited with the definition of the sentimental novel in *Siervo libre de amor* (composed 1438 to 1440; The Emancipated Slave of Love), Juan Rodríguez del Padrón also celebrated women in *El triunfo de las donas y Cadira del honor* (1438; Triumph of Women and the Seat of Honor), in the *Bursario* (1438; Pocket Novel), and in his poetry dedicated to the themes of *courtly love. As Paz y Melia pointed out in his edition of Rodríguez's complete works (1884), the poet carried the religion of courtly love to an extreme in "Siete gozos" (Seven Joys) and "Los diez mandamientos del amor" (The Ten Commandments of Love). The latter outlines the ideal lover's qualities including loyalty, disinterest, chastity, courage as well as gentility, being well groomed, wealth, generosity, presence, and extroversion. "Siete gozos" laments the poet's lack of love's pleasures and deplores his five wounds for love (jealousy, hopeless love, etc.). The lady is equated with the sun and with fate. The source of all virtues, she should show mercy in pardoning or killing him. Despite her elevation, the lover nurses the hope that his love will overcome her cruelty. Rodríguez associates himself with Macías, his friend and fellow Galician, as a victim of love. In the courtly love system the cause of the lady's attraction, her superior status and virtue, are the very things she would lose were she to yield to the lover's importunities.

In the amusing poem "Ham, ham, huyd que rauio" (Damn and Double Damn; Flee for I Grow Rabid), the poet is reduced to howling when his lady spurns him. Other short poems develop themes of the lover's suffering and his desire for death, could he arise again in three days to see the lady's reaction to his demise. In one set of poems

Rodríguez gently curses his lady for the misery she has cost him, while she replies only with the plea that he accept their separation. Lida points out that Rodríguez introduced the insult of the lady to the love themes developed in the Spanish fifteenth-century *cancioneros* (songbooks). His traditional palinode abjures youthful pastimes of seeking pleasure and favor at court with the ladies. Yet even as he abjures them, Rodríguez requests that the ladies pray for him, a sinner.

Poems attributed to Rodríguez include a fervent paean to the Virgin who paid in suffering for her dead son what she escaped in his painless birth. Serés argues that "Planto que fizo la Pantasilea" (Lament Made by Pantasilea) is the work not of the Marqués de *Santillana but of Rodríguez. Serés contends that the poem's Ovidian tone as well as the handling of the motifs of love and fame indicate Rodríguez's authorship. Pantasilea has attributes of the court gentleman as well as of the lady, that is, nobility, merit, valor, power, goodness and generosity.

Rodríguez's *Bursario* translates Ovid's (43 B.C.–A.D. 17?) Heroides, epistles written by legendary women and by three men (Paris, Leandro, Acunti). Pointing to their usefulness in showing diverse manners of loving, Rodríguez added introductions identifying the author's purpose of reprehending *loco amor*, that is to say, physical lust (Felis, Oenoe, Islifle, Dido, Daymira, Adriana, and Medea), condemning illicit love (Fedra, Canace, Elena), or praising licit love (Penelope, Laudomia, Ipermesta, Hero, Cedipe) or chastity (Briseyda). Rodríguez attributed to Ovid three of Rodríguez's own letters, revealing mastery of Ovid's technique. Writing to Brecaida/Briseyda (Cressida), Troilus upbraids her for disloyalty. Brecaida answers with a defense of her fidelity and an attack that Troilus's interest in spoils prevented him from rescuing her. Rodríguez reclaims the Grecian woman from detractors such as Boccaccio (1313–1375) and Chaucer (1340?–1400), who depict her as the classic unfaithful woman as in the *Roman de Troie*.

The turning of the tables to make men rather than women the perpetrators of infidelity informs Madreselva's letter to Manseol. Rodríguez juxtaposes the good to the evil woman in the characterizations of Madreselva and the enchantress Artemisa. Madreselva argues that marriage vows voluntarily assumed take precedence over forced ones. Impey sees the tale of Madreselva as the precursor of *Siervo libre de amor*, the mother-daughter tension of the first anticipating the father-son animosity of the second. She also perceives Troilus as foreshadowing the sentimental Siervo. The *Bursario* shows both men and women active in the pursuit of licit and illicit love. Woman as an object of exchange, subject to man's domination, is also portrayed in the letters. Nevertheless, Rodríguez's characters retain independent judgment, and the author depicts with sympathy the injustice of woman's subservient status. Impey argues that Rodríguez relied heavily on *Alfonso X's presentation of Ovid's ladies in the *General historia*, where social class, laments, and internal analysis are emphasized. Alfonso's original views on love and marriage are spread through the *Bursario*. Furthermore, Rodríguez created the lamenting male counterpart to the spurned Ovidian lady and emphasized male as well as female chastity.

Critics have argued more about genre than about gender in studies of Rodríguez's sentimental novel or *tratado* (treatise), *Siervo libre de amor*. Brownlee perceives it as an antisentimental novel or an erotic pseudoautobiography. Menéndez y Pelayo, Paz y Melia, Gilderman, Andrachuk and Herrero argue for the novel's incompleteness, while Dudley, Impey, Fernández Jiménez, and Cocozzella argue its completeness. The novel is supposedly based on Rodríguez's own love for a lady-in-waiting to María of Aragón, wife of Juan II. The lady's ire spurred Rodríguez to join the Franciscan order. The novel presents three paths: "loving well and being loved"; "loving but being unloved"; and "neither loving nor being loved." As Prieto points out, the typical courtly situation of a high-born lady dallying secretly with a dependent lover prevails here in contradistinction to Boccaccio's bourgeois world.

The narrator introduces the story of Ardanlier and Liessa to illustrate "loving and being loved"; the theme of loyalty predominates in this intercalated tale in juxtaposition to the disloyalty of the narrator's story. Spinelli has documented its rather heavy use of chivalric vocabulary. To escape the ire of his father who forbids their marriage, Ardanlier and Liessa travel through many European courts. At one, Yrena falls in love with the gallant and excellent knight Ardanlier. He remains true to Liessa, whom he takes into the forest to live an idyllic life. His father discovers them and kills the pregnant Liessa, in Impey's description, a woman in her full potential as lover, wife, and mother who exemplifies courtly, marital, and maternal love. Ardanlier commits suicide; according to Impey this is the first death caused by love in original Castilian prose. Yrena establishes and serves in a shrine for the dead lovers. The shrine brings fame to the town of Padrón; Macías is the first to penetrate its depths. Herrero characterizes Yrena's purified love as Christian self-sacrificing charity that makes her imitate the Virgin Mary (*Marianism) in dedicating her soul to saving those of Ardanlier and Liessa. Grieve points out that Rodríguez broke the sex/sin/downfall parallel by associating Liessa with Inés de *Castro (1325?–1355) and the Virgin Mary, especially with the legend of the Virgin of Liesse. He avoided the good/bad woman dichotomy by associating Yrena with the Virgin Mary and emphasizing her loyalty. Finally the primary dates of the love story (May 1, June 24, and July 25) are associated with important pagan and Christian festivals.

The narrator awakens from his dream of Ardanlier and Liessa to see an old woman with her seven maids-in-waiting. He identifies her as Synderesis, knowledge. Now cured of love, he recounts his adventures to her. Brownlee points out that Synderesis is based on Boethius's Lady Philosophy. Gilderman believes Rodríguez presents love as a relationship between equals and as a rebellious act leading to death. Forcadas has shown the influence of Rodríguez's novel on the *Celestina.

The apotheosis of Rodríguez's praise of women occurs in *Triunfo de las donas* where the nymph Cardiana lists 50 reasons for women's superiority to men. Dedicated to Queen María, the work answers the criticisms of women put forward by Boccaccio and his follower the Arcipreste de Talavera (1398?–1468?), author of the *Corbacho. Paz y Melia says Rodríguez wrote it to receive a pardon from Queen María so that he might return to court. Rodríguez holds women to be more temperate, pious and merciful, prudent, cleaner, more just, and more amorous than men. They are less vain and stronger-willed than men, for they can resist men's attempts at seduction. Using arguments still cherished by feminists, Rodríguez declares that women have not excelled in intellectual pursuits only because men forbade them the right to study. Women have been excluded from history by the men who wrote it. He urges men to respect women from gratitude to their own mothers who brought them into the world and reared them. Rodríguez puts a positive gloss on biblical stories of woman's secondary creation and the Fall. He also praises woman's modesty, condones the use of *cosmetics through the biblical precedent of Judith and Hester, and insists that men are more vain in dress than women. Rodríguez goes so far as to say that a delightful odor emanates from the womb, a statement that foreshadows French feminists' desire to cherish the female body. He points out the inequality of adultery laws and of laws assigning nobility by paternity and servility by maternity. He points out that women are less inclined to criminal acts and credits women with invention of the innocent domestic arts of carding and weaving. He appeals to religion by pointing out that God chose to be born of woman but took the form of man who most needed redemption. Christ, Rodríguez reminds the reader, was given succor by women while he was persecuted, tried, and condemned by men. Rodríguez adds quaint biological ideas such as the highest animal, the eagle, being female, and the lowest, the basilisk, being male. He also entertains the notion that ferocious animals like the lion do not attack women. In Rodríguez's opinion women drown less swiftly than men, and they are less afraid of heights. Finally he cites the Bible, Aristotle, and Seneca about the praise due the virtuous woman.

A companion work, the *Cadira del honor* defines inherited and earned nobility in men. Honor is the product of virtue and nobility. As Paz y Melia points out, Rodríguez advises young men not to use love to overcome social barriers and concedes great importance to wealth, which makes the cultivation of noble qualities easier. Virtue in itself does not constitute nobility, which requires: (1) princely authority; (2) clarity of lineage; (3) good customs; and (4) ancient wealth. Rodríguez claims that women value a lower nobility of longer lineage more than a higher but recent nobility.

As well as praising women, Rodríguez wrote on the love themes interesting to them. While he urged subjecting love to reason, which meant taking into account the likelihood of success when initiating a courtship, he wrote primarily of unrequited love. Indeed, he made such love a defining characteristic of the sentimental novel. The virtuous noble lady remained his feminine ideal while Macías was his model of the ideal courtly lover.

Work by

Bursario. Intro., ed., and notes Pilar Saquero Suárez-Somonte and Tomás González Rolán. Madrid: Universidad Complutense, 1984.

Obras. Ed. Antonio Paz y Melia. Madrid: Sociedad de Bibliófilos Españoles, 1884.

Siervo libre de amor. Ed. Antonio Prieto. Madrid: Castalia, 1976.

Work about

Andrachuk, Gregory Peter. "A Further Look at Italian Influence in the *Siervo libre de amor.*" *Journal of Hispanic Philology* 6 (1981–1982): 45–56.

———. "A Re-Examination of the Poetry of Juan Rodríguez del Padrón." *Bulletin of Hispanic Studies* 57 (1980): 299–308.

Brownlee, Marina Scordilis. "The Generic Status of the *Siervo libre de amor*: Rodríguez del Padrón's Reworking of Dante." *Poetics Today* 5 (1984): 629–643.

Coccozzella, Peter. "The Thematic Unity of Juan Rodríguez del Padrón's *Siervo libre de amor.*" *Hispania* 64.2 (May 1981): 188–198.

Dudley, Edward J. "Court and Country: The Fusion of Two Images of Love in Juan Rodríguez' *El siervo libre de amor.*" *PMLA* 82 (1967): 117–120.

Fernández Jiménez, Juan. "La estructura del *Siervo libre de amor* y la crítica reciente." *Cuadernos Hispanoamericanos* 388 (Oct. 1982): 178–190.

Forcadas, Albert M. "Implicaciones de la 'afinidad de los opuestos' entre Acto I de *La Celestina* y el *Triunfo de las donas.*" *Josep Maria Solà-Solé: Homage, Homenaje, Homenatge.* Ed. Antonio Torres-Alcalá. Zaragoza: Puvill, 1984. 1: 251–265.

Gerli, E. Michael. "Towards a Poetics of the Spanish Sentimental Romance." *Hispania* 72 (1989): 474–482.

Gilderman, Martin S. *Juan Rodríguez de la Cámara.* Boston: Twayne, 1977.

Grieve, Patricia E. *Desire and Death in the Spanish Sentimental Romance (1440–1550).* Newark, DE: Juan de la Cuesta, 1987.

Herrero, Javier. "The Allegorical Structure of the *Siervo libre de amor.*" *Speculum* 55 (1980): 751–764.

Impey, Olga Tudorica. "The Literary Emancipation of Juan Rodríguez del Padrón: From the Fictional 'Cartas' to the *Siervo libre de amor.*" *Speculum* 55 (1980): 305–316.

———. "Ovid, Alfonso X, and Juan Rodríguez del Padrón: Two Castilian Translations of the *Heroides* and the Beginnings of Spanish Sentimental Prose." *Bulletin of Hispanic Studies* 57 (1980): 283–297.

Lida, María R. "Juan Rodríguez del Padrón: Influencia." *Nueva Revista de Filología Hispánica* 8 (1954): 1–38. Reprinted with articles "Juan Rodríguez del Padrón: Vida y Obras, Influencia, Adiciones." *Estudios sobre la literatura española del siglo XV.* Madrid: José Porrúa Turanzas, 1976.

Menéndez y Pelayo, D.M. *Orígenes de la novela.* Vol. 1. Madrid: Bailly/Bailliére, 1925.

Nozick, Martin. "The Inez de Castro Theme in European Literature." *Comparative Literature* 3 (1951): 330–341.

Olivetto, Georgina. "Apuntes sobre el manuscrito del *Siervo Libre de amor*." *Incipit* 17 (1997): 229–244.

Pampin Barral, Mercedes. " 'Por ser más limpia' y 'más honesta': Juan Rodríguez del Padrón y la visión de la sexualidad femenina en el *Triunfo de las donas*." *Medievalia* 26 (December 1997): 26–34.

Salvador Miguel, Nicasio. *La poesía cancioneril: El Cancionero de Estúñiga*. Madrid: Alhambra, 1977.

Serés, Guillermo. "La elegía de Juan Rodríguez del Padrón." *Hispanic Review* 62 (1994): 1–22.

Spinelli, Emily. "Chivalry and Its Terminology in the Spanish Sentimental Romance." *La Corónica* 12 (1984): 241–253.

Judy B. McInnis

Rojas, Fernando de

See Celestina, La. Comedia o tragicomedia de Calisto y Melibea

Romero, Concha (1945–   )

Dramatist Concha Romero studied classical languages at the Universities of Seville and Salamanca, participating actively in theater groups, and later attended the Madrid School of Cinematography and collaborated in writing screenplays for film and television while teaching Latin at the secondary level. Romero began to write for the stage in the 1980s, publishing in 1983 her first play, *Un olor a ámbar* (A Smell of Amber). She currently resides in Madrid where she combines playwriting and scripting for movies and television with teaching at the Royal Academy of Dramatic Art. Although only one of her dramatic works had been staged commercially by the mid-1990s, many of her full-length plays and her two monologues have been successfully produced by university and independent groups. Some of her works have been translated and staged in Germany, Belgium, and Brazil.

Romero's dramatic production has taken two fundamental directions: plays based on historical or mythological events and char-

acters and those that focus on the situation of women in contemporary Spain. Works from either tendency, however, center on relationships of all kinds and dramatize the conflicts women face in a world dominated by masculine power structures and values. Female characters often take center stage to tell their own stories, challenging the official versions of history that have silenced or misrepresented the feminine point of view. Through metatheater, intertextuality, and irony, Romero's works question traditional gender roles and present on stage women's search for their own identity and voice in a patriarchal society.

Set in sixteenth-century Spain, Romero's *Un olor a ámbar* recreates the events surrounding the death of Saint *Teresa of Avila (1515–1582) and the conflict over the possession of her mortal remains. While remaining faithful to historical documents, Romero combines contemporary dialogue and humor with the representation of past events, shedding light on the abuse of masculine authority and the silencing of the female voice. *Así aman los dioses* (1991; Thus Love the Gods) analyzes romantic love from many perspectives, both masculine and feminine. By representing classical mythology, Romero's play shows that little has changed in the arena of amorous conduct and sentiment over the years. Due perhaps to its length and many characters and subplots, *Así aman los dioses* has not received the critical attention enjoyed by Romero's other dramatic works. It has in common with her other plays, however, the presentation of female characters who are strong, rebellious women that struggle to establish their own identity in spite of the many obstacles placed in their paths by the masculine power structure.

Two of Romero's plays are based on historical events in the lives of Spain's Queen *Isabel I (1451–1504), her brother Henry IV, and her daughter *Juana *la Loca* (1479–1555). Like *Un olor a ámbar*, these works remain true to historical accounts of their fifteenth-century characters while focusing on their motives and inner lives. Both plays examine tensions that arise between individuals and power structures and the divided consciousness that is the result of the conflicting demands of public and private lives. *Las bodas de una princesa* (1988; The Nuptials of a Princess) portrays the struggles of a young and naive Isabel to escape victimization at the hands of manipulative political forces and to achieve some degree of control over her own destiny. By the play's conclusion she has learned to affirm her personal identity and assert her feminine point of view. *Juego de reinas* (unpublished, staged 1991; Game of Queens) portrays a much older Isabel and focuses on her daughter Juana's path to madness and silence. A dialogue between the two women, this play confronts Isabel's "masculine" reason that gives primary importance to matters of state with the much younger Juana's "feminine" sentiment that wants to reconcile her personal needs with the demands of her public position. Left alone in a locked cell, Juana begins to imagine her husband's infidelity and exhibits signs of her future madness, understood here as the inability to transcend the limits of gender and the result of the silencing of her feminine perspective. Although the mature Isabel is depicted as a woman who has been successful in both public and private life, the play points to the tension and interior strife that she has endured through the years as a result of her conflicting roles as mother and political leader.

To date, Romero has written one full-length play and two monologues that are set in contemporary Spain. *Un maldito beso* (1989; An Accursed Kiss) makes use of a variety of metatheatrical techniques to create a fascinating look at male-female relationships in the 1980s. The play revolves around the world of acting and the theater. Protagonist María is a professional actress married to a successful director. The fateful kiss of the title is part of a theatrical improvisation in which the director-husband tests the abilities of an aspiring young actress. María's misin-terpretation of this kiss brings about a series of plays within the play, both voluntary and involuntary, in which the couple examines their relationship. Metatheater in this work provides interesting insights into male and female roles in contemporary society and sexist attitudes that persist in spite of legislative victories for gender equality.

The theme of gender roles in contemporary society is further examined in Romero's two monologues, written to be presented together. *¿Tengo razón o no?* (1995; Am I Right or Not?) gives voice to Carlos, an aging Don Juan whose discovery that his wife has abandoned him for another man destroys his self-confidence and causes him to reject the reality of his situation by retreating into an alcohol-induced fantasy. The female protagonist of *Allá él* (1994; That's His Affair) faces a similar dilemma. Pepa is a housewife who has been cast aside by her husband of many years, but her monologue leads her to determine a very different course of action from that of Carlos. Through the help of a sister's phone call and the imagined visit of an old friend, Pepa comes to see her new situation as an opportunity to search for her own identity. When her husband calls at the play's conclusion, she thanks him for leaving. Unlike Carlos, who clings to his donjuanesque role even after coming to the realization that it is a charade, Pepa embraces change. Now that her eyes have been opened she is willing, like so many of Romero's female characters, to accept the truth about her situation and to struggle to grow as a person while holding fast to her feminine values. *See also* Drama by Spanish Women Writers: 1970–2000; Feminist Theory and the Contemporary Spanish Stage.

Work by

Allá él. Estreno 20.2 (1994): 8–14. Also in *Esencia de mujer. Ocho monólogos de mujeres para mujeres.* Ed. Charo and Joaquín Solanas. Madrid: J. García Verdugo, 1995. 43–60.

Así aman los dioses. Madrid: Clásicas, 1991.

Las bodas de una princesa. Madrid: Lucerna, 1988.

Un maldito beso. Murcia: Universidad de Murcia, 1994. Also in *Gestos* 8 (1989): 109–144.

Work about

Floeck, Wilfried. "Entre el drama histórico y la comedia actual: El subtexto femenino en el teatro de Concha Romero." *Estreno* 23.1 (Spring 1997): 33–38.

Harris, Carolyn. "Concha Romero y Paloma Pedrero hablan de sus obras." *Estreno* 19.1 (Spring 1993): 29–35.

———. "Isabel y Juana: Protagonistas históricas del teatro de Concha Romero." *Estreno* 19.1 (Spring 1993): 21–25.

———. "La perspectiva femenina en escena: *Allá él* de Concha Romero." *Estreno* 20.2 (Fall 1994): 5–14.

Leonard, Candyce. "Los niveles de ficción en *Un maldito beso* de Concha Romero." *De lo particular a lo universal: El teatro español del siglo XX y su contexto*. Frankfurt/Vervuert/Madrid: Iberoamericana, 1994. 188–195.

———. "Role-Playing in Concha Romero's *Un maldito beso*." *Estreno* 20.2 (Fall 1994): 15–17, 44.

Carolyn Harris

Romo Arregui, Josefina (1913–)

Born in Madrid, poet, critic, and educator Josefina Romo Arregui studied at the University of Madrid, where she received a Doctorate in Letters (1944). A member of the Center for the Studies of Lope de Vega in the Royal Academy of the Spanish Language, she was also affiliated with the Consejo Superior de Investigaciones Científicas, where she served as secretary of the journal *Cuadernos de Literatura*. After competing successfully for the position of adjunct professor to the chair of Spanish Language and Literature, she taught at the University of Madrid and founded the poetry magazine *Alma*. In the mid-1950s she became a professor of Spanish at the University of Connecticut, teaching there until her retirement. Romo Arregui held several distinguished positions in the United States, including serving as president of the Academy of the Spanish Language in New York and vice-president of the Puerto Rican Athenaeum in New York.

The Puerto Rican Culture Institute in San Juan de Puerto Rico also bestowed its highest award on her.

Romo began writing poetry while very young with her book *La peregrinación inmóvil* (1934; The Motionless Pilgrimage). She acknowledges that her work reaches maturity in the 1950s and 1960s and from that period come the texts she includes in her *Autoantología* (1968; Autoanthology): *Cántico a María sola* (1954; Canticle to María Alone), *Isla sin tierra* (1955; Landless Island), *Elegías desde la orilla del triunfo* (1964; Elegies from the Shore of Triumph), *Poemas de América* (1967; Poems of America), and *Monólogos del bosque* (n.d., Monologues from the Woods). In 1979, she was reportedly working on a volume to be titled "Larga soledad definitiva" (Long Definitive Solitude).

Romo wrote from her early years as a university student to the end of her professional days. Her outstanding doctoral dissertation on Núñez de Arce, awarded the distinction of summa cum laude, opened academic opportunities for her at the University of Madrid. Nonetheless, it was in the United States where she attained fulfillment of a long, distinguished career in university teaching. Her poetry, scarcely included in the canon by male critics, has been judged as intimist and sentimental. Her poems voice solitude with a melancholic nostalgia of known and distant places and a search for peace. Passionate love is perceived as sorrow, an incurable affliction and insanity, while true love is identified with tenderness, submissiveness, oneness. In Romo's quest for transcendence, God remains a distant voice.

Work by

Autoantología. New York: Academia de la Lengua Española de Nueva York, 1968.

Work about

Sáinz de Robles, Federico Carlos. *Historia y antología de la poesía española*. Madrid: Aguilar, 1984.

Torres, Esteban. "Aproximaciones al estudio del

poema 'Isla sin tierra' de Josefina Romo Arregui."
Punto 7 1.6 (August–December 1985): 23–26.

Pilar Sáenz

Rossetti, Ana (1950–)

Born in Cádiz, Ana Rossetti is most known for her poetry. The majority of her books deal with sensual love and form part of the neobaroque return to classical meters of the 1980s; however, a recent book belongs to the essentialist Spanish poetry movement of the 1990s. Like other Spanish feminine writers of the last two decades, Rossetti revises patriarchal stereotypes of women in her poetry. Taking the theme of Eros as the central one of her first work, Rossetti produces a poetic voice that, in a subversive manner, transgresses the norm of phallocentric discourse by deconstruction of the traditional subject (male)/ object (female) pattern into a new one that portrays the female as a subject and the male as the object of seductive gaze and sexual desire. Ugalde has affirmed that Rossetti's poetry represents an example of how women can simultaneously write against, of, and within the phallocentric tradition.

Rossetti's first works (*Los devaneos de Erato*; 1980 [The Frenzies of Erato, muse of lyric poetry]; and *Dióscuros*; 1982 [Dioscuri, an allusion to Castor and Pollux]) were collected in *Indicios vehementes* (1985; Vehement Signs). Rossetti's best-known poetic work is *Devocionario* (1985; Devotionary). In this book the theme of Eros is framed with the Catholic liturgy. Like San *Juan de la Cruz (1542–1591), who used sensual love to describe divine love, Rossetti uses divine love to portray human love, demonstrating her belief that religious prayer offers the best way of expressing passion. This is how St. Augustine's "Divinas palabras" (Divine Words) become prayers of sensual love in the verses of *Devocionario*. Through use of religious intertextuality, these poems subvert traditional mystic discourse to impose the pleasures of the body. *Yesterday* (1988) is a bilingual collection of poems that continue her previous tone but at the same time have a more concentrated voice that foreshadows the poems of "Quinteto" (1989; Quintet) and "Virgo potens" (1994; Potent Virgin).

Punto umbrío (1995; Shaded Point) is a book of reflection. The poetic voice abandons the playful erotic tone of the first poems and the seduction of the Eros-dominated poetry in order to seek the essence of existence. Universal themes of time, love, and death are unveiled through a discourse that no longer needs eroticism or mystic imagery. The poetic voice is mature, reflexive, and temperate; nevertheless, these poems continue to provide the Rossettian poetic seduction. Rossetti's selected poetry works have been collected in two bilingual anthologies—*Imago Passionis* (1994), Spanish-Italian, and *Hubo un tiempo . . . / There Was a Time . . .* (1997), Spanish-English.

Rossetti wrote three plays: *El saltamontes (Monologue)* (1974; The Grasshopper), *Sueño en tres actos* (1975; Dream in Three Acts), and *La casa de las espirales* (1977; The House of Spirals). She also has three novels, *Plumas de España* (1988; Plumes of Spain), *Prendas íntimas* (1989; Undergarments), and *Mentiras de papel* (1994; Paper Lies), plus *Prosa erótica, Alevosías* (1991; Erotic Prose. Betrayals) and an opera, *El secreto enamorado* (1993; The Secret Lover), with music by Manuel Balboa. *See also* Eroticism in Contemporary Spanish Women Writers' Narrative; Short Fiction by Women Writers: 1975–1998, Post-Franco

Work by

Alevosías. Barcelona: Tusquets, 1991.
Los devaneos de Erato. 2nd ed. Valencia: Prometeo, 1980.
Devocionario. Madrid: Visor, 1986.
Indicios vehementes. Madrid: Hiperión, 1985.
Una mano de santos. Madrid: Siruela, 1997.
Mentiras de papel. Madrid: Temas de Hoy, 1994.
Plumas de España. Barcelona: Seix Barral, 1988.
Prendas íntimas. Madrid: Temas de Hoy, 1989.
Pruebas de escritura. Madrid: Hiperión, 1998.
Punto umbrío. Madrid: Hiperión, 1995.

Recuento: Cuentos Completos. Madrid: Páginas de Espuma, 2001.

Yesterday. Madrid: Torremozas, 1988.

Work about

Ciplijauskaite, Biruté. "De Medusa a Melusina: Recuperación de lo mágico." *La Chispa '97: Selected Proceedings.* Ed. and prol. Claire J. Paolini. New Orleans: Tulane UP, 1997. 91–100.

Escaja, Tina F. "Liturgia del deseo en el *Devocionario* de Ana Rossetti." *Letras Peninsulares* 8.2–3 (Fall 1995–Winter 1996): 453–470.

Ferradáns, Carmela. "La seducción de la mirada: Manuel Vázquez Montalbán y Ana Rossetti." *Revista Canadiense de Estudios Hispánicos* 22.1 (Fall 1997): 19–31.

Kruger Robbins, Jill. "Poetry and Film in Postmodern Spain: The Case of Pedro Almodóvar and Ana Rossetti." *Anales de la Literatura Española Contemporánea* 22.1 (1997): 7–8, 165–179.

Nantell, Judith. "Writing Her Self: Ana Rossetti's 'Anatomía del beso.' " *Anales de la Literatura Española Contemporánea* 22.2 (1997): 196, 253–263.

Newton, Candelas. "Retales y retórica: Jugando a las prendas con Ana Rossetti." *Romance Languages Annual* 8 (1996): 615–620.

Ríos Font, Wadda. "To Hold and Behold: Eroticism and Canonicity at the Spanish *Fines de siglo.*" *Anales de la Literatura Española Contemporánea* 23.1–2 (1998): 14–15, 355–378.

Robbins, Jill. "Seduction, Simulation, Transgression and Taboo: Eroticism in the Work of Ana Rossetti." *Hispanófila* 128 (January 2000): 49–65.

Ugalde, Sharon Keefe. "Erotismo y revisionismo en la poesía de Ana Rossetti." *Sigloxx/20th Century* 7 (1989–1990): 24–29.

Zaldívar, María Inés. *La mirada erótica en algunos poemas de Ana Rossetti y Gonzalo Millán.* Santiago de Chile: RIL; Barcelona: Café Central, 1998.

Yolanda Rosas

Rubio, Fanny (1949–   )

Combining her career as a prestigious scholar and literary critic with that of poet, as a professor at the University of Madrid (Complutense), Fanny Rubio has focused mainly on contemporary Spanish literature. Rubio has also taught at the Universities of Fez and Granada. She has written several books on criticism such as *Las revistas poéticas españolas (1939–1975)* (1976; Spanish Poetry Magazines [1939–1975]), and *Poesía española contemporánea* (1981; Contemporary Spanish Poetry). Although Rubio does not subscribe to any particular group or generation of poets, her work has been considered to show affinities to the so-called group of the *novísimos*, characterized by their experimentation with poetic language. Rubio identifies herself as a woman within the text, and her work is an inquiry of herself as she relates with other women and men. Although her books are not specifically feminist, they deal with women's issues in a way that explores female identity as well as the lack of true female representation in a discourse traditionally dominated by men.

Rubio is the author of several books of poems such as: *Acribillado amor* (1970; Love Riddled with Holes), *Retracciones* (1982; Retractions), *Reverso* (1987; Reverse), and *Dresde* (1990; Dresden). *Acribillado amor* is linked with the tradition of Spanish postwar social poetry in that it tries to incorporate personal experience and to bring colloquial language into the realm of the poem. *Retracciones* and *Reverso* are especially open to poetical experimentation. The author alternates verse and prose in an attempt to erase traditional boundaries between literary genres. *Dresde* takes the city of the same name as reference and mirror as the poet establishes a dialogue with herself articulated through elements such as culture and language. Rubio sees in the fragmentary condition of this destroyed and later reconstructed town a special point of reference from which her poetical discourse departs. The city becomes an alter ego through which the author structures her dialogic process. In 1992, Rubio published her first novel, *La sal del chocolate* (Salt of the Chocolate), which reflects the Spanish democracy and the social and individual changes this process entailed. This novel stands as a snapshot of contemporary Spanish history. Rubio has written other narrative works, including short stories such as "A Madrid por capricho" (To Madrid on a Whim).

Work by

La casa del halcón. Madrid: Santillana, Alfaguara, 1995.

Dresde. Griñón, Madrid: J. Pastor, 1990.

El embrujo de amar. Amantes, pasiones y desencantos. Madrid: Temas de Hoy, 2001.

"Novelas y transiciones: 1978–1995." *Historicidad en la novela española contemporánea*. Cádiz: Universidad de Cádiz, 1997. 81–88.

Retracciones. Madrid: Ayuso, 1982.

Reverso. Granada: Exma. Diputación Provincial de Granada, 1987.

Work about

Ferradans, Carmela. "Fanny Rubio o el anverso y reverso de lo cotidiano." *Romance Languages Annual* 7 (1995): 456–461.

Keefe Ugalde, Sharon. *Conversaciones y poemas. La nueva poesía femenina española en castellano*. Madrid: Siglo Veintiuno de España, 1991.

Violeta Padrón

Ruiz, Sor Beatriz Ana (1666–1735)

A member of the Tertiary Order of St. Augustine, Beatriz Ana Ruiz was born in Guardamar (Alicante) to Pedro Ruiz and Juana Ana Guill. She married Pedro Celdrán at age 14. Following his early death, she married a second husband, a jealous and abusive man who left her widowed by age 33, with four children to care for. She was a visionary who claimed to have been present in spirit at the Battle of Almansa, where she helped the forces of Philip V. Desperately poor, she led an exemplary life but was nonetheless vilified and persecuted by her fellow villagers, who accused her of carrying on an illicit affair with Miguel Pujalte, the mayor's secretary. Pujalte helped her and recorded many pages of religious visions dictated to him by the illiterate Beatriz. Upon her death, the townspeople recognized the error of their judgment, proclaimed her a saint, and honored her with a magnificent funeral.

Beatriz's texts consist of a series of doctrines or revelations, written to save souls, to correct vices, and to stimulate virtues. Her intelligence and her direct, simple, frequently elegant style have surprised critics, who have suggested that her writings were improved by Miguel Pujalte. Some critics deem certain sections of her writings worthy of inclusion in religious anthologies. Beatriz also wrote a vision entitled "Para la Madre Priora del Convento de Religiosas de San Sebastián" (For the Mother Prioress of the Convent of Religious of San Sebastián) that describes her view of purgatory. Her poetry includes a poem to Christ's Passion and many verses reflecting her religious raptures. Her manuscripts have been preserved in Orihuela and Guardamar.

Many of Beatriz's doctrines and revelations became part of her biography, written in first draft by Pujalte and completed by Father Thomás Pérez.

Work by

Pérez, Fr. Thomás. *Vida de la Venerable Madre Sor Beatriz Ana Ruiz*. Valencia: Pascual García, 1744.

Work about

Serrano y Sanz, Manuel. *Apuntes para una biblioteca de escritoras españolas desde el año 1401 al 1833*. 2 vols. Madrid: Rivadeneyra, 1903.

María A. Salgado

Sabuco de Nantes Barrera, Oliva (1562–1622?)

The daughter of Miguel Sabuco y Alvarez, who held the degree of *bachiller* (roughly, bachelor) in pharmacy, and Francisca de Cózar, residents of Alcaraz, the full name by which she became known to posterity omitted the particle *de*. Properly, she was, with her marriage to Don Acacio de Buedo at age 18, Luisa Oliva Sabuco Cózar de Buedo. The book *Nueva filosofía de la naturaleza del hombre . . .* (1587; New Philosophy of the Nature of Man . . .) was published under the name of Doña Oliva Sabuco. A second edition of 1588 (as well as, possibly, a fraudulent or phantom edition of the same year) and a 1622 edition, published in Lisbon in Spanish, likewise gave the author as plain Doña Oliva Sabuco. Dr. Martín Martínez (1684–1734), who edited the 1728 edition, gave currency to the name that heads this entry.

From 1587 to 1903—over 300 years—Oliva Sabuco enjoyed undisputed the attribution of *Nueva filosofía*. She is listed as an authority on the language in volumes 4–6 of the *Diccionario de autoridades* (1734–1739). Men from the sixteenth to the nineteenth centuries marveled that a woman by age 25 could write so perspicacious a treatise on human psychology and medicine. Still, her dedicatory letter to King Philip II, her letter to the king's councilor Francisco Zapata asking for support against adversaries, the copyright, dated July 23, 1586, awarded by the king, and two sonnets by an admiring resident of Alcaraz, Don Juan de Sotomayor, lend credence to the attribution on the title page. Then in 1903, José Marco Hidalgo, who three years before had published a biography of Oliva Sabuco, reported on documents he had subsequently found. They led him to declare in the title of his article that "Doña Oliva Sabuco was not a writer," asserting that the book was written by her pharmacist father Miguel. The researcher published his findings in the official organ of Spanish archives, libraries, and museums. Around the world, librarians hastened to despoil Doña Oliva of the attribution that she had so long enjoyed.

Many critics have found the evidence to be convincing; others, such as Waithe, ask pointed questions regarding the puzzling series of events known about the family dispute. The documents are as follows. In legal papers dated September 11, 1587—the very year that the first edition was published—Miguel Sabuco declares that he is "the author of the book entitled *Nueva filosofía*. And father of Doña Oliva Sabuco, my daughter, whom I named as author only to give her the honor but not the profit or the gain." He awards to his eldest son Alonso the right for 10 years to publish the book in Portugal for distribution there and in the Portuguese Indies. In his will, signed on February 20, 1588, he states that he "put her name as author . . . only to give her fame and honor," warning her not to meddle in the affair "under the penalty of my curse," and reaffirms that "I am the author and not she."

Sabuco's motives are unclear. Why in 1586 did he engage in an elaborate deception involving the king of Spain, Councilor Zapata, and a local poet, only to renounce all that less than a year after the book had been published? In a first marriage of more than 30 years, he had had eight children, of whom only Alonso and Oliva survived in 1587. In a second marriage, he had one boy, 4 years old, separated from his siblings by more than 20 years. Was Sabuco under pressure from his oldest son and his wife? Was the elderly father with a young wife concerned for the well-being of their child? Why had his relationship with Oliva and her husband deteriorated so notably in a short time? A later biographer, Torner, suggests a dysfunctional family.

Who were the adversaries from whom Doña Oliva sought the protection of king's Councilor Zapata? Could they have been members of her family or her community? Or were they, perhaps, familiars of the Inquisition? Torner notes that the Holy Office did indeed, at a later date, examine the *Nueva filosofía* and require the deletion of certain statements relating to free will, an excision made by Dr. Martín Martínez in the 1728 edition. Did Sabuco, near the end of his life, vehemently affirm his authorship in order to protect a beloved daughter from dangers that might assail her because of the book that bore her name? These questions remain unanswered.

In the four centuries since it was published, the *Nueva filosofía* has been esteemed as a work written with style and replete with innovative ideas. It is compared favorably with a better-known contemporary treatise, *Examen de ingenios para las ciencias* (1575; Examen of Men's Wits for the Sciences), by the physician Juan Huarte de San Juan (1530?–1591?). Both texts move from dependence on Aristotle, Hippocrates, and Galen toward reliance on experience and observation. The Sabuco work is divided into seven unequal parts. The first four are called colloquia, for they purport to be conversations among three shepherds named Antonio, Veronio, and Rodonio. It is this feature that earned the *Nueva filosofía* a place in *belles lettres* as well as in the history of ideas. Antonio is older and responds discursively to the briefer questions or comments of his companions. The first colloquium, called "El conocimiento de sí mismo" (Knowledge of One's Self), is the most substantial with 70 chapters (*títulos*). It deals for the most part with human nature and the human psyche. There follow two briefer colloquia, a total of 15 chapters, that treat the world man lives in and its improvement. The fourth part introduces the extensive and significant fifth, called the "Diálogo de la vera medicina y vera filosofía" (Dialogue of True Medicine and True Philosophy). Antonio and another shepherd discuss with a medical doctor aspects of medicine and philosophy that were unknown to the ancients. The final two parts are made up of pronouncements in Latin (*Dicta brevia*), by Antonio and the doctor, on medicine and philosophy.

The book is respected; the issue of authorship to date remains unresolved.

Work by

"Coloquio del conocimiento de sí mismo . . ." "Coloquio de las cosas que mejoran este mundo y sus repúblicas." *Obras escogidas de filósofos*. 1873. Ed. Adolfo de Castro. BAE 65. Madrid: Sucesores de Hernando, 1922. 325–376.

Nueva filosofía de la naturaleza del hombre, no conocida ni alcanzada de los grandes filósofos antiguos, la qual mejora la vida y salud humana. Compuesta por doña Oliva Sabuco. Madrid: P. Madrigal, 1587.

Obras. Ed. Octavio Cuarteto. Madrid: Ricardo Fe, 1888.

Work about

Marco Hidalgo, José. *Biografía de Doña Oliva de Sabuco*. Madrid: Antonino Romero, 1900.

———. "Doña Oliva de Sabuco no fue escritora." *Revista de Archivos, Bibliotecas y Museos* Series 3, 7 (1903): 1–13.

Torner, Florentino M. *Doña Oliva Sabuco de Nantes. Siglo XVI*. Madrid: Aguilar, after 1935?

Waithe, Mary Ellen. "Olivia Sabuco de Nantes Barrera." *A History of Women Philosophers*. Ed. Mary Ellen Waithe. Dordrecht: Kluwer Academic Publishers, 1989. 2: 261–284.

John Dowling

Sáenz-Alonso, Mercedes (1917–): *Don Juan y el donjuanismo*

Born in 1917 to a noble family of San Sebastián, Mercedes Sáenz-Alonso credits her learned father as her mentor. Her university studies in philosophy and letters were interrupted by the Spanish Civil War; then she began her career as a journalist. A professor at the University of Navarra, she became an internationally known lecturer on art, history, and literature as well as a literary critic known for her book on Don Juan. She has also written newspaper correspondence, essays, short stories, travel books, and postwar realist novels. Her essays, criticism, short stories, and journalism have won several prizes.

Sáenz-Alonso's *Don Juan y el donjuanismo* (Don Juan and the "Latin lover" Phenomenon), a thesis work that she considers her best, won the Premio Guipúzcoa in 1969. In 38 chapters of objective and erudite examination she deals with all that Don Juan encompasses in Spain and other countries, resisting previous definitions of the phenomenon. She considers Don Juan as a type of man, both the literary character and actual persons, whose reason for being directs him toward women who, in turn, represent the destiny of his existence. Taking her cue from Ortega y Gasset's (1883–1955) concept of *donjuanismo* as an immense quarry of inspiration where distinct works can be created, Sáenz-Alonso contemplates numerous interpretations of Don Juan that discourse across centuries through literature, the fine arts, philosophy, and science.

Thus, Sáenz-Alonso launches her argument with the plurality of Don Juan because he has occupied writers, composers, painters, essayists, analysts, and philosophers for centuries. The hundreds of works written on him palpably demonstrate the inexhaustible facets of his character. Once Tirso de *Molina (1580?–1648) established the prototype, interpreters from the world over came to reshape Don Juan to their own creative ideas. Don Juan was to go on wandering across time and national boundaries, conserving in all these migrations the unique point of departure that identifies and qualifies him as Don Juan: woman. Even when Sáenz-Alonso entertains others' theories of wickedness, dominance, or ridicule as the principal drive behind Don Juan's behavior, she maintains that his clear objective is woman.

Sáenz-Alonso also views Don Juan's valor as absolutely necessary to his character—a reckless valor, which scorns life but *loves*, as do all Dionysian beings. Another essential qualification emerges in her initial considerations as she mediates upon the ruses of Tirso's Don Juan. She finds in him a lively, brilliant intelligence common to all versions of the type and even attributes amazing brilliance to Lord Byron as a flesh-and-blood Don Juan. The essayist's final analysis of Don Juan is the logical outcome of her initial considerations of the type. Having dealt with such topics as love, the Spanish psychology of Don Juan, the painterly and musical versions of the universal lover, she then traces his literary origins. She assumes that Tirso de Molina's *El *burlador de Sevilla* engendered the "larva" that would bring about centuries of literary proliferation. From that point she examines comprehensively the multiple creations Don Juan inspired in world literature, from seventeenth-century Spain to twentieth-century England and Belgium, as well as central Europe, Russia, and Denmark. Ultimately, Sáenz-Alonso deals with her personal interpretation of Don Juan by presenting her findings on the inward nature of all Don Juan variants. Additionally, she admits that she, a woman given to fighting for lost causes, is defending this literary hero. In this case she stands alone for a figure attacked by many writers, both men and women. Sáenz-Alonso presents six conditions essential to the Don Juan type and then illustrates how each conceptual characteristic she sets forth is indispensable. She identifies the fundamentals of the Don Juan type as intelligence, amorality, pride, valor, and the polygamous direction of the male sexual drive. Don Juan's gallant and manly bearing are also added to this list. If one of these elements is subtracted, Don Juan does not exist.

In the systematic approach of her analysis, Sáenz-Alonso's interpretation of Don Juan remains a personal, feminine one. She not only defines the character in terms of his relationship to women but also interprets seduction as a mutual phenomenon. Women surround and attract Don Juan; he yields to the attraction by selecting who he will seduce next. While some have compared Don Juan to Lucifer, seeing him as blasphemer, iconoclast, and rebel, Sáenz-Alonso notes that today's social circumstances differ from those of the Golden Age, seventeenth-century France, or the time of English Romanticism. With the exception of royal courts, Sáenz-Alonso observes that these societies possess a common feature: the lack of freedom for women. Because of it, Don Juan had to use the special boldness of reckless valor, since all attempts to approach women supposed danger. The concept of woman-as-conquest surely echoes the aristocratic lexicon of war, which was man's business on the battlefield as well as in love. The Don Juan phenomenon of that time was founded on personal valor, contempt for life, pride in defying God and even all those who believed. Sáenz-Alonso also notes that in the present day amorous entreaty no longer exposes life to any threat; social circumstances and the context of sexuality have changed to the degree that few worry or believe in the eternal damnation pursuant to blasphemous or amoral conduct. In those earlier times, women without freedom were women vulnerable to marriages of convenience or family arrangement. For those women Don Juan represented a devastating phenomenon. Unable to forget him, the woman who loved Don Juan was inexorably destined to love him forever, somehow believing that she might prove herself unique by producing the miracle of being loved in return by him. However, Sáenz-Alonso insists that Don Juan avoids loving, for he knows that his objective is to deliver love but not himself. Thus, Don Juan in love with one woman indicates the occurrence of a miracle, and for Sáenz-Alonso, women are apt to believe in such miracles; to end Don Juan's career stimulates feminine vanity. Yet if one woman stops the course of the inconstant lover by converting him to monogamy, Don Juan would cease to exist.

Sáenz-Alonso's passion to study a type of man blinded by women, to analyze how he developed through the passage of time, caused her to close her eyes to his indefensible amorality. Seeking another moral ground, she concentrates on the principle of life that turns her toward the possible nullification of any and all Don Juans. Since he is marked by destiny from his very inception, Sáenz-Alonso searched for the appropriate ending for every Don Juan within the framework of "donjuanismo." After establishing a set of indispensable fundamentals Sáenz-Alonso goes beyond the theatrical conventions of damnation and repentance. What she ultimately determines derives from Don Juan's lack of complete, fulfilling love, for such engagement on his part would threaten his existence as she has conceived it. *See also Burlador de Sevilla, El* (1627–1629): Its Women Characters; Zorrilla y Moral, José (1817–1893): His View of Women

Work about

Don Juan y el donjuanismo. Madrid: Guadarrama, 1969.

Glenn Morocco

Sáez de Melgar, Faustina (1834?– 1895)

As author of *folletos* (pamphlets), Sáez de Melgar recommended the traditional virtues of submission and obedience, upholding patriarchal values that demanded that the only feminine role in life should be that of conventional wife and mother. Her manuals for young women are filled with a conviction of the inferiority of her own gender and suggest submission to men in the most self-contemptuous manner.

According to the biographical account of Enríquez de Salamanca, Sáez de Melgar became a prominent figure in the field of female education. Although she successfully produced fictional works between 1850 and 1880, Sáez de Melgar did not enjoy the recognition of her contemporaries among canonical writers and instead was classified as a secondary author. The three dominant themes of her works consist of political views that mirror her own support of the liberal constitutional monarchy, domesticity as the solution to social-class conflict, and middle-class woman as **ángel del hogar*. The limited number of critical studies dealing with Sáez de Melgar's work reflects the general exclusion of women writers of the mid-nineteenth century. Andreu and Enríquez de Salamanca find an emphasis on the feminine literary tradition of late-nineteenth-century Spain in her writing and also identify the relation of Sáez de Melgar's *La cruz del olivar* (1868; The Olive Grove Cross) and *Rosa la cigarrera de Madrid* (1872; Rosa the Madrid **Cigarrera*) with **Pérez Galdós's La desheredada* and **Pardo Bazán's La tribuna*, respectively. Studies by Ferreras, Simón Palmer, and Enríquez de Salamanca provide further insights regarding the general role of women writers in the nineteenth century, while the theme of domesticity is discussed by Aldaraca, Kirkpatrick, and Andreu (*Galdós*). Among Sáez de Melgar's biographers, Simón Palmer and McNerney have stated that in following the literary practices of her time the role of female protagonists mirrors their role in reality. As a model of literary creation, femininity is encompassed by domesticity, which in turn fuels the continuance of a patriarchal society.

Work by

La cadena rota. Drama en tres actos. Madrid: F. Macías, 1879.

La cruz del olivar. Novela original. Madrid: F. Peña, 1868. Rpt. in *Anales galdosianos* Suplemento 14 (1980): 1–68.

La higuera de Villaverde. Leyenda tradicional. Madrid: Bernabé Fernández, 1860.

Un libro para mis hijas. Educación cristiana y social de la mujer. Barcelona. Librería de Juan y Antonio Bastinos, 1877.

Las mujeres españolas, americanas y lusitanas pintadas por sí mismas. Obra dedicada a la mujer por la mujer . . . bajo la dirección de Faustina Sáez de Melgar. Barcelona: n.p., 1885.

Rosa la cigarrera de Madrid. Gran novela original de las señora Doña Faustina Sáez de Melgar. 2 vols. Barcelona: Biblioteca Hispano-Americana, 1872.

Work about

Aldaraca, Bridget. "El ángel del hogar: The Cult of Domesticity in Nineteenth-Century Spain." *Theory and Practice of Feminist Literary Criticism.* Ed. Gabriela Mora and Karen S. Van Hooft. Ypsilanti: Bilingual Press/Editorial Bilingüe, 1982. 62–87.

Andreu, Alicia G., ed. and intro. "*La cruz del olivar* por Faustina Sáez de Melgar: Un modelo literario en la vida de Isidora Rufete." *Anales galdosianos* Suplemento 14 (1980): 7–16.

———. *Galdós y la literatura popular.* Madrid: Sociedad General Española de Librería, 1982.

———. "Maternal Discourse in *La cruz del olivar*, by Faustina Sáez de Melgar." *Revista Canadiense de Estudios Hispánicos* 19.2 (Winter 1995): 229–240.

Enríquez de Salamanca, Cristina, "Faustina Sáez de Melgar." *Spanish Women Writers. A Bio-Bibliographical Source Book.* Ed. Linda Gould Levine, Ellen Engelson Marson, and Gloria Feiman Waldman. Westport: Greenwood, 1993. 460–472.

Ferreras, Juan Ignacio. "La novela decimonónica escrita por mujeres." *Escritoras románticas españolas.* Ed. Marina Mayoral. Madrid: Fundación Banco Nacional, 1990. 17–24.

Kirkpatrick, Susan. "The Female Tradition in Nineteenth-Century Spanish Literature." *Cultural and Historical Grounding for Hispanic and Luso-*

Brazilian Feminist Literary Criticism. Ed. Hernán Vidal. Minneapolis: Institute for the Study of Ideologies and Literature, 1989. 344–370.

————. "*Rosa la cigarrera de Madrid* como modelo literario de *La tribuna.*" *Continental, Latin-American and Francophone Women Writers. Vol. 3. Selected Papers from the Sixth Annual Wichita State University Conference on Foreign Literatures April 13–16, 1989.* Ed. Ginette Adamson and Eunice Myers. Lanham, MD: UP of America, 1993.

Scanlon, Geraldine. *La polémica feminista en la España contemporánea: 1868–1974.* Madrid: Akal, 1986.

Simón Palmer, María del Carmen. *Escritoras españolas del siglo XIX: Manual bio-bibliográfico.* Madrid: Castalia, 1991.

Lisa Nalbone

Sáiz y Otero, Concepción (1851– c.1930)

When Adolfo González Posada published his book *Feminismo* (1899), which treats the question of women's franchise from an international perspective, he quoted Concepción Sáiz y Otero's articles on Spanish feminism and referred to her as "a distinguished professor of the Central Normal School for Women Teachers." Thus Sáiz, who pursued an eminent career in the field of education, became an early point of reference for Spanish feminism. She belonged to the Asociación para la Enseñanza de la Mujer and the feminist group Unión Iberoamericana and, was a chair of Spanish Language and Literature at Central Normal; she was the professor of many eminent future professional women.

As a pedagogue she wrote several professional works: *Cartas . . . ¿pedagógicas? Ensayo de psicología pedagógica* (1895; Pedagogical? Letters. Essay on Pedagogical Psychology), coauthored with the well-known educator Urbano González Serrano, professor at Madrid University; the influential *Teoría y práctica de la educación y la enseñanza* (1908; Theory and Practice of Education and Teaching); *Dos meses por las escuelas de Londres* (1911; Two Months in the Schools of London); *El método de la escuela renovada de Milán* (1930; The Method of the Reformed School of Milan); and *Las nuevas escuelas italianas* (1930; The New Italian Schools), which treat her experience with other national education systems. Her commitment to feminist issues is documented in articles published in the pedagogical magazine *La Escuela Moderna* (1893–1902). The book that commands more interest, however, is *Un episodio nacional que no escribió Pérez Galdós: La Revolución del 68 y la cultura femenina* (A National Episode Pérez Galdós Didn't Write: The 1868 Revolution and Feminine Culture), an autobiography/memoir she published in 1929.

In the prologue, Sáiz defines the book's purpose as setting straight the historical record for women. She was prompted by the need to repudiate the version of women's access to education given by Pérez Galdós in *Cánovas,* the last volume of his *Episodios nacionales.* Sáiz felt that Galdós denigrated the first woman inspector of state schools. Claiming that as a rule Galdós's accounts deal with atypical women, she then observes that "honest" women have no history of their own, even though they contribute to the writing of men's history. Thus she sets about narrating the story of women as professional educators. In the process, what she really vindicates is her own case, for she dwells on her own documented and detailed recollections, first as a young student and then as an educator, creating in this way a very original autobiography.

Sáiz's career was fraught with political and ideological obstacles that turned women into pawns. Devoted primarily to explaining her personal struggles to establish herself as an independent professional educator in the difficult field of policymaking, the book provides a view of education from a female perspective, as she tells the story of an upwardly mobile woman at the turn of the century. It is therefore an essential primary source for the identification and understanding of women's entry into the professional world. It was this consideration of women as a social collective that brought about the awaking of female consciousness, and women then began the process of securing full possession of their rights as human beings by winning their right to education.

Thus Sáiz narrates her own personal story intertwined with a historical account of women's access to education. Taking as its point of departure the information provided by the official census of 1860, which stated that 90.42 percent of women were illiterate, the book traces the real impetus of a modern approach to teaching and learning by women not so much to the official Normal Schools (the first of which was founded in Badajoz in 1851) as to the founding of the Asociación para la Enseñanza de la Mujer (Association for the Instruction of Women) that originated in the wake of the 1868 "Glorious Revolution." The Asociación was sponsored and inspired by Fernando de Castro (1814–1874), a leader in the democratization of Spanish education who was appointed rector of the Central University after the Revolution of 1868. At this point, new views seemed to come together and it became possible to implement some of the philosophical doctrines of Sanz del Río (1814–1869), which Castro did regarding the education of a vast sector of middle-class women. By 1882 the Asociación, through its Escuela de Institutrices (School for Governesses), managed to change the inefficient, ignorance-ridden Madrid Escuela Central Normal and over the next 25 years lifted the culture of Spanish teachers and with it Spanish women's culture from a state of absolute ignorance to one of conscious knowledge.

From a general perspective the book provides inside details, or the human face, of many historical figures, revealing aspirations, achievements, frustrations, and even rivalries. Prominent individuals discussed include Fernando de Castro, Concepción *Arenal (1820–1893), Ramona Aparicio, Carmen Rojo (c. 1846–1915), and María *Goyri (1873–1954), along with others now com-

pletely forgotten; all were protagonists of the first stage of Spanish women's emancipation. At the same time the curricula, faculty, and atmosphere of several schools and teaching institutions are described as Sáiz narrates her educational itinerary. She received her degree as elementary teacher in 1877 after one year of study (1876–1877) at the Madrid Central Normal School, and the following academic year, she completed her studies for the degree of advanced teacher. Next she began her teaching career in 1878 working in a private school for girls while continuing to study in the evenings to become an *institutriz* (governess), receiving her diploma in 1881. That same year a National Examination was called to select a replacement for Ramona Aparicio (1800–1880), director of the Normal Central de Maestras.

The examinations were open to the public and commanded great interest among those devoted to education and public welfare, including Concepción Arenal, educators from the Institución Libre de Enseñanza, and its founder, Francisco Giner de los Ríos (1839–1915). Sáiz's performance was outstanding, but as she later explains, she did not get the position due to political manipulations for which the said Institución was partially responsible. The position went to Carmen Rojo, and this incident marked the beginning of a lifelong rivalry between the two women. Nevertheless, in 1882 she was admitted as a teacher to the Normal, and in 1884 her performance at the earlier examination won her the official appointment of teacher of languages, literature, and fine arts at that institution. Previously (in 1883), she had been appointed director of the Primary Grade School, founded by the Asociación para la Enseñanza de la Mujer, following another outstanding performance in 1882 with a paper read at the First International Conference on Education that took place in Madrid. In 1889 she became tenured as professor of language and literature at the Normal Central.

Throughout her career, Sáiz continued to

be linked to the progressive and creative Asociación para la Enseñanza de la Mujer, which was directed by members of the Institución Libre de Enseñanza, Ruiz de Quevedo first and later Gumersindo de Azcárate. In 1906, following retirement of the respected pedagogue Pedro de Alcántara, she became professor of pedagogy at the Escuela de Institutrices. With the 1909 founding of the Escuela de Estudios Superiores de Magisterio, a coeducational university-level pedagogy school with fields of concentration in either sciences or letters, Sáiz applied for the position of literature professor. Here again another professional conflict emerged that her self-confidence and tenacity overcame. The position in fact was assigned to María Goyri, the first woman to obtain a Ph.D. from Central University and Sáiz's former student at the Normal Central. Goyri belonged to the inner cluster of the Institución Libre de Enseñanza and was Ramón Menéndez Pidal's (1869–1968) wife. Sáiz challenged the assignment and won her case, thus securing her chair as professor as well as vice-director of the New School. Her strong opinions about the duties of teachers and students in elementary and secondary education, as opposed to university-level studies, generated ongoing tension with colleagues.

The book also provides invaluable documentation of a single woman's solitary fight against general prejudices and, especially, political and administrative inequities faced by women. It is in this context that the above-mentioned conflicts with Carmen Rojo, María Goyri, and other colleagues such as María de *Maeztu (1882–1948) should be judged. While her rivals were firmly backed by political and ideological organizations, Concepción Sáiz is exemplary in her independence of judgment, self-assurance, courage, and clarity of mind. Her position is that of a moderate feminist, fiercely liberal and an ardent defender of the importance of women teachers. Even though she wrote this text when the debate for women's franchise and the politicization of women was at its height

(1929), as a feminist she belongs to the first period of the awakening of female consciousness, when education was stressed as the door to real emancipation. She was right in her assessment of the importance of teacher's education. Most of the women who educated working-class women, who in turn would become political activists or feminists, were directly or indirectly influenced by her or by instructors like her. *See also* Women's Education in Spain: 1860–1993 Women's Situation in Spain: 1786–1931; The Awakening of Female Consciousness

Work by

Cartas. . . . ¿pedagógicas? Ensayo de psicología pedagógica. With Urbano González Serrano. Madrid: Suc. de Rivadeneyra, 1895.

Dos meses por las escuelas de Londres. Madrid: Suc. de Hernando, 1911.

Un episodio nacional que no escribió Pérez Galdós. La Revolución del 68 y la cultura femenina (Apuntes del natural). Madrid: Victoriano Suárez, 1929.

"El feminismo en España." *La Escuela Moderna* 13 (1897): 248–260, 321–334.

El método de la escuela renovada de Milán. Madrid: Ministerio de Instrucción Pública, 1930.

"La mujer en el Congreso Pedagógico." *La Escuela Moderna* 4 (1893): 88–91.

Las nuevas escuelas italianas. Madrid: Ministerio de Instrucción Pública, 1930.

Teoría y práctica de la educación y la enseñanza. Madrid: Suc. de Hernando, 1908.

Work about

Bravo, María Elena. "La Revolución de 1868 y el feminismo español: Una escritora al margen." *La balsa de la Medusa* 53 (1995): 87–106.

María Elena Bravo

Salamanca, Concha de

See Zardoya González, María Concepción (1914–   )

Salas Barbadillo, Alonso

See Hija de Celestina, la ingeniosa Elena, La (1612–1614)

Salisachs, Mercedes (1916–   )

Born in Barcelona of a wealthy and conservative family, convent-educated Mercedes Salisachs earned a degree in merchandising from Barcelona's Escuela de Comercio and later established herself as a radio journalist, cultural commentator, and novelist, also operating an interior decorating business with a partner. She married in 1935 and had five children. In 1958, one of Salisachs's sons died in an accident, an incident that affected her profoundly and often echoes in her works. Her writing, generally ironic and intelligent, reflects not only her education and varied experience but her extensive travels.

In Spain as well as elsewhere, Salisachs is a well-known author. Her novel *Una mujer llega al pueblo* (1957; trans. as *The Eyes of the Proud*, 1960) won the Premio Ciudad de Barcelona in 1956 and was translated into seven languages. Five of her novels have appeared in French translation. A finalist for the Premio Planeta in 1956 for *Carretera intermedia* (Second-Class Highway) and again for the same award in 1973 for *Adagio confidencial* (Confidential Adagio), she won the 1975 Planeta for *La gangrena* (Gangrene). A commercial success during a good part of her literary career, Salisachs has received slight attention from reviewers and critics, who often labeled her a common writer of commercial middle-class novels—a classification that fails to describe her works accurately or fairly. Salisachs has published long and short works of fiction and memoirs; they reveal fantasy, rural settings, fables, biblical and religious themes, and contemporary social issues. What is more, the techniques and structures Salisachs employs reveal a penchant for innovation, seen in several works that defy linear narrative and pay homage to Faulkner with inventive approaches to point of view. In her early works, Salisachs pursued moral issues. Later novels, set in a cosmopolitan milieu, focus on the failure of love in marriage as a result of moral decay in the materialist world that followed the Civil War. From this follows her disposition to observe and satirize the middle class. As one of the first postwar generation of writers, Salisachs probes Spain's restricted social environment, notably the impact of the bygone Falangist national program of instruction and training for women called the Sección Femenina (Women's Section). By the time her first book was published in the 1950s, the Section's code of conduct for women had been firmly and deliberately imposed in Spain.

Salisachs's writings present social criticism on all fronts. In a satire of sexual stereotypes daring for the 1950s, two sections of *Adán Helicóptero* (1957; Adam Helicopter) lampoon the prevailing attitudes and behavior of both sexes. "La escuela internacional de mujeres" (The International School for Women), a caricature of the Sección Femenina, trains girls to become subservient women by giving them classes consisting of indoctrinating decrees; the unique goal of a woman's life is her man. One of the most blatant proclamations states that women must not write because female writers are "amputated mammals." "La escuela internacional masculina" (The International School for Men) teaches men to be egotistical, unjust, and unfaithful to their wives in order to show their masculinity.

In her later autobiographical work, *Derribos: Crónicas de un tiempo saldado* (1981; Demolition: Intimate Chronicle of a Liquidated Time), she confesses that Catholic education did not motivate her. The discovery of Fernán Caballero (Cecilia *Böhl de Faber) was a revelation for Salisachs and changed her attitude about studies for a while. *Derribos* is not a formal autobiography or history but rather selected, significant moments from her childhood, emphasizing personal contacts with famous people including Dalí and guitarist Andrés Segovia and concentrating upon those aspects seen as having influenced her artistic development. Although she dedicated *Derribos* to her grandchildren, Salisachs exposes her past errors and present feelings of guilt, seemingly without guile;

some of her most painful memories emanate from her lack of love and attention to her handicapped sister.

In the 1950s, social realism flourished in Spanish literature, and with it came technical innovation. *Primera mañana, última mañana* (1955; First Morning, Last Morning), Salisachs's first novel (signed with her pseudonym María Ecín), showed such inventiveness. Its protagonist-narrator, artist Rómulo Dogimasia, relates his present and past in alternate sections. These 430 pages of smallish print depict the artistic, human, and societal aspects of Spanish life, including Madrid aristocracy and Catalan upper-class society. Rómulo, from Madrid, marries Clara, of a wealthy Barcelona family. His situation allows him to be estranged and yet devote himself to artistic philosophizing and to a variety of love affairs. Communicating neither with his daughters nor his wife, whose aging and obesity he describes as though reviewing the work of an unknown, unskilled artisan, Rómulo functions as a detached literary viewpoint on the first half of this century. Salisachs reputedly spent five years (1948–1953) writing this first novel, which covers five decades of Spanish life "in all its aspects, social, artistic and human," according to critic Eugenio de Nora.

A dominant current inhabits Salisachs's realistic, cosmopolitan novels: to present a sociological base of Spain (frequently Barcelona) in the years before and after the Spanish Civil War. Some of her novels have broad historical aspirations; others are stories of individuals; all depict a central theme: failure of love in marriage. One of Salisachs's expressed intentions is to expose the defects, disorientation, and senseless life of the upper-middle class. In this endeavor she outlines a materialistic society that destroys morality and disguises ennui and infidelity as marriage. *La sinfonía de las moscas* (1982; Symphony of the Flies) is set in Barcelona during the 1950s, when it was written; the author withheld it for some three decades in fear of censorship. Julio, almost 60 and em-ployed in a publishing house, receives news that he has won approximately 2 million pesetas in the lottery; the novel treats the expectations of change introduced by this windfall. His sordid personal life (a triangle involving his sister-in-law, which leads his daughter to attempt suicide) is little worse than that of his "successful" sister, Juana, mistress of a financier, or the alcoholic grandmother who fancies herself an opera star. Julio, with delusions of grandeur (echoed by his sister and mother) dreams of becoming a novelist but instead wastes most of the lottery money with a prostitute. The novel ends disastrously, with the protagonist's son in the morgue, victim of a suspicious auto accident, his niece jailed, and daughter Julita jilted, and Julio himself seriously ill. While Salisachs ostensibly treats dreams, hopes, and illusions and their importance, each character is also to some extent the victim of those illusions.

Carretera intermedia, set on the Riviera, features a female chemist, Bibiana, an unusual protagonist for the period. While feminist issues are not at the forefront here, her unfaithful husband blames her for their daughter's death and abandons her. Now a mature woman, Bibiana awakens to sexuality but is rejected by the man she loves when he breaks up the relationship on religious grounds. This novel could be designated feminist in its consideration for the protagonist's dilemma: loss of roles of wife and mother compounded by questions of profession and sexuality. *Una mujer llega al pueblo*, one of Salisachs's more eminent works, translated into eight languages, departs radically from prior works with its rural setting. The repercussions prompted by the return of the illegitimately pregnant Eulalia to her village generate an acute portrayal of small-town sexual hypocrisy. The novel was originally prohibited by censors and eventually published with numerous cuts. Male critics in Spain belittled the book, but reviewers grounded in the American novel have found in it technical and thematic reflections of

Faulkner and Dos Passos. Between 1955 and 1957, Salisachs published six works, some now inaccessible. *Más allá de los raíles* (Beyond the Rails), *Adán helicóptero*, and *Pasos conocidos* (Well-Known Footsteps) all appeared in 1957, the last identified as a collection of two novels and nine stories.

Vendimia interrumpida (1960; Interrupted Wine Harvest) tells the story of a small-town priest; Salisachs considers this her most authentic book. *La estación de las hojas amarillas* (1963; The Season of the Yellow Leaves) presents a love story, an intimate analysis of Cecilia, a haughty soul deprived of all decent emotions. The major conflict arises when she degrades the attachment she feels for the boy put in her custody; what should have been his salvation becomes inexpressible passion. *El declive y la cuesta* (1966; The Cliff and the Hillside) takes as its point of departure the "good thief," Dimas, who converted to Christianity upon the cross when he was crucified next to Jesus. The narrative concentrates on his mother who questions the meaning of her life's devotion to someone who died crucified. *La última aventura* (1967; The Last Adventure) links psychological study to social problems through the story of a man in quest of impossible happiness. An egotistical and shortsighted dreamer, he abandons his wife for the sake of a new love, destined for failure. Also during this period, Salisachs published a "do-it-yourself" decorating manual, *El gran libro de la decoración* (1969; The Great Book of Decorating).

One of her most successful bestsellers, *Adagio confidencial* explores the casual encounter between a man and a woman who have not seen each other for 20 years. The dialogue between the couple, mature adults who evoke a past they can never quite forget, takes place during a few hours in an airport lounge and constitutes an analysis of their frustrated relationship, as well as a clarification of many vague or misunderstood points concerning their mutual circle of friends in former years. Another famous and popular work, *La gangrena* (1975; Gangrene) deals

with the story of Carlos Honderos, a successful but morally reprehensible man. Jailed on suspicion of murdering his second wife, Serena, Carlos looks back on his life. Born to a ruined aristocratic Madrid family, he climbs the ladder of social and financial success, aided greatly by his first marriage to Alicia, daughter of a wealthy Catalan financier. The historical framework, which moves from the advent of Spain's second Republic to the 1970s, provides a backdrop for Salisachs's avidly critical view on morality. Through the historical network and about 100 characters, she traces economic development and social change in Spain, mostly Barcelona, during the first half of the twentieth century. Salisachs combines internal monologue and dialogue and shifts continually between past and present with the intent to satirize the aspirations, bourgeois hypocrisy, and moral decay of the *nouveau riche*. Starting with the protagonist's beautiful mother (and her lover, Carlos's "uncle"), two wives, and a series of love affairs, the women in this panorama form a symbolic chain that lends significance to his trajectory. His "gangrene" is the relentless ambition that impels him. Ultimately, his sense of guilt for his hateful treatment of Alicia leads him to offer no defense against accusations of responsibility for Serena's murder. He is not convicted, but Salisachs indicates that his daughter will inherit a similarly afflicted life. Between its publication in December 1975 and March 1976, this novel went through 12 editions and sold more than 400,000 copies—extraordinary success for Spain at that time.

Viaje a Sodoma (1977; Trip to Sodom) has as its protagonist a boy, Jacobo, the hapless victim of his parents' divorce, who goes to spend time with his uncle, a bohemian painter who lives a dissolute existence on the Costa Brava. The picturesque site on the seashore and the adventure of meeting and associating with mature people captivate Jacobo, especially the formation of a bond with his uncle. The psychological depiction of the boy's sensibility and Salisachs's use of his perceptions to present the corrupt and decadent world surrounding the painter are among her best novelistic achievements. The people in the uncle's circle live from orgy to orgy, inevitably leaving Jacobo's childlike consciousness in a conflict that spoils the happiness of his new world. In *El volumen de la ausencia* (1983; Volume of Absence), Ida Sierra, a middle-aged married woman with three children, has been diagnosed as terminally ill. She has an inoperable brain tumor, and with the prognosis of only a few months to live, Ida walks the city of Barcelona. As she walks, she reviews her life and wonders if she should leave her husband Daniel for the painter she once loved. Ida's frame of reference is a happy home and marriage, but she has never felt at home with her husband; he and his mother have made Ida their subordinate. Daniel, once part of Franco's army, is now a publicity agent and author of some bad highbrow novels. Ida lives in the Calle de Aribau with her family, the domineering mother-in-law, her saintly mother; her eldest son, Rodolfo, and sometimes her daughter, Andrea. As Ida reflects on her life, layers of complications emerge. Her husband is having an affair with Ida's feminist friend who accidentally killed Ida's younger son in a drunk-driving spree; her older son is gay and gets caught up in a police raid, and her daughter Andrea is having an affair with the father of her best friend. For all its resemblance to soap opera or *novela rosa* (romance novel), *El volumen de la ausencia* presents a set of contradictions that modify and surpass so-called women's literature. Salisachs, it seems, has chosen to construct Ida's story as a dig at male avant-garde novels and at the same time a tribute to Carmen *Laforet. That is, Daniel flops as a novelist (and as recalcitrant husband) on the very street of Barcelona where Laforet's *Nada* (1944; Nothing) takes place. Several American women scholars have attributed critical neglect of Salisachs to her commercial and popular success and her specialization in what some male critics might call a feminine sub-

genre. The innovative female critics have shown that Salisachs successfully challenged established views about men and women and altered a traditional female narrative model to chart her satirical offensive.

La danza de los salmones (1988; The Dance of the Salmon), subtitled *Una fábula novelada* (a novelized fable), presents a story about salmon with human attributes and names. Some, like Trueno and Patricio, strive to deny the preordained swim upstream to mate; that is the symbolic *danza*. This fable of vital struggle and love is probably the only one Salisachs ends on a happy note when Patricio and his mate, Potámide, fulfill their destiny. After long silence, Salisachs published *Bacteria mutante* (1996; Mutant Bacteria), a continuation of *La gangrena*, which recalls the format of *El volumen de la ausencia* insofar as the protagonist's attempts to recuperate from the past. Perhaps exemplifying Sancho Panza's dictum that "never were second parts any good," the sequel failed to duplicate the success of *La gangrena*, and it is unlikely that Salisachs, in her eighties, will return to the literary fray. While somewhat scorned by critics of the Franco era because she seldom portrayed the plight of the lower classes, she occasionally approached "social criticism" from the upper extreme, examining the parasitic existence of the bourgeoisie. An independent writer whose narrative accomplishments deserve better treatment, she has been undervalued by feminists as well, given the absence of explicit feminist theses and overt indictments of the patriarchy. *See also* Short Fiction by Women Writers: 1900–1975

Work by

Adagio confidencial. Barcelona: Planeta, 1973.

Derribos: Crónicas de su tiempo saldado. Barcelona: Argos Vergara, 1981.

La estación de las hojas amarillas. 4th ed. Barcelona: Argos Vergara, 1980.

The Eyes of the Proud. Trans. Delano Ames. New York: Harcourt Brace, 1960.

La gangrena. Barcelona: Planeta, 1975.

Una mujer llega al pueblo. Barcelona: Planeta, 1977.
El volumen de la ausencia. Barcelona: Planeta, 1983.

Work about

Castillo, Debra A. "Mercedes Salisachs, Ideal Womanhood, and the Middlebrow Novel." *Intertextual Pursuits: Literary Meditations in Modern Spanish Narrative.* Ed. Jeanne P. Brownlow and John W. Kronik. Lewisburg, PA: Bucknell UP; London: Associated UP, 1998. 97–125.

Espadas, Elizabeth. "*Adagio confidencial* de Mercedes Salisachs: ¿Novela rosa o novela de testimonio feminista?" *Ensayos de literatura europea e hispanoamericana.* Ed. Felix Menchacatorre. Spain: Universidad del País Vasco, 1990. 145–150.

Lado, María Dolores. "Mercedes Salisachs y la novela católica." *Letras Femeninas* 12.1–2 (Spring–Autumn 1986): 114–120.

Masanet, Lydia. *La autobiografía femenina española contemporánea.* Madrid: Fundamentos, 1998.

Zatlin, Phyllis. "Childbirth with Fear: Bleeding to Death Softly." *Letras Femeninas* 16.1–2 (Spring–Fall 1990): 37–44.

Zatlin Boring, Phyllis. "Mercedes Salisachs, novelista de su época." *Novelistas femeninas de la postguerra española.* Ed. Janet Pérez. Madrid: José Porrúa, 1983. 7–17.

Glenn Morocco and Janet Pérez

San Alberto, Sor María de (?–1640)

A Discalced Carmelite who rose to the position of prioress of the convent in Valladolid, she was known as a musician and held to be saintly. She is considered to be the author of the following religious works: *Carta a un religioso, acerca de San Juan de la Cruz* (1614; Letter to a Religious Person, on St. John of the Cross), *Diario de sus visiones y favores divinos* (no date; Diary of Her Visions and Divine Favors), *Testimionio acerca de la vida y virtudes de San Juan de la Cruz* (1615; Testimony about the Life and Virtues of St. John of the Cross), *Visiones de la Madre Catalina Evangelista Monja de Valladolid* (no date; Visions of Mother Catalina Evangelista, Valladolid Nun). We may also conjecture, based on the two dates given, that she was born in the late 1500s (c. 1580–

1585), as she could surely not have written them when younger than about 30.

Work by

Carta a un religioso, acerca de San Juan de la Cruz. Rioseco, original, 1614.
Diario de sus visiones y favores divinos. Villiers Bibliotheca Carmelitana, n.d.
Testimonio acerca de la vida y virtudes de San Juan de la Cruz. Autographed ms. dated 1615.
Visiones de la Madre Catalina Evangelista Monja de Valladolid. N.O., n.d.

Work about

Serrano y Sanz, Manuel. *Apuntes para una biblioteca de escritoras españolas desde el año 1401 al 1833.* Madrid: Revista de Archivos, Bibliotecas y Museos, 1905. 2:223.

Elena Cámara

San Bartolomé (García y Manzanas), Ana de (1549–1626)

This Discalced Carmelite nun, reformer, and writer was born to *ricos labradores* (well-to-do peasants) in the province of Toledo. After overcoming family resistance, Ana de San Bartolomé entered the newly established house of Santa *Teresa's Carmelite reform at San José de Avila in 1570, becoming the first lay sister of the reform and professing her vows in 1572. During Santa Teresa's life, she served as cook, nurse, and eventually traveling secretary to the foundress. Although only partially educated as a youth, Ana learned to write in the convent, subsequently authoring a large number of works, including two autobiographies, books on spirituality, instructions for nuns of the reform, and numerous letters. In 1605 she professed as a choir sister and in 1608 took up the first of many posts as prioress at Pontoise in France. Ana later held the same office in Paris, Tours, and finally Antwerp, where she died.

Her contributions to the reform were many. After the death of Santa Teresa, she incorporated the example of the foundress into her instructive writings aimed at new members of the Carmelites, urging novices to study both the writings and the example of the foundress. Much of her correspondence dealt with the business of founding new convents throughout Europe, an activity that she helped further in France and the Low Countries. Ana also had a hand in establishing the first English Carmelites, whose house by necessity was founded in present-day Belgium. She also devoted a large part of her letter writing to the struggle over the Constitutions of the order that followed the death of Santa Teresa.

Work by

Obras completas de la beata Ana de San Bartolomé. Ed. Julián Urkiza, OCD. 2 vols. Rome: Teresianum, 1981, 1985.

Work about

Jiménez Duque, D. Baldomero. *Ana de San Bartolomé (1549–1626)*. Madrid: n.p., 1979.

Manero Sorolla, María Pilar. "Cartas de Ana de San Bartolomé a Monseñor Pierre de Berulle." *Criticón* 51 (1991): 125–140.

Urkiza, Julián. "San Juan de la Cruz en los escritos de la beata Ana de San Bartolomé." *Actas del Congreso Internacional Sanjuanista, II: Historia*. Ed. A. García Simón. Intro. Teofanes Egido López. Valladolid, Spain: Junta de Castilla y León, Consejería de Cultura y Turismo, 1993. 437–455.

Elizabeth T. Howe

San Félix, Sor Marcela de (1605–1687)

Daughter of the famed dramatist and poet Lope de *Vega y Carpio, Marcela del Carpio was born in 1605 to the actress Micaela de Luján, who at the time was married to an actor. Two years later a brother, Lope Félix, was born of the same parents. When their mother died or disappeared (perhaps along with five siblings also born to the pair), the two children were raised by a trusted servant until the death of Lope de Vega's second wife, Juana de Guardo, at which time they came to Madrid to live with their father and his new love, Marta de Nevares. The young del Carpio thus had a turbulent childhood, moving from one caretaker to another and

finally living in the unconventional household of her renowned father. In addition to the instability of her situation, she was stigmatized by her illegitimate birth, making it tempting to surmise that the desire for permanence formed part of her motivation to leave her father's house and enter a convent in February 1621. Del Carpio, renamed Sor Marcela de San Félix, professed her final vows a year later. Her father visited her in the convent daily, except for occasional short absences, until he died in 1635. Sor Marcela served as superior of the convent three times before her own death in 1687.

Arenal and Schlau suggest that Sor Marcela found more freedom to write and to be her own self in the cloister than out of it. Over the years, she wrote, directed, and acted in six one-act allegorical religious plays, the *Coloquios espirituales* (Spiritual Colloquies). She also wrote 24 *romances* (ballads), seven *loas* (short dramatic panegyrics), miscellaneous other poems, and a short prose biography of Madre Catalina de San José, a Trinitarian nun. Sor Marcela is reported to have written four other books, including a spiritual autobiography, all of which she subsequently burned at the request or instruction of her confessor.

Sor Marcela's poems and plays evidence a strong sense of humor, being full of lively, irreverent jokes about the clergy, the court, and convent life. At the same time, her religious devotion was clearly intense and sincere. Arenal and Schlau attribute to her an "aesthetic of asceticism," derived from St. *Teresa of Avila, according to which poetic eloquence comes not from literary artifice but from the speech of the Holy Spirit to the self in solitude. Certainly one of Sor Marcela's loveliest poetic contributions is the *romance* "A una soledad" (To a Solitude), in which she praises solitude for affording her opportunity for contemplation and spiritual life. *See also* Autobiographical Self-Representation of Women in the Early Modern Period; Nuns who Wrote in Sixteenth- and Seventeenth-Century Spain.

Work by

Arenal, Electa, and Georgina Sabat de Rivers, eds. *Literatura conventual femenina: Sor Marcela de San Félix, hija de Lope de Vega. Obra completa.* Barcelona: Promociones y Publicaciones Universitarias, 1988.

Work about

Arenal, Electa, and Stacey Schlau. *Untold Sisters: Hispanic Nuns in Their Own Works.* Trans. Amanda Powell. Albuquerque: U of New Mexico P, 1989.

Olivares, Julián, and Elizabeth S. Boyce, eds. *Tras el espejo la musa escribe: Lírica femenina de los Siglos de Oro.* Madrid: Siglo Veintiuno de España, 1993.

Elizabeth S. Boyce and Julián Olivares

San Jerónimo, Sor Ana de (1696–1771)

Known outside the convent as Ana Verdugo y Castilla, Ana de San Jerónimo was the daughter of the distinguished neoclassic poet Pedro Verdugo, count of Torrepalma, and his wife Isabel de Castilla. The count instilled in both his children, Ana and her brother Alfonso, his refined spirit and love of learning. Ana was well versed in Greek, Latin, Italian, and Spanish literature and became an excellent painter. In 1729, she entered the Convent of the Franciscas Descalzas del Santo Angel de Granada, against her parents' wishes.

Extraordinarily learned, Ana composed many excellent eclogues and *canciones* (a type of poem using 7- and 11-syllable lines), mostly on religious subjects. In addition, she left a manuscript titled "Afectos de un alma religiosa" (Affections of a Religious Soul). Her works were published posthumously.

Work by

Obras poéticas. Córdoba: Oficina de Juan Rodríguez, 1773.

Work about

Serrano y Sanz, Manuel. *Apuntes para una biblioteca de escritoras españolas desde el año 1401 al 1833.* 2 vols. Madrid: Rivadeneyra, 1903.

María A. Salgado

San Pedro, Diego de (fifteenth century)

His sentimental novels dissect love, the subject considered most appropriate for women in the fifteenth century. Diego de San Pedro directed his novels to the court ladies who were fascinated with the dilemmas of *honor and passion arising within the complicated system of *courtly love. According to strict rules, courtly love had to be a passion outside the materialistic considerations of marriage. Spanish puritanism prohibited treating adulterous passion of the kind emblemized in the story of Lancelot and Guinevere: Diego de San Pedro considered only young unmarried lovers separated by the political or economic interests of their elders who controlled the choice of marriage partners. Included within *Tractado de amores de Arnalte y Lucenda* (probably written in 1481 and printed in 1491; Treatise on the Loves of Arnalte and Lucenda) is a long poem praising Queen *Isabel (1451–1504). It underscores the importance of a powerful woman and indirectly reminds the reader of the necessity of subordinating personal to state interests, as Isabel had done in her marriage to Ferdinand. The author praises her for prudence, piety, beauty, knowledge, and valor. The beauty of other ladies is like Good Friday to the Easter of her glory, and he foresees the joy of Mary and Christ welcoming her to heaven.

The mixture of sacred and profane motifs, of erotic and sacred love, characterizes San Pedro's work. *La pasión trovada* (Christ's Passion Versified), composed around 1474, was addressed to a nun for whom the poet wrote the poem to help himself overcome his love for her. These verses were deleted in printings after 1530. This poem emphasizes the gory details of the Crucifixion and the anguish of the Virgin, who places herself in the category of all women who have lost sons or husbands. *Las siete angustias de Nuestra Señora* (The Seven Sorrows of Our Lady), appearing first in an anthology around 1480, was included in *Arnalte y Lucenda.* The poem places the hero's agony in perspective by comparing it to the far greater pain of the Virgin, who witnessed her son's death. The poem was cut from the 1522 edition of the novel.

The suggestion of the lover's assimilation to Christ in the first novel became quite explicit in the second novel, *Cárcel de amor* (*Prison of Love*, 1979), which was written in 1488 and first published in 1492. Here the imperfect, egotistical Arnalte has been transformed into the perfect courtly lover Leriano. The latter remembers the need of secrecy and sacrifices his life to help his lady Laureola retain her reputation as a virtuous (i.e., chaste) woman. As much as Arnalte exalted Lucenda, he seemed to expect the return of his love with specific favors as his due. These lovers' relationship ended with Arnalte killing the false friend who, acting as intermediary, had himself wooed and won the lady. Leriano, on the other hand, is depicted as a Christ figure with crown of thorns in the allegorical prison at the novel's beginning. At the end, instead of withdrawing to the wilderness to continue his suffering or entering a religious establishment like Lucenda, Guinevere, and Lancelot, Leriano commits suicide through fasting: His only food is Laureola's letters, which he eats to prevent their publication. A.A. Parker describes Leriano's action as a eucharistic communion. Leriano carries his passion to the grave, possibly to hell. The author does not analyze this death as the capital sin it is within a Christian context. He veils the act of suicide through its passive nature and presents it as an exaltation of earthly love. Whinnom points out that Leriano, in his defense of women against Tefeo's misogynistic attack, cites two women who were viewed as suicides for love—Lucretia and Doña Isabel de las Casas. In San Pedro's *Sermón* (Sermon) about love, written in the mid-1480s at the request of the court ladies, he reported Thisbe's words to the dead Piramus. Without making the inference explicit, San Pedro suggests that suicide for love is justified; he makes his secular lovers

follow Christ's example of the pure soul voluntarily dying for the sake of the other. Kurtz attributes the pleasure of San Pedro's works precisely to the tension between their religious and profane contexts.

The *Sermón*, a fictitious gospel attributed to St. Infatuation, presents the lady as a goddess whose excellence elicits the lover's suffering in silent humility. Dudley observes that to love is to suffer in San Pedro's code. However, the lady, lest she be guilty of the sins of pride, avarice, anger, and sloth, should be merciful to the worthy lover by rewarding him with small tokens of her esteem. Throughout his works this author endorsed the position that women, eliciting love through their virtue, were the civilizers of men. Chorpenning, in his analysis of the rhetorical structure of *Cárcel de amor*, shows San Pedro's debt to Diego de *Valera's (1412–1488?) *En defensa de virtuosas mugeres* for much of Leriano's defense of women. From his occasional poetry written to various ladies in the court, the reader surmises that San Pedro regarded courtly love as a game appropriate to youth. Chorpenning traces the trajectory of San Pedro's work: The commonplaces of the courtly love tradition are suggested in *Arnalte y Lucenda*, codified in the *Sermón*, and exemplified in *Cárcel de amor*. This trajectory can be related to modern depth psychology's process for individuation. As Tejerina-Canal points out, erotic pleasure springs from breaking rules, including those of courtly love, in rebellion against the tyranny of honor.

Like the Marqués de *Santillana (1398–1458), San Pedro ended his career by abjuring his love stories and embracing a serious work praising the stoic virtue that allows one to show *Desprecio de fortuna* (composed around 1498; Contempt of Fortune). Critic Gascón Vera points out that despite the real power of women in Isabel's court, San Pedro continued to view women as objects created by men to provide a mirror of their performance as perfect lovers. Besides her functions as wife or mother, woman existed only to receive the praise or blame of man. The double standard that brought a woman public condemnation for loss of honor forced her to be an object rather than a subject. Her entire virtue was wrapped up in her strength in defending her chastity. Honor and fame make a king's daughter like Laureola more subject than an ordinary woman to society's constrictions. Grieve observes that physical love always leads to violence in the sentimental novel. Weissberger concurs that the *Cárcel de amor* exemplifies patriarchal ideology since it reveals masculine rivalry to control the woman who provides access to power, status, and wealth.

Work by

Obras completas, I: Tractado de amores de Arnalte y Lucenda y Sermón. Ed. Keith Whinnon. Madrid: Castalia, 1973.

Obras completas, II: Cárcel de amor. Ed. Keith Whinnom. Madrid: Castalia, 1971.

Obras de Diego de San Pedro. Ed. Samuel Gili y Gaya. Madrid: Espasa-Calpe, 1958.

Work about

Chorpenning, Joseph F. "Loss of Innocence, Descent into Hell, and Cannibalism: Romance Archetypes and Narrative Unity in *Cárcel de amor*." *Fifteenth Century Studies* 2 (1985): 37–49.

———. "Rhetoric and Feminism in the *Cárcel de amor*." *Bulletin of Hispanic Studies* 54 (1977): 1–8.

Dudley, Edward. "The Inquisition of Love: *Tratado* as a Fictional Genre." *Mediaevalia: A Journal of Mediaeval Studies* 5 (1979): 233–243.

Granados, Pedro. "La *Cárcel de amor* como exemplum." *Lexis* (Peru) 22.2 (1998): 267–272.

Grieve, Patricia E. *Desire and Death in the Spanish Sentimental Romance (1440–1550).* Newark: Juan de la Cuesta, 1987.

Ihrie, Maureen. "Discourses of Power in the *Cárcel de amor*." *Hispanófila* 125 (January 1999): 1–10.

Kurtz, Barbara E. "La ambigüedad en el concepto del amor y de la mujer en la prosa castellana del siglo XV." *Boletín de la Real Academia Española* 59 (1979): 119–155.

———. "The Castle Motif and the Medieval Allegory of Love: Diego de San Pedro's *Cárcel de amor*." *Fifteenth Century Studies* 2 (1985): 37–49.

Parker, A.A. *The Philosophy of Love in Spanish Literature 1480–1680.* Edinburgh: Edinburgh UP, 1985.

Tejerina-Canal, Santiago. "Unidad en *Cárcel de amor*: El motivo de la tiranía." *Romance Quarterly* 31 (1984): 51–59.

Weissberger, Barbara E. "The Politics of *Cárcel de amor*." *Revista de Estudios Hispánicos* 26 (1992): 307–326.

Whinnom, Keith. *Diego de San Pedro.* New York: Twayne, 1974.

Judy B. McInnis

Santa Isabel, Sor María de

See Belisarda, Marcia (seventeenth century)

Santas

See Women's Professions in Early Spanish Literature: *Santas, Rameras, Casadas, Amas,* and *Criadas,* (Saints, Whores, Wives, Governesses, and Servants)

Santa Teresa, Sor Gregoria de (1658–1736)

Born in Seville and named Gregoria Francisca de la Parra y Queinogher, Gregoria de Santa Teresa was the daughter of lawyer Diego García de la Parra and Francisca Antonia Queinogher, his Flemish wife. Given a strict Christian upbringing, she grew up to become a Barefoot Carmelite. At age 6 she had a vision in which Christ appeared to her, and at 15 she entered the convent. Her biographer Diego Torres de Villarroel states that she learned Latin by divine grace. Within the convent walls, Gregoria grew in prominence. She became prioress and teacher of novices and in 1706 founded a convent at Puente de Don Gonzalo.

Gregoria wrote beautiful mystical poetry and *coloquios* (colloquies). Her poems express her desire to transcend limitations of the body in order to enjoy God's presence. Her growing fame, and in particular a *coloquio* she wrote for the beatification of San *Juan de la Cruz, provoked the envy of her sisters in religion. To avoid further anguish, she burned her texts (those that still remain are preserved in manuscript form at the National Library). Her confessor chastised her for this action. He also forbade her to write poetry and ordered her to compose her life story, which she completed in 1693. Diego de Villarroel's biography quotes extensive passages from this autobiography.

Her virtuous, exemplary life and her inspired, deeply felt mystical poems have moved some critics to compare her life and works to those of the sixteenth-century mystics. In fact, some consider her the last and the best woman mystic poet in Spain. Her deceptively simple style exemplifies the best traits of lyrical poetry. *See also* Autobiographical Self-Representation of Women in the Early Modern Period; Nuns Who Wrote in Sixteenth- and Seventeenth-Century Spain

Work about

Serrano y Sanz, Manuel. *Apuntes para una biblioteca de escritoras españolas desde el año 1401 al 1833*. 2 vols. Madrid: Rivadeneyra, 1903. Rpt. Madrid: Atlas, 1975.

Sherman, Alvin, Jr. "The Lover and the Captive: Sor Gregoria Francisca de Santa Teresa's Mystical Search for the Feminine Self in 'El pajarillo.'" *Dieciocho* 19.2 (Fall 1996): 191–201.

Torres de Villarroel, Diego. *Vida ejemplar, virtudes heroicas y singulares de la venerable madre Gregoria de Santa Teresa*. Salamanca: Xavier de Santa Cruz, 1738.

María A. Salgado

Santiago Fuentes, Magdalena de (1876–1922)

Born in Cuenca, author Magdalena de Santiago Fuentes was a teacher, first in Huesca and later in Barcelona and Madrid. Fuentes collaborated on several magazines, including *Blanco y Negro, Nuevo Mundo, Diario Universal, El Imparcial, Escuela Moderna,* and *Feminal.* Her literary production includes: novels—*Emprendamos una nueva vida* (1905; Let's Start a New Life), *El tesoro de Abigail, narraciones de Tierra Santa* (1898; Abigail's Treasure, Narrations from the Holy Land); short stories—*Cuentos del sábado* (1909; Sat-

urday's Stories), *Cuentos orientales* (1908; Stories from the East); and pedagogical essays.

Work by

Aves de paso. Huesca: L. Pérez, 1909.
Cuentos del sábado. Einsieden: Benziger, 1909.
Cuentos orientales. Barcelona: Antonio J. Bastinos, 1908.
Emprendamos una nueva vida. Barcelona: Henrich, 1905.
Mi primer libro. Barcelona: Sopena, 1923.
El tesoro de Abigail, narraciones de Tierra Santa. Barcelona: Herder, 1898.

Carmen de Urioste

Santillana, Marqués de (1398–1458): His Portrayal of Women

Don Iñigo López de Mendoza, the first Marqués de Santillana, moved in the highest circle of Aragonese and Castilian societies where he experienced the power wielded by high-ranking women. According to Amador de los Ríos, Santillana's mother, Doña Leonor, had to protect his landed inheritance from marauding lords; his grandmother, Doña Mencía de Cisneros, with whom he lived in his youth, instilled in him the love of learning. In maturity he was involved in prolonged litigation with his older half sister, Doña Aldonza de Mendoza, over the possession of certain lands. The accounts of his life reveal that noblewomen could inherit property and, as widows, act legally in their families' interests.

Lapesa declares Santillana the first to attribute high virtues to common as well as to noblewomen. Composed according to Lapesa from 1423 (IV) to at least 1440 (X), the *serranillas* (short, lyrical pastoral poems) depict love encounters between a noble traveler and a *serranilla* (mountain girl). (All references to Santillana's works refer to Amador de los Ríos's edition.) The woman's presence in the poems and her interaction in dialogue with the lover distinguish these poems from those of the *courtly love tradition. In his book and article Lapesa points out that even the crudest *serranilla* (IV) is more refined than *serranillas* found in the *Libro de buen amor, by the Arcipreste de Hita Juan Ruiz (1283?–c. 1350). Toledano assigns the more idealized poems to Provenzal origin (III, V, VI, VII, IX, X) and the more realistic and disputatious to Castilian (I, II, IV). The poems begin with a truncated stanza in which the male narrator gives a flashback of the *serrana*'s incomparable beauty. As Terrero has elucidated, Santillana locates her in a geographically precise place and gives details of her dress. Villegas perceives the narrator's attitude as the derogatory one of *droit du seigneur*. However, most critics stress the independence of the *serranas* who may invite the narrator to become a lover as in "Serranilla I" or challenge him to an amorous duel (IV). They accept him as lover (IV), reject him (II, V, VI), impose certain conditions like his joining them in the shepherd's life (IX), or simply answer his compliments (III). Sexually sophisticated, they immediately recognize the narrator's seductive intention and often reply insolently (II). Lapesa points out that the narrator may resist the *serrana* in fidelity to his lady (V, X). Marino argues that "la Finojosa" (VI) is a dream vision, although she is a true *vaquera* (cowgirl) and not a courtly lady in disguise, as Foster contends. Bratosevich, using speech act theory, elucidates the astuteness of the "Mozuela de Bores," who in "Serranilla IX" rejects the gentleman's false elevation of her social status for a firm avowal of her equality with her two shepherd swains. Bratosevich emphasizes the ambiguity of woman's position in a society that placed her on a pedestal within the courtly love tradition but displaced and undervalued her in economic and social spheres.

Santillana's "Villancico que hizo el marqués a tres hijas suyas" (1444 or 1445; Poem That the Marquis Wrote for Three of His Daughters) relates a man's observation of three young girls who sing popular song fragments of longing for their lovers. Since the title identifies the narrator as father of the

girls, the reader perceives his wish not to be supplanted by their lovers. Durán identifies this poem as Santillana's most Renaissance-like work, for the poet avoids the allegorical devices that usually distance him from feminine beauty and sexual love. The poem may be the work of Suero de Ribera (Lapesa). In another poem Santillana envisions two daughters as bejeweled shepherdesses and expresses his joy in their sexual maturation.

Santillana's *decires* (poems in traditional Spanish verse forms) refine the courtly love tradition of Galician-Portuguese, French, and Provenzal origins. The lady is perceived as a paragon of beauty and virtue superior to the lover. Her "cruelty" lies in not rewarding the lover with a token of esteem. Santillana's comparisons of himself to Narcissus in two *decires* inadvertently reveal the self-reflectiveness of the courtly love tradition. Another *decir* compares the lady to Christ, but such explicitly Christian comparisons are not typical. His religious attitude toward the lady is more pagan than Christian, for he prays to her and to Love personified. Santillana sometimes comments upon the lady's having chosen or captured him as her lover. Salvador Miguel praises the greater lyrical sensitivity and more spiritualized tone of Santillana in comparison to other lesser poets in the *Cancionero de Estúñiga*.

Santillana's *decires* include three longer poems that reveal Italian as well as French influence. Critic Alan Deyermond places the *Triunfete de amor* (Triumph of Love) in the late 1420s or early 1430s and the *Sueño* (Dream) as well as the *Infierno de los enamorados* (Lovers' Inferno) in or shortly before 1437. The *Triunfete* is modeled on Petrarch's *Trionfi*. While hunting beneath the auspices of chaste Diana, the narrator witnesses a parade of Love's victims following Venus and Cupid. He becomes another victim as his cruel lady fells him with a poisoned arrow. The list of male victims includes mythological, chivalric, biblical, and historical figures, Dante among them. The female list is limited to mythological figures except for Cleopatra and Semiramis. In the *Sueño* the narrator has a prophetic dream of falling victim to Love. To assert his free will, he goes in search of Diana, who fails to roust Venus and Cupid in the battle between his lady's attractions (Beauty, Prudence, Skill, Cheerfulness, and Youth) and his ineffectual soldiers of resistance (Laziness, Understanding, Purity). The narrator compares himself to Dido and Proserpine. Lapesa points out that Santillana suppresses the antifeminism of the sources of the *Sueño* (Boccaccio's *Fiammetta* and Bernat Metge's *Lo Somni*) and of the *Infierno* (Seneca).

The *Infierno* opens on a dark night in Diana's wood where such martyrs for chastity as Lucretia reside. When the lovesick narrator awakens, he sees Hypolitus killing a pig, symbol of lust. Hypolitus takes the narrator to Venus's castle where, by witnessing the sad fate of those who yielded to passion (mythological couples, Dante, Francesca da Rimini, Macías, etc.), he overcomes his own. In Santillana's evenhanded treatment men and women are equally able to maintain chastity or fall victim to passion. Love occurs within a cycle dominated by female deities and may be conquered through time and reflection.

In another long allegorical *decir*, the *Querella de amor* (Complaint of Love), Santillana presents an abandoned, dying lover as a warning against love that admits no remedy and that afflicts people at its own whim. "Visión" presents the lament of Firmness, Loyalty, and Chastity, presented as three beautiful women who have abandoned inhospitable Spain. The narrator showers praise on his own lady, who outshines Lucretia and the Grecian nymphs. Although the cardinal virtues serve her and Philosophy and Gentility befriend her, he is uncertain that they recommend him to her.

In the "Planto de la Reina Margarida" (Lament for Queen Margarita), Santillana combines amorous and funereal themes to lament the death of Margarita de Prades. Lapesa (points out that for her virtuous conduct she

was regarded as the ideal lady by contemporary poets. Santillana compliments both Margarita and his own lady while revealing his association of love with his feminine side. While Santillana relates to lovesick women, as in comparisons of himself to Medea, he does not adopt their personae. "El planto que fiço Pantasilea" (Lament That Pantasilea Made), in which a woman directly presents her complaint, is now regarded as the work of Juan *Rodríguez del Padrón (de la Cámara) (1399?–1450).

The scope of *La comedieta de Ponza* (composed c. 1436 and transmitted to Doña Violante de Prades in 1444; Comedy of Ponza) permits Santillana to speak in women's voices. In 120 stanzas of *arte mayor* (verses of 7, 11, and 14 syllables), Santillana presents the queen mother Doña Leonor waiting with her three daughters-in-law to learn the outcome of the Battle of Ponza in which three of her sons (King Alfonso V of Aragón-Cataluña, King Juan of Navarra, and Don Enrique, maestre of Santiago) were captured by the Genoese and one (Don Pedro) escaped. Boccaccio is summoned to immortalize them like the women in his *De claris mulieribus* (1360–1374), a function Santillana accomplishes with the help of Jove and the muses through his poem. Aubrun also points to the influence of Alain Chartier's *Livre des quatre Dames*. Santillana paints portraits of all the participants, but those of the four sons are more detailed than those of the women. He limits his presentation of the three grieving wives to mythological comparisons and to a description of their shields, which establish their nobility and lineage. He gives a more complete portrait of the Queen Mother Leonor. She recounts her birth to high station, her good marriage, and her joy in her children including Doña María, queen of Castile, and Doña Leonor, queen of Portugal. They are praised for beauty, virtue (especially chastity and good reputation), and intelligence. Santillana's *decires* dedicated to Queen María and to noble ladies like Doña Johana de Urgel celebrate similar exemplary qualities.

Santillana evokes the intensity of maternal love when Leonor reveals a prophetic dream in which she was thrown out of a boat in a stormy sea and consumed by predatory fish. The image startles with its implied presentation of the sons as "flesh of her flesh." Leonor falls dead upon receipt of the letter relaying her sons' capture. In fact, she died in December, a month after she had learned of their release, according to Kerkhof and Martín Baños. While Santillana's alteration of history evokes greater pathos, he succumbs to the stereotype of woman's tender weakness in assimilating tragedy. The essential powerlessness of passive women who can only lament the misadventures that befall their active menfolk dominates the poem. All humans are subject to Fortune, a female deity who manipulates human events according to God's plan. This conception differs from Santillana's presentation of Fortune in *Bias contra Fortuna* (1448; Bias against Fortune), where she is a malicious woman deliberately and willfully attempting to destroy the tranquillity of the stoic Bias.

With their alternating praise and blame, Santillana's sonnets (composed 1438–1458) present the same range of attitudes toward love and the lady as his *decires*. Foster elucidates among others the topoi of the divine lady and the *belle dame sans merci* to conclude with Menéndez y Pelayo and Lapesa that Santillana failed to spiritualize the lady to the degree of Dante (1265–1321), Petrarch (1304–1374), and the *dolce stil nuovo* poets. The patriotic "Sonnet XVII" reveals an underlying antifeminism in its association of *armas femeniles* (feminine weapons) with weakness. "Sonnet XXI" employs *femenil* in a positive sense in the context of the poet's irresistible attraction to the lady's angelic beauty. In "Sonnet V" the poet speaks in the person of the Infante Don Enrique, who laments the death of his wife, Doña Catalina. There is an implied comparison to Orpheus and Eurydice in the king's wish to regain his wife, whom he refers to as "dulçe mia Idea" (my sweet Idea). Sonnet XXXV praises the Virgin Mary as the pure temple where the Word was made flesh. Other religious sonnets include six in praise of male saints and one in honor of the Virgin Saint Clara (XXXVII), an example to saintly women in her humble poverty. Santillana's devotion to the Virgin Mary (*Marianism), to whom his banners referred in the motto "Dios e Vos" (God and You), can also be seen in the 12 happy moments described in "Los Goços de Nuestra Señora" (Joys of Our Lady). His "Coplas a Nuestra Señora de Guadalupe" (Verses to Our Lady of Guadalupe) praise the Virgin's grace, humility, and power.

In the *Proverbios* (1437; Proverbs), Santillana's most popular work according to Menéndez y Pelayo, Santillana presents the Virgin as model for women in his discussion of chastity and also singles out Saint Catherine for truth and beauty, Esther for beauty and nobility, and Judith for beauty and "virile virtue." He speaks of the value of pagan women, listing Evadnes, Diana, Lucretia, Daphne, Anna (a reference both to the mother of the Virgin Mary and to Dido's sister), and Virginia. In his glosses on the *Proverbios* Santillana points out the fictitiousness of Dido's alliance with Aeneas as described by Virgil. In "Sonnet XLVII" Santillana informs us that the *estado femenil* (feminine state) is neither useless nor of little scope. Nevertheless, in the 16 chapters and 100 stanzas of the *Proverbios* women are mentioned only as wives in the discussion of chastity, an essential virtue for women but not for men. Women bring additional value if they possess noble lineage and beauty, but a reasonable and virtuous wife is preferred to a merely rich or beautiful one.

Santillana presents both common and noblewomen as mistresses of love. He also recognizes the abilities and intelligence of queens and noblewomen. Within the *Comedieta de Ponza* and in its dedication to Doña Violante de Prades, he praises women for their discriminating literary taste. His pagan mythology is dominated by women: They control chastity (Diana), love (Venus), and fortune (Dame Fortune). In the *Prohemio y carta* (Prologue and Letter) he relegates his amorous poetry to his youth. Male maturity necessitates extricating himself from the feminine world of love poetry to undertake manly works about politics, war, and philosophy.

Work by

La Comedieta de Ponza; Sonetos del Marqués de Santillana. Ed. Maxim P.A.M. Kerkhof. Madrid: Cátedra, 1986.

Obras de don Iñigo López de Mendoza. Ed. José Amador de los Ríos. Madrid: José Rodríguez, 1852.

Poesías completas del Marqués de Santillana. Ed. Manuel Durán. 2 vols. Madrid: Castalia, 1975, 1980.

Work about

Aubrun, Charles V. "Alain Chartier et le Marquis de Santillana." *Bulletin Hispanique* 40 (1938): 129–149.

Bass, Laura R. "Crossing Borders: Gender, Geography and Class Relations in Three *Serranillas* of the Marqués de Santillana." *Corónica* 25.1 (1996): 69–84.

Bratosevich, Nicolás. "Entornos y efectos de enunciación en una serranilla de Santillana." *Homenaje a Ana María Barrenechea.* Ed. Lía Schwartz Lerner and Isaías Lerner. Madrid: Castalia, 1984. 207–217.

Durán, Manuel. "Santillana y el Prerenacimiento." *Nueva Revista de la Filología Hispánica* 15 (1961): 343–363.

Foster, David William. *The Marqués de Santillana.* New York: Twayne, 1971.

Kuzma, Mary Kathryn. "The Feminine Literary Figures in the Works of the Marqués de Santillana." Diss. Case Western Reserve, 1977.

Lapesa, Rafael. *La obra literaria del Marqués de Santillana.* Madrid: Insula, 1957.

———. " 'Las serranilllas' del Marqués de Santillana." *El comentario de textos, 4: La poesía medieval.* Ed. Manuel Alvar et al. Madrid: Castalia, 1984. 243–276.

Marino, Nancy F. "The Vaquera de la Finojosa: Was She a Vision?" *Romance Notes* 26.3 (Spring 1986): 261–268.

Martín Baños, Pedro V. "La muerte de doña Leonor y la 'Comedieta de Ponza.' " *Boletín de la Real Academia Española* 72.257 (September–December 1992): 445–461.

Menéndez y Pelayo, D. Marcelino. *Historia de las ideas estéticas en España.* 9 vols. Madrid: Hijos de M. Tello, 1920.

Salvador Miguel, Nicasio. *La poesía cancioneril: El Cancionero de Estúñiga.* Madrid: Alhambra, 1977.

Terrero, José. "Paisajes y pastoras en las 'serranillas' del marqués de Santillana." *Cuadernos de Literatura* 7 (1950): 169–202.

Toledano, Jerónimo. "Las serranillas del Marqués de Santillana." *Síntesis* 4.11 (1928): 67–86.

Villegas Morales, Juan. "Acerca de lo cortesano en las 'Serranillas' del Marqués de Santillana." *Anales de la Universidad de Chile* 117.113 (1959): 164–167.

Judy B. McInnis

Santo Domingo, Sor María de (c. 1468/1474–c. 1524)

Also known as the "Beata of Piedrahita," this daughter of illiterate laborers led a tumultuous, controversial life as an outspoken religious reformer and visionary who rejected the concept of silence as an essential virtue for devout women. María de Santo Domingo showed evidence of extreme piety since childhood, and by age 17 she had joined the Third Order Dominicans. As a visionary she experienced public raptures (occasionally on request—provoking accusations of fakery from detractors), in which she lauded the Inquisition, answered questions learned men posed about theology, and criticized the local Provincial. Additionally, she heard confessions (coming dangerously close to the role of priest) and referred to the Virgin Mary as her mother-in-law. As a reformer, she vigorously promoted stricter observance, especially increased fasting, abstinence, and penance in the order.

Both her charismatic religious fervor and her reformist activities provoked strong reactions, positive and negative. She reportedly inspired devotion in many, causing their return to the sacraments, and counted King Fernando and Cardinal Cisneros among her supporters. Her reform activities, however, coincided with a crisis in the Dominican Order, which was on the verge of splitting entirely over the reform/no reform issue; thus, her outspoken activism earned her many political enemies. The situation came to a head around 1508–1509, and no fewer than three Inquisitorial proceedings were conducted regarding her activities (a fourth proceeding—second in the series—was not allowed to take place). The items considered heretical included: whether the raptures were real or feigned; her claim that she spoke with the Virgin Mary, the saints, and Jesus, and then uttered prophesy on secular and religious matters; whether she was stigmatic; a charge that men sometimes spent nights alone with her; and her manner of dress, which included a fondness for little hats and bracelets, her liking of dance and games, her frequent illnesses, and penchant for fasting.

The first proceeding rendered a favorable judgment for María, prompting the Provincial Magdaleno to travel to Italy and personally request a new tribunal from Pope Julius II. The second proceeding was not allowed to take place. The third tribunal, called in response to Pope Julius's orders, was composed of judges hostile to María's situation; although the investigation went forward, it was never completed because in 1509 a new brief from the pope arrived, ordering that the third tribunal be disbanded and allowing the king to participate in naming a new, final tribunal, which exonerated María from any wrongdoing. After her examination, she lived as foundress/abbess of an endowed monastery in Aldeanueva, her birthplace.

The *Libro de la Oración de Sor María de Santo Domingo* (Sister María de Santo Domingo's Book of Prayer) was published sometime after the final, 1509–1510 tribunal, but the work was rediscovered only recently when the manuscript was found in the University of Zaragoza archives and reprinted in 1948. It contains printed transcriptions of her visionary experiences (which Cardinal Cisneros ordered) as recorded by an unidentified scribe/confessor who is clearly very close to her. He reminds potential readers of the Church's traditional respect for inspired teachings imparted to her illiterate holy men and women. Blecua and Giles observe that María's theology is solidly mainstream: In her narration of the soul's quest for union with God she specifically rejects illuminist tenets by honoring religious orders, valuing vocal and mental prayer, and supporting the existence of hell, the value of the sacraments and mortification of the flesh, the authority of the saints, the special role of the Virgin Mary, and so on. The text is divided into four parts corresponding to the four ways in which María speaks and teaches: enraptured by sacrament; enraptured by contemplation; enraptured and answering questions posed by theologians, and alone, writing letters. Giles has also explored some of the very interesting ways in which this text of ecstatic moments corresponds to twentieth-century understandings of "holy theater." *See also* Autobiographical Self-Representation of Women in the Early Modern Period; Nuns Who Wrote in Sixteenth- and Seventeenth-Century Spain

Work by

The Book of Prayer of Sor María of Santo Domingo. Study and trans. Mary E. Giles. Albany: State U of New York P, 1990.

Libro de la Oración de Sor María de Santo Domingo. Facs. ed. and study José Manuel Blecua. Madrid: Hauser y Menet, 1948.

Work about

Bilinkoff, Jodi. "Establishing Authority: A Peasant Visionary and Her Audience in Early Sixteenth-Century Spain." *Studia Mystica* 18 (1997): 37–59.

Giles, Mary E. "The Discourse of Ecstasy: Late Medieval Spanish Women and Their Texts." *Gender and Text in the Later Middle Ages.* Ed. and intro. Jane Chance. Gainesville: UP of Florida, 1996. 306–330.

———. "Holy Theatre/Ecstatic Theatre." *Vox Mystica. Essays on Medieval Mysticism in Honor of Professor Valerie M. Lagorio.* Ed. Ann Clark Bartlett, Thomas H. Bestul, Janet Goebel, and William Pollard. Cambridge: D.S. Brewer, 1995. 117–128.

Surtz, Ronald E. "The 'Sweet Melody' of Christ's Blood: Musical Images in the 'Libro de la oración' of Sister Maria de Santo Domingo." *Mystic Quarterly* 17.2 (June 1991): 94–101.

Maureen Ihrie

Sau Sánchez, Victoria (1930–)

An essayist and author of children's fiction, Victoria Sau Sánchez is an active feminist and lecturer who cites among significant influences the names of Betty Friedan and Simone de *Beauvoir. She holds a professorial appointment as a psychologist at Barcelona's Central University in addition to her career as a practicing psychologist in that city, in connection with which Sau Sánchez founded a group dubbed "Permanent Investigative Seminar for New Women's Psychology." Most of her writing is of a professional nature, rather than "creative," and her children's books appear to be adaptations of Russian and Yugoslav legends. Other titles unrelated to her profession suggest the domestic manual, for example, *La decoración del hogar* (1967; Home Decorating) and *Aprenda a cocinar sin errores* (1971; Learn to Cook without Mistakes). There can be little question that these aim at a female readership. In other volumes, Sau Sánchez treats varied, miscellaneous themes, including religion, popular songs, and the Catalan separatist movement: *Sectas cristianas* (1971; Christian Sects); *Historia antropológica de la canción* (1972; Anthropological History of Song); and *El catalán, un bandolerismo español* (1973; Catalanism as Spanish Banditry).

Sau Sánchez has authored several titles of specific relevance to feminism and the study of women's condition in Spain: *Manifiesto para la liberación de la mujer* (1975; Manifesto for Women's Liberation), written after extensive background study of women's issues and feminine types, comprises treatments of a number of key themes: marriage, adultery, incest, prostitution, and virginity. She examines various female archetypes, including the witch, the old maid, the priestess/ prophet, the devourer of men, and the frigid woman. *Mujer, matrimonio y esclavitud* (1976; Woman, Marriage and Slavery) is an indictment of the institution of matrimony on social, economic, and sexual grounds. Sau Sánchez argues that woman is an unequal partner, disenfranchised, without freedom to seek her self-realization. Especially interesting is *La suegra* (1976; The Mother-in-Law), a continuation of the writer's investigation of feminine types and stereotypes. Her approach to this often mistreated figure is novel, insofar as she begins at the earliest stages of the life cycle, when each mother-in-law was a naive, romantic bride, later becoming a young mother, and perhaps a disenchanted wife, making of her children her central reason for living, only to see them eventually marry and abandon her, now become a *suegra*. This negative stereotype, characteristically feared and unloved, traditional rival of the bride, recurs in a self-renewing cycle with each new generation. In yet another treatise extending her examination of feminine types, *Mujeres lesbianas* (1979; Lesbian Women), Sau Sánchez contributes a historical overview of lesbianism, stressing its existence as a political phenomenon. The author also studies ideological differences between lesbians and male homosexuals and identifies relationships between feminism and lesbianism. In *Un diccionario ideológico feminista* (1981; A Feminist Ideological Dictionary) she attempts to provide or derive feminist definitions of significant terms involving sexuality, sexual politics, family relationships, and other concepts necessary for analyzing or understanding male-female relationships (e.g., dominance and exploitation) and the scientific explanations of these.

Work by

Aprenda a cocinar sin errores. Barcelona: Aura, 1971.

El catalán, un bandolerismo español. Barcelona: Aura, 1973.

Un diccionario ideológico feminista. 2nd ed. Barcelona: Icaria, 1990.

Historia antropológica de la canción. Barcelona: Picazo, 1972.

Manifiesto para la liberación de la mujer. Barcelona: Bruguera, 1975.

Mujeres lesbianas. Madrid: Zero, 1979.

Ser mujer, el fin de una imagen tradicional. 2nd ed. Barcelona: Icaria, 1993.

La suegra. Barcelona: Ediciones 29, 1976.

*El vacío de la maternidad: Madre no hay más que nin-
guna.* Barcelona: Icaria, 1995.

Janet Pérez

Sedano, Dora (1902–   )

Born in Madrid to a very conservative, upper
middle-class family, she was groomed by her
parents to be a concert pianist. From childhood, however, Dora Sedano wanted to be a
writer. Many of her early novelettes and
short stories were published in a magazine
devoted to children's literature, *Pulgarcito*
(Tom Thumb). So numerous were her contributions to that periodical that her picture
appeared on its cover when she was 13. She
was especially attracted to the theater, but
because she had no family connections and
dramaturgy was very much closed to women,
she began writing in collaboration with two
established playwrights, Luis Fernández
de Sevilla and Luis Tejada. Her plays were
primarily domestic comedies and political
melodramas of conservative sociopolitical
orientation, performed largely during the
Franco years, the bulk of them from 1940
through 1960. Her major work *La diosa de
arena* (The Sand Goddess) won the prestigious Pujol Prize in 1952. In this political
melodrama set in the 1930s, just prior to the
outbreak of the Spanish Civil War, a young
woman who has been brainwashed by com-
munism undergoes a conversion after "seeing
the light," thanks to her marriage into a pious Catholic family.

Sedano also cultivated the novel, but her
works are little known and of difficult access;
as a general rule, writers complacent about
the Franco regime found little favor with
critics. Except for helping, by her own moderate success, to ameliorate slightly the difficulties besetting women wishing to write for
the theater in this period, Sedano contributed in somewhat negative fashion to
women's liberation. Her works, however, can
be considered representative of the dominant
mentality of the Franco era and serve as a
source for those wishing a better understand-

ing of the difficulties Spanish women faced
at that time. *See also* Women's Situation in
Spain: 1931–1975: The Second Spanish Republic, the Spanish Civil War and Its Aftermath

Work by

Mercaderes de sangre. Madrid: A. Aguado, 1945.
Nuestras chachas. Madrid: Arba, 1955.

Work about

O'Connor, Patricia W. "The 'Dark Double' and the
Patriarch in Dora Sedano's *La diosa de arena*." *Crit-
ical Essays on the Literatures of Spain and Spanish
America.* Ed. Luis T. González del Valle and Julio
Baena. Boulder, CO: Society of Spanish and
Spanish-American Studies, 1991. 181–186.
———. "Encuesta: Por qué no estrenan las mujeres
en España?" *Estreno* 10.2 (1984): 24–25.
———. "¿Quiénes son las dramaturgas españolas, y
qué han escrito?" *Estreno* 10.2 (1984): 9–12.

Janet Pérez

Serranillas

See Santillana, Marqués de (1398–1458): His
Portrayal of Women

Serrano García, Emilia, Baronesa de Wilson (1834?–1923)

A prolific, cosmopolitan journalist, travel
writer, and novelist whose writings offer
unique insights into social history of the day,
Emilia Serrano García was the only child of
Ramón Serrano y García and María de la
Purificación García Cano. The father was an
active-duty army officer and a partisan of
Queen Isabel II, whose succession, after she
became queen in 1833 at age three, was being disputed by her uncle during the first
Carlist War (1836–1839). The child was
born in Granada on January 4, probably in
1834, although her penchant for taking years
off her age has left the date in doubt. She
was baptized months later in Valladolid,
where the mother spent those tumultuous
years with her family, suffering concern for
the well-being of her husband.

In the 1840s Serrano's parents resided in Paris, and she was educated at the College of the Sacred Heart, where her classmates called her "Mademoiselle Minerve" because of her love of reading. There, she encountered the poet José *Zorrilla when, in 1850 or 1851, he visited the school in the company of French poet Alphonse de Lamartine. Later, he met her at a performance of Verdi's *Rigoletto*, and because of mutual friendships, her family received Zorrilla into their home. Estranged from his wife, Zorrilla (the author of *Don Juan Tenorio*) seduced the teenage girl. A child was born, Marguerite Aurore, but on November 28, 1854, Zorrilla bade farewell to Serrano to pursue his fortunes in America. She then married a certain Baron Wilson, half English and half German, thus acquiring the name Baroness Wilson by which she is best known. On their honeymoon, the couple made a grand tour of Europe, but the baron died within two years. The daughter by Zorrilla died in 1858.

Baroness Wilson went on to have a remarkable career for more than 50 years as a journalist, poet, novelist, translator, founder of periodicals, and indefatigable traveler. The young widow expressed her religious bent in two books of poetry: *Las siete palabras de Cristo en la cruz* (1858; The Seven Words of Christ on the Cross) and *El camino de la cruz* (1859; The Road to the Cross). She also essayed narrative poems: *Alfonso el Grande* (1860; Alfonso the Great), "a historic poem"; and *¡Pobre Ana!* (1861; Poor Ana), "a historic legend." Years later she again paid tribute to Zorrilla's predilection for Moorish Spain with *Almeraya* (1883), "an Arab legend."

A travel article that she wrote in the 1850s on her visit to the cathedral of Bourg in Bresse, published in *La Iberia*, launched her on a journalistic career during which she wrote in Spanish and French. Before her daughter's death, she had started her Parisian monthly *La caprichosa*, "a journal of good taste," which ran for 20 issues in 1857–1858. Another early article was called "La mujer de hoy" (Today's Woman). She went on to publish the book for which she was famous over the years, *Almacén de las Señoritas* (1860; Young Women's Department Store), "a work devoted to young Spanish and American women containing lessons on skills, history, moral examples, advice, etc." The seventh edition appeared in 1874. There was also an 1880 Mexican edition and a new Paris edition of 1883 with 10 engravings and 12 colored plates. As late as 1924 there was a Madrid edition.

Serrano was a widely traveled woman while still in her twenties and took advantage of her experience to compose two guide books, both in 1860, to accommodate the Spanish and Spanish American trade of her publisher, Rosa and Bouret: *Manual, o sea Guía de los viajeros en Francia y Bélgica: Geografía, historia, monumentos* (Manual or Guide for Travelers in France and Belgium, Geography, History, Monuments) and *Manual, o sea Guía de los viajeros en la Inglaterra, Escocia e Irlanda . . . para uso de los americanos* (Manual or Guide for Travelers in England, Scotland and Ireland . . . for Use by Americans). To this period belong also her translations of Alexander Dumas's father, whom she had known as a girl. Of his son she translated, the same year it appeared in French, *Le Fils naturel* as *El hijo natural* (1858; The Illegitimate Son). Her own novels were *La familia de Gaspar* (1867; The Family of Gaspar) and *Los pordioseros del frac* (1875; The Beggars in Swallow-Tailed Coats).

As a girl, Serrano writes, a family friend allowed her to read in his personal library, which was rich in books on the discovery and exploration of the Americas. The deep interest in the New World that they awakened in her combined with her concern regarding women's role to become the dominant themes of her life and work. Traveling in southern Spain in the 1860s, she met Fernán Caballero (Cecilia *Böhl de Faber) and also cemented a friendship with Cuban Gertrudis *Gómez de Avellaneda. She made her first trip to the Americas on the spur of the moment, visiting Cuba, Puerto Rico, and Santo Domingo during a year and a half. Serrano made five more trips to the New World, some lasting several years. From them, she developed a substantial collection of books on America. *América y sus mujeres* (1890; America and Her Women) is characteristic of her travel literature; combining the experience of several journeys, she covers countries from the Straits of Magellan to Niagara Falls, featuring a historical or contemporary woman of each country she describes: in Argentina, novelist Juana Manuela Gorriti, whom she interviewed; in Mexico, poet Sor Juana Inés de la Cruz (1651–1695); in the United States, first lady Martha Washington.

In her journeys, Serrano went directly to the heads of states, often staying in their homes and palaces. Thus, when she writes of Porfirio Díaz and his wife in Mexico, it is with intimate knowledge of their lives and personalities. But, she asserts, too, and the evidence is in her writings, that she was in touch with the people of the Americas. Her mission was to acquaint Spaniards with those lands and peoples where the language and culture of Iberia still prevailed during the new epoch of political freedom from the mother country, and social historians would do well to consult her for insights into life at all levels in nineteenth-century Latin America. The hardships she experienced on journeys seemed only to strengthen her. Married and widowed a second time, she lived to a ripe old age, dying in Barcelona on January 1, 1923, just short, it would seem, of her eighty-ninth birthday.

Work by

América en fin de siglo: Actualidades, sucesos, apreciaciones, semblanzas, datos históricos. 'Barcelona: Henrich, 1897.
América y sus mujeres. Barcelona: Fidel Giró, 1890.
Americanos célebres: Glorias del Nuevo Mundo. 2 vols. Barcelona: Suc. de N. Ramírez, 1888.
Lágrimas y sonrisas: Poesías líricas. Mexico: Ireneo Paz, 1884.

La ley del progreso: Páginas para los pueblos americanos. 2nd ed. San Salvador: La Concordia, 1883.
Maravillas americanas: Curiosidades geológicas y arqueológicas, tradiciones, leyendas, algo de todo. 2 vols. Barcelona: Maucci, 1910.
México y sus gobernantes de 1519 a 1910. Biografías, retratos y autógrafos . . . 2 vols. Barcelona: Maucci, 1910.
El mundo literario americano: Escritores contemporáneos, semblanzas, poesías, apreciaciones, pinceladas. Barcelona: Maucci, 1903.
Las perlas del corazón: Deberes y aspiraciones de la mujer en su vida íntima y social. 4th ed. Quito: M. Rivadeneira, 1880.

Work about

Alonso Cortés, Narciso. *Zorrilla: Su vida y sus obras.* 2nd ed. Valladolid: Santarén, 1943.
Elices Montes, Ramón. *La Baronesa de Wilson: Su vida y sus obras.* Mexico: El Centinela Español, 1888.
Monner Sans, Ricardo. *La Baronesa de Wilson: Apuntes biográficos y literarios.* Barcelona: Suc. de N. Ramírez, 1888.

John Dowling

Serrano y Balañá, Eugenia (1918–)

Born in Madrid from a family with roots in Andalucía, Catalonia, and Castile, Eugenia Serrano identified herself with Madrid where she lived, studied, and received her degree in romance philology and literature from the University of Madrid. A conservative but of liberal leanings, she did not belong to any party in particular nor could she be identified with the postwar generation of writers of the 1950s. She was a contributor to *Fantasía*, a magazine where the young generation (*Cela [1916–], Cunqueiro [1911–1981?], among others) as well as the older writers (*Azorín [1873–1967], Gerardo Diego [1896–1996]) were equally welcomed. Serrano wrote novels and contributed short stories and essays to newspapers and magazines, among them *Medina, La Estafeta Literaria, Arriba, Artes y Letras, Semana, Fotos,* and *Mundo Hispánico.* She published essays in *Revista Finisterre* and was in charge of specific sections in newspapers: "La pequeña crónica" in *Arriba*, "Una dama" in *El Español*, and "Público" in *Vida Española*. She also wrote many radio scripts.

Serrano's first novel *Chamberí-Club* (n.d., Club Chamberí) was published in serial form as a pamphlet inserted in the newspaper *Pueblo*. Other novels are *Retorno a la tierra* (1945; Return to the Land), *Perdimos la primavera* (1952; We Lost Spring), and *Pista de baile* (1963; Dance Floor). Her interest in feminine concerns is manifest in *El libro de las siete damas* (1943; Book of Seven Ladies), a collection of seven fictionalized biographies. All her novels are focused from a feminine perspective through the eyes of the main character, a woman. *Retorno a la tierra* is the feminine approach to life of Delfina Avellano, the main character, who in a rural setting goes through the successive life stages of losing her parents, adolescence, experiencing love, marriage, suffering widowhood, and a hope for future happiness in a projected second marriage. *Perdimos la primavera* approaches the feminine problematic through the different life stages of a woman, now a middle-class city dweller, viewed successively in her school days, adolescence, and first love against the backdrop of a portion of the Spanish Civil War in 1936–1937. All that leads to disappointment, maternity, and early death. The last novel, *Pista de baile*, again deals with a feminine problem and its feminist approach, as Serrano confronts the societal changes of the 1960s through a young heroine who immerses herself in a life among bohemians and marginal characters. Finally she comes to the realization that time takes a toll both on youth and beauty and that those facts have repercussions on her love relationships.

Serrano's active and constant contributions to newspapers and to magazines as well as to the radio no doubt detracted from her potential development and greater productivity as a writer of novels.

Work by

Perdimos la primavera. Barcelona: Plaza y Janés, 1952.
Pista de baile. Madrid: Bullón, 1963.
Retorno a la tierra. Madrid: Nacional, 1945.

Work about

Gallego Díaz, J. "Eugenia Serrano: *Retorno a la tierra*." Insula (May 1946).

Pilar Sáenz

Sex in Spanish Golden Age Literature (1500–1700)

Sex as a literary subject appears abundantly in premodern Spanish literature. The most literal, and rarest, representation is in satiric erotic poetry and in picaresque fiction (**pícaras*). In these types of carnivalesque literature, references to sexual matters are written in through words with double meaning and avoidance of complicated metaphors that would dissociate the reader from the meaning of the text. Writers' primary concern was to provoke humor. Early examples of this semiliteral representation are found in lyric poems of Juan del Encina (1468?–1529/30) and in Francisco Delicado's (1480?–1534) *El retrato de la *Lozana andaluza (1528; Portrait of Lozana: The Lusty Andalusian Woman,* 1987). Both writers were influenced by burlesque Italian authors such as Teofilo Folengo (1491–1544), Francesco Berni (1497/1498–1535), and Pietro Aretino (1492–1556).

Sex is an important component of the didactic tradition. In this instance the body is represented as the origin of sin and condemnation—the weak flesh that carries a soul always at risk of falling into eternal damnation. Preachers would present the feminine body as an evil symbol of temptation; women's weakness was the origin of humankind's condemnation to death. Francisco de **Quevedo's* (1580–1645) poems provide a good example of the negative vision of the body as "grave of the soul" and of beauty as the victim of time. Sex is also connected to the topic of **honor*. A man's honor depended greatly on the behavior of his female family members. Any female behavior that would suggest even minimally any action or thought related to sexual matters was grounds for male members to lose their honor. Many Golden Age plays by Lope de *Vega (1562–1635), *Calderón de la Barca (1600–1681), Tirso de *Molina (1582–1648), and others use misunderstandings in matters of honor as a nucleus for their plots.

Because mainstream literature was closely censored by the Catholic church, reference to sexuality was made through very discriminatory selective language: *blanquísima mano* (the whitest hand), *gallarda figura* (elegant figure), and *gracia de talle y porte* (grace of figure and carriage) are stock references to a woman's beauty that would not impugn her virtue. The presence of a body in a woman's character depiction automatically meant dishonor for the woman and the male authority figure above her—her father, husband, brother, or other male relative. Examples of this topic are found in the feminine picaresque, *La *pícara Justina*, and Cervantes's character Dorotea, from *Don Quijote*. Theatrical works that dealt with individual honor versus the legitimacy of power, as in Calderón de la Barca's *El alcalde de Zalamea* or Lope de Vega's *Fuenteovejuna*, used illegitimate sex such as the rape of a virtuous virgin as a vehicle to emotionally move the public. The sexual act or offense thus loses relevance as such and becomes a symbol of social struggle.

Representation of the body and matters related to corporal pleasures were limited by the religious and moral culture of this particularly strict period of the Counterreformation. During this time in Spain the Catholic Church ruled over the private lives of subjects and even more over the public representation of private acts. There were ways to evade Church censorship—in writing moralistic or didactic texts, writers described the sin they would prevent in the sinner. This modality of moralistic literature was the pillar that supported didactic literature and, in an indirect way, fictional works possessing moral intention, such as the picaresque novel or narratives inspired by Fernando de Rojas's (1474?–1541) *La *Celestina*. The symbolism

of sex appeared frequently in Spanish Golden Age writing, but explicit language, glorification of the body, and erotic writings are not common in traditional literature of the period.

Work about

Alzieu, Pierre, and Jammes, Robert. *Poesía erótica del Siglo de Oro*. Madrid: Nacional, 1983.

Damiani, Bruno. *Francisco Delicado*. New York: Twayne, 1974.

Delicado, Francisco. *Portrait of Lozana: The Lusty Andalusian Woman*. Tr., intro., and notes Bruno Damiani. Potomac, MD: Scripta Humanistica, 1987.

———. *Retrato de la Lozana andaluza*. Ed. Claude Allaigre. Madrid: Cátedra, 1985.

Encina, Juan del. *Poesía lírica y Cancionero musical*. Ed., and notes R.O. Jones and C.R. Lee. Madrid: Castalia, 1990.

Hurtado y Mendoza, Diego. *Poesía erótica*. Archidona, Málaga: Aljibe, 1995.

María Luisa García-Verdugo

Sexuality in the Golden Age: Fray Gaspar de Villarroel (?–after 1659)

This Augustinian gives the lie to the notion that in the seventeenth century the clerical estate was unanimously opposed to public theater. Named the first bishop of Santiago de Chile in 1651 and archbishop of Lima in 1659, Villarroel was one of the highest "princes of the church" to defend, in theory at least, commercial theater. In *Gobierno eclesiástico pacífico* (Peaceful Ecclesiastical Governance), which was composed before April 30, 1646, and published in Madrid in 1656, he confronted extremist interpretations of biblical texts and writings of the Church Fathers that were being employed to condemn as per se obscene, therefore illicit, any dramatic representation of sexual desire and/or endorsement of sexual activity, even in marriage. What (Foucault termed) "la 'mise en discours' du sex" included, in this instance, theatrical discourse as well as critical discourse on theater. In opposing what was subsequently labeled "the Jesuit theme," unrelenting hostility toward female performers and the dramatic representation of love affairs (*amores*), Villarroel relied and expanded upon a theological tradition established by other members of his order, Fray Alfonso de Mendoza (in 1587), Fray Marco Antonio de Camos (in 1692), and Fray Juan González de Critana (in 1610).

Jesuits, Dominicans, Discalced Carmelites, and others, including many laypersons, had routinely charged over the years that the Spanish *comedia* (play) failed to meet the requirements of ecclesiastical censure both for public performance and for subsequent publication, that is, that it not contravene the purity of Catholic faith and good mores. Villarroel contested the views of Doctor Juan Machado de Chaves, whose *Perfecto confesor* (Perfect Confessor) had charged that Spanish plays were indecent and obscene (*torpes*). Villarroel's response was unequivocal, rejecting Machado de Chaves's contention that all amatory material is obscene.

Villarroel upheld the morally indifferent nature of amatory affection traditionally represented in Spanish theater, even when performed by actresses before a public composed of men and women, as long as the manner of performing those actions, especially the love scenes, did not degenerate into obscenity. As a defender of Lope de *Vega (1562–1635), Villarroel echoed, in a theological vein, what the great dramatist had enunciated in the *Arte nuevo de escribir comedias* (New Art of Writing Plays) as a major principle of the Spanish *comedia*, that ladies not be "unworthy of their name." Marc Vitse has identified this Spanish sense of decorum, along with a commitment to theatrical verisimilitude, as the two principles governing the writing of plays in the Lopean manner. However, decorum, especially as it related to the behavior of women, tended to idealize dramatic action and thus affect the limit to which verisimilitude could be pushed by writers.

Spanish attitudes toward decorum deter-

mined, to a large extent, the nature and character of debates on the lawfulness of public theater. Some believed that the mere presence of women on stage constituted at least an occasion of sin, if not serious sin in and of itself. Citing the authority of the Augustinian master Mendoza, Villarroel, with a moral equanimity not common in the period, challenged traditional misogynous assumptions regarding the dangers that actresses presented: After doubting that men sin because they see a woman on stage, he further comments that women must run the same risk when watching men perform. Regarding the morality of attending Spanish plays, Villarroel expressed confidence in the maturity of Christian men and women alike, perhaps the most surprising opinion issued by the Augustinian in this age of governmental and ecclesiastical intervention. He rejected the commonplace that women were the morally weaker members of society, finding that "because neither are strengths equal nor are conditions the same," both male and female theatergoers who were able to distinguish "with good judgment" between actors and actresses and the roles they played "will be able to see plays without sin."

Villarroel confronted forthrightly the new campaign against the theater that, as Antonio García Berrio has noted, began in 1630 and was led by Jesuits. The major figure in this assault on theater was the theologian Padre Pedro Puente Hurtado de Mendoza, whose moral inflexibility particularly displeased the Augustinian. To demonstrate that Spanish plays were immoral and therefore unlawful, Hurtado advanced the argument that, when clerics, religious, and bishops attended them, they gave scandal to the faithful. Villarroel observed that the Jesuit had spoken "wisely but narrowly" on this point; however, his "argument about scandal is a bit weak, and thus does not oblige very much." Based on his experiences in Madrid, Lima, and other large cities, Villarroel denied that clerics and prebendaries gave scandal; religious only did so when they were seen in theaters or present in indecent locales; and bishops could only attend plays in the presence of the king, great lords, and grandees of Spain.

Villarroel's approach to the lawfulness of dramatizing human sexuality evidenced an analytical methodology, which Foucault found to be characteristic of discourse in the classical age, in contradistinction to the textual-commentary practices of adversaries who only discovered immodesty and obscenity in the performances of women and in the representations of human love. *See also* Sexuality in the Golden Age: Fray Manuel de Guerra y Ribera (seventeenth century)

Work by

Gobierno eclesiástico pacífico . . . Sel. and prol. González Zaldumbide. Quito: Ministerio del Gobierno, 1943.

Work about

Cotarelo y Mori, Emilio. *Bibliografía de las controversias sobre la licitud del teatro en España.* Madrid: Est. Tip. de la "Rev. de Archivos, Bibl. y Museos," 1904.
Foucault, Michel. *The History of Sexuality. Volume I: An Introduction.* Trans. Robert Hurley. New York: Vintage Books, 1990.
———. *The Order of Things: An Archaeology of the Human Sciences.* New York: Vintage Books, 1970.
García Berrio, Antonio. *Intolerancia de poder y protesta popular en el Siglo de Oro: Los debates sobre la licitud moral del teatro.* Málaga: Universidad de Málaga, 1978.
Vitse, Marc. *Eléments pour une théorie de théâtre espagnol du XVIIe siècle.* Toulouse: France-Iberie Recherche, 1988.

Thomas Austin O'Connor

Sexuality in the Golden Age: Fray Manuel de Guerra y Ribera (seventeenth century)

On April 14, 1682, this Trinitarian signed a 47-page ecclesiastical censure, which appeared in the *Verdadera quinta parte de comedias de Don Pedro Calderón de la Barca* (True Fifth Part of Plays by Don Pedro Calderón de la Barca), that constituted a theologicodramaturgical treatise dealing with the

major points raised over the years by those who opposed the *Comedia* (theater). Responding in particular to political machinations of the 1670s, Guerra issued a theological opinion that stated that "the *Comedia* is indifferent in Christian terms" and then quickly added that "it is profitable politically speaking." The clarity, force, and extensive nature of the opinion was intended to respond to attempts by Spanish elites, such as the Marquis of Montealegre (president of the Supreme Council of Castile) and Don Francisco Ramos del Manzano (president of the Council of the Indies), who, for various reasons, had failed to obtain from the monarchy the permanent banishment of the *Comedia* during a period of dynastic and political instability. In 1677, during that turbulent time of political and ecclesiastical putsches, Ramos made the startling claim "that the prohibition of [plays] corresponds to civil and ecclesiastical authorities." That delicate balance between theological consultation and political action, maintained since the times of Felipe II (1527–1598), was now upset; and Ramos mentioned that matters had gotten to the point where some authors were encouraging bishops to bypass civil authorities altogether and prohibit plays in their dioceses on their own authority. This ecclesiastical juggernaut was rolling along, gathering momentum with time, until Guerra appeared on the scene. In and of itself Guerra's *aprobación* (official approval) would today stand as little more than an interesting document in Spanish theatrical history, were it not for a startling opinion that cut through more than 100 years of rhetorical excess and theological misrepresentation: for this official preacher of Carlos II stated that all of *Calderón de la Barca's (1600–1681) plays, and the *Comedia* as a whole, "are so tightly-bound to the laws of modesty that they present no danger, but [supply] doctrine." Guerra moved the debate, for the *Comedia*'s advocates, from essentially defensive reactions to a positive position that upheld the sanctity and divine origin of what

Oliver has termed a "conjugal spirituality," a "popular spirituality" often found, among other locations, in secular literature.

For his own part Guerra rejected the imposition on laics of what some religious leaders considered appropriate conduct primarily for those pursuing a monastic calling. In the first place, he openly challenged the opinion of some Jesuits, Carmelites, Dominicans, and others who found the mixing of the sexes in public theaters to be morally objectionable, due to its provocative nature, if not in fact per se immoral. Secondly he declared that the public representation of amatory emotions by actors and actresses, which the *Comedia*'s critics charged incited lust (*ad libidinem*) in spectators, was an opinion held by them and not an official position of the Church based on doctrinal or disciplinary evidence. But the most far-reaching opinion of this Trinitarian came in the above-cited statement that upheld the sanctity of the embodied state and lawfulness of the proper exercise of sexuality for those called to live fully their conjugal love. In a shorter statement to the same effect, he declared that Calderón's plays, in particular, combined "the amatory with the decent," thus affirming the goodness of marital love and reelevating its practice to the place already conceded to it in Christian tradition, especially in the Deutero-Pauline letters of the New Testament. One reason Jesuit writers in particular so fiercely attacked Guerra in 1682–1683, and continued to do so even in the eighteenth century, in what Cotarelo classified as "a silent war of manuscript satires," was the Trinitarian's open and reasoned rejection of their "sexualized" political agenda for Spanish society. For many traditionalists were shocked by the presence of actresses in Spain's public theaters and fearful that women in general would break out from the seclusion that both religion and culture had imposed on them.

The "Guerra Affair" brought to a head the theological controversies that had pitched, in the main, Jesuits against Augustinians in the discussion of what constituted legitimate recreation (*eutropelia*). One of the traditional instruments in theological debate, in addition to declared Christian doctrine, was the *magisterium* of the Church, its teaching authority. The writings of the Church Fathers were frequently consulted to identify traditionally orthodox positions on a variety of moral matters, and many opponents of the *Comedia* were wont to cite their scathing opinions of theater in imperial Rome as representative of what occurred on the Spanish stage. Guerra, like Fray Gaspar de Villarroel before him, chose to contest the use to which Padre Pedro Hurtado de Mendoza put patristic sources, demonstrating the essential differences between the two dramatic traditions. For this disputative methodology had been employed to great effect by Padre Pedro de Rivadeneira (1526–1611) in 1589 and by that most influential Jesuit intellectual, Padre Juan de Mariana (1535/1536–1624), in 1609, among others, thus establishing a kind of self-confirming discursive authority beyond the reach of the opposition. With detailed analysis and precise citation, Guerra permanently problematized this approach as the unquestionable source that condemned plays as morally illicit and therefore in opposition to Christian faith and good morals. Guerra stated unequivocally that "the amatory [cape-and-sword] plays" constituted an "innocent diversion without danger," and the *Comedia*'s " 'mise en discours' du sex," a doctrine for the laity. *See also* Sexuality in the Golden Age: Fray Gaspar de Villarroel (?–after 1659)

Work by

Verdadera quinta parte de comedias de don Pedro Calderón de la Barca. Madrid: Francisco Sanz, 1694.

Work about

Cotarelo y Mori, Emilio. *Bibliografía de las controversias sobre la licitud del teatro en España.* Madrid: Est. Tip. de la "Rev. de Archivos, Bibl. y Museos," 1904.

Foucault, Michel. *The History of Sexuality. Volume I:*

An Introduction. Trans. Robert Hurley. New York: Vintage Books, 1990.

Oliver, Mary Anne McPherson. *Conjugal Spirituality: The Primacy of Mutual Love in Christian Tradition.* Kansas City: Sheed & Ward, 1994.

Thomas Austin O'Connor

Short Fiction by Women Writers: 1800–1900

Though most critics find that her sermonizing and moralizing detracts from her stature as a writer, Cecilia *Böhl de Faber y Larrea (1796–1877), pseudonym Fernán Caballero, enjoys a prominent place in the development of the modern short story. Born in Switzerland, the daughter of Hispanophile Johann Niklaus Böhl von Faber, her attempt at anonymity is further seen in her use of the name León de Lara for the story "Callar en vida y perdonar en muerte" (1850; To Keep Silent in Life and to Pardon in Death). She first published her novel *La gaviota* (1856; *The Sea Gull*, 1965) in the newspaper *El Heraldo*. Then followed *Clemencia* (1852), *Cuadros de costumbres populares andaluces* (1852; Sketches of Popular Andalusian Customs), *La farisea* (1853; The Pharisee Woman), *Lágrimas: Novela de costumbres populares* (1853; Tears: Novel of Popular Customs), and *La familia de Alvareda: Novela original de costumbres populares* (1856; The Alvareda Family: Original Novel of Popular Customs). Böhl de Faber was also an inveterate letter writer (her correspondence has been published in *Cartas* [1919], *Epistolario* [1922], and *Cartas inéditas* [1961]).

Her short stories and sketches are deeply rooted in Spanish folklore and often set against an Andalusian background, as seen in "Callar en vida y perdonar en muerte," *Una en otra* (1849; One and Another), *Con mal o con bien a los tuyos te ten* (1851; Stick to Your Own Good), *Un servilón y un liberalito, o tres almas de Dios* (1855; A Loyalist and a Liberal or Three Good Souls of God, 1882); and *Relaciones* (1857; Tales). Böhl de Faber collected *Cuentos y poesías populares*

andaluces (1859; Popular Andalusian Short Stories and Poems), which are a tribute to her fervent love of the Andalusian folklore, of which the Spanish Catholic faith is a strong component. Her religiosity as well as her "Spanishness" can be traced at least partly to her deeply rooted Romanticism, which was antirevolutionary and strongly reactionary. Together with her compilation of *Cantos, coplas y trobas populares* (Popular Songs, Poems and Verses), her *Refranes y máximas populares recogidos en los pueblos de campo* (Proverbs and Popular Sayings Collected in Country Villages), and her *Cuentos, oraciones, adivinas y refranes populares e infantiles* (1877; Children's Popular Stories, Prayers, Riddles and Proverbs), she offers a wide range of observations of the legendary, traditional region of Andalusia. Critics have classified Fernán Caballero's novels and short stories as romantic, *costumbrista* (local color writing), or simply realist, for she partakes of all these tendencies to varying degrees. For instance, "Una paz hecha sin preliminares, sin conferencias y sin notas diplomáticas" (A Peace Made without Preliminaries, without Meetings and without Diplomatic Notes), which bears the subtitle *escenas populares andaluzas* (popular Andalusian scenes), is a dramatic sketch in which the narrator adopts the standpoint of a stenographer (*taquígrafo*) who records street conversations in the Andalusian town of Chiclana. In the conversations, disagreements on the subject of nationality build up to a chaotic fight but are then put to a sudden end by the unexpected presence of a running bull. In general, Böhl de Faber aimed to provide an accurate painting of Spain based on *naturalidad* (naturalness) by using techniques found in the most orthodox narrative folklore. According to Williams, the mutual collaboration and influence of Washington Irving and Böhl de Faber may have influenced Irving's Spanish interests and fiction. Böhl de Faber enjoyed national and international acclaim, but her tendency to moralize may explain the wane of her popularity toward the end of her life.

Her work also exerts great demands on the modern reader averse to folklore or to exemplary and religious stories. Böhl de Faber wrote a good part of her work when European romanticism was already at a low ebb. After her heyday in the 1850s and 1860s, she maintained a definite, if declining, popularity by publishing a flood of short stories in magazines. Both the quality and abundance of her popular children's stories also kept her name in the public view during her later years.

The first two editions of her *Obras completas* were printed in 16 volumes by Mellado (1861–1864), and there have been several subsequent editions, all in Madrid. There is also José María Castro Calvo's edition, *Obras de Fernán Caballero* (1961). The absence of a reliable edition of her works adds to the critical obstacles in cross-listing her references. Furthermore, classifications of her short fiction present difficulties, because in the first half of the nineteenth century the *cuadro de costumbres* (local-color sketch) was not clearly delineated from the legend and the short story. The *cuadro* described a picturesque human type or scene and differed from the short story in that it either lacked a plot or tended to minimize it. Legends, which were often set in the past, stressed the fantastic or supernatural. The short story as we know it today through its originators—Poe, Maupassant—had practically no history before the nineteenth century, *Alarcón being the writer who introduced the modern form of the genre to Spain. Böhl de Faber endeavored to classify some tales as *relaciones* (relations), which supposedly differed from novels of customs (*romans de moeurs*) and from short novels. The traits she attributes to this uncertain term is that the *relación* must have an ethical component, be truthful, and create its effect—in accord with Poe's tenets—through a surprise ending. Critics have yet to chart the dividing line between local color sketches, *nouvelles*, popular tales based on folklore, vignettes, *ejemplos* (examples), and *juguetes dialogados* (diversions in

dialogue). Böhl de Faber attempted to distinguish the local color sketch from the short story, insisting that the former departs from invention by adhering to an exact reproduction of the life and traditions of the Andalusian people. Even so, the stories gathered under a particular series do not fall conveniently into any set classification. To add to the confusion, stories such as "Con mal o con bien a los tuyos te ten" and "No transije la conciencia" (Don't Compromise Conscience) have been described as possible novels; "Estar de más" (To Be in the Way) as a *nouvelle*. Böhl de Faber herself wrote to Hartzenbusch in 1850 that she was working on "una novelita o relato llamado 'El exvoto' " (a little novel or story called 'The Votive Offering'), which points to the fact that the term *novela corta* (short novel) was not common and often used interchangeably with *relato* or *cuento*. Thus, it is not surprising to see critics throw up their hands in despair, as Montesinos does when faced with "Jessica la Judía" (Jessica the Jewess), a piece he describes as "que no sé qué pueda ser" (I don't know what it might be). *Relaciones* (1857) contains: "Justa y Rufina," "Más largo es el tiempo que la fortuna" (Time Lasts Longer Than Luck), "No transije la conciencia," "La flor de las ruinas" (The Best Ruin), "El exvoto," and "Los dos amigos" (The Two Friends), based on the true fate of Cadalso. The 1868 edition contains two additional *relaciones*: "La hija del sol" (Daughter of the Sun) and "La Estrella de Vandalia" (Star of Vandalia). These dramatic and often tragic stories either fall into moralizing digressions or propose an explicit Christian solution.

Her local color writing is extensive: *Cuadros de costumbres populares andaluces* (1852), which contains "La noche de navidad" (Christmas Night), "El día de Reyes" (Twelfth Night), "¡Pobre Dolores!" (Poor Dolores!), "Lucas García," and "El ex-voto"; *Cuentos y poesías populares andaluzas* (1859); *Cuadros de costumbres* (1857 and 1862), which contains "Simón Verde," "Más vale honor que honores" (Honor Is Worth More

Than Being Honored), "Lucas García," and "Obrar bien, que Dios es Dios" (To Do Good, For God Is God). The Valencia edition of that work (1878) contains two additional stories: "El último consuelo" (The Last Comfort) and "Dicha y suerte" (Happiness and Luck). "Más vale honor que honores" is a piece of sentimental literature that resorts to the *feuilleton*. "Obrar bien, que Dios es Dios" embeds a popular children's tale within an Andalusian sketch. Böhl de Faber's love of folklore and the defense of traditional values in these *cuadros* are obvious and the moral of the stories emphatic. *Deudas pagadas* (1860; Debts Paid) also contain *cuadros de costumbres*.

Böhl de Faber's contribution to children's literature is collected in *Cuentos, oraciones, adivinanzas y refranes populares e infantiles* (1877), *El pájaro de la verdad y otros cuentos* (1969; The Bird of Truth and Other Stories); and *Cuentos de encantamiento infantiles* (1911; Children's Fantasy Stories). *Diálogos* (Dialogues) contains six unrelated stories, apparently modeled after Don Juan Manuel's fourteenth-century work **Conde Lucanor*, where the dialogue between the nobleman and his adviser, Patronio, provide a frame for the stories they introduce. Some appear to be character studies and resemble the local sketch in their absence of conflict; all exhibit Fernán Caballero's ever-present religious orientation and her defense of the traditional Andalusian spirit: "El albañil" (The Bricklayer), "El marinero" (The Sailor), "El sochantre de lugar" (The Local Subchanter), "El general" (The General), "El quinto" (The Fifth One), and "Un tío en América" (An Uncle in America).

Relatos breves are epigrammatic stories best described as *proverbios en acción* (proverbs in action), a subtitle used for one of the stories. They include: "La noche de Navidad," "El día de Reyes," "El ex-voto," "Matrimonio bien avenido, la mujer junto al marido" (A Harmonious Marriage [Needs] the Wife Next to the Husband), "Promesa de un soldado a la Virgen del Carmen" (A Soldier's Promise

to the Virgen of Carmen), "Deudas pagadas" (Debts Repaid), "La corruptora y la buena maestra" (The Perverted Woman and the Good Teacher), "La maldición paterna" (The Father's Curse), "La viuda del cesante" (The Unemployed Man's Widow), "Las mujeres cristianas" (Christian Women), "Los dos memoriales" (The Two Written Requests), "Un vestido" (A Dress), and "Los pobres perros abandonados" (The Poor Abandoned Dogs). The latter story refers explicitly to Cervantes and triggers an association with his exemplary novel *El coloquio de los perros* (Canine Colloquy). There are several translations of her short fiction available in French, English, and German.

Born in Puerto Príncipe, Cuba, playwright, poet, and novelist Gertrudis *Gómez de Avellaneda (1814–1873) is a major figure of nineteenth-century letters and often referred to as the Georges Sand of Hispanic literature. From 1836 she lived almost exclusively in Spain, where she obtained recognition and popularity. In 1863 she returned to Cuba and reestablished her roots in Cuban literature. An author of impressive range, she wrote poetry, novel, drama, short stories, essays, and epistles. The breadth, quality, and variety of Avellaneda's literary achievements may have been unmatched by any woman writer of her day. Her poetry can be found in *Poesías selectas* (1966) or in her *Obras* (1914–1918). Her dramatic works include historical plays, such as her famous *Alfonso Munio* (1844), and biblical themes, in such works as *Baltasar* (1858) and *Saúl* (1849). Her romantic comedies, such as *La hija de las flores, o todos están locos* (1852; The Daughter of the Flowers, or Everyone Is Mad) or the farce *El millonario y la maleta* (1869; The Millionaire and the Suitcase), reflect contemporary social themes that represent a fresh departure from the customary approaches to drama at the time. Avellaneda's novels include *Sab* (1841); *Dos mujeres* (1842; Two Women); and *Guatimocín* (1846; Cuauhtemoc). She also wrote prayer books, *Manual del cristiano. Nuevo y completo devocionario* (The Christian's Manual. New Complete Devotionary), written in 1846, and a second *Devocionario nuevo y completísimo en prosa y verso* (New and Most Complete Devotionary in Prose and Verse), published in 1867. Her contribution to epistolography shines in the deeply moving letters she wrote to her reluctant lover, Don Ignacio de Cepeda, from 1839 to 1854. Her books have been translated into English, French, Italian, German, Russian, and Hungarian.

The status of women in society was a major concern for Gómez de Avellaneda—or Tula, as she used to be called—and she gave that subject a prominent position in her plays and prose works. Her article "La mujer" (1860; Woman), published in Cuba, denounces, among other things, the exclusivity of the Royal Spanish Academy, which had excluded her on the grounds that women had never been appointed to the Academy other than as honorary members. The outspoken, passionate case the article made for the dignity of women represents an important document for feminist studies. Among her shorter prose works, critics have distinguished what the author herself called *leyendas* (legends) from her short stories and short novels. The legends are based on folk traditions, and Gómez de Avellaneda uses the well-established literary device of a narrator who transcribes oral tales. Her brother, Manuel, recounted the Swiss legends to the author, and she may have heard the stories of the Basque regions and the Pyrenees while traveling in that region with her second husband, Verdugo. Several legends are set in the Jura mountains of France, and in Switzerland, while others are based on material drawn from American history. All explore the fantastic and the supernatural and clearly belong to the tradition of romantic medievalism and the Gothic novel. For example, "La ondina del lago azul" (1859; The Water Nymph of the Blue Lake) shares many similarities with the well-known legend on which Gustavo Adolfo *Bécquer based "Los ojos verdes." It carries the subtitle "Recuerdo

de mi última excursión por los Pirineos" (Memory of My Last Excursion in the Pyrenees). "La bella Toda" (The Beautiful All) and "Los doce jabalíes" (1858; The Twelve Wild Boars) in turn are subtitled "Dos tradiciones de la plaza del mercado de Bilbao" (Two Traditions from the Market Square of Bilbao). "La flor del ángel" (1859; The Angel's Flower) is a Basque legend, as is "La dama de Amboto" (1858; The Lady of Amboto). "La baronesa de Joux" (The Baroness of Joux) is based on a poem by French author Demesnay and dates from 1844. "Una anécdota en la vida de Hernán Cortés" (An Anecdote in the Life of Hernán Cortés) develops an incident drawn from *Guatimozín* and is often thought to be an epilogue to the novel. "La velada del helecho o El donativo del diablo" (1845 or 1846; The Fern's Soiree or the Devil's Gift) is based on a Swiss tradition, as is "La montaña maldita" (1859; The Cursed Mountain). "El donativo del diablo" was later expanded into a full-length play that opened in 1852.

Gómez de Avellaneda uses American materials for her legends in "El cacique de Turmequé" (The Chief of Turmequé) and "El aura blanca" (The White Dawn), the latter of which bears the subtitle "Suceso extraño ocurrido en nuestros días" (Strange Event [Which] Occurred in Our Day). The first work could be considered a short novel because of its length and is often acclaimed as a masterpiece of short fiction. Set in New Granada (now Colombia) in the second half of the sixteenth century, "El aura blanca" recounts a story of Avellaneda's birthplace, Puerto Príncipe, Cuba. Avellaneda's unconventional life has been the subject of various biographies, and it is only recently that critical studies on this author have begun to liberate themselves from the autobiographical references in her writing.

Born in La Coruña to a noble family, Emilia *Pardo Bazán (1852–1921) received the standard education available to women at her time, but she read voraciously. Her literary achievements warranted her title of condesa (countess). Next to "Clarín" and Palacio Valdés, Pardo Bazán represents one of the most brilliant representatives of brief fiction writing. Her achievements in the short story may have been obscured only by her splendid novel *Los pazos de Ulloa* (1886; *The Son of the Bondswoman*, 1908). Pardo Bazán had already acknowledged that a novelist does not necessarily know how to write a short story, commenting in her essay on naturalism that the short story is a subgenre virtually ignored by critics, but not all great novelists are capable of composing a well-wrought short story. She first became known as a writer with her critical essay on *Feijóo, who inspired her campaign to advance female emancipation throughout her distinguished career. Pardo Bazán then wrote articles for magazines, particularly about the education of women, and her interest in science and pedagogy led her to explore kraussist ideas. She wrote several volumes of literary essays. Her essay "La cuestión palpitante" (The Burning Question), which she wrote after reading Zola, is often credited with introducing naturalism to Spain. She became a prolific writer of novels, short stories, and articles and today continues to be one of the best-known female authors of Spain.

Among her best novels are *Los pazos de Ulloa* (1886; trans. as *The Son of The Bondswoman* 1908) and its sequel *La madre Naturaleza* (1887; Mother Nature). Her later novels, which have not received equal critical attention, include a linked pair, *Una cristiana* (1890: A Christian Woman) and *La prueba* (1890; The Test); *La piedra angular* (1891; The Angular Stone); *Doña Milagros* (1894); *Memorias de un solterón* (1896; Memories of a Bachelor); *La quimera* (1905; The Chimera); *La sirena negra* (1908; The Black Siren); *La tribuna* (1882: The Rostrum); and many others. During 1891–1893 she produced a collection of solid essays and short stories in the *Nuevo Teatro Crítico*, and after 1890 she wrote over 500 stories in an impressive range of styles and content, most of which appeared in newspapers (*El Impar-*

cial, *El liberal*, *El Heraldo*, *Blanco y Negro*, *La Esfera*, *La Ilustración Española y Americana*, among others).

The nineteenth-century short story in Spain is inextricably tied to the proliferation of newspapers and literary magazines, in which it developed its modern form as we know it today, and Pardo Bazán contributed to the short story more than any other writer of that time. In addition to her outstanding output of some 800 high-quality short stories, she wrote critical works on the genre and studies on the major French short story masters, such as Daudet and Maupassant. Pattison states that Pardo Bazán "chose Maupassant as her chief model for the technique of the short story," for she believed the writer should compress an action, drama, or comedy in a brief space. According to her, short story writers should stick to their subject, avoiding extraneous elements and proceeding rapidly in swift development of the narrative. Sainz de Robles claims that her achievements in this genre cause the rest of her fiction—its merit notwithstanding—to pale in comparison. The 41 volume of her *Obras completas* contain most of her work—20 novels, 13 religious depictions, seven plays, literary criticism, and 544 short stories—classified thematically by the editors as: "Cuentos de la vida moderna" (Stories of Modern Life), "Cuentos de épocas pasadas" (Stories of Past Ages), "Cuentos de Galicia" (Stories of Galicia), "Cuentos de humor y tristeza" (Humorous and Sad Stories), "Cuentos de fantasía" (Fantasy Stories), "Cuentos de amor y pasión" (Stories of Love and Passion), "Cuentos de Navidad y Año Nuevo" (Christmas and New Year's Stories), "Cuentos de la tierra" (Stories of the Land), and "Cuentos trágicos" (Tragic Stories). Hundreds of other stories, published in newspapers and magazines, were not included in her *Complete Works*, and many remain scattered. Juan Paredes Núñez in his four-volume edition of Pardo Bazán's *Cuentos completes* (1990) collected some 800 stories.

Pardo Bazán herself grouped her short stories after a fashion, particularly in the beginning. At times the only purpose seems to have been that of simply collecting the stories she had already published in newspapers up to a certain date, as is the case with *La dama joven, Sud-exprés, Cuentos escogidos, Cuentos nuevos, Lecciones de Literatura*, and *Arco Iris*. These compilations were followed by collections she grouped thematically according to subject matter. Given their great variety, critics such as Baquero Goyanes have attempted elaborate classifications of her stories. Paredes Núñez, also recognizing the fact that the various classes frequently overlap, categorizes her short stories using larger thematic clusters. One category he uses, "Cuentos de objetos y seres pequeños" (Stories about Objects and Small Beings), highlights Pardo Bazán's ability to structure a story around a small object or animal.

Until 1902, very few of Pardo Bazán's stories had been gathered in a single volume. Book editions of short stories were not too popular in the first decade of the twentieth century, since they had to compete with lower-cost, special-interest magazines such as *El Cuento Semanal, La Novela Corta, El Libro Popular*, or *Los Contemporáneos*, which were preferred by short story readers. Reading habits were also turning toward the novel, a phenomenon that Pardo Bazán regarded as detrimental to the genre. Her own output of short stories decreased as she turned to the short novel after 1906.

Work by Fernán Caballero

Obras completas. 16 vols. Madrid: Mellado, 1861–1864.

Obras de Fernán Caballero. Ed. and study José María Castro Calvo. 5 vols. Madrid: Atlas, 1961.

Work about Fernán Caballero

Cantos Casenave, Marieta. "Los relatos de Fernán Caballero entre costumbrismo y realismo." *Siglo Diecinueve* 2 (1996): 187–200.

Chevalier, Maxime. "Inventario de los cuentos folklóricos recogidos por Fernán Caballero." *Revista de Tradiciones Populares* 26 (1878): 49–65.

Gabriel y Ruiz de Apodaca, Fernando de. *Estar de*

más, relación, y Magdalena, obra inédita, precedida de una nota biográfica. Sevilla: Gironés y Orduña, 1878.

Grillo, Rosa María. "La confusión reinante: Definición y estructuras de la prosa breve de Fernán Caballero." *Siglo Diecinueve* 2 (1996): 201–212.

Herrero, Javier. *Fernán Caballero: Un nuevo planteamiento*. Madrid: Gredos, 1963.

Klibbe, Lawrence H. *Fernán Caballero*. New York: Twayne, 1973.

López Martínez, Isabel. "Fernán Caballero y la leyenda popular." *Cuentos y leyendas de España y Portugal/Contos e lendas de Espanha e Portugal*. Mérida, Spain: Regional de Extremadura, 1997. 95–99.

Montesinos, José F. *Fernán Caballero: Ensayo de justificación*. México: El Colegio de México, 1961.

Williams, Stanley T. "Washington Irving and Fernán Caballero." *Journal of English and Germanic Philology* 29 (1930): 352–366.

Work by Gómez de Avellaneda

Manual del cristiano: Nuevo y completo devocionario. Ed. and intro. Carmen Bravo-Villasante. Madrid: Fundación Universitaria Española, 1975.

Obras de doña Gertrudis Gómez de Avellaneda. Ed. and study José María Castro y Calvo. 4 vols. Madrid: Atlas, 1974–1981.

Work about Gómez de Avellaneda

Bravo Villasante, Carmen. *Una vida romántica: La Avellaneda*. Barcelona: Enrique Granados, 1967.

Cotarelo y Mori, E. *La Avellaneda y sus obras: Ensayo biográfico y crítico*. Madrid: Tipografía de Archivos, 1930.

Harter, Hugh A. "Shorter Prose Works." *Gertrudis Gómez de Avellaneda*. Boston: Twayne, 1981. 157–168.

Homenaje a Gertrudis Gómez de Avellaneda. Ed. Gladys Zaldívar and Rosa Martínez de Cabrera. Miami: Universal, 1981.

Rosello Selimov, Alexander. "La verdad vence apariencias: Hacia la ética de Gertrudis Gómez de Avellaneda a través de su prosa." *Hispanic Review* 67.2 (1999): 215–241.

Work by Pardo Bazán

Cuentos completes. Ed. and study Juan Paredes Núñez. 4 vols. La Coruña: Fundación "Pedro Barrie de la Maza Conde de Fenosa," 1990.

Obras completas. 41 vols. Madrid: Aguilar, 1947, 1957, 1964, 1973.

Work about Pardo Bazán

Bravo Villasante, Carmen. *Vida y obra de Emilia Pardo Bazán*. Madrid: Revista de Occidente, 1962.

Chevalier, Maxime. "Cuento folklórico y cuento literario (Pereda, Pardo Bazán, Palacio Valdés)." *Anuario de Letras* 18 (1980): 193–208.

Hannon, Harold. "Algunos aspectos estilísticos en los cuentos de Emilia Pardo Bazán." *Kanina: Revista de Artes y Letras de la Universidad de Costa Rica* 7.2 (1983): 83–92.

Hoffman, Joan. " 'Torn Lace' and Other Transformations: Rewriting the Bride's Script in Selected Stories by Emilia Pardo Bazán." *Hispania* 82.2 (May 1999): 238–245.

Livingston, Dana. "First Love? Marginal Sexualities in a Short Story by Emilia Pardo Bazán." *Letras Peninsulares* 10.2 (Fall 1997): 265–279.

McKenna, Susan. "Recalcitrant Endings in the Short Stories of Emilia Pardo Bazán." *Letras Peninsulares* 11.2 (Fall 1998): 637–656.

Osborne, Robert E. "Doña Emilia y el cuento." *Emilia Pardo Bazán: Su vida y sus obras*. México: Stadium 42, 1964.

Paredes Núñez, Juan. *Los cuentos de Emilia Pardo Bazán*. Granada: Universidad de Granada, 1979.

Pattison, Walter T. *Emilia Pardo Bazán*. New York: Twayne, 1971.

Pérez, Janet. "Subversion of Victorian Values and Ideal Types." *Hispanófila* 113 (1995): 31–43.

Pozzi, Gabriela. "Usos de la histeria, el discurso científico y la sexualidad en tres cuentos fantásticos de Emilia Pardo Bazán." *Boletín de la Biblioteca de Menéndez Pelayo* 73 (January–December 1997): 83–97.

Sánchez, P. "How and Why Emilia Pardo Bazán Went from the Novel to the Short Story." *Romance Notes* 11 (1970): 309–314.

Work about Nineteenth-Century Short Story

Blanco García, F. "Cuentos y narraciones cortas." *La literatura española en el siglo XIX*. Madrid, 1891. 2: ch. 16.

Charnon-Deutsch, Lou. *The Nineteenth-Century Spanish Story. Textual Strategies of a Genre in Transition*, London: Tamesis, 1985.

El cuento español en el siglo XIX. Madrid: Consejo Superior de Investigaciones Científicas, 1949.

Ezama Gil, Ángeles. "El relato breve en las preceptivas literarias decimonónicas españolas." *España Contemporánea* 8.2 (1995): 41–51.

Sainz de Robles, F.C. *Cuentistas españoles del siglo XIX*. 3rd ed. Madrid: Aguilar, 1962.

Simón Palmer, María del Carmen. *Escritoras españolas del siglo XIX. Manual bio-bibliográfico*. Madrid: Castalia, 1991.

Ana Rueda

Short Fiction by Women Writers: 1900–1975

Perhaps we are still too close to the literature of the twentieth century to discern periods in the way we do for the nineteenth century. The quick succession and simultaneous development of different literary currents or "isms" that are characteristic of modern literary history frustrate critics' attempts toward periodization. For lack of a better perspective, one might say that the coexistence of many different currents is a distinctive feature of this century. Yet women writers fail to fit within the tidy critical categories of competing "isms." Critical classifications tend to exclude women writers from the five generations traditionally established for twentieth-century Spanish literature—those of 1927, 1936, mid-century, 1968, and the *postnovísimos*. Certainly, many writers—both male and female—can fall outside the rigidities of chronological studies, but it is unjustifiable that Rosa *Chacel, María Teresa *León, and Elisabeth *Mulder should find no place in most studies of the Generation of 1927, to which they rightly belong. Carmen *Kurtz or Mercedes *Salisachs, who published in the decade immediately following the Spanish Civil War (1936–1939), are only recently receiving proper attention in revisionist studies of the "Postwar Generation." Clearly, women writers of earlier generations do not enjoy the same prestige as their male compatriots, even if they did enjoy public acclaim in their day. As a corollary to this cultural amnesia, critical studies generally disregard the contribution of the short story to narrative discourse. Since the short story shares common elements with other genres, most theoreticians have tried to assert its uniqueness in opposition to the poem or, more commonly, to the novel, of which the short story had wrongly been considered a subset. However, this approach has failed to yield more than vague descriptions. Furthermore, even though length may not be the crucial issue for the genre, brevity has often been associated with "minor" genres—the type of value judgment from which the genre is still recovering, as Pratt has cogently argued. The problem of literary criticism proves especially vexing when women's short fiction is assessed against the standards and textual norms set by the male writer and reader. As a result, the contribution of female short story writers to Spanish literary history suffers a double neglect. For practical purposes, this entry is divided into two major periods, each marked by its conspicuous production and consumption of short stories. The section dedicated to the first third of the century includes authors whose work is published before the Civil War (1936–1939). The section treating the years following the Civil War (1940–1975) is composed of writers who were initially, though not exclusively, associated with what has been called "social realism" (*realismo social*).

Not many women have advanced a theory of the short story, although there are several studies of the genre and many studies of particular authors. Oversights of the past are being addressed by both Spanish and non-Hispanic theoretical explorations in short fiction theory and criticism. Among them are Baldeshwiler, who published an article on the lyrical short story in 1969, which was later included in Hanson's book, *Re-Reading the Short Story*. The same volume also contains Hanson's article "Things out of Words: Towards a Poetics of Short Fiction." Hanson also is the author of *Short Stories and Short Fictions, 1880–1980*. Lohafer and Clarey map out the field conceptually in a valuable collection of essays, *Short Story Theory at a Crossroads*. Argentine fiction writer Bullrich has refuted Horacio Quiroga's famous "Decálogo del perfecto cuentista" (Decalogue for the Perfect Short-Story Writer) in her book *Carta a un joven cuentista* (Letter to a Young Short-Story Writer). Theoretical concerns

centered on the short story have hardly reached Spain. Brandenberger's *Estudios del cuento español contemporáneo* (Studies of the Contemporary Spanish Short Story) is one of the pioneer studies of the contemporary Spanish short story. Litvak's work focuses on the anarchist short story, *El cuento anarquista: 1880–1911*; while Ezama Gil covers the nineteenth-century short story in its accustomed medium—the press—with *El cuento de la prensa y otros cuentos. Aproximación al estudio del relato breve entre 1890 y 1900* (The Story of the Press and Other Stories. Approximation to the Study of the Short Story between 1890 and 1900). *Martín Gaite offers her personal reflections on the genre in *El cuento de nunca acabar* (The Never-Ending Story), while Lida de Malkiel analyzes the popular short story, *El cuento popular y otros ensayos* (Popular Short Story and Other Essays). Finally, Rueda's *Relatos desde el vacío* (Stories from the Void) examines connections between the peninsular Spanish and Spanish American short story, providing a theoretical focus for a body of fiction published between 1970 and 1985.

First Third of the Twentieth Century: 1900–1939

The short story enjoyed great popularity in this period, owing in large part to the journal *El Cuento Semanal* (The Short-Story Weekly), founded in 1908 and directed by Eduardo Zamacois. Subsequent publications devoted to the genre include *Los Contemporáneos*, *El Libro Popular*, and *La Novela Corta*, which contributed to creating a great demand for short pieces that could be read at one sitting. Hundreds of excellent short stories were published and read until an avid readership reached its saturation point the short story per se ceased being marketable, and it was relegated to newspapers and general-interest magazines. Joaquín Millán Jiménez claims that one of the possible reasons for this deflation of the genre is that the same story would appear in various journals, at times under a different title. Another reason might be that some writers switched to other genres, which forced editors of these journals to hire short story writers. During this period, the short story is still largely dependent on the press. Collections of short stories are difficult to publish and are often compiled by the author. An exception to this tendency is the compilation *Cuentistas españolas contemporáneas* (1946), with a forward by Francisco Sainz de Robles. A collection of short stories by one author is still a rare event, and such collections of works are by male writers (Vicente Soto, Julián Ayesta, for example). The writings of women of this period reflect their position with regard to the turn-of-the-century women's movement. Although Concha Espina turned her back on this historical phenomenon and fluctuated in her political sympathies, Caterina Albert (pseudonym Victor Catalá), Carmen de *Burgos, and Sofía Casanova fought for women's education, civil rights, and the status of women in society. Regardless of their ideological orientations, all these writers created a vast body of literature in need of assessment. The inattention by critics and historians to their work is as regrettable as it is commonplace. Some efforts are being made to remedy this neglect, such as Castalia's 1989 editions of short fiction by women writers of this period. However, the editorial effort is limited, and women's production of short stories during this period is still in dire need of critical investigation.

Carmen de Burgos Seguí (1867–1932), who used the pseudonym Colombine, focused sharply on the short novel, publishing 105, and the short story. Her short stories include: *La hora del amor* (1917; The Hour of Love), *Cuentos de Colombine* (1908; Stories by Columbine), *Ellas y ellos, o ellos y ellas* (1917; Females and Males, or Males and Females), and *Los anticuarios, Mis mejores cuentos* (1923; The Antiquarians. My Best Stories). She actively campaigned for women's suffrage, women's education, and the civil rights of women, which won her the presidency of the Liga Internacional de Mujeres Ibéricas e Hispanoamericanas. These interests are reflected in her 1921 short story "El artículo 438" (Article 438, in *Mis mejores cuentos*), which deals with adultery and the murder of a woman by her husband, who ends up vindicated for having defended his *honor.

Best known as a poet and short story writer, Sofía Casanova (1862–1958) also published travelogues, war episodes, and a play. She collaborated assiduously with the Spanish press and published several novels written outside Spain. *El pecado* (1911; Sin) is a collection of stories set mostly in Galicia that presents the themes of love and marriage from a psychological angle. Casanova also published many short stories in short novel collections: *Sobre el Volga helado* (1903; On the Frozen Volga), *Triunfo de amor* (1919; Triumph of Love), *Princesa rusa* (1922; Russian Princess), *Kola, el bandido* (1923; Kola, the Bandit), among others.

Concepción Espina (1869–1955), better known as Concha Espina, is recognized primarily as a novelist. Her numerous works reflect both realism and the sentimental novel of late romanticism. Although at times Espina demonstrates sensitivity to feminist issues, she has acquired a reputation of being politically conservative, due to a series of politicized novels written during the period of the Spanish Republic, the Spanish Civil War, and the early postwar years. Some of her works do reveal a Falangist rhetoric, but her nationalistic fervor is also counterbalanced in many of her early works by a more objective narrative style. Even so, her style may seem dated to some contemporary readers. Her first book was a collection of poems, followed by 17 long novels and several volumes of short stories, among them *Cuentos* (1922; Stories) and *El fraile menor* (1942; The Minor Priest), written between 1920 and 1942. The earliest stories are an apposite reflection of the belief that love leads to disillusionment. Some stories focus on the need for social reform in this period of Spanish history, while a few of the war stories reveal

Espina's nationalistic or rightist sympathies. *Llama de cera* (1925; Wax Flame) contains two stories and a short novel. This work reflects a more objective and less traditional Espina.

From very early on, Blanca de los *Ríos (1862–1956) used the anagram Carolina del Boss. As a creative writer, she wrote poetry and drama but excelled in the narrative: short novels and short stories. The latter include: *La rondeña. Cuentos populares* (1902; Ronda Woman. Popular Stories), *El Salvador. Cuentos varios* (1902; The Savior. Various Stories), *El tesoro de Sorbas. Cuentos* (1914; The Treasure of Sorbas. Stories), and *La saeta. El molino de los Gelves. La rondeña* (n.d.; The Saeta [The Arrow, or Andalusian Dance]. The Gelves Mill. The Native of Ronda).

Mid-Century: 1940–1975

According to Anderson Imbert, two generations of short story writers were publishing during the decades following the beginning of the Spanish Civil War: those born between 1900 and 1915 and those born between 1915 and 1930. Medardo Fraile extends this conventional classification to yet another generation, to include those born between 1930 and 1945. Either classification should also encompass those writers of the *España Desterrada* (Exiled Spain) or *España Peregrina* (Wandering Spain), exiled Spanish writers dispersed throughout Europe, Latin American, and North America—notably, Francisco Ayala, Max Aub, Rafael Dieste, Arturo Barea, Ramón Sender, M. Rodoreda, and Rosa Chacel. Their stories, published abroad, reached Spain only sporadically and in clandestine fashion. Thus, the decade of the 1940s, immediately following the Spanish Civil War, offers certain peculiarities due to the sociopolitical circumstances of exile, cultural isolation, and harsh censorship within the peninsula. After a fashion, Spain participates in the world war taking place outside its borders. Extraliterary circumstances lead Spanish writers to focus on the

peninsula and to search in history for a Spanish tradition. Thus, they arrive at a social or testimonial realism also found in the so-called mid-century generation comprising mostly writers born between 1915 and 1930. Daily life becomes the focus of Spanish authors, and the short story traces the life of a particular character, a city, or a human or spiritual ideal. In this way, the short story enlists Spanish realism in its depiction of a social reality, no matter how unfortunate and sordid it may be.

By the 1950s, the short story genre had reached maturity, yielding works of high caliber that were first published in newspapers and magazines, then gathered in anthologies such as García Pavón's (1959), which brought together a wide range of authors. Literary prizes in postwar Spain represent an important institutional and commercial source of support. Significant prizes for the short story include: Sésamo, Café Gijón, Leopoldo Alas, Juventud, and those supported by the Cajas de Ahorro (Savings and Loan Associations), such as the Hucha de Oro, or the Puerta de Oro. Publishing houses—Taurus, Seix Barral, Ínsula, and Destino, among others—additionally have given decisive support for the genre. Literary journals have also exercised an important role, including *Clavileño, Escorial, La Hora, Cuadernos Hispanoamericanos, Índice, Papeles de Son Armadans, Agora, Revista Española*, and many others. The thematics of love become standard, particularly in women's magazines, whose publications exalt traditional virtues associated with femininity. Slowly, psychological and existential problems appear in the work of writers publishing short stories on a regular basis.

The decade of the 1960s brings a limited degree of renovation in narrative techniques, for the short story continues to deploy dialogue as an effective tool of social realism. Monologues and monodialogues are used to express life as a sad and irreparable flux. Oneiric and more ludic aspects, at first limited to juvenile literature, are slowly incorporated into the genre, eventually seduced by the possibilities of the fantastic. Humor and tenderness toward persons of humble station, a staple of the brief fiction of the 1940s and 1950s, give way to other themes by writers employing fable, myth, and symbol. The next generation, that of the 1950s, shows an abundance of writers whose primary work is in this genre: Ignacio Aldecoa, Ana María *Matute, Juan Benet, Carmen Martín Gaite, Medardo Fraile, Jesús Fernández Santos, and many others. This generation's testimony reveals the state of affairs in Francoist Spain of the 1950s but also absorbs foreign influences, such as existentialism, Marxism, and American literature. Its writers provide a graphic inventory of daily life, while exploring literary techniques more akin to those of other cultures. They open the door to the next generation—that of 1968—which will coincide even more with the cultural horizons and artistic experimentation prevalent in other European cultures.

A member of the Generation of 1927, Rosa Chacel (1898–1994) wrote novels, essays, poetry, and short stories from 1930 onward. In *Icada, Nevda, Diada,* Chacel combined the stories from two collections published abroad during her exile (*Sobre el piélago* [1952; On the High Sea] and *Ofrenda a una virgen loca* [1961; Offering to a Crazy Virgin]), in addition to some stories published in journals and other formerly unpublished works. The title is based on three variations on the word *nada,* nothingness.

A novelist and short story writer, Eulalia *Galvarriato's (1905–) best-known short story is "Raíces bajo el agua" (1953; Roots Underwater), which was awarded a prize as a film script. It can be found in *Eulalia Galvarriato: Raíces bajo el tiempo* (1985; Eulalia Galvarriato: Roots under Time), a compilation of her short stories and other pieces classified as "Momentos vividos" (Moments Lived), "Poemillas en prosa" (Little Poems in Prose), "Sueños" (Dreams), and "Recuerdos de viaje" (Travel Memories). Her

work depicts a poetic and nostalgic world, seen through eyes of delicate sensibility.

Born in Córdoba, Concepción Gutiérrez Torrero (1913–) uses the pseudonym Concha *Lagos. She has published many poetry collections, a short novel, a fictionalized diary, and a collection of sketchlike narrations entitled *La vida y otros sueños: Cuentos* (1969; Life and Other Dreams: Stories). The style is direct and realistic and deals with everyday life.

Cristina *Lacasa's (1929–) primary work is in poetry, but she also penned two collections of short stories. *Jinetes sin caballo* (1979; Horseless Riders) contains stories dated from 1955 to 1977 depicting the marginalization suffered by characters of the lower social class and effects of the Spanish Civil War. Her second book of stories, *Los caballos sin bridas* (1981; Horses without Bridles), gathers stories dated from 1955 to 1981. Its prose is permeated with lyricism.

The Condesa de *Campo Alange, María de los Reyes Laffitte y Pérez de Pulgar (1902–1986) has distinguished herself primarily as a historian, sociologist, novelist, and critic of art and literature. She also composed a book of short stories, *La flecha y la esponja* (1959; The Arrow and the Sponge), which explores intimate relationships and sexual difference.

After the Spanish Civil War, Carmen *Laforet received national acclaim with publication of her novel *Nada* (Nothing), which received the first Premio Nadal in 1944. Her novels and short stories are written in the so-called social realism vein, depicting Spanish life in the 1940s and 1950s. Laforet's conversion to Roman Catholicism in 1951 marks a change in her style. The stories in *La llamada* (1954; The Call) and the novel *La mujer nueva* (1955; The New Woman) depict heroines transmuted by conversion and religious sentiments. Laforet is the author of two other short story collections. *La muerta* (1952; The Dead Woman) contains stories written from 1942 to 1952 and depicts such women's concerns as motherhood. Several stories reflect religious themes, Christian charity in particular. Others treat childhood and misery in post–Civil War Spain. *La niña y otros relatos* (1970; The Girl and Other Stories) contains some stories previously included in *La muerta*. Laforet is much admired for her characterization of women and adolescents, and her short stories are the most highly praised aspect of her work.

María Teresa *León (1903–1988) explored many genres, but her first publication was a collection of short stories for children, *Cuentos para soñar* (1929; Stories for Dreaming). The lyric stories in *La bella del mal amor* (1930; The Beauty Wrongly Loved) are set in an atemporal rural Castile and have a traditional air. *Rosa Fría, patinadora de la luna* (1934; Rosa Fría, Moon Skater), a beautiful collection that transcends juvenile literature, includes drawings by her husband, poet Rafael Alberti, and the images of its prose owe much to the poetics of the Generation of 1927. *Cuentos de la España actual* (1937; Stories of Today's Spain) represents social realism and reflects a Marxist ideology. *Una estrella roja* (1979; A Red Star) comprises a selection of short stories from *Cuentos de la España actual*, *Morirás lejos* (1942; You Will Die Far Away), and *Fábulas del tiempo amargo* (1962; Fables from the Bitter Time). The latter, first published in Revista de Poesía Universal Ecuador 0° 0'0" (1962), uses a very poetic prose to denounce injustice and violence. The thematics of *Morirás lejos* (1942) include the Civil War and exile but also Mexican myths. The nine stories comprising *Las peregrinaciones de Teresa* (1950; Teresa's Pilgrimage) depict women and explore feminine psychology, with Teresa as the central character.

One of Spain's leading poets, Susana *March (1918–1993) is also a novelist and short story writer. *Cosas que pasan* (1983; Things That Happen) is a collection of short stories that gives particular importance to women figures coping with societal constraints. Her short story "Mi tía Clara" (My Aunt Clara) was selected for *Los mejores cuentos*, an anthology of the best stories

awarded the Hucha de Oro prize before 1969. "Mi tía Clara" vindicates the apparently uneventful life of a spinster devoted to helping others.

Carmen Martín Gaite (1925–2000), a prolific and renowned author, first became known as a social realist writer during the postwar. She amassed a series of prestigious literary awards, among them: Café Gijón short story award for *El balneario* (1954; The Spa); Premio Nadal for her novel *Entre visillos* (1957; Between the Blinds); the Premio Anagrama de Ensayo for *Usos amorosos de la postguerra española* (1987; Customs of Love in Postwar Spain); Príncipe de Asturias de las Letras; Castilla de León de las Letras; and the Premio Nacional de Literatura for *El cuarto de atrás* (1978; The Back Room, 1983). She produced literary criticism, short stories, scripts, and essays, in addition to novels. Her personal reflections on the short story were crystallized in *El cuento de nunca acabar* (1983; The Never-Ending Tale). Short stories by Elena *Fortún provided the base for Martín Gaite's screenplays for the TV series *Celia*, directed by José Luis Borau. *El balneario* and *Las ataduras* (1960; Bonds) each contain a title novella and seven short stories. All of her short stories to that date are collected in the anthology *Cuentos completos* (1978), which groups the short stories from *El balneario* and *Las ataduras* by theme rather than chronologically. According to the author's prologue, the themes are routine, the opposition between urban and rural life, the first disillusions of childhood, lack of communication, the gap between what people do and what they envision, and fear of freedom. Martín Gaite adds that women are more affected by their inability to reconcile their dreams with their actual lives, to the point that this collection could bear the title "Cuentos de mujeres" (Stories by Women). Martín Gaite also wrote markedly feminist short stories for children, including *El castillo de las tres murallas* (1982; The Triple-Walled Castle) and *El pastel del diablo* (1985; The Devil's Cake), both of which were subsequently published as *Dos relatos fantásticos* (1986; Two Fantasy Tales). *Lo que queda enterrado* (1987; What Lies Buried) and *Caperucita en Manhattan* (1990; Red Riding Hood in Manhattan) are likewise stories for younger readers. All of Martín Gaite's juvenile fiction subtly inculcates the female's right to education and liberty.

Ana María Matute (1926–   ) excels as a novelist and writer of short stories and children's literature. Subsequent to *Los Abel* (1948; The Abel Family) and *Primera memoria* (Premio Nadal 1959; First Memoirs), she was awarded the Premio Nacional de Literatura for *Los hijos muertos* (1958; The Lost Children). Author of a vast body of works, her short stories deal with social concerns, the effects of the Spanish Civil War, and the passage of time—in particular, lost childhood and the sadness connected to rites of passage from innocence to adulthood. They resort to symbolism and some fantasy, aptly depicting the emotions, fantasies, suffering, and frustrations of children. *El tiempo* (1957; Time) touches upon many themes and subjects but tends to center on childhood and adolescence. The last story in the Destino edition, "Los cuentos vagabundos" (Vagabond Stories), should be read as a personal reflection on the art of storytelling and on the genre in general. *Algunos muchachos* (1968; trans. as The Heliotrope Wall and Other Stories, 1989), *El arrepentido* (1961; The Penitent), and *Historias de la Artámila* (1961; Stories of Artamila) are other collections. The latter contains 22 tragic stories set in the fictional region of Artámila (actually the impoverished area of La Rioja). Belying its title, *Libro de juegos para los niños de los otros* (1961; Book of Games for the Children of Others) is not written for children. It contains a series of pieces that escape classification as they describe "games" of street children that provide fantasy outlets for their negative feelings and emotions—a response to the harsh reality they live in. *Los niños tontos* (1981; The Stupid Children) includes 21 short sketches of a fantastic nature, about

children. *Tres y un sueño* (1961; Three and a Dream) are three stories of three characters, two children and one adult who thinks she is still a child. Unable to cope with adult life, they live (or die) in their own private worlds. *La Virgen de Antioquía y otros relatos* (1990; The Virgin of Antioquía and Other Tales) includes the title short story and 11 earlier short stories. Matute has also written close to a dozen stories for children, many in the form of fairy tales resembling those of Hans Christian Andersen, and has won several prizes for her juvenile fiction.

Best known for her novels and short stories, Dolores *Medio (1911–1996) composed her fiction within the tradition of social realism. She depicts realistic, emotionally charged situations as they affect lower-class protagonists. *Compás de espera* (1954; A Time of Waiting), Medio's first collection of short stories, deals primarily with the pathetic circumstances of lower-class people, portrayed as victims of their surroundings. *Andrés* (1967), which received the Premio Sésamo, contains stories dealing with children or young boys placed in unhappy circumstances. Without deviating much from her usual realistic approach, *El babanch* (1974) explores science fiction and the supernatural. *El urogallo* (1982; The Grouse) comprises three long stories, two of which had been published previously. The story that lends its title to the collection was written during the Civil War but went unpublished due to censorship.

Elisabeth Mulder de Daumer (1904–1987) was born in Barcelona to a Dutch father and a South American mother. Well traveled and the product of a refined education, she wrote many novels, several books of poetry, and the short story collection *Este mundo* (1945; This World).

Carmen de Rafael Mares Kurz (1911–   ) uses the pen name Carmen Kurz. From Barcelona, Kurz is an award-winning writer of novels and short stories, receiving the Premio Ciudad de Barcelona in 1954 and the Premio Planeta in 1956, among others. She is known for her stories for adults and younger audiences as well. *El último camino* (1961; The Last Road) focuses on the theme of death and its attendant feelings of loneliness and alienation. *Siete tiempos* (1964; Seven Epochs) is a collection of 27 short stories, divided into seven *tiempos* or periods of time that encompass thematic categories such as death, love, and the impact of the war.

Since 1955, Mercedes *Salisachs (1916–), who initially used the pseudonym María Ecín, has published 12 novels over a 20-year period, the most famous being *La gangrena* (Premio Planeta 1975; Gangrene). A winner also of the Premio Ciudad de Barcelona (1957) and the Premio Ateneo de Sevilla (1983), her short stories include *Pasos conocidos: Dos novelas y nueve relatos* (1958; Familiar Steps: Two Novels and Nine Tales) and *El proyecto y otros relatos* (1978; The Project and Other Tales).

Concha *Suárez del Otero (1908–) has written novels, poetry, essays, and short stories and has collaborated with various journals, garnering numerous literary awards. Her stories stress the existential plight of unusual women in search of self-definition and revelation. *Mi amiga Andrée* (1954; My Friend Andrée) gathers 10 short stories, some of which were previously published in *La vida en un día* (1951; Life in One Day), a collection of 12 stories that obtained the Premio Álvarez Quintero.

Born in Madrid, Ana Voyson first published stories and articles under a pseudonym. After the Civil War she became prominent as a writer of essays, biography, and newspaper articles. She published four novels, novelettes, and a collection of short stories titled *Cuentos de misterio* (1952; Mystery Stories), some of which are science fiction.

Finally, María de la Concepción *Zardoya González (1914–) used the pseudonym Concha de Salamanca until 1946, thereafter adopting the pen name Concha Zardoya. Born of Spanish parents in Valparaíso, Chile, she returned to Spain in 1932. Zardoya is considered one of the most prominent contemporary Spanish women poets. She is also a well-known literary critic, especially for her work on contemporary Spanish poetry and also on Gil Vicente and Ercilla. Zardoya additionally has translated Walt Whitman and published a history of North American literature. Her only book of short stories is *Cuentos del Antiguo Nilo (Las dos tierras de Hapí)* (1944; Stories from the Ancient Nile [The Two Lands of Hapi]), in which she still uses the pseudonym Concha de Salamanca. Set in Egypt, these stories create a mythic and exotic world. *See also* Short Fiction by Women Writers: 1975–1998, Post-Franco.

Work by

Anthologies

Cuento español contemporáneo. Ed. María Angeles Encinar and Anthony Percival. Madrid: Cátedra, 1993.

Cuentos de este siglo. Varias autoras. Ed. María Angeles Encinar. Barcelona: Lumen, 1995.

Doce relatos de mujeres. Comp. by Ymelda Navajo. Madrid: Alianza, 1982.

The New Catalan Short Story. Washington, DC: UP of America, 1983.

On Our Own Behalf. Women's Tales from Catalonia. Ed., intro., and notes Kathleen McNerney. Lincoln: U of Nebraska P, 1988.

Individual Authors

Burgos Seguí, Carmen de. *Mis mejores cuentos.* Sevilla: Editoriales Andaluzas Unidas, 1986.

Espina, Concha. *Obras completas.* Madrid: FAX, 1972.

Laforet, Carmen. *La muerta.* Madrid: Rumbos, 1952.

———. *La niña y otros relatos.* Madrid: Magisterio Español, 1970.

Martín Gaite, Carmen. *Cuentos completes y un monólogo.* Barcelona: Anagrama, 1994.

Ríos, Blanca de los. *La rondeña. Cuentos populares. El Salvador. Cuentos varios.* Madrid: Idamor Moreno, 1902.

———. *El tesoro de Sorbas.* Madrid: Bernardo Rodríguez, 1914.

Work about

Baldeshwiler, Eileen. "The Lyric Short Story: The Sketch of a History." *Studies in Short Fiction* 6

(1969): 443–453. Rpt. in Hanson, Clare. *Re-Reading the Short Story*. New York: St. Martin's P, 1989.

Brandenberger, Erna. *Estudios del cuento español contemporáneo*. Madrid: Nacional, 1973.

Bullrich, Silvina. *Carta a un joven cuentista*. Buenos Aires: Santiago Rueda, 1968.

Ezama Gil, Angeles. *El cuento de la prensa y otros cuentos. Aproximación al estudio del relato breve entre 1890 y 1900*. Zaragoza: Universidad de Zaragoza, 1992.

Fraile, Medardo. Introduction to *Cuento español de posguerra*. 5th ed. Madrid. Cátedra. 1994. 13–48.

Hanson, Clare, ed. *Re-Reading the Short Story*. New York: St. Martin's P, 1989.

————. *Short Stories and Short Fictions, 1880–1980*. London: Macmillan, 1985.

————. " 'Things out of Words.' Towards a Poetics of Short Fiction." *Re-Reading the Short Story*. Ed. Clare Hanson. New York: St. Martin's P, 1989.

Jackson, Rosemary. *Fantasy: The Literature of Subversion*. New York: Methuen, 1981.

Lida de Malkiel, Rosa María. *El cuento popular y otros ensayos*. Buenos Aires: Losada, 1976.

Litvak, Lily. *El cuento anarquista: 1880–1911*. Madrid: Taurus, 1982.

Lohafer, Susan, and Jo Ellyn Clarey, eds. *Short Story Theory at a Crossroads*. Baton Rouge, LA: UP, 1989.

Martín Gaite, Carmen. *El cuento de nunca acabar*. 2nd ed. Madrid: Trieste, 1983.

Millán Jiménez, Joaquín. "El cuento literario español en los años 40. Un género a flote." *Las Nuevas Letras* 8 (1988): 80–86.

Percival, Anthony. "El cuento en la posguerra." *Las Nuevas Letras* 8 (1988): 87–93.

Pratt, Mary Louise. "The Short Story: The Long and the Short of It." *Poetics* 10 (1981): 175–194.

Redondo Goicoechea, Alicia, ed. *Relatos de novelistas españolas 1939–1969*. Madrid: Castalia, Instituto de la Mujer, 1993.

Rueda, Ana. *Relatos desde el vacío*. Madrid: Orígenes, 1992.

Ana Rueda

Short Fiction by Women Writers: 1975–1998, Post-Franco

In the last three decades of the twentieth century, women have radically altered their literary discourse, creating their own literary models. The thematics of feminist issues plus the need to find voices of their own have led women authors to a serious self-examination at the metanarrative level, raising the question of difference in women's writings. A subversive or parodic quality has emerged in many short stories as a result of increased consciousness of women's marginal status and the discovery of ways to recover their own word and to create their own language. A great part of this short fiction engages in a new dialogue with the female body, and with silence, as it attempts to free its discourse from restrictive codes and classifications. The concept of *l'écriture féminine*, as developed by French feminist theory, figures among influential countervoices of poststructuralism and aptly suits women's recently developed modes of expression. Cixous, Leclerc, Irigaray, and other French theoreticians have exerted an influence on the writing of many of these women, although their familiarity with the work of Julia Kristeva or Robin Lakoff, for instance, indicates that such an influence is not limited to French critical theory. Ymelda Navajo states in her introduction to *Doce relatos de mujeres* (1982) that contemporary women writers in Spain are more influenced by Virginia Woolf, Simone de *Beauvoir, or Mary MacCarthy than they are by the generations of Spanish women writers that precede them. This sense of being severed from their own tradition may explain, at least partly, the battles these writers often face in their creative process; it may also help us appreciate the universal scope of their work.

The short story has become revitalized as women offer new sexual models, a renewed language, and a personal search that resist the critic's tendency to seek common elements. In this multivocal panorama of female voices, the only common impulse might be their insistence on their own discourse. Women's short fiction confronts the nature of being a woman and conveys with great force a uniquely female sensibility. "Difference" is inextricably connected to the conditions that allow writing itself. For instance, Cristina Peri Rossi (born in Uruguay) is one of many self-exiled Latin American writers who live and publish in Barcelona and whose language and influx of ideas have expanded discursive boundaries for the genre. Influences from all over the world have flooded the literary scene in Spain, and differences of cultural heritage have ceased to be a barrier for communication. In turn, the revival of regional autonomous states and the diaspora of geographical writing centers in Spain—once limited to Madrid and Barcelona—has spurred the use of several vernacular languages including Catalan, Gallego, and Basque. The literary and linguistic renaissance in Catalonia is well reflected in the short stories written by women: Margarida Aritzeta, Silvia Aymerich, María Barbal, Mercè Canela, Montserrat Canela, Maite Carranza, Lali Cistaré, Mercè Company, Joana Escobedo, María Jaén, Empar de Lanuza, Gemma Lienas, Anna Llauradó, M. Mercè Marçal, M. Antònia Oliver, María Josep Raqué, Carme Riera, M. Mercè Roca, Montserrat Roig, Isabel-Clara Simó, Elena Valentí, Antònia Vicens, and many others. Francisca Herrera Garrido, one of the first women to publish narrative in Galician, has been followed by Margarita Ledo Andión (*Mama-Fé* [1983; Mother Faith]), Ursula Heine (*Remuiños en coiro* [1984; Whirlpool of Pain]), and María Xosé Queizán (author of many uncollected short stories). Arantxa Urretabizkaia writes in Basque and has published, among other works, a collection of short stories, *Aspaldian espero zaitudalako ez nago sekula bakarrik* (1984; I Am Never Alone Because I Have Been Waiting for You for a Long Time). Basque and Galician representation suffer particularly when the market cannot offer works in translation.

Although not every woman writer in Spanish society enjoys "a room of one's own"—Virginia Woolf's metaphor for a woman's living space in which her intimate dramas unfold—one must admit that, compared with earlier generations, women writers today enjoy fewer restrictions as they attempt to maintain a separate selfhood.

Still, much of women's fiction is devoted to mastering the smaller aspects of life and to finding a comfortable space for the self. Women's voices of "difference" constitute a polyphonic and pluralistic body of literature. Among significant recent features of recent short stories by women writers is a twofold concern for genre and gender. In these writers' concern for genre, one notes the following traits: (1) A marked lyrical quality is found in the work of poets who write short stories. Examples are Pilar Cibreiro who, in 1985, published a cycle of stories on life in a small village in Galicia, and Ana *Rossetti, Elena Santiago, Clara *Janés, and many others, whose stories demand to be read as poems. (2) There is a modest attempt to recover neglected or unusual "subgenres" in Spanish short narrative, such as the detective story (Soledad *Puértolas, Rosa María Pereda), the ghost story (Cristina *Fernández Cubas), and science fiction (Beatriz de Moura, Ana Voyson). (3) Various explorations of the fantastic challenge standard portraits of women in fantasy literature written by males. The work of Mercè Rodoreda, Ana María *Moix, Isabel del Río, Cristina Fernández Cubas, and several others shows the insufficiencies of traditional theories of the fantastic, such as Todorov's, confirming the need for new theories of the fantastic in the feminine mode, such as Rosemary Jackson's perspectives on cultural meanings in the fantastic. (4) There is a ludic appropriation of and experimentation with other genres: drama, diary, the travelogue, and the letter. Letter writing in particular appears ubiquitous in brief fiction by contemporary women, a phenomenon suggesting women are reconnecting with a literary tradition often associated—rightly or not—with women. Writers attracted by the possibilities of letter writing in the short story context include Nuria Amat, Carme Riera, Elena Santiago, and Mercedes *Abad. (5) there is the presence of a female erotica as evidenced in the work of Mercedes Abad or Ana Rossetti, which attempts to overcome phallocentric alienation through the articulation of female desire. The collection *Cuentos eróticos*, although not limited to women authors, includes pieces by Lourdes *Ortiz, Paloma *Díaz-Mas, Cristina Peri Rossi, and Ana Rossetti.

Furthermore, one notes the following traits regarding these writers' concern for gender: (1) Language centered on women's body (*escritura del cuerpo*) runs through many short stories. In general, one senses less reticence to discuss women's biological processes and greater exploration and emancipation in sexuality through various love configurations: marriage, lesbianism, *ménage a trois*, or other triangular settings of desire (Esther *Tusquets, Helena Valentí, Marina *Mayoral, Ana Rossetti, Mercedes Abad, and many others). (2) There is a thematics that attempts to recover a matrilineal line from mother to daughter, woman to woman, in an attempt to move beyond the patriarchal, paternal, or phallocentric confines. Laura Freixas, author of the short stories *El asesino en la muñeca* (1988; The Assassin on the Wrist), has brought together in *Madres e hijas* (1996; Mothers and Daughters) 14 short stories on the mother-daughter relationship. This anthology on the gender theme includes works by Rosa *Chacel, Carmen *Laforet, Ana María *Matute, Carmen *Martín Gaite, Josefina R. *Aldecoa, Esther *Tusquets, Cristina Peri Rossi, Clara Sánchez, Paloma Díaz-Mas, Mercedes Soriano, Almudena *Grandes, and Luisa Castro. Clearly, the conjunction of a feminist thematics and linguistic experimentation has led to a ludic metanarrative that speaks particularly to women. (3) There is a strong focus on contemporary Spanish society from a uniquely female point of view (Montserrat Roig, Esther Tusquets, Nuria Amat) but also new perspectives on history (Angeles Irisarri, *Siete cuentos históricos y siete que no lo son* [1995; Seven Historical Stories and Seven That Aren't]; Paloma Díaz-Mas, *Nuestro milenio* [1987; Our Millennium]); a revision of myths (Lourdes Ortiz, *Los motivos de Circe* [1991;

Circe's Reasons], Mercè Rodoreda, *Mi Cristina y otros cuentos* [1982; My Cristina and Other Stories]); and fairy tales (Isabel del Río, *La duda* [1995; Doubt]). (4) There is a recovery of links with women's literary history, such as marginal discourses based on oral tradition. Critic Marta Traba relates women's writing to memory and oral structures, such as repetitions, interruptions for clarification, and so on; the often-ignored genre of children's stories is an example of this tradition. Carmen Eva *Nelken (Magda Donato), born in 1900, contributed greatly to children's stories with her collection *La protegida de las flores* (n.d.; Protegée of the Flowers) and particularly with her presence in the children's section of periodicals such as *Los Lunes del Imparcial*. María Teresa *León's *Cuentos para soñar* (1929; Stories for Dreaming), Carmen *Conde's *Zoquetín y Martina* (1979), Ana María *Navales's *Mi tía Elisa* (1983; My Aunt Elisa), and the entire work of María Angeles Ollé offer examples of this tradition. Lourdes Ortiz, Carmen *Kurtz, and Esther Tusquets, among others, have also written children's stories.

Mercedes Abad (1961–   ) writes fiction and journalistic pieces for the leading Spanish newspapers. Actively involved in theater, film, and radio, she became known in the literary world with the collection of erotic short stories *Ligeros libertinajes sabáticos* (Frivolous Weekend Libertines), for which she won the VIII Premio La Sonrisa Vertical in 1986. In 1989 she published a second collection entitled *Felicidades conyugales* (Conjugal Happiness). Its 13 stories portray couples in absurd or grotesque scenarios that reveal the cruelty, noncommunication, and hidden obsessions underlying conjugal relationships.

Although she is mainly a novelist, in 1957 Concha *Alós (1922–   ) was awarded a prize by the Mallorcan magazine *Lealtad* for her short story "El cerro del telégrafo" (Telegraph Hill). A resident of Barcelona, her short stories are published under the title *Rey de gatos. Narraciones antropófagas* (1972; Cat King. Cannibal Stories).

Writer, librarian, and expert in computer science Nuria Amat (1950–   ) is the author of novels, short stories, essays, and technical books, and she also publishes research studies and regularly writes for Spanish newspapers. Her world travels give her novels and brief fiction a cosmopolitan worldview and provide fascinating reflections on travel and literature in her essay book *Viajar es muy difícil. Manual de ruta para lectores periféricos* (1995; Traveling Is Very Hard. Route Guide for Marginal Readers). She has published the short story collection *Amor breve* (1990; Brief Love), which contains 25 brief, imaginative stories, experimenting with various writing modalities. Amat's concise, witty style draws the reader effectively and intelligently to the harshness of contemporary daily life.

Author of numerous short stories published in literary magazines (*Sur-Express, Puro Cuento*), Bárbara Aranguren (n.d.) has also written scripts for film and TV. *Bajo la sombra de cualquier árbol* (1990; Under the Shade of Any Tree) gathers 17 of her best stories and includes a prologue by Soledad *Puértolas. Most of the stories have a female protagonist and reveal *un extrañamiento del presente* (alienation from the present). Some stories include marginalized figures—the madman, the retarded child, the gypsy—seen by guileless eyes.

Paloma Díaz-Mas (1954–   ), professor of Spanish Golden Age and Sephardic literature, published her first collection of short stories in 1973 and since then has become an award-winning novelist with *El rapto del Santo Grial* (1984; The Sequestering of the Holy Grail), *Tras las huellas de Artorius* (Premio Cáceres de Novela, 1985; Following the Footsteps of Artorius), and a play, *La informante* (Premio Ciudad de Toledo de Teatro, 1983; The [Female] Informer). She is also the author of the essay *Los sefardíes: Historia, lengua y cultura* (1986; The Sephardim: History, Language and Culture). Her short stories are published under the title *Nuestro milenio* (1987; Our Millennium); they explore linguistic, spatial, and historical displacements that invite the reader to reflect upon our fast-paced millennium.

One of the most inventive writers in Spain is Cristina Fernández Cubas (1945–   ), who became known in the literary community with *Mi hermana Elba* (1980; My Sister Elba). Three years later she published *Los altillos de Brumal* (The Highlands of Brumal), which inspired Cristina Andreu to produce a movie featuring actors Lucía Bosé and Paola Dominguín. Although Fernández Cubas has explored the novel, she continues to find in the short story the perfect medium to explore the mirages of time and memory, dreams and nightmares, which envelop her characters. A master of the *Doppelgänger* phenomenon (the double), many of her stories explore obsessive images of the other in mirror effects, interior duplications, and transmigrations of personalities. Her contribution to the fantastic short story is important. Fernández Cubas's stories were reedited in a single collection, *Mi hermana Elba y Los altillos de Brumal* in 1988. *El ángulo del horror* (1990; The Angle of Horror), a collection of four short stories, portrays the strange hidden in the commonplace. A more recent collection of short stories is *Con Ágata en Estambul* (1994; With Agatha in Istanbul).

A prolific, well-known contemporary poet, Clara Janés (1940–   ) has published several collections of poems, novels, essays, and other writing; she is also the author of one collection of short stories, *Tentativa de olvido* (n.d.; Attempt to Forget).

Another professor of Spanish literature, Marina Mayoral (1942–   ) centers her scholarly work on the poetry of Rosalía de *Castro and Emilia *Pardo Bazán. She has also written textual commentaries and published novels in Spanish and in Galician. *Morir en sus brazos y otros cuentos* (1989; To Die in His Arms and Other Stories) is a short story collection whose characters discover unsuspected aspects and disturbing ambiguities regarding love and friendship.

Ana María Moix (1947–   ) alternates between poetry and prose. Her poetry was published mostly between 1969 and 1972. Moix's work uses complex literary forms and often hybrids of poetry and prose. *No time for flowers y otras historias* (1971) combines interior monologues with popular songs and references to the work of *García Lorca and Tennessee Williams. Her short story collection *Ese chico pelirrojo a quien veo cada día* (1972; That Red-Headed Boy I See Every Day) portrays innocent characters who defend their odd lives in spite of what others may think of them. These strange, disturbing stories begin with insignificant events or anecdotes that build gradually to a plot. Some stories resort to Ovidian metamorphoses that transform ordinary reality into suprareal phenomena: Children become animals, vampires are humanized, and so on. This results in a symbiosis of the fabulous and the familiar. A wide range of everyday circumstances is reasoned through a poetic logic aimed at critiquing the loneliness and disillusionment in contemporary society. The collection was reprinted in 1995 by Lumen. *Las virtudes peligrosas* (1985; Dangerous Virtues), another collection, contains five elaborately written stories.

Ana María Navales has published three collections of short stories, *Dos muchachos metidos en un sobre azul* (1976; Two Boys Stuffed in a Blue Envelope), *Paseo por la íntima ciudad y otros encuentros* (1987; Stroll through the Intimate City and Other Encounters), and *Kot o la muñeca japonesa* (1988; Kot or the Japanese Doll). She is also the author of several novels, books of poems, and a children's book and has published two anthologies of Aragonese writers and several studies on contemporary literature.

Lourdes Ortiz (1943–) has dedicated much of her professional time to teaching—history, sociology, communication theory, art history—and to writing fiction. She also takes an active role in Spanish cultural life and in political activities, such as the coalition Izquierda Unida. Some of Ortiz's short stories in *Los motivos de Circe* (1991) have been anthologized in *Doce relatos de mujeres* and *Relatos eróticos escritos por mujeres*. The protagonists in *Los motivos de Circe*, Eve, Circe, Penelope, Bathsheba, Salomé, and Gioconda, emerge from their silence through Ortiz's pen.

Marta Pessarrodona (1941–) has translated the work of women writers from English and French and published poetry, drama, short stories, scripts, and critical studies. Her short stories *Nessa. Narracions* (1988), written in Catalan, exist also in Spanish translation, *Nessa. Narraciones* (1988; Nessa. Stories). One of her stories is also anthologized in *Doce relatos de mujeres* (1982).

At present, Soledad Puértolas (1947–) combines fiction writing with articles in Spanish newspapers. Her essay *La vida oculta* (1993; The Hidden Life) won the XXI Premio Anagrama de Ensayo. Puértolas's three collections of short stories, which have earned her as much fame as her novels, are *Una enfermedad moral* (1982; A Moral Illness), *Todos mienten* (1988; Everyone Lies), and *La corriente del golfo* (1993; The Gulf Current). According to the author's preface, the stories in the first collection revolve around a moral problem. The question of whether every story is ultimately a moral one is also posed in the preface. Puértolas is anthologized in *Doce relatos de mujeres* with her story "A través de las ondas" (Across the Waves), which injects a battle of the sexes into the detective genre by recounting a successful crime story.

Carme Riera Guilera (1949–) has received important prizes: Premio Prudenci Bertrana (1981) for her novel *Una primavera per a Domenico Guarini* (A "Primavera" for Domenico Guarini) and the Premi de Novella Ramon Llull (1989) for *Joc de miralls* (*Mirror Images*, 1993). Her first short story collection, *Te deix, amor, la mar com a penyora* (1975; I Leave You, Love, the Sea as Token), became a Catalan bestseller. It portrays social misfits and was followed by *Jo pos per testimoni les gavines* (1977; Let the Seagulls Be My Witness), which brings together

12 lyrical short stories centered on female characters. *Palabra de mujer, bajo el signo de una memoria impenitente* (1980; The Woman Speaks, under the Sign of an Unrepentant Memory) is the Spanish version of several short stories included in *Te deix, amor, la mar com a penyora* and *Jo pos per testimoni les gavines*. The tone of these stories is melancholy despite their vibrant language. Several stories explore epistolarity, such as "El reportaje" (The Report), which offers an interesting case of intertextuality with "Mallorca," a story by Anaïs Nin. Riera's stories tend to present female central characters who experience a wide range of emotions. *Epitelis tendríssims* (1981; Exquisite Epithelia), a collection of 7 stories also written in Catalan, combines humor and eroticism. *Contra el amor en compañía* (1991; Against Accompanied Love) displays characters immersed in reading or writing. Riera's work is both feminist and erotic.

Isabel del Río (1945–) has published translations, biographical vignettes, and poetry, but her collection of short stories *La duda* (1995; Doubt) is her only book of fiction to date. It contains 14 short stories, of which "La duda," the title piece, portrays a princess overcome by doubts after she endures the test mandated by the king, her father, and the lecherous miser who seeks her affections. Doubt emerges as the central theme in these stories exploring human contradictions, obsessions, dreams, and nightmares. The subtitle, "y otros apuntes para escribir una colección de relatos" (and other notes for writing a collection of tales), points to the stories' metanarrative aspect. Fantasy blends into daily existence with constant references to and reflections on the writing and reading process. Fantasy is evoked through fairy tales, the oriental tradition in the genre, and the medieval author of frame stories, Don Juan Manuel.

Mercè Rodoreda i Gurgui (1908/1909–1983), recognized as one of the greatest modern Catalan writers, received the most important prizes of Catalan literature (Creix-

elles, 1937; Víctor Català, 1957; Premi d'Honor de las Lletres Catalanes, 1980; Ciudad de Barcelona, 1981). Her short stories are suggestive and full of lyricism and fantasy. *Vint-i-dos contes* (1957; Twenty Two Stories), printed in *Obres completes* (1976–1978), uses the social/cultural milieu of postwar Spain to create a strong thematic unity. *La meva Cristina i altres contes* (1967; My Christina and Other Stories, 1984) contains modern fantasies grounded in myth, traditional tales, and folklore. The lyricism and fantasy of *Semblava de seda i altres contes* (1978; It Seemed Like Silk and Other Stories) brings together various short stories without chronological or thematic unity. Some stories in *Viatges y flors* (1980; Travels and Flowers) were written in Geneva during Rodoreda's exile, and some in Spain. A deep pessimism pervades this work.

Montserrat Roig i Fransitorra (1946–1991) was known for her journalistic work and feminist essays as well as for her fiction. In the 1970s she wrote four novels and a book of short stories, all of which have been translated from Catalan, with numerous reprintings. *Molta roba i poc sabó* (1971; Lots of Clothes and Little Soap), reprinted at least five times and translated into Spanish as *Aprendizaje sentimental* (1981; Sentimental Apprenticeship), comprises short stories on contemporary Spanish society, specifically on the Catalonian middle class, and critiques the dead-end upbringing of its young people during the Franco regime. Roig's creative works almost always feature women characters who reflect the mentality of females at critical historical moments over the course of the century.

Ana Rossetti (1950–), primarily known as a poet, has also written several plays, novels, and essays. Her short story collection *Alevosías* (1991; Betrayals) received the Premio La Sonrisa Vertical, a collection devoted to erotica. Her poetic use of erotic images in *Alevosías* is evocative of a certain Georgia O'Keefe quality. A recurrent theme in Rossetti's stories is religiosity and the potential dangers of derailing from mystic aspirations, as sin and prohibition open the door to a latent sexuality.

Elena Santiago (1941–) combines creative writing with journalism. Although she has won major literary prizes for her short stories, her literary work in this genre remains largely unknown. *Relato con lluvia y otros cuentos* (1986; Tale with Rain and Other Stories), a collection of short stories marked by a lyrical tone, rescues the language of country people and maids, without turning it into local color or depriving it of dignity. The stories exhibit a marked obsession with time and explore new avenues for the genre. "Ni título" (Not Even a Title) is a good-bye letter that refuses to conform to typographical writing conventions because the sender, a woman failed by her husband and lover, has reached the conclusion that nothing makes sense anymore.

The best approach to Elena Soriano's (1918–1998) life and works may be *Testimonio materno* (1985; Maternal Testimony), a long autobiographical account of her son's death. In 1969 she founded the major literary journal *El urogallo*, which she edited and directed single-handedly until 1975. Carlos Saura based his film *Ana y los lobos* (1972; Ana and the Wolves) on Soriano's first novel, *Caza menor* (1951; Small Game Hunting). Her trilogy, formed by *La playa de los locos*, *Espejismos*, and *Medea* (1955; Beach of Madmen, Mirages, Medea), was published under the general title "Mujer y Hombre" (Woman and Man) since the three texts explore in lucid fashion the problems facing lovers. Soriano's participation in the "Año Internacional de la Mujer" in Madrid in 1976 indicates her interest in women's issues. *La vida pequeña* (1989; The Small Life) is a selection of previously published and unpublished stories by Soriano. Since they are dated, these 11 stories give a sense of the author's trajectory in the genre, from "El perfume" (The Perfume), written in 1949, to "El vídeo perfecto" (The Perfect Video),1989. This lesser-known facet of Soriano's writing

confirms her indebtedness to Ortega y Gasset's formulations concerning the human condition, that is, the combination of an innate sense of being and the social and historical circumstances that affect it.

Esther Tusquets (1936–) has directed Lumen publishing house since the early 1960s. Tusquet's fiction tends to explore monolithic taboos regarding sex and genre and to subvert rigid sexual demarcations. Besides her three novels, Tusquets has written the short story collection *Siete miradas en un mismo paisaje* (1981; Seven Gazes at One Landscape). The structure of the book challenges modern genre delimitations, as the tales appear interrelated by their common protagonist, Sara, a member of the Catalonian bourgeoisie observed with a keen eye at critical moments of her life. Another story, "La niña lunática" (The Lunatic Little Girl), is anthologized in *Cuentos eróticos* (1988), while "Las sutiles leyes de la simetría" (The Subtle Laws of Symmetry) appears in *Doce relatos de mujeres* (1982). *See also* Basque Women Writers: 1804–1997; Catalan Women Writers: A Brief History; Eroticism in Contemporary Spanish Women Writers' Narrative; Galician Women Writers: A Brief History

Work by

Anthologies

Cuento español contemporáneo. Ed. María Angeles Encinar and Anthony Percival. Madrid: Cátedra, 1993.

Cuentos de este siglo. Varias autoras. Ed. María Angeles Encinar. Barcelona: Lumen, 1995.

Cuentos del mar. Lisbon: Pabellón de España, 1998.

Cuentos eróticos. Barcelona: Grijalbo, 1988.

On Our Own Behalf. Women's Tales from Catalonia. Ed., intro., and notes Kathleen McNerney. Lincoln: U of Nebraska P, 1988.

Individual authors

Freixas, Laura. *Madres e hijas.* Barcelona: Anagrama, 1996.

Puértolas, Soledad. *Burdeos.* Trans. Francisca González-Arias. Lincoln: U of Nebraska P, 1998.

Riera, Carme. *Mirror Images*. Trans. Cristina de la Torre. New York: Peter Lang, 1993.

Rodoreda, Merce. *My Christina and Other Stories*. Trans., and intro. David H. Rosenthal. Port Townsend, WA: Graywolf, 1984.

Tusquets, Esther. *La niña lunática y otros cuentos*. 2nd ed. Barcelona: Lumen, 1997.

Work about

Encinar, Angeles. "Escritoras españolas actuales: Una perspectiva a través del cuento." *Hispanic Journal* (Spring 1992): 181–192.

López, Aurora, and María Ángeles Pastor, eds. *Crítica y ficción literaria: Mujeres españolas contemporáneas*. Granada: Universidad de Granada, 1989.

Pérez, Janet. "Characteristics of Erotic Brief Fiction by Women in Spain." *Monographic Review/Revista Monográfica* 7 (1991): 173–195.

———. *Contemporary Women Writers of Spain*. Boston. Twayne, 1988.

60 Catalan Language Women Writers Today. Generalitat de Catalunya: Institució de les Lletres Catalanes, 1990. Bio-bibliography.

Ana Rueda

Short Story
See Short Fiction entries

Sí de las niñas, El (1806)

El sí de las niñas (*The Maiden's Consent*, 1962), the quintessential neoclassical comedy by Leandro Fernández de *Moratín (1760–1828), is the literary masterpiece of the Spanish Enlightenment. The title refers to the tacit consent of young women to marriages arranged by their parents, an often suspect "yes" born of filial obedience that requires respectable daughters to repress their own opinions, wishes, and desires regarding matrimony. In this play, the reform-minded *ilustrado* (enlightened) Moratín criticizes three common social ills: the abuse of parental authority in coercing dutiful daughters into unwanted or unsuitable marriages, the refusal to allow women an active role in selecting a husband, and the limited education that in essence forces women to become hyp-

ocrites to please their parents, spouse, and community.

The play's action, which begins one evening and ends the following morning, takes place at an inn on the outskirts of Madrid. Don Diego, a wealthy, 59-year-old gentleman, has been persuaded by the manipulative, self-serving Doña Irene that he would make the perfect husband for her convent-educated, 16-year-old daughter Doña Francisca. Don Diego believes that Paquita (as she is nicknamed) wants to marry him of her own free will; however, the young woman appears to acquiesce to make her mother happy and financially secure. Yet unbeknown to Diego and Irene, Paquita has fallen in love with her fiancé's nephew, Don Carlos, to whom she appeals for help to avoid the unwanted marriage. When Carlos arrives at the inn, Paquita's hopes for deliverance initially rise, only to fall shortly thereafter as he abruptly departs. Eventually the elder suitor discovers the young couple's secret, and as the darkness of night and his irrational desires give way to the clear light of dawn and reason, Don Diego arranges the engagement of Carlos and Paquita and reconciles Doña Irene to the new, suitable match. During the final joyful scene, Don Diego voices the work's moral, warning the audience of the disastrous consequences of parental oppression combined with the cultivation of ignorance in young women.

Moratín deftly employs neoclassical aesthetics in *El sí de las niñas* to create a comedy that both instructs and entertains. While the author adheres to the Aristotelian unities in the play's composition, he balances witty repartee, aspects of farce, and the broad humorous strokes of the caricaturesque Doña Irene with moments of overt didacticism. Moratín attains the neoclassical ideals of harmony and proportion through the repetition of constitutive elements in units of two and three. Rita, Paquita's maid, accurately describes the unfolding dramatic situation as a *contradanza* (contredance). In this study in equipoise, the playwright juxtaposes an older with a younger couple, mismatch with love match, mother-daughter with uncle-nephew relationships, the selfless, rational Diego with the selfish, irrational Irene. Moratín's comedy also features three acts, a trio of servants, and three conversations in which Don Diego plumbs the depths of Doña Francisca's heart. Such repetitions endow *El sí de las niñas* with dramatic symmetry and an almost musical rhythm.

The play's plot and social themes invite comparison with Marivaux's *L'Ecole des mères* (1732) and Molière's *L'Ecole des femmes* (1662) even as its language and humor suggest the influence of Beaumarchais. Whatever their impact may have been, *El sí de las niñas* shows Moratín's profound commitment to the Bourbon monarchy's reform program concerning the status and education of women. The playwright, like the preponderance of Spain's *ilustrado* (enlightened) minority, recognized the primacy of the domestic sphere in molding individuals for their social roles and responsibilities. As teaching models of civility, morality, and industrious citizenship, wives and mothers occupied a privileged position in social reform and the development of the new Spanish middle class. The elite accordingly acknowledged that women were human beings with thoughts and feelings worthy of respect. Moratín's Paquita is denied this basic dignity when she is not permitted to participate in choosing her husband. Overbearing elders push her into deceit and dissimulation, perversely making the revelation of her genuine sentiments and true personality a potential source of shame and degradation. Don Diego, acting as a man of reason, frees Paquita from the prison of hypocrisy and secures for her the position of happy, virtuous wife.

Yet even as Moratín condemns societal vices, the social changes he advocates in the comedy pose no threat to the status quo for Spanish women. Paquita's modesty, passiveness, and obedience—traditional female virtues—are rewarded with the fulfillment of her fondest wishes. And while a woman's opinions should figure into the selection of her husband, Moratín indicates that these opinions should arise in frank discussions in which father and daughter strive to achieve a rational compromise on the matter, like those that occur between Don Diego and Doña Francisca. A female's place clearly remains in the home, where she discharges her duties as a loving, honorable wife and mother. An innocent maiden with a kind and gentle nature, Paquita offers the perfect, conventional complement for Carlos, a worldly officer, mathematics professor, and gentleman. In the world of Moratín's theater, the only acceptable alternative for respectable women is life in the convent, the option chosen by the protagonist Isabel at the end of his first play, *El viejo y la niña* (1790; The Old Man and the Girl). Indeed, the independent Agustina of Moratín's *La comedia nueva* (1792; The New Comedy), a rebellious bluestocking who rejects traditional female responsibilities, meets only with ridicule and frustration at the end of the work.

As his final and finest original play, *El sí de las niñas* embodies Moratín's belief in the power of the theater to educate and reform the public. This didactic comedy synthesizes the themes and aesthetic practices of the author's previous dramatic works, all of which, to a greater or lesser degree, focus on women's issues. Significantly, in *El sí de las niñas* Moratín lavishes the same compassion and sense of humanity on the older, comic Doña Irene (one example of the female character role he introduced to the Spanish stage) and the young ingenue Doña Francisca that he bestows on their male counterparts. By modern standards his views on women and social reform might seem limited or conventional, but in his plays Moratín consistently presents women as complex individuals worthy of sympathy and respect, rails against limited educational opportunities that foster ignorance and immorality in females, and argues for the right of women to lead useful, virtuous, happy lives, albeit anchored in the domestic structure of marriage and family that formed the pillar of Enlightenment society.

Work by

La comedia nueva. El sí de las niñas. Ed. John Dowling and René Andioc. Madrid: Castalia, 1978.

The Maiden's Consent. Trans. Harriet de Onís. New York: Barrons, 1962.

Teatro completo. Leandro Fernández de Moratín. Ed. Manuel Fernández Nieto. 2 vols. Madrid: Nacional, 1977.

Work about

Andioc, René. "Sobre Goya y Moratín hijo." *Hispanic Review* 50 (1982): 119–132.

———. *Teatro y sociedad en el Madrid del siglo XVIII.* 2nd ed. Madrid: Castalia, 1987.

Di Pinto, Mario. "La tesis feminista de Moratín: Una hipótesis de lectura de *El viejo y la niña.*" *Coloquio internacional sobre Leandro Fernández de Moratín—Bolonia, 27–29 de octubre 1978.* Abano Terme: Piovan, 1980. 75–91.

Dowling, John. "El comerciante gaditano: El Don Roque de Moratín." *Dieciocho* 16 (1993): 67–76.

———. "Moratín's Creation of the Comic Role for the Older Actress." *Theatre Survey* 24 (1983): 55–63.

———. "Words and Music: Moratín and the Musical Culture of His Age." *Modern Language Studies* 14 (1984): 84–95.

Froldi, Rinaldo. "El sentimiento como motivo literario en Moratín." *Coloquio internacional sobre Leandro Fernández de Moratín—Bolonia, 27–29 de octubre 1978.* Abano Terme: Piovan, 1980. 137–146.

Kish, Kathleen. "A School for Wives: Women in Eighteenth-Century Spanish Theater." *Women in Hispanic Literature: Icons and Fallen Idols.* Ed. Beth Miller. Berkeley and Los Angeles: U of California P, 1983. 184–200.

Llanos M., Bernardita. "Integración de la mujer al proyecto de la Ilustración en España." *Ideologies and Literature* 4 (1989): 199–223.

Maravall, José Antonio. "Del despotismo ilustrado a una ideología de clases medias: Significación de Moratín." *Coloquio internacional sobre Leandro Fernández de Moratín—Bolonia, 27–29 de octubre 1978.* Abano Terme: Piovan, 1980. 163–192.

———. "The Idea and Function of Education in Enlightenment Thought." *The Institutionalization of Literature in Spain.* Trans. Terry Cochran. Ed. Wlad Godzich and Nicholas Spadaccini. Minneapolis: Prisma Institute, 1987. 39–99.

Marías, Julián. "Moratín y la originalidad del siglo XVIII español." *Coloquio internacional sobre Leandro Fernández de Moratín—Bolonia, 27–29 de octubre 1978.* Abano Terme: Piovan, 1980. 193–199.

Martín Gaite, Carmen. *Usos amorosos del dieciocho en España.* Madrid: Siglo Veintiuno de España, 1972.

Menton, Seymour. "La contradanza de Moratín." *Romance Notes* 23 (1982–1983): 238–244.

Sebold, Russell P. "Autobiografía y realismo en *El sí de las niñas.*" *Coloquio internacional sobre Leandro Fernández de Moratín—Bolonia, 27–29 de octubre 1978.* Abano Terme: Piovan, 1980. 213–227.

Sherman, Alvin F., Jr. "Leandro Fernández de Moratín: Distanciamiento y silencio autorial." *Dieciocho* 14 (1991): 69–79.

Marsha S. Collins

Siete partidas, Las

See Alfonso el Sabio (1221–1284): Women in *Las siete partidas*

Silva, Beatriz de (1424–1491)

Blessed Beatriz de Silva y Meneses was born in Ceuta, a Christian enclave on the Moroccan coast near Gibraltar. She received an extensive education in Campo Maior (Portugal) and became a lady-in-waiting to Princess Isabel of Portugal. When the princess married Juan II de Castilla in 1447, Beatriz moved to Spain with her mistress. There, according to the popular legends dramatized by Tirso de *Molina (1582–1648) in *Doña Beatriz de Silva* and Lope de *Vega (1562–1635) in *El milagro de los celos*, she was courted by the king, which provoked so much jealousy in her mistress that Isabel had her locked in a chest. During her confinement, Beatriz received a vision of the Virgin Mary (*Marianism), who instructed her to persevere because she had been chosen to serve a higher mistress. When she was released, Beatriz fled the court and lived as a cloistered nun for the next 30 years in the Dominican monastery of Santo Domingo el Real (Toledo). She became a close friend of Queen *Isabel la Católica (1451–1504), and the two planned the foundation of a new order in honor of the Immaculate Conception. Isabel ceded the famous Palaces of Galiana in Toledo to Beatriz for use as a convent, and in 1484 Pope Innocent VIII recognized the new group as Franciscan Conceptionists under the rule of Cister but subject to the archbishop of Toledo. The order now has over 130 monasteries (90 in Spain) and approximately 3,000 sisters.

Work about

Abad, A. "Beatriz de Silva." *Diccionario de historia eclesiástica de España.* Madrid: CSIC, 1975.4: 2478–2479.

David H. Darst

Sinués de Marco, María del Pilar (1835–1893)

Unquestionably the most representative Spanish woman writer of domestic literature, Sinués's portrayal of the nineteenth-century stereotype known as the "domestic angel" (**ángel del hogar*) is particularly interesting for the influence she ascribes to the aristocracy in configuration and support of this middle-class role model. María del Pilar Sinués was born in Zaragoza and moved to Madrid after her sight-unseen marriage to the journalist D. José Marco, with whom Sinués started her career as a writer. In 1861, in an emotional preface to *Fausta Sorel*, Sinués dedicated the novel to her husband and remembered the happy years of working together. Paradoxically, theirs was far from being the ideal family she used to write about; her husband finally abandoned her, and she died alone in Madrid.

Sinués was an extremely prolific writer. Sometimes under the pseudonym "Laura," but most of the time under her own name, she published around 100 books, hundreds of contributions to newspapers and magazines such as *El Imparcial, El correo de la moda, La Tribuna, La correspondencia de España, La familia,* and *La moda elegante,* as well as several translations from French and English. She was also director of the journal *El ángel*

del hogar. Her literary production ranged from domesticity and historical novels to short stories, legends, and essays. The education of women is a characteristic shared by all her works, with the most important writings being those dealing with women's social conduct. Sinués's writings found a great acceptance among middle-class bourgeois families because of their didactic tone and the exemplary, submissive female characters of her novels, which became very popular in Spain, America, and some European countries. The impact of Sinués's moralizing books was such that, for example, *La ley de Dios* (1858; The Law of God) and *A la luz de la lámpara* (1862; By the Light of the Lamp) were required readings in some schools. Some of her works were translated into foreign languages or published in the original Spanish by international publishing houses.

In spite of the sociological interest of her works, the extremely conservative ideology expressed in them, the questionable literary quality of her novels and short stories, and the traditional discrimination received by women's literary production contributed to Sinués's gradual fall into oblivion. Until recently, she was only mentioned in a few literary dictionaries and in some essays dealing with her version of the nineteenth-century domestic angel concept. However, new studies on nineteenth-century Spanish women writers are beginning to approach Sinués's production from different angles.

Work by

El ángel del hogar. Madrid: Nieto, 1859.
Cortesanas ilustres. Madrid: Calleja, 1878.
Doña Urraca Queen of Leon and Castile. Trans. Reginald Huth. Bath: Wilkinson, 1890.
Fausta Sorel. Madrid: Española, 1861.
La misión de la mujer. Barcelona: Manero, 1886.
Mis vigilias. Zaragoza: Cristóbal Juste y Olana, 1854.
Morir sola. Madrid: Giménez, 1890.
La mujer en nuestros días. Madrid: Jubera, 1878.

Work about

Charnon-Deutsch, Lou. *Narratives of Desire: Nineteenth-Century Spanish Fiction by Women.* University Park: Pennsylvania State UP, 1994.

Simón Palmer, María del Carmen. *Escritoras espa ñolas del siglo XIX: Manual bio-bibliográfico*. Madrid: Castalia, 1991.

Joan Torres-Pou

Sobrino, Cecilia (late sixteenth century–1646) a.k.a. Cecilia del Nacimiento

The daughter of Antonio Sobrino and Cecilia Morillas, Cecilia Sobrino was born in Valladolid. She studied Latin, humanities, painting, and poetry, professed in the Discalced Carmelite order, and rose to become abbess of the Calahorra Convent. In 1612 she returned to Valladolid.

Sobrino wrote poetry and short tracts (*opúsculos*) about biblical scripture and in defense of the Immaculate Conception (*Marianism). She composed a biography of her sister María de *San Alberto, prioress of the Valladolid convent, and also painted her portrait. Her *Canciones* (Songs) use those of San *Juan de la Cruz (1542–1591) as their model.

Work by

Obras completas. Notes and study Father José M. Díaz Cerón. Madrid: Editorial de Espiritualidad, 1970.

Work about

Arenal, Electra and Stacey Schlau. *Untold Sisters, Hispanic Nuns in Their Own Works*. Trans. by Amanda Powell. Albuquerque: U of New Mexico P, 1989. 131–189.

Serrano y Sanz, Manuel. *Apuntes para una biblioteca de escritoras españolas desde el año 1401 al 1833*. 2 vols. Madrid: Rivadeneyra, 1903. Rpt. Madrid: Atlas, 1975.

Elena Cámara

Sopetrán Julie (twentieth century)

This Guadalajara-born journalist spent 10 years in California before returning to Madrid. She has published six volumes of poetry to date and received the fourth Carmen Conde Prize for Women's Poetry for *Los

Dioses y el Anfora* (1987; The Gods and the Amphora).

Julia Sopetrán writes an unstructured, lyrical verse that is at once introspective and exploratory in nature. She presents herself as very comfortable in her role as writer; several poems discuss her situation as that of a vessel waiting to be filled by an unspecified presence so that she in turn may pass on the resulting verses to her audience. Her favorite themes include art, nature, the relationship between the two, and how that relationship can connect humanity to the world and the forces around it. One book of poems, *Silvas de mi selva en ocaso* (1985; Poems from My Forest at Dusk), is a unified collection, with each poem carrying an art term or tool as the title in a thorough examination of the creative process. For Sopetrán, art and the act of creation are the basis for the existence of this world and all that inhabit it.

Work by

Amorismos. Barcelona: Rondas, 1984.
Los Dioses y el Anfora. Madrid: Torremozas, 1987.
En Hita hoy es otoño y se oye el mar. By Juanita González Barba [Julie Sopetrán]. Guadalajara: Avena Loca, 1990.
Polvo luminoso. Guadalajara: Gacela, 1984.
Un siglo en Atherton. Barcelona: Rondas, 1984.
Silvas de mi selva en ocaso. Madrid: Torremozas, 1985.

Work about

Wing, Helen. "Julie Sopetrán and Jorge Guillén: Poetry of Harmony?" *Women Writers in Twentieth-Century Spain and Spanish America*. Ed. and intro. Catherine Davies. Conclusion Montserrat Ordóñez. Lewiston, NY: Mellen, 1993. 177–194.

Shannon W. Sudderth

Suárez del Otero, Concha (1908–)

Novelist, poet, essayist, critic, and short story writer, Concha Suárez del Otero was born in the village of Luarca in northwestern Spain, in the picturesque province of Asturias. She later studied at the province's prestigious, historic University of Oviedo and returned to teach Spanish literature there after receiving her doctorate from the University of Madrid. Suárez scored an early success with her first novel *Mabel* (1928), published when she was barely 20, recreating the life of a young schoolteacher in a remote Asturian mountain village who struggles to adapt successfully to the loss of her family's once-comfortable lifestyle and to communicate with people whose backgrounds and culture differ greatly from her own. In *Vulgaridades* (1930; Ordinary Things), the author traces the friendship of two Asturian girls, Marta and Carmen, dreamy adolescents whose aspirations are slowly modified by reality. The two novels have in common their study of young women's process of maturation and adjustment. Following a 19-year hiatus in her publishing (1930–1949), Suárez returned to writing in a variety of genres—the essay, poetry, novel, and short story—publishing a poetry collection, *Vida plena* (1949; Full Life). It is composed of three sections corresponding to developmental stages in her life—a more or less autobiographical poetic journal of maturation. *La vida en un día* (1951; Life in a Day) contains a dozen stories analyzing mostly feminine viewpoints and treating themes such as love, domesticity, and loneliness. A second story collection, *Mi amiga Andrée* (1954; My Friend Andrée), reiterates many themes (and repeats four of the stories) of the first volume but enlarges upon the author's exploration of feminine existential quandaries, the conflict between self-realization and the need for security, and the search for happiness.

Among her mature novels is *Satanás no duerme* (1958; Satan Doesn't Sleep). One month before the outbreak of the Spanish Civil War in July 1939, six high school friends in Madrid vow to meet again in 10 years. The narrative traces their lives and loves in the intervening decade, from the traumatic civil conflict and its bitter aftermath to their eventual reunion, at which time the friends realize how much they have changed and how little they now have in common. A more recent work featuring a female protagonist is *Me llamo Clara* (1968; My Name is Clara), considered by most commentators to be the writer's best achievement. Stylistically, it belongs to the postneorealist trend toward modified experimentalism. The protagonist of this metafictional romance is writing an autobiographical novel for which the publisher has paid a cash advance, and the first part comprises a lengthy fragment of her manuscript—a novel within a novel. Clara's vocation is not as a novelist, but having lost her teaching job, she needs the money; the manuscript is interrupted when she becomes a tour guide for a Madrid travel agency, setting off in pursuit of adventure across half a dozen countries. Following an ill-fated romance and frustrated marriage plans, Clara returns to Spain for an inconclusive ending that seems to leave the door open for a sequel. Apparently the writer subsequently abandoned Clara, perhaps because relaxing of constraints in the twilight years of the Franco regime began to make it possible for many young women to seek adventures on their own rather than merely read about them.

Suárez del Otero's work is feminine rather than feminist but is noteworthy for being written about and for young women; the first two novels hold special interest because of the picturesque Asturian environment and depiction of a bygone age. Although her works today seem a bit quaint and nostalgic, "old-fashioned" beside the works of younger feminists, Suárez herself provides an early example of the independent "careeer woman," something of a rarity for her generation in Spain. *See also* Short Fiction by Women Writers: 1900–1975

Work by

Mabel. Madrid: Biblioteca Patria, 1928.
Me llamo Clara. Madrid: Quevedo, 1968.
Mi amiga Andrée. Madrid: Afrodisio Aguado, 1954.
Satanás no duerme. Madrid: Prensa Española, 1958.
La vida en un día. Madrid: S. Aguirre, 1951.
Vida plena. Madrid: Afrodisio Aguado, 1949.

Janet Pérez

Suffrage in Spain: 1908–1931

Spain did not have a full-blown suffrage movement. The reasons usually given for this absence are the country's undeveloped capitalism that failed to establish a broad middle class, a social structure that resisted the integration of women into higher education and the workforce, and an enduring ideological conservatism vigorously perpetuated by the Catholic Church. During the nineteenth century, the defenders of women centered their discussions on educational and labor issues rather than on civil rights. While women in England and the United States wrote manifestos and held meetings to demand the right to vote, the first public recommendation of suffrage for women in Spain was made by male legislators in 1908. Even in an amended and diminished form, this early proposal failed. After his assumption of power in 1923, the dictator Miguel Primo de Rivera displayed a paternalistic interest in the rights of women and made a number of political concessions to them. Having granted suffrage to unmarried women over 23, in 1927 he appointed 13 women to the national assembly, an ineffective advisory body.

After the declaration of the Second Republic in 1931, the question of women's suffrage surfaced during the debates on the new constitution. Many male politicians of the Right as well as the Left opposed the measure because they sensed a political advantage in it for their ideological opponents. The parties of the Left, however, had greater cause for concern because upbringing and inexperience had conditioned most Spanish women to embrace conservative thought. Among liberal women, the notion of suffrage did not receive universal support. Of the two women elected to Parliament, Victoria *Kent (1898–1987) argued that women lacked the preparation necessary for political involvement, while Clara *Campoamor (1888–1972) championed the cause of women's right to vote. Despite passionate arguments against suffrage for women, the Republican Parliament granted them the vote in October 1931. It was in effect nullified by the Franco regime (1939–1975), which held no free elections. *See also* Women's Situation in Spain: 1931–1975: The Second Spanish Republic, the Spanish Civil War and Its Aftermath

Work about

Capel, Rosa María. *El sufragio femenino en la 2a república española*. Granada: Universidad de Granada, 1975.

Fagoaga, Concha. *La voz y el voto de las mujeres. El sufragismo en España. 1877–1931*. Barcelona: Icaria, 1985.

Scanlon, Geraldine. *La polémica feminista en la España contemporánea: 1868–1974*. Madrid: Siglo XXI, 1976; Madrid: Akal, 1986.

Catherine G. Bellver

Syphilis as Sickness and Metaphor in Early Modern Spain: 1492–1650

After 1492 there appeared in Europe the first literary references to a new venereal disease later known as syphilis. This new plague exposed intimate sins publicly. It carried a heavy load of meanings: body, dirt, filth, sin, and sex. The new nameless illness was related to a capital sin that was becoming a favorite topic in European churches: lust. And lust brought upon humankind the deadliest punishment, variously called the "morbo gálico," the "serpentine evil," the "pestilential scorra," the "Neapolitan evil," the "French evil," the "grande verole," the "greñimón," until finally it was given a mythical name: Syphilis. This new malady became a symbol of the fallen body and the fallen soul, and as such a symbol it found its place in literature.

The first references to venereal diseases appeared in a sober literature of transition between medieval and reformist Renaissance moral satire. The focus was representation of social and individual vices and sins; the style was simple; the Bible was the source of inspiration. There was a feeling of proximity between the writer and the reader. By the end of the fifteenth and beginning of the sixteenth century, three Spaniards had published scientific poems on the subject—a venereal disease already identified. The three writers, all medical doctors, chose poetry as a medium, and Spanish as the language rather than Latin, the usual language for medical publications. During the aegis of European humanism, medicine and literature were not separate subjects, since both were used as complementary disciplines to study the human being. This literature of exploration studied syphilis, placing the new sickness in historical and cultural context. Although these texts are primarily informative, their authors were also concerned with the aesthetics of their writings. The sickness carried a stigma in moral literature—as well as in artistic and informative literature—related to the paradox of its origin: Syphilis is death that starts during copulation and therefore is the product of an act of creation of life. It was not perceived as a simple mistake of nature, since sexuality carried a heavy burden of political connotations in the European Reformation and Counterreformation period.

Syphilis entered Reformation and Antireformation literary loci as an illness transmitted mainly by women; therefore, it was a useful theme for misogynist literature. There were implications of spiritual weakness in having the "pestilential scorra," as syphilis was also known. The sufferer of syphilis was a sinner, lustful, and at the mercy of the lowest passions of the flesh, thus good material for humor and literary creation.

During the 1500s syphilis acquired a diversified semantic value in social culture. It was not only a divine punishment but also the immediate consequence of unnatural unions between old and young, sex out of wedlock, or sex in an unlawful union—for instance, if one of the spouses is deceiving the other. Syphilis was to love what the anti-Christ was to Jesus: a condemnation with the appearance of salvation. In literature, syphilis

moved from scientific literature to nonutilitarian artistic literature. In the process it was dehumanized to become a perfect symbol for the marginal. Its presence moved from poetry to prose. The symbol acquired a value of its own, separated from the social and medical reality that originated it. Now the writer could create a particular vision of the world writing through the experience of a man or a woman who suffered syphilis or suggest a pure world of health and beauty via expressing the absence of syphilis. Venereal disease, associated with madness, was invited to participate in the construction of perspective in the text. Finally, by the 1600s the representation of syphilis acquired other connotations, reflecting the need for representation of deceit and disappointment. In the Spanish Baroque, a time of social despair, syphilis served to represent the feeling of internal destruction that afflicted the individual, the social decay, and a world captured in the process of self-destruction.

In 1498, Francisco López Villalobos described the arrival of the disease thus: "A terrible pestilence never seen before and never written neither in verse or in prose, or in science or in history, for which there is no cure and that starts in the most 'lowly place that we have' [meaning of course the genitals], because it is a lowly illness." López de Villalobos expressed surprise that this curse had fallen upon Spain, which, according to the writer, was at the summit of success; God was on Spain's side but nevertheless allowed this catastrophe to happen to His people. In 1494, Juan de Vigo described the symptoms of a new illness that he called "the French disease"—as did Italian doctors Cumanus and Benedetto—and gave some ideas about cures (the usual at the time): mercury, boiling baths, and purges. The disease also had been named "the Neapolitan evil" in France, "the Spanish evil" in England, always depending upon the transnational antipathies of kingdoms. Ruy Díaz de Isla, in 1514, was the first to tie the new sexual disease to the discovery of the New

World. He described in Spanish a new illness that men on the first expedition led by Christopher Columbus had contracted in the Americas. Díaz de Isla also suggested the possibility that it was a mutation of an already existing malady. He called the new illness the "serpentine evil."

Girolamo Francastoro invented the word *syphilis* in his long mythical explanatory poem *Syphilis, sive Morbus Gallicus* (1530), published in Verona with the approval of Pietro Bembo. Francastoro's hexameters narrated that the illness was brought by Spaniards from America, that it could appear spontaneously in some people, but it could also be transmitted through coitus. The process was determined by the position of the stars and the planets, particularly those known as carriers of misfortune: Saturn and Mars. Francastoro dedicated a fragment of his work to the cures common at the time, and in the last part of his poem he created the myth of Syphilus. Syphilus cursed the good Sun, and his punishment was to suffer burning wounds. He asked Calirrhoe for help. Being aware that Syphilus's pain could not be cured under the Sun light, Calirrhoe sent him to a dark cave where the nymph Lipari awaited him. In the cave Lipari guided Syphilus to a river of mercury, from which, after submerging himself 10 times, he emerged cured of his sickness. Francastoro gathered in his poem all that was known about the illness, but most important he transmitted a vision of a world where individual destiny was determined by the planets: History and astrology were inseparable concepts.

Published in Spain, the *Chistes del Greñimón* (1552–1610; Jokes of Greñimón) are moral poems representing men who have suffered syphilis. The authors (these are collective poems) gave sufficient information about victims to allow contemporary readers to identify them. We see a clear intention of offense: The purpose of these *Chistes* is not to warn but to destroy the social prestige of those included in the poems. Mockery and social scorn of the ill predominate, with cruel, detailed descriptions of the physical features of the victims, lack of hair, lack of eyebrows, dysfunctional bodies. Chronologically, the *Chistes del Greñimón* belongs fully to the Spanish Baroque, although it is a continuation of medieval moral poetry written for the masses, using vernacular languages and possessing an exemplary intent.

A little-known book written in Spanish and published in Venice, the *Retrato de la *Lozana andaluza* (1528; Portrait of the Lusty Andalusian Woman) is the most important piece of literature that contains syphilis not only as a secondary topic but as a part of the process of creation of literature itself. In the prologue to his novel, Francisco Delicado (1480?–1534) introduces a character he names "the author" who is in a hospital recovering from the *morbo gálico*. He decides to write a book to forget his suffering and for the amusement of those that "Fortune made passionate like me." Later we see the same author writing at home, with his protagonist Lozana thanking him for composing a fair portrayal of her and for immortalizing her. After the Sack of Rome in 1527, the fictitious "author" leaves Rome, as does his character Lozana. Lozana is a young woman who engages in all types of business, licit and illicit, to survive the underworld of Roman streets. Being a woman of grace and beauty, one of her main assets is her body, and one of her physical characteristics is a sagging nose. The nose seems to be an important element since it recurs in the text. Physical description of someone with syphilis is a novelty of *Lozana*: The writer specifies that the syphilitic loses his hair, the body is in pain, and the sexual organs are sore. Lozana's clients as prostitute are also her clients for a cure or remedy that will alleviate their suffering. The parade of Lozana's patients includes cardinals, soldiers, merchants, and prostitutes. The *Retrato de la Lozana andaluza* is not a canonical book. Critics do not consider it theater, although it is written as dialogue; though written in Spanish, it was not published or recognized by the literary world in Spain until the nineteenth century. It is difficult to classify because it follows no specific literary tradition. Delicado published the *Lozana* anonymously, at least partly because he was a Catholic priest running away from Spain first, and from the Sack of Rome later, in 1527. The stigma of marginalization is inherent in this particular representation of syphilis.

In the Spanish feminine picaresque, there are two novels in which male authors introduce their feminine protagonists with a physical description that connotes their immoral characters: in *Retrato de la Lozana Andaluza*, as we have seen already, and in the **Pícara Justina* (1605), by López de Ubeda. Justina is not as young and beautiful as Lozana; an older woman, she narrates the history of her life after joining in unholy matrimony with another well-known character in the Spanish picaresque, Guzmán de Alfarache. As Justina writes her story, a hair falls from her head and sticks to her pen. The author uses this excuse to have Justina meditate about her sad destiny and the "bitter memories of her French baldness." Justina relates that she went to bed healthy in Spain and awoke sick in France, continuing in a chain of phrases about dirt, putrid hidden sickness, and apparent health. She is by her own definition a peach, rosy on the outside and rotten within.

Miguel de Cervantes uses syphilis in his exemplary novel *El casamiento engañoso* (1613; The Deceitful Marriage). *El casamiento engañoso* is the literary prologue intercalated in another exemplary novel, *El coloquio de los perros* (The Dogs' Colloquy). Each text contains a picaresque autobiography, and each presents the topics of deceit and disillusionment, representing Cervantes's notion of these problems in the social world. Deceit results from the individual evils of selfishness and greed. In *El casamiento engañoso*, the man of letters Peralta runs into his old friend Campuzano, a soldier, in the streets of Valladolid, by the Hospital de la Resurrec-

ción. Peralta notices how pale and sick Campuzano looks. Campuzano, just out of the hospital, complains about his illness, *bubas* in Spanish, given to him by a woman he had married. When Peralta inquires whether he married for love, Campuzano answers that he does not know but that he definitely married for pain. Peralta further explains that his physical illness can be treated, but his soul will not heal. As the two friends go to eat, Campuzano relates to Peralta how he married an apparently wealthy lady, Doña Estefanía, who lured him into marriage. Afterwards, Campuzano learned that she had lied about her income, her properties, and her social status. Worse still, Doña Estefanía escaped with all of Campuzano's belongings, particularly his thick, flashy gold chain. Even though this jewelry was fake, he was hurt because this woman he had thought to be an angel had outsmarted him. He lost not only the anticipated dowry but also his health and, most important of all, his control of the situation.

Cervantes brings into his exemplary novel the biblical idea of lust but also treats a contemporary situation within its social and cultural framework. What moves Campuzano first is the sight of the "white as snow" hand of Doña Estefanía. But after that first lusty impulse, what concerns the soldier is securing his material well-being. In *El casamiento engañoso* Cervantes presents a situation that transcends the individual to represent a collective vision of the moment. Early-seventeenth-century Spanish society suffered a depressed economy resulting from the political unrest in Spain and Europe plus the bad health of a population reduced one-third by the "plagues." The baroque person is an agonic, lonely individual, thrown into a fight for survival. Therefore, the principle motivating Campuzano is selfishness, and the result of his scheme is self-destruction. The irony of this exemplary novel is that the individual does not acknowledge the moral lesson that could be drawn from his experience.

The soldier Campuzano functions as a mediocre intelligence, unaware of the situation and lacking concern for others, trapped by the dishonesty of his intentions concerning his estranged wife. His resolution vis-à-vis his sexual relations for the future constructs an accurate portrait of an unprincipled antisocial individual. The punishment for his deceitful intentions, while not immediate, is fatal. Campuzano married his own death. By using syphilis and fake jewelry, Cervantes symbolically satirizes the ultimate exchange of matrimonial vows. The connotations of this exchange are a double folly, in the material world: the hollowness of material goods, including sex as origin of death; and in the spiritual realm, the death of the soul as consequence of lack of *caritas*/love and the sin of deceit. *See also* Misogyny in Medieval and Early Modern Spain; *Pícaras* and *Pícaros*: Female and Male Rogues in the Spanish Picaresque Canon

Work about

Casalduero, Joaquín. *Sentido y forma de las* Novelas Ejemplares. Madrid: Gredos, 1962.

Cervantes, Miguel de. *Novelas ejemplares*. Intro. and notes Juan Bautista Avalle-Arce. Vol. 3. Madrid: Clásicos Castalia, 1982.

Delicado, Francisco. *Portrait of Lozana: The Lusty Andalusian Woman*. Trans., intro., and notes Bruno Damiani. Potomac, MD: Scripta Humanistica, 1987.

———. *Retrato de la Lozana andaluza en Roma*. Ed., notes, and intro. Giovanni Alegra and Bruno Damiani. Madrid: Porrúa, 1975.

Farrell, Anthony. "Sebastián de Horozco y la tradición poética de la cofradía de Greñimón." *Hispanófila* 71–73 (1981): 1–10.

López de Ubeda, Francisco. *La pícara Justina*. Madrid: Sociedad de bibliófilos madrileños, 1912.

Maravall, José Antonio. *La cultura del Barroco*. Barcelona: Ariel, 1975.

Scheiner, Winfried. "Infection and Cure through Women: Renaissance Construction of Syphilis." *Journal of Medieval and Renaissance Studies* 24.3 (Fall 1994): 499–517.

María Luisa García-Verdugo

Tapada

See Cubiertas *and* Tapadas

Téllez, Gabriel

See Molina, Tirso de, Pseudonym of Gabriel Téllez (1582–1648): Women in His Theater

Tercera

La tercera, also known in Spanish by the names *medianera* or *alcahueta*, or in English by the term *go-between*, is a name given to the literary character who arranges illicit amorous relations between a man and his would-be lover. This character, most prevalent during the medieval and Renaissance periods, is typically portrayed as an older woman who is frequently a former prostitute. She is astute and uses her knowledge of human nature to manipulate her victims. Occasionally she employs witchcraft and other trickery as well.

The type originated in the works of Ovid and Eastern literature and was first developed in Spanish literature by Juan Ruiz, archpriest of Hita, in El *libro de buen amor* (1335, 1343; *The Book of Good Love*, 1972). In this work, Don Melón seeks the aid of Urraca, the *trotaconventos* or convent-trotter, to seduce Doña Endrina. After successfully arranging this liaison, she suggests he might also enjoy the favors of a nun, Doña Garoça. Doña Garoça and the *trotaconventos* die shortly after Don Melón possibly enjoyed the nun's favors. Upon the *trotaconventos's* death, in one of the most ironic passages in the book, the archpriest states his "saintly bawd" has a place with the martyrs in Heaven due to her suffering and service on Earth.

The quintessential *tercera* in Spanish literature is the masterfully depicted character Celestina in Fernando de Rojas's *Tragicomedia de Calisto y Melibea* (1499; La **Celestina*, 1969). In this work, Celestina convinces Melibea to accept Calisto's advances through manipulation and magic spells in dialogues that reveal Celestina's exceptional psychological penetration and ability to manipulate others.

Celestina was imitated heavily in later works. Celestine characters appear in a wide range of texts from the *comedia* (theater) to picaresque novels. Notable examples are the go-betweens Eritea and Fulgencia in Juan del Encina's *Eglogas* (c. 1510), Brígida Vaz in Gil Vicente's *Barca de Infierno* (c.1520), Teodora and Terecinda in the *Comedia del infamador* (1581) by Juan de la Cueva, Fabia in Lope de **Vega's* The Knight of Olmedo (c. 1620), and Teresa in Alonso de Castillo Solórzano's La **niña de los embustes* (1632), who boasts of the riches she accumulates as her mistress's go-between.

Spanish authors of both fiction and essay throughout the Middle Ages and Renaissance warn against the dangers of employing a *tercera* or falling victim to her wiles. Although the bawd was usually colorfully portrayed, she was included in fiction primarily as an example of the type of person to be avoided. She was seen as an individual that could cloud man's reason and cause him to fall into sin. Worse still, if such a person were admitted into a man's house, she could lead his wife, daughters, or sisters astray and damage his *honor*. See also *Pícaras and Pícaros: Female and Male Rogues in the Spanish Picaresque Canon*

Work about

Dunn, Peter N. *Fernando de Rojas*. TWAS 368. Boston: Twayne, 1975.

Gilman, Stephen. *The Art of the Celestina*. Madison: U of Wisconsin P, 1956.

————. *The Spain of Fernando de Rojas*. Princeton, NJ: Princeton UP, 1973.

Lida de Malkiel, María Rosa. *Two Spanish Masterpieces: The "Book of Good Love" and the "Celestina."* Urbana: U of Illinois P, 1961.

Rojas, Fernando de. *The Spanish Bawd*. Trans. J.M. Cohen. Harmondsworth and Baltimore: Penguin, 1964.

————. *La Celestina*. Ed. D.S. Severin. Intro. S. Gilman. Madrid: Alianza, 1969.

Karoline J. Manny

Teresa de Jesús, Santa (1515–1582)

The first person to write an autobiography of any length in Spanish, Santa Teresa de Jesús provides vital information on attitudes toward women in sixteenth-century Spain. She also serves as model of the achieving woman for her administrative and literary work. Her manuscripts, published posthumously, include *Libro de su vida* (1562–1565; *The Life of Santa Teresa*, 1960), *Camino de perfección* (1562; *Way of Perfection*, 1964), *Libro de las fundaciones* (1573–1576–1582; *Foundations*, 1979), *Moradas del castillo interior* (1577; *Interior Castle*, 1961), *Relaciones espirituales/Cuentos de conciencia* (1560–1581; Spiritual Relations/Stories of Conscience), *Exclamaciones del alma a Dios* (1569; Exclamations of the Soul to God), *Meditaciones sobre los Cantares/Conceptos del amor de Dios* (1566–1575; Meditations on the Song of Songs/Concepts of the Love of God), 31 poems, and 458 letters. Luis de *León (1527–1591), who undertook publication of her works, considered it a miracle that a woman could have accomplished so much.

She was born Teresa de Cepeda y Ahumada on March 28, 1515, in Avila to a wealthy merchant family and died on October 4, 1582. Canonized in 1622, her feast day is October 15. Recognition of her authority in mystical theology came belatedly in 1970 when the Roman Catholic Church named her its first female doctor. In Castro's view, Teresa overcame alienation springing from the Jewish origin of the Cepeda family through her "spontaneous" mystical writing. Teresa regarded reading romances and falling (after her mother's death) into a mild flirtation with a cousin as the major sins of her preconvent life. The favorite child of her father and a person who easily found favor with others throughout her life, Teresa defied his wishes to enter the Carmelite Convent of the Incarnation at Avila in 1534. Following a life-threatening illness in 1537, she began to study and practice the instructions in Francisco de Osuna's *Tercer Abecedario*, a treatise on mental prayer. For 20 years she lived quietly in the liberal Carmelite convent. Then, following her reading of Saint Augustine's *Confessions*, she underwent a spiritual reawakening and began with renewed vigor to practice mental prayer. Teresa rose to ever greater heights of spiritual life, which she described as the four waters of the *Vida* and the seven interior mansions of the *Moradas*.

Teresa began the reform of the Carmelite Order in 1558, establishing her first convent, St. Joseph's, in 1562, where she instituted cloistering of the nuns for devotion to prayer and imposed the rule of poverty. Her convents depended on public alms rather than on the nobles' private endowment. She endured protest from religious and municipal authorities by identifying with the persecuted Christ. Through an active letter campaign, she persuaded the pope to send his emissary John Baptist Rossi, the Carmelite prior general, to Avila in 1567. Receiving permission to continue her foundations, she established 16 more convents and enlisted San *Juan de la Cruz to establish reformed monasteries. Ordered to retire to her Sevillian convent in 1575 because of a jurisdictional dispute with the regular Carmelites, Teresa appealed to Philip II and Pope Gregory XIII. She returned to her reform in 1580, gaining the nickname *la Andariega* (The Gadabout) for her journeys throughout Spain. She died, possibly of uterine cancer, in 1582.

Investigated by the Inquisition several times during her life and after her death, Teresa managed to thread her way through the politics of sixteenth-century Spain. The coquettish tone of her letters reveals that she owed success to beauty and a forceful personality as well as to intelligence and expressive power. De la Virgen del Carmen, describing the "human Teresa," points to her "feminine" qualities of sincerity, delicacy of feeling, and affection apparent in her concern for the physical and emotional health of others. She valued these same characteristics in her nuns, openly stating her refusal of accepting "homely" novices. Despite her oft-stated humility and allegiance to the Church, she dared undertake exegesis of the Song of Songs, the most controversial biblical text of her day.

In post-Tridentine Spain pietistic works were often suspected of unorthodox Protestant tendencies. Oñate in the 1930s emphasized Teresa's humble submission to the confessors who directed her writing. In Oñate's view, "the sainted mother" wrote for the edification of the nuns in the reformed Carmelite convents and strove to improve their deficient education. Ostensibly Teresa bowed to the prevailing view of women as inferior to men; she frequently affirmed her own lowly status and spoke of feminine weakness in general (*Vida*, ch. 23; *Fundaciones*, ch. VI, etc.). Nevertheless, she also insisted that Christ respected women (*Camino de perfección*, ch. 3), that women had done heroic deeds (*Vida*, ch. 21), and that parents err in regretting the birth of daughters (*Fundaciones*, ch. 20).

More recent critics have expanded Oñate's interpretation. Rodríguez and Donahue tally 13 negative comments about women in the *Vida* but two qualitatively important positive comments disassociating women from evil. Deneuville, judging that Teresa was neither feminist nor antifeminist, points to the 13 times she used the phrase "nosotras, mujeres" (we, women), sometimes to deplore female ignorance but also to offer hope of knowledge. Quitsland points out that Teresa encouraged her nuns to avoid petty rivalries. Díaz Castañón, Weber, Comas, and Dobhan stress Teresa's drive toward the spiritual emancipation of women that depended upon their spiritual instruction and growth. In the other-worldly thrust of Teresa's mystic program, worldly honors, wealth, and fame held no value. Contemporary critics usually credit Teresa with deliberate strategy for gaining her ends. She managed to have things both ways: to play the obedient daughter while acting the ambitious spiritual reformer. Laguardia points out that Teresa consistently undermined patriarchal authority. Instead of accepting her father's direction she replaced him with the ambiguous paternal figure of Saint Joseph, then relished bossing her biological father in his final days. Teresa affirmed that the nun must accept her confessor's decision about her spiritual growth, but she also insisted on the nun's right to choose her own confessor. Teresa frequently attacked "unlettered" confessors who fettered spiritual progress. Tylus shows how Teresa tended to displace the authority of her earthly fathers (confessors) onto Christ who spoke to her personally. Márquez Villanueva points out that the length and number of her works indicate that she wrote from a personal impetus, not merely from obedience, and that she astutely manipulated her confessors into requesting her treatises. Sullivan documents the expansion of Teresa's audience from her confessors to a large audience of believers to God. Carreno, declaring the *Vida* the first great defense of woman's dignity as a woman, traces the creation of her ideal autobiographic "I" from the triple "I" of author, narrator, and character. Chorpenning finds a parallel between the *Vida* and the romance plot: Teresa begins in the paradise of childhood, descends to the "hell" of forgetfulness of God, then returns to union with God in spiritual marriage. Slade argues that Teresa transformed the judicial confession into a self-defense of the heroic life. Intelligence and knowledge of politics and psychology enabled Teresa to achieve her own purposes.

Recent criticism has sought to disentangle Teresa's writing from sexist premises. Praising Menéndez Pidal for his enlightening studies of Teresa's deliberate use of some colloquial, "uneducated" words, they question his and other earlier critics' insistence on her "feminine" style. Márquez Villanueva perceives Teresa's laments about her "confused" style as a rhetorical trope developed for self-protection. Her "spontaneous" style avoids technical, theological, and pedagogical vocabulary in favor of colloquial, sometimes illiterate language, homely metaphors, and words with sensorial connotations. Carreter perceives Teresa as a complex writer who used both sophisticated and rustic forms as well as the tropes of humility and divine inspiration. He, following Pope, credits her with inventing the genre of the self-portrait in Spanish. Analyzing her subversive rhetoric, Trépanier points out that in mysticism stereotypically female traits are valued above stereotypically male characteristics; Teresa's confessors excised some of Teresa's claims for women from her works.

Bernini's statue in the Cornari Chapel in Rome commemorates the much-discussed "transverberation" when an angel appeared to Teresa and thrust his dart into her heart,

seeming to draw out her entrails as she was filled with love of Christ. Teresa places this event on August 27, 1559, and describes it in the *Vida*, chapter XX; *Relaciones*, chapter V; and *Moradas*, Book VI, chapter 4, and Book VI, chapter 6. The sexual vividness of her description led the female Mexican acting troupe, the Compañía Divas, to use a reproduction of Bernini's statue as symbol of insatiable sexual desire in their 1980s play on the Don Juan (**Burlador*) figure. The correspondence of the transverberation with the likely time of the menopausal climactorium strengthens Breuer's classification of Teresa as an hysteric. Matus points out that Breuer stressed Teresa's accomplishments to correct the stereotype of the listless hysteric by showing that religious enthusiasm does not preclude achievement. Dombrowski analyzes William James's classification of Teresa not as an hysteric but as a "shrew," that is, an active rather than a sensorial person. James praised Teresa as the first mystic to minutely describe the psychosomatic effects of contemplative life, but he condemned her "flirtatious" relationship with Christ. Slade analyzes French psychoanalysts' interpretations of Teresa's mysticism, which they relate to pre-Oedipal experience. Interpreting Bernini's statue, Jacques Lacan extended Teresa's supplementary *jouissance*, or sexual pleasure, to womankind. Luce Irigaray relates mystical experience to woman's connatural union with other women and the loss of self-identity. Smith and Slade believe Julia Kristeva's theory most closely approximates Teresa's similarity in difference between self and God in the mystic union where the soul regresses to infantile maternal love. Kristeva, like Teresa herself, characterizes the sickness of some nuns not as hysteria but as melancholia. Swietlicki and Kindelán analyze the *Castillo interior* in relation to Kristeva and Lacan, while Kamboureli applies Derrida and Lacan to the transverberation, declaring that it is a profanity only if one regards woman's body thus. The multiple interpretations of Santa Teresa's texts by feminists, theologians, and psychoanalysts from the sixteenth century through the twentieth bear witness to her ability to engage the reader in every age. *See also* Autobiographical Self-Representation of Women in the Early Modern Period; Nuns Who Wrote in Sixteenth- and Seventeenth-Century Spain

Work by

Collected Works of St. Teresa of Avila. Trans. and ed. Kieran Kavanaugh, and Otilio Rodríguez. 3 vols. Washington, DC: Institute of Carmelite Studies, 1976–1985.

Complete Works of Teresa of Avila. Ed. and trans. E. Allison Peers. 3 vols. London: Sheed and Ward, 1944–1946.

Santa Teresa de Jesús: Obras completas. Ed. Efrén de la Madre de Dios and Otger Steggink. Madrid: BAC, 1954.

Work about

Barrientos, Alberto, et al., eds. *Santa Teresa de Jesús: Obras completas.* Madrid: Espiritualidad, 1984.

Bradburn Ruster, Michael. "The Lovely Face Aflame: An Ambiguity of Angels in St. Teresa of Avila's Visions." *Studia Mystica* 19 (1998): 68–77.

Carreno, Antonio. "Las paradojas del 'yo' autobiográfico: El *Libro de la vida* de Santa Teresa de Jesús." *Santa Teresa y la literatura mística: Actas del I Congreso Internacional sobre Santa Teresa y la mística hispánica.* Ed. Manuel Criado de Val. Madrid: EDI-6, 1984. 255–264.

Castro, Américo. *Teresa la Santa y otros ensayos.* Madrid: Alfaguara, 1972.

Chorpenning, Joseph F. "Santa Teresa's *Libro de la vida* as Romance: Narrative Movements and Heroic Quest." *Revista Canadiense de Estudios Hispánicos* 14.1 (Fall 1989): 51–64.

Comas, Antonio. "Femina inquieta y andariega." *Cuadernos hispánicos* 53 (1963): 509–520.

De la Virgen del Carmen, Salvador. *Teresa de Jesús.* 2 vols. Vitoria: Franciscus, Epp. Victoriensis, 1968.

Deneuville, Dominique. *Santa Teresa de Jesús y la mujer.* Barcelona: Herder, 1966.

Díaz Castañón, Carmen. "Teresa de Ahumada: Un vivir desviviéndose en un castellano vivido." *Boletín de la Asociación Europea* 14.27 (1982): 79–88.

Dobhan, Ulrich. "Teresa de Jesús y la emancipación de la mujer." *Congreso internacional teresiano: 4–7 octubre, 1982.* Ed. Teofanes Egido Martínez, Victor García de la Concha, and Olegario González de Cardedal. Salamanca: U of Salamanca, 1983. 1: 121–136.

Dombrowski, Daniel A. "Was Saint Teresa a Shrew?" *The Downside Review* 109.374 (January 1991): 35–43.

Kamboureli, Smaro. "Chapter 3: St. Teresa's Jouissance: Toward a Rhetoric of Reading the Sacred." *Silence, The Word and the Sacred.* Ed. E.D. Blodgett and H.G. Coward. Waterloo, Ontario, Canada: Wifrid Laurier UP, 1989. 51–63.

Kindelán, Magdalena Velasco. "Motivaciones y destinatarios del *Libro de la vida* de Santa Teresa de Jesús." *Revista de Literatura* 54.108 (July–December 1992): 645–651.

Kristeva, Julia. *In the Beginning Was Love: Psychoanalysis and Faith.* Trans. Arthur Goldhammer. New York: Columbia UP, 1987.

Laguardia, Gari. "Santa Teresa and the Problem of Desire." *Hispania* 63 (1980): 523–530.

Lázaro Carreter, Fernando. "Lección inaugural: Santa Teresa de Jesús, escritora (El *Libro de la vida*). *Congreso internacional teresiano: 4–7 octubre, 1982.* Ed. Teofanes Egido Martínez, Victor García de la Concha, and Olegario González de Cardedal. Salamanca: U of Salamanca, 1983. 1: 11–27.

Márquez Villanueva, Francisco. "Avila, ciudad morisca y cuna de espiritualidad." *Mélanges María Soledad Carrasco Urgoiti/Tahiyyat taqdir lil-dukturah María Soledad Carrasco Urgoiti, I-II.* Zaghouan, Tunisia: Fondation Temimi pour la Recherche Scientifique et l'Information, 1999. 209–219.

———. "La vocación literaria de Santa Teresa." *Nueva Revista de Filología Hispánica* 23.1 (1983): 355–379.

Matus, Jill L. "Saint Teresa, Hysteria, and *Middlemarch.*" *Journal of the History of Sexuality* 1.2 (October 1990): 215–240.

Menéndez Pidal, Ramón. "El estilo de Santa Teresa." *La lengua de Cristóbal Colón y otros estudios sobre el siglo XVI.* By Ramón Menéndez Pidal. Madrid: Espasa-Calpe, 1958. 119–142.

Oñate, María del Pilar. *El feminismo en la literatura española.* Madrid: Espasa-Calpe, 1938.

Pope, Randolph. *La autobiografía española hasta Torres Villaroel.* Bern, Frankfurt: H. and P. Lang, 1974.

Quitsland, Sonya. "Elements of a Feminist Spirituality in Saint Teresa." *Carmelite Studies* (1984): 19–50.

Rodríguez, Alfred, and Darcy Donahue. "Un ensayo de explicación razonada de las referencias de Santa Teresa a su propio sexo en *Vida.*" *Santa Teresa y la literatura mística. Actas del I Congreso internacional sobre Santa Teresa y la mística hispánica.*

Ed. M. Criado de Val. Madrid: EDI-6, 1984. 309–313.

Slade, Carole. *St. Teresa of Avila: Author of a Heroic Life.* Berkeley: U of California P, 1995.

Smith, Paul Julian. "Writing Women in Golden Age Spain: Saint Teresa and María de Zayas." *Modern Language Notes* 102.2 (March 1987): 220–240.

Sullivan, Marcy C. "From Narrative to Proclamation: A Rhetorical Analysis of the Autobiography of Teresa of Avila." *Thought* 58 (1983): 453–471.

Swietlicki, Catherine. "Writing 'Femystic' Space: In the Margins of Saint Teresa's *Castillo interior.*" *Journal of Hispanic Philology* 13.3 (Spring 1989): 273–293.

Trépanier, Hélène. "L'incompétence de Thérèse d'Avila: Analyse de la rhétorique mystique du *Chateau Interieur.*" *Études Littéraires* 27.2 (Autumn 1994): 53–65.

Tylus, Jane. *Writing and Vulnerability in the Late Renaissance.* Stanford: Stanford UP, 1993.

Weber, Alison. "Saint Teresa's Problematic Patrons." *Journal of Medieval and Early Modern Studies* 29.2 (Spring 1999): 357–379.

———. *Teresa of Avila and the Rhetoric of Femininity.* Princeton, NJ: Princeton UP, 1990.

Judy B. McInnis

Teresa de Manzanares

See *Niña de los embustes, Teresa de Manzanares, La* (1632)

Theater

See Drama entries

Tía Tula, La (1921)

The fifth novel of Miguel de *Unamuno y Jugo (1864–1936), *La tía Tula* (Aunt Gertrude), begun as early as 1902 and published in 1921, conforms to the skeletal but readerly style that predominates after his more writerly experiments with narratology published prior to 1915. Its anecdote deals with Gertrudis (Tula), sister-in-law to Ramiro, who rejects a life of conjugal and motherly fulfillment in order to become surrogate mother to his children when their mother dies. Ramiro, drawn to Gertrudis by an unconscious sexual attraction, has nevertheless married her sister

Rosa, who tenuously duplicates Gertrudis's provocation without the liability of her stern independence. A time passes without children, and the puritanical Gertrudis accuses the couple of marrying for sex and of a refusal to shoulder responsibilities. Intimidated by her, they conceive a son and, after a difficult birth, Gertrudis moves in to care for the child. She proves to be a tyrant, both ordering Ramiro to beg his wife's forgiveness for sullying her purity and demanding that Rosa service Ramiro's sexual needs in order to lessen his lust for Gertrudis and other women. She also orders the couple to keep producing children to keep their surrogate mother busy and to stifle the libido that might prompt either of the parents to elevate their sexuality to an end rather than a means. Two more children are born, greatly weakening Rosa, and Gertrudis accosts Ramiro for his selfishness and immorality in seeking sex from a woman during her periods of exhaustion and postpartum infertility. She accuses Ramiro of poisoning the children's capacity for purity through a sensual contamination of Rosa's breast milk. When the exhausted Rosa finally dies, Gertrudis, instead of recognizing her own degree of culpability, fully blames Ramiro and moves in as permanent mother to the children and guardian of their home's sanctity. Claiming a responsibility to the children, she turns down marriage proposals from both Ramiro and an old boyfriend. She expresses her abomination of society's practice of making women submit to the whims of men rather than seeking out mates of their own. Her confessor, recognizing danger in Ramiro's lack of a sexual partner and pathology in Gertrudis's unhappy purity, counsels marriage between them, but Gertrudis is infuriated by his notion that her life be reduced to the level of a holy remedy for the male sexual desires that may lead her brother-in-law to burn in hell. Gertrudis's unwitting provocation and asceticism finally prompt Ramiro to sexual relations with the servant, Manuela, and Gertrudis forces them to marry, thus occasioning a repetition of the cycle. Gertrudis is a completely self-sacrificing mother to the children, and they dearly love her, but her refusal to permit the acknowledgment of sexuality in their otherwise happy upbringing causes them to search for sexual identity with almost a vengeance. At long last, Ramiro and Manuela die, leaving a daughter, Manuelita, determined to emulate her "aunt" Tula in caring for the younger children. However, on her deathbed, Gertrudis confesses that she would do things differently if her life could begin again. She would soil her hands with the "slime" of life instead of emulating the Pauline message of spirituality. She acknowledges her sexual frustration but confesses that something about sex had always repelled her. She urges Manuela's children not to fear a loss of spirituality by a willful surrender to another human being's drives, especially if that surrender will "save" the other person from a spiritual or psychological abyss. Nevertheless, in a final conversation, Manuelita and her sister Rosita are filled with admiration for the strength and goodness of their "aunt."

Early commentary on the novel emphasized its intense and accurate depiction of the drama and conflict of motivations occurring within a simple home. Unfortunately, this was often combined with a useless debate (frequent in dealing with Unamuno's female characters) over whether Gertrudis was a saint or a monster and whether Unamuno had employed strategies to effect either one judgment or the other. Guided by Unamuno's frequent statements that his own wife, Concepción (Concha), had been his refuge and "mother" in times of spiritual crisis and by his apparent fixation on distinguishing between "motherly and "non-motherly" characters in his books, there was a consensus that Unamuno had designed to depict Gertrudis as a monster, albeit one with clay feet. A contemporary reading of Gertrudis shows a continual dialogy of charitable, selfish, and legitimately self-centered motivations. She is highly sexualized but re-

sents prevailing attitudes (social and ecclesiastical) that her sexuality and life's accomplishments be channeled and sacrificed to meet the "needs" of a man. Ironically and with almost no reflexivity, she passes on these same attitudes in her dealings with her sister and her brother-in-law's second wife. She is a far more involved parent than any of the other adults in the novel, and the children reward her with intense love and an echoing of her values. Yet though she recognizes that no man or men can fulfill all the needs in her life, she is incapable of recognizing her own incapacity to arrange, on her own terms, all the educational and sexual needs of others. She and Manuelita are head and shoulders above all the other characters in their acknowledgment that adulthood brings difficult choices. They make adult decisions, and they are willing to accept the consequences. All of the novel's adult males, who believe that women exist to "save" them by silencing their eschatological and machoistic anxieties through sexual release, have very little stature. It can scarcely be doubted that Unamuno is writing here squarely against his own well-documented fantasies and desires, but it is more important to note that his text posits an objective solution in the new generations of males who will be raised by Gertrudis, not perfectly, but with a sense that their own perfectibility depends on a male internalization of the "feminine" motherliness that Gertrudis incarnates. The novel clearly argues that "all male" and "all female" are not only undesirable opposites but clear impossibilities.

Work by

La tía Tula. 18th ed. Madrid: Espasa-Calpe, 1990.

Work about

Caballé, Anna. Introduction to La tía Tula. 18th ed. Madrid: Espasa-Calpe, 1990. 9–34.

Gullón, Ricardo. Autobiografías de Unamuno. Madrid: Gredos, 1964. 204–217.

Hynes, Laura. "La tía Tula: Forerunner of Radical Feminism." Hispanófila 117 (May 1996): 45–54.

Nozick, Martin. Miguel de Unamuno. The Agony of

Belief. Princeton, NJ: Princeton UP, 1982. 154–157.

Thomas R. Franz

Ticiano Imab

See Biedma y la Moneda de Rodríguez, Patrocinio de (1848–1927)

Tiempo de silencio (1962): Its Portrayal of Women

Tiempo de silencio (1962; *Time of Silence*, 1974) has been heralded as the critical turning point toward the "new" novel of the late 1960s and 1970s in Spain. Within Luis Martín-Santos's ambitious text, the vision of women is inextricably linked to a method that he christened "dialectical realism," which exposes human and societal complexities regardless of class or gender. Like other characters in *Tiempo de silencio*, traditional female roles such as mother, wife, widow, prostitute, society woman, and marriageable woman are presented and questioned through an ironic lens. In line with Martín-Santos's mission to break with the oversimplification of the 1950s objectivist novel, his "new" novel offers a dense portrayal of Spain and Spanish women from all socioeconomic backgrounds.

Female fragmentation is one strategy that Martín-Santos's narrator(s) employs to discuss gender roles. Female characters are described as fragmented body parts, rather than whole beings with individualizing characteristics, raising critical questions about women's roles in Spanish society in 1949. Typical of the younger female characters in *Tiempo de silencio*, Pedro's girlfriend Dorita is young and beautiful, with angelic facial features, abundant hair, firm thighs, and a well-proportioned build. Her voluptuousness attracts comments from other characters and the narrator. Her looks render the reader incapable of experiencing her as an individual because Dorita becomes her stereotypical representation. Woman is portrayed as the ironic sum of her sexual attractiveness (or unattractiveness). Pregnant Florita is another young, comely character represented through her breasts, smooth skin, and sexy carriage. Impregnated by her father, during her abortion and death scene, her body is clinically positioned and her physical parts are surveyed. At the autopsy, Florita's fragmentation becomes both literal and figurative. Both Florita and Dorita are not whole; rather, they are young women playing gender-based roles in patriarchal post–Civil War Spain. Focusing on young women's body parts effectively illustrates their traditional lot. It is not just young women's bodies that are scrutinized; older characters such as the brothel madam, Doña Luisa, have their bodies appraised. Her flabby thighs, sagging eyelids, wrinkled skin, and heavy feet indicate age and station. Regardless of their ages, in *Tiempo de silencio* women's societal functions are limited and well defined. The technique of fragmentation also underscores women's alienation in Franco's Spain. Female alienation runs parallel to protagonist Pedro's much-studied existential alienation in the city. The well-studied doubling of Madrid itself runs parallel to the doubling of alienated female characters (Florita-Dorita, Doña Luisa–Ricarda), which exposes dualities, uncovers contradictions, and enlivens Martín-Santos's dialectic.

Mueca's illiterate wife Ricarda (also referred to as Encarna) is an archetypal Jungian Earth-mother. When Pedro is unjustly imprisoned for the abortion and death of Ricarda's daughter Florita, Ricarda succeeds in obtaining his release. A coarse, round, Toledan peasant woman dressed in earthen-colored rags, as an immigrant to Madrid she represents a significant wave of settlers during the 1940s and 1950s. Ricarda creates a home for her family in Madrid's *chabolas* (shanty towns), using the earth and the city's discards. Ricarda feeds her daughters by scouring the land during the notable *años de hambre* (years of hunger) in Madrid. Abused by her husband, her representation is filthy, physically repugnant, and inarticulate, but despite her circumstances, she is above all a mother. Casting her as the Earth-mother gives her dignity, intuitive wisdom, and moral ability to liberate Pedro. At the same time, Ricarda truly grieves the loss of her daughter Florita. Literary critics have pointed out that the empowerment of this near-mute female character with the most pivotal words in the novel, words that vindicate Pedro, is significant.

Equally important, the *celestineo* (matchmaking efforts) of the widow, Dorita's grandmother and keeper of the boarding house where Pedro resides, successfully entraps Pedro in a plot to force the marriage of her only granddaughter Dorita to the young research physician. Dorita, a virgin, prepares herself for the tired, drunken Pedro on the Saturday night around which most of the action in the novel revolves. Prompted by the widow, Dorita and Pedro have sexual relations. An astute matchmaker, the widow knows that Pedro is obligated to marry Dorita. From the widow's viewpoint, their union is both socially and economically attractive. In the widow's Joycean interior monologue, she reveals that she orchestrated their relationship to save the family's reputation. Dorita and Pedro's marriage would render them financially secure and help vindicate the widow for allowing her own daughter to have a child out of wedlock. The widow's *celestineo* lies in contrast to the pimping of Doña Luisa, who also arranges matches, but her motivation is strictly economic.

Female characters are largely defined by their reproductive functions. Reproductive women are erotic objects and reliable breeders. The physical descriptions of premenopausal women parallel descriptions of Pedro's copulating laboratory mice throughout the novel. Dorita, Florita, the prostitutes, the *tagalas* (young Philippine girls), and other young women are victimized due to the aggressive male sex drive. Reproductivity is exchanged for economic security and stability; therefore, young women are objectified

through sexual exploitation. Because they become objects, these women are collectively "silenced." Given these pressures, menopausal characters show anxiety as their fertility wanes. The widow states that the process of menopause drove her to drink and caused her to commit strategic errors in family management. Likewise, Matías's high-society mother (beginning menopause) exhibits paranoid behavior to maintain her sophisticated good looks and feminine beauty. She constantly inspects herself in the mirror and labors to achieve the illusion of youth. Her eroding youthfulness diminishes the power society has vested in her, trading on her good looks for social and economic position. Menopausal and premenopausal women contrast with postmenopausal women; with age they are no longer objectified, and they develop matriarchal power within the patriarchy. Doña Luisa manages a brothel. The widow runs a boarding house, and Ricarda maintains a family. These three older women exhibit control over women and men. As matriarchs, they have their own domain; nevertheless, they are continually mocked by the narrator for their aging bodies. Nonreproductive women display greater independence and individuality within the fictional world of *Tiempo de silencio*. Young females are one-dimensional, in contrast to the more mature and complex characters of Ricarda, Doña Luisa, and the widow, all presented as individual women.

Martín-Santos was a psychiatrist with a documented interested in psychoanalysis. Woven into the narrative of *Tiempo de silencio*, the Freudian technique of free association leaves male characters contemplating "the mother." Oedipal complexes lie just beneath the surface. Rooted in feelings for his own mother, the main character Pedro recognizes his attraction to his best friend's mother. Similarly the drunk Matías makes sexual advances toward the head madam of the brothel, Doña Luisa. She is old enough to be his mother, but he confesses that the oedipal urge is the attraction.

Because women and men are represented in traditional gender roles, they are polarized. However, Martín-Santos's rich, ironic language stands as the centerpiece for analysis of females and their bodies, exposing the limited individual, personal, and societal possibilities that even fictitious women possess. It is significant that in the early editions of the novel censors recommended elimination of much of Florita's abortion scene and parts of the brothel scenes. Ultimately these attempts to suppress the female experience during this period failed. Despite censors' efforts, the novel was fully restored in a definitive edition (1981); thus the study of women's fictional roles in *Tiempo de silencio* continues to give voice to Spain's "silence" during the Franco period.

Work by

Tiempo de silencio. Study and notes, Alfonso Ray. Barcelona: Crítica, 2000.
Tiempo de silencio. Edición definitiva. 17th ed. Barcelona: Seix Barral, 1981.

Work about

Anderson, Christopher. "Mueca's Consort: The Great Mother Archetype in *Tiempo de silencio.*" *Revista Canadiense de Estudios Hispánicos* 12 (1988): 287–295.
Díaz, Janet Winecoff. "Luis Martín-Santos and the Contemporary Novel." *Hispania* 51 (1968): 232–238.
Freire, Silka. "Luis Martín-Santos: *Tiempo de silencio*: Ricarda, un instinto hacia la libertad." *Hispanic Journal* 11 (1990): 155–164.
García Ronda, Angel. "El sexo en *Tiempo de silencio.*" *Journal of Basque Studies* 8 (1987): 36–38.
Holdsworth, Carole. "The Scholar and the Earth Mother in *Tiempo de silencio.*" *Hispanófila* 92 (1988): 41–48.
Knickerbocker, Dale F. "*Tiempo de silencio* and the Narrative of the Abject." *Anales de la Literatura Española Contemporánea* 19 (1994): 11–31.
Martínez Carbajo, A. Paloma. "La (des)composición del espacio matritense: Del 98 a *Tiempo de silencio.*" *Nuevas perspectivas sobre el 98.* Ed. John P. Gabriele. Madrid: Iberoamericana; Frankfurt: Vervuert, 1999. 121–130.
Pérez Firmat, Gustavo. "Tumors and Twins." *Literature and Liminality: Festive Readings in the Hispanic Tradition.* Durham, NC: Duke UP, 1986. 109–162.

Sheri Spaine Long

Tobacco Factory Worker
See Cigarrera

Tormento (1884)

One of Benito Pérez Galdós's *Novelas españolas contemporáneas*, the novel takes its title from the main character, Amparo Sánchez Emperador, who is called "Tormento" (Torment) by his lover, the priest Don Pedro Polo.

Tormento is the second novel in a trilogy formed by *El doctor Centeno* and *La de Bringas* (*The Spendthrifts*, 1951). In *El doctor Centeno*, the orphan Amparo is seduced by her protector, Don Pedro. In the sequel, she regrets giving herself to the priest and tries to keep an honest, respectful social conduct. However, Don Pedro still loves Amparo and insists on seeing her. With Amparo's refusal to run away with him, and lacking the strength to rebuild his life as a priest, Don Pedro collapses physically and mentally. Amparo struggles between her compassion for the priest and her sense of guilt and shame. At the same time, the *indiano* (person returning rich from South America) Agustín Caballero is seduced by Amparo's charms and asks her to marry him. Rosalía Pipaón, Amparo's envious aunt, arranges for Agustín to find out about her niece's past. Faced with confronting Agustín and telling him the truth, Amparo decides to commit suicide and takes a medicine she believes to be poison. Agustín arrives in time to stop Amparo and convinces her to go to France and live with him as an unmarried couple. The novel ends with the triumph of social conventions that deny "fallen" women the possibility of having a respectful life.

As he later did in *Tristana* (1892), Galdós insists in *Tormento* on the condemnation of a society that does not allow women the possibility of supporting themselves with decent jobs and makes them victims of abusive situations. In order to emphasize this point, Amparo's portrayal is similar to those of Galdós's female characters representing the simple, natural qualities of Spanish people. Amparo is described as a hardworking, serious, unselfish, and caring woman of classic and romantic beauty. Her personality is sweet and prone to melancholy; she is feeble and weak in her acts and determination but always inclined to be kind and patient with others. This characterization of Amparo, added to the identity of her two lovers, an immoral priest and an industrious self-made man, is why *Tormento* has been read as a metaphor of Spain's fight for emancipation from clerical subjugation and her embrace of modern moral standards that characterize economically developed societies.

Work by

Torment. Trans. J.M. Cohen. New York: Farrar, Straus & Young, 1953.

Tormento. Dir. Pedro Olea. With Concha Velasco, Paco Rabal, and Ana Belén, 1974. Film.

Tormento. *Obras completas*. Madrid: Aguilar, 1970.

Work about

Aldaraca, Bridget. "*Tormento*: La moral burguesa y la privatización de la virtud." *Texto y sociedad: Problemas de historia literaria*. Amsterdam: Rodopi, 1990. 215–229.

Andreu, Alicia. "El folletín como intertexto en *Tormento*." *Anales galdosianos* 17 (1982): 55–61.

Bly, Peter. "Al perder la virginidad tres heroínas galdosianas." *Insula* 48 (1993): 11–13.

Macciuci, Raquel. "Representación femenina y política doméstica en *Tormento* de Galdós." *Filología* (Buenos Aires, Argentina) 28.1–2 (1995): 209–216.

Ribbans, Geoffrey. "Amparando/desamparando a Amparo: Some reflections on *El doctor Centeno* and *Tormento*." *Revista Canadiense de Estudios Hispánicos* 17 (1993): 495–524.

Rogers, Douglass M. "Amparo o la metamorfosis de la heroína galdosiana." *Selected Proceedings of the Mid-America Conference on Hispanic Literature*. Lincoln: Society of Spanish & Spanish-American Studies, 1986. 137–146.

Vázquez, Luciana Elena. "De/construcción de la institución literaria en *Tormento* de Benito Pérez Galdós." *Filología* (Buenos Aires, Argentina) 28.1–2 (1995): 217–223.

Joan Torres-Pou

Torre, Josefina de la (1907–before 1989)

Writer, singer, and actress Josefina de la Torre was born in Las Palmas, Grand Canary. She began her singing lessons and poetry writing at a very early age. Her first published poem appeared in 1920, and between 1927 and 1935, she gave frequent singing recitals in Madrid. After moving there permanently in 1935, de la Torre shifted her artistic activities to the theater. In the Canary Islands, she and her brother, playwright and novelist Claudio de la Torre, had earlier formed their own theater company, "Teatro Mínimo." After 1940, she became known for her work as an actress of stage, movies, radio, and television. She became the lead actress of the Teatro Nacional, at the María Guerrero Theater, and married the actor Ramón Carroto. She again formed her own theater company with her brother as director.

Introduced into the literary circles of the day by her brother, de la Torre developed friendships with many leading poets of the Generation of 1927 and became one of the two women included in the landmark anthology of contemporary poetry published by Gerardo Diego in 1934. While still in her teens, she wrote the compositions of her first book, *Versos y estampas*, (Verses and Illustrations), published in 1927 with an introduction by Pedro Salinas. It is a short volume of 16 prose sketches alternated with an equal number of poems plus a seventeenth final poem and a composition entitled "Romance del buen guiar" (Ballad of Good Guidance) at the middle of the book. Written in short lines of free verse, the poems display a preference for themes of nature, particularly of the sea, and a sense of unity between the natural and human world. Salinas, Juan Ramón *Jiménez, *García Lorca, and her Canary compatriots seem to have influenced the structure and imagery of Torre's poetry. In her second collection, *Poemas de la isla* (1930; Island Poems), nature continues to provide sensorial richness and a joyful atmosphere, but a new concern for language, love, and time surfaces. Vocabulary from the fields of sport, technology, and cinematography links the book to experimental poetry of the period. In the rest of her poetry, consciousness of the outside world gives way to anguish and retrospection, imagery becomes simplified, and her initial exuberance fades into strains of nostalgia and desolation.

De la Torre continued to write after 1940. She finished the collection *Marzo incompleto* (Incomplete March), published first in 1947 in the magazine *Fantasía*. The poems of *Medida del tiempo* (Measure of Time), written between 1940 and 1980, remained unpublished until appearance of her posthumous complete works, *Poemas de la isla*. She also published a short story titled "En el umbral" (1954; On the Threshhold) and a short novel, *Memorias de una estrella* (1954; Memory of a Star), that tells of a beautiful but frivolous woman who searches for stardom but finally finds happiness as an anonymous housewife.

Work by

Poemas de la isla. Islas Canarias: Gobierno de Canarias, 1989.

Poemas de la isla: Poems. Trans. Carles Reyes, Spokane: Eastern Washington UP, 2000.

Work about

Bellver, Catherine G. *Absence and Presence. Spanish Women Poets of the Twenties and Thirties*. Lewisburg, PA and London: Buckhell UP and Associated UP, 2001.

Cole, Gregory Keith. "Josefina de la Torre. Women Poets of the Generation of 1927." Diss. U of Kentucky, 1993. 109–132.

Landeira, Joy Buckles. "Josefina de la Torre." *Women Writers of Spain. An Annotated Bio-Bibliographical Guide*. Ed. Carolyn L. Galerstein and Kathleen McNerney. Westport, CT: Greenwood P, 1986. 313–314.

Radtke, Rosetta. "Josefina de la Torre." *An Encyclopedia of Continental Women Writers*. Ed. Katharina M. Wilson. New York: Garland P, 1991. 1246–1247.

Santana, Lázaro. Introduction to Josefina de la Torre. *Poemas de la isla*. Islas Canarias: Gobierno de Canarias, 1989. 9–20.

Catherine G. Bellver

Torrente Ballester, Gonzalo (1910–1999): Women in His Works

The future novelist was born in the port city and shipbuilding center of El Ferrol (Galicia), the eldest child in the family of a career naval officer. Galicia, the seacoast, and the middle-class professional milieu of his formative years all become constants in his fiction, although much of his mature life was spent in Madrid, where he taught history and established himself as a prominent and insightful critic before becoming known for his creative writing. After years of literary obscurity, Torrente became Spain's most successful novelist of the 1970s and 1980s, garnering all the country's most prestigious awards. He produced some two dozen novels, eight plays, two collections of short stories, 10 volumes of essays and criticism, and about a dozen books of miscellany, including journalistic articles, memoirs, and diaries.

The early novelette *Ifigenia* (1948; Iphigeneia) and *El golpe de Estado de Guadalupe Limón* (1945; Guadalupe Limón's Coup d'État) have feminine protagonists, although their personality development is constrained by the mythic original of the former and the demythologizing intent of both works. Torrente subverts the traditional masculine heroes, more interested in their own fame than in ethical questions. A major constant in Torrente's works is his burlesquing of historiography: History typically is written by the victors, and he observed firsthand how idealization by Franco historiographers was converting the victorious Falangists into mythic heroes. He pulls the carpet from beneath the exalted fascist machismo of the Falangists by having women supplant the masculine rev-olutionaries: The conspirators are largely controlled by their erotic urges and the women in their lives, with feminine rivalries displacing all social and political ideologies. While not necessarily a "liberated" vision of women, Torrente's demythologized version shows the women to be generally more eth-ical, less vain, more admirable than their male counterparts—and at least as intelli-gent.

Three interesting women appear in the trilogy *Los gozos y las sombras* (Pleasures and Shadows), comprised of *El señor llega* (1957; The Landlord Arrives); *Donde da la vuelta el aire* (1969; Where the Air Turns); and *La pascua triste* (1972; Sad Easter). Doña Mari-ana represents the old system, relatively pa-ternalistic and benevolent in contrast to the economic tyranny of the new industrial cap-italist, Cayetano, political boss of the town of Pueblanueva. A proud, beautiful, myste-rious, stoic old spinster, Mariana, owner of the fishing fleet, defends the fishermen's rights against Cayetano's total monopoly; she dies of pneumonia after abandoning her sick-bed to beg Cayetano for help to save the crews of several fishing boats during a hur-ricane. Although a bit old-fashioned, Mari-ana is a woman of principles and strength, decisive, independent, and admirable. Rosa-rio, an attractive, sensual seamstress and daughter of sharecroppers, has been handed over by her family to obtain economic favors from Cayetano, who beats and abuses her; aware of the risk, she offers herself to Dr. Carlos Deza, an indecisive psychiatrist and local landowner recently returned from many years abroad, hoping that he will lead the villagers' resistance to Cayetano's tyranny. Her own plan, however, is to marry Ramón, a young farm laborer, and when Carlos leaves, he presents Rosario with the farm on which her family lives. On her wedding night, Rosario evicts her parents and broth-ers, her revenge for their selling her to Cay-etano. The third woman, Clara Aldán, a distant relative of Carlos, lives a Cinderella-

like existence, mistreated by her brother and sister who hate her (as the only legitimate child of their father, a traditional nobleman who has lost most of the family fortune, she is his heir); they maliciously spread rumors that she is an "easy woman." Clara represents feminine initiative, autonomy, and indepen-dence; she begins a small business and by dint of hard work achieves modest success, helping to care for her siblings and their al-coholic mother. Cayetano proposes marriage, but she has fallen for Carlos and refuses, upon which Cayetano first attempts to pur-chase her as a concubine, then brutally rapes her, leaving her badly hurt. On the eve of the Civil War, Carlos sells his property in Pueblanueva and escapes with Clara and her mother to Portugal. Clara is by far the most admirable character of the trilogy, always generous and authentic in her relationships. Torrente's women are usually more decisive, autonomous, and sympathetic than his male characters, who tend to be intellectuals, often vacuous or conceited, either weak or malevolent or else well intentioned but in-effective. Cayetano with his strength and vigor constitutes the exception, but his amo-rality and abusiveness make him a negative character.

Off-Side (1969), an extensive novel of in-trigue involving Madrid's world of high fi-nance and the marginal characters of the *Rastro* (flea market), offers several variations in narrative perspectives on woman's condi-tion in Spain, undermining certain stereo-types such as that of the prostitute, usually portrayed as a poor, uneducated woman of little taste (unlike *Cela, Torrente rarely de-picts prostitutes). María Dolores, a high-priced call girl of aristocratic appearance, holds a university degree, speaks several lan-guages, dresses discreetly, and lives elegantly. Her obvious talent and intelligence consti-tute an implied critique of the sexism of Spain's establishment of the period, wherein women hoping for anything more than an ill-paid job as a secretary or schoolteacher found doors to advancement closed. With her many clients from the "official" capitalist sphere, María Dolores decisively influences various important banking operations. Although several female characters play significant parts, she is the most original and memorable.

La saga/fuga de J.B. (1972; J.B.'s Fugal Saga), a long, dense novel with multiple plots, mythic and millennial structure, and numerous fantastic or outrageously idiosyncratic characters, is perhaps the most influential exponent of postmodernism in Spain. Although it has no really important female characters, its numerous parodies and satires include some very funny jokes at the expense of the patriarchal establishment, one of them alluding to the nation's patron saint, Santiago (St. James); legend holds that his uncorrupted corpse is buried beneath the cathedral of Santiago de Compostela, and this Torrente transforms to a female, "Santa Lilaila, Martyr," with her suspiciously similar cathedral and legend, and equally miraculous corpse, which like that of the Apostle, appeared a thousand years earlier. Torrente also creates a secret matriarchal order of Rosicrucian-like priestesses whose primary function is the selection of wombs to bear the next of the periodically reincarnated J.B.s; while supposedly they guarantee the legitimacy of the J.B. descendants, the genealogy is complicated by centuries of adulterous contributions. The sacrosanct male institution, the "Round Table," a parody of phallocentric knighthood and heroism, has allowed the search for the Holy Grail to degenerate into a sacrilegious adoration of genital attributes. Torrente comically subverts pornography, as well, both in *La saga/fuga* and its equally hilarious successor, *Fragmentos de Apocalipsis* (1977; Fragments of Apocalypse), whose protagonist invents an ideal, imaginary lover, Lenutchka, a young communist intellectual who critiques his manuscripts but has absolutely prohibited that he think about her sexuality. Another object of Torrente's satire is religious repression and its puritanical intrusion into matrimonial rela-

tions (again attacked, with similarly comic results, in *Crónica del rey pasmado* [1989; Chronicle of the Amazed Monarch]), but he also defrauds the expectations of readers of erotic tales in *Quizá nos lleve el viento al infinito* (1984; Perhaps the Wind Will Carry Us to Infinity) when the object of the protagonist's affections proves to be an android.

Torrente has portrayed several women among the university professors appearing in works such as *La isla de los jacintos cortados* (1980; The Isle of Cut Hyacinths) and *Yo no soy yo, evidentemente* (1987; Evidently, I'm Not Myself), both comic, postmodern novels depicting the proliferation of professional women as commonplace—at least in countries other than Spain. Torrente further subverts the phallocentric cult of machismo in *Las islas extraordinarias* (1991; The Extraordinary Isles) whose protagonist, a private investigator and thus a supermacho by definition, turns out to be both inept and easily duped, manipulated and used by his "guide," Gina, who apparently has masterminded an intricate plot leading to the PI's assassination of the very man he was hired to protect. Still more humiliating for the masculine ego, Gina then rescues him following the assassination, driving a motorcycle among a hail of bullets and jumping the cycle across a deep strait while the detective faints. Torrente, however, does not deform gender realities to the point of presenting a world (even a fictional one) ruled by women. In fact, he shows very realistically in works such as *La muerte del Decano* (1992; Death of the Dean), *La novela de Pepe Ansúrez* (1994; Pepe Ansúrez's Novel), and *La boda de Chon Recalde* (1995; Chon Recalde's Wedding) the extent to which exceptionally talented women found their talents not only unrecognized but almost unusable in Franco Spain and were forced by lack of alternatives into marriages with men in many ways inferior to themselves but who would at least trust them, treat them with respect, and allow them a measure of autonomy.

Although ludic aspects of Torrente's pictures of the war of the sexes may be more noteworthy, he does present a serious side, what might be termed an idealized relationship of equality between the sexes, wherein mutual love and respect enable man and woman to "save" each other. Frequently, women also quite literally save men in Torrente's works, from their folly, their penury, or their solitude. Seldom does he present a simple female stereotype, and if there is a cluster of traits shared by a majority of his women characters, these would include superior intelligence, sensitivity, valor, generosity, and initiative.

Work by

La boda de Chon Recalde. Barcelona: Planeta, 1995.
Crónica del rey pasmado. Barcelona: Planeta, 1989.
Dafne y ensueños. Barcelona: Destino, 1982.
Donde da la vuelta el aire. Barcelona: Bruguera, 1981.
Don Juan. Barcelona: Orbis, 1982.
Filomeno, a mi pesar. Barcelona: Planeta, 1988.
Fragmentos de Apocalipsis. Barcelona: Destinolibro, 1982.
El golpe de Estado de Guadalupe Limón. Barcelona: Plaza y Janés, 1985.
Ifigenia. Barcelona: Destino, 1988.
La Isla de los jacintos cortados. Barcelona: Destino, 1980.
Las islas extraordinarias. Barcelona: Planeta, 1991.
Javier Mariño. Historia de una conversión. Barcelona: Seix Barral, 1985.
La muerte del Decano. Barcelona: Planeta, 1992.
La novela de Pepe Ansúrez. Barcelona: Planeta, 1994.
La pascua triste. Barcelona: Bruguera, 1981.
La princesa durmiente va a la escuela. Barcelona: Plaza y Janés, 1983.
Off-Side. Barcelona: Destinolibro, 1981.
Quizá nos lleve el viento al infinito. Barcelona: Plaza y Janés, 1984.
La rosa de los vientos. Barcelona: Destino, 1985.
La saga/fuga de J.B.. Barcelona: Destinolibro, 1980.
El señor llega. Barcelona: Bruguera, 1981.
Yo no soy yo, evidentemente. Barcelona: Plaza y Janés, 1987.

Work about

Ambitos literarios. Barcelona: Anthropos, 1987. Collected essays and extracts.
Anthropos 66–67 (Extraordinario 9) 1986. Volume devoted to Torrente.

Becerra, Carmen. *Guardo la voz, cedo la palabra.* Barcelona: Anthropos, 1990. Interviews.
———. *Los mundos imaginarios de Gonzalo Torrente Ballester.* Madrid: Espasa-Calpe, 1994.
Colahan, Clark. "Two Post-Franco Visions of Women's Mysticism: Gonzalo Torrente Ballester and María Teresa Alvarez." *Studia Mystica* 18 (1997): 172–181.
Giménez, A. *El autor y su obra. Torrente Ballester.* Barcelona: Barcanova, 1981.
———. *Torrente Ballester en su mundo literario.* Salamanca: Universidad, 1984.
Knickerbocker, Dale. "Ideología y sujeto en *La saga/fuga de J.B.*" *Hispanic Journal* 16.2 (Fall 1995): 399–416.
———. "Of Narrative Strategies and Practical Jokes: A Meta-Reading of *La saga/fuga de J.B.*" *Romance Languages Annual* 7 (1995): 527–531.
Loureiro, Angel. *Mentira y seducción: La trilogía fantástica de Torrente Ballester.* Madrid: Castalia, 1990.
Miller, Steven. "Structuring Probability, Possibility, and Ultimate Questions: Theory and Practice of Fantastic Fiction in Torrente Ballester." *The Fantastic Other: An Interface of Perspectives.* Ed. Brett Cooke, George E. Slusser, and Jaume Marti Olivella. Amsterdam, Netherlands, and Atlanta, GA: Rodopi, 1998. 87–100.
Pérez, Janet. *Gonzalo Torrente Ballester.* Boston: Twayne, 1984.
———. "The Impotence of Power in Recent Novels of Torrente." *Revista Hispánica Moderna* 40.1 (June 1995): 160–170.
Pérez, Janet, and Stephen Miller. *Critical Studies on Gonzalo Torrente Ballester.* Boulder, CO: Society of Spanish and Spanish-American Studies, 1989.
Ruiz Baños, Sagrario. *Itinerarios de la ficción en Gonzalo Torrente Ballester.* Murcia: Universidad, 1992.
Torrente Malvido, G. *Gonzalo Torrente Ballester, mi padre.* Madrid: Temas de Hoy, 1990.

Janet Pérez

Torres, Inés de (c. 1390)

Inés de Torres is the subject of the *Laudatio Agnetis Numantinae* (1440; Eulogy of Zamoran Inés), one of the first biographical texts on a Spanish woman.

Born in Zamora to a wealthy family, she was most likely of *converso* (Jewish convert) descent. She bore seven illegitimate children by Luis de Guzmán, master of Calatrava, with whom she refused to live. As *privada* (favorite) of the Queen Regent Catherine of Lancaster during the minority of Juan II of Castile (1414–1416), Torres wielded some political influence in the Castilian court along with her friend Leonor *López de Córdoba (c. 1362) until she was forced into exile in Cordoba by a conspiracy, accused of having intimate relations with Juan Alvarez de Osorio.

The *Laudatio* was written by the Florentine humanist Giannozzo Manetti (1396–1459) and dedicated to Torres's youngest son, the bibliophile Nuño de Guzmán. She is portrayed as an example of the humanist *femina erudita* (learned woman) who conjoined *ingenium et eloquentia* (talent and learning). Following the ideal characteristics of the cultivated woman outlined in Leonardo Bruni's *De studiis et litteris* (c. 1425), a manual for the education of girls, Manetti praises Torres's beauty, chastity (the seven illegitimate children are decorously overlooked), and piety by comparing her to an array of classical heroines, all of them persevering housewives. On the other hand, Torres's intellectual accomplishments—her love of reading, discriminating taste, and intelligence—although the predictable result of a noble upbringing, are presented as manly attributes. In the end, the humanist praise of Torres's manliness as a *monstrum* (miracle) continues the old prejudice against educated women depicted in Juvenal's *Sixth Satire* and authorized by the Pauline precepts: A woman's place is in the home, and her learning is an insolent threat to the established order.

Work about

Lawrance, J.N.H. *Un episodio del proto-humanismo español: Tres opúsculos de Nuño de Guzmán y Giannozzo Manetti.* Salamanca: Biblioteca Española del Siglo XV, 1989.
———. "Transgressions of Order: The Universities at the End of the Middle Ages." *Atalaya* 6 (1995): 15–37.

Sol Miguel-Prendes

Tórtola Valencia, Carmen (1882–1955)

One of Spain's most controversial women, Carmen Tórtola Valencia was a talented avant-garde dancer and a pioneer Spanish feminist of the twentieth century. Her life was a constant striving toward personal and artistic freedom. According to a copy of her birth certificate conserved at the Institut del Teatre of Barcelona, she was born in Seville on June 18, 1882, to a Catalan father, Florenc Tórtola Ferrer, and an Andalusian mother, Georgina Valencia Valenzuela. When she was three years old her family moved to London, where they later left her, for reasons unknown, in the care of a wealthy British family. Her parents both died between 1891 and 1894 in Oaxaca, Mexico, where they had settled.

Tórtola generally refused to discuss her early years, and when she did she gave contradictory versions of her story, encouraging the air of mystery that eventually grew around her. Some critics speculated that her lineage could be traced to the Spanish royal family; others thought she was the daughter of a British nobleman. In *Tórtola Valencia and Her Times* (1982), Odelot Solrac, one of her first biographers, describes a youthful, unconventional Tórtola who rejected formal dance training and tradition, in order to develop her own personal style based on the free expression of emotion through movement. Her disdain for conventionality was also mirrored in her private life, which she always protected from public scrutiny.

Better educated than most women of the day, she learned several foreign languages and read extensively. Although she never forgot Spanish, she spoke it with a foreign accent. Influenced by the North American dancer Isadora Duncan, Tórtola took the Greek ideals of beauty and the passion of Greek tragedy as inspiration for her innovative use of movement and mime. Her interests soon extended to the study of other cultures and their dance forms. Whenever not dancing, she was in museums or libraries, discovering the images and ideas that would stimulate her imagination. Tórtola was an anthropologist of dance and particularly fascinated by African, Arab, and Indian cultures, which she reinterpreted in her own expressive art form. She was profoundly aware of her role as an avant-garde artist who spoke to her audience in a universal language. Among her extraordinary creations were the *Danza del incienso* (Dance of Incense), *La bayadera* (Hindu Ballerina), *Danza africana* (African Dance), the *Danza de la serpiente* (Dance of the Serpent), and *Danza árabe* (Arab Dance).

Tórtola made her first public appearance in 1908 at the Gaiety Theatre in London, as part of the show *Havana*. The *Morning Post* of London reported that her dancing was very animated. That same year she was invited to dance at the German Wintergarten and the Folies Bergères of Paris. She quickly became known as the "La Bella Valencia," a new favorite of Parisian audiences along with Carolina Otero ("La Bella Otero") and Raquel Meller.

The following year she danced in Nuremberg and again in London. She was invited to join the "Cirkus Varieté" of Copenhagen with Alice Réjane. Her Spanish debut took place in 1911 at the Romea Theatre of Madrid, where she again danced in 1912. In 1913 she began a tour of Spain, which included the Ateneo of Madrid. In 1915 she performed with Raquel Meller in Barcelona. Tórtola's artistic originality was understood by only a minority of the Spanish public. While some considered her to be truly talented, others thought her dance was more lascivious than artistic. In 1916 Tórtola was satirized by the Catalan humorist weekly *Papitu* and presented as another Mata-Hari. Despite her recognition that the Spanish public did not understand her art, she kept trying to gain public acceptance on the Spanish stage and eventually she did. Spanish intellectuals who praised her talent include Jacinto *Benavente, Ramón *Pérez de

Ayala, Miquel dels Sants Oliver, Pio *Baroja, and Ramón del *Valle-Inclán. Emilia *Pardo Bazán declared Tórtola the personification of the Orient and the reincarnation of Salome.

An eclectic and multitalented artist, in 1917 she acted in the films *Pasionaria* and *Pacto de lágrimas*, both directed by José María Cortina. That same year she traveled to New York, dancing at the Century Theatre. In 1920 the Laietanes Gallery of Barcelona exhibited 45 of her excellent paintings on the subject of dance. The following year she began a series of trips that would take her throughout Latin America, visiting Brazil, Chile, Uruguay, Mexico, Guatemala, El Salvador, Panama, and the Dominican Republic. Between 1921 and 1930 she performed throughout Latin America, enjoying great popularity.

Tórtola's independence, both in her art and her life, was often perceived as a menace to the stability of traditional Spanish society. Like contemporaries such as Isadora Duncan, Virginia Woolf, and Sarah Bernhardt, Tórtola was a pioneer in advancing women's liberation. She made many unorthodox choices such as becoming a vegetarian and advocating abolition of the corset that constricted women's bodies and impeded freedom of movement. Although she was known to have taken lovers from the intellectuals of her time, she chose to remain single and lived many years of her life with another woman, Angeles Magret Vilá. We know very little about the dynamics of this relationship because Tórtola defended her right to privacy as much as her autonomy.

Suddenly, at the height of her career, after performing in Venezuela, Bolivia, and Cuba, with no explanation or justification, she decided to abandon the stage. She danced for the last time on November 23, 1930, in Guayaquil, Ecuador. In 1931 she declared herself Catalan and Republican and moved to Barcelona with her beloved Angeles. She was then 48 years old and above all a free woman. Tórtola dedicated the last years of her life to reading and collecting stamps. She also became a Buddhist. Tórtola died on February 14, 1955, after a heart attack, in her home at Sarrià. She is buried in the cemetery of Poblenou in Barcelona.

Work about

Archives of the Institut del Teatre of Barcelona.
Peypoch, Irene. *Carmen Tórtola Valencia*. Barcelona: Editions de Nou Art Thor, 1984.
Solrac, Odelot. *Tortola Valencia and Her Times*. New York: Vantage, 1982.

Carlota Caulfield

Tratado en defensa de las virtuosas mujeres (before 1448)

This small treatise was one of several that may have been written at the general request of Queen Doña María, first wife of King Juan II. Upon reading *El *Corbacho* (written 1438), the Archpriest of Talavera Alfonso Martínez de Toledo's misogynous attack on women, she was sufficiently offended to request that other writers respond to restore the sullied honor and good name of women. Court historian, soldier, and moralist Diego de Valera (1412–1488?) penned the *Tratado en defensa de las virtuosas mujeres* (Treatise in Defense of Virtuous Women) as such an answer.

Valera constructs his defense via a conversation the narrator directs to "a friend," in which he refutes three basic arguments held by women's detractors, namely: that by their very nature women are bad; that all humans are sinful but women are more so because they are weaker than men; and that all women practice adultery, at least in their thoughts. Van Veen observes that although Valera refutes these antifeminist beliefs, he does not challenge the basic, traditional definition of women as inferior creatures, weaker vessels who, by virtue of their ability to provoke lust, are essentially temptresses; thus his essay implicitly reinforces traditional views, challenging only what might be termed an excessive negativity. Montoya Ramírez likewise detects a lack of zeal in Valera's position and speculates that the treatise was penned out of a sense of obligation to the queen or even as an act of political opportunism, rather than from personal convictions.

Work by

Tratado en defensa de las mujeres virtuosas. Ed., study and notes, María Angeles Suz Ruiz. Madrid: El Archipiélago, 1983.

Work about

Montoya Ramírez, María Isabel. "Observaciones sobre la defensa de las mujeres en algunos textos medievales." *Medioevo y literatura. Actas del V Congreso de la Asociación Hispánica de Literatura Medieval*. Ed. Juan Paredes. 4 vols. Granada: Universidad de Granada, 1995. 4: 397–406.
Van Veen, Manon. "La mujer en algunas defensas del siglo XV: Diego de Valera y Juan Rodríguez del Padrón y los mecanismos de género." *Medioevo y literatura. Actas del V Congreso de la Asociación Hispánica de Literatura Medieval*. Ed. Juan Paredes. 4 vols. Granada: Universidad de Granada, 1995. 4: 465–473.

Maureen Ihrie

Tristana (1892)

The eponymous protagonist of this novella by Benito Pérez Galdós is a beautiful orphan who becomes the ward of her family's benefactor, Don Lope Garrido, nearly 40 years her senior. An inveterate womanizer, Don Lope quickly seduces Tristana. The story's action begins eight months into the affair, which has grown increasingly distasteful to Tristana. A chance meeting with a young artist, Horacio, provides her with an emotional release from her elderly guardian's oppressive control. The love between Horacio and Tristana remains unconsummated until a threat by the jealous Don Lope causes Tristana to defy his authority through a series of afternoon trysts in Horacio's studio. Although the young lovers are happy together, their intimate conversations reveal a fundamental incompatibility in their attitudes concerning gender roles. Horacio wants to marry Tristana despite her public dishonor, but she totally rejects both the institution of marriage (which she views as a form of slavery) and society's definition of dishonor. For Tristana, a career would bring her respectability as well as independence. Since it is this *libertad honrada* (honorable freedom) to which she aspires, she laments that her parents gave her "la educación insustancial de las niñas" (a vapid girls' education). The strength of Tristana's convictions makes Horacio uneasy, and they quarrel when Tristana states that any child of theirs would bear her surname alone since Nature gives a woman the greater claim to her children. Their relationship is interrupted when Horacio leaves Madrid to care for his ailing aunt. Over the next several months their letters evidence a growing dissimilarity in tastes and opinions. Whereas Horacio finds contentment in the simplicity of country life and urges Tristana to become his docile bride, Tristana seeks fulfillment in pursuing her professional goals. Don Lope now encourages Tristana's ambitions by hiring an English tutor and providing her with reading materials. There, in Lady Macbeth's words "Unsex me here," Tristana finds a profound expression of her frustration with gendered social constraints. Meanwhile, Tristana's mind gradually transforms the absent, unsupportive Horacio into her ideal man. Suddenly, Tristana's life is changed by a malignant tumor that requires her leg to be amputated. Don Lope continues to develop Tristana's intellectual, artistic, and musical talents after the operation in order to strengthen his hold over her. When Horacio returns to Madrid, Tristana is surprised at the difference between the real Horacio and her idealized version. After the lovers' awkward reunion, Horacio arranges with Don Lope to send Tristana an organ with sheet music as a parting gift. Tristana finds spiritual solace in playing religious music and attending mass. Finally, the aging Don Lope marries Tristana because his aunts promise them financial security if they legalize their relationship. The story ends in a pastoral setting with Don Lope planting trees and raising chickens while Tristana busies herself with the art of pastry making.

Emilia *Pardo Bazán's (1852–1921) review of this novel lauded Galdós for his initial characterization of Tristana as a woman denouncing the gender-based limitations placed on her by society. But Pardo Bazán also criticized Galdós for abandoning this feminist focus midway through the plot. Recent critical studies of this novel contend, however, that through the destruction of Tristana's aspirations Galdós presents a portrait of wasted human potential that powerfully argues for a reevaluation of women's roles. The key to Galdós's feminist orientation in this text rests in its ironic narration, which covertly exposes the intolerance, injustice, and arbitrary nature of conventional social codes. The final triumph of patriarchal order with the grotesque union of Tristana and Don Lope not only parodies the traditional "happy ending" in literature but also questions its validity in life. The last line of the novel invites the reader to evaluate the marriage of Tristana and Don Lope by asking: *¿Eran felices uno y otro?* (Was each one of them happy?). By having the question posed in a way that causes the reader to consider the situation of each character independently, Galdós underscores the degree to which Tristana's desire for autonomy has been denied and the extent to which Don Lope's quasi-incestuous exploitation of Tristana has been socially sanctioned. The narrator's ironic answer, *Tal vez* (Perhaps), points to the sham of domestic tranquillity based on sexual inequality. The crippled Tristana personifies the proverb *La mujer honrada, pierna quebrada y en casa* (The honorable woman [is the one] at home, [with a] broken leg). It has been suggested that Galdós signaled his feminist intentions in this novel by naming his heroine after Flora Tristán, the famous Hispano-French advocate for woman's rights. Also, letters written to Galdós by actress Concha-Ruth Morell reveal that she and Galdós were involved in a love triangle similar to the one depicted in *Tristana*.

Luís Buñuel's 1970 film adaptation retains the basic concept of a young woman seduced by an older man before taking a young lover, but Buñuel changes many of the details and completely alters the dynamics among the three major characters. Don Lope is made more sympathetic as the man left behind by Tristana when she goes away with Horacio after he physically assaults Don Lope. Tristana voluntarily returns to Don Lope when she becomes ill, and after her surgery she becomes the dominant figure in the relationship, with Don Lope passively resigned to their sexless marriage. In the final scene Tristana duplicitously withholds medical attention from Don Lope as he suffers a fatal heart attack. Buñuel's manipulative and vengeful Tristana has none of the spirituality of the Galdosian original, and the novel's exploration of women's issues is sacrificed to the game of psychological warfare played by Buñuel's characters.

Work by

Tristana. Ed., intro., notes, and bibliography Gordon Minter. London: Bristol Classical, 1996.
Tristana. Trans. R. Selden Rose. Peterborough, NH: R.R. Smith, 1961.

Work about

Aldaraca, Bridget A. *El ángel del hogar: Galdós and the Ideology of Domesticity in Spain*. Chapel Hill: UNC Department of Romance Languages, 1991.
Friedman, Edward H. " 'Folly and a Woman': Galdós' Rhetoric of Irony in *Tristana*." *Theory and Practice of Feminist Literary Criticism*. Ed. Gabriela Mora and Karen S. Van Hooft. Ypsilanti: Bilingual Press/Editorial Bilingüe, 1982. 201–228.
Jagoe, Catherine. *Ambiguous Angels: Gender in the Novels of Galdós*. Berkeley: U of California P, 1994.
Pardo Bazán, Emilia. *Obras completas*. Vol. 3. Madrid: Aguilar, 1973.
Rodríguez, Alfred. "Un título y una protagonista." *Anales Galdosianos* 15 (1980): 129–131.
Smith, Gilbert. "Galdós, *Tristana*, and Letters from Concha-Ruth Morell." *Anales Galdosianos* 10 (1975): 91–120.
Sobejano, Gonzalo. "La prosa de *Tristana*." *Pensamiento y literatura en España en el siglo XIX: Idealismo, positivismo, espiritualismo*. Ed. Yvan Lissorges.</br>

Ed. and afterword Gonzalo Sobejano. Toulouse, France: PU de Mirail, 1998. 189–199.

Linda M. Willem

Triunfo de las donas

See Rodríguez del Padrón (de la Cámara), Juan (1399?–1450)

Trotaconventos

See Celestina, La. Comedia o tragicomedia de Calisto y Melibea; Tercera

Tusquets, Esther (1936–)

Born in Barcelona, Esther Tusquets completed her primary and secondary education at the Colegio Alemán and studied philosophy and letters with a specialization in history at the Universities of Barcelona and Madrid. She later taught literature and history at the Academia Carrillo and in the early 1960s became director of the Editorial Lumen, a Barcelona publishing house, a position she still holds. Tusquets has two children, Milena and Néstor, both in their twenties now, whom she considers a very positive influence on her life. Her love for storytelling goes back to her childhood, when she would listen to stories told by various members of her household, especially by her mother, whom she credits for having created a magical world for her and her brother (see "Carta a la madre" [1996; Letter to Mother]). An avid reader from her early years, it seems that literature, movies, and her own fantasy provided an outlet for her shyness and loneliness.

Tusquets grew up within the confines of her bourgeois Catalan family and friends, and she says that it was not until her university years that she learned the true facts about the Spanish Civil War. She has referred to her father's side of the family as rightist, albeit not her mother's. Her sympathetic feelings toward the "losers" in the conflict are detectable in the sociocultural subtext of her fiction, in her ironic treatment of her own bourgeois-class—"her tribe"—and her overt alliance with "outsiders." The difficult relationship between Tusquets and her mother is common knowledge, and literary critics have amply explored the theme of the mother/daughter failed relationship and its impact on female characters in her novels, especially her first, *El mismo mar de todos los veranos* (1978; The Same Sea as Every Summer). Unlike most post-Franco Catalan writers, Tusquets writes in Castilian.

Tusquets's first published work was a book of adolescent poetry, *Balbuceos (Poesías)* (1954; Mutterings [Poems]). It was not until 24 years later that *El mismo mar de todos los veranos* appeared. The novel created a stir in the literary world because of its frank portrayal of lesbian love and its explicit eroticism, but it is important to underscore that the work received high praise for its artistic and lyrical prose and the author's skillful use of a variety of narrative techniques. The novel tells the story of a woman—a university professor—who in the midst of a marital crisis finds refuge in the house of her childhood in an attempt to revisit her past and recover her true identity. During her brief separation from her husband, she finds love in Clara, one of her young students, in whom she sees the woman she once was. They engage in a passionate relationship that comes to an end when the woman's errant husband returns from his trip and reclaims her. *El mismo mar* explores the subjects of bisexuality, love/power relations, and female midlife awakening and self-search against the backdrop of the Catalan upper class; it also serves as testing ground for the author's creativity. In the novel, Tusquets draws upon mythological figures and *fairy tales to weave her plot and also creates a complex network of literary, sociohistorical, and cultural intertexts that place the story in its proper time and space, all of which account for the rich texture of its narrative tapestry. By telling her stories to Clara, the protagonist/narrator adopts the role of a modern-day Scheherazade who finds her narrative voice and entertains her captive audience (Clara and the readers) until her husband's inevitable return.

Tusquets's second novel, *El amor es un juego solitario* (1979; Love Is a Solitary Game), received the Premio Ciudad Barcelona. Here the protagonist/narrator of the previous novel is replaced by a third-person omniscient narrator. Elia, the protagonist, is much younger than the unnamed protagonist of *El mismo mar*, but her background is again upper-class Catalan society. The reader is made aware that Elia has a husband and children, although they are not with her. Elia emerges as a narcissistic, self-centered woman who can only fill her aloneness and boredom through sexuality. The mating game at the center of the narrative is preempted by Elia's memories of a book of adventures she had read as a child in which primates in the jungle responded to the springtime call of sexual desire of their female counterparts. Once again there is a character named Clara in the novel, also depicted as a young university student who has a fixation on the older woman. She keeps Elia company and runs errands for her. Their lesbian relationship is not explicit as in *El mismo mar*. Elia seems to take for granted Clara's adoring and servile attitude and is amused by Clara's role as matchmaker for a fellow student, Ricardo, and Elia. Ricardo, insecure in his manhood, fancies being sexually initiated by Elia, although he claims to be in love with Clara. Both Clara and Ricardo belong to an impoverished middle class typical of postwar Spain. Elia, due to her age, her experience, and her wealth, is in the position of the master vis-à-vis her two "slaves." The representation of Elia's decadent life and the suffocating world the other characters inhabit calls attention to Tusquets's social consciousness. Elia is amused by Ricardo's proposal and accepts his challenge. The climactic moment in the novel finds the trio in bed—Elia in the middle—after a night of champagne and pills. The expected gender/power play results in a reversal of the master/slave positions as previously established, yielding power to Ricardo, who, having consummated his initiation, pleads with Elia to induce Clara to respond to him sexually. Clara, drunk and hurt by Elia's betrayal, manages to escape the sordid scenario. At the conclusion of the novel, Elia meditates on her fear of death and growing old. Although she admits to the banality of her life, she finds herself incapable of renouncing the only stimulus that counteracts her neurotic depression. For Elia, the solitary game of sexual gratification must continue, since she affirms her own existence through the existence of others.

After writing her second novel, Tusquets decided that a third novel was needed to bring closure to the cycle she had started with *El mismo mar*, making the novels part of a trilogy. That third novel was to be *Varada tras el último naufragio* (1980; Stranded). Here Elia, the protagonist, is a woman in her late thirties who, after having been happily married for some 15 years, is unexpectedly rejected by her husband, Jorge, who, exasperated with her notion of undying, romantic love, asks her how long must they play the roles of Abelard and Héloïse. Elia falls into a deep depression and seeks the help of a psychiatrist friend who tries to make her understand the shortcomings of her total dependency on Jorge's love and encourages her to face the challenge of life without him. Elia had idealized Jorge to the extent of believing that he held the key to her life, her happiness, her sexuality, and even her literary inspiration and now is reminded that she was a writer in her own right before she met him. She is particularly disconcerted by having to decide what to do with the rest of her life. While her adolescent son, Daniel, is at summer camp, Elia goes to the beach house she and Jorge had shared for many years with their friends, Eva and Pablo. Unable to write

or to communicate her feelings to her friends, she drinks, takes pills, and even tests her sexuality with a young man she meets in a beach cafe. She soon realizes that the marriage of her friends is also in trouble; Eva is distraught when hearing of Pablo's infidelity and proposes that they divorce, but when the couple weigh the consequences of their separation—socially and financially—they decide against it. Elia and Eva actually represent the two sides of the same woman. Eva, like the protagonist of the first novel, feels humiliated by her husband's adventure with a younger woman, falls victim of depression, wants to break away from him, but later accepts the status quo. Elia, on the other hand, aware that she can respond to sexual love after her tryst with the young man from the beach cafe, and motivated by her son's love and support, decides to take responsibility for her own life. She will live with her son and continue her career as a writer. In the last 21 pages of the novel, the protagonist's stream of consciousness replaces the omniscient narrator, allowing the reader to partake in her exalted state of mind. The trilogy thus closes on an optimistic note as a prelude to female independence, an option not considered in the previous novels.

After the publication of *Para no volver* (1985; Never to Return, 1999), some critics called attention to certain common grounds between the new novel and the trilogy and began to refer to Tusquets's novelistic cycle as a tetralogy. However, during her talk at the Modern Language Association meetings on December 30, 1996, Tusquets insisted on the notion of the trilogy and disclosed that in a new edition of *El mismo mar* currently in preparation by Castalia, she has (re)named the protagonist Elia, as in the other two novels, to further confirm the connectedness of the trilogy.

Para no volver signals a departure from the trilogy, mainly because in this novel irony turns into outright humor. As Elena, the protagonist, approaches age 50, she faces the perspective of the irretrievable loss of her youth (alluded to in the title—a fragment from Rubén Darío's famous verses). Her uneasiness about her age is compounded by the realization that she has never lived her own life, having settled for a rather parasitic relationship with her husband. Furthermore, she is presently alone in her house; her two grown sons now have their own lives and have settled outside of Spain, and her husband has taken his young female assistant, not her, on a trip to America to promote his latest film. All this leads her to fall into a manic-depressive state: She cries and laughs, describes her predicament with self-deprecating humor, and imagines outrageous fantasies. She seeks the help of a male analyst, and her resistance to submit herself entirely to his control unravels into a parody of Freudian psychoanalytical theories, as Tusquets subverts Freud's male-centered concept of human sexuality in her ludic, carnivalesque discourse. The setting of the novel is Barcelona at the end of the Francoist period, looking retroactively to the late 1950s and 1960s, and the characters belong to the Catalan bourgeoisie, as in Tusquets's earlier works. At the novel's conclusion, Elena, who has shielded herself from criticism by not publishing her manuscripts, becomes aware of her friends' and her own husband's vulnerability to failure and compromise. They have taken risks and thus lived more fully, while she passively looked on from the sidelines. Her pledge to psychoanalysis in the last lines of the text presupposes Elena's desire to seek self-knowledge and change.

In addition to her four novels, Tusquets has published a collection of short stories, *Siete miradas en un mismo paisaje* (1981; Seven Glances at the Same Landscape), whose protagonist—Sara—serves as a common thread. Although the stories are not arranged in chronological order, they present crucial moments in Sara's life from age 9 to 18, as she goes through rites of passage at various stages of her development and experience. The character is a bourgeois child growing up in post–Civil War Spain, like the

author, who acknowledges the autobiographical content of the stories.

Tusquets has also authored two stories for children, *La conejita Marcela* (1980; Marcela the Little Rabbit) and *La reina de los gatos* (1993; The Queen of the Cats), articles for periodicals, and various stories that have been published in journals, periodicals, or as part of collections of short narratives. Of special interest is "Carta a la madre," which appeared in *Madres e hijas* (1996; Mothers and Daughters), a collection of works by female authors on the subject of their mothers. The story is openly autobiographical, a poignant letter to an elderly mother in which the mature daughter attempts to come to terms with old wounds and settle accounts. Shortly after this story appeared, Tusquets compiled most of her short stories in a volume under the title *La niña lunática y otros cuentos* (1996; The Lunatic Girl and Other Stories). It includes the following: "El hombre que pintaba mariposas" (The Man Who Painted Butterflies), "Las sutiles leyes de la simetría" (The Subtle Laws of Symmetry), "Recuerdo de Safo" (Memory of Sappho), "A Love Story," "La niña lunática," "La conversión de la pequeña hereje" (The Conversion of the Little Heretic), "La increíble, sanguinaria y abominable historia de los pollos asesinados" (The Incredible, Bloody and Abominable Story of the Murdered Chickens), and "Carta a la madre."

Tusquets has earned an important place in contemporary Spanish letters, and her literary merits have been recognized in Europe and in the United States, where her fiction has been the focus of extensive and serious scholarship. Her works have been translated into English, French, German, and Italian. *See also* Eroticism in Contemporary Spanish Women Writers' Narrative; Short Fiction by Women Writers: 1975–1998, Post-Franco

Work by

El amor es un juego solitario. Barcelona: Lumen, 1979.
La conejita Marcela. Barcelona: Lumen, 1980.

Love Is a Solitary Game. Trans. Bruce Penman. New York: Riverrun Press; London: J. Calder, 1985.

El mismo mar de todos los veranos. Barcelona: Lumen, 1978.

Never to Return. Trans. and afterword Barbara Ichiishi. Lincoln: U of Nebraska P, 1999.

La niña lunática y otros cuentos. Barcelona: Lumen, 1996.

Para no volver. Barcelona: Lumen, 1985.

La reina de los gatos. Barcelona: Lumen, 1993.

The Same Sea as Every Summer. Trans. Margaret E.W. Jones. Lincoln: U of Nebraska P, 1990.

Siete miradas en un mismo paisaje. Barcelona: Lumen, 1981.

Stranded. Trans. Susan E. Clark. Elmwood Park, IL: Dalkey Archive P, 1991.

Varada tras el último naufragio. Barcelona: Lumen, 1980.

Work about

Bellver, Catherine. "The Language of Eroticism in the Novels of Esther Tusquets." *Anales de la Literatura Española Contemporánea* 9.1–3 (1984): 13–27.

Buck, Carla Olson. "With Needle and Pen, Making Women's Art: *Siete miradas en un mismo paisaje*." *Letras Peninsulares* 3.2–3.3 (1990): 233–245.

Dolgin, Stacey L. "Conversación con Esther Tusquets: Para salir de tanta miseria." *Anales de la Literatura Española Contemporánea* 12.3 (1988): 397–407.

Gascón Vera, Elena. "El naufragio del deseo: Esther Tusquets y Sylvia Molloy." *Un mito nuevo: La mujer como sujeto/objeto literario*. Madrid: Pliegos, 1992. 91–97.

Gil Casado, Pablo. *La novela deshumanizada española, 1958–1988*. Barcelona: Anthropos, 1990. 432–452, 475–482.

Gold, Janet N. "Reading the Love Myth: Tusquets with the Help of Barthes." *Hispanic Review* 55 (1987): 337–346.

Ichiishi, Barbara F. *The Apple of Earthly Love: Female Development in Esther Tusquets' Fiction*. New York: Peter Lang, 1994.

Lecumberri, María Esther. " 'Siete miradas en un mismo paisaje' de Esther Tusquets: ¿Una novela o siete relatos?" *Monographic Review/Revista Monográfica* 4 (1988): 85–96.

Lee-Bonanno, Lucy. "The Renewal of the Quest in Esther Tusquets' 'El mismo mar de todos los veranos.' " *Feminine Concerns in Contemporary Spanish Fiction by Women*. Eds. Robert Manteiga, Carolyn Galerstein, and Kathleen McNerney. Potomac, MD: Scripta Humanística, 1988. 134–151.

Levine, Linda Gould. "Reading, Rereading, Misreading and Rewriting the Male Canon: The Narrative Web of Esther Tusquets' Trilogy." *Anales de la Literatura Española Contemporánea* 12 (1987): 203–216.

Molinaro, Nina L. *Foucault, Feminism, and Power: Reading Esther Tusquets*. Lewisburg, PA: Bucknell UP, 1991.

Navajas, Gonzalo. "Repetition and the Rhetoric of Love in Esther Tusquets' 'El mismo mar de todos los veranos.' " *Nuevos y novísimos: Algunas perspectivas críticas sobre la narrativa española desde la década de los sesenta*. Ed. Ricardo Landeira and Luis T. González-del-Valle. Boulder, CO: Society of Spanish and Spanish-American Studies, 1987. 13–129.

Nichols, Geraldine Cleary. "Esther Tusquets." *Escribir, espacio propio: Laforet, Matute, Moix, Tusquets, Riera y Roig por sí mismas*. Minneapolis: Institute for the Study of Ideologies and Literature, 1989. 71–101.

———. "The Prison-House (and Beyond): 'El mismo mar de todos los veranos.' " *Romanic Review* 75.3 (1984): 366–385.

Ordóñez, Elizabeth. "A Quest for Matrilineal Roots and Mythopoesis: Esther Tusquets' 'El mismo mar de todos los veranos.' " *Crítica Hispánica* 6.1 (1984): 3–46.

Rodríguez, Mercedes M. (Mazquiarán) de. "Conversación con Esther Tusquets." *Letras Peninsulares* 1.1 (1988): 108–116.

———. "Narrative Strategies in the Novels of Esther Tusquets." *Monographic Review/Revista Monográfica* 7 (1991): 124–134.

———. " 'Para no volver': Humor vs. Phallocentrism." *Letras Femeninas* 16.1–2 (1990): 29–35.

Schumm, Sandra J. " 'El amor es un juego solitario': Loss of Identity through Metaphors and Provocative Mirrors." *Letras Peninsulares* 8.1 (1995): 147–167.

Servodidio, Mirella d'Ambrosio. "Esther Tusquets' Fiction: The Spinning of a Narrative Web." *Women Writers of Contemporary Spain: Exiles in the Homeland*. Ed. Joan L. Brown. Newark: U of Delaware P, 1991. 159–178.

———. "Perverse Pairings and Corrupted Codes: 'El amor es un juego solitario.' " *Anales de la Literatura Española Contemporánea* 11.3 (1986): 237–254.

Smith, Paul Julian. "The Lesbian Body in Tusquets's Trilogy." *Laws of Desire: Questions of Homosexuality in Spanish Writing and Film 1960–1990*. Oxford: Clarendon P., 1992. 91–128.

Tsuchiya, Akiko. "Theorizing the Feminine: Esther Tusquets's 'El mismo mar de todos los veranos' and Hélène Cixous's écriture féminine." *Revista de Estudios Hispánicos* 26. 2 (May 1992): 183–199.

Vázquez, Mary S. "Tusquets, Fitzgerald and the Redemptive Power of Love." *Letras Femeninas* 14.1–2 (1988): 10–21.

———, ed. *The Sea of Becoming: Approaches to the Fiction of Esther Tusquets.* Westport, CT: Greenwood P, 1991. 157–172.

Vosburg, Nancy B. " 'Siete miradas en un mismo paisaje' de Esther Tusquets: Hacia un proceso de individuación." *Monographic Review/Revista Monográfica* 4 (1988): 97–106.

Mercedes Mazquiarán de Rodríguez

U

Uceda, Julia (1925–)

One of the finest women poets of the so-called Spanish generation of the 1950s, Julia Uceda was born in Seville, receiving her doctorate from and later teaching at the University of Seville. From 1965 to 1973 she taught at Michigan State University. After that she traveled to Ireland, finally returning in 1976 to Spain, where she lives today. Her literary trajectory, mainly in the poetry genre, started in 1959 with publication of *Mariposa en cenizas* (Butterfly in Ashes). Her poetry, as a true and complete art, is not merely conditioned by "female" questions but focuses on a deep preoccupation for the human being in the world; thus her work interests feminists and others. Uceda's poetry is compelling and personal because of its existential themes and the peculiar way in which she treats life, death, time, transcendence, and divinity. All are elaborated with careful consideration of the formal features of poetic language. Peñas-Bermejo's 1991 study and edition of Uceda's poetry includes both an introduction and a fundamental analysis (the most reliable, accurate one) of Uceda's poetic value.

The love theme in her first books, mainly *Mariposa en cenizas*, belongs to the tradition of Spanish poet Miguel Hernández: the absent lover. Gradually, Uceda's interests generalize to embrace the human being, human

rights, solidarity, social aspects, and Spain. All are treated from an ethical (not political) position, as seen in some poems in *Poemas de Cherry Lane* (1968; Cherry Lane Poems) and *Campanas en Sansueña* (1977; Bells in Sansueña). But Uceda's greatest theme, and primary concern, deals with existential matters: the search for meaning in life and death, the questioning of human transcendence. In this existential thematic Uceda uses poetic symbols such as the sea, the tide, the dream, fire, ashes, and others, to understand the world, time and childhood, unavoidable death, and the anguish of nothingness. Facing death, her poems attempt to transcend, to continue being although in another reality, and this is especially important in relation to nature and light. Uceda's poetry never denies God; the divine existence of God is accepted, although sometimes rebelliously questioned and importuned, as with Spanish poets such as *Unamuno, Dámaso Alonso, or Blas de Otero.

Viejas voces secretas de la noche (1981; Old Secret Voices of the Night) is perhaps Uceda's best book in which the symbol of dream takes on important meaning. The dream allows Uceda to order chaos and even return to the past, offering dream as a way and path of knowledge. In the final analysis, her poetry attempts to explain human presence in the world in a way where even traditional concepts of time and space lose their conventional limits and harmonize with poetic discourse. Uceda's value must be found precisely in her will to stay away from the exclusively feminine or masculine debate and her attempt to universalize the problem of humanity in the world.

Work by

Campanas en Sansueña. Madrid: Dulcinea, 1977.
Del camino de humo. Seville: Col. "Calle del Aire," 1994.
Extraña juventud. Madrid: Adonais, 1962.
Mariposa en cenizas. Arcos de la Frontera: Arcaraván, 1959.
Poemas de Cherry Lane. Madrid: Agora, 1968.
Sin mucha esperanza. Madrid: Agora, 1966.
Viejas voces secretas de la noche. Ferrol: Esquío, 1981.

Work about

Molina Campos, Enrique. "Nocturna luz de la poesía de Julia Uceda." *Nueva Estafeta* 41 (1982): 80–84.
Peñas-Bermejo, Francisco J., ed. *Julia Uceda. Poesía.* Esquío-Ferrol: Colección Esquío de Poesía, 1991.
Valis, Noël. *The Poetry of Julia Uceda.* New York: Peter Lang, 1994.
———. "Translation as Metaphysics: Working on Julia Uceda's Poetry." *Letras Peninsulares* 10.3 (1997–1998): 403–413.

Alberto Acereda

Uceta Malo, Acacia (1927–   )

Born in Madrid just before the outbreak of the Spanish Civil War, poet Acacia Uceta received her *bachillerato* (secondary school degree) and studied drawing and painting in the Escuela Central de Artes y Oficios de Madrid as well as programming techniques for broadcast media. She also earned a degree in the history and art of Spanish America from the Instituto de Cultura Hispánica. Uceta has collaborated in literary programs of Spain's National Radio, Televisión Española, and various literary journals in Spain and the Americas. Closely linked to the cultural life of the city of Cuenca, she has served as an officer of the Academia Conquense de Artes y Letras. Her poems have been translated to English, French, Portuguese, Italian,

and Arabic. A recipient of subsidies from the Fundación Juan March and Spain's Ministerio de la Cultura, she has received poetry prizes such as Luisa Soriano, Contraluz, Fray Luis de León, Ciudad de Cuenca, Amigos de la Poesía de Valencia, and others.

At a very early age Uceta revealed a considerable artistic temperament and was a painter until her inclination for poetry prevailed. As a poet, she made herself known in poetry readings organized by diverse groups and in literary reviews of Spain during the 1950s. She participated in recitals of the so-called café poets, a postwar generation who affirmed their presence by opposing the stiff "official" poetry of that period. Uceta also writes novels and stories but has left much of her prose in manuscript form. She has published only two novels: *Quince años* (1962; Fifteen Years), a finalist for prizes awarded to the short novel; and the long novel *Una hormiga tan sólo* (1967; Only an Ant).

Uceta classifies her poetry in stages and considers the first entirely autobiographical. Having shed the fear of intimacy, she talks of her own life, of the people and circumstances of her childhood and adolescence. At first this poetry is realistic, but little by little it becomes more transcendent, religious, and humanistic, approaching more general themes without leaving the realm of the personal. That aspect delineates her own life cycle; the poem "Introit" announces her birth with a shout of pain. The title *El corro de las horas* (1961; The Ring of Hours), her first book, takes up that cyclical concept of the ring of hours as its creative principle. Like a timeless circle of children singing, the course of time crystallizes in scenes of a little girl's maturation to adolescence, love, then motherhood.

In *El corro de las horas*, the poem "Hombre cansado" (Tired Man) announces a new stage as the poet's voice moves to another level, opening herself to the suffering of all people, their failures, their illusions, but her tone is not disheartened. She writes of individual existence and collective solidarity, furthering the central conflict of all her poetry: the struggle between ultimate nothingness that overshadows life and the affirmative will to live. This intense period takes form in her second book of poems, *Frente a un muro de cal abrasadora* (1967; Facing a Wall of Burning Lime).

Uceta's third stage emanates from another autobiographical work, *Detrás de cada noche* (1970; Behind Every Night). She divided this long poem into the parts of the day, which symbolize life's path from joy to nothingness. The personal aspect becomes a struggle between hope and total anguish in death, a lonely agony she learned in childhood from the terror of the Civil War. However, Uceta ends this poem with her amazement at being alive. Thus, her first two phases melt into a passionate vitalism, a continuous, tenacious song to life in all its dimensions. One of the poems of *Al sur de las estrellas* (1976; South of the Stars) proclaims that the main thing in life is to be born. Uceta agrees that those who have judged her poetry as "vitalist" knew exactly what they were saying; she has made of her writing a source of life. When writing *Cuenca, roca viva* (1980; Cuenca, Living Rock), Uceta continued in this direction, effecting a complete fusion of that city's spirit and her own experiences. She identifies with Cuenca as the model of staying power and titanic effort against the rigors of time. The poetic conversation allows her to gather fortitude as she, like the rock of Cuenca, stands fast before the abyss.

Uceta's vitalism heightens in *Intima dimensión* (1983; Intimate Dimension) as she moves toward the interior of her being in order to be in contact with all that lives. The book is composed of three sections that recall Uceta's earlier cyclical concept, "Esfera" (Sphere), "Círculo" (Circle), and "Espiral" (Spiral). Here, using more abstraction than in previous poetry, Uceta expresses her strength as solitude, a concept she envisions as a diminutive universe that she dominates.

One of her principal motifs is the invincibility of her dimension, for within it she possesses the fortitude to close the door on the fear of nothingness and open her dimension of hope. As a vitalist, she finds herself engaged in the defense of life that has never been so threatened. She considers it a duty to cry out for peace, to rebel against those who put our very existence in danger, to fight for everyone's right to carve out a destiny.

Uceta maintains that she never had any concern for metrical structure in her poetry. Her poetry slowly became more refined as she advanced in thought and aesthetic demands. She has tried to reach the metaphysical by way of everyday life and to express its deepest part in simple language because she has always believed in the transparency of the transcendent. She feels free when using blank verse and loves the music of the 11-syllable line. All the same, while she feels that one must know poetic technique, she states that above all one must have something to say.

In her poetry Uceta deals with hope and transcendence, but in lectures and interviews she has been very forthright on women's issues. She believes that if a male writer has two distinct tasks in life, creativity and subsistence, the female writer has three. Besides working as a writer and earning a living in or outside her home, a woman writer must assume moral responsibility in managing a family and raising children. She asserts that no matter what is said to the contrary, that Spanish men barely participate in family matters. For Uceta, marriage has made very few advances in the social revolution under the new Spanish democracy. Spain is still emerging from a repressive phase that started in 1936 and reversed any social progress women had made. The reversal produced several generations of docile women who have recently been appeased by material improvements such as the latest electric appliances. Uceta believes that women's rights are still systematically denied while only a very small number of activists continue to fight for their equality before the law.

Work by

Al sur de las estrellas. Cuenca: Colección Gárgola, 1976.

El corro de las horas. Madrid: Agora, 1961.

Cuenca, roca viva. Cuenca: Colección El Toro de Barro, 1980.

Detrás de cada noche. Madrid: Nacional, 1970.

Frente a un muro de cal abrasadora. Cuenca: El Toro de Barro, 1967.

Intima dimensión. Cuenca: Colección El Toro de Barro, 1983.

Glenn Morocco

Unamuno y Jugo, Miguel de (1864–1936): Archetypes of the Mother and Immature Males in His Works

Miguel de Unamuno lost his father before reaching his sixth birthday. All his works of fiction attest to the absence of a strong father figure, if, in fact, such a figure is present in his novels at all. Unamuno grew up in a matriarchal household presided by his mother, to whom he was very attached. For a man in whose life the mother plays a dominant role, quite often the love of all women becomes maternal in nature, as is evident in Unamuno's adolescent attachment to Concepción Lizárraga, whom he later married and subsequently metamorphosed, both in life and in fiction, into a mother substitute, frequently referring to her as "mi esposa-madre" (my wife-mother). During Unamuno's religio-existential crisis of 1897, Concha Lizárraga cradled her husband in her arms, calling him "hijo mío" (my child), a cry recreated in nearly all the creative work Unamuno published after his first novel, *Paz en la guerra* (1897; *Peace in War* 1983). For Unamuno, Woman became synonymous with Mother, and the son's role that his male protagonists prefer to assume before their wife-mothers is clearly a relationship operative in their creator's psyche as well. Perhaps it was also an unconscious response to the

incest taboo that led Unamuno to transform his fictional wife-mothers into virgin-mothers, thereby avoiding the implication of consummated incest between mother and son.

The struggle of the Unamuno protagonists, or *agonistas* as he called them, is undoubtedly linked to Unamuno's own inability to complete what Swiss psychologist Carl Gustav Jung (1875–1961) described as a "process of masculine individuation." Jung posited that a man takes a first step toward psychic independence by freeing himself from the anima fascination of his mother. Metaphorically this is described as a confrontation between the conscious, or male, contents of the psyche with its unconscious, or female, counterparts. In practice a male "liberates" his anima from subordination to the Mother archetype by recognizing his unconscious, female nature in a woman from outside the family circle. He must then integrate the female characteristics that the anima represents into his own consciousness. Only at this point can a man achieve a true capacity for relating to women. Men such as the Unamuno protagonists, however, for whom the feminine is irrevocably identified with the Great Mother, are not prime candidates for a total process of self-realization, since their inability to distinguish the anima from mother leaves them in an infantile state of psychic dependence upon her. Under such conditions the male projects the mother-imago directly onto his wife-lover, who is then unable to fulfill her liberating, complementary function and instead is cast into the role of wife-mother or virgin-mother to her husband/son.

Unamuno's first three novels—*Paz en la guerra, Amor y pedagogía* (1902; *Love and Pedagogy*, 1996), and *Niebla* (1914; *Mist*, 2000)—all explore the process of masculine individuation in which youthful male protagonists struggle to liberate themselves from the magnetism of the unconscious symbolized by the chthonic, maternal element. In all three cases, love is the catalyst that leads to the kind of self-knowledge implicit in a process of individuation, the closest fictional equivalent of which is the formation of personality at the core of any typical *bildungsroman*. In *Paz en la guerra*, the external, physical conflict of the Third Carlist War provides a metaphorical backdrop against which Unamuno sets the internal, metaphysical struggle for individuation of his two young heroes, Pachico Zabalbide and Ignacio Iturriondo. Representing *intrahistoria* (intrahistory)—the everyday, uneventful life of the common people unaffected by History—Ignacio sheds his intellectual lethargy by going off to fight in the war, thus becoming swept up in historical events. The confrontational, well-read Pachicho, on the other hand, who does not participate in the civil conflict, gradually loses himself in philosophical ruminations. The Great Mother in this novel is emblematized by the rural, communal nature of Carlism and Catholic tradition. Ignacio first awakens to consciousness and separation from undifferentiated containment in the Mother by falling in love, an act that typically leads men and women alike to first recognize their individuality and subsequently to affirm the characteristics of the "other." But just as he begins to acquire awareness of himself through a strengthening of his ego, and to develop an identity apart from the collective, Ignacio is killed in battle. Death has had a long association with the notion of a return to the Great Mother's womb, often described as both cradle and tomb: a shelter for the unborn and a vessel that receives the dead. Ignacio's death therefore is a literal return to Mother Earth and to the collective unconscious of which She is a universal symbol. Pachico Zabalbide, who began as a character firmly established in the masculine world of reason, extroversion, and action, also fails to fulfill his promise of potential wholeness, experiencing in the last scene of the novel a pantheistic vision of the Godhead through a mystical union with Mother Nature; although he returns from the mountaintop vowing to "arouse in people the

discontent which is the prime mover of all progress and all good," a character like Pachico never again surfaces in Unamuno's novels.

Augusto Pérez, the protagonist of *Niebla*, is an older, more complex version of Ignacio Iturriondo and Apolodoro Carrascal, protagonist of *Amor y pedagogía*. Like Apolodoro, Augusto lacks a psychologically acceptable father, develops an unusually strong attachment to his mother, and falls in love with a woman similar to mother in appearance and character. In the first pages of *Niebla*, we are apprised of Señora Pérez's recent death: an auspicious beginning, since elimination of mother's influence in a young man's life should theoretically open the door to the self-discovery that is coincidental to severing ties with the mother-imago, as well as rejecting ego containment in the unconscious "mist" that she symbolizes. Augusto's choice of love object unfortunately is a woman as domineering and manipulative as his mother, and because his only previous relationship to a woman was the quasi-symbiotic existence he led as an extension of his own mother, Augusto can only relate to Eugenia on a submissive level, as an inferior son rather than adult lover. Eugenia uses him to obtain a financially secure position for her own fiancé, with whom she elopes the night before her "wedding" to Augusto.

Although this wound to his psyche gives Augusto a final push toward self-consciousness, and he confesses to a friend that the pain and humiliation he suffers have made him "give birth" to a more mature Self, Augusto, nevertheless, resolves to commit suicide. The idea of death by suicide haunted Unamuno almost as much as it did the lives of his male characters, a number of whom die by their own hand (Eugenia's father, for example). Although the transformative process of individuation undeniably set in motion a series of changes in Augusto's personality, the abrupt end of his life is not unusual in men who find it impossible to resist the mother archetype and choose to regress to the unconscious world that she represents by way of suicide.

The process of individuation clearly tempts Unamuno at the same time that it inspires terror of complete removal from the sphere of maternal influence. Augusto Pérez represents what Jung called a "positive shadow" archetype, frequently rejected not because of the typically negative connotations associated with the shadow; but because its positive incarnation represents that which is "unknown," it also tends to inspire terror. Unamuno banishes the urge to individuation from his consciousness by projecting the positive shadow archetype out of himself and onto Augusto, whose life he then proceeds to snuff out when he proves to be excessively eager to achieve psychological independence and autonomy from mother. Augusto's attempt at self-realization is routed by his creator, the Great Mother/Unamuno who overwhelms the hero, defeating him in his battle of deliverance from the mists of the female matrix. Unamuno often toyed with the idea that God does not assure human beings immortality; rather, it was the cyclical aspect of female nature that presided over birth, death, and regeneration, guaranteeing humankind perpetual life, and he frequently compared artistic creation to motherhood. Augusto Pérez's last cries—"madre mía . . . Eugenia . . . Unamuno"—are, in fact, a progression from biological mother to mother substitute to Unamuno, his god-creator and fictional "mother."

The novels Unamuno produced in the second half of his life—*Nada menos que todo un hombre* (1916; Nothing Less Than Every Inch a Man), *Abel Sánchez* (1917), and *Como se hace una novela* (1925–1927; How to Write a Novel)—study the progressive disintegration of the splintered male personality. This series of male protagonists no longer attempts processes of individuation, almost as if hope for completion no longer exists, and perhaps reflecting Unamuno's own inability to resolve the polarities within his psyche, they suffer full-blown neuroses. The short novel

Nada menos que todo un hombre inaugurates this new approach to masculine characterization with special emphasis on the psychological impasse that arises when a male rejects the mediating influence of his female nature (the anima), while allowing the ego to enter into conflict with his public persona. According to Jung, for a process of individuation to be completed successfully, the human being must learn to distinguish between who she/he is and how she/he appears to others. In a split personality, cleavage will occur between a subject's outward compliance to what one fancies oneself to be and inner rebellion against having to maintain that compliance. Psychic dualism of this kind frequently leads to the construction of a persona meant to camouflage internal divisions as well as to hide a fragmented self even from one's own psyche. When the artificially constructed persona overwhelms the ego, as Unamuno feared it did in *Como se hace una novela*, and as it actually does in the case of Alejando Gómez in *Nada menos*, a man becomes susceptible to personality fragmentation. This accounts for the role-playing and accusations of hypocrisy that dominate the lives of male characters Unamuno created in the second half of his life.

According to Jung, the man who comes closest to achieving self-realization is the one who most successfully minimizes the function of his persona. On the other hand, a male fused to the false aspects of his mask is known as a "personal man," and just as the man who cannot divest himself of a dominant mother archetype, the personal man carries a tremendous psychological burden that prevents him from attaining complete individuation. The mask assumed by Alejandro Gómez not only disguises a social inferiority complex, it also prevents him from recognizing his wife Julia as the anima and mediator of the unconscious contents of his psyche to consciousness.

To ensure the healthy survival of a heterosexual pair, the male partner must willingly relate to his anima and rescue her, as it were, from repression into the unconscious. Initially it is normal for a male to resist the numinosity of this archetype, primarily because it represents all the traits a patriarchal value system tends to diminish: irrationality, creativity, earthiness, the instincts, and the unconscious; it is common for men to fear being "invaded" or "weakened" by a woman's femininity, and only during the integrative stages of individuation are they able to accept and reclaim the feminine side of the Self rejected in earlier stages of development. Alejandro's tragedy lies in excluding the anima archetype from his life and in the mental cruelty he showers upon Julia as a symbol of that archetype. For all his outward show of bravado and strength, after Julia's untimely death, Alejandro succumbs to his hidden weakness by committing suicide: The attraction of the feminine proves to be stronger than he, and Alejandro opts to reunite with his wife in death rather than to continue living without her.

The conflict between the Self and its increasingly rebellious "other," or rival personality, is also at issue in *Abel Sánchez*. Human beings often relegate negative character traits they perceive in themselves to an unconscious existence in what Jung called the "shadow" personality. These incompatibilities are normally projected out of the Self onto someone who seems to embody the undesirable character traits. *Abel Sánchez*, a novel about fraternal discord, metaphorizes the competition between the light and dark sides of the personality that is one of the oldest archetypal motifs in human history. Unamuno's growing fascination with twins and personality splitting perhaps had its basis in his own inability to resolve successfully the now-famous conflict between his contemplative but repressed self and the aggressive public figure he had permitted to become his dominant personality.

One keystone of the individuation process is the recognition of one's dark personality (the shadow) and, in the case of men, its assimilation to consciousness through the mediating role of the female anima. When the anima is denied her role as facilitator, the shadow splinters away from the personality and begins a rival existence as an autonomous psychic entity. The case of Joaquín Monegro, however, presents the more unusual case in which the positive qualities normally attributed to the ego are rejected, while the negative traits of the shadow are permitted to seize hold of the ego, causing it to appropriate the negative features as its own. Joaquín's inability to accept his wife Antonia as a mediating force between his ego and his shadow, his insistence on separation rather than relatedness, his reduction of Antonia to an object to be used for vengeful purposes (Joaquín's only interest in his wife is that she bear a male child), causes Monegro to go through life an unwell man. Hate and rejection of some aspects of the Self—personified by the shadow or double (in this case, represented by Abel Sánchez)— often culminates in suicide intended as a death for the pursuing double. Joaquín's role in Abel's "accidental" death is a clear attempt to excise that part of his own psyche that he finds bothersome and tormenting. This characteristic elimination of the "other" is tantamount to suicide since the ego cannot survive long without the complementary presence of its opposite. Joaquin's deathbed confession that Antonia had not been able to "cure" him because he could not bring himself to love her completely is a delayed recognition of his failure to accept his wife as mediatrix. Unamuno's stories of male, and not infrequently, female doubling (e.g., *Las dos madres, La *tía Tula*), are often pretexts through which he seeks to experience the fully integrated, yet perpetually elusive Self. Although Joaquín and Abel, like their biblical counterparts Cain and Abel, are essentially indivisible, neither is able or willing to surrender autonomy in the interests of harmonious coexistence. They remain, like Unamuno's own personality, an ego forever at odds with its shadow.

Unamuno's last important work of fiction,

San Manuel Bueno, mártir (1933; *St. Manuel Bueno, Martyr*, 1973), returns to the unconscious collective life of *intrahistoria* first novelized in *Paz en la guerra*. A thoroughly matriarchal order rules this novelistic universe: As the work unfolds, its narrator, Angela Carballino, evolves from a surrogate daughter to Don Manuel, the saintly priest of Valverde, to the recipient of a series of female archetypes that he projects upon her. Her function as "deaconess" to Manuel leads Angela to develop a "maternal affection" for her spiritual father. Later, when Manuel asks for and receives absolution from Angela, she also assumes numinous qualities characteristic of the Virgin Mary; however, she is an inverted Mary who intercedes not with Christ on behalf of humankind but with God the Father on behalf of her son Manuel. As Don Manuel's spiritual guide and confessor, Angela is likewise comparable to the highest form of the anima archetype: the Gnostic Sophia, symbol of wisdom and most evolved partner of the male ego. Because Sophia is often associated with the Holy Ghost, the concept acquires, in Unamuno's hands, a feminine connotation that reinforces Angela's angelic role as mediator and messenger between the "unseen" regions of Don Manuel's psyche and the "seen" world of his conscious biography as she records it for posterity.

Angela thinks of her Don Manuel as a "varón matriarcal" (matriarchal man) since as a priest he fulfills a maternal function by sheltering his flock in an unconscious state of existence far removed from the trials of History, while voluntarily sacrificing his own well-being by never revealing, other than to Angela's brother, his personal disbelief in the resurrection of Christ. Ironically, Manuel himself longs for peaceful, untrammeled sleep in a mother's arms, and his temptation to commit suicide by drowning in the Lake of Valverde reflects a basic need to resolve the contradictory tendencies of his psyche through escape to the amniotic waters of the Great Mother whose womb is a gateway that

leads to peace and the unconsciousness of the underworld. Convinced as he is that there is no life after death, when Don Manuel feels his own end drawing near, he nevertheless asks to be taken into the "womb" of his church and to be interred in a casket made of planks from the "matriarchal walnut tree" beneath which he says he played as a child. He thereby assures himself an allegorical return to the great container vessel that is Mother Church. Unable to resolve the problems posed by the patriarchal nature of Catholic dogma, in life as well as in death, Don Manuel advocates instead the superiority of unconscious containment in the chthonic world of the archetypal feminine. And by espousing matriarchal values, he completes the circle of Unamuno protagonists whose preference for an unconscious existence within the Great Mother indicates a psychological immaturity characteristic of the masculine ego in an arrested state of development. Consonant with this type of personality is a rejection of the male spiritual principle that typically devalues the feminine as negative and evil. Thus in Manuel's new theology, the notion of apocatastasis—the restoration to wholeness through God—is not related to God the unsubstantiated Father but rather to the heterodox idea of immortality attained through the eternally cyclical womb of the Mother, symbol of eternity, equilibrium, and perpetual regeneration.

Unamuno's return to Mother is not unique in and of itself but exemplifies Jung's position that any work of art can adapt ancient myth to contemporary sensibility. At the foundation of many world religions lies a belief in personal renewal through symbolic death, regression to the female underworld, an ensuing battle of deliverance from the Terrible Mother, followed by ascension to a patriarchal society of ego-affirmation, light, and consciousness. Since the human urge to self-realization is the most basic of archetypes, it is impossible for Unamuno not to have responded to its prompting: His entire novelistic corpus appears to explore attempted and failed processes of individuation, failed because, in Unamuno's recasting of the story, the symbols of transformation that typically accompany a hero's symbolic death and resurrection are wholly absent from his personal idiolect.

While at first glance the feminine archetype operative in Unamuno's fiction gives the impression of being a benevolent, nurturing mother, she quickly proves herself to be a devouring mother whose magnetism the male child finds irresistible. When a man allows himself to be overwhelmed in this fashion by the Great Mother's numinosity, he is unable to separate his anima archetype from the mother-imago, and deprived of the anima's liberating function, he remains in a truncated state of development in which, as Neumann states, the Feminine is dominant over the Masculine, as is the unconscious over the ego and consciousness. Death, in Unamuno's fiction, is thus not a symbolic road to enlightenment and renewal but a permanent escape from life, as well as a demonstrated preference for psychologically involuted states of existence within the "realm of the mothers." Unable to complete a process of individuation, the Unamuno protagonist, especially in the mature novels, is a man who suffers ontological illness and split personality, or what Unamuno referred to on more than one occasion as the *pavoroso problema de personalidad* (the terrifying problem of personality).

Work by

Abel Sánchez. Ed., intro., and notes José Luis Abellán. Madrid: Castalia, 1985.

Abel Sanchez, and Other Stories. Trans. and intro. Anthony Kerrigan. Chicago: Gateway, 1970.

Love and Pedagogy. Trans. Michael Vande Berg. New York: P. Lang, 1996.

Mist: A Tragicomic Novel. Trans. Warner Fite. Foreword Theodore Ziolkowski. Urbana: U of Illinois P, 2000.

Niebla. Prol. Gonzalo Torrente Ballester. Album by A. Ramoneda. Madrid: Alianza, 1998.

Obras completas. Ed. and prol. Ricardo Senabre. 4 vols. Madrid: Turner, 1995–1999.

Obras selectas. Prol. Julián Marías. Madrid: Espasa-Calpe, 1998.

Peace in War. Annotated Allen Lacy and Martin Nozick. Princeton, NJ: Princeton UP, 1983.

St. Manuel Bueno, Martyr. Trans. Mario J. Valdés and María Elena de Valdés. Chapel Hill: U of North Carolina P, 1973. Spanish and English.

Work about

Franz, Thomas. Parallel But Unequal. The Contemporizing of Paradise Lost in Unamuno's Abel Sánchez. Valencia: Albatrós, 1990.

Hall, Nor. The Moon and the Virgin: Reflections on the Archetypal Feminine. New York: Harper and Row, 1980.

Jung, C.G. Symbols of Transformation. Vol. 5 of The Collected Works of C.G. Jung. Trans. R.F.C. Hull. Ed. William McGuire. 2nd ed. Princeton, NJ: Princeton UP, 1970.

Jurkevich, Gayana. The Elusive Self: Archetypal Approaches to the Novels of Miguel de Unamuno. Columbia/London: U of Missouri P, 1991.

———. "The Sun-Hero Revisited: Inverted Archetypes in Unamuno's Amor y pedagogía." MLN 102 (1987): 292–306.

Lauter, Estella, and Carol Schriet Rupprecht, eds. Feminist Archetypal Theory. Interdisciplinary Re-Visions of Jungian Thought. Knoxville: U of Tennessee P, 1985.

Neumann, Erich. The Great Mother: An Analysis of the Archetype. Trans. Ralph Mannheim. New York: Pantheon, 1955.

Ouimette, Victor. Reason Aflame; Unamuno and the Heroic Will. New Haven, CT: Yale UP, 1974.

Gayana Jurkevich

Urraca de Castilla y León (1080–1126)

The daughter of Alfonso VI de Castilla, Urraca was married to Raimundo de Borgoña, count of Galicia, at age seven. Their only offspring was Alfonso Raimúndez, the future Alfonso VII, born in 1105. When Raimundo died in 1107, Urraca became the sole ruler of Galicia, and when Alfonso VI died in 1109 she assumed the title of queen of Castile y León and contracted matrimony with Alfonso I de Aragón y Navarra, *el Batallador* (The Battler), forming thereby an alliance of all the Christian kingdoms in the peninsula. The two monarchs never liked each other, however, and in 1114 they annulled their marriage and released their respective kingdoms from their national alliances. Urraca then turned her attention to consolidating her power in Galicia, signing an agreement with the powerful Church leader Diego Gelmírez, whom she later appointed the first archbishop of Santiago de Compostela.

Urraca was an independent, strong-willed woman whose primary interest was the protection of her hereditary interests. She was successful in maintaining the unity of Castile and León, and her authority in Galicia permitted a growth in the economy from the influx of foreigners in Santiago de Compostela as a result of its promotion as a pilgrimage site.

Work about

Reilly, Bernard F. *The Kingdom of León-Castilla under Queen Urraca: 1109–1126*. Princeton, NJ: Princeton UP, 1982.

David H. Darst

Valderrama Alday, Pilar de (1889–1979)

Valderrama is a poet and dramatist in her own right; however, her work has attracted wider attention because of her sentimental friendship with the poet Antonio Machado (1875–1939). Born in Madrid to a conservative, Catholic family, Pilar de Valderrama spent her early infancy in Zaragoza, where her father was governor. Being of a very sensitive nature, she suffered with the loss of her father at the age of 6, and subsequently from the presence of a stepfather and stepbrothers. Moved by the desire to distance herself from the family situation, she married very young—she was only 19—a friend of her brother after a courtship of only six months. Interested in music, she took voice lessons, assiduously attended musical events of Madrid, and participated in cultural activities of the *Lyceum Club Femenino (an organization founded in 1926 and in existence through 1936, whose first president was María de *Maeztu). The principal function of the Lyceum was to provide a meeting place for cultural events attended by this small group of cultivated women, among them Carmen Baroja, Zenobia Camprubí, Ernestina *Champourcín, Carmen Monné, María Teresa *León, and María de la O Lejárraga, wife of Gregorio Martínez Sierra. Such an organization reflected the impetus to *women's edu-

cation given by the Krausists, the increased presence of *feminism in Spanish life, and the fertile years in literary and artistic creativity that characterized the Second Republic.

Valderrama confesses in her memoirs that writing poetry for her was a vocation, an inner need to express herself, rather than a profession or a means of attaining fame. She started writing poetry in her childhood to overcome feelings of sadness while in boarding school at the Sacred Heart. In the early years of her marriage, deeply involved in motherhood, she felt a yearning for fulfillment not met by the daily demands of family life; again she sought solace in writing, which served as a spiritual escape from melancholy and solitude. She took refuge in her poetry writing almost secretly in the privacy of her sitting room as if it were a wrongdoing, feeling that her literary inclinations were not favorably viewed by her husband. Her first book, *Las piedras de Horeb* (1923; The Stones of Horeb), written in a short time, is a collection of poems dedicated mostly to her children, dealing with emotions of tenderness, profound affection, and anxiety concerning their illnesses. Persistent feelings of solitude caused by a distant husband prompted her to continue writing, seeking as solace the contact with writers and artists who frequented the studio of his brother-in-law, sculptor Victorio Macho. Her second book, *Huerto cerrado* (1928; Closed Garden), whose title was inspired by the biblical King Solomon's Song of Songs, was well received by literary critics. She even sent a copy to Machado, already a famous poet, whom she had not met at the time. Following discovery of her husband's infidelity, she distanced herself to reflect, making a short trip to Segovia. There she met Machado, and the two developed a Platonic friendship between 1928 and 1936. Once more, depression and melancholy were overcome by writing. The next collection of poems, *Esencias* (1930; Essences), is marked by spiritual communication with Machado, including the textual interpolation of two of his stanzas that was reciprocated by his insertion of two poetic lines by Valderrama in his play *La Lola se va a los puertos.*

The last postwar collection of poems, *Holocausto* (1943; Holocaust), dedicated to the memory of her dead son, includes a sonnet by Manuel Machado as a prologue, followed by poems of memory, love, solitude, and finally solace in God. The volume *Obra poética* (1958) is a compilation of Valderrama's poetry with selections from *Huerto cerrado*, most of *Esencias*, and some unpublished poems collected as "Espacio" (Space) reputedly written in different periods of the poet's life. Those poems, not published until 4 years after the death of her husband and 19 years after Antonio Machado died in Collieure, are revealing songs to the beloved, where Valderrama lets her unveiled voice speak at last. *Las piedras de Horeb* (1922) and *El tercer mundo* (1930; The Third World) are omitted from the volume.

Valderrama's interest in dramatic art led her to establish in her own house a chamber theater, "Fantasio," for the entertainment of her children. Later it broadened its repertoire and, in its two short years of existence, it attracted the attention of many artists and writers in Madrid. She also wrote for the theater. *El tercer mundo* is a dramatic poem in three acts (two in prose, the last in verse)

thematically inspired by the mutual affection of Valderrama and Machado. The characters live and explore reality, dream, will, and artistic creation, with a feminine character who deals with the problem of unhappiness at the level of reality by escaping to the level of dreams in quest of fulfillment of her desires. "La vida que no se vive" (c. 1930; Life That Is Not Lived) remains unpublished, although Machado tried to have it staged by Lola Membrives; it was read publicly at the Ateneo in the post–Civil War years.

Valderrama reveals herself in her autobiography *Sí, soy Guiomar* (1981; Yes, I Am Guiomar) as a nonliberated woman, subject to a social code she could not or did not know how to escape. In the correspondence of Machado included in the text, Valderrama emerges as restraining Machado with a secrecy that only her death could break. The epistolary itself bears witness to Valderrama's autocensorship resulting in a fragmentary correspondence due to her intervention (partial deletion of texts, alteration of dates, artificial sequential order). The result is an intimate but cryptic message, not easily deciphered. Valderrama mirrors women's experience when ambivalence, hesitation, and submission occur in the defiance of rigid social codes. The well-kept secret of Guiomar's identity slowly began to unravel after Valderrama confided the existence of Machado's correspondence to writer Concha Espina, who subsequently published the semifictitious novel *De Antonio Machado a su grande y secreto amor* (1950?; From Antonio Machado to His Great, Secret Love). Disclosure climaxed with the guarded admission by Valderrama in her posthumous autobiography.

In the posthumous volume *De mar a mar* (1984; From Sea to Sea) Valderrama's poetic voice appears without restraint. This collection includes poems written since publication of her compilation *Obra poética* in 1958 up until her death. The volume, in addition to poems of the last 30 years of her life, incorporates many written previously but that

Valderrama, exercising self-imposed censorship, had refrained from publishing until after her death. The title of the volume is already an homage to Machado, since it comes from the initial verse of one of Machado's last sonnets written in 1938 when, due to the Civil War, Valderrama was in Portugal, by the Atlantic Ocean, and Machado near Valencia, beside the Mediterranean Sea. While some poems of the collection are an implicit allusion to Machado, others are openly dedicated to him; her true feelings for Machado appear unmasked, and the lyric voice of Valderrama reaches authenticity.

Work by

De mar a mar. Madrid: Torremozas, 1984.

Holocausto. Madrid: Artegrafía, 1943.

Obra poética. Madrid: Siler, 1958.

Sí, soy Guiomar. Memorias de mi vida. Barcelona: Plaza y Janés, 1981.

El tercer mundo. Teatro de mujeres. Madrid: Aguilar, 1934.

Work about

Cotres Ibáñez, Emilia. "La autodiégesis en Pilar de Valderrama, Josefina Manresa y Felicidad Blanc." Escritura autobiográfica: Actas del II Seminario Internacional del Instituto de Semiótica Literaria y Teatral. Ed. José Romera Castillo. Madrid: Visor, 1993. 159–167.

Machado, Antonio. Cartas a Pilar. Madrid: Anaya, 1994.

Moreiro, José María. Guiomar, un amor imposible de Machado. Madrid: Espasa-Calpe, 1982.

Nieva de la Paz, Pilar. Autoras dramáticas españolas entre 1918 y 1936. Madrid: CSIC, 1993.

Pérez, Janet. Modern and Contemporary Spanish Women Poets. New York: Twayne, 1996. 59–62.

Ruíz de Conde, Justina. Antonio Machado y Guiomar. Madrid: Insula, 1964.

Pilar Sáenz

Valera, Juan (1824–1905): Women in His Novels

Padre Piñón, a character of Valera's *Las ilusiones del doctor Faustino* (1875; Dr. Faustino's Illusions), states at one point: "Dominus, inter caetera potentiae suae miracula, in sexu fragil victoriam contulit" (God, among other miracles of his power, gave victory to the weak sex). Juan Valera's women characters are in general strong, proud, and possessed of a powerful will to achieve their goals in life. At the same time, they resemble Jane Austen's characters in that they are conscious of the limitations imposed on women by the fin-de-siècle *Restauración* society, the Spanish equivalent of the Victorian period. Valera's female characters resemble those of Pérez Galdós, the master of Spanish realism. They belong to all social classes and form part of a diverse array of families (nuclear, single mother, widow, extended), and like Galdós, Valera did not favor any kind of family over the others, although many of his novels end with conventional marriages, often to an older man.

Pepita Jiménez (1874) is Valera's *opera prima* and his masterpiece. Its protagonist Pepita fulfills both conservative and liberal male fantasies of the perfect rural woman after the 1868 revolution. Young, blonde, extremely beautiful and rich, she is also very cultured and learned but knows the proper position of a woman in society; ever religious, she is never a "goody-goody." Her status as widow affords her the social freedom of a male and the ability to hold properties and manage her own financial affairs without seeming mannish. Pepita knows how to manipulate social norms of courtship to her own advantage, having learned well how to read social codes and benefit from them. Valera's originality resides in including sexual desire as an attribute of this perfect nineteenth-century *ángel del hogar (angel of the house).

The problem of portraying female characters in a society that is experiencing revolutionary changes is perhaps most clearly revealed in *Las ilusiones del doctor Faustino*. Valera demonstrates how difficult it was for a young man of the upper middle class to ascend socially and how easy it was to slide downwards; the constraints that class and caste norms impose on Faustino help explain the even greater difficulty women faced when attempting to improve their social status. The novel has three very interesting female characters: Doña Costanza, a young, confident heiress who controls her father's will and acknowledges her own sexual desires; Rosita, the 28-year-old daughter of the town solicitor, who states that she is free to do whatever she pleases because the only person who exercises control over her is her father, who demands no explanation of her behavior; and Manolilla, Costanza's chambermaid, who transforms herself into Etelvina Mercier, a famous dressmaker. The conclusion of the novel constitutes a farce of the adultery novel so typical of nineteenth-century realism. In this case, the adulteress is not punished, nor does she commit suicide.

The action of *El comendador Mendoza* (1876; Commander Mendoza) unfolds in 1744 in a small Andalusian town. The narrator explains that women of that day were denied access to education; middle-class women were taught to read religious books but were forbidden to learn to write. The village is ruled with an iron hand by Doña Blanca, the archetypal *beata (devout woman). She controls her household, the family business, and her daughter's education and exemplifies religious fanaticism (presented as a female characteristic). Because she fails to control her daughter's destiny, she ends defeated. Two interesting secondary characters of the novel are Nicolasa, a very determined social climber, and Lucía, who falls in love with her uncle, the *comendador*, because both share a passion for astronomy and botany.

Pasarse de listo (1877; Trying to Be Too Clever) combines features of two popular nineteenth-century subgenres—the bureaucrat's wife (e.g., Pérez Galdós's *Miau*) and adultery—with the story of two female social climbers, Doña Beatriz and her younger sister Inesita. Beatriz escapes poverty by marrying Don Braulio, a humble bureaucrat who manages to secure a position in Madrid. Once there, Beatriz convinces her sister to stroll with her in the Buen Retiro gardens so that possible suitors may admire Inesita's youth and beauty. The weak, effeminate Don Braulio becomes convinced his wife is having an affair with Count Alhedín el Alto. After Braulio forgives his wife and commits suicide, the reader discovers that Inesita was the real lover of the count. A charming secondary character of the novel is Rosita, another social climber described as "the queen of chichi."

Set in Villafría, yet another mid-nineteenth-century Andalusian town, *Doña Luz* (1878) dramatizes the constraints society imposed on women who depart from accepted social mores. An orphaned, illegitimate daughter of a marquis, Doña Luz's sophistication, education, and small inheritance cannot erase the stigma of her birth circumstances. Caballero Pozo commented that Doña Luz gives the two saddest kisses in the history of erotic and mystic Spanish literature, one to the image of a suffering Christ and the second to the dying priest she loved. Like Pepita Jiménez, Doña Luz's main characteristic is pride, but unlike Pepita, she ends tragically.

Juanita la Larga (1895; Formidable Juanita) offers the finest example of Valera's ideal of personal freedom, irrespective of gender. Juana is a single mother and businesswoman who lives in a medium-sized Andalusian city; she caters all the town's banquets, does all the fancy baking and sewing in town, and even slaughters pigs, earning a good living with her many entrepreneurial activities. Her well-educated daughter Juanita wants to use her money and education to become part of the upper class in the city. Juanita falls in love with Don Francisco López, lawyer and secretary to the political boss. She is opposed by another social climber, Francisco's daughter Doña Inés, a very pious woman married to the local aristocrat. Inés controls all social and religious activities of the city, down to choosing the names, jobs, and spouses for all the townspeople, especially the lower class. The novel presents the struggle between these two strong but very different women, each of whom knows how to read social codes and ascend socially; in this case, the illegitimate woman overcomes her stigma through marriage and triumphs in society, thanks to her older husband's position.

Rafaela *la Generosa* (the Generous), protagonist of *Genio y figura* (1897; A Leopard Never Changes Its Spots), is a **pícara* (female rogue) who evolves from working as a dancer and prostitute in Cádiz to becoming the most sought-after lady of Río de Janeiro and Parisian society and a matriarch who rules over her husband, estate, servants, and lovers. The conclusion to this example of the "adultery subgenre" is more conventional than that of *Pasarse de listo* because Rafaela, like Anna Karenina, commits suicide when one of her lovers, English diplomat Juan Maury, refuses to legitimize their daughter. Rafaela decides to die the day of her fiftieth birthday, a moment when her beauty begins to fade. Valera stated that *Genio y figura* refuted the thesis of Alexandre Dumas's *The Camelia-Lady*, that redemption through human and sexual love was possible.

Morsamor (1899), Valera's last novel, treats the baroque theme of *desengaño* (disillusion) via the adventures of Miguel de Zuheros and Tiburcio de Simahonda. There are three women characters in the work. Doña Sol de Quiñones, a typical lady of the court as depicted in romantic novels, symbolizes the conservative nostalgia for the *ancien régime*'s aristocratic woman. More interesting are the two high-class courtesans, Doña Olimpia de Belfiore and her companion, Teletusa la Culebrosa. These Renaissance women are represented in terms of metamorphosis, a Renaissance cliché. Olimpia is always someone else; her ductility and cross-dressing prefigure the mobility of the modern woman, and she contradicts the essentialism of the Victorian woman as she prefigures the twentieth-century woman.

Valera's attitudes about women are wonderfully summarized in his short story "El pájaro verde" (The Green Bird, 1999). Written like a traditional fairy tale with some varia-

tions, protagonist Princesa Venturosa (Princess Fortunate) cannot find the right husband. As she evaluates possible candidates, she has two erotic encounters with a green bird. In the first, the bird steals her garter while she is in the forest fixing it and showing her "well-shaped leg"; in the second, the bird steals her locket and a kiss when she is wearing only her undergarment. Princess Fortunate actively tries to discover the true identity of the bird and discovers he is an enchanted prince. To break the spell holding him, she, her maid, and her washerwoman must stare at three naked, handsome men, without feeling sexual desire while falling in love with them. This short story reveals the hidden erotic content of *fairy tales and denounces the impossible contradiction that fairy tales advocate by repressing female desire within the context of romantic love. Valera sends the same message in his novels: Nineteenth-century men wanted angels (**ángel del hogar*) but found mostly strong women with sexual desires and energy who also wanted to improve their social lot. Often, nevertheless, male fantasies were realized via the marriages of older men to young beauties. Despite the prominence of women in his novels, Valera's credentials as an advocate for women are at best ambiguous.

Work by

Doña Luz. Ed. Enrique Rubio. Madrid: Espasa-Calpe, 1990.

Doña Luz. Trans. Mary J. Serrano. 1891. New York: H. Fertig, 1975.

Genio y figura. Ed. Cyrus DeCoster. Madrid: Cátedra, 1975.

"The Green Bird." Trans. Robert M. Fedorchek. *Marvels and Tales: Journal of Fairy Tale Studies* 13.2 (1999): 211–233.

Las ilusiones del doctor Faustino. Ed. Cyrus DeCoster. Madrid: Castalia, 1981.

Juanita la Larga. Ed. Enrique Rubio. Madrid: Castalia, 1985.

Morsamor. Ed. Leonardo Romero Tobar. Barcelona: Plaza & Janés, 1984.

Obras completas. Madrid: Aguilar, 1947.

El pájaro verde. Ed. Carmen Bravo-Villasante. Madrid: Escuela Española, 1986.

Pepita Jiménez. Ed. Carmen Martín Gaite. Madrid: Taurus, 1982.

Pepita Jiménez. Trans. Harriet de Onís. New York: Barron's, 1964.

Work about

Caballero Pozo, Luis. "Valera y el embrujo andaluz." *Revista de la Universidad de Buenos Aires* 12 (1953): 135–202, 403–460.

DeCoster, Cyrus. *Juan Valera.* New York: Twayne, 1974.

González López, Luis. *Las mujeres de don Juan Valera.* Madrid: Aguilar, 1934.

Rupe, Carole J. *La dialéctica del amor en la narrativa de Juan Valera.* Madrid: Pliegos, 1986.

Taylor, Teresia Langford. *The Representation of Women in the Novels of Juan Valera. A Feminist Critique.* New York: Peter Lang, 1997.

Salvador A. Oropesa

Valle-Inclán, Ramón María del (1866–1936): The Image of Women in His Theater

Despite all the recognition Valle-Inclán has received, he has never been celebrated for his characterization of women. Valle-Inclán neither embraced nor was sympathetic to the notion of feminism. His theater, like his work in general, suggests a pervasively male view of the world. His male characters are always central to the action, while female characters appear to contribute only marginally to the overall critical picture. Characteristically, Valle-Inclán's women are victims of circumstance, of the corrupt and degraded social order in which they find themselves, and may be grouped under the two archetypal categories traditionally assigned to literary female characters, that of the fallen woman and angelic figure. Their secondary importance notwithstanding, the evolution of Valle-Inclán's female characters is indicative of an attempt by the Spanish playwright to integrate the feminine into the greater social and artistic context of his unique dramatic expression.

Valle-Inclán's first play, *Cenizas* (1899; Ashes), and its subsequent revision, *El yermo de las almas* (1908; The Barrenness of Souls), are the first examples of the playwright's intention to assign the female figure a certain measure of importance. The action of the play revolves around Octavia Santino's adulterous affair with Pedro Pondal. Octavia is the victim of her husband Don Juan Manuel, of her lover, and to a lesser degree, of other patriarchal figures as represented in the doctor and the priest. The men in the play make demands on Octavia that eventually lead to her death. Despite her victimization at the hands of the patriarchy, Octavia adopts a heroic stance in her confrontation of authority, most vividly expressed in her decision to escape her house, which she equates with a jail. The freedom from oppression that Octavia seeks outside the house symbolizes Valle-Inclán's own defiance of authoritative social structure and positions a female character at the center of his critical discourse.

In *Aguila de blasón* (1907; The Emblazoned Eagle) and *Romance de lobos* (1907; Ballad of the Wolves), two of the three plays that comprise the trilogy *Comedias bárbaras* (Barbaric Plays), Doña María and Sabelita continue the pattern evinced by Octavia, that of challenging through action the traditionally conceived and otherwise prescriptive place of women within the social order. Don Juan Manuel Montenegro is the undisputed central figure of the *Comedias bárbaras*, yet the action of the plays signifies a shift in the importance of women. Both Doña María and Sabelita display rebellious attitudes. Once again, the motif of the house symbolizes feminine entrapment. In response to her husband Don Juan Manuel's adultery, Doña María retaliates by leaving the family abode. Similarly, Sabelita leaves the home of her adulterous lover in protest. Their actions signify a break from their enclosure (**encierro*) within a patriarchal social order.

The victimization of women escalates in Valle-Inclán's later dramatic works, the *esperpentos* (a genre invented by the author, featuring absurd characters, who speak and dress like caricatures). As Valle-Inclán's exploration of the individual's relation to society at large is heightened to acerbically critical proportions in *Luces de bohemia* (1920; Lights of Bohemia), *Los cuernos de don Friolera* (1921: The Horns of the Cuckold, Don Friolera), *Las galas del difunto* (1926; The Regalia of the Deceased), and *La hija del capitán* (1927; The Captain's Daughter), the significance of his women characters increases proportionately. The image of woman in Valle-Inclán's *esperpentos* evolves to include that of woman as the object of male desire and takes on crucial significance in the author's elaboration of a new aesthetic dimension more in line with reflecting the grotesque realities of contemporary Spanish society. The concave mirrors of the *esperpento* not only distort social reality as traditionally perceived but also imply a revolutionary view of gender.

The notion of women as innocent and hopeless victims of a corrupt, even reckless and savage society persists in *Luces de bohemia*. In one scene, a woman cries out and runs through the streets holding her dead child, killed innocently by stray gunfire. The play is populated with prostitutes and spinsters. The only moral dimension in the play comes in the character of Madame Collet. At Collet's insistence, her blind poet-husband, Max Estrella, sets out on his nocturnal odyssey through the streets of Madrid in search of justice and retribution for the wrong he has suffered, the basis for Valle-Inclán's elaboration of a social satire that eventually leads to a definition of his *visión esperpéntica*. In *Los cuernos de don Friolera* it is Doña Loreta's victimization by an antiquated, senseless notion of *honor that leads Valle-Inclán to posit his critical view of the institutional degradation of modern Spain. Preoccupied by the accusation of adultery leveled against his wife Loreta, Don Friolera is unable to separate his personal convictions from social expectations, resulting in the tragic death of their innocent daughter. What is conveyed through action in *Luces de bohemia* and *Los cuernos de don Friolera* is ar-

ticulated in *Las galas del difunto* by la Daifa, who, driven to prostitution by her father, openly calls for rebellion against the injustices of society against individuals. In all three cases, the female figure plays a crucial role in Valle-Inclán's criticism of Spain's national reality.

Women in the *esperpento* move from the margin of critical discourse to the center. *La hija del capitán* in particular proves that issues of gender serve both an ideological premise and an aesthetic precept in Valle-Inclán's theater and explicitly demonstrates the author's attempt to integrate the feminine into his biting exposé of Spanish institutional decadence. The play comes as close to a defense of a feminist ideal by the Spanish playwright as any contemporary feminist dramatic text. Protagonist Sinibalda Pérez is driven by a strong desire for self-determination and autonomy, concepts that both challenge the idea and the fact of male dominance. Her father's decision to prostitute her in order to avoid prosecution for a murder he committed is suggestive of Sinibalda's objectification and entrapment at the hands of a patriarchal social structure. The motif of the house is once again the unifying nexus for the dramatic structure. Characters in this play allude to *el domicilio paterno* (the paternal domicile) as a place of confinement. Sinibalda's desire is to break free of the house in order to control her destiny. What transpires corresponds to the elaboration of a feminine consciousness, as Sinibalda takes the necessary actions to establish her autonomy: She succeeds in blackmailing her father, which ultimately leads to her escape from the house, at which point the focus shifts from Sinibalda as object to Sinibalda as subject of the narrative, thereby supplanting the conventional view of woman as passive with one of woman as aggressively prone to action. Sinibalda's rebellious action culminates the rising curve begun with Octavia Santino. Her rebellion against patriarchal domination brings about a break with the popular stereotype of female as a submissive figure.

Seeking harmony between perception and representation, Valle-Inclán's evolution as a playwright is characterized by a personal determination to find adequate means of artistic expression to convey the sordid social and political condition of contemporary Spain. Reality, as depicted in his theater, is corrupt and demoralized, a world of artifice and contrivance, populated by nefarious and self-indulgent individuals whose penchant for treachery categorically undermines heroic action and hampers any coherent representation of society. The theme of female exploitation that runs through Valle-Inclán's theater reflects the general corruption of early twentieth-century Spain, a parallel that permits him to arrive at the universal through the feminine particular and take into account the relations between art, gender, and social change. It is difficult to separate the function of Valle-Inclán's women characters from the overall critical picture he conveys, yet their rebellious actions both constitute an expression of morality and righteousness that opposes the unscrupulous behavior of their oppressors and exemplify feminist notions of self-reaffirmation and self-preservation. *See also* Valle-Inclan, Ramón María del (1866–1936): Women in His Short Fiction and the *Sonatas*

Work by

Luces de bohemia; Bohemian lights; esperpento. Trans. A. Zahareas and G. Gillespie. Intro. A. Zahareas. Austin: U of Texas P, 1976. English and Spanish.
Obras completas de Ramón María del Valle-Inclán. Madrid: Plenitud, 1952.

Work about

Andrews, Jean. "Saints and Strumpets: Female Stereotypes in Valle-Inclán." *Feminist Readings on Spanish and Latin-American Literature.* Ed. Lisa P. Condé and Stephen M. Hart. Lewiston: Edwin Mellen P, 1991. 27–35.
Gabriele, John P. "Gender in the Mirror: A Feminist Perspective on the *Esperpento de la hija del capitán.*" *Revista Hispánica Moderna* 48.2 (December 1995): 307–314.
Johnston, David. "Valle-Inclán: The Mirroring of the Esperpento." *Modern Drama* 41.1 (Spring 1998): 30–48.
Leonard, Candyce. "Gendered Spaces in Two Dramatic Works by Valle-Inclán: *Cenizas* and *El Yermo de las Almas.*" *Nuevas perspectivas sobre el 98.* Ed. and pref. John P. Gabriele. Madrid: Iberoamericana; Frankfurt: Vervuert, 1999.
Paolini, Claire J. "Valle-Inclán's Modernistic Women: The Devout Virgin and the Devout Adulteress." *Hispanófila* 88 (1986): 27–40.
Predmore, Michael P. "The Central Role of Sabelita in *Aguila de blasón*: Toward the Emergence of a Radical Visión of Women in the Later Art of the Esperpento." *Ramón del Valle-Inclán: Questions of Gender.* Ed. Carol Maier and Roberta L. Salper. Cranbury: Associated U Presses, 1994. 177–190.
Salper, Roberta L. "Las dos Micaelas de Valle-Inclán: Un arquetipo de mujer." *Divergencias y unidad: Perspectivas sobre la Generación del '98 y Antonio Machado.* Ed. John P. Gabriele. Madrid: Orígenes, 1990. 141–159.
———. "Vínculos rotos: Hijas y padres en *Martes de carnaval* de Valle-Inclán." *De lo particular a lo universal: El teatro español del siglo XX y su contexto.* Ed. John P. Gabriele. Frankfurt am Main: Vervuert, 1994. 56–67.

John P. Gabriele

Valle-Inclán, Ramón María del (1866–1936): Women in His Short Fiction and the *Sonatas*

The role of women in the works of a complex writer such as Ramón del Valle-Inclán (1866–1936) is not easy to define even if one's assessment of this topic is limited, as is the case here, to a few of his early works. Part of the problem with this subject is that too many questions can be asked of these texts, and the act of framing these questions will, undoubtedly, result in somewhat different answers reflecting certain preconceived notions affecting interpretation of these tales. Furthermore, the forthcoming reflections on these texts cannot be completely comprehensive in that Valle wrote too many short stories that include diverse realities not fully coalescing with one another. In sum, it is within the limitations discussed previously that this brief study will take up the sensitive topic of women in certain works by Valle-Inclán.

Even though on average the works that concern us on this occasion are not mimetic in nature (that is, they do not reproduce concrete and specific, documentable realities), Valle-Inclán's brief narratives and *Sonatas* do reflect certain cultural beliefs concerning women during the last part of the nineteenth century and the first decade of the twentieth. Often, these texts mirror attitudes of the period as they proceed to question them in critical terms and in ways too complex to be fully explored at this time. On other occasions, however, preponderant cultural views are expressed without challenging them in order to facilitate the development of Valle-Inclán's other aesthetic preoccupations. The *Sonatas*, for instance, document a parodic treatment of the "Don Juan" theme. In so doing, these novels illustrate aspects of Valle-Inclán's negative position toward the stereotype of a seducer who interacts with women he views as objects for his own gratification. The aforementioned parody occurs because Bradomín is a "Don Juan" whose artificiality is clearly perceptible to the implied reader of the *Sonatas*. In this context, Bradomín's Don Juan role is undermined as the implied reader realizes that all is not what it appears to be in these novels, a conclusion facilitated by the autobiographical format of the *Sonatas* and the fact that most autobiographies are motivated by a desire to justify one's self before one's narratee. In sum, as the implied reader comes to terms with the fact that the autobiographical elements of these works are a strategy to distract the reader and to absolve the narrator, he/she concludes that these novels are examples of narrative with unreliable narrators whose views on women cannot be accepted at face value. Bradomín is a dandy, and the dandy is a modernist icon demonstrating, most vividly, that human identity and human perceptions are a matter of self-construction. In this sense, Bradomín, as is the case with other dandies, makes evident human follies that

cultures usually attempt to hide or ignore, acts that reaffirm that the human body is never naked of its cultural clothing.

The Don Juan/dandy preoccupation of the *Sonatas* concerns Spanish reality in the sense that it reflects certain cultural and artistic stereotypes in the Hispanic world as they are subverted and undermined before the implied reader of these novels. In the *Sonatas*, Bradomín is an "admirable" Don Juan in that he shows the careful reader many of the flaws associated with stereotypical constructs. Some of these can be seem in *Sonata de Otoño* (1902; Autumn Sonata) in the way Bradomín reacts to the dying Concha: As he is sexually attracted to her sickly beauty, the implied reader witnesses how unnatural his behavior is even though Bradomín does his best in the first and last chapters of the novel to excuse himself of all blame as he attempts to justify his actions before his potential readers. Something similar occurs as well in *Sonata de Invierno* (1905; Winter Sonata) when he is less concerned with the effects of his seduction of his illegitimate daughter, Maximina, than with hiding his own decadent and flawed stereotypical attitudes toward women (in *Sonata de Invierno* he fails to succeed, in part, as a result of Sor Simona's reminder of the terrible nature of his misdeeds).

But not all female characters in the *Sonatas* function in terms of revealing Bradomín's limitations as a stereotypical Don Juan in his relations to women. At times, what has been subverted are certain traditional moral values espoused by women like Príncesa Gaetani in *Sonata de Primavera* (1904; Spring Sonata), a character who avails herself of less than exemplary means to achieve her "lofty" objectives. On other occasions in the *Sonatas*, however, women are assigned masks reminiscent of the one worn by Bradomín in order to hide deeper conflicts. An excellent example of this is afforded by Niña Chole in *Sonata de Estío* (1903; Summer Sonata). To a large extent, her sensual and immoral behavior allows this character to hide a deeper problem in her life: namely, the incestuous relationship she has with a tyrannical and abusive father concerned with his physical appetites. In this case, Niña Chole fails to face reality as she hides behind the promiscuity she demonstrates toward Bradomín, just as Bradomín hides his lack of courage when he meets Niña Chole's father as he finds reasons for not having a physical confrontation with this man in order not to lose his self-respect and sense of courage, traits essential to his Don Juan role in the four *Sonatas*.

Valle-Inclán's views on women as documented in his early writings are not an affirmation of the equality of the sexes. Above all, he is preoccupied with the stereotypical roles preassigned to the sexes in that to him said roles often lack authenticity. A case in point is provided by the short story "Tula Varona" (1895). In it, Tula assumes the traditional Don Juan role associated with the male in Spanish literature, and as a result, the implied reader derives a most negative view of her. Logically, one may assume the implied author of this story is simply criticizing the characteristics associated with the Don Juan stereotype when, in fact, the implied author is emphasizing as well the incompatibility of the Don Juan stereotype with the stereotypical view society has reserved for women. That is why Tula becomes substantially more reprehensible to the implied reader than Bradomín has ever been. It is as if the guiding consciousness of this story not only criticizes Tula's Don Juan–like behavior but points to certain limitations society has assigned to women even in their exercise of reprehensible behavior (in this context, the equivalent will be the effeminate characteristics of Sandóval in "La generala" [1892; The Lady General]).

Finally, even if only in passing, one must remember that women often have other important roles in Valle-Inclán's early fiction. In these texts, he develops certain philosophical and aesthetic preoccupations that have little to do with gender issues. In this

fashion, in *Augusta* (1897/1903), Nelly functions in terms of the expression of certain recurring internal forces in humanity through her initiation in the sexual, whereas in "Rosita" (1899/1903), the protagonist of this story participates in a ludic situation reflecting the prevailing absurdity and grotesqueness of life. Other times, however, certain female characters facilitate a representation of situations not fully comprehensible to them nor to the implied reader in that what transpires may have been motivated by the violation of cultural codes affecting women and by supernatural forces that may victimize them ("Beatriz" [1900, 1903] is an example of this in that its protagonist was sexually abused by a priest in her household, a morally deficient servant of God whose diabolic powers allowed her victimization in the eyes of some and made her morally reprehensible to others).

In conclusion, Valle-Inclán was not misogynistic in his early works regardless of what we know of his personal life. The previous statement does not mean, however, that he did not reflect many of the cultural biases that surrounded him in the patriarchal world in which he lived, biases against which he often reacted ironically and that on other occasions were depicted so as to express some of his other concerns. *See also Burlador de Sevilla, El (1627–1629): Its Women Characters Sáenz-Alonso, Mercedes (1917–): Don Juan y el donjuanismo*

Work by

Obras completas. 2nd ed. Madrid: Plenitud, 1952.

Work about

Gullón, Ricardo, ed. *Valle-Inclán: Centennial Studies*. Austin: U of Texas P, 1968.

Nickel, Catherine. "Pale Hands and a Trickle of Blood: The Portrayal of Women in Valle-Inclán's *Rosarito* and *Beatriz*." *Nuevas perspectivas sobre el 98*. Ed. John P. Gabriele. Madrid: Iberoamericana; Frankfurt: Vervuert, 1999.

Zahareas, Anthony. *Ramón del Valle-Inclán: An Appraisal of His Life and Works*. New York: Las Américas, 1968.

Luis T. González-del-Valle

Vázquez de la Cruz, Juana (1481–1534)

A Franciscan nun, she was the subject of Tirso de *Molina's dramatic trilogy *La Santa Juana* (1613–1614). When she was 15, Juana was supposed to marry into a noble family but instead entered the convent of Santa María de la Cruz on the outskirts of Madrid. She soon became popular as a speaker and spiritual counselor and was credited with many miracles, prophecies, and speaking in tongues. She become known before her death as *la santa Juana* and retained the popular title throughout the sixteenth and seventeenth centuries, even though she was never canonized by the Church. Her popularity as a cult figure in the Madrid area led to a biography by Antonio Daza in 1610 (*Historia, vida y milagros de Santa Juana de la Cruz*), upon which Tirso de Molina based his three plays.

Work about

del Campo, Agustín, ed. *Tirso de Molina: La Santa Juana.* Madrid: Castilla, 1948.

Mayberry, Nancy K. "On the Structure of Tirso's Santa Juana Trilogy." *South Atlantic Bulletin* 41.2 (1976): 13–21.

David H. Darst

Vega y Carpio, Lope de (1562–1635): Women in His Drama

As the most prolific dramatist of Golden Age Spain, and renovator of the national theater, Lope de Vega exhibited intense interest in romantic love and women, mirroring many diverse social attitudes in his life and his art. Celebrated as a national treasure during his life, he had two wives, three longtime mistresses (one of whom he cared for, through blindness and insanity, until her death), and numerous short liaisons. Counting only his drama, he is estimated to have written around 800 full-length plays, about half of which survive. Women of many types populate them: queens, noble ladies, servants, peasants, *terceras*, nuns, saints, bandits, scholars, wives, widows, sisters, and daughters. They come from urban and rural environments and may be Christian or Moor. His preferred ideal woman character, however—the model most meant for emulation—is Christian, of high nobility and outstanding beauty, such as Inés in *El caballero de Olmedo* (*The Knight of Olmedo*, 1961). This entry will focus on some of the ways that women characters figure in his extensive dramatic output.

In his treatise on playwriting, the *Arte nuevo de hacer comedias* (written c. 1604; New Style of Writing Plays), Lope does not discuss specifics regarding male characters (with the exception of a few references to kings), but he does indicate that women characters should be treated with *el debido decoro* (due respect), that *damas no desdigan de su nombre* (ladies live up to their name), and recommends the *disfraz varonil* (male disguise, which revealed a woman's legs), as a perennial crowd pleaser. Unlike England, where male adolescents were used to perform female characters' roles, Spain permitted actresses on stage; nonetheless, the mere sight of a woman "on public display" rather than enclosed (*Encierro*), expressing opinions rather than maintaining silence, or performing erotic dances such as the *zarabanda*, ran counter to contemporary mores, provoking strong attacks from moralists. The government issued edicts forbidding the *diszfraz varonil* in 1587, 1600, 1603, 1605, 1641, 1646, 1672, and 1675—clearly with limited effect.

The key tenet of the *Arte nuevo* that determines women's roles in Lope's theater is the statement that *los casos de la honra son mejores,/ porque mueven con fuerza a toda gente* (plots about honor are best, because they strongly affect all people). The concept of *honor and honra*, a ubiquitous concern of seventeenth-century Spanish society, is defined by Larson as the esteem and respect of one's peers; it is derived from illustrious lineage and, more immediately, the perceived chastity of one's wife, sister, daughter, or other female relative. Personal worth and virtues were assumed to flow innately and inevitably from noble blood. A women's honor also consisted in her conjugal fidelity or chastity, which reflected primarily on her husband or father. A man also took pride in the beauty of his wife or daughters; beauty, however, was a double-edged sword, for it also provoked desire in other males, and since the double standard admired and encouraged such appetite in a man, beautiful women were aggressively pursued by men, placing that husband or father's honor at risk. Thus, women were closely guarded in the home as much as possible and valued for the "feminine" virtues of chastity, silence, and *verguenza* (sense of shame). In general, the good wives of Lope's theater, like Casilda in *Peribáñez y el Comendador de Ocaña* (*Peribáñez*, 1961), willingly accept these standards and struggle to control the liability their beauty represents to their husbands' honor. In the case of *El perro del hortelano* (*The Dog in the Manger*, 1961), the noblewoman Diana's high lineage is not complemented by the virtues appropriate to her station and gender, as Fernández notes, and she is harshly criticized by Lope. In *Los comendadores de Córdoba* (The Commanders of Cordoba), one of the infrequent cases where *women's* sexual desire cannot be contained, this attribute is negatively portrayed and punished fiercely at the work's conclusion.

Maravall, Díez-Borque, and others have argued convincingly that the honor code in seventeenth-century Spain functioned as propaganda to maintain the elite nobility's power over an increasingly fragmented society. The theater represented a primary avenue for disseminating social ideals and patterns of behavior that validated this closed power base, offering spectators a way to equate themselves to nobility by adopting the personal virtues associated with illustrious lineage but still maintaining the status quo for the elite minority. A return to traditional order is routine at the conclusion of Lope's theater; many plays close with multiple marriages, reaffirming Lope's basic sense of the "natural order" of the universe, in which a woman's correct, *divinely* ordained role is that of wife and devoted partner of her man. McKendrick, Yarbro-Bejarano, Stoll, and others have refined this view, pointing out that even though the status quo is generally reasserted at any given play's conclusion, Lope gave serious and often sympathetic voice to elements challenging the status quo and that stock characters like the *mujer varonil* (a woman possessing virtues or strengths traditionally associated with males) and a key subtype, the *mujer esquiva* (a women averse to love, men, and/or marriage), represent more than controlled models of social behavior, as they question at length and even challenge the prevailing social structure.

Much recent criticism has been devoted to uncovering these areas of resistance to the idealized patriarchal ideology. McKendrick pioneered study of Lope's *mujer varonil*, the woman who departs significantly from social norms of the day. Between 1595 and the early 1600s, he produced at least one play a year featuring this character type; she appears in over 50 of his surviving plays, some of the most memorable being the protagonists of *La moza de cántaro* (The Girl with a Jug), *Fuenteovejuna* (*Fuenteovejuna*, 1961), and *La vengadora de mujeres* (The Avenger of Women). McKendrick finds that Lope's characterizations of such women are largely quite positive, providing they comply with their divinely ordained roles as wives and lovers, following traditional Aristotelian ideas of woman as "matter" craving and needing man (in marriage) as "form," to guide and instruct her. Still, they are spirited, determined heroines who defend their right to choose which mate they will have, and they challenge the double standards of a society that admires male philandering but rejects seduced or raped women. The *mujer varonil* is a type with many superficial variations (career woman, *mujer esquiva*, scholar, amazon, bluestocking, warrior, female bandit), but in Lope she always follows the pattern of the woman recognizing her error, her pride, or vanity, and accepting the proper marriage by the work's end, functioning ultimately as a vehicle through which the playwright could expound his views on women, love, and marriage.

In her study of feminism in 46 of Lope's honor plays, Yarbro-Bejarano defines the honor play as one in which a husband believes that a rival is pursuing his wife—a situation that allowed for infinite variations—and explores how gender and sexuality function as structuring principles of these texts. The inherent "ideal" male construct is noble, of pure blood, brave to the point of aggressive, a predator of other men's sexual property (women), and protector of his own (woman/women); the "ideal" female is noble, of pure blood, compassionate, chaste, self-effacing, lacking in sexual appetite, motivated by shame to protect her honor. Again, Yarbro-Bejarano finds that most female characters in the honor plays of Lope conform to this ideal; those who deviate, evading male control for part or all of the text, exhibiting sexual desire, rejecting the need for a man, donning the *disfraz varonil* to act upon their desires, document cultural resistance to the excessively programmed ideals of the day. The phenomenon of *disfraz varonil*, in which a woman character creates access to power by appropriating male attire and thereby escaping confinement to pursue her own will, was not generally a last recourse of outcasts or rebels, by any means. Never used by peasant women or what Yarbro-Bejarano terms "sexual outlaws," the majority of cross-dressers were wives intent on influencing outcomes in their lives, who resumed traditional roles when their goals were secured at a play's conclusion. For playgoers, cross-dressing could be received in various ways: It emphasized the novelty of exceptional women; it could be seen as pleasingly titillating or as temporarily destabilizing to traditional social roles; or it could represent a challenge to male viewers who would vicariously enjoy the woman's inevitable return to the traditional role and attire of wife

by a play's conclusion. As McKendrick astutely notes, any *mujer esquiva* of Lope is ultimately a sophisticated variation of Sleeping Beauty, waiting for the right man to awaken her to the joys of love and life that divine providence has destined for her. Nonetheless, these female independents articulate a sharp dissatisfaction of social roles and limits ascribed to them and offer successful models for rejecting such strictures when necessary.

In addition to the above-mentioned character types and general conventions of Lope's theater, a variety of other works offer specific vindications or defenses of women. Starting from the position that discourse serves to variously define, empower, and oppress, Heigle has detected a feminist subtext in Lope's popular comedy *La dama boba* (The Stupid Lady, adapted as *At Wit's End*, 2000). It is the story of two beautiful sisters, the bright *mujer esquiva* Nise, who writes poetry and resists the idea of marriage, and dimwitted Finea, who has been given the sole dowry in the household to compensate for her apparent inability to apprehend more than the most basically literal meaning of words. A poor noble, Laurencio, who earlier had set his sights on Nise, opts for the economic security that Finea represents and sets out to train (or mold) her, following Neoplatonic ideas about love and marriage. Finea reveals herself to be a more than apt pupil, mastering multiple levels of meaning encoded in discourse and then turning the tables on the men around her, first cleverly mocking Laurencio's (supposedly pure) Neoplatonic love for her, and then exploiting the possibilities of metaphor to resist her father's will. In a similar work, titled *La boba para los otros y discreta para sí* (Simpleton to Others and Clever to Herself), Hicks studies how the protagonist Diana likewise exploits the multiple meanings of linguistic and social codes to confuse and deflect enemies so she may rise from her condition of shepherdess to assume the position of duchess.

Heiple has analyzed how *La prueba de los ingenios* (The Test of Wits) presents Lope's systematic rejection of Juan Huarte de San Juan's extremely popular and influential work, the *Examen de ingenios* (1585; Examination of Men's Wits). Huarte's text maintains that women's inferior intellect is determined by her biology, as explained by the theory of the four humors. According to it, the male sex is hot and dry, while the female sex is wet and moist. Since intellect needs a hot, dry environment to flourish, it then follows that all women possess severely inferior intellectual abilities, compared to men, because of their physical makeup. Lope clearly rejects this position and defends women's intellectual parity to that of men. In the play, two women organize a competition of letters to test suitors' intellect against their own via a debate, the deciphering of enigmas, and a labyrinth. At the play's conclusion, the women are judged winners of the competition.

In yet other examples where women triumph over men, Case has studied the female protagonists of two historical plays, *Las almenas de Toro* (The Ramparts of Toro) and *Las famosas asturianas* (The Famous Asturian Women). Each heroine surpasses male leadership through superior integrity, leadership, and independence, leading Case to suggest that the texts could represent an indirect rebuke to the notoriously weak Philip III, king from 1598 to 1621, during which time the two plays were written. And in the mythological play *Las mujeres sin hombres*, which McGaha terms the most ardently feminist drama by Lope, women's ability to live alone in harmony, to organize society, and to make war when necessary is defended, the double standard of society is attacked, and any flaws that women may have are attributed to men's refusal to provide them adequate education.

In conclusion, the relationship between life and art is particularly intense in theater, which applauds the convictions of a society, examines its flaws, and purges its demons; Lope created many women characters who participated vigorously in the current social debate over women's rights, roles, and abilities. *See also:* Invisible Mistress

Work by

Five Plays. Trans. Jill Booty. London: MacGibbon and Kee; New York: Hill and Wang, 1961. (*The Knight from Olmedo, Justice without Revenge, Fuenteovejuna, Peribáñez, The Dog in the Manger*).

Friedman, Edward H. *Wit's End: An Adaptation of Lope de Vega's La dama boba.* New York: Peter Lang, 2000.

The Knight of Olmedo. Trans. and ed. Willard F. King. Lincoln: U of Nebraska P., 1972. Spanish and English.

Obras de Lope de Vega. Ed. study M. Menéndez y Pelayo. *Biblioteca de autores españoles.* Various vols. Madrid: Atlas, various years.

Work about

Case, Thomas. "A Time for Heroines in Lope." *The Perception of Women in Spanish Theater of the Golden Age.* Ed. Anita K. Stoll and Dawn L. Smith. Lewisburg, PA: Bucknell UP, 1991. 202–219.

Díez Borque, José María. *Sociología de la comedia española del siglo XVII.* Madrid: Cátedra, 1976.

Fernández, Jaime, S.J. "Honor y libertad: *El perro del hortelano* de Lope de Vega." *Bulletin of the Comediantes* 50.2 (Winter 1998): 307–316.

Fothergill Payne, Louise. "Taming Women on the Spanish Stage: Lope on Women, Love and Marriage." *Prologue to Performance. Spanish Classical Theatre Today.* Lewisburg, PA: Bucknell UP, 1991. 67–82.

Heigle, Michaela. "La representación de la mujer en *La dama boba.*" *Bulletin of the Comediantes* 50.2 (Winter 1998): 291–306.

Heiple, Daniel. "Profeminist Reactions to Huarte's Misogyny in Lope de Vega's *La prueba de los ingenios* and María de Zayas's *Novelas amorosas y ejemplares.*" *The Perception of Women in Spanish Theater of the Golden Age.* Ed. Anita K. Stoll and Dawn L. Smith. Lewisburg, PA: Bucknell UP, 1991. 157–169.

Hicks, Margaret R. "Lope's Other dama boba: The Strategies of Incompetence." *The Perception of Women in Spanish Theater of The Golden Age.* Ed. Anita K. Stoll and Dawn L. Smith. Lewisburg, PA: Bucknell UP, 1991. 135–153.

Larson, Donald R. *The Honor Plays of Lope de Vega.* Cambridge: Harvard UP, 1977.

Maravall, José A. *Teatro y literatura en la sociedad barroca.* Madrid: Seminarios y Ediciones, 1972.

McGaha, Michael. "The Sources and Feminism of

Lope's *Las mujeres sin hombres*." *The Perception of Women in Spanish Theater of the Golden Age*. Ed. Anita K. Stoll and Dawn L. Smith. Lewisburg, PA: Bucknell UP, 1991. 157–169.

McKendrick, Melveena M. *Theatre in Spain 1490–1790*. Cambridge: Cambridge UP, 1989.

———. "Woman against Wedlock. The Reluctant Brides of Golden Age Drama." *Women in Hispanic Literature: Icons and Fallen Idols*. Ed. Beth Miller. Berkeley and Los Angeles: U of California P, 1983. 115–146.

———. *Woman and Society in the Spanish Drama of the Golden Age. A Study of the* Mujer Varonil. Cambridge: Cambridge UP, 1974.

Rozas, Juan Manuel. *Significado y doctrina del* Arte Nuevo *de Lope de Vega*. Madrid: S.G.E.L., 1976.

Smith, Marlene K. *The Beautiful Woman in the Theater of Lope de Vega. Ideology and Mythology of Female Beauty in Seventeenth-Century Spain*. New York: Peter Lang, 1998.

Stoll, Anita K., and Dawn L. Smith, eds. *The Perception of Women in Spanish Theater of the Golden Age*. Lewisburg, PA: Bucknell UP, 1991.

Sumner, Gordon. "Astraea, the Pax Christiana, and Lope de Vega's Santa Casilda." *A Star-Crossed Golden Age: Myth and the Spanish Comedia*. London: Associated UP; Lewisburg, PA: Bucknell UP, 1998. 150–161.

Yarbro-Bejarano, Yvonne. *Feminism and the Honor Plays of Lope de Vega*. West Lafayette, IN: Purdue UP, 1994.

Maureen Ihrie

Veiled Women
See Cubiertas and *Tapadas*

Versos con Faldas (1951)

In 1951, according to Gloria *Fuertes (1918–1998), poets were running about Madrid carrying verses under their arms, hoping to read them aloud in some café or *tertulia* (social literary gathering). In March of that same year, recognizing the great number of women poets whose work needed to be heard, Fuertes, Adelaida Las Santas, and María Dolores de Pablos took steps to put a stop to the old-boy system of the *tertulias* organized by male poets. Certain that their output was as good as or better than the male

counterpart, these three women decided to end the injustice by organizing a series of recitals that they called *Versos con faldas* (Verses in Skirts). In 1983, when Fuertes wrote a short prologue to commemorate the *tertulia*, she recalled this name as the only one she could think of back then. Ultimately, *Versos con faldas* came to represent a truly feminist cultural group for Fuertes, although she had not thought so initially.

As part of the same commemoration, Las Santas remembered that with the help of the literary society of the Teatro Gallego the women were able to have a place to conduct their sessions. *Pueblo*, one of the daily newspapers of the time, covered their first presentation held on March 5, 1951, in that theater on Madrid's Carrera San Jéronimo. Headed by a caption stating that Fuertes, de Pablos, and Las Santas had put poetry in skirts and a photograph of the three, the article reported that the founders were fed up because women were not invited to read in poetry recitals programmed by men. For *Versos con faldas*, the first session was a great success. The auditorium, on the theater's lower level, was filled by other literary groups as well as newspaper reporters and photographers.

In 1959, Las Santas published a novel, *Poetas de café* (Café Poets), which relates the literary activity and frenzy of the early 1950s that Fuertes spoke of, especially of the poets whose only outlet was promoting and taking part in public poetry readings. In her novel, partially autobiographical, Las Santas presents a female protagonist who participates in this literary scene. Thus, this book becomes a human document of post–Civil War Spain in which Las Santas communicates her sincerest thinking about the struggle of women on both social and literary levels. Additionally, Las Santas assumes the position of a chronicler who narrates the history of café recitals and the formation of poetry groups. At certain moments in the novel she suspends the story of her protagonist in order to recount her enthusiastic appraisal of the spring of 1951 as an epidemic of poetry. New groups were forming, and one of them was *Versos con faldas*, the first women's *tertulia* to be introduced in that poetic movement. Fuertes and Las Santas had concurred that a series of poetry recitals exclusively for and by women was sorely needed.

In her novel, Las Santas indicates how great an impact the news of their *tertulia* had on the other poetry groups; *Versos con faldas* received some negative commentary, even on the choice of the name the women had given to their association. Las Santas again justifies the new women's group, founded because women poets had been unfairly excluded from the men's *tertulias*. If they did invite women to participate, the men most often behaved more like connoisseurs of pretty faces than of poetry. When Las Santas depicts her group's first recital, she incorporates not only real events but also herself and her colleagues by name in the text, thereby establishing a significant pattern of blending fiction and history. With this technique she represents the innermost reality of a poet's life experience. Her protagonist, Lalia, probably modeled on Las Santas herself, reveals a woman poet who lives a double bind in which literary calling and prescribed female roles clash as if irreconcilable in a woman.

Las Santas reports that *Versos con faldas* held 11 recitals during the year 1951. There were also two extraordinary sessions held in honor of the Asociación para la Enseñanza de la Mujer. The story seems to be a great success for Fuertes, Las Santas, and de Pablos who joined forces with other women and were heard in public performances. They meant to set up a poetry network because they envisioned their association as one that encompassed women poets throughout Spain. Women of Madrid were therefore linked to those who wrote poetry in other Spanish cities and provinces. They forwarded their poetry to Madrid where it was presented in performance, often interpreted by another woman, in the public forum established by Las Santas and her colleagues.

In her introduction to *Versos con faldas*,

complete with reproductions of newspaper articles, Las Santas illustrates that the three founders enjoyed success. Adversity, however, was to confront them within a few short months after the inauguration of their women's poetry association. A sympathetic newspaper columnist, Julio Trénas, who wrote for *Pueblo*, relates in May 1951 how the women were prevented from convening one night because the administrators of the Teatro Gallego showed one documentary movie after another until many of the people who had come to attend a presentation by *Versos con faldas* departed. In May 1952, *El boletín* printed an interview with Fuertes in which she revealed another obstacle. A type of pinball machine was placed in their way so that they could not use the recital hall, and no one on the theater's staff would take responsibility for it. Additionally, the newspaper took Fuertes's words out of context and put them on the front page. As a result it seemed that Fuertes was insulting Las Santas. The journalist also wrote that the interview exposed the difficulty for an assembly of women to get along with each other. An exchange of letters and articles ensued, but no party found satisfaction in it. Years later Las Santas expressed her certainty of bad intentions on the part of that newspaper and its reporter.

Ultimately, 1952 was to turn out as a disastrous year for poetry recitals. By order of the Spanish government's director de Seguridad, all poetry recitals were outlawed. The prime of *Versos con faldas*, then, was in 1951 when the three founders endeavored to bring the women poets of Spain together.

Just as significant as the inception of the *tertulia* is the way Las Santas revisits its collective history. In 1959 she looked back to 1951 to review and narrate the past history of *Versos con faldas* in *Poetas de café*. Then, in 1983, by that time in charge of her own small press, Aquacantos, she revived the *tertulia* as a printed anthology and reenlisted Fuertes as writer of the prologue. In looking back, Las Santas focused on what might have otherwise been considered a brief historical episode, but her revisions have become acts of survival that now keep the past performances of the historical recitals alive.

Work about

Las Santas, Adelaida. *Versos con faldas: Breve historia de una tertulia fundada por mujeres en el año 1951.* Madrid: Aguacantos, 1983.
Poetas de café. Madrid: Aguacantos, 1992.

Glenn Morocco

Villarroel, Fray Gaspar de

See Sexuality in the Golden Age: Fray Gaspar de Villarroel (?–after 1659)

Villarta Tuñón, Angeles (1921–)

With the advantages of having been educated in Switzerland, this Spanish novelist, journalist, and essayist brings her cosmopolitan upbringing into play in her fiction; it also stood her in good stead in her editorial work: Angeles Villarta Tuñón edited the second series of *La novela corta* as well as the comic magazine *Don Venerando*. Her most productive period corresponds to the first quarter century following the Spanish Civil War, approximately 1940 to 1965, after which her production has diminished markedly.

Villarta's novels include *Un pleno de amor* (1942; a play on words, meaning Full Moon of Love, Love Dance, and Complete Love), *Por encima de las nieblas* (1943; Above the Fog), *Muchachas que trabajan* (1944; Working Girls), *Ahora que soy estraperlista* (1949; Now That I'm a Black Marketeer), and *Con derecho a cocina* (1950; With Cooking Privileges). The latter two titles refer specifically (and somewhat satirically) to the economic difficulties and restrictions of the early postwar years under Franco when real reconstruction had not begun, most necessities were in short supply, and the housing shortages in many areas were severe. Although Villarta's

use of humor sets them apart from the more typical "social novel" of the period year (usually quite serious about social criticism and the implicit denunciation of socioeconomic injustices), she subsequently moves away from her initial works, which were more in the vein of the sentimental romance (*novela rosa*) and pulp fiction in the direction of "social" literature and politicosocial engagement. Growing feminist concerns also emerge in her writings of the mid-1950s, and with *Una mujer fea* (1954; An Ugly Woman), she won the Premio Femina Prize for 1953, as she made connections between her Asturian origins and her increasing interest in women's issues. She has also written short stories and poetry and in 1953 published *La taberna de Laura—Poemas del mar* (Laura's Tavern—Poems of the Sea). It is unfortunate that most of Villarta's works were not widely distributed and are of difficult access, for she is an interesting writer.

Work by

Con derecho a cocina. Madrid: n.p., 1950.
Muchachas que trabajan. Madrid: Espasa-Calpe, 1944.
Una mujer fea. Madrid: Calenda, 1954.
Un pleno de amor. Barcelona: Hymsa, 1942.
Por encima de las nieblas. Madrid: A. Aguado, 1943.
La taberna de Laura—Poemas del mar. Madrid: n.p., 1953.
Yo he sido estraperlista. Madrid: n.p., 1950.

Janet Pérez

Viñas, Celia (1915–1954)

This poet grew up speaking Catalan, the language of the mountainous province of Lérida at the western edge of Catalonia, where she was born; her name is sometimes listed as Vinyes, with the Catalan spelling. However, even though one of her books of poetry is written in Catalan, she is associated almost exclusively with Castilian-speaking Almería, where she spent her adult life and which she celebrates in the majority of her lyrics, composed in Castilian. For the provincial capital and Mediterranean port where she completed her university degree in modern romance philology and obtained a teaching post in 1943, Viñas became an adoptive daughter and something of an official poet. She married educator and writer Arturo Medina, who edited and published her posthumous works.

Best known for her poetry, Viñas also cultivated the short story, wrote children's literature and vignettes, and even tried her hand at theater. Poetry collections published before her untimely death include *Trigo del corazón* (1946; Wheat from the Heart), *Canción tonta del sur* (1948; Silly Song in the South), *Palabras sin voz* (1953; Voiceless Words), all in Castilian, and in Catalan, *Del foc i la cendra* (1953; Of Fire and Ashes). Posthumous poetry collections are *Como el ciervo corre herido* (1955; As the Deer Runs Wounded), *Canto* (1964; Song), *Antología lírica* (1976; Lyric Anthology), and *Poesía última* (1980; Final Poems). Prose works, mainly intended for children, include *Estampas de la vida de Cervantes* (1949; Scenes from the Life of Cervantes), *El primer botón del mundo y trece cuentos más* (1976; The World's First Button and 13 Other Stories), and the play, *Plaza de la Virgen del Mar* (1974; Plaza of Our Lady of the Sea). Her posthumously published *Antología lírica* (1976), drawing upon her earlier out-of-print and generally unavailable collections, offers the best sampling of Viñas's works.

Given that the primary audience of her prose works is children and adolescents, Viñas's fame rests mostly on her poetry, which features several reiterated themes. In addition to her love for Almería, Viñas developed a very special attachment to the island of Mallorca, and her fondness for both places is expressed in numerous poems (she is considered among those who contributed to renovating Mallorcan poetry in the post–Civil War period). Another thematic nucleus of her poetry centers around her teaching experience, including the classroom itself, and her young students' wide-eyed attention to stories. Viñas adored children, and their games, laughter, innocence, and questions

become another significant cluster of themes. Most often she employs an implicit dialogue form, with frequent rhetorical questions, addressing interlocutors (usually juveniles or her beloved) in the familiar *tú* form, creating effects of tenderness, warmth, and intimacy. Another thematic nucleus involves poems of religious inspiration: Viñas was ardently religious, professing Franciscan poverty, humility, and love of all living things. Her poetry thus exudes gentleness and humanizes all creation, both flora and fauna, attributing life and sentiments even to inanimate objects such as wine and almonds.

Although Viñas is not an experimental poet and does not employ free verse, her poetry usually follows no discernible metric or strophic pattern, although occasional sonnets appear in her last collection. She is especially fond of popular forms, shorter lines (*arte menor*), intercalating neopopular song, elements of games, and bits of fantasy. Her major poetic devices are repetition, cadence, alliteration, and metaphor, with occasional remarkable, original imagery (a spider with a bridal veil, for example, or swallows with tiny musical bones; the wind with its desert whiskers of broken glass and dead silver; a simple stone dressed in workclothes). Freshness, simplicity, a deceptive naïveté, and elements of Spain's popular poetic tradition combine with rare cosmopolitan intertextuality (e.g., allusions to Heine) to create a very personal, profoundly lyric voice.

Viñas's voice and themes are strongly gendered feminine and with her love of children would have almost certainly created a body of poetry celebrating pregnancy, childbirth, and maternity, as did Angela *Figuera. Viñas died while expecting her first child, and the city of Almería dedicated a small plaza and bust in her name after her early death—an uncommon tribute for women poets in Spain. Without voicing concerns usually deemed feminist (equality of the sexes, abortion, prostitution, abuse or neglect of women and children, etc.), Viñas contributes to women's history by her depiction of a special woman's life and work, her lyric sensibility, and her way of looking at the world.

Work by

Antología lírica. Madrid: Rialp, 1976.
Canción tonta del sur. Almería: Peláez, 1948.
Del foc i la cendra. Palma de Mallorca: Moll, 1953.
Estampas de la vida de Cervantes. Madrid: Gredos, 1949.
Trigo del corazón. Almería: La Independencia, 1946.

Janet Pérez

Vindicación feminista (1976–1979)

Lidia *Falcón (1935–) and Carmen *Alcalde (1936–) founded this feminist journal, whose all-woman staff of regular and occasional contributors contains a stellar group of lawyers, scholars, journalists, and creative writers (among others, Rosa *Montero [1951–], Marta *Pessarrodona [1941–], Cristina Peri-Rossi, Ana María *Moix [1947–], Monserrat Roig [1946–1991], and Nuria Beltrán). Its purpose is to discuss a wide range of subjects from a feminist perspective: culture (reviews of art, literature, theater, cinema, etc.); international features (particularly about Third World countries); and interviews, editorials, and problems of particular concern to women (adultery, divorce, desertion, etc.). National issues receive the heaviest coverage, including information on politics, labor, legal rights, and changes in the law. Individual numbers often feature an exposé of a specific problem (pornography, divorce, women in prison, prostitution, abuse).

The journal addresses inequities underlying the traditional patriarchal structure. Articles condemn the political opportunism of the early post-Franco years, detailing how emerging sectors take advantage of women's support but refuse them access to positions of influence and power. A Marxist-inspired feminism underlies some of the theoretical questions, expanding the definition of female oppression and initiating an ongoing debate concerning whether to categorize women as a class as well as a gender, an idea that implicates the family structure in the discussion of economic exploitation.

On a less critical note, the journal also conveys a sense of solidarity by regularly supplying information on women's organizations in Spain and other countries and offering sections such as "Sin miedo a volar" (Without Fear of Flying, an obvious rejoinder to Erica Jong's *Fear of Flying*), which gives a brief account of women who were not afraid to take risks or reclamations of forgotten or unsung women. Whenever possible, the articles emphasize the role of active women who could offer an alternative to the passive, compliant helpmate who was the national role model during the Franco regime.

The same objectives appear in a more humorous vein: "Pepitina," the "hero" of a regular comic strip, is a stick-figure sketch of an ill-humored young person who questions authority and accepts nothing at face value. A monthly column by Ana María Moix ("Nena no t'enfilis: Diario de una hija de familia") serializes the relationships of a quirky, dysfunctional family. This witty caricature of the traditional bourgeois family structure (and the place of women within it) uses stereotype and droll touches as the vehicle for the "message."

Vindicación feminista ran from 1976 until 1979, when it ceased publication because of financial problems. Its radical, confrontational tone alienated those in authority; a considerable percentage of the female population was also disaffected. Not surprisingly, these included traditional Spanish women of the "silent majority," but even some of the more committed feminists disagreed with the theoretical bases or the direction of the journal.

Vindicación feminista is a time capsule of information about Spain, about woman's place in it, and about the directions that feminism was taking during the period immediately following Franco's death. Its contents allow a glimpse into Spanish social and political history from the minority perspective of feminism. *See also* Feminism in Spain: 1900–2000

Work about

Levine, Linda Gould, and Lidia Falcón. "*Vindicación feminista* o el ideal compartido." *Revista de Estudios Hispánicos* 22 (1988): 53–65.

Margaret E. W. Jones

Visconti, Silvia

See Ballesteros, Mercedes (1913–   )

Vives, Luis (1492–1540): His View of Women

One of the most influential Spanish humanists of his day, Luis Vives was born in Spain but left in 1509 to study in Paris, where he met Erasmus of Rotterdam (1465–1536), Guillaume Budé (1467–1540), and Jacques Lefevre d'Etaples (c. 1455–1536) at the College of Montaigu. These northern European humanists deeply influenced Vives's writings and the development of his ideas. In 1512 Vives moved to Bruges in the Low Countries, then part of the Spanish Empire, and married Margarita Valdaura. Five years later he moved to Louvain, whose university was one of the most important intellectual institutions of Europe and a focus of the ongoing Reformist versus Catholic struggle.

In 1523 Vives traveled to England, teaching in the Corpus Christi College of Oxford. There he also entered the private circle of Queen *Catalina de Aragón, first wife of Henry VIII, tutoring her young daughter Princess Mary. During his stay in England, Vives also became a close friend and confidant of Thomas More (1478–1535). The relation with Princess Mary inspired Vives to compose his didactic book *De Institutione Feminae Christianae* (written 1523; *The Instruction of a Christian Woman* 2001). This work conveyed Vives's ideas about women's position in society, their roles in the family, and their rights and obligations; it also de-

fined the ideal woman's behavior and offered criticism of behavior and fashions of young bourgeois girls in the Low Countries, England, and Spain. Vives's advice, like that of Fray Luis de *León's *La perfecta casada*, represents the humanists' concern with education and information in general, and that of women in particular, and also the perceived need to establish limits of freedom—to define rules of social and private behavior during a critical period when values and customs were shifting. It is appropriate to recognize that Vives also wrote a manual for the education of young boys in the Tudor schools, and his writings on the instruction of young children and his book on urban poverty in Bruges represent early precedents for the study of developmental psychology and social welfare.

In *The Instruction of a Christen Woman*, Vives organizes his teachings in three sections that correspond to the three fundamental stages in women's lives: the virgin, the wife, and the widow. The criterion for this division of time is the position of a woman in the private universe of men, as daughter, as wife, and as survivor. The text assigns the first stage to the childhood and early youth of women, the second stage to postpuberty, and the final one to maturity and old age. However, the behaviors that Vives teaches—chastity for the virgin, obedience for the wife—are really independent of their ages since Vives, like the vast majority of his contemporaries, did not believe that women ever matured as men did. The first part of the text, devoted to the early years of life, is the longest and richest in information.

The "Instruction of the Virgins" (Chapters 1–18, First Book) begins with the life of baby girls, whose early childhood is separated from that of boys. Vives demonstrates deep concern with the importance of virginity and its preservation, thoroughly treating topics like feminine hygiene, clothing and ornamentation, and the virtues of virginal solitude. Deeming modesty and chastity the most important virtues for a woman, the avoidance of exposure was paramount. Vives emphasized that women must get an education, considering ignorance a social evil, but this education must come from other women. This idea contradicts the preaching of the apostle Paul, who banned women from teaching. In Vives's opinion, the more educated a woman was, the more virtuous she would be, a clear benefit to husbands and children. The mere idea of teaching women to read and allowing them to develop their own minds was revolutionary and represents a point of departure for a new concept of the ideal bourgeois wife and mother in the Low Countries and Tudor England. Women were still to function only as housekeepers and child caregivers, but post-Reformation society needed a partner for the humanist-man who, following the new Erasmist ideas in favor of marriage, should have a companion appropriate to his intellectual and social status. Vives intended to contribute to the education of these new women without abandoning traditional Catholic ideas. He recommended a very specific type of literature for women (hagiographies, writings of the Church Fathers, and other religious literature) and expressly condemned chivalry books (*novelas de *caballerías*) and leisure books that might induce young girls to entertain vain and sinful ideas. When reading Vives one must remember that the practices he criticized were probably common behavior and that the model of feminine comportment he advocated—the invisible, quiet, wise wife, always ready to serve her husband—was neither abundant nor realistic.

The Second Book, the "Instruction of Married Women" (Chapters 1–14 or 19–33), reiterates that the most important virtues of the married woman comprise modesty and chastity in addition to love and obedience to the husband. Other duties of the good wife include maintaining peace and harmony among family members. The Third Book, which deals with widows (Chapters 1–7 or 34–41) limits itself to reminding these women of their obligation, again, to remain

modest and chaste if they are young and to be aware of the dangers involved in dealing with men, servants and sons included.

The main value of *The Instruction of a Christen Woman* for women's studies resides in the fact that by criticizing women's behavior Vives leaves a rich testimony of women's actual way of life and what was expected of them; women's behaviors in the Low Countries, Spain, France, and England are compared and contrasted. Although the manual was originally written for Mary Tudor, it reached a wide public, being translated from Latin into English by Richard Hyrde in 1540 and into Spanish by Juan Justiniano in 1528. In Spain, together with Luis de León's *La perfecta casada*, it has been the required reading for young women since the 1500s until very recently. The text's teachings do not deal with a woman as a figure of authority, as one might expect since it was written for a princess, but with women as a "difficult to manage" entity to be limited to the domestic domain, defined in relation to men and subordinated to their authority.

Work by

The Instruction of a Christen Woman. Ed. Virginia Walcott Beauphamp, Elizabeth H. Hageman, and Margaret Mikesell. Urbana: U of Illinois P, 2001.

La mujer cristiana, De los deberes del marido, Pedagogía pueril. Trans. and study Lorenzo Riber. 2nd ed. Madrid: Aguilar, 1949.

On Assistance to the Poor. Trans., intro., and commentary Alice Tobriner. Toronto and Buffalo: U of Toronto P and Renaissance Society of America, 1999.

Tratado de la enseñanza. Trans. José Otañón. Prol. Foster Watson. Madrid: La Lectura, 1923.

Tratado del socorro de los pobres. Trans. Juan de Gonzalo. Madrid: Ministerio de Asuntos Sociales, 1991.

A Very Fruitfull and Pleasant Boke called the Instruction of A Christen Woman. Trans. Richard Hyrde. London, 1540. Micropublished in *History of Women*. New Haven, CT: Research Publications, 1975.

Vives and the Renascence Education of Women. Ed. Foster Watson. New York: Longmans, Green; London: Edward Arnold, 1912.

Vives: On Education; A Translation of the De tradendis disciplinis of Juan Luis Vives. Intro. Foster Watson. Foreword Francesco Cordasco. Totowa, NJ: Rowman and Littlefield, 1971.

Work about

Bergmann, Emilie L. "La exclusión de lo femenino en el discurso cultural del humanismo." *Actas del X Congreso de la Asociación de Hispanistas, I-IV.* Ed. Antonio Vilanova, Foreword Josep María Bricall. Pref. Elias L. Rivers. Barcelona: Promociones y Pubs. Universitarias, 1992.

Mikesell, Margaret. "The Place of Vives's *Instruction of a Christen Woman* in Early Modern English Domestic Book Literature." *Contextualizing the Renaissance: Returns to History.* Ed. and intro. Albert H. Tricomi. Binghamton, NY: Brepols, 1999.

Miller, Nancy Weitz. "Metaphor and the Mystification of Chastity in Vives's *Instruction of a Christen Woman.*" *Menacing Virgins. Representing Virginity in the Middle Ages and Renaissance.* Ed. Kathleen Coyne Kelly and Marina Leslie. Newark: U of Delaware P; London: Associated U Presses, 1999.

Vigil, Mariló. *La vida de las mujeres en los siglos XVI y XVII.* Madrid: Siglo XXI, 1986.

Wayne, Valerie. "Some Sad Sentence: Vives' *Instruction of a Christian Woman.*" *Silent But for the Word; Tudor Women as Patrons, Translators and Writers of Religious Works.* Ed. Margaret Patterson Hannay. Kent, OH: Kent State UP, 1985. 15–29.

María Luisa García-Verdugo

Women's Deceits: Medieval Approaches to the Topic

The literary tradition of recording women's deceits is a universal one, often expressed in the form of humorous or cautionary tales of women's cunning methods of attaining financial or sexual gratification illicitly. The pre- and early medieval sources of such tales and attitudes are numerous: Much Sanskrit, Latin, theological, popular, and folkloric material on women is organized around the conviction that the female—especially when married—is fickle, ambitious, and vain. In the Western world, many early Christian writers repeatedly refer to woman as intrinsically evil, while in the East, the Indian collection of narratives known as the *Panchatantra* (third century) contains numerous stories of women's deceits, making its way to the West via translations in the twelfth and thirteenth centuries. The variants, glosses, offshoots, and continuations of didactic and artistic expositions of women's flawed character abound in the European Middle Ages, and Spain participates fully in the tradition.

In the case of medieval Spain, the intertextual link with both Latin and Eastern sources is particularly dynamic in light of the peninsula's close interaction with both Near Eastern and Western literary traditions. Accounts of women's deceits appear in a variety of genres in medieval Spanish literature: Ex- empla, poems, and didactic treatises deal with the topic, stating as their purpose the blending of entertainment with moralizing postures.

In the twelfth century, the collection of tales known as the *Disciplina clericalis* (Instruction on Life for the Educated) by the converted Jewish scholar Pedro Alfonso (fl. 1106) appeared in Latin; among his tales, translated from Arabic and meant as didactic *exempla* on such issues as the evils of lying, the importance of good friends, and the virtues of discretion, a number of narratives expose the crafty skills of women who lie to their husbands to hide their adulterous behavior; other tales show the cunning ways in which old women go about facilitating adultery for younger ones. The collection of tales translated from Sanskrit and Persian via Arabic—the *Calila e Digna* (translated 1251)—also contains anecdotes on the wiles of women. Similarly, the thirteenth-century *Libro de los engaños y assayamientos de las mujeres* (translated 1253; Book of Women's Deceits and Habits)—also known as the *Sendebar*—presents a series of prose narratives translated from Arabic on women's ingenious tactics for indulging in immoral acts. Both collections begin with a frame story and relate the subsequent tales in the typical "Chinese box" structure of Eastern stories. The work of wisdom literature entitled *Libro de los buenos proverbios* (late 13th c.; Book of Good Proverbs) presupposes the evil nature of woman, while the exposure of women's deceits and wiles constitutes one of the main components of the lyric genre of medieval Gallego-Portuguese poetry known as *cantigas de escarnio*, satirical and narrative poems, many of which mock women.

Between 1400 and 1421 the canon of León cathedral, Clemente Sánchez de Vercial (1370?–1426?), compiled the collection of 438 *exempla* under the title *Libro de los exenplos por a.b.c* (Book of Examples by A.B.C); here stories from a variety of sources (such as the *Disciplina clericalis*) address a number of issues, among them women's duplicity and their talent for deceiving their husbands. Another prominent example of attacks on women is the didactic work entitled *El *corbacho*, also referred to as *El arcipreste de Talavera* (1438) by Alfonso Martínez de Toledo (likewise known as the Archpriest of Talavera [1398?–1482?]), divided into four parts, the second part of which is a vehement criticism of women, using satire as the main form of expression. The writer makes use of anecdotes, *exempla*, lively dialogue, and frequent generalizations to drive home his points on the misfortunes that befall men from interacting with women.

References to women's skill in deception can be found in other works of the medieval period whose principal aim is not to expose women's cunning but to mention this attribute in the context of each work's own thematic priorities. In both *El *libro de buen amor* (mid-fourteenth century; Book of Good Love) by Juan Ruiz, archpriest of Hita (1283?–1353?) and *La *Celestina* (1499) by Fernando de Rojas (1465?–1541) the old *alcahueta* (go-between) displays a number of traits that recall the clichéd associations of old women's cunning placed at the service of illicit sexuality: The *vieja's* (old woman's) use of colorful and manipulative speech is portrayed in both texts from an ambivalent standpoint that at once admires and condemns her skill with words. The hints at her

familiarity with sorcery and nonacademic medicinal practices further confirm her image as an untrustworthy agent for the perpetuation of illicit sexual contacts.

The basic idea underlying narratives on women's deceits is that women are by nature fickle, defective, and imperfect. In the Middle Ages, while many writers and genres extolled the virtues of women, concomitantly a variety of sources promoted the literary conviction that women have an exaggerated interest in money, prevarication, excess chatter, intrigue, and sexual gratification. Medical, philosophical, and religious interpretations of woman's nature often concurred in the view that she was fatally flawed, even if such sources articulated this conviction in diverse ways. Female anatomy in particular played a crucial role for such a conviction, for it was on the basis of her sole purpose in life—procreation—that doctors and theologians alike inferred a natural order that placed her in an inferior position. The fact that woman was regarded as a sexual being with little or no control over her corporeal desires helped elaborate the general notion that she represented nature without the advantageous access to a rational mind. Thus, some theologians and medical authorities saw woman's reproductive function as the cause for her irrational behavior and linked this fact to her role in Creation. Since she had been created after man, and represented a flawed mirror image of his body, she was prone to ailments and conditions that did not affect the superior male. Medical writings, inspired by Galen (c. 130–200) and other Greek doctors as well as medieval Arab physicians, discussed factors such as female emissions, the condition known as the wandering womb, and the sensitivity to vapors as principal features of the female anatomy. The Church Father Saint Isidore of Seville (560?–636) discussed the functions of the female body in one section of his vast encyclopedic work known as the *Etymologies* (mid-seventh century), purely in terms of reproduction. Those theologians and writers who were inscribed in the tradition of misogynist thought reappropriated this knowledge to account for woman's frailty, inferiority to man, and natural disposition to misbehavior.

The depictions of women's deceits is one offshoot of such convictions, set into a popular and narrative tradition that thus draws on popular medicine, sermons, and Near Eastern as well as Latin sources, with a special focus on the narration of tricks and ploys used by women in urban settings to deceive their husbands or other community members.

Some scholars have warned against the interpretation of such tales solely in the context of *misogyny. The argument that these tales have a purely entertaining purpose, free of any didactic aim, has been put forward; elsewhere, it has been asserted that tales that depict women's cunning alongside men's gullibility do indicate, albeit implicitly, some admiration for the woman's skill and talent and are therefore not as straightforwardly antifeminist as one may think. Thus, the critical responses to collections such as *El libro de los engaños* or the *Disciplina clericalis* have been diverse, taking into account the many resonances of such tales on the didactic and artistic levels. *See also* Cosmetics in Medieval and Renaissance Spain

Work about

García Teruel, G. "Medieval Misogyny and Other Views of Women in Various Medieval Narratives (12th–13th-Century)." *Moyen Age* 101 (1995): 23–39.

Keller, John Esten. *Collectanea hispanica: Folklore and Brief Narrative Studies.* Ed. Dennis P. Seniff. Newark, DE: Juan de la Cuesta, 1987.

Lacarra, María Jesús. *Cuentística medieval en España: Los orígenes.* Zaragoza: Universidad de Zaragoza, 1979.

Marsan, Rameline E. *Itinéraire espagnol du conte médiéval: VIIIe-XVe siècles.* Paris: Klincksieck, 1974.

Miller, Beth, ed. *Women in Hispanic Literature: Icons and Fallen Idols.* Berkeley and Los Angeles: U of California P, 1983.

Picerno, Richard A. *Medieval Spanish Ejempla: A Study of Selected Tales from "Calila y Dimna," "El libro de los engaños de las mujeres"* and the *"Libro de los exemplos por A.B.C."* Miami: Ediciones Universal, 1988.

Leyla Rouhi

Women's Education in Spain: 1860–1993

Although a few thinkers of the Enlightenment publicly recognized the intellectual capacity of women, formal education for women in Spain was essentially neglected until the second half of the nineteenth century. The reforms that began to emerge did not arise from a desire for equality between the sexes but rather as a means to enhance women's traditional roles as wives and mothers. The disinterest and restrictions surrounding women's education reflect the dominance of the Catholic Church in Spain, the weakness of its middle class, and its underdeveloped feminist consciousness. The little education available to girls focused on domestic skills, religion, and subjects considered helpful to the development of social graces. Slowly, certain academic courses were added to the curriculum, but its intellectual substance was rudimentary. Middle schools were not opened to girls until 1868. The Normal School of Madrid was created in 1856, and the Escuela de Institutrices (Governesses' School) in 1869. Fernando de Castro, a follower of the liberal philosophers and pedagogues known as *krausistas* (followers of German philosopher Karl Christian Friedrich Krause [1781–1832]), founded the Asociación para la Enseñanza de la Mujer (Association for the Instruction of Women) in 1870, as well as a number of trade schools for women. Only a select few profited from the reform efforts of the *krausistas*. Working-class women received little, if any, schooling, and women of the upper middle classes who attended school went to institutions run by nuns. Nonetheless, the question of women's education became a widely debated issue. Two important national pedagogy congresses were held during this period, one in 1882 and the other in 1892, where both Concepción *Arenal (1820–1893) and Emilia *Pardo Bazán (1852–1921) spoke on the need to improve women's education. Despite isolated support for higher education for women, between 1880 and the beginning of the twentieth century only 15 women received university degrees, and in 1900, 71 percent of females in Spain were still illiterate.

At the end of the nineteenth century the issues of secularization, centralization, and coeducation were debated on the national level. At the beginning of this century the government of Spain began to take a more active part in reforming the nation's school system. It created nonreligious schools, a council of public instruction, and the Junta de Ampliación de Estudios (Council for Extended Studies), in 1907, which granted scholarships (mostly to males) for study abroad. Coeducation in the primary grades was established in 1909, and schooling to 12 years of age was made obligatory in the same year. In 1910, the law requiring women to secure government permission to attend the university was abolished. Also after this date a number of schools and centers, such as the Residencia de Señoritas (Young Women's Residence), were opened to women. In response to these measures, the Church established reform programs that did not threaten its basic conception of womanhood. All these advancements along with the growing need for middle-class women to seek employment* fostered the improvement in women's education through the years of the Second Republic. Between 1900 and 1930 university enrollment for women multiplied a thousandfold, but the overall level of education for women remained lamentably low. The mission of education, when not the preparation for socially acceptable vocations for women, continued to be the instillment of religiosity, feminine social virtues, and a love of domesticity.

After 1940, the fascist agenda of dictator Francisco Franco (1892–1975) set back this modest development in women's education. Coeducation was eliminated, women's pursuit of careers was obstructed, and indoctrination in domesticity was carried out through the schools and the "Sección Femenina" (Feminine Section) of the Spanish Falange. The democracy that replaced Franco after 1975 supported the expansion of women's education. By 1993 half of university students were female; but women continue to study the traditional programs associated with females, and education in rural areas is still inferior to that of urban areas. *See also* Women's Situation in Spain: 1600–1700; Women's Situation in Spain: 1700–1800; Women's Situation in Spain: 1786–1931: The Awakening of Female Consciousness

Work about

Capel Martínez, Rosa María. *El trabajo y la educación de la mujer en España (1900–1930)*. Madrid: Ministerio de Cultura, 1986.

Folguera, Pilar. *Vida cotidiana en Madrid. El primer tercio del siglo a través de las fuentes orales*. Madrid: Comunidad de Madrid, 1987.

Martín Gaite, Carmen. *Usos amorosos de la postguerra española*. Barcelona: Anagrama, 1987.

Scanlon, Geraldine. *La polémica feminista en la España contemporánea: 1868–1974*. Madrid: Akal, 1986.

Zulueta, Carmen. *Cien años de educación de la mujer española. Historia del Instituto Internacional*. Madrid: Castalia, 1992.

Zulueta, Carmen, and Alicia Moreno. *Ni convento ni college. La Residencia de Señoritas*. Madrid: Consejo Superior de Investigaciones Científicas, 1993.

Catherine G. Bellver

Women's Professions in Early Spanish Literature: *Santas, Rameras, Casadas, Amas,* and *Criadas* (Saints, Whores, Wives, Governesses, and Servants)

The most important profession for women in early Spanish literature was that of being a woman created by a (generally male) writer's imagination; therefore, she had to be dependent and subordinate to development of the story and to the male character: Doña *Jimena in the *Poema de Mío Cid* (Poem of the Cid) exists because she is secondary and highlights the character of her *señor*, her sire, and her profession is to be a wife. The most common profession for women in Spanish literature, famous wives include Alisa, Melibea's mother in Fernando de Rojas's *La *Celestina*, and Teresa Panza, Sancho's spouse in Miguel de Cervantes's *Don Quijote de la Mancha*. A key component of being a good wife was to stay in the background, almost unnoticed.

Fray Luis de *León describes extensively and with abundant examples and anecdotes his ideal for a wife's behavior in *La perfecta casada* (1583; The Perfect Wife). Although his purpose was to educate women through his biblical commentary, he also offered a detailed description of the idea writers held of what a good woman, or a good wife, should be. Fray Luis advised women to be homebound, silent, servile, self-denying, hardworking, attentive as mothers, faithful and protective of family honor, and competent as administrators and to fulfill their role in life as wives with appreciation of God's will. Good women in literature are symbols of these virtues. Any transgression of these duties represented the beginning of a tragic story where male *honor is jeopardized, or the beginning of a picaresque story, or another exemplary or moralistic work. In *Don Quijote I* (1605) Cervantes introduces the character of Dorotea, a beautiful young girl who has been dishonored by the noble Don Fernando. Dorotea is instrumental in achieving the return of Don Quijote to his village and the end of his adventures in the first part of the book. Her power over the knight is based on her beauty but most of all on her word. Whenever a woman or a wife is presented in the story with a long speech, it indicates that her intentions are dubious.

The model for the female character is found in Aristotle's *Poetics*. It demands a low-key presentation; should the female character become more active and noticeable, thereby playing a more important role in the story, she is not a positive role model or a good woman. The existence of a female protagonist immediately represents a transgression; the natural order of society is broken and that rupture becomes the main motivation of the story. This is the case in *La Celestina* (1499?), in Francisco Delicado's *La *lozana andaluza* (1528), in López de Ubeda's *La *pícara Justina* (1605), and in other protagonists of the feminine picaresque (*Pícaras) where the main character exerts control over her literary existence. Professions exercised by these female protagonists—prostitution and sorcery, for example—are marginal and illegal for the most part. *La lozana andaluza* lists some jobs of its protagonist: to make *cosmetics, wash clothes and linen, cook, prepare brides for their weddings (closing their hymens), prepare concoctions and remedies for sundry illnesses but especially venereal diseases, sing, entertain guests, and be a prostitute.

As professionals, picaresque women are very active since their survival depends on their own skills rather than a man's economic power. In some cases, they created "schools," as seen in *La Celestina*, where the old sorceress has several apprentices. Writers are relatively explicit when explaining their abilities and the ways these women use their skills, to make clear the dangers that lie in wait to ambush the male protagonist and also to demonstrate to readers that the more a woman knows, the more dangerous she is.

Cervantes did elaborate female characters who were "working girls," primarily to add verisimilitude to a story. His country peasant girls take care of livestock and are short, dark, and strong. Far from the Petrarchan ideal of fair, passive beauty, the dark strong woman adds humor to the narration, mocking the ideal "*Dulcinea" and including in the fictional space a realistic depiction of working women. Doña Rodríguez, in *Don Quijote II* (1615), represents the older female servant, or *dueña, in a rich household of the

Spanish aristocracy. As she herself explains to Don Quijote, young girls from aristocratic families who did not inherit enough money to keep their status ended up as waiting-maids or dames of honor to richer aristocrats, receiving "miserable salaries and scanty favors" and constantly subjected to the wishes and moods of their masters. Their aristocratic upbringing permitted them to become tutors or caregivers for offspring of richer families. The conflict between their pride or "honor" and their dependent economic position creates the problems that brought Doña Rodríguez to seek Don Quijote's "help" in correcting the abuses of the rich peasants who dishonored them.

In her *Escritos autobiográficos* Luisa de *Carvajal y Hurtado de Mendoza (1566–1614) describes her governess Ayllon, an older single woman who, after the parents' deaths, was given charge of raising Carvajal when she was six years old. Carvajal describes how Ayllon spanked and pinched her when she did not follow Ayllon's wishes but praises her sense of duty and fidelity. Carvajal herself is an example of the holy path some women chose as their profession. Some women who possessed the education and economic ability to do so chose celibacy but then lived independent of religious orders. Like Carvajal, they fought male relatives to preserve their independence and follow their beliefs. Carvajal decided to become a missionary and traveled to England to convert the English back to Catholicism, channeling self-denial toward religious sacrifice in hope of changing the world. She was imprisoned several times and finally died in London. Her autobiography and that of St. *Teresa de Jesús and other women contemporaries preserve firsthand information about women's professions that were ignored by male writers. See also Autobiographical Self-Representation of Women in the Early Modern Period; Nuns Who Wrote in Sixteenth- and Seventeenth-Century Spain; Syphilis as Sickness and Metaphor in Early Modern Spain: 1492–1650; *Tercera*

Work about

Carvajal, Luisa de. *Escritos autobiográficos de la Venerable doña Luisa de Carvajal y Mendoza*. Intro. and notes Camilo María Abad. Barcelona: Juan Flors, 1966.

Cervantes, Miguel de. *Don Quixote* Trans. J.M. Cohen. London: Penguin, 1950.

Delicado, Francisco. *Portrait of Lozana: The Lusty Andalusian Woman*. Trans., intro., and notes Bruno Damiani. Potomac, MD: Scripta Humanistica, 1987.

Rojas, Fernando de. *La Celestina*. Madrid: Bruno, 1995.

Vigil, Mariló. *La vida de las mujeres en los siglos XVI y XVII*. Madrid: Siglo XXI, 1986.

María Luisa García-Verdugo

Women's Situation in Spain: 1250–1400

See Alfonso el Sabio (1221–1284): Women in *Las siete partidas*

Women's Situation in Spain: 1400–1600

In the fifteenth and sixteenth centuries, Spanish women were viewed as frail physically, spiritually, and emotionally and as such were considered susceptible to temptation. This attitude was supported by the clergy who pointed out that it was Eve who brought Adam to sin, and not the reverse. Because of such weaknesses, women were seen as inferior and even dangerous to men. Conversely, women were also seen as the receptacle of their family's *honor. A maiden's honor resided in her virginity, which her father guarded, and a wife's in her fidelity to her husband. The combination of these factors—women's perceived physical, spiritual, and emotional inferiorities, and feminine responsibility for the family honor—explain much of the treatment women received in this time period.

All women were defined in terms of their sexual state. Upper-class women held four positions: maiden, wife, nun, or widow. Chastity was considered their highest virtue, followed closely by obedience and modesty. Unmarried noblewomen rarely left their parent's houses, except to go to mass, to fulfill other religious duties, to go to the bullfight, or to attend the theater. When they did go out, they were always chaperoned and frequently segregated from men—as in the case of the theater, where women sat in a separate seating area known as the *cazuela* (stewpot). If, despite her seclusion, a maiden dishonored her family by having an affair or other indiscretion, she was forced into marriage by her father or confined to a convent.

Female children rarely received any formal education. Some learned reading, writing, and the four basic mathematical rules, but typically a girl's education consisted of domestic skills such as sewing, knitting, and weaving. Parents, normally the father, had complete authority over their children. Upon reaching the age to marry, the upper-class woman was expected to marry the man chosen for her by her father for economic or political reasons. Because financial considerations were paramount, a noblewoman would carry with her into marriage a large dowry.

Once married, a woman passed from the charge of her father to that of her husband. Her dowry remained her separate property, but her husband administered it. He had the right to liquidate any part of it, only needing her permission to sell lands. Like fathers, a husband enjoyed complete authority over his wife. He could seclude her (*encierro), if he chose, to protect the family honor. When a wife was unfaithful, it was not uncommon or illegal for her husband to kill her. Men possessed a variety of legally and socially approved recourses for dissolving an unsatisfactory marriage. They could kill an unfaithful wife or divorce one they claimed was infertile. Women, however, had no right to expect fidelity or kind treatment from their husbands. Instead, women were to understand that husbands were their superiors and as such had more freedom and privileges. A wife's duty was to bear all her husband did and never speak to him in anger. Religious

writers reminded women that when they married, they made themselves subject to their husbands and were no longer the owners of their own bodies. However, wives were obligated to resist their husbands' sexual advances during menstruation or if the husband was motivated solely by lust. A woman could only separate from her husband by becoming a nun. Even then, the marriage was not dissolved until the death of one marriage partner.

A married woman's daily life was primarily domestic. She cared for the young male children and the female children, sewed, embroidered, and read prayer books or fiction. She might, if permitted by her husband, receive female guests. At meals, only men sat at the table. Women and children sat on cushions at the side of the table. After the meal and siesta, men went out to socialize and conduct business while women stayed at home. Since women were expected to be silent and remain in their homes, it goes without saying that they could not hold positions of public authority.

Women with insufficient dowries found it difficult to marry well. Families who knew they would have trouble providing dowries for their daughters often put them out to work as domestic servants at a very early age to accumulate money for a dowry. Organizations also existed to provide dowries for well-born but poor women; *Isabel I (1451–1504) left in her will a sum of money to provide such women dowries to marry or enter the convent. Many families who lacked the economic means to arrange appropriate marriages for their daughters forced them into the convent, whether they had a vocation or not, to protect their family honor. Other women entered the convent to avoid unwanted marriages or simply because they could not support themselves in any other respectable manner. Because so many women without true vocations lived in the convents, the *galán de monjas* (nuns' beau), who courted nuns, was a common figure.

Nevertheless, life in the convent had its

advantages. Women in the convent were significantly more educated. Many could read and write Latin and were exposed to a variety of culture through their readings. Women who became abbesses, although they did not enjoy the power of the male clergy, did experience considerably more freedom and authority than the average woman.

Finally, widowhood was a potentially liberating, albeit difficult, state for women in the fifteenth and sixteenth centuries. A widow without sons of age inherited from her husband control over her dowry as well as part of her husband's estate. Widows also had charge of their children, enjoying the right to arrange marriages for sons and daughters. When a woman with sons of age was widowed, her dowry was considered part of their estate, but she retained control over her lands and could inherit a part of her husband's estate. Widows of tradesman could inherit their husband's guild membership, even when guild membership for individual women was prohibited. Widows could conduct business, and file, benefit from, and testify in legal suits. Widows retained these rights until they chose to remarry. On the other hand, upper-class widows were expected to be even more circumspect than maidens and wives. Standards of decent behavior required that they spend their days secluded and grieving the death of their husbands. The merry widow of literature was a disgraceful figure, seen as a corrosive element in society. Widows left without the financial means to support themselves had few ways of earning their living: charity, service as *dueñas*, prostitution, or the nunnery. Begging and prostitution were not uncommon.

Despite their cloistered lives, women of the fifteenth and sixteenth centuries in Spain made enough social appearances to inspire controversy regarding their attire. Women in these centuries are most commonly ridiculed for their use of makeup (*cosmetics). Ceruse, a pink or red foundation cream, was applied to the cheeks for color. The lips were covered with a thin layer of wax to make them

shine. Powder was also used on the face, neck, hands, and shoulders to produce white skin and to hide blemishes. Many women used perfumed waters, and women's clothing also generated controversy. One notably controversial garment was the *guardainfante*, a framework of hoops that held the petticoats and gown in a bell-shape. The hoops eventually reached such a width as to inhibit a woman's ability to pass through doors. This outfit was banned by royal decree in 1633, except for use by prostitutes, but was so popular that many ladies risked being mistaken for disreputable women in order to continue wearing it.

Outside their homes, women wore a cloak and veil that covered them from head to foot (*cubiertas* and *tapadas*). This garb was also criticized for various reasons. The cloak was occasionally made of tulle, or other see-through fabrics, considered to be too seductive. The veil might modestly cover the face, or it might be used to conceal the identity of prostitutes or to aid flirtatious or adulterous behavior. Distinctions were made in writings of these centuries between the *cubierta, who allowed her cloak to cover her face naturally and modestly, and the *tapada*, who folded her veil to reveal one eye and took advantage of the anonymity this costume provided for dishonorable behavior. Attempts were made to ban the veil, most notably in 1590 and 1639, with little success.

The lives of upper-class women in the fifteenth and sixteenth centuries had not changed significantly since the Middle Ages. Seen as weak and dangerous, they spent their lives cloistered by their male relatives, with few rights or privileges. *See also Encierro*

Work about

Defourneaux, Marcelin. *Daily Life in Spain in the Golden Age.* New York: Praeger, 1966.

Perry, Mary Elizabeth. "Crisis and Disorder in the World of Maria de Zayas." *Maria de Zayas, the Dynamics of Discourse.* Ed. A. Williamsen and J. Whitenack. London: Associated UP, 1995. 23–29.

———. *Gender and Disorder in Early Modern Seville.* Princeton, NJ: Princeton UP, 1990.

Vigil, Mariló. *La vida de las mujeres en los siglos XVI y XVII.* Madrid: Siglo veintiuno, 1986.

Karoline J. Manny

Women's Situation in Spain: 1600–1700

Any discussion of history, and women's history in particular, in seventeenth-century Spain must be framed within the context of the decline of the Spanish empire (beginning with the defeat of the Spanish Armada in 1588 at the hands of the British Navy) and the "Santo Oficio," or Spanish Inquisition. These two phenomena had an overwhelming influence on daily life in Spain and contributed to a climate of repression that affected women especially. Women's sphere of activity in society became restricted as economic and social pressures contributed to an atmosphere of conservatism, forcing women to become more active "behind the scenes." Within these confines, however, women were able to exert considerable influence, as evidenced by the writings of women from all social classes and the activities of women in high positions, either within religious orders or because of noble birth. The influence of women's voices heard "behind closed doors" was especially true for queens and other noblewomen, who could influence those in power during the period of weak monarchies that characterized the seventeenth century in Spain.

The history of the Bourbons and Hapsburgs and the intermarriage of first cousins within the Spanish line is well known for the succession of mentally and physically weak monarchs it produced. From the time of the marriage of Philip III to Margarita of Austria in 1599 (he ascended to the throne in 1598) until the death of Charles II in 1700, women wearing the Spanish crown exerted a great influence on politics. During that time a succession of Austrian queens, together with the Royal Council, determined the direction of Spanish foreign policy: Margarita of Austria (queen from 1598 to 1611), Mariana of Austria (queen from 1623 to 1665, regent from 1665 to 1675), and María Ana of Neuborg (queen from 1689 to 1700). These women were instrumental in maintaining the strong ties of Catholicism between the two nations (both Margarita and Mariana brought their confessors from Austria to the Spanish court, where these men exercised considerable political influence) and assured continued Spanish military support to the Hapsburg Empire in its fight against the Turks. With Spain involved in three major military enterprises (against the Dutch, who defeated them in 1648, the French, who defeated them in 1659, and the English, who defeated them in 1667), many noblemen and kings had to be absent from Madrid, leaving their wives to rule with the *junta*, or conciliar government. Not only did their wives (and in the case of Charles II, his mother, Queen Mariana) have a considerable amount of political influence, but also certain women religious influenced their policy decisions: the Descalzas Reales convent in the case of Philip III, where both his aunt and cousin were sisters, and in the case of Philip IV, Sor María de *Agreda, whose influence in political matters was considerable. All these women used the traditional women's realms of family and religion as a source of power exercised in traditional men's realms.

Family life varied according to social class, but one constant was the confinement of women (*encierro*), affecting especially members of the middle and upper classes. These women could only leave the house to attend mass or for religious or other holidays and were always chaperoned. When they were in public, restrictions were imposed on their manner of dress and travel. Philip III, in an effort to stem prostitution, forbade the wearing of veils (*cubiertas* and *tapadas*) in public and riding in covered carriages. Lower-class women had the most freedom to move about on the streets, largely due to the necessity of earning a living. Among those women found on the streets were the class of merchant women and the lower-class women who worked as maids or prostitutes.

Almost all families had servants of one kind or another, and many families had African slaves. In Cádiz in 1654 there were more than 1,500 slaves, used mostly to load and unload ships, while in other parts of Spain they were domestic servants. In 1623 Philip IV prohibited titled families from having more than 18 servants, and those of councilors or ministers from having more than 8. In general, servants of families were treated well and often considered part of the extended family. The women who worked as servants in the *posadas*, or inns, however, reportedly had a very bleak existence, suffering physical and sexual abuse. Another common occupation of lower-class women was as *nodrizas*, or wet nurse and nanny.

Prostitution and vagrancy (often two sides of the same coin) were the most serious problems affecting women for the civil authorities in Spain. Seville had the most activity, counting 20 houses of prostitution in 1601, and some 3,000 prostitutes. This situation sparked the establishment of "casas de recogidas" (foundling homes) for younger girls who it was thought could be saved, and the first female prisons for adult women, with the idea that they too could be "reinserted" into society after having been "corrected." Magdalena de San Jerónimo wrote an important treatise on the punishment and rehabilitation of women, titled "Razón y forma de la Galera" (1608; Reason for and Functioning of Women's Prisons), addressed to Philip IV, in which she suggested the establishment of women's prisons for vagrants, thieves, go-betweens, and other women of ill repute. The treatise is extremely detailed, describing how they should live, what they should wear and eat, and what type of activities they should engage in. In many cases, convents were established next door to foundling homes, with the professed purpose of offering these women a basic education, but some sources indicate that in many cases there was more penitence than education involved.

Another important chapter in women's occupations in the seventeenth century was that of the witches, who were also seen as social deviants. Contrary to popular belief, the Spanish Inquisition did not prosecute witches unless they challenged religious ideology or were involved in major crimes. The professions of most witches revolved around arranging or reviving amorous relationships and healing, which on the whole were not considered serious challenges to Church or secular authorities. To give an example of how witchcraft was treated compared to other crimes "against the faith," one can look at an *auto de fe* celebrated in Madrid in 1680, where 7 men and 3 women were lightly punished for witchcraft, 2 women were lightly punished for polygamy, 28 men and 23 women were punished harshly, and 13 men and 5 women were burned alive for suspicion of practicing Judaism.

Women working in artisanry or other professions were not recognized as workers in their own right but rather as family members of the men involved in those professions. Some evidence suggests that women formed groups, especially textile workers. In 1628, in Barcelona, a group of women spinners burst in on the city council meeting to protest the drapers' practice of sending wool outside the city to be spun, which was taking away their jobs. In Barcelona, women were encouraged to participate in the workforce but not allowed to participate in guilds, of which only masters could be members, and only men could be masters (those with their own businesses and apprentices). Many of these women actually ran the shops of their husbands and fathers, but the official records bear no witness to this; all businesses were cataloged under the name of the male owner.

The education of women began to be seen as more common and acceptable in the seventeenth century as compared with the century before, when Counterreformation ideology created an atmosphere of repression concerning women's education. Two notable sixteenth-century treatises on women's education are Fray Luis de *León's *La perfecta casada* (1583; The Perfect Wife) and Luis *Vives's *Instrucción de la mujer cristiana* (1540; *The Instruction of a Christien Woman*, 2001), both of which continued influencing the way people thought about women's education in the following centuries. While León opposed the idea of educated women, Vives, influenced by the ideas of Erasmus, supported it, if only in a limited context. For middle- and upper-class women, it was generally considered appropriate for them to learn to sing, dance, play instruments, sew, and do enough reading to be able to follow a book of hours or other such books of spiritual instruction—in other words, enough education to make them desirable, decorative wives. They were not permitted to read scripture and were not admitted to the university. The upper-class women who were truly educated (and who often became writers or—exceptionally—taught at the university) were taught in the home, usually being daughters or wives of intellectual men with formidable libraries. The convent did offer some opportunities for women, especially upper-class women, to study and dedicate themselves to intellectual pursuits, as well as create positions of leadership for those who rose in the convent's administration. *See also* Sexuality in the Golden Age: Fray Gaspar de Villarroel (?–after 1659); Sexuality in the Golden Age: Fray Manuel de Guerra y Ribera (seventeenth century); Women's Professions in Early Spanish Literature: *Santas, Rameras, Casadas, Amas,* and *Criadas* (Saints, Whores, Wives, Governesses, and Servants)

Work about

Alcalá-Zamora, José, ed. *La vida cotidiana en la España de Velázquez*. Madrid: Temas de Hoy,1989.

Barbeito, María Isabel. *Cárceles y mujeres en el siglo XVII*. Madrid: Castalia Biblioteca de la Mujer, 1991.

Davis, Natalie Zemon. *Culture and Identity in Early Modern Europe (1500–1800)*. Ann Arbor: U of Michigan P, 1993.

Davis, Natalie Zemon, and Joan Wallach Scott. *Women's History as Women's Education*. Essays by Natalie Zemon Davis and Joan Wallach Scott from a Symposium in Honor of Jill and John Conway. Northampton: Smith College (Sophia Smith Collection and Archives), 1985.

Defourneaux, Marcelin. *Daily Life in Spain in the Golden Age*. Stanford: Stanford UP, 1970.

Dewald, Jonathan. "Deadly Parents: Family and Aristocratic Culture in Early Modern France." *Culture and Identity in Early Modern Europe (1500–1800)*. Ed. Barbara Diefendorf and Carla Hesse. Ann Arbor: U of Michigan P, 1993. 223–236.

Domínguez Ortiz, Antonio. *La sociedad española en el siglo XVII*. Madrid: CSIC, Instituto Balmes de Sociología, 1984.

Elliot, J.H. *Imperial Spain*. London: Penguin, 1963.

Sánchez, Magdalena S., and Alain Saint-Saens, eds. *Spanish Women in the Golden Age: Images and Realities*. Westport, CT: Greenwood P, 1996.

Shorter, Edward. *The Making of the Modern Family*. New York: Basic Books, 1975.

Voltes, María José, and Pedro Voltes. *Las mujeres en la historia de España*. Barcelona: Planeta, 1986.

Nancy Cushing-Daniels

Women's Situation in Spain: 1700–1800

The situation of women in Spain during the eighteenth century greatly differed from that of the previous centuries, and these changes were closely related to the new political situation following the end of the Habsburg dynasty. The death of Charles II in 1700 marked the end of a historic period and the beginning of a new era in which Spain would lose its hegemony. France, victorious in war and highly reputed as a cultural center, imposed upon Europe the fashion of Versailles. During the first half of the eighteenth century new philosophical trends stressing worldly happiness and a tendency to disregard spiritual values appeared. The style of Versailles would be closely imitated in Spain; its main characteristics—the lack of interest in moral concerns, gallantry, and ludic superficiality—were to dictate Spanish social life. In this new hedonistic society women were encouraged to enjoy life freely, functioning as society's indispensable adornment. Women's main duty of introducing the image of pleasure in society required learning a new role. A first step was to discard the past's coyness and reserve, which greatly improved the lives of Spanish women, since for centuries they had been indoctrinated to curb inclinations and reduce them to minimal expression. During the eighteenth century a remarkable subversion of values took place: The right to enjoy a luxurious life was gradually recognized in Spain, encouraging spending and magnificence. Spanish women learned how to dress up, entertain in their homes, and socialize. They also contributed decisively to creation of new demands and needs as they eagerly received fashions from abroad. To meet the new social standards, women also needed to acquire certain abilities: Singing, dancing, or playing an instrument were essential attributes for a lady, replacing the traditional attributes of economy and dedication to the family.

In part because of the frivolous role for women that fashion imposed, women's education suffered serious neglect. Society had a very specific idea of what a woman should be, and cultivation of the intellect did not fit this model. Many texts of the period describe women with a single word: frivolous. While this frivolity was much criticized by writers (almost all men), nothing was done in terms of education or treatment to change their role. On the contrary, superficiality, vanity, and lack of knowledge were deemed fashionable for women, and the purpose of whatever education they received was for selecting a husband. From childhood on, women were encouraged to make personal adornment a main objective in their lives; the preoccupation with beauty was both habitual and demanding, and beautifying ceremonies became more and more complicated, multiplying into numberless needs that overwhelmed women. The richness and profusion of feminine adornments were commonly criticized in the writings and graphic art of the period.

Church and home were the primary education sources for women, and intellectual growth falling outside this realm was considered inappropriate and actively discouraged. Women were to provide for the well-being of their men and children and nothing else. Moreover, women who yearned to learn and tried to react against the inertia and superficiality imposed upon them were judged subversive by men and by female friends and relatives. These reactionary women were derogatorily called *bachilleras* (bluestockings). Nonetheless, by mid-century some changes emerged for those women not wishing to dedicate their lives entirely to family, Church, or social activity. First, the distorted education women received began to be recognized, and then their mentors began to be held responsible. Many writers of this period insisted that fault was not in women (who were really victims of a faulty system) but in men, since it was a male ideal of feminine behavior that was being imposed.

During these years debates about women's inferiority or superiority to men became common. One of the first was initiated by Fray Benito Jerónimo *Feijóo (1676–1764). As a main defender of the feminist cause, he dedicated one of the longest chapters of his *Teatro crítico universal* (1726–1739) to the "Defense of Women." His treatise defended women from unfair male criticism of the day and also proclaimed the intellectual equality of the sexes. After comparing the general qualities of each sex, Feijóo concluded that women surpassed men in the realm of private virtues but men were better suited for the civic life. Like most intellectuals of his day and good intentions notwithstanding, Feijóo expressed clear preference for the subjection of women to men. Almost all enlightenment intellectuals worried about women's education only in terms of proper training for their domestic mission rather than a personal need for intellectual fulfillment.

From the middle of the eighteenth century on, what society expected from women changed noticeably, because the political thought of enlightened despotism stressed the need for women as useful members of society. The educational system that fostered superficiality, frailty, and pusillanimity as fashionable characteristics for women was now viewed as flawed. Especially during the reign of Charles III, intellectuals closely associated with government policymaking believed that frail or fainthearted women could neither be good mothers nor good citizens. From the beginning of his reign, Charles III tried to lay foundations for a more reasonable education of women. In 1785 he decreed for the first time in Spanish history that a woman be granted the Doctorate in Humanities. In spite of the event's aristocratic and exclusive character, it showed an effort to integrate women into university studies. The young lady, María Isidra Quintina *Guzmán (1768–1803), was admitted as a member of the Royal Academy of the Language at age 17. In August 1787, by royal decree, 14 distinguished ladies were admitted and also nominated as meritorious members of the Madrid Economic Society. But the question of women's education focused not so much on opening the world of knowledge to them as on correcting vitiated behavior. By admitting these 14 ladies, the king wanted to promote virtue and industriousness among them, to inculcate a love for work, to eradicate a love of luxury that had ruined many a patrimony and discouraged men from marrying, and to induce purchase of national articles instead of imported luxury items. As the decree clearly states, admittance of these 14 women to the Society was done not to instruct them but to politicize them and win them over to the cause of enlightened despotism, a policy based on economy and administration. Women were to educate themselves, to correct their sisters' defects and love of luxury and splurging—but always on behalf of men, that is to say, to correct men's negative attitude toward marriage that was so harmful to the country.

In the cultural arena, Spanish literary salons began to resemble those of their French counterparts. Literary salons were now presided over by women like the widow countess of Lemos, who hosted the famous "Academia del buen gusto" (Academy of Good Taste) in her palace. It comprised a small court of the most illustrious writers and intellectuals of the time. Such literary inclinations were now seen as an excellent complement to the education every upper-class Spanish woman ought to receive. Meanwhile, the majority of Spanish women, who hardly knew how to read and write, dedicated their lives entirely to domestic duties.

Despite the good intentions of enlightened intellectuals and the new social and intellectual freedom women enjoyed, they remained subjected to men and had little, if anything, to say in relevant matters. In general, women's two options were either to marry, at a very early age, the husbands selected unilaterally by their parents or enter the religious life, with or without religious vocation. A few women did freely dedicate themselves to a literary career, but they constituted the exception and not the rule.

Until the last quarter of the eighteenth century, Spanish women were excluded from all intellectual professions and manual trades. The political thought of enlightened despotism tried to change this situation by stressing the need to incorporate all idle individuals into the workforce, and women numbered among them. The *Informe* (Report) that Gaspar Melchor de Jovellanos (1744–1811) presented to the Junta General de Comercio y Moneda in 1785 is a general defense of the free exercise of liberal professions, impeded then by unionlike organizations. The author applied the same principle to women, which would allow them to exercise any trade that did not undermine their natural delicacy and decorum. Once again, despite his defense, Jovellanos was really proposing an arrangement that did not challenge the common belief that women belonged in their homes. This new "job opportunity" would only provide women with useful tasks to replace the nonlucrative idleness that earlier had been so fashionable.

The efforts of the enlightened minority were not strong or sincere enough; thus the ideal women of the last quarter of the eighteenth century remained very close to the ideal of the seventeenth century. Women were mainly restricted to the home environment: They should be good wives and mothers, hardworking, and modest; they must not slavishly follow the dictates of fashion; they must exercise common sense but under no circumstance be "Miss Know-It-Alls." Everything was to be done with moderation, even more so when referring to the acquisition of knowledge and culture.

Despite this reality, a group of women writers did emerge in the second half of the century. Impassioned feminists, they vehemently defended the need to appreciate women. The ideas of most had been nourished by a long polemic that began in 1726 with Feijóo's "Defense of Women." Among those writers were Margarita *Hickey (1753–after 1793), poet and translator of Racine and Voltaire, and Josefina *Amar y Borbón (1753–1833), author of several pedagogical treatises. Amar y Borbón's two best-known works were the ones she presented to the Economic Society of Madrid in 1786, entitled *Discurso en defensa de las mujeres y de su aptitud para el gobierno y otros cargos en que se emplean los hombres* (Defending Women's Talent and Aptitude for Government and Other Jobs Employing Men) and the treatise she published in 1790 with the title *Discurso sobre la educación física y moral de las mujeres* (Discourse on the Physical and Moral Education of Women). Even though this intelligent lady was one of the most combative feminist writers of the period, she too perpetuated the female model imposed on women by men; the second part of the latter work states that the mission of women is found in the home. Women could dedicate their free time to cultivation of the spirit only provided they did not neglect their domestic duties.

Several other feminist writers of the period penned defenses of women. At the end of her novel *El príncipe de Abisinia* (1798; The Prince of Abyssinia) Inés Joyes y Blake added a section defending women, using the format of a letter addressed to her daughters. In the letter she complains about the unfair destiny imposed on women, deploring their ill treatment by men. While accepting male supremacy in government of the house, she stipulates that this supremacy does not imply an essential inequality between the sexes. Joyes y Blake also maintained that woman's destiny was her home. For Joyes, women should be educated in order to educate their sons and daughters. Other feminist writers who penned diatribes honoring women's attributes were María de las Mercedes Gómez Castro de Aragón, who wrote *Pintura del talento y carácter de las mujeres* (Portrait of Women's Talent and Character), and actress María de Laborda, whose play *La dama misterio, capitán marino* (Lady Mystery, Sea Captain) included a prologue full of feminist statements.

As one can see from eighteenth-century feminist writings, male domination and woman's exclusive role in the home were deeply ingrained even in those who actively embraced the feminist case. Thus began a long, arduous path toward achievement of equality; yet much more time and frustrated lives passed before fulfillment of one's own destiny could be pursued by women. *See also Encierro*

Work about

Kaminsky, Amy Katz, ed. *Water Lilies. An Anthology of Spanish Women Writers from the Fifteenth through the Nineteenth Century*. Minneapolis: U of Minnesota P, 1995.

Martín Gaite, Carmen. *Love Customs in Eighteenth-Century Spain*. Trans. Maria G. Tomsich. Berkeley: U of California P, 1991.

Oñate, María del Pilar. *El feminismo en la literatura española*. Madrid: Espasa-Calpe, 1938.

María Alejandra Zanetta

Women's Situation in Spain: 1786–1931: The Awakening of Female Consciousness

The publication in 1868 of *La mujer del porvenir* (Future Woman) by Concepción *Arenal (1820–1893), linked to liberal attitudes, has traditionally marked the emergence of modern feminism in Spain, and the franchise of women during the Second Republic in 1931, its eventual culmination. The achievements gained from 1868 to 1939 were practically forgotten during the Franco years (1939–1975) even if their spirit did not fully die, as Mercedes *Fórmica (1918–), María Laffitte (known as Condesa de *Campo Alange [1902–1986]) or Lidia *Falcón (1935–) demonstrate. With the return of democracy in 1975, militant new groups and associations were scarcely acquainted with any previous efforts. For a full understanding of Spanish feminism it is, therefore, essential to return to the earlier stages of women's emancipation to clarify the necessary links with the subsequent stages.

The beginning of Arenal's work, in which she envisions a possibly hostile reader, points to tense and difficult gender relations. Yet the political and literary perspective of 1860, eight years before the Revolution, might seem to contradict Arenal's fears. From the viewpoint of social and political significance, some women embodied progress and liberalism. Beginning with Infanta Carlota de Borbón—who in 1833 smacked King Fernando VII's minister, Francisco Calomarde, for his opposition to the liberal regency of her sister María Cristina de Borbón (1806–1878), and the accession to the throne of her niece and future daughter in law, Queen Isabel II (1830–1904)—the hopes of Spanish liberals were placed on female royal persons. The popularity of the little girl Isabel and her sister (the princess of Asturias) is charmingly highlighted by Pérez Galdós (1843–1920) in his *Episodios nacionales*. Yet those same years denied women any political or social personality. Arenal considers these contradictions to be grounded in error and powerlessness, stating that a woman may be a queen or a tobacco seller, but nothing in between.

The same extremes prevailed on the cultural front during the 1840s: Gertrudis *Gómez de Avellaneda (1814–1873) was an intellectual celebrity in Madrid, acclaimed by the most distinguished writers, yet Arenal had to attend university dressed as a man. The literary perspective of the 1860s and 1870s again emphasized this contradiction. Great women writers included: Fernán Caballero (pseudonym of Cecilia *Böhl de Faber) (1796–1877), Gómez de Avellaneda, Carolina *Coronado (1820–1911), Rosalía de *Castro (1837–1885), and Emilia *Pardo Bazán (1852–1921), yet according to the census of 1860, 90.42 percent of women were illiterate. Such paradoxes, contradictions, and in sum errors, as Arenal puts it, point to the need to reexamine Spanish cultural history from a feminist perspective. As another early feminist scholar and educator, Concepción *Saiz (1851–c. 1930) argued in her book *La revolución del 68 y la cultura femenina* (1929; The 1868 Revolution and Women's Culture) that "honest women" lack their own history, for their role was to contribute to the history of men. Traditionally, one turns to literature to explore the first documentation of women's consciousness, but in fact, the hidden threads that connect and explain this issue are first visible in pedagogical and social records. Learning more about women as subjects and objects of education, and as agents of social welfare, opens new vistas on the earliest stages of modern *feminism, eventually allowing a more accurate literary understanding and a fuller view of women's status.

Liberal ideology in its progressive branch (as opposed to its moderate branch and the conservative Absolutist Party) offers a perspective that helps to identify the origins of Spanish women's emancipation. Laffitte refers to the friendship between Juana de Vega (countess of Mina, 1805–1872) and Arenal in her introduction to the *Memories of the Countess of Mina* (1977). Though they were 15 years apart in age, both women shared essential traits that define the dawn of modern female consciousness. Both came from the middle class, and their fathers were advanced liberals who suffered the consequences of confrontation with absolutist repression. In 1841, Arenal's liberal militancy led de Vega to be appointed *aya* (governess) of the queen and the Infanta María de las Mercedes, during the regency (1841–1843) of the progressive leader Espartero (1792–1879). After the moderates gained control in 1843, de Vega resigned and was appointed Vice-protector of Welfare in Galicia, where she worked with indigent women. It seems that some aspects of this liberal spirit of the nineteenth century came directly from the Enlightenment. At the end of the eighteenth century, new attitudes towards *women's education and their social and political responsibility (as exhibited by de Vega and later by Arenal) can already be recognized in Josefa *Amar y Borbón (1753–1833), an early modern advocate for women's inclusion in social, scientific, and cultural institutions. With her work *Memoria sobre la admisión de señoras en la Sociedad* (1786; Report on the Admittance of Ladies to the Society), she contributed to women's subsequent membership in the Sociedad Económica Madrileña. From this debate and admission, the Junta de Damas de Honor y Mérito (Council of Honorable and Worthy Ladies) was born. This association, in turn, provides a link between the Enlightenment and the educational efforts of liberalism in the first half of the nineteenth century. At the same time, the new model of education sponsored by the Progressive Liberal Party had its roots precisely in the lay centers of the late eighteenth century, such as *juntas de comercio* (business councils) or *sociedades económicas* (economic societies) as well as in the doctrine of the 1789 Revolution. In consequence, Amar y Borbón's view of women's education can be linked to the countess of Mina's, establishing a link that culminates in Concepción Arenal, for in all three cases education, philanthropy, and political awareness from a middle-class stance are stressed, all of which characterize progressive liberal ideology.

Another important connection between this incipient feminist awareness and nineteenth-century liberalism is the founding of the Lancasterian School of Madrid in 1821, during the Liberal Triennia. Ramona Aparicio (1800–1880) was appointed director of the school; her long career helps connect the major educational reforms of the nineteenth century. Teaching was the first job for women to require some academic training. The law generally credited for shaping the educational structure in Spain, the Moyano Law of 1857, was a Liberal Unión achievement. The law established that elementary education was obligatory for all citizens and regulated the establishment of Normal Schools (Article 7). Concepción Sáiz connects the Central Normal School for Women, founded in Madrid in 1858, and previous liberal efforts, stating that the new school had at its base the old primary Lancasterian School. It should also be pointed out that the new school was placed under the protection of the Junta de Damas de Honor y Mérito, the institution born out of the Enlightenment and indirectly related to Josefa Amar y Borbón. The mature and by then moderate liberal Aparicio, director of the Lancasterian School, was appointed director of the Madrid Normal School. Her death in 1880 ended the oscillations in education as well as the contradictions between progressive policies constantly dampened by the moderates and effectively opened education to modern, twentieth-century attitudes.

Before the 1868 Revolution, university education was out of the question for women.

In her biography of Arenal, Laffitte states that the famous criminologist, so very vocal on questions concerning her profession and vocation, was extremely private in what concerned her own life, never addressing the question of her own formal training. Arenal attended classes in silence, dressed as a man, wearing coattails and a top hat. Once discovered, she had to take an entrance exam and was given permission to remain in the university. Doménech considers Concepción Arenal's initiative as groundbreaking. Official permission for women to attend classes was granted after the 1868 Revolution, but a special request had to be filed; when they joined the classes they had to sit in separate chairs, near the professor's, and they had to be ushered in and out by him.

Attorney Arenal was appointed Women's Penitentiary Inspector in 1863. She was revered both by the international community of criminologists and by women, whether workers, prisoners, or educators. The "Glorious Revolution" of 1868 thus forged women's access to universities and secondary schools, albeit with special permission. When they were officially admitted into these two levels of education, most prepared themselves with private tutors and only took final exams at the actual institutions. Laffitte gives an approximate account of the first diplomas granted to a number of women, but the diplomas or degrees that these women received could not be used professionally. As late as 1892, such was precisely the situation denounced by Pardo Bazán in the paper she delivered at the 1892 Education Conference, in which she decries as unjust the laws that allow women to study for a profession but forbid them to be professionals.

The real social impact of 1868 on women's education was linked to the university in a more modest but rather effective way; it came from another strand of progressive thought, *krausismo*, a philosophy school founded by Julián Sanz del Río (1814–1869) following the doctrines of German thinker Karl Christian Friedrich Krause (1781–

1832). A disciple of Sanz del Río, Fernando de Castro (1814–1874) was appointed rector of the Central University by the new government, and from this position he implemented some Krausist principles concerning the education of a vast sector of middle-class women. His first step was taken in 1869, when he involved a considerable number of university professors in the question of women's education through an initiative called Las Conferencias Dominicales (Sunday Lectures). At this point, a growing interest in feminist questions on the part of men contributed to a debate that slowly but surely gathered momentum as the fight for women's rights became apparent. Most of these men held Krausist views, believing that marriage was a harmonious integration of men and women as beings of the same human quality. In this way, the feminist question became a common concern for men and women. The lectures were a conspicuous success, producing as an immediate consequence the founding of El Ateneo Artístico y Literario de Señoras (Women's Artistic and Literary Athenium) in February 1868 by a group of women attendees encouraged by de Castro. Arenal was a member of its board of directors. The president of this Ateneo, Faustina *Sáez de Melgar (183?–1895), was a deeply committed activist for women's education. Author of over 18 very popular novels, several books of poems, and a number of books concerning women and their education and an assiduous contributor to more than 18 journals, she founded and directed a journal for women, *La Mujer*, in 1871. This publication was one of the first run exclusively by women. Sáez de Melgar also directed compilation of a book, *Las mujeres españolas, americanas y lusitanas pintadas por sí mismas* (Madrid, 1885; Spanish, American and Lusitanian Women Depicted by Themselves), and she represented Spain in the Feminist Pavilion of the Chicago Colombian Exhibition of 1894.

At the same time, it was obvious that the cultural/literary character of this Ateneo would not prepare women as independent breadwinners, and so with this team of men and women, in 1869 de Castro founded the influential Escuela de Institutrices. An active participant and witness of this period, Sáiz wrote that this school was where all advances in women's education from 1875 to 1925 began. Aparicio was again appointed supervisor, and she offered the Central Normal School building as a location for the new institution, thereby facilitating the eventual update of Central Normal's old-fashioned, flawed curriculum. In the evenings the future governesses attended classes that were volunteered by freethinking university professors such as de Castro and Sanz del Río, a circumstance that made the school somewhat suspicious to traditional audiences since it was said to be run by Freemasons. Most were Krausists, followers of Sanz del Río, and future members of the Institución Libre de Enseñanza. This success prompted the next step: foundation of La Asociación para la Enseñanza de la Mujer (Association for Women's Education) in June 1871. This association, in turn, created the training that incorporated women into modern professions by founding the School of Accounting (1878), the School for Post Office and Telegraphy (1883), Modern Languages, Drawing and Music (1878), and Primary Schools (1884), and 10 years later, the School of Library Sciences and Archives (1894). When de Castro died in 1874, Manuel Ruiz de Quevedo was appointed president of the association, followed by Gumersindo de Azcárate; both were associated with the Institución Libre de Enseñanza.

Between 1882 and 1892, three prestigious national and international conferences devoted to education, female training, accreditation, and the work of women in general were held. Besides that of women of the working class, so actively defended by Arenal, there was the work of an increasing population of young middle-class women. Those coming out of the recently established schools found themselves being denied job opportunities; when they could get them, they received a considerably lower salary than men. The topic of women's education and training and their right to work was discussed in the earlier-mentioned, splendid paper by Pardo Bazán at the 1892 Conference. Pardo Bazán denounced the pervading animosity toward emancipation of women based on their role as mothers, observing that all women bear ideas, but not all bear children. Just as Arenal had, Pardo Bazán felt a deep gender solidarity, and her literary production was but one branch of her professional activism. She understood herself first as a woman, then a writer; she assumed equal capacities in any woman given the opportunity: "Make the conditions even [for both sexes] and free evolution will take care of the problem." These words implied a complete revolution, since every aspect would have to be revised: legal codes, marriage as an institution, prostitution, and work.

In this fashion, Spanish public opinion entered into a long debate in which women and men alike intervened. In his *Feminismo* (1899), Adolfo Posada (1860–1944) deemed this phenomenon one of the greatest revolutions of the century. In 1868 Arenal had denounced the myth that confuses real working women with the patriarchal feminine archetype. Some 30 years later, Posada, a professor of sociology, admirer of Arenal, Pardo Bazán, and Sáiz, and member of the Institución Libre de Enseñanza, reiterated the same ideas about the necessary economic independence for women, which for many boils down to having or not having food to eat. What the twentieth century brought was a new, very militant, aggressive approach consonant with the new political scenario; old ideologies were left behind, new parties and new perspectives led women and men to an eventual Republican Spain and with it to the Constitution of 1931 and the full incorporation of women into national life.

For Sáiz the educator, the real transformation of the larger sector of underprivileged Spanish women was due to schoolteachers, the dedicated, well-prepared professionals coming out of the Escuela Normal Central and other Normal Schools. Their goal was to instruct the population of Madrid as well as the whole population of Spain. Dolores *Ibarruri (1895–1989), the legendary communist activist, secretary general and president of the Spanish Communist Party, seemed to agree with Sáiz when recalling in her memoirs her school days in the Basque village of Gallarta, where state compulsory education began at age seven. Ibarruri recalled that these women schoolteachers she affectionately and respectfully describes had attended the provincial Normal Schools and were bringing a considerable amount of human dignity into the lives of their young students. Sáiz also commented on the effect these first women workers scattered all over the country had, offering the possibility of some education to every girl. She states that from 1882 to 1901, 313 teachers graduated from the Central School, subsequently dispersing throughout Spain, bringing cultural advancement, integrative learning, and improvement in instruction at the primary level. Girls who received this education became the future leaders of the political parties and organizations as the social climate became progressively more sensitive.

Anarchists, together with the budding PSOE (Partido Socialista Obrero Español [Spanish Socialist Workers' Party]), had rejected the sexist views of Mikhail Bakunin (1814–1876), who sought to "liberate" women from any work other than the domestic one and actively promoted enrolling women in the party. Teresa *Claramunt (1862–1931), a textile worker, is considered the first revolutionary woman of nineteenth-century Spain. In 1884 she organized an anarchist labor union for women in Sabadell (Barcelona). A gifted public speaker, she was incarcerated several times from 1885 on and eventually sent into exile. During the early years of the century, Claramunt and anarchist Belén Sárraga were role models for the young Ibarruri, who admired their rhetoric at

party rallies. Besides them, many other women workers gave public speeches and took an active part in the success of miners' and peasants' strikes during the 1920s. In 1898, anarchist couple Juan Montseny (1864–1942) and Teresa Mañé (1866–1939) founded the *Revista Blanca* (White Magazine). Writers from the Institución Libre de Enseñanza, such as Francisco Giner de los Ríos (1839–1915) and Manuel Bartolomé Cossio (1858–1935), as well as independent men such as Miguel de *Unamuno (1864–1936), published in this journal that supported feminism during its first period, 1898 to 1906. During its second period (1908–1936), however, the radicalization of ideas and the need to close ranks led the party to reject feminism as disturbing. Federica *Montseny (1905–1994), daughter of Juan Montseny and Mañé, put social issues as a whole before feminist issues; for her, feminism belonged in the realm of the middle class. She regarded the war between the sexes as immoral and absurd since the ideal society should concern itself with humans without gender considerations. Nevertheless, during the war, anarchist women founded the journal *Mujeres Libres* (Free Women), and Montseny, appointed Minister of Public Health in 1936, favored legislation to legalize abortion and family planning.

Although in theory socialists opposed indissoluble marriages and were suspicious of feminist attitudes, they upheld women's right to work and equal salaries; feminism in their eyes, just as in those of later-stage anarchists, was a bourgeois aspiration. Society as a whole had to be changed; salaries had to be increased both for men and women. August Bebel's views, explained in his *Die Frau und der Sozialismus* (1879; translated by Pardo Bazán as *La Mujer ante el Socialismo* [1883; Women and Socialism]), were widely accepted. Bebel (1840–1913) equated the subjection of women with subjection of the proletariat. Pardo Bazán, very active as a feminist when the PSOE was founded (1879), was far more attracted to Stuart Mill as a thinker. In the prologue to her translation of Bebel's work, she pointed out that female and male workers cannot be equated, because women are servants by law and men are not.

By 1891 the "woman issue" had practically disappeared from the Socialist Party's agenda. Nevertheless, at the end of the 1920s socialists María Lejárraga (1874–1974), Margarita *Nelken (1896–1968), and Luis Jiménez de Asúa (1889–1970) were defending the rights of women; they tried to convince women and men that working was a privilege and an obligation for both sexes. Both Lejárraga and Nelken were elected representatives to the Republican Cortes (Congress). Jiménez de Asúa, a lawyer and university professor, pushed for contraception, abortion and euthanasia and favored free unions rather than permanent marriage. He was the main designer of constitutional rights for women in the 1931 Constitution (article 34), directing a commission for that purpose. Another member of that commission was radical lawyer and ex-school teacher Clara *Campoamor (1888–1972); her intervention in the chamber won *suffrage for Spanish women.

On the Catholic front, María de Echarri (1878–1955) played an important role regarding women's labor and women's franchise, organizing a campaign supporting women's right to vote in 1918 from the pages of the right-wing paper *El Debate*. It is noteworthy that right-wing parties also favored the right to vote; in November 1919, a conservative representative presented the Cortes a project requesting suffrage for all Spaniards, regardless of gender. The women's association Acción Católica was very influential and tried to present a truly feminist platform in conservative version; they defended women's rights as a workforce but also defended patriarchal marriage.

By the 1920s the feminist debate assumed a prominent place in the public forum, and women organized themselves in a variety of associations. Some of these organizations were moderate in their demands, attempting to promote dialogue rather than confrontation; this category includes the Junta de Damas de la Unión Iberoamericana, whose members organized very popular debates in the Ateneo in 1903 and again in 1913. Concepción Jimeno (1850–c. 1910), founder and director of this group, was very aware of the need to raise women's level of social consciousness. She considered herself a leader of *feminismo conservador* (conservative feminism), which believed not in revolution but rather in evolution. To this end the Centro Iberoamericano de Cultura Popular Femenina was established; it held classes for women from all social strata. The Center helped locate jobs, organized consumers leagues, and founded a journal, *La Ilustración de la Mujer*, with three issues a month.

La Liga Internacional de Mujeres Ibéricas e Ibero-americanas, on the other hand, led by Carmen de *Burgos (1879–1932), was a very militant group of women who, along with another radical association, Cruzada de Mujeres Españolas, fought for civil and political rights. These women, much like the English suffragettes, gathered thousands of signatures in the streets. In 1921 they took them to the president, Manuel Allende Salazar (1856–1923). Unlike their British sisters, they were received very positively, and by 1927, 12 percent of the members of the Asamblea Nacional Consultiva, established by Miguel Primo de Rivera, were women who had been elected indirectly via municipalities.

In 1918, María Espinosa de los Monteros, businesswoman and author of *Influence of Feminism in Contemporary Legislation* (1920), founded the respected feminist organization Asociación Nacional de Mujeres Españolas, ANME, and delivered a famous lecture on feminism at the Royal Academy of Jurisprudence. Monteros also served as president of the Confederación de Asociaciones de Mujeres in Spain (also called Consejo Supremo Feminista), which was composed of five associations: La Mujer del Porvenir, La Progresiva Femenina de Barcelona, The League for

Women's Progress and the Concepción Arenal Society in Valencia, along with ANME itself. These feminist associations had no links to any political party and were run exclusively by women. Their agendas promoted an idea of women who would not lose that identity when acting as mother and pillar of the family; they wanted to clarify that women were not exclusively mothers but also citizens in their own right. Although the question of suffrage was not explicitly mentioned in their set of goals, it was implicitly favored. Nevertheless, ANME avoided seriously controversial topics. Contraception, abortion, and divorce had little room in their agenda, which was totally devoted to the promotion of women in the workforce and in professional ranks. To carry out this project with a greater degree of political independence, they created their own political party in the 1930s, La Acción Política Femenina Independiente, whose president was Julia Peguero. This group rejected violent, aggressive methods; although they were not monarchists, they did not agree with the Republic's hostility toward religion and toward a class system that included their own. On the other hand, they were aware that the Republic supported women's rights. Both right-wing and leftist parties mistrusted this independent women's party whose platform included promotion of women in the labor ranks, a system of retirement pensions, state-run hospitals and sanitariums, preschool and day-care centers, as well as orphanages, equal pay, expropriation of idle latifundia, freedom of conscience and religion, and separation of church and state. This quite modern, tolerant program disagreed with the intolerance of the other factions. Such middle-of-the-road solutions were the result of the efforts of those waves of women—middle-class women—who had attended the university.

In 1907, the Junta para la Ampliación de Estudios was created by royal decree. This institution consisted of a postgraduate program for improvement of education by providing an independent body, outside the rigid university regulations, that would indirectly enrich the quality of the teaching body. The idea and the persons who ran it came directly from Francisco Giner de los Ríos and the Institución Libre de Enseñanza. To ensure official approval, its bylaws included all ideological positions of the moment that were concerned with education, including the Catholic Church. Santiago Ramón y Cajal (1851–1934) was president of the first Junta, and José Castillejo served as secretary for its 30 years of existence. Castillejo wanted to send as many students as possible abroad. Carmen de Zulueta quotes the number of grantees to study in foreign universities as 1,594 during the years the Institution lasted. In 1910, women were accepted into the university automatically, no longer needing individual authorization. A number of university women were sent to work and study in the United States, mostly through the Instituto Internacional.

María de *Maeztu (1882–1948) was one of those women. In 1919 she was invited to lecture at Columbia University and other colleges, all of them related to the Instituto Internacional. When, as a response to the famous Residencia de Estudiantes, the Residencia para Señoritas opened in 1918, María de Maeztu was appointed its director. The Residencia was soon full of medical, pharmaceutical, legal, pedagogy, and humanities students. By 1919 there were 300 women enrolled as students in Spanish universities, with 100 of them in Madrid. Many of her students became feminists who fought for the civil rights of women during Primo de Rivera's (1870–1950) dictatorship and during the Second Republic. In 1926, Maeztu founded the *Lyceum Club Femenino, made up of feminist professional women whose objective, according to their statutes, was to create a climate where women help one another and participate in social and cultural issues. One section of the club was devoted to the change of legal treatment of women. The first Spanish woman lawyer, Victoria *Kent (1898–1987), was vice-president of the club, and along with other lawyer club members, she wrote an address to the government requesting the reform of a number of laws and articles of the civil and penal codes that were particularly offensive to women. Maeztu also helped organize the Spanish chapter of the International Association of University Women. Politically, Maeztu carried much weight; in 1926 she, along with Carmen Cuesta, Natividad Domínguez, and nine other women, was appointed to the National Assembly by Primo de Rivera and later named Counselor of Public Instruction. In 1936 Maeztu was awarded the highly coveted title of *catedrática* (chaired professor) of the School of Pedagogy.

In 1931 the Constituent Congress debated the question of women's suffrage, with two women lawyers taking opposite views: Clara Campoamor, of the Radical Party, and a delegate from Madrid, defended the motion (article 34), and Victoria Kent, from the Republican Left (Izquierda Republicana), a delegate from Jaén, opposed it. The rationale offered by Kent was based on what she considered caution: According to her, Spanish women were still immature beings governed by males; to assign suffrage to women was, then, an act that would endanger the very existence of the Republic. Campoamor vigorously defended the principle of justice implied in the recognition of women as human beings and as full citizens of the Republic. The article carried by a fairly close margin: 161 favored, 121 opposed the vote for women. The Chamber's decision on this important issue was based on the debate of the two women lawyers as well as on formulation of the question as it appeared to the public at the onset of the Second Republic. The state of the question was, in turn, the result of a long struggle toward women's emancipation. Unfortunately the cataclysm of the Civil War and the intellectual stagnation of the postwar years submerged all these achievements in what seemed an endless oblivion. *See also Cigarrera;* Women's Education in Spain: 1860–1993

Work about

Amar y Borbón, Josefa. *Discurso sobre la educación física y moral de las mujeres.* Ed. Maria Victoria López Cordón. Madrid: Cátedra, 1994.

Arenal, Concepción. *La emancipación de la mujer en España.* Ed. Mauro Armiño. Madrid: Akal, 1974.

Campo Alange, Condesa de (Maria Laffitte). *Concepción Arenal 1820–1893. Estudio biográfico documental.* Madrid: Revista de Occidente, 1973.

———. *La mujer en España. Cien años de su historia.* Madrid: Aguilar, 1964.

Capel Martínez, Rosa María, ed. *Mujer y sociedad en España 1700–1975.* Madrid: Ministerio de Cultura, Instituto de la Mujer, 1982.

Espadas Burgos, Manuel. *La España de Isabel II.* Barcelona: Historia 16, 1985.

Espoz y Mina, Condesa de (Juana de Vega). *Memorias.* Ed. Condesa de Campo Alange. Madrid: Giner, 1977.

Nelken, Margarita. *Las escritoras españolas.* Barcelona: Labor, 1930.

Pardo Bazán, Emilia. *La mujer española y otros artículos feministas.* Ed. Leda Schiavo. Madrid: Nacional, 1971.

Pérez Galdós, Benito. "Los ayacuchos." *Episodios Nacionales.* III Madrid: Aguilar, 1941.

Posada, Adolfo. *Feminismo.* Ed. Oliva Blanco. Madrid: Cátedra, 1994.

Sáiz, Concepción. *La revolución del 68 y la cultura femenina (Apuntes del natural).* Madrid: Librería General de Victoriano Suárez, 1929.

Scanlon, Geraldine. *La polémica feminista en la España contemporánea: 1868–1974.* Madrid: Akal, 1986.

Simón Palmer, María del Carmen. *Escritoras españolas del siglo XIX.* Madrid: Castalia, 1991.

Zulueta, Carmen de. *Misioneras, feministas y educadoras.* Madrid: Castalia, 1987.

María Elena Bravo

Women's Situation in Spain: 1931–1975: The Second Spanish Republic, the Spanish Civil War and Its Aftermath

During the Second Republic (1931–1936), many social reforms were planned, and some came to fruition, several of which would directly affect the female population. Through the centuries, Spanish women had been both sheltered and abused. Their virginity was a matter of *honor for fathers, brothers, or other males who had charge of them. They had no civil rights, no economic means, and even in 1930, over half of Spanish women were still illiterate.

In 1931, the Republic's constitution recognized women as citizens with legal rights and sexual equality; it was a unique moment in Spanish history. More women became literate, and some from the middle and upper class became teachers or pursued other professions. There were "visible" women involved in policymaking. Congresswoman and writer Margarita *Nelken (1896–1968) had recognized the "disconsolate" status of women in the early 1920s, when she published a unique treatise on their plight. During the Republic she strove for a feminist agenda within the Socialist and, later, the Communist Parties. Anarchist Federica *Montseny (1905–1994) became the first female Minister (of Health) in Spain. Communist leader and head of Mujeres Antifascistas, Dolores *Ibarruri (1895–1989) was the first Spanish female to merit political attention from the male power structure in the 1930s. Other women in Congress were working toward improvements for women: Clara *Campoamor (1888–1972) fought and won the battle for female suffrage in 1931; lawyer and director of Spanish prisons Victoria *Kent (1898–1987) created a model prison for women; playwright María Lejárraga (1874–1974) championed women's rights in both her writing and her activism; others, like Matilde de la Torre, called for birth control, divorce, and abortion rights.

Such important social changes—which could have catapulted the medieval-minded country into the twentieth century—were to be truncated in 1936. The military, aided by the conservative monolith that had governed Spain for millenia, staged a coup. They unleashed an apocalyptic confrontation that would last three years and result in a dicta-

torship that only ended in 1975 with the death of Franco.

In 1936, there were some 12 million women and 11 million men in Spain; until recent years, though, little was known about the role of more than half of Spain's citizens during that class struggle that pitted rich against poor and left the country devastated for decades to come. During the war, nevertheless, Spanish women experienced a "flash of freedom" that was facilitated by the rarefied atmosphere of political strife: The men had gone to the fronts and women entered the workforce, taking over jobs and responsibilities they had never dreamed possible.

With their newfound freedom, a number of these formerly "invisible" women acquired a sense of empowerment and became aware of role models—the "visible" female leaders who had played important roles in the Republic and were now impacting on war matters. This is, for example, the case of Montseny, Nelken, and Ibarruri. When the war broke out, Madrid and Barcelona remained loyal to the legitimate government. By November 1936, Franco was pushing his way north to take over Madrid and declare victory over the Republic. These three women were key figures during the siege on Madrid; they kept up radio broadcasts day and night, inspiring the people of Madrid to resist invasion by the insurrectionists.

The female supporters of the nationalist rebels were largely Catholic, middle- and upper-class women. One group, called the Margaritas (Daisies), was part of the monarchist Comunión Tradicionalista Española, which emphasized obedience to "God, Country, and King." The more politically active group, the Sección Femenina, was established in 1934 by the Nazi-inspired Falangist leader José Antonio Primo de Rivera. Headed by his sister Pilar, the organization embraced the patriarch-imposed belief that women were inferior to men. By 1939, there were some 500,000 members. The only conservative women at the front lines went as nurses; the majority played a passive role in the rearguard preparing supplies and lending moral support to the troops.

On the other end of the spectrum were the Republican women and those of the Left. Theirs was a vastly different experience, given that they were primarily from the working class. Also, their life choices were not dictated by the Catholic Church but rather by their political affiliations or those of their men. Like the women of the Right, they collected and made food and clothing for the troops, set up laundry and meal facilities, and established hospices for children victimized by bombs, starvation, and the loss of parents. Yet their presence was much more visibly aggressive than that of the Margaritas or of the members of the Sección Femenina.

Some leftist women went to the front lines to fight at the beginning of the war as part of the militias, though they were recalled after several months. These *milicianas* were considered distracting to the troops. Above all, they were targeted as the chief cause of venereal diseases; in fact, some prostitutes had infiltrated the ranks of the militias, which caused all women at the front to be looked upon as tainted. Others joined leftist organizations such as the anarchist group Mujeres Libres, the Marxist Mujeres Antifascistas, and their youth organization, Muchachas, which counted some 70,000 among their numbers. For the first time, proletariat women began to dress in "unisex" garb, donning the blue overalls of male workers.

Female leaders were mobilizing women in these and many other organizations around the country. Those who joined the International Red Cross, mostly youngsters, took to the streets to collect money for the front. Even women not affiliated with any political group were, for the first time, visible in the streets of cities and towns making barricades and organizing neighborhood groups against the encroaching enemy. They not only provided moral and material support to the soldiers but often—especially in small towns—

replaced them at the front lines while the men rested.

In those three years, women began to break through the patriarchal "steel ceiling" that had kept them doubly oppressed for centuries as poor, powerless citizens and as subjugated females. Although women took over many factory jobs, men feared that women would compete for their jobs at the end of the war; therefore, female workers received minimal training. In spite of this, the war provided a unique educational opportunity for young girls; for many of the young activists, it was the only training or instruction in the "three R's" they would ever enjoy.

The war endured because of the bravery of those women and men who resisted fascism in Spain. They were undaunted in the face of hunger, death, and persecution. The women who were protecting their men in hiding from the Franco forces were often tortured or otherwise persecuted. They fought to keep their families together and to nourish them. In the cities, as food became more scarce, women would stand in endless lines for staples while dodging bombs; in the countryside, they bravely fought tooth and nail to grow crops or forage to feed their loved ones.

In spite of the destruction caused by Hitler's and Mussolini's intervention in the war, in spite of the demoralization overtaking the Republic with every bloody battle that Franco's troops and Moorish mercenaries won, the loyalists resisted until early 1939. By then all was lost and the government surrendered; Franco proclaimed himself the sole leader of Spain on April 1, 1939.

By January, the Spanish exodus into France had begun. Some 500,000 women, men, and children made the cold, exhausting trip through the Pyrenees to what they saw as their only hope for survival. They were not prepared for the double apocalypse many of them would suffer from the indifference of the French and then the ferocity of Hitler's Gestapo. They were met with hostility and, in some cases, sent back across the border. A few managed to escape to America. Most were incarcerated in war camps, where they continued to suffer as they had in the war. Many Spaniards, including some women, were sent to Nazi prison camps. Women were separated from children, husbands, and other family members. Pregnant women gave birth in subhuman conditions.

Women forced to remain in Spain who were implicated in the war through their activism or that of their men usually faced even more frightening realities. Labeled "red whores," in the best of cases women were punished with head shavings and cod liver oil and paraded through the streets. In the worst scenarios, they were imprisoned, tortured, and in many cases, executed. Over 23,000 women were incarcerated in 1939, the majority being political prisoners. Thousands passed through Madrid's Ventas Prison alone during the worst repression, which lasted until 1946. But many of the activist women who survived prison returned repeatedly because they resumed their underground activities each time they were released. Some women, like activist and now writer Juana *Doña Jiménez (1919–), spent as many as 20 years in prison.

The numerous testimonies and autobiographical works that testify to life in prison for female activists reveal the most frightening and disheartening themes of prison existence: loss of youth and reproductive abilities, death of babies in prison, mental and physical illness caused by tainted food, rats, lack of hygiene, and the ravages of war. The prisoners joined together in solidarity to combat the victimization they experienced because of state and Church repression. They were considered sexually and mentally aberrant creatures; they were not only punished through incarceration but also through the mental and physical abuse they suffered at the hands of prison guards, doctors, and Church officials intent on "reforming" them.

Civil rights for all women were revoked after the war. Single females were required to join the Sección Femenina and to perform six months of social service. Through the ef-

forts of the Sección Femenina and the Gestapo-like Spanish police, women, especially in urban areas, were cloistered in the home and indoctrinated to become the "new women": silent, abnegated, sexually irreproachable, content to assume their subservient role as wives and propagators of the species; they were old rules bearing a modern label.

For centuries, the female population of Spain lived in a state of, at best, subjugation, conformity, and inferiority, with only a brief hiatus of freedom during the turbulent 1930s. The reversal of fortune could not have been more complete; after 1939, abortion rights, legal divorce, and suffrage for all Spaniards were eliminated. The Church-state-military monolith was restored, and any verbal or physical form of attack on its institutions met swift punishment. It would only be in the late 1960s and early 1970s that Spain would begin to climb out of its period of totalitarian hibernation and reawaken to the need for women's rights. With the death of Franco in 1975, swift advances were made, and women began to enjoy a new status. *See also:* Alfonso el Sabio (1221–1284): Women in *Las siete partidas*, *Versos con Faldas* (1951)

Work about

Acklesberg, Martha. *Free Women of Spain: Anarchism and the Struggle for the Emancipation of Women*. Bloomington: Indiana UP, 1991.

Capel Martínez, Rosa María. *El trabajo y la educación de la mujer en España (1900–1930)*. Madrid: Ministerio de Cultura, 1982.

Capel Martínez, Rosa María, et al. *Mujer y sociedad en España 1700–1975*. Madrid: Ministerio de Cultura, 1982.

Doña Jímenez, Juana. *Desde la noche y la niebla (mujeres en las cárceles franquistas)*. Madrid: Ediciones de la Torre, 1978.

Gallego Méndez, María Teresa. *Mujer, Falange y Franquismo*. Madrid: Taurus, 1983.

Mangini, Shirley. *Memories of Resistance: Women's Voices from the Spanish Civil War*. New Haven, CT: Yale UP, 1995.

Martínez Sierra, María. *Una mujer por caminos de España*. Buenos Aires: Losada, 1952.

Las mujeres y la Guerra Civil Española: [ponencias]. III

Jornadas de Estudios Monográficos, Salamanca, Oct. 1989. Madrid: Ministerio de Asuntos Sociales, Instituto de la Mujer, 1991.

Nash, Mary. *Mujer y movimiento obrero en España, 1931–1939.* Barcelona: Fontamara, 1981.

Nelken, Margarita. *La condición social de la mujer en España.* Barcelona: Minerva, 1921.

Roig, Mercedes. *A través de la Prensa. La Mujer en la Historia. Francia, Italia, España. Siglos XVIII–XX.* Madrid: Ministerio de Asuntos Sociales, 1989.

Scanlon, Geraldine. *La polémica feminista en la España contemporánea: 1868–1974.* Madrid: Siglo XXI, 1976.

Shirley Mangini

Women's Situation in Spain: 1975–2000, Post-Franco

The death of Francisco Franco in November 1975 had a profound impact on women's lives in Spain. Franco's disappearance from the political arena, together with the United Nations' proclamation of 1975 as International Women's Year, led to an explosion of feminist activity that would quickly rival the political activism of sister movements in the United States and other countries of western Europe. While the UN initiative provided the impetus for feminist groups in Spain to organize a wide spectrum of seminars on issues pertaining to women, Franco's death and the political climate that followed enabled them to convert such issues into demands passionately articulated in the streets and meeting rooms of Spain.

The first manifestation of the new wave of Spanish *feminism was felt in December 1975, when more than 400 women from all regions of the country gathered for an illegal three-day conference in Madrid called the Primeras Jornadas Nacionales por la Liberación de la Mujer (First National Days for Women's Liberation). This historic gathering, sponsored by the Democratic Movement of Women, a section of the Spanish Communist Party, grappled with a controversial ideological issue that would be passionately discussed by women's groups in Spain in

years to come: the relationship between the feminist struggle and the general political struggle. While no consensus was reached concerning prioritization of the two, different political positions were clearly delineated in a climate of healthy debate. In May 1976, Barcelona and the Jornades Catalanes de la Dona (Catalan Women's Days) provided the site for a gathering of more than 4,000 women who attended forums on such issues as women and the class struggle, women and family, women and work, and the relationship between women's marginalization and capitalism (Falcóns "Spain"). In the same year, women's groups gathered at the female prison, Yeserías, to demand amnesty for women convicted of political crimes and crimes related to their gender. They demonstrated against large stores such as Simago to call for equal pay for equal work. They fought to legalize divorce and to recover this essential right granted to them under the Second Spanish Republic in 1931 and abolished following Franco's victory in 1939. University women banded together in Madrid to denounce the lack of day-care centers for faculty, students, and staff. Gay women marched proudly in the streets affirming their right to sexual difference. On Mother's Day 1976, women joined together in Barcelona to demand legalization of abortion, unrestricted sale of contraceptives, and equal rights for illegitimate children. As feminist Lidia *Falcón (1935–), founder of the magazine *Vindicación feminista, so aptly summarized, in 1976, "to vindicate" was a verb conjugated on the streets of Spain.

The struggle to achieve essential civil liberties arduously articulated in the months following Franco's death was a prolonged and heated one achieved in some measure through the 1978 Constitution and various reform laws passed during the government of the transition leader, Adolfo Suárez. In 1978, contraceptives were legalized and adultery, which was considered a crime only in regard to women, was decriminalized. It would take an additional three years for women to obtain a divorce law with equal responsibility for both spouses regarding child custody; essential to this law was the modification of the archaic *patria potestad* (male parental authority) clause that previously granted fathers sole authority in family matters. The year 1981 also saw legalization of the Feminist Party, founded by Falcón. Noticeably absent from these legislative reforms that overturned the unequal status of women during the Franco regime was the depenalization of abortion. It was not until 1985—despite the 1982 victory of the Socialist Party—that abortions would be legalized in the case of rape, a malformed fetus, and threats to the life and health of the mother. Credit for these successes must be attributed in great measure to a coalition of feminist groups organized under such general rubrics as the Feminist Platform of Madrid, the Feminist Coordinatorship of Barcelona, the Front for the Liberation of Women, and the Union for the Liberation of Women, as well as to hundreds of splinter groups throughout Spain concerned with individual issues. Many of these organizations were dissolved at the beginning of the 1980s, but their role in championing feminist demands in the early years of the post-Franco regime cannot be underestimated. Political parties of the Left and the Moderate Left including the Communist Party, the Socialist Party, and the National Confederation of Workers were also instrumental in the feminist fight, skillfully capitalizing on the energy and dynamism of the feminist movement during national elections of 1977 and 1979 while maintaining sexist political and social practices consolidated during years of clandestinity.

Yet despite major legal victories during the first decade following Franco's death, and despite the increased level of consciousness toward women's issues promoted during that time, certain questions were repeatedly raised as Spain approached the mid-1980s and the specter of *desencanto* (disillusionment) infiltrated all sectors of Spanish political life: Were women really equal to men? Did they

have the same opportunities for advancement in the workforce and traditional male positions? Had they gained access to power in Parliament? Were they attaining positions as ministers in the government of Felipe González where they could shape power? Did they live with men who shared domestic and child-rearing responsibilities? Were there shelters where they could seek refuge if they were the victims of domestic violence? And most significantly, when would they be granted control over their own reproductive rights? That is, did the legal victories of the late 1970s and early 1980s change the daily lives of women in Spain? Why was it that only 27 percent of the active female workforce in Spain in 1984 was employed? Why was it that in that same year only 6 percent of the representatives in the Senate and Chamber of Deputies were women?

The attempt to address these questions together with the impetus provided by the planning for the Nairobi conference celebrating the tenth anniversary of International Women's Year led to founding of the Instituto de la Mujer in 1984. With Carlota Bustelo as its first director, the Instituto undertook surveys to assess attitudes toward women, domestic violence, and birth control matters. It also issued a series of publications to inform women about their legal and personal rights, it organized forums and symposia to educate the public, it published an extensive bibliography and list of services for women, and it provided grants to feminist groups in need of state support. While clearly fulfilling many important functions with regard to women's rights and issues, the Instituto was viewed by some as a vehicle used by the Socialists to package, process, and sell feminism.

In 1988 the government initiated a two-year Plan for Equal Opportunities for Women, followed by a second phase to consolidate the objectives recommended in the initial phase and to provide for further integration of women into positions of power in society, the military, the world of finance, and government. Bustelo's successor, Carmen Martínez Ten, acknowledged in 1990 that women constituted the one group in society that had realized the most radical changes in attitudes and expectations, without reaping significant reforms in the job market, in merit systems, or in child care services, as reported in the journal *Mujeres* (1). Gains for women were noted, however, in employment opportunities; in 1990, 34 percent of the female active workforce was employed, a jump of 7 percent from five years before. In the same year, *Mujeres* (1) wrote that women constituted 13 percent of the Senate and Chamber of Deputies, a 7 percent increase from the previous five-year period but well below the Socialists' pledge to have 20 percent of higher-level positions filled by women.

With regard to social interaction and communal living, a study undertaken by the Instituto de la Mujer revealed that 60 percent of all males over age 18 had never participated in any domestic work in the home. The attempt to radicate such entrenched forms of sexism resulted in diverse and often ingenious campaigns to raise male consciousness. One mass publicity campaign initiated by the Instituto de la Mujer and targeted at the concept of shared domestic responsibilities featured a picture of a man, described as an active and liberal professional, a modern and responsible father, a good companion. Accompanying the photo was the caption: "This man has never broken a plate in his life . . . because when he arrives home he is not used to doing anything." The concluding lines of the text exhorted men to find new goals in life, to participate in domestic responsibilities, and to "break now—with inequality" (*Mujeres*, 1). Other campaigns run by the Instituto against sexist advertisement offered a prize for the best nonsexist ad for children's toys during the 1990 Christmas season. The prize was symbolically named the First National Cassandra Prize. Similar campaigns were waged by the Ministry of Social Affairs and the Institute for Youth

against unwanted pregnancies and sexually transmitted diseases with suggestive pictures of condoms and crossed-out words such as "unwanted pregnancies, gonorrhea, AIDS, fungi, Hepatitis B, vaginitis, and genital herpes" inscribed on a condom followed by the caption: "Put it on yourself, put it on him" (*Mujeres*, 3). A 1991 analysis published by SAL, the magazine of the Movement for the Liberation and Freedom of Women, criticized this pro-condom campaign, which, despite all good intentions, had two basic shortcomings: The condoms that were to be distributed free through youth organizations were insufficient to meet the demand, and the campaign was not accompanied by adequate sex education.

Also included among the services available to women highlighted by the Instituto de la Mujer in its 1990 publication was a list of 30 shelters for women who were victims of domestic abuse. By the late 1980s, Falcón's Feminist Party estimated that there were 500,000 cases of violence committed against women each year, yet in Barcelona alone, the first shelter for battered women was not available until 1988. The Instituto was also instrumental in publicizing (in 1989) 11 centers where women could obtain information on their legal rights; in that year alone, 60,000 consultations were requested by women.

Despite social and economic advances, various surveys and studies conducted in the first half of the 1990s confirmed the degree to which Spanish society still carried the weight of centuries-old traditions. With regard to shared domestic responsibilities in the home, reports produced by feminist organizations disclosed that little had changed since the previous decade: 63 percent of Spanish men never washed dishes, 64 percent never prepared a meal, and the average time men spent on domestic work was six minutes a day, as compared to the one and one-half to four hours spent by their female counterparts who also worked outside the home. Also cited in conferences organized by women's groups was the high percentage of Spanish housewives (80 percent) who took antidepressants and other drugs to help boost their lack of self-esteem and social worth. Accompanying this dismal view of the domestic sphere was the more chilling reality of abuse within the home. While difficult to verify because of the secretive nature of domestic abuse and the fact that many women do not report such abuses to the police, Falcón's 1991 book *Violencia contra la mujer* (Violence against Women) estimated that as few as 200,000 and as many as 2 million women throughout Spain had been abused. In 1992, the Institut Catalá de la Dona published a further study on female victimization that disclosed that 10 percent of the female population in Catalonia suffered daily abuse.

The issue of abuse of minors also received much-needed attention in the 1990s. A 1994 report by the Federation for Assistance to Abused Women revealed that sexual attacks against minors had increased 30 percent since 1993 and that 31 percent of these attacks occurred in the home, 91 percent of the victims were females between the ages of 4 and 17, and 40 percent of the attackers were the biological father. A June 17, 1996 article published in the Spanish newspaper *El Periódico* further publicized the results of a study undertaken by the National Commission on Children's Day that cited that 500,000 minors suffered from physical assault each year and that 800,000 suffered from psychological abuse. Feminist groups have consistently pressed for specific legislation to deal with domestic violence and for punishments that address the crime committed.

With regard to the complex issues of job opportunities for women and equal pay for equal work, Falcón's 1996 book. *Trabajadores del mundo, ¡rendíos!* noted that only 9.5% of managerial positions in Spain were held by women and that women earned 39% less than men for jobs of equal worth. As reported in "Gabinete," it has also been determined that 63 percent of women in Spain did not possess the professional qualifications necessary to obtain well-paying jobs because of illiteracy (7 percent), lack of formal studies (18 percent), or completion of only elementary school (38 percent). This reality, coupled with the fact that in cases of divorce 70 to 80 percent of men do not pay child support, led sociologists to conclude in the mid-1990s that 8 percent of divorced women live in extreme poverty. While a 1990 article of the Penal Code called for punishment by fine and the detention of men who don't pay for child support during three consecutive months or six nonconsecutive months, this article has rarely been invoked.

The political arena in post-González Spain reveals an absence of women in positions in authority. An article published in the Spanish newspaper *El País* on May 26, 1996, and suggestively entitled "Escaparate de Mujeres" (Showcase of Women), highlighted the political games played by Manuel Aznar's Popular Party (PP) with regard to positions of leadership. While the PP has named four female ministers to the cabinet, one more than the three women who occupied such positions during the government of González, they are all from the political Right. Further, the PP has not named a single female secretary of state (out of 21 positions) and only two under secretaries or secretary generals (out of 27), and 12 general directors (out of 154). These statistics compare unfavorably to the five secretaries of state, three under secretaries or secretary generals, and 38 general directors appointed during the González government.

On a more positive note, a 1996 reform of the Penal Code has resulted in notable changes affecting women's lives. Increases in punishments for perpetrators of sexual aggression have been legislated, and a mild punishment for sexual harassment has been instituted, consisting of a prison term of 24 weekends. However, the attempt to add an additional clause to the abortion law that would legalize abortion in the case of socioeconomic considerations was rejected by a vote of 166 to 176, with the Popular Party outvoting the Socialist Party and United Left. Ever more advanced than the rest of Spain, Catalonia passed a law in 1996 to legalize the union of individuals of different sexes, preparing the way, it is believed, for the legalization of unions among gays and lesbians.

Much remains to be accomplished to equalize the status of Spanish women in the beginning of the new millennium. The defeat of the expanded abortion law by a narrow minority suggests the possibility of a future victory in this area, although Aznar's conservative government and other interest groups will no doubt use all their political influence to oppose this reform. Expansion of opportunities for women in the working world and the political arena are ever-pressing concerns as is protection against sexual abuse and violent crimes. Official government statistics released in the late 1990s confirmed Falcón's earlier estimate of violence against women and revealed that 2 million women are annual victims of domestic abuse. Although legislative reforms during 1998 and 1999 include protection for victims of domestic abuse, reductions of penalties have also been legislated in areas relating to sexual abuse. A law addressing child pornography has yet to be passed. Furthermore, Spain is suffering, much as other countries in Europe and North America, from the current backlash against feminism and the erroneous perception that women have achieved equality. Despite much-needed advances in these areas, Spain has witnessed since Franco's death a surge of feminist activity and consciousness that has left its mark on society and has been instrumental in the reform and transformation of laws and social practices pertaining to women.

Work about

Falcón, Lidia. "Spain: Women Are the Conscience of Our Country." Trans. Gloria Waldman. *Sisterhood Is Global*. Ed. Robin Morgan. New York: Anchor P, 1984. 626–631.

———. *Trabajadores del mundo, ¡rendíos!* Madrid: Akal, 1996.

———. *Violencia contra la mujer*. Madrid: Vindicación Feminista Publicaciones, 1991.

"Gabinete jurídico y psicológico para la mujer." Publications of Lidia Falcón's legal practice in Barcelona include "Delitos contra la mujer" and "El trabajo doméstico."

González, Anabel, et al. *Los orígenes del feminismo en España*. Madrid: Zero, 1980.

Levine, Linda Gould, and Gloria Feiman Waldman, eds. *Feminismo ante el franquismo: Entrevistas con feministas de España*. Miami, FL: Universal, 1980.

Moreno, Amparo. *Mujeres en lucha. El movimiento feminista en España*. Barcelona: Anagrama, 1977.

Mujeres, 1, 1990. [Publication of the Instituto de la Mujer.]

Mujeres 3, 1990. [Publication of the Instituto de la Mujer.]

Ortiz Corulla, Carmen. *La participación política de las mujeres en la democracia (1979–1986)*. Madrid: Instituto de la Mujer, 1987.

Sal 5, 1991.

Linda Gould Levine

Women Writers in Spanish Literary History: 1500–1996

Before the twentieth century, few women authors appear in canonical Spanish literary history. This finding is not unexpected in a culture whose ethic of masculine superiority precludes the recognition of great achievement by women. From the biased perspective of the modern age, Spanish literature by women can be divided into three arbitrary periods: before Franco (1100 to 1936), during the Franco era (1936–1975), and after Franco (1975 to the present). The first period, lasting eight centuries, saw the fewest writers, while during the most recent two decades there have been the most. In the intervening 39-year interval, women began contributing to Spanish literature in substantial numbers. This uneven distribution over time reflects Spanish women writers' recent productivity. It also highlights women's near-total exclusion from previous literary history.

Measured by prevalence in traditional literary histories and "masterwork" anthologies, only a handful of women writers of the past are as well known as their male contemporaries. The first is still the most famous: Santa *Teresa de Cepeda y Ahumada (1515–1582), who wrote prayers, autobiography, poems and reflections. In the seventeenth century, María de *Zayas y Sotomayor (1590–after 1647?) was a popular contributor to the *novela corta* (short novel) genre. The eighteenth century yielded no female creative writers of renown, although Josefa *Amar y Borbón (1753–1833) achieved fame as an intellectual. In the nineteenth century, four first-class female writers have achieved enduring recognition. Two were novelists: Cecilia *Böhl de Faber (1796–1877), who wrote under the pseudonym Fernán Caballero, and professor Emilia *Pardo Bazán (1852–1921). Two nineteenth-century female masters were recognized primarily for their poetry: Cuban-born Gertrudis *Gómez de Avellaneda (1814–1873) and Rosalía de *Castro (1837–1885).

Because of the paucity of famous women authors, any attempt to trace a female literary tradition in Spanish necessitates a search outside the received canon. Such investigations are worthwhile. They indicate that outstanding women writers did exist prior to the present century and that the reason for their absence from the canon was exclusion. Editors Carolyn L. Galerstein and Kathleen McNerney's seminal *Women Writers of Spain: An Annotated Bio-Bibliographical Guide* (1986), building on older sources such as Manuel Serrano y Sanz's *Apuntes para una biblioteca de escritoras españolas desde el año 1401 al 1833* (1903–1905), compiled a roster of authors whose neglect was unwarranted. Including both poets and writers of narrative fiction, this guidebook lists 91 women authors in Spain who published in Castilian before the twentieth century: 1 in the fourteenth century, 4 in the fifteenth century, 8 in the sixteenth century, 10 in the seventeenth century, 7 in the eighteenth century, and 61 in the nineteenth century. Some 70 additional writers (not subdivided by cen-

tury) produced literature in Catalan. A more detailed resource is *Spanish Women Writers: A Bio-Bibliographical Source Book* (1993), edited by Linda Gould Levine, Ellen Engelson Marson, and Gloria Feiman Waldman. This volume offers full chapters on writers whose importance is demonstrated by leading feminist critics. Two writers from the fifteenth century are featured, 3 from the sixteenth, 3 from the seventeenth, 2 from the eighteenth, and 12 from the nineteenth century.

Women's presence in Spanish literary history from 1936 to the present is many times greater than that of the preceding five centuries. Comprehensive source books substantiate this change: Galerstein and McNerney's guide features 198 authors; the Levine, Marson, and Waldman reference includes 27. Janet Pérez's overview of *Contemporary Women Writers of Spain* features 51 narrators, including major and minor Spanish women authors who wrote in Castilian and the vernacular languages. Scholarly publications on literature by women also have increased. Books of specialized scholarship devoted to contemporary women writers chronicle the diversity and excellence of their literature and especially their prose fiction. Edited volumes and dedicated journal issues reflect a trend toward separate examinations of literature by women. A review of annual *Bibliography* listings compiled by the Modern Language Association of America confirms that scholarship on women increased from 3 percent of all studies of Spanish literature in 1978 to roughly 10 percent in 1988. The number of pages devoted to women writers in histories of the contemporary Spanish novel also has risen from less than 10 percent of all pages in major "first-generation" histories published in the 1960s and 1970s to over 25 percent in "second-generation" literary histories of the 1980s. The continually increasing representation of women in scholarly publications and surveys of literature indicates that women's presence in Spanish literary history in the future will be different from that of the past. Beginning with the twentieth century, women authors eventually will be well represented in the mainstream of Spanish literary history. *See also* Autobiographical Self-Representation of Women in the Early Modern Period; Basque Women Writers: 1804–1997; Catalan Women Writers: A Brief History; Drama by Spanish Women Writers: 1500–1700; Drama by Spanish Women Writers: 1770–1850; Drama by Spanish Women Writers: 1860–1900; Galician Women Writers: A Brief History; Nuns Who Wrote in Sixteenth- and Seventeenth-Century Spain; Poetry by Spanish Women Writers: 1800–1900; Short Fiction by Women Writers: 1800–1900; Short Fiction by Women Writers: 1900–1975; Short Fiction by Women Writers: 1975–1998, Post-Franco.

Work about

Brown, Joan L. "Women in Spanish Literary History: Past, Present and Future." *Revista Canadiense de Estudios Hispánicos* 14 (1990): 553–560.

———. "Women Writers of Spain: An Historical Perspective." *Women Writers of Contemporary Spain: Exiles in the Homeland.* Ed. Joan L. Brown. Newark: U of Delaware P, 1991. 13–25.

Galerstein, Carolyn L., and Kathleen McNerny, eds. *Women Writers of Spain: An Annotated Bio-Bibliographical Guide.* Westport, CT: Greenwood P, 1986.

Levine, Linda Gould, Ellen Engelson Marson, and Gloria Feiman Waldman, eds. *Spanish Women Writers: A Bio-Bibliographical Source Book.* Westport, CT: Greenwood P, 1993.

Martín Gaite, Carmen. *Desde la ventana: Enfoque femenino de la literatura española.* Madrid: Espasa-Calpe, 1987.

Pérez, Janet. "Status of Women Writers in Spain." *Contemporary Women Writers of Spain.* Boston: Twayne, 1988. 1–4.

Serrano y Sanz, Manuel. *Apuntes para una biblioteca de escritoras españolas desde el año 1401 al 1833.* Madrid: Rivadeneyra, 1903; Rpt. Madrid: Atlas, 1975.

Joan L. Brown

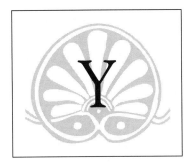

Yerma

See García Lorca, Federico (1898–1936):
Women in His Rural Trilogy

Zambrano, María (1904–1991)

Philosopher and essayist, author of some 20 volumes of writings, she was born in Vélez Málaga (Andalusia) to a family of educators. María Zambrano was greatly influenced by her father, who upheld the aesthetic and ethical ideals that characterized the teaching reform movement of the day, rooted in the innovative system of the Institución Libre de Enseñanza (founded 1876; Free Pedagogical Institute). As a child María benefited from the friendship of her father with Antonio Machado (1875–1939), and at the university she was taught by the eminent philosophers Ortega y Gasset (1883–1955), García Morente (1886–1942), and Zubiri (1898–1983). Then she herself taught at the Instituto Escuela and the Residencia de Señoritas where, in a more direct way, she experienced the influence of the Institución. Soon after finishing her studies at the University of Madrid, she was offered the position of assistant to the chair of metaphysics, a post she held until 1936. After going into exile in 1939, she successively taught at universities in Havana, Mexico, and Puerto Rico through 1953. She then moved to Europe, living in Italy, France, and Switzerland. Only in 1984 did she finally return to Spain.

An intensely private person, Zambrano never revealed what made her abandon the teaching profession in a discipline traditionally held to be a male bastion but that she exercised with distinction. After 1953 she dedicated herself to writing and held a fellowship from the Fundación Fina Gómez to continue her work in philosophy. Always highly regarded by her peers, she was given public recognition after her return to Spain: She was made a Doctor *honoris causa* by the University of Málaga (1983), she was awarded the Premio Príncipe de Asturias (1981) and the Premio Cambio 16 (1986), and she was the first woman to receive the Premio Cervantes (1988).

Zambrano's professionalism and commitment to writing began very early with collaborations in newspapers (*El Liberal*) and periodicals (*Revista de Occidente, Cruz y Raya*). Her first book, *Horizontes del liberalismo* (Horizons of Liberalism), was published in 1930. Zambrano was a modern, enlightened woman, a product of post–World War I liberal Spain, when women began to have access to liberal professions previously closed to them, a time when their intellectual capabilities were beginning to be recognized as equal to those of men. In 1931, Spanish women won the right to vote and thereby participate in political life. In the years prior to the Spanish Civil War, Zambrano entered into the intellectual life of the country. During the war she worked actively on the publication *Hora de España* with some of Spain's most distinguished writers (Emilio Prados, Gil Albert, Sánchez Barbudo, Serrano Plaja, Rafael Dieste, and even Antonio Machado). She was beginning to be included in the canon with other contemporary women such as Carmen *Conde, Concha *Espina, and Rosa *Chacel, but her absence from Spain during the long years of the Franco regime limited her recognition to a relatively minor group of intellectuals. General recognition came only after her return to Spain.

Influenced by Ortega's teachings and doctrine, Zambrano advocates a ratio-vitalism with a *sui generis* interpretation of her master. The most outstanding ideas in her system include a distinction between ideas and beliefs, and formulation of the notion of hope as an underlying element in human life, more profound and fundamental than beliefs themselves. From her early writings, Zambrano saw philosophy as a "knowledge of the spirit." Philosophy is considered a fundamental event in human life that nevertheless is not sufficient to fulfill hope, leaving always an inherent element of despair. Her work reflects an interest in the ways in which philosophy and poetry oppose and complement each other. She is also concerned with the relationship between philosophy and Christianity, where the divine is considered not from the viewpoint of sociology but metaphysics. In her view the stoics illustrate the concept of reason as mediator. Her prose, beautiful and clear, abounds in metaphors.

Hacia un saber sobre el alma (1934; Toward a Knowledge of the Soul) is a seminal work laying the ground for future development. Starting from Ortega's doctrine of ratio-vitalism, she holds that reason as integrated in man will make it possible to gain knowledge about the spirit and thus to achieve a certain order in our interior life. Zambrano claims that knowledge of the spirit, defined as a portion of the cosmos between nature and the individual, cannot be gained via rationalism or scientific psychology; the spirit dwells in a sphere of its own, between the individual and the cosmos, where it enjoys a certain independence to explore the motivations of its heart in solitude and abandon.

Zambrano affirms a commitment to philosophy and also the vocation of a writer—thus her work couples poetry to philosophy. In *Filosofía y poesía* (1939; Philosophy and Poetry) she states that both poetry and philosophy share an aspiration to eternity and perdurability—thus salvation—but they differ in the means of achieving their end. While philosophy works through reflection that requires a distancing from worldly manifestations, poetry seeks the world's diversity and the variations of passing time. Philosophy depends on meditation; poetry rests on intuition. Poetic intuition, called "poetic reason" by Zambrano, is for her the only way to gain knowledge of the spirit.

The "preoccupation with Spain" is not absent from Zambrano's work. *Pensamiento y poesía en la vida española* (1939; Thought and Poetry in Spanish Life) was originally a series of three lectures delivered in Mexico shortly before the end of the Civil War. There she tries to penetrate the essence of Spain, its history, its meaning. She dwells on European rationalism and the crisis created by it as well as the problems of Spain, omitted by that rationalism and with its own natural values left intact, such as the preponderance of spontaneity that characterizes Spanish realism. The closeness to the world that Spanish realism fosters also functions as a detriment to objectivity, systematization, and abstraction. Therefore, concludes Zambrano, the only way to reach the essence of Spanish thought and what it is to be a Spaniard is through the interpretation of its literature by means of "poetic reason." Zambrano discovers two Spanish peculiarities: "self-willedness" and stoicism, where the latter is halfway between the extremes of self-willedness (absolute affirmation) and quietism (absolute negation). Stoicism, seen as a suicide of the will that paralyzes all activity to live, is for Zambrano perhaps the most characteristic form of Spanish thought, and it is responsible for producing an isolation from history and the flow of time, and in that sense it becomes a form of suicide.

In one of her early books, *El hombre y lo divino* (1955; Man and the Divine), Zambrano explores the possibility of reaching a religious plateau within poetic knowledge, which in turn leads to approaching piety as a philosophical problem. She solves the conflict between the piety of antiquity and what may be the philosophy of being by means of stoicism, where she finds a persistence of the sacred world of antiquity within the realm of being and thought.

Claros del bosque (1977; Clearings in the Forest) is a mature formulation of Zambrano's poetic theory. Via the title's metaphor of clearings in a forest, she confronts the elusive nature of light and the passing of time as a twilight where knowledge and life become one. Her method consists of glimpses, imperfect views, discontinuous appearances. This method includes logic and life and implies a contradiction in terms by incorporating logic's continuity and life's discontinuity, but the result is the perpetuation of instantaneousness, of discontinuity. Birth is conceived as an awakening that links itself to a preexistent love. The word, hesitant, hardly articulated at first, is later substituted by forms that express the awakened intelligence. Humans inhabit several bodies: the earth, the universe, their own individual corporeal frames. In the depths lies the zone of logic; the universe houses the volition of the human heart, the renewal of nature, the presence of life as a gift. With death, life enters a wider and undefined domain. Although time flows with discontinuous steps, there is a synchronization between life and being that is accomplished by a unitive pathway. Time is not suspended but transcended, thus becoming a flow without events.

The word exists even before the possibility of being articulated; thus, it is destined not to communicate but to commune. As the light in a clearing within the woods, the true word does not wear out nor disappear. However, it may hide itself, and, if so, it becomes dormant as a seed found in unexpressed feelings, in hope, in an unfulfilled love, in death. The word may be retained by humans as their own substance, becoming part of their own being, as in the case of poets and writers who leave their word in their work, be it poetry, metaphysics, or revelation.

Signs of that being appear in the universe, in beauty, in images, in forms, that guide toward an unreachable aim, an absolute point where knowledge resides. Death takes place beyond reality where a remote gaze sustains solitude and silence. Zambrano formulates in this book her principle that "thinking is above all to decipher feelings," and man/woman is the being who suffers his/her own transcendence in the constant process between passivity and knowledge, between being and life. The true life can only be apprehended in some clearing in the woods between sky and earth, and in the remote horizon where heaven and earth, being and living, life and death, submerge.

Zambrano seldom revealed her intimate self in her work. *Delirio y destino: Los veinte años de una española* (1989; Delirium and Destiny: Twenty Years of a Spanish Woman) is her only autobiographical text. Here the self appears, but only in its relationship to collective identity. By using the third-person voice, personal references are diluted in a self-effacing account of events, people, and places. Although none of her books deals exclusively with women's issues it is revealing that in her essays on Pérez Galdós only two of his female characters are considered at length: Jacinta from the novel *Fortunata y Jacinta*, and Benigna, the main character in *Misericordia*. Fortunata, a working-class woman of the Madrid people, and Benigna, the servant girl from the Alcarria village, embody the essence of two females who rise above the constraints of society and thus acquire heroic proportions.

Work by

Claros del bosque. Barcelona: Seix y Barral, 1990.
Delirio y destino: Los veinte años de una española. Madrid: Mondadori, 1989.

La España de Galdós. Barcelona: La Gaya Ciencia, 1982.

Hacia un saber sobre el alma. Madrid: Alianza, 1987.

Obras reunidas. Primera entrega. Madrid: Aguilar, 1977.

Senderos. Barcelona: Anthropos, 1986. Includes extensive primary and secondary bibliography.

Work about

Abellán, José Luís. *Filosofía española en América (1936–1966).* Madrid: Guadarrama, 1967. 169–189.

Anthropos 70–71 (1989). Special journal issue.

Cuadernos Hispano-Americanos 413 (1984). Special journal issue.

Donahue, Darcy. "National History as Autobiography: María Zambrano's *Delirio y destino.*" *Monographic Review/Revista Monográfica* 9 (1993): 116–124.

Hart, Anita M. "Poetry and Philosophy: Amparo Amorós and María Zambrano." *Anales de la Literatura Española Contemporánea* 18.1 (1993): 211–223.

Insula 509 (May 1989). Special journal issue.

Johnson, Roberta. "María Zambrano as Antigone's Sister: Towards an Ethical Aesthetics of Possibility." *Anales de la Literatura Española Contemporánea* 22.1 (1997): 181–194.

Litoral 121–126 (1983). Special journal issues.

Nimno, Clare E. "The Poet and the Thinker: María Zambrano and Feminist Criticism." *Modern Language Review* 92.4 (October 1997): 893–902.

Ortega Muñoz, Juan Fernando. *Introducción al pensamiento de María Zambrano.* México: Fondo de Cultura Económica, 1994.

Pérez, Janet. "Circunstancia, Reason and Metaphysics: Context and Unity in the Thought of María Zambrano." *Spanish Women Writers and the Essay: Gender, Politics and the Self.* Ed. and intro. Kathleen Glenn and Mercedes Mazquiarán de Rodríguez. Columbia: U of Missouri P, 1998. 144–171.

Pilar Sáenz

Zapatera prodigiosa, La (written 1926): The Representation of Honor

Written by Federico *García Lorca and first performed in 1930, *La zapatera prodigiosa* (The Shoemaker's Prodigious Wife) is a lyric farce in two acts depicting the exasperation of a rich, aging bachelor of 58 who marries a destitute, pretty orphan of 18. This marriage of convenience, based on aversion to solitude, was induced by relatives of the couple, and within three months it proves unsatisfactory. The play's unforgettable female protagonist, like so many of Lorca's *dramatis personae*, constitutes a "poetic example of the human soul." When asked why many of his characters were female, Lorca replied that women possess greater passion, are less intellectual, more human and vital. The *zapatera* is denied a loving emotional reward as well as the possibility of having children. She longs for both, as seen in her relationship with the *niño* (little boy) in whom she sublimates her maternal feelings. The episode in which the *zapatera* and the boy child chase a butterfly reflects her unconscious desire to be reborn with her own child. Her infertility carries social implications, since friends and neighbors view childlessness as a curse. In her role as wife, the *zapatera* must keep her marital fidelity and *honor intact. After an absence of four months, the husband, tired of being alone, decides to come home. Significantly, his lack of trust motivates a ruse: He returns in disguise, impersonates a younger, more "exciting" male, and attempts to seduce the wife he abandoned, leaving her in desperate economic straits. Failing ludicrously, he deems his wife's rejection a proof that the family honor is intact, and the two are reconciled. Once reunited, they again begin to fight, although each feels less vulnerable when living with the other.

All art consists of an opposition between reality and fantasy, and the *zapatera* personifies a poetic vision that enters into conflict with the environment besieging her. Lorca termed this piece a violent farce because, in spite of the comic element associated with the genre, there is a dramatic factor that makes the *zapatera* a victim of circumstances. Her disillusionment carries philosophical implications about the need to balance the struggle between reality and fantasy. With *zapatera*, fantasy is synonymous with daydreams, a meditation in which consciousness gives free rein to imagination and desire. The *zapatera* does not personify an abstract feeling since her contradictions emanate from reality. In Act I, while with her husband, she fantasizes about her suitors (*alcalde* [mayor], *mozo* [young man], Don Mirlo), and when her admirers are close, she longs for her missing husband, bestowing on him many of the imaginary attributes she associates with her suitors. However, she always must return to reality, for if she stays in her fantasy, she will go mad. Although at the end the *zapatera* is reconciled with her husband, their marriage cannot endure without dreams and fantasy. When disappointed, they return to reality to begin again the existential struggle against oppressive social conditions. *Zapatera* and *zapatero* do compromise at the end since they are able to accept the fact that the presence of one restricts the freedom of the other.

Work by

La zapatera prodigiosa. Ed. Arturo del Hoyo. Madrid: Libertarias, 1999.

Work about

Massel, Adrian Pablo. "Belisa y la zapatera o las cadenas de la imaginación: Para una relectura de los códigos genéricos en dos dramas de Federico García Lorca." *Ariel* 9.1 (1993): 39–64.

Matus Romo, Eugenio. "*La zapatera prodiosa* de García Lorca: Tradición y originalidad." *Alpha* 8 (1992): 9–22.

Roles, Cary Talbot. "The Making of a Tragic Heroine: *La zapatera prodigiosa*." *Mester* 21.1 (1992): 73–83.

José Ortega

Zardoya González, María Concepción (1914–)

Born in Valparaiso to immigrant Spanish parents, poet and literary critic María Concepción [Concha] Zardoya spent her childhood in her native Chile but as an adolescent went to Spain when her family returned in 1932. Prior to the Spanish Civil War (1936–1939) she enrolled at the University of Madrid (School of Philosophy and Letters) while tutoring younger students. Her studies were interrupted by the war, but later she finished her Licenciatura (1947) and then went to the United States. Zardoya worked as a professor of Spanish at various universities from 1948 until 1977. When she retired, she returned to Spain, her country by choice if not by birth. Zardoya's North American years were very fruitful both as a poet as well as a literary critic, and the excellence of her literary criticism led to wider recognition of her poetry.

A prolific writer who authored some 25 books of poetry between 1946 and 1987, she is one of the best examples of lyric women's voices in twentieth-century Spain. Recognized by other men and women poets (Dámaso Alonso, Rafael Alberti, Vicente Aleixandre, Manuel Durán, Leopoldo de Luís, as well as Carmen *Conde, Concha *Castroviejo, and María Gracia Ifach, among others), she won several prizes for her poetry: *Dominio del llanto* (Premio Adonais, 1947; Domain of the Mournful Cry); *Los signos* (Premio Ifach, 1952; The Signs); *Debajo de la luz* (Premio Boscán, 1955, pub. 1959; Beneath the Light); *El corazón y la sombra* (Premio Fémina, 1975; Heart and Shadow); *Manhattan y otras latitudes* (Premio Opera Optima, 1983; Manhattan and Other Latitudes); and *Ritos, cifras y evasiones* (Premio Poesía Café Marfil, 1985; Rites, Figures and Evasions). Nevertheless, Zardoya's work is seldom included in anthologies, although her male counterparts are abundantly represented. Several facts undoubtedly contributed to the oversight and slow recognition of Zardoya's poetic work. Her first poems appeared in *Hora de España*, a short-lived literary periodical published intermittently during the Spanish Civil War, thus identifying herself with the Spanish Republic, whose ideals she ardently shared. When the war ended, with Spain under the government of Franco she felt compelled to publish under the pseudonym "Concha de Salamanca," no doubt a tribute to Miguel de *Unamuno

(1864–1936) whom she greatly admired. During the North American years of her spiritual self-exile, she became recognized first for her literary criticism, and then, through it, public attention moved to her own poetry. The 1977 return to Spain finally allowed her to dedicate herself fully to her poetry and become well known there. Given the circumstances that surround her poetic work, very little research has been undertaken and published on Zardoya's poetry to date, despite the quality of her work.

Zardoya's poetry joins a Castilian stoicism with a tendency to guarded privacy, spiritual intimacy, and a feeling of solitude with the attempt to overcome it. All are elements that traditionally may be identified as feminine. However, in *Diotima y sus edades* (1981; Diotima and Her Ages), a collection of poems rich in autobiographical elements such as memories of personal experiences, places known, events witnessed, readings, meditations, and thoughts, Zardoya claims not to wish to emphasize the subjective strain but to maintain a universal content. Her quest for universality is evident in *Los engaños de Tremont* (1971; Deceptions of Tremont), where metaphysical and existential elements are prevalent. Zardoya's poetry conveys a universal as well as a feminine view of the world, and her poetic work constitutes a feminine history of the poet where universal themes of death, love, and solitude appear regularly together with subjects more personally related to her life, especially exile and her nostalgia for Spain. Early poems, published in the wartime Republican periodical *Hora de España*, are only partially available, mostly in books published before her residence in the United States and under the pen name Concha de Salamanca. *Pájaros del nuevo mundo* (1946; Birds of the New World) and *Dominio del llanto* both reflect the rigorous postwar days in Spain with the presence of hunger, repression, and spiritual chaos. Feelings of desperation and fear, anguish for the victims, and a sense of interior exile are expressed graphically in the poems by un-

conventionally using punctuation such as the question mark. This stylistic device, part of Zardoya's poetics, becomes one of her most distinctive characteristics. It can convey an inquisitive intention, an interior doubt, a probing of the surrounding reality of the world, an existential doubt. *La hermosura sencilla* (1953; Simple Beauty) represents a process of catharsis and expresses a desire to overcome the painful memories leading toward an interior mysticism.

Those sentiments are intensified in *Los signos* where the yearning to conquer death is manifested. *El desterrado ensueño* (1955; The Exiled Daydream), a hymn to the lost Spain dreamed of by the poet, is a spiritual journey filled with the ardent desire for return, where nostalgia serves as a mean of evasion and dreams are the result of memories blending with reality. The rhetorical questions used convey feelings of uncertainty and restlessness. *Mirar al cielo es tu condena: Homenaje a Miguel Hernández* (1957; To Look Skyward Is Your Sentence: Homage to Miguel Hernández) is a poetic homage to the young poet and father whose untimely death in a Francoist prison outraged intellectuals and stands as testimony to the endurance and salvation of the creator by means of his/her creation. It also advances Zardoya's search concerning the nature of artistic creativity. *La casa deshabitada* (1959; The Uninhabited House) sounds an existentialist tone. The absence of love in the soul gives way to a sense of physical solitude, fear, and loss. Alone, with no one else in the uninhabited house, the body feels like an abandoned home and perceives the emptiness of not having borne another human being. *Debajo de la luz* is a quest for love, wherein the art of creation is equaled to the art of love. Grief for the loss of beloved family with the separation that exile imposes permeates the collection of poems *Elegías* (1961; Elegies) that Durán categorizes in three phases as personal, civic and intimate, or philosophical elegies.

One of Zardoya's most distinctive collections of poems is *Corral de vivos y muertos*

(1965; Corral of Living and Dead), a title evoking Unamuno, whom Zardoya quoted in the book's dedication. The poems persistently deal with the exile's dream of return and the constant sense of rupture that exile entails. However, nostalgia helps to endure absence and to strengthen faith in the distant land. In the end personal grief supersedes desperation and transcends to the sphere of shared human destiny where a return is possible via the collective hope of humanity. This collection incorporates some poems that originally were part of *Dominio del llanto* and whose publication was prevented by Francoist censorship in 1947. It abounds in themes representative of Zardoya's poetics: death in war and postwar Spain and the suffering of innocent children; Spain in war and in its aftermath; its cities and villages, its mountains and forests; love contemplated in nature and humans; sorrow in fleeing the homeland and in exile; the afflictions of Spain in lullabies that celebrate everyday manifestations of life (water, wine, olive, oil, wood, metal, orange, geranium, fish, eagle, fog, poplar, woodcutter, shepherd, shadow, search, roof). Language provides the last refuge for a lost homeland ("My only country is in my language").

Between 1968 and 1983 several collections appear that convey feelings elicited by geography, either as result of a journey or of residing in a particular place. Such are the cases of *Donde el tiempo resbala* (1966; Where Time Slips), a series of ballads inspired by a trip to Belgium that brings forth a happy and optimistic experience; *Hondo Sur* (1968; Deep South) deals with impressions and memories of 10 years spent in Louisiana while teaching at Tulane University where feelings of sadness prevail jointly with human and social concerns; *Los engaños de Tremont* (1971), prompted by years of residence in Boston, expresses in sonnets a theoretical approach to what poetic reality is for the poet; *Manhattan y otras latitudes*, inspired by the big metropolis, conveys the perception of isolation and detachment; *Retorno a Magerit*

(1983; Return to Magerit) deals with the conflict between life as imagined and the encountered reality on return to the homeland. Another important collection where nostalgia prevails is *Diotima y sus edades*, a lyric biography of the poet in quest of capturing the flow of life through childhood and adolescence, youth, maturity, and old age, each representing a different phase of solitude: initial at first, growing with the war, increasing in exile, and finally conquered in old age with resignation and melancholic acceptance. Other collections are *Las hiedras del tiempo* (1972; The Ivy of Time), *El corazón y la sombra; Los ríos caudales. Apología del 27* (1982; Flowing Rivers; Apologia for [the Generation of] 1927), *Poemas a Joan Miró* (1984; Poems to Joan Miró), *No llega a ser ceniza lo que se arde* (1985; What Burns Won't Become Ash), *Ritos, cifras y evasiones, Forma de esperanza* (1985; Form of Hope), *Los perplejos hallazgos* (1986; Perplexing Finds), *Altamor* (1986), and *Gradiva y un extraño héroe* (1987; Gradiva and a Strange Hero). Some of the last collections incorporate unpublished poems written in 1937–1938.

No stereotyped feminist traits appear in Zardoya such as defiance of her condition as a repressed human being, nor a conscience of submission to a patriarchal structure that would entail a preconceived and oppressive role. There is likewise no evidence that she associates the act of writing with authority. In fact, as Bellver has observed, in one poem Zardoya views the thimble and the pen as a double symbol serving neither to defend nor to defy nor to give victories but to serve as soothing instruments for living. Nevertheless, Zardoya is a strong, independent woman who is not restricted to a domestic environment. If Zardoya's poetry suggests the possibility of liberation through literature, writing is not defiance of a traditional domain reserved to males but rather the means to triumph over inner exile and feelings of solitude. The poet makes no overt mention of repression. Zardoya does not emphasize feminism in her writing, nor does she place a particular feminist importance on the creative act. But her poetic creativity and her accomplishments as a literary critic attest to a different feminism that varies from traditional or ideological feminine expectations. Her autonomous existence, her poetic vocation, her constant search to transcend narrow realities prove the legitimacy of Zardoya's conquest of a nontraditional feminine reality. *See also* Short Fiction by Women Writers: 1900–1975

Work by

La casa deshabitada. Madrid: Insula, 1959.
Corral de vivos y muertos. Buenos Aires: Losada, 1965.
El desterrado ensueño. New York and Madrid: Hispanic Institute, 1955.
Diotima y sus edades. Barcelona: Ambito Literario, 1981.
Hondo Sur. Madrid: El Bardo, 1968.
Manhattan y otras latitudes. El Ferrol: Sociedad de Cultura Valle-Inclán, 1983.

Work about

Bellver, Catherine. "Tres poetas desterradas y la morfología del exilio." *Cuadernos Americanos* 4 (1990): 163–177.
Fagundo, Ana María. "La guerra civil en la poesía de Concha Zardoya." *Insula* 392–393 (1979): 13, 17.
Pérez, Janet. *Modern and Contemporary Spanish Women Poets.* New York: Twayne, 1996. 90–100.
Persin, Margaret. "Reading Goya's Gaze with Concha Zardoya and María Victoria Valencia." *Anales de la Literatura Española Contemporánea* 22.1 (1997): 75–90.
Rodríguez Pequeño, Mercedes. *La poesía de Concha Zardoya: Estudio temático y estilístico.* Valladolid: Universidad de Valladolid, 1987.
Sin Nombre. Homenaje a Concha Zardoya 9.3 (1978). Contains several articles.
Wilcox, John. *Women Poets of Spain, 1860–1990: Towarda Gynocentric Vision.* Chicago and Urbana: U of Illinois P, 1997.

Pilar Sáenz

Zayas y Sotomayor, María de (1590–after 1647?)

Very little is known about the life of Golden Age novelist María de Zayas y Sotomayor. The daughter of a military captain, she is believed to have been born in Madrid and spent a good part of her life there, although it is possible that she went with her father and the Spanish court to Naples. She was well known to her contemporaries and active in literary circles. Both Lope de *Vega (in *Laurel de Apolo*) and Pérez de Montalbán (in *Para todos*) praise her writings, and Zayas mentions other women writers in her works, Ana *Caro Mallén de Soto being the most widely published of those mentioned. For an apparently noble woman, it is unusual that there is no record of either a marriage or entry into a convent, which would have been the path most frequently chosen by unmarried women of her time and one that she herself advocates in her second collection of novellas.

María de Zayas is known primarily as a novelist, although she also published poetry and at least one play. Her poetry consists of poems written for special occasions and poems included in her prose works, some of which are superb examples of baroque love poetry. She also wrote for poetry competitions and to grace the novels or plays written by friends (one written to Miguel Botello in 1621 is the earliest of these). By 1632 she was known in Madrid as a poet and playwright and had written the first version of her *Novelas amorosas ye jemplares* (Amorous and Exemplary Novels), containing eight novellas. The extant play *Traición en la amistad* (c. 1632; Betrayal in Friendship), focuses on two issues: the importance of female friendship and the difficulty for a woman to break out of the strict role stereotypes available to her. The female protagonist in the play, Fenisa, resembles many of Lope de Vega's heroines in her vindication of her right to have as many lovers as she wishes, although she is ultimately criticized for her capricious behavior.

Zayas published two collections of novellas: *Las novelas amorosas y ejemplares* (1634; Amorous and Exemplary Tales) and *Los desengaños amorosos* (1647; Disillusions in

Love). Zayas was extremely popular in her time and in the following century, as we know from the number of editions and translations of her works published, but fell into relative obscurity for the nineteenth and most of the twentieth centuries, being rediscovered by feminist critics in the late 1970s. With the advent of gender and queer studies, her works are becoming popular once again not only with Hispanists but among those in the field of comparative literature. There is no record of Zayas, either of a literary or social nature, after publication of her second collection of novellas.

Each of these collections contains 10 stories, narrated in the context of a frame story involving the same group of people. In the tradition of Boccaccio's *Decameron*, the stories are told by a group of young people who have gathered as a result of illness: In Zayas, their purpose is to lift the spirits of the hostess, Lysis, who is convalescing. One of the major differences between the collections of Zayas and the *Decameron* is the importance of the frame story in the interpretation of the tales told, which in Zayas does not become evident until the second collection. As their names indicate, the first collection of stories has happy endings, having no overt purpose other than to entertain. In the second book, however, the men present are not given a voice. Lysis instructs the women to tell stories of men's deceits, as she herself has been deceived by one of the men present and is now engaged to be married to another of the group. This time her illness is directly related to the *engaño* (deception) she has suffered. At the end of the second collection, Lysis, along with her widowed mother, has decided to enter a convent instead of marrying. She makes it clear in the final frame narrative that she will thus "save herself" from men's deceits, as have several of the heroines in the stories. The *desengaños* themselves are full of grisly events, including the murder or torture of wives, sisters, and daughters at the hands of male relatives. At several times during the frame narrative an authorial voice intervenes

to relate stories of real-life women to those of the women in the tales and to reinforce the moral message of the stories. At the end of the *desengaños*, this same voice declares she has taken the pen, and will take the sword, in defense of women who have been wronged like those in the stories, leading many to believe that this is the voice of Zayas the writer.

Zayas's writings have been described by critics as anywhere from socially reactionary to progressive, and often she is cited as Spain's first feminist. There is no doubt that she takes a firm stance on the need for proper formal education for women, and she directly criticizes marriage as the "enslavement" of women. Conservative elements in her works include apparent adherence to the male code of **honor*, and a yearning expressed for earlier times—when men were chivalrous, kept their word, and protected women. Perhaps most original in her works is the portrayal of a world in which laywomen and religious women function together to play an important role in the education of women. Often the religious women are catalysts for the laywoman's entrance into the convent, but just as often the convent is presented as a place of refuge and repose, from which the laywomen emerge again to take their place in society.

Work by

The Enchantments of Love. Trans. and intro. Patsy Boyer. Berkeley: U of California P, 1990.

Novelas amorosas y ejemplares. Ed. Agustín G. de Amezúa. Madrid: Aldus, 1948.

Parte segunda del sarao y entretenimiento honesto: Desengaños amorosos. Ed. Alicia Yllera. Madrid: Cátedra, 1983.

La Traición en la amistad. Intro., ed., and notes Alessandra Melloni. Verona: n.p., 1983.

Work about

Arenal, Electa. " 'Leyendo Yo y Escribiendo Ella': The Convent as Intellectual Community." *Journal of Hispanic Philology* 13.3 (Spring 1989): 214–229.

Barass, Tina. "El llamado feminismo en las novelas de María de Zayas." *Estudis Romanics* 16 (1971–1975): 119–152.

Barbeito, María Isabel. "El Amor Barroco en María de Zayas." Separata of *Anales del Instituto de Estudios Madrileños.* Madrid: Consejo Superior de Investigaciones Científicas, 1989. 27: n.p.

Boyer, Patsy. "La visión artística de María de Zayas." *Estudios sobre el siglo de oro en homenaje a Raymond R. MacCurdy.* Madrid: Cátedra, 1983. 253–264.

Brownlee, Marina S. "Cultural Authority in Golden Age Spain." Introduction to *Cultural Authority in Golden Age Spain.* Ed. Marina S. Brownlee and Hans Ulrich Gumbrecht. Baltimore: Johns Hopkins UP, 1995. ix–xvii.

———. *The Cultural Labyrinth of María de Zayas.* Philadelphia: U of Pennsylvania P, 2000.

———. "Postmodernism and the Baroque in María de Zayas." *Cultural Authority in Golden Age Spain.* Ed. Marina S. Brownlee and Hans Ulrich Gumbrecht. Baltimore: Johns Hopkins UP, 1995. 107–127.

Cocozzella, Peter. "María de Zayas y Sotomayor: Writer of the Baroque 'Novela Ejemplar.'" *Women Writers of the Seventeenth Century.* Ed. Katharina M. Wilson and Frank J. Warnke. Athens: U of Georgia P, 1989. 189–200

Cruz, Anne J. "Studying Gender in the Spanish Golden Age." *Cultural and Historical Grounding for Hispanic and Luso-Brazilian Feminist Literary Criticism.* Ed. Hernán Vidal. Minneapolis: Institute for the Study of Ideologies and Literature, 1989. 193–222.

Cruz, Anne J., and Mary Elizabeth Perry, eds. *Culture and Control in Counter-Reformation Spain.* Minneapolis: U of Minnesota P, 1992.

El Saffar, Ruth. "Ana/Lysis/Zayas: Reflections on Courtship and Literary Women in María de Zayas's 'Enchantments of Love.'" *Indiana Journal of Hispanic Literatures* 2.1 (Fall 1993): 1–28.

Ferreras, Juan Ignacio. *La novela corta en el siglo XVII.* Madrid: Taurus, 1988.

Gossy, Mary S. "Skirting the Question: Lesbians and María de Zayas." *Hispanisms and Homosexualities.* Ed. and intro. Silvia Molloy and Robert McKee Irwin. Durham: Duke UP, 1998. 19–28.

Greer, Margaret Rich. *María de Zayas Tells Baroque Tales of Love and the Cruelty of Men.* State College: Penn State UP, 2000.

Grieve, Patricia E. "Embroidering with Saintly Threads: María de Zayas Challenges Cervantes and the Church." *Renaissance Quarterly* 44.1 (Spring 1991): 86–106.

Soufas, Teresa. "María de Zayas's (Un)Conventional Play, 'La traición en la amistad.'" *The Golden Age Comedia: Text, Theory, and Performance.* Ed.

Charles Ganelin, West Lafayette: Purdue UP, 1994. 148–164.

Wilkins, Constance. "Subversion through Comedy?: Two Plays by Sor Juana Inés de la Cruz and María de Zayas." *The Perception of Women in Spanish Theater of the Golden Age.* Ed. Anita Stoll and Dawn L. Smith. Lewisburg, PA: Bucknell UP, 1991. 107–120.

Williamsen, Amy, ed. *María de Zayas: The Dynamics of Discourse.* Rutherford: Fairleigh Dickinson UP, 1995.

Wilson, Katharina, and Frank J. Warnke, eds. *Women Writers of the Seventeenth Century.* Athens: U of Georgia P, 1989.

Nancy Cushing-Daniels

Zorrilla y Moral, José (1817–1893): His View of Women

At age 19, Romantic poet José Zorrilla y Moral abandoned law studies in his native Valladolid and fled to Madrid, thus incurring the displeasure of a severe and righteous father. Thereafter, five women loomed large in his life and art: his wife, a mistress in Paris and another in Mexico, the character Doña Inés in his drama *Don Juan Tenorio*, and the Virgin Mary.

The poet, still not 20 years old, leaped to fame in Madrid when, on February 15, 1837, he read a poem at the funeral of a suicide, the controversial Romantic journalist Mariano José de *Larra. The next day a boyhood friend introduced him to another youth, Antonio Bernal O'Reilly, and his widowed mother, Florentina Matilde O'Reilly. Drawn to Zorrilla, young Bernal observed that the poet was ill clothed and ill fed. He persuaded Zorrilla to take some of his own clothes and begged his mother to invite his friend to dinner. The poet became a regular guest, and from Matilde O'Reilly's board, he moved to her bed. Two years after they met, she was pregnant, and the couple married on August 22, 1839. Six weeks later a daughter, Plácida Ester, was born; and Antonio Bernal, a witness at the wedding, became godfather to his infant half sister.

The relationship of Zorrilla and Matilde

O'Reilly was not a happy one, but the couple remained together during the short life of the child and through Zorrilla's most productive years in Madrid. Matilde never trusted her husband, and he felt restive when she insisted on attending rehearsals at the theater to protect her marriage from the wiles of actresses. He went to France in 1850 and she followed him, but the break came in Paris, and she returned to Spain. In 1854, Zorrilla went to Mexico, spending the next 11 years there and returning to Spain only after receiving word of his wife's death.

In Paris, Zorrilla had met Emilia *Serrano, a teenage girl. Zorrilla, an older, married, "real-life" Don Juan Tenorio, was in his thirties. When he departed for the New World, he left Emilia with an infant in her arms. She, in turn, married a young but sickly half-English, half-German baron and acquired the title of Baroness Wilson. Neither her husband nor Zorrilla's child survived, but Emilia herself had an astonishing career in journalism, living to a ripe old age and secretly cherishing the knowledge that she was the Leila of passionate poems that Zorrilla published in *La flor de los recuerdos* (1857; Bouquet of Memories).

In the Republic of Mexico, where his fame preceded him, he was warmly received by the literary world and moved easily from it to the society of wealthy landowners, either Spanish emigrés or Mexicans with close Spanish ties, writing about them in a long essay "México y los mexicanos," addressed to Angel de Saavedra, duke of Rivas, and published in *La flor de los recuerdos*. José Gómez, count of La Cortina, introduced him to his cousin, José Adalid, owner of the vast Hacienda de los Reyes northeast of the capital. Adalid's wife was Concepción Sánchez de Tagle, who had inherited from her father, poet Francisco Manuel Sánchez de Tagle (whom Zorrilla discusses in his essay), a 90,000-acre estate, the Hacienda de los Goicoechea in San Angel, near the capital. Zorrilla was already friends with Adalid's two brothers, and after returning to the capital

from a visit to her estate, he became a long-term guest at the San Angel home. In reality, Zorrilla was more than a houseguest, for he became the lover of Doña Concepción. It is a measure of Mexican society at mid-century that the lovers' relationship was known and accepted in the Spanish and Creole circles in which they moved. We may speculate that José Adalid was a complacent (rather than Calderonian) husband because he had more compelling interests elsewhere and was glad enough to have his wife entertained. She figures in Zorrilla's poems of this period as Rosa, Paz, Luz, or, in tribute to a fine horsewoman, as *la campirana*, the country girl. When Maximilian and Carlota arrived in Mexico in 1864, Doña Concepción became a lady-in-waiting to the empress. Zorrilla was later named director of the national theater and reader to the emperor, but he and his *campirana* saw less and less of each other. By his departure in 1866, their passion was spent.

Whatever Zorrilla's relationship with women may have been and/or may appear to have been, he was the creator of one of the loveliest women characters of the Spanish stage and one that all men can love. Doña Inés de Ulloa is the intended victim and then savior of Don Juan Tenorio. Tirso de *Molina's seventeenth-century Don Juan is a youth driven by sex and the fun of playing tricks. The Don Juan of Mozart and Da Ponte is a mature rake, pestered by women he has seduced. The protagonist of Zorrilla's *Don Juan Tenorio* (1844)—one of the most popular Spanish plays of all time—is an expert seducer who truly falls in love with a pure and beautiful woman who then saves his soul. During 150 years, thousands of Hispanic males have played the role on stage as professionals or amateurs before thousands more who have sinned but find consolation in the belief that the love of a pure woman, adorable and adored, can save a man, whatever his sins of the flesh, from eternal damnation. Feminist readers might argue that the poet—unrepentant seducer and irresponsible father—created the self-abnegating Inés in the hope that her salvation of Don Juan might somehow bolster his own chances of redemption.

After the creation of Doña Inés, Zorrilla began a long poem, a tribute to the Virgin Mary, entitled *María, corona poética de la Virgen* (1849; Maria, Poetic Crown of the Virgin). He had intended to collaborate with an older friend, Manuel Joaquín de Tarancón, bishop of Córdoba, whose episcopal duties prevented his participation. The publisher, having offered the work to the public by subscription, arranged for a collaborator, José Heriberto García de Quevedo, a Venezuelan and facile versifier, in case Zorrilla should be unable to make his periodical contributions. Zorrilla began his poem hoping once again to placate a stern and devout father by placing his poetic gifts at the service of religion. Word reached him of his father's death when he had finished 2,187 verses of a poem that came to more than 7,000. Zorrilla never went back to it. García de Quevedo wrote the other 5,000. Zorrilla's "poetic crown" was not this offering to the Virgin but his creation of Doña Inés, a pure woman who saved a sinful man that he might enter with her into the kingdom of Heaven. *See also Burlador de Sevilla, El* (1627–1629): Its Women Characters; Marianism; Sáenz-Alonso, Mercedes (1917–   ): *Don Juan y el donjuanismo*

Work by

Don Juan Tenorio. Ed. Salvador García Castañeda. Textos Hispánicos Modernos, 33. Barcelona: Labor, 1975.

La flor de los recuerdos. Ofrenda que hace a los pueblos hispano-americanos Don José Zorrilla. María, corona poética de la Virgen, poema religioso. With José Heriberto García de Quevedo. Madrid: Operarios, 1849.

Obras completas. Ed. Narciso Alonso Cortés. 2 vols. Valladolid: Santarén, 1943.

Work about

Alonso Cortés, Narciso. *Zorrilla: Su vida y sus obras.* 2nd ed. Valladolid: Santarén, 1943.

Cardwell, Richard A. "Specul(ariz)ation on the Other Woman: Don Juan Tenorio's Inés." *José Zorrilla, 1893–1993.* Ed. Richard A. Cardwell and Ricardo Landeira. Nottingham: Nottingham U, 1993. 41–57.

Dowling, John. "José Zorrilla en el Parnaso mexicano." *Actas del IX Congreso de la Asociación Internacional de Hispanistas: 18–23 agosto 1986, Berlin.* Ed. Sebastian Neumeister. Frankfurt am Main: Vervuert, 1989. 2: 527–533.

———. "José Zorrilla y la retórica de la muerte." *Hispanic Review* 57 (1989): 437–456.

———. "The Poet and the Emperor: José Zorrilla in Maximilian's Mexico." *Homage to Faye LaVerne Bumpass.* Ed. Roberto Bravo et al. Lubbock: Texas Tech U, 1981. 6–18.

———. "Traditional Spain in the Works of José Zorrilla." *Crítica Hispánica* 2 (1980): 97–108.

Dowling, John, and Russell P. Sebold. "Las singulares circunstancias de la publicación de la María de Zorrilla." *Hispanic Review* 50 (1982): 449–472.

Feal, Carlos. "El Don Juan Tenorio de Zorrilla: Una carta, una apuesta y dos salvaciones." *Salina Revista de Lletres* (Tarragona, Spain) 11 (November 1997): 93–99.

Gabriele, John P. "From Assimilation to Liberation: Reassessing Inés's Role in José Zorrilla's *Don Juan Tenorio.*" *Letras Peninsulares* 10.1 (Spring 1997): 111–131.

Gies, David Thatcher. "Don Juan contra Don Juan: Apoteosis del romanticismo español." *Actas del Séptimo Congreso de la Asociación Internacional de Hispanistas celebrado en Venecia del 25 al 30 de agosto de 1980.* Ed. Giuseppe Bellini. Rome: Bulzoni, 1982. 545–551.

———. "Don Juan Tenorio y la tradición de la comedia de magia." *Hispanic Review* 58 (1990): 1–17.

———. "José Zorrilla and the Betrayal of Spanish Romanticism." *Romanistiches Jahrbuch* 33 (1980): 339–346.

Sebold, Russell P. "Larra y la misión de Zorrilla." The *American Hispanist* 3.26 (April 1978): 7–12.

John Dowling

Appendix

For readers wishing to focus upon a specific time period, this appendix provides an approximate chronological grouping of entries by century. Each century is arranged alphabetically. Women authors are indexed by their date of birth; entries on literary works are grouped by their composition or publication date. Entries which treat women characters or the depiction of women in works of male authorship are indexed by publication dates of the work or works discussed. Entries with information spanning more than one century are listed in each pertinent time period. Brief definitions of terms are listed in pertinent centuries.

1000–1099

Alba

Cantiga de amigo

Courtly Love

Cubiertas and *Tapadas*

Disciplina clericalis (eleventh century)

Encierro

Hispano-Arabic Poetry by Women

Honor and *Honra*

Jarcha

Jimena (1056?/1058?–1104?/1122?)

Marianism in Spain

Misogyny in Medieval and Early Modern Spain

Urraca de Castilla y León (1080–1126)

Women's Professions in Early Spanish Literature: *Santas, Rameras, Casadas, Amas* and *Criadas* (Saints, Whores, Wives, Governesses, and Servants)

1100–1199

Alba

Berenguela de Castilla la Grande (1181–1246)

Cantiga de amigo

Courtly Love

Cubiertas and *Tapadas*

Dueña

Encierro

Hispano-Arabic Poetry by Women

Honor and *Honra*

Jarcha

Marianism in Spain

Misogyny in Medieval and Early Modern Spain

Poema de Mio Cid (twelfth–thirteenth centuries): Its Portrayal of Women

Women's Deceits: Medieval Approaches to the Topic

Women's Professions in Early Spanish Literature: *Santas, Rameras, Casadas, Amas* and *Criadas* (Saints, Whores, Wives, Governesses, and Servants)

1200–1299

Alba

Alfonso el Sabio (1221–1284): Women in *Las siete partidas*

Beata

Cantiga de amigo

Cosmetics in Medieval and Renaissance Spain

Courtly Love

Cubiertas and *Tapadas*

Dueña

Encierro

Hispano-Arabic Poetry by Women

Honor and *Honra*

Jarcha

Libro de Apolonio (late 1200s): Its Portrayal of Women

Marianism in Spain

Misogyny in Medieval and Early Modern Spain

Molina, María de (1259–1321)

Women's Deceits: Medieval Approaches to the Topic

Women's Professions in Early Spanish Literature: *Santas, Rameras, Casadas, Amas* and *Criadas* (Saints, Whores, Wives, Governesses, and Servants)

1300–1399

Alba

Beata

Cantiga de amigo

Castro, Inés de (1325?–1355)

Catalan Women Writers: A Brief History

Comadrona

Conde Lucanor, El (1335)

Cosmetics in Medieval and Renaissance Spain

Courtly Love

Cubiertas and *Tapadas*

Dueña

Eiximenis, Francesc (1330?–1409): His Views on Women

Encierro

Hispano-Arabic Poetry by Women

Honor and *Honra*

Jarcha

Leonor de Navarra (1350–1415), Queen of Navarre

Libro de buen amor (1335, 1343): Its Portrayal of Women

López de Córdoba, Leonor (late fourteenth–early fifteenth century)

Marianism in Spain

Misogyny in Medieval and Early Modern Spain

Tercera

Torres, Inés de (c. 1390)

Women's Deceits: Medieval Approaches to the Topic

Women's Professions in Early Spanish Literature: *Santas, Rameras, Casadas, Amas* and *Criadas* (Saints, Whores, Wives, Governesses, and Servants)

1400–1499

Alba

Beata

Beltraneja, Juana la (1462–1530)

Cantiga de amigo

Cartagena, Teresa de (c. 1420–after 1460?)

Catalan Women Writers: A Brief History

Catalina de Aragón (1485–1536)

Celestina, La. Comedia o tragicomedia de Calisto y Melibea

Comadrona

Corbacho, El (1438)

Cosmetics in Medieval and Renaissance Spain

Courtly Love

Cruz, Juana de la (1481–1534)

Cubiertas and *Tapadas*

Dueña

Encierro

Galindo, Beatriz (1475–1534)

García, Antona (?–1476)

Grisel y Mirabella (pub. c. 1495)

Hispano-Arabic Poetry by Women

Honor and *Honra*

Isabel I, Queen of Castile: The Vision of the Queen in *Converso* Poetry (c. 1474–c. 1480)

Isabel I de Castilla (1451–1504)

Jarcha

Jardín de las nobles donzellas (written c. 1468)

Juana *la Loca* (the Mad One; 1479–1555)

Libro de las virtuosas y claras mujeres (fifteenth century)

Marianism in Spain

Medrano, Luisa (Lucía) de (1484?–1527?)

Misogyny in Medieval and Early Modern Spain

Pinar, Florencia (late 15th c.?)

Repetición de amores (c. 1495–1497)

Ribera, Suero de (c. 1410–c. 1480)

Rodríguez del Padrón (de la Cámara), Juan (1399?–1450)

San Pedro, Diego de (15th c.)

Santillana, Marqués de (1398–1458): His Portrayal of Women

Santo Domingo, Sor María de (c. 1468/1474–c. 1524)

Silva, Beatriz de (1424–1491)

Syphilis as Sickness and Metaphor in Early Modern Spain: 1492–1650

Tercera

Tratado en defensa de las virtuosas mujeres (before 1448)

Vásquez de la Cruz, Juana (1481–1534)

Women's Deceits: Medieval Approaches to the Topic

Women's Professions in Early Spanish Literature: *Santas, Rameras, Casadas, Amas* and *Criadas* (Saints, Whores, Wives, Governesses, and Servants)

Women's Situation in Spain: 1400–1600

1500–1599

Abencerraje y la hermosa Jarifa, El (1561–1565)

Antigua, Sor María de la (1566–1617)

Autobiographical Self-Representation of Women in the Early Modern Period

Beata

Caballerías, novelas de: Their Treatment of Women

Cantiga de amigo

Caro Mallén de Soto, Ana (1565?/1600?–1652?)

Carvajal y Mendoza, Luisa de (1566–1614)

Catalan Women Writers: A Brief History

Comadrona

Cosmetics in Medieval and Renaissance Spain

Courtly Love

Cubiertas and *Tapadas*

Diálogo de mujeres (1544)

Diálogo en laude de las mugeres (1580)

Diana, La (1559)

Drama by Spanish Women Writers: 1500–1700

Dueña

Eboli, Princess of, doña Ana de Mendoza y de la Cerda (1540–1592)

Encierro

Enríquez de Guzmán, Feliciana (late sixteenth–early seventeenth centuries)

Erauso, Catalina de (1578?/1585?/1592?–after 1630)

Fernández de Alarcón, Cristobalina (1576?–1646)

Guevara, Antonio de (1481?–1545): Women's Roles in the *Epístolas familiares*

Honor and *Honra*

Invisible Mistress

Juan de la Cruz, San (1542–1591)

León, Fray Luis de (1527–1591)

León, Fray Luis de (1527–1591): Admiration and Misogyny in *La perfecta casada*

León, Fray Luis de (1527–1591): Women in His Poetry

Lesbianism in Early Modern Spanish Literature: 1500–1700

Liaño, Isabel de (1570–after 1604)

Lozana andaluza, La (1528)

Marianism in Spain

Marimacho

Misogyny in Medieval and Early Modern Spain

Montemayor, Jorge de (c. 1520–1561)

Nebrija (or Lebrija), Francisca de (sixteenth century)

Nuns Who Wrote in Sixteenth- and Seventeenth-Century Spain

Padilla Manrique y Acuña, Luisa María de, Condesa de Aranda (1590–1646)

Pícaras and *Pícaros*: Female and Male Rogues in the Spanish Picaresque Canon

Sabuco de Nantes Barrera, Oliva (1562–1622?)

San Alberto, Sor María de (?–1640)

San Bartolomé (García y Manzanas), Ana de (1549–1626)

1600–1699

Vega y Carpio, Lope de (1562–1635): Women in His Drama

Women Writers in Spanish Literary History: 1500–1996

Women's Deceits: Medieval Approaches to the Topic

Women's Professions in Early Spanish Literature: *Santas, Rameras, Casadas, Amas* and *Criadas* (Saints, Whores, Wives, Governesses, and Servants)

Women's Situation in Spain: 1600–1700

1700–1799

Amar y Borbón, Josefa (1749–1833)

Beata

Böhl de Faber, Cecilia, Pseud. Fernán Caballero (1796–1877)

Catalan Women Writers: A Brief History

Cienfuegos, Beatriz de (eighteenth century)

Cigarrera

Defensa de las mujeres (1726)

"Discurso en defensa de las mujeres . . . " (1786)

Drama by Spanish Women Writers: 1770–1850

Encierro

Feminism in Spain: 1700–1800

Gálvez de Cabrera, María Rosa (1768–1806)

Guzmán y de la Cerda, María Isidra Quintina (1768–1803)

Helguero y Alvarado, María Nicolasa de (?–after 1805)

Hickey y Pellizone, Margarita (1753–after 1793)

Hore y Ley, María Gertrudis (1742–1801)

Lorenza de los Ríos, María, Marchioness of Fuerte Hijar (c. 1768–after 1817)

Marianism in Spain

Marimacho

Maturana y Velázques de Gutiérrez, Vicenta (1793–1859)

Moratín, Leandro Fernández de (1760–1828): His Portrayal of Women

Pensadora Gaditana, La (1763–1764)

Women Writers in Spanish Literary History: 1500–1996

Women's Situation in Spain: 1700–1800

Women's Situation in Spain: 1786–1931: The Awakening of Female Consciousness

1800–1899

Acuña y Villanueva de la Iglesia, Rosario de (1851–1923)

Alarcón, Pedro Antonio de (1833–1891): Women in His Works

Ángel del hogar

Arenal, Concepción (1820–1893)

Basque Women Writers: 1804–1997

Beata

Bécquer, Gustavo Adolfo (1836–1870): Women in His Works

Biedma y la Moneda de Rodríguez, Patrocinio de (1848–1927)

Blasco Ibáñez, Vicente (1867–1928): His Portrayal of Women

Bridoux y Mazzini de Domínguez, Victorina (1835–1862)

Burgos, Carmen de (1867–1932)

Campoamor, Clara (1888–1972)

Castro, Rosalía de (1837–1885)

Catalan Women Writers: A Brief History

Cigarrera

Claramunt, Teresa (1862–1931)

Contreras y Alba de Rodríguez, María del Pilar (1861–1930)

Coronado, Carolina (1823–1911)

Dama de Elche, La

Doña Perfecta (1876)

Drama by Spanish Women Writers: 1770–1850

Drama by Spanish Women Writers: 1860–1900

Encierro

Espronceda, José de (1808–1842): His Portrayal of Women

Estevarena y Gallardo, Concepción (1854–1876)

Fortún, Elena, Pseud. of Encarnación Aragoneses Urquijo (1886–1952)

Galician Women Writers: A Brief History

García Balmaseda, Joaquina (1837–1883)

García de la Torre, Ana (fl. nineteenth century)

Gimeno de Flaquer, Concepción (1860–1919)

Gómez de Avellaneda, Gertrudis (1814–1873)

Goyri y Goyri, María (1873–1954)

Grassi, Angela (1823–1883)

Ibarruri Gómez, Dolores (1895–1989)

Icaza, Carmen de (1899–1979)

Kent Siano, Victoria (1898–1987)

Larra, Mariano José de (1809–1837): Women in His Works

Maeztu y Whitney, María de (1882–1948)

Marianism in Spain

Marimacho

Méndez, Concha (1898–1986)

Millán Astray, Pilar (1879–1949)

Mojigata, La (1804)

Nelken y Mausberger, Margarita (1896–1968)

Palacio Valdés, Armando (1853–1938): Women in His Works

Palencia, Isabel de (1878–1974)

Pardo Bazán, Emilia (1852–1921): Reception of Her by Male Colleagues, 1870–1921

Pereda, José María de (1833–1906): His Portrayal of Women

Pérez de Ayala, Ramón (1880–1962): His Portrayal of Women

Poetry by Spanish Women Writers: 1800–1900

Regenta, La (1885): Female Enemies in the Novel

Regenta, La (1885): Protagonist Ana Ozores

Ríos Nostench de Lampérez, Blanca de los (1862–1956)

Sáez de Melgar, Faustina (1834?–1895)

Sáiz y Otero, Concepción (1851–c.1930)

Santiago Fuentes, Magdalena, (1876–1922)

Serrano García, Emilia, Baronesa de Wilson (1834?–1923)

Short Fiction by Women Writers: 1800–1900

Sí de las niñas, El (1806)

Sinués de Marco, María del Pilar (1835–1893)

Tormento (1884)

Tórtola Valencia, Carmen (1882–1955)

Tristana (1892)

Valderrama Alday, Pilar de (1889–1979)

Valera, Juan (1824–1905): Women in His Novels

Women Writers in Spanish Literary History: 1500–1996

Women's Education in Spain: 1860–1993

Women's Situation in Spain: 1786–1931: The Awakening of Female Consciousness

Zorrilla y Moral, José (1817–1893): His View of Women

1900–2000

Abad, Mercedes (1961–   )

Aguirre, Francisca (1930–   )

Alberca Lorente, Luisa (1920–   )

Albornoz, Aurora de (1926–1990)

Alcalde, Carmen (1936–   )

Aldecoa, Josefina R(odríguez) (1926–   )

Alfaro, María (1900–   )

Alós, Concha (1922–   )

Alvarez de Toledo, (Luisa) Isabel, Duchess of Medina Sidonia (1930–   )

Amorós, Amparo (twentieth century)

Andrés, Elena (1931–   )

Andreu, Blanca (1960–   )

Atencia, María Victoria (1931–   )

Azorín (1873–1967): Feminism in His Novel *Doña Inés* (1925)

Badell, Ana María (1932–   )

Ballesteros (Mercedes (1913–   )

Barberá, Carmen (twentieth century)

Barbero, Teresa (1934?–)

Baroja, Pío (1872–1956): Women Characters in His Works

Basque Women Writers: 1804–1997

Beata

Beauvoir, Simone de (1908–1986): Her Influence in Spain

Benavente, Jacinto (1866–1954): His Portrayal of Women in *La noche del sábado* and *La malquerida*

Beneyto Cunyat, María (1925–   )

Blasco Ibáñez, Vicente (1867–1928): His Portrayal of Women

Boixadós, María Dolores (1919?–)

Bravo-Villasante, Carmen (1918–1995)

Buero Vallejo, Antonio (1916–2000): His Vision of Women

Cajal, Rosa María (1920–   )

Calvo de Aguilar, Isabel (1916–   )

Campo Alange, Condesa de (1902–1986)

Canelo Gutiérrez, Pureza (1946–)

Capmany i Farnés, Maria Aurèlia (1918–1991)

Casas, Borita (1911–1999)

Castro, Juana (1945–)

Castroviejo Blanco-Cicerón, Concha (1912–)

Catalan Women Writers: A Brief History

Cela, Camilo José (1916–2002): Women in His Works

Chacel, Rosa (1898–1994)

Champourcín, Ernestina de (1905–1999)

Cigarrera

Colmeiro Laforet, Carlos (1906–1986)

Conde, Carmen (1907–1996)

Dama de Elche, La

Delibes, Miguel (1920–): Women in His Novels

Detective Fiction by Spanish Women Writers

Díaz-Mas, Paloma (1954–)

Doña Jiménez, Juana (1919–)

Drama by Spanish Women Writers: 1970–2000

Encierro

Eroticism in Contemporary Spanish Women Writers' Narrative

Escolano, Mercedes (1964–)

Fagundo, Ana María (1938–)

Fairy Tales in Novels by Spanish Women

Falcón, Lidia (1935–)

Feminism in Spain: 1900–2000

Feminist Theory and the Contemporary Spanish Stage

Fernández Cubas, Cristina (1945–)

Figuera Aymerich, Angela (1902–1984)

Forest, Eva (1928–)

Fórmica, Mercedes (1918–)

Fuentes Blanco, María de los Reyes (1927–)

Fuertes García, Gloria (1918–1998)

Gala, Antonio (1936–)

Galician Women Writers: A Brief History

Galvarriato, Eulalia (1905–)

García, Consuelo (1935–)

García Diego, Begoña (1926–)

García Lorca, Federico (1898–1936): Women in His Rural Trilogy

García Morales, Adelaida (194?–)

Gatell, Angelina (1926–)

Gómez Ojea, Carmen (1945–)

Grandes, Almudena (1960–)

Guilló Fontanills, Magdalena (194?–)

Janés, Clara (1940–)

Jiménez, Juan Ramón (1881–1958): Women in His Works

Jiménez Faro, Luzmaría (1937–)

Kurtz, Carmen, Pseudonym of Carmen de Rafael Marés de Kurz (1911–)

Laborda Medir, Clemencia (1908–1980)

Lacaci, María Elvira (1928–1997)

Lacasa, Cristina (1929–)

Laforet, Carmen (1921–)

Lagos, Concha (1913–)

León, María Teresa (1903–1988)

Linares, Luisa-María (1915–)

Luca, Andrea (1957–)

Lyceum Club Femenino (1926–1936)

Madera, Asunción ["Chona"] (1901–after 1980)

March Alcalá, Susana (1918–1993)

Marco, Concha de (1916–)

María Fontán (novela rosa) (1944)

Marianism in Spain

Marías Aguilera, Julián (1914): On Female Human Condition in Spain, 1965–1992

Marimacho

Martel, Carmen (1915–)

Martín Gaite, Carmen (1925–2000)

Martín Recuerda, José (1925–): *Salvajes, Arrecogías* and Other Women in His Theater

Martín Vivaldi, Elena (1907–)

Martínez Mediero, Manuel (1939–): Women in His Theater

Masoliver, Liberata (1911–)

Matute, Ana María (1926–)

Maura, Julia (1906–1971)

Mayoral, Marina (1942–)

Medio, Dolores (1911–1996)

Mieza, Carmen Farrés de (1931–1976)

Moix, Ana María (1947–)

Montero, Rosa (1951–)

Montseny y Mañé, Federica (1905–1994)

Mora y Maura, Constancia de la (1906–1950)

Mujeres libres (1936–1938)

Mujer moderna y sus derechos, La (1927)

Mulder, Elisabeth (1904–1987)

Navales, Ana María (1945–)

Nelken, Carmen Eva, Pseudonym. Magda Donato (1900–1966)

Ojeda, Pino (1916–)

Olmo, Lauro (1921–1994): *La soltera* (Spinster) and Other Female Characters in His Drama

Ortiz, Lourdes (1943–)

Palou, Inés (1923–1975)

Pardo Bazán, Emilia (1852–1921): Reception of Her by Male Colleagues, 1870–1921

Pasamar, Pilar Paz (1933–)

Pedrero, Paloma (1957–)

Pompeia, Nuria (1938–)

Portal, Marta (1930–)

Puértolas Villanueva, Soledad (1947–)

Quiroga, Elena (1921–1995)

Resino, Carmen (1941–)

Rico Godoy, Carmen (1939–2001)

Rincón Gutiérrez, María Eugenia (1926–)

Rivera Garretas, María-Milagros (1947–)

Romero, Concha (1945–)

Romo Arregui, Josefina (1913–)

Rossetti, Ana (1950–)

Rubio, Fanny (1949–)

Sáenz-Alonso, Mercedes (1917–): Don Juan y el donjuanismo

Salisachs, Mercedes (1916–)

Sau Sánchez, Victoria (1930–)

Sedano, Dora (1902–)

Serrano y Balañá, Eugenia (1918–)

Short Fiction by Women Writers: 1900–1975

Short Fiction by Women Writers: 1975–1998, Post-Franco

Sopetrán Julie (twentieth century)

Suárez del Otero, Concha (1908–)

Suffrage in Spain: 1908–1931

Tía Tula, La (1921)

Tiempo de silencio (1962): Its Portrayal of Women

Torre, Josefina de la (1907–before 1989)

Torrente Ballester, Gonzalo (1910–1999): Women in His Works

Tusquets, Esther (1936–)

Uceda, Julia (1925–)

Uceta Malo, Acacia (1927–)

Unamuno y Jugo, Miguel de (1864–1936): Archetypes of the Mother and Immature Males in His Works

Valle-Inclán Ramón María del (1866–1936): The Image of Women in His Theater

Valle-Inclán Ramón María del (1866–1936): Women in His Short Fiction and the *Sonatas*

Versos con Faldas (1951)

Villarta Tuñón, Angeles (1921–)

Viñas, Celia (1915–1954)

Vindicación feminista (1976–1979)

Women's Education in Spain: 1860–1993

Women's Situation in Spain: 1786–1931: The Awakening of Female Consciousness

Women's Situation in Spain: 1931–1975: The Second Spanish Republic, The Spanish Civil War and Its Aftermath

Women's Situation in Spain: 1975–2000, Post-Franco

Women Writers in Spanish Literary History: 1500–1996

Zambrano, María (1904–1991)

Zapatera prodigiosa, La (written 1926): The Representation of Honor

Zardoya González, María Concepción (1914–)

Selected Bibliography

Acklesberg, Martha. *Free Women of Spain: Anarchism and the Struggle for the Emancipation of Women.* Bloomington: Indiana UP, 1991.

Aguado, Ana María, et al. *Textos de la historia de las mujeres en España.* Madrid: Cátedra, 1994.

Alcalde, Carmen. *La mujer en la guerra civil española.* Madrid: Cambio 16, 1976.

Amar y Borbón, Josefa. *Discurso en defensa del talento de las mujeres y su aptitud para el gobierno.* Madrid, 1786.

———. *Importancia de la instrucción que conviene dar a las mujeres.* Zaragoza, 1784.

Amorós, Celia. *Feminismo e ilustración. Actas del Seminario Permanente, 1988–1992.* Madrid: Universidad Complutense y Comunidad Autónoma, 1992.

Antología de poetisas del 27. Ed. and intro. Emilio Miró. Madrid: Castalia, 1999.

Arana, María José. *La clausura de las mujeres. Una lectura teológica de un proceso histórico.* Bilbao: Universidad de Deusto, 1992.

Archer, Robert, and Isabel de Riquer. *Contra las mujeres: Poemas de rechazo y vituperio.* Barcelona: QuadernsCrema, 1998.

Arenal, Concepción. *La emancipación de la mujer en España.* Ed. Mauro Armiño. Madrid: Akal, 1974.

———. *La mujer del porvenir* (1861); *La mujer de su casa* (1881); *La educación de la mujer* (1892). In *Obras completas.* 23 vols. Madrid: Sucesores de Rivadeneyra, 1894 (I); Madrid: V. Suárez, 1895–1898, 1913.

Arenal, Electa, and Stacey Schlau. *Untold Sisters: Hispanic Nuns in Their Own Words.* Trans. Amanda Powell. Albuquerque: U of New Mexico P, 1989.

Barbeito, Maria Isabel, ed. *Cárceles y mujeres en el siglo XVII.* Madrid: Castalia/Biblioteca de la Mujer, 1991.

Beltrán, Nuria. *¿Muerte civil de la española?* Barcelona: Plaza y Janés, 1975.

Benegas, Noni, and Jesús Muñárriz, eds. *Ellas tienen la palabra: dos décadas de poesía española: antología.* 2nd ed. Madrid: Hiperión, 1998.

Benería, Lourdes. *Mujer, economía y patriarcado durante la España franquista.* Spanish trans. Angels Martínez Castells. Barcelona: Anagrama, 1977.

Birriel Salcedo, Margarita María, ed. *Nuevas preguntas, nuevas miradas: fuentes y documentación para la historia de las mujeres, siglos XIII–XVIII.* Granada: Universidad de Granada, Instituto de la Educación, Servicio de Publicaciones, 1992.

Bordonada, Angela Ena, ed. *Novelas breves de escritoras españolas (1900–1936).* Madrid: Castalia/Biblioteca de Escritoras, 1989.

Borreguero, Concha, et al. *La mujer española: De la tradición a la modernidad, 1960–1980.* Madrid: Tecnos, 1986.

Brown, Joan L., ed. *Women Writers of Contemporary Spain: Exiles in the Homeland.* Newark: U of Delaware P, 1991.

Butler, Judith, et al. *Feminismos literarios.* Madrid: Arco Libros, 1999.

Calvi, Giulia. *La mujer barroca.* Spanish trans. José Luis Gil Aristu. Madrid: Alianza, 1995.

Calvo de Aguilar, Isabel. *Antología bibliográfica de escritoras españolas.* Madrid: Biblioteca Nueva, 1956.

Campo Alange, María. *La mujer como mito y como ser humano.* Madrid: Taurus, 1961.

———. *La mujer en España: Cien años de su historia. 1860–1960.* Madrid: Aguilar, 1964.

———. *La mujer española: De la tradición a la modernidad, 1960–1980.* Madrid: Tecnos, 1986.

Capel Martínez, Rosa María. *El trabajo y la educación de la mujer en España (1900–1930)*. Madrid: Ministerio de Cultura, 1986.

Capmany, Maria Aurèlia. *Cartas impertinentes*. Palma de Mallorca: Francesc de B. Moll, 1971.

———. *El feminismo a Catalunya*. Barcelona: Nova Terra, 1973.

———. *El feminismo ibérico*. Barcelona: Oikos-Tau, 1970.

Charnon-Deutsch, Lou, ed. *Estudios sobre escritoras hispánicas en honor de Georgina Sabat-Rivers*. Madrid: Castalia, 1992.

Charnon-Deutsch, Lou, and Jo Labanyi, eds. *Culture and Gender in Nineteenth-Century Spain*. Oxford: Clarendon P, 1995.

Conde, Carmen. *Poesía femenina española (1939–1950)*. Barcelona: Bruguera, 1967.

———. *Poesía femenina española (1950–1960)*. Barcelona: Bruguera, 1971.

Criado y Domínguez, Juan Pedro. *Literatas españolas del siglo XIX: Apuntes bibliográficos*. Madrid: Pérez Dubrull, 1889.

Cruz, Anne J. *Discourses of Poverty: Social Reform and the Picaresque Novel in Early Modern Spain*. Toronto: U of Toronto P, 1999.

Cuevas García, Cristóbal, ed. *Escribir mujer. Narradoras españolas hoy*. Málaga: Publicaciones del Congreso de Literatura Española Contemporánea, 1999.

De Armas, Frederick A. *The Invisible Mistress: Aspects of Feminism and Fantasy in the Golden Age*. Charlottesville: Biblioteca Siglo de Oro, 1976.

Delgado, María José, and Alain Saint Saëns, eds. *Lesbianism and Homosexuality in Early Modern Spain*. Sewannee, TN: UP of the South, 2000.

Diaz-Diocaretz, Myriam, and Iris M. Zavala, coord. *Breve historia feminista de la literatura española*. 6 vols. Madrid: Dirección General de la Mujer, Consejería de la Comunidad de Madrid; Barcelona: Anthropos, 1993–2000.

Dillard, Heath. *Daughters of the Reconquest. Women in Castilian Town Society, 1100–1300*. Cambridge: Cambridge UP, 1984.

Durán, María Angeles. *El feminismo en España: Dos siglos de historia*. Madrid: Fundación Pablo Iglesias, 1989.

———. *La investigación sobre la mujer en la universidad española contemporánea*. Madrid: Ministerio de Cultura, 1982.

———. *Mujeres y hombres. La formación del pensamiento igualitario*. Madrid: Castalia, 1998.

———. *Mujer y sociedad en España 1700–1975*. Madrid: Dirección General de Juventud y Promoción Socio-Cultural, 1982.

Durán, María Angeles et al. *La mujer en la historia de España (siglos XIV–XX)*. Madrid: Universidad Autónoma de Madrid, 1984.

El Saffar, Ruth. *Rapture Encaged: The Suppression of the Feminine in Western Culture*. London: Routledge, 1994.

Enders, Victoria Lorée and Pamela Beth Radcliff, eds. *Construction Spanish Womanhood. Female Identity in Modern Spain*. Albany: SU of New York, 1999.

Escario, Pilar, et al. *Lo personal es político. El movimiento feminista en la transición*. Madrid: Ministerio de Asuntos Sociales, 1996.

Estreno 10.2 (1984). Special journal issue devoted to Spanish women playwrights.

Fagoaga, Concha. *La voz y el voto de las mujeres. El sufragismo en España, 1877–1931*. Barcelona: Icaria, 1985.

Falcón, Lidia. *Los derechos civiles de la mujer*. Barcelona: Nereo, 1963.

———. *Los derechos laborales de la mujer*. Madrid: Montecorvo, 1965.

———. *En el infierno. Ser mujer en las cárceles de España*. Barcelona: Ediciones de Feminismo, 1977.

———. *Mujer y poder político. Fundamentos de la crisis de objetivos e ideología del Movimiento Feminista*. Madrid: Vindicación Feminista, 1992.

———. *Mujer y sociedad*. Barcelona: Fontanella, 1969.

———. *La razón feminista. 1. La mujer como clase social y económica. El medio de producción doméstica. 2. La reproducción humana*. Barcelona: Fontanella, 1981–1982.

Fernández Quintanilla, Paloma. *La mujer ilustrada en la España del siglo XVIII*. Madrid: Ministerio de Cultura, 1981.

Ferrandiz, Alejandra, and Vicente Verdú. *Noviazgo y matrimonio en la burguesía española*. Barcelona: Cuadernos para el Diálogo, 1974.

Ferreras, Juan Ignacio. *Catálogo de novelas y novelistas del siglo XIX*. Madrid: Cátedra, 1979.

Folguera, Pilar. *Vida cotidiana en Madrid. El primer tercio del siglo a través de las fuentes orales*. Madrid: Comunidad de Madrid, 1987.

Fórmica-Corsi, Mercedes. *A instancia de parte*. Ed., intro., and notes María Elena Bravo. Madrid: Castalia/Instituto de la Mujer, 1991.

———. *Escucho el silencio*. Barcelona: Planeta, 1984.

———. *Visto y vivido, 1931–1937*. Barcelona: Planeta, 1982.

Galerstein, Carolyn L., and Kathleen McNerney, eds. *Women Writers of Spain. An Annotated Bio-Bibliographical Guide*. Westport, CT: Greenwood P, 1986.

Gallego Franco, María H. *Femina dignissima: Mujer y sociedad en Hispania Antigua.* Valladolid: n.p., 1991.

Gallego Méndez, María Teresa. *Mujer, falange y franquismo.* Madrid: Taurus, 1983.

García de León, María A., et al. *Sociología de las mujeres españolas.* Madrid: Universidad Complutense, 1996.

Garrido, Elsa. *Historia de las mujeres en España.* Madrid: Síntesis, 1997.

Glenn, Kathleen, and Mercedes Mazquiarán de Rodríguez, eds. *Spanish Women Writers and the Essay: Gender, Politics and the Self.* Columbia: U of Missouri P, 1998.

Graña Cid, María del Mar, ed. *Las sabias mujeres, I: Educación, saber y autoría (siglos III–XVII).* Madrid: Asociación Cultural Al-Mudayna, 1994.

———. *Las sabias mujeres, II: Homenaje a Lola Luna.* Madrid: Asociación Cultural Al-Mudayna, 1995.

Hegstrom, Valerie, and Amy R. Williamsen, eds. *Engendering the Early Modern Stage: Women Playwrights in the Spanish Empire.* New Orleans: UP of the South, 1999.

Jiménez Faro, Luzmaría, ed. *Panorama antológico de poetisas españolas. Siglos XV al XX.* Madrid: Torremozas, 1987.

———. *Poetisas españolas, Tomo II: De 1901 a 1939. Antología general.* Madrid: Torremozas, 1996.

Kaminsky, Amy, ed. *Water Lilies. An Anthology of Spanish Women Writers from the Fifteenth through the Nineteenth Century.* Minneapolis: U of Minnesota P, 1995.

Kirkpatrick, Susan. *Las Románticas: Women Writers and Subjectivity in Spain, 1835–1850.* Berkeley and Los Angeles: U of California P, 1989.

Letras femeninas 12. 1–2 (1986). Special journal issue on Spanish women writers and the Civil War.

Levine, Linda Gould, Ellen Engelson Marson, and Gloria Feiman Waldman, eds. *Spanish Women Writers. A Bio-Bibliographical Source Book.* Westport, CT: Greenwood P, 1993.

Levine, Linda Gould, and Gloria Feiman Waldman, eds. *Feminismo ante el franquismo: Entrevistas con feministas de España.* Miami, FL: Universal, 1980.

López, Elsa, ed. *La poesía escrita por mujeres y el canon.* Lanzarote, Canarias: Cabildo Insular, 1999.

López Beltrán, María T., et al. *Realidad histórica e invención literaria en torno a la mujer.* Málaga: Servicio de Publicaciones, Diputación Provincial de Málaga, 1987.

Mangini, Shirley. *Memories of Resistance. Women's Voices from the Spanish Civil War.* New Haven, CT: Yale UP, 1995.

Manteiga, Robert, Carolyn Galerstein, and Kathleen McNerney, eds. *Feminine Concerns in Contemporary Spanish Fiction by Women.* Potomac, MD: Scripta Humanística, 1988.

Martínez Sierra, María/Gregorio. *Feminismo, feminidad, españolismo.* Madrid: Renacimiento, 1917.

Martín Gaite, Carmen. *Desde la ventana: Enfoque femenino de la literatura española.* Madrid: Espasa-Calpe, 1987.

———. *Love Customs in Eighteenth-Century Spain.* Trans. Maria G. Tomsich. Berkeley: U of California P, 1991.

———. *Usos amorosos de la postguerra española.* Barcelona: Anagrama, 1987.

———. *Usos amorosos del dieciocho en España.* Barcelona: Anagrama, 1987.

Martín-Gamero, Amalia. *Antología del feminismo.* Madrid: Alianza, 1975.

Masanet, Lydia. *La autobiografía femenina española contemporánea.* Madrid: Fundamentos, 1998.

McKendrick, Melveena M. *Woman and Society in the Spanish Drama of the Golden Age. A Study of the Mujer Varonil.* Cambridge: Cambridge UP, 1974.

McNerney, Kathleen, and Cristina Enríquez de Salamanca, eds. *Double Minorities of Spain. A Bio-Bibliographic Guide to Women Writers of the Catalan, Galician and Basque Countries.* New York: Modern Language Association, 1994.

Mieza, Carmen. *La mujer del español.* Barcelona: Ediciones Marte, 1977.

Miguel, Amando de. *El miedo a la igualdad. Varones y mujeres en una sociedad machista.* Barcelona: Grijalbo, 1975.

———. *Sexo: Mujer y natalidad en España.* Barcelona: Cuadernos para el Diálogo, 1974.

Miller, Beth, ed. *Women in Hispanic Literature: Icons and Fallen Idols.* Berkeley and Los Angeles: U of California P, 1983.

Mirrer, Louise. *Women, Jews and Muslims in the Texts of Reconquest Castile.* Ann Arbor: U of Michigan P, 1996.

Mujeres en la historia de Andalucía, Las. Actas del II Congreso de Historia de Andalucía. Cordoba: Junta de Andalucía, 1994.

Muñoz Fernández, Angela. *Las mujeres en el cristianismo medieval.* Madrid: Asociación Cultural Al-Mudayna, 1989.

Nash, Mary. *La mujer en las organizaciones políticas de izquierda, 1931–1939.* Barcelona: Universidad, 1980.

———. *Mujer, familia y trabajo en España, 1875–1936.* Barcelona: Anthropos, 1983.

———. *Mujer y movimiento obrero en España, 1931–1939.* Barcelona: Fontamara, 1981.

Navarro, Ana, ed. *Antología poética de escritoras de los*

siglos XVI y XVII. Madrid: Castalia/Biblioteca de escritoras, 1989.

Nelken, Margarita. *La condición social de la mujer en España*. Madrid: CVS Ediciones, 1975.

———. *Las escritoras españolas*. Barcelona: Labor, 1930.

O'Connor, Patricia W., ed. *Mujeres sobre mujeres. Teatro breve español*. Madrid: Fundamentos, 1998. (Spanish-English bilingual edition)

Olivares, Julián, and Elizabeth S. Boyce, eds. *Tras el espejo la musa escribe: Lírica femenina de los Siglos de Oro*. Madrid: Siglo Veintiuno de España, 1993.

Oñate, María del Pilar. *El feminismo en la literatura española*. Madrid: Espasa-Calpe, 1938.

Parada y Barrera, Diego Ignacio. *Escritoras y eruditas españolas*. Madrid, 1881. Rpt. Madrid: CVS Ediciones, 1975. Prologue by Maria Aurèlia Capmany.

Pardo Bazán, Emilia. *La mujer española y otros artículos feministas*. Ed. Leda Schiavo. Madrid: Nacional, 1971.

Pérez, Janet. *Contemporary Women Writers of Spain*. Boston: Twayne, 1988.

———. *Modern and Contemporary Spanish Women Poets*. New York: Twayne, 1996.

———. *Novelistas femeninas de la postguerra española*. Ed. Janet Pérez. Madrid: José Porrúa, 1983.

Pérez Priego, Miguel A., ed. *Poesía femenina en los cancioneros*. Madrid: Castalia/Biblioteca de escritoras, 1989.

Perry, Mary Elizabeth. *Gender and Disorder in Early Modern Seville*. Princeton, NJ: Princeton UP, 1990.

Redondo Goicoechea, Alicia, ed. *Relatos de novelistas españolas 1939–1969*. Madrid: Castalia/Instituto de la Mujer, 1993.

Rivera-Garretas, María Milagros. *Nombrar el mundo en femenino. Pensamiento de las mujeres y teoría feminista*. Barcelona: Icaria, 1994.

Rodrigo, Antonina. *Mujeres de España. Las silenciadas*. 2nd. ed. Barcelona: Plaza y Janés, 1979.

Salas, María. *Nosotras, las solteras*. Barcelona: Juan Flores, 1955.

———. *Solteras de hoy*. Madrid: PPC, 1996.

Sánchez, Magdalena S., and Alain Saint-Saens, eds. *Spanish Women in the Golden Age: Images and Realities*. Westport, CT: Greenwood P, 1996.

Scanlon, Geraldine. *La polémica feminista en la España contemporánea: 1868–1974*. Madrid: Siglo XXI, 1976; Madrid: Akal, 1986.

Segura Graíño, Cristina, ed. *Las mujeres en las ciudades medievales*. Madrid: Seminario de Estudios de la Mujer, Universidad Autónoma de Madrid, 1989.

———. *La voz del silencio, I: Fuentes directas para la historia de las mujeres (siglos VII-XVII)*. Madrid: Al-Mudayna, 1992.

———. *La voz del silencio, II: Historia de las mujeres: Compromiso y método*. Madrid: Al-Mudayna, 1993.

Serrano y Sanz, Manuel. *Antología de poetisas líricas*. 2 vols. Madrid: Revista de Archivos, Bibliotecas y Museos, 1915.

———. *Apuntes para una biblioteca de escritoras españolas desde el año 1401 al 1833*. 2 vols. Madrid: Rivadeneyra, 1903. Rpt. Madrid: Atlas, 1975.

Servodidio, Mirella, ed. *Reading for Difference: Feminist Perspectives on Women Novelists of Contemporary Spain*. In *Anales de la Literatura Española contemporánea* 12.1–2 (1987). Special journal issue.

Simón Palmer, María del Carmen. *Escritoras españolas del siglo XIX: Manual bio-bibliográfico*. Madrid: Castalia, 1991.

———. *La Biblioteca Nacional de Madrid: Escritoras españolas 1500–1900*. Madrid: Chadwick-Healey España, 1992. Microfiche.

Soufas. Teresa Scott. *Dramas of Distinction. A Study of Plays by Golden Age Women*. Lexington: UP of Kentucky, 1997.

———, ed., intro. *Women's Acts. Plays by Women Dramatists of Spain's Golden Age*. Lexington: UP of Kentucky, 1997.

Sponsler, Lucy. *Women in the Medieval Spanish Epic and Lyric Traditions*. Lexington: U of Kentucky P, 1975.

Stoll, Anita K., and Dawn L. Smith, eds. *The Perception of Women in Spanish Theater of the Golden Age*. Lewisburg, PA: Bucknell UP, 1991.

El trabajo de las mujeres pasado y presente: Actas del congreso internacional del Seminario de Estudios Interdisciplinarios de la Mujer. Ed. María Dolores Ramos Palomo and María Teresa Vera Balanza. 4 vols. Servicio de Publicaciones, Diputación Provincial de Málaga, 1996.

El trabajo de las mujeres. Siglos XVI-XX. VI Jornadas de Investigación Interdisciplinaria sobre la Mujer, 2–3 Abril 1987. Madrid: Universidad Autónoma de Madrid, Seminario de Estudios de la Mujer, 1987.

Vázquez de Aldana, Enrique. *Safo en Castilla. Antología de más de doscientas poetisas españolas, en sonetos ortodoxos*. Madrid: Ediciones Studium de Cultura, 1953.

Vigil, Mariló. *La vida de las mujeres en los siglos XVI y XVII*. 2nd ed. Madrid: Siglo Veintiuno, 1994.

Vollendort, Lisa, ed. *Recovering Spain's Feminist Tra-*

dition, New York: Modern Language Association, 2001.

Voltes, María José, and Pedro Voltes. *Las mujeres en la historia de España*. Barcelona: Planeta, 1986.

Wilcox, John. *Women Poets of Spain, 1860–1990: Toward a Gynocentric Vision*. Chicago and Urbana: U of Illinois P, 1997.

Yarbro-Bejarano, Yvonne. *Feminism and the Honor Plays of Lope de Vega*. West Lafayette, IN: Purdue UP, 1994.

Zulueta, Carmen de. *Cien años de educación de la mujer española. Historia del Instituto Internacional*. Madrid: Castalia, 1992.

Zulueta, Carmen de, and Alicia Moreno. *Ni convento ni college. La Residencia de Señoritas*. Madrid: Consejo Superior de Investigaciones Científicas, 1993.

Index

Page numbers of primary entries appear in **bold face** type.

Contributors

Alberto Acereda, Arizona State University

Concha Alborg, St. Joseph's University

Eric V. Alvarez, Tampa, Florida

Alma Amell, Pontifical College Josephinum

Frederick A. de Armas, Penn State University

Mindy Badía, University of Arkansas, Fayetteville

Catherine G. Bellver, University of Nevada, Las Vegas

Elizabeth S. Boyce, Houston Baptist University

María Elena Bravo, Dominican University

Joan L. Brown, University of Delaware

Elena Cámara, Madrid, Spain

Carlota Caulfield, Mills College

Jean S. Chittenden, Trinity University

Francesca Colecchia, Duquesne University

Marsha S. Collins, University of North Carolina, Chapel Hill

Reyes Coll-Tellechea, University of Massachusetts, Boston

José F. Colmeiro, Michigan State University

Nancy Cushing-Daniels, Gettysburg College

David H. Darst, Florida State University

John Dowling, emeritus, University of Georgia

Thomas R. Franz, Ohio University

John P. Gabriele, College of Wooster

Candelas Gala, Wake Forest University

María Luisa García-Verdugo, Purdue University, Calumet

Linda S. Glaze, Auburn University

Kathleen M. Glenn, Santa Barbara, California

Luis T. González-del-Valle, University of Colorado, Boulder

Roberta Gordenstein, College of Our Lady of the Elms

Patricia V. Greene, Michigan State University

Martha T. Halsey, emeritus, Penn State University

Carolyn Harris, Western Michigan University

Juana Amelia Hernández, emeritus, Hood College

Deborah Hirsch, Durham, North Carolina

Joan M. Hoffman, Western Washington University

Elizabeth T. Howe, Tufts University

Maureen Ihrie, Elon University

Estelle Irizarry, Georgetown University

Margaret E.W. Jones, University of Kentucky

Gayana Jurkevich, Baruch College, CUNY

Gregory B. Kaplan, University of Tennessee, Knoxville

Susan Kirkpatrick, University of California, San Diego

Jennifer Rae Krato, University of Alabama, Tuscaloosa

Jill Kruger-Robbins, Florida Atlantic University

Eva Legido-Quigley, University of Montana, Missoula

Linda Gould Levine, Montclair State University

Elizabeth Franklin Lewis, Mary Washington College

Marina A. Llorente, Saint Lawrence University

Sheri Spaine Long, University of Alabama, Birmingham

Shirley Mangini, California State University, Long Beach

Karoline J. Manny, Seminole Community College

Kathleen March, University of Maine, Orono

Delmarie Martínez, University of Central Florida

María Jesús Mayans Natal, University of the South

Mercedes Mazquiarán de Rodríguez, emeritus, Hofstra University

Judy B. McInnis, University of Delaware

Kathleen McNerney, West Virginia University

Sol Miguel-Prendes, Wake Forest University

Stephen Miller, Texas A & M University

Nina L. Molinaro, University of Colorado, Boulder

Glenn Morocco, Philadelphia, Pennsylvania

RoseAnna Mueller, Columbia College

Eunice Myers, Wichita State University

Lisa Nalbone, University of Central Florida

Maite Núñez-Betelu, University of Missouri, Columbia

D.J. O'Connor, University of New Orleans

Thomas Austin O'Connor, Binghamton University, SU of New York

Julián Olivares, University of Houston

Salvador A. Oropesa, Kansas State University

José Ortega, emeritus, University of Granada, Spain

Jeffrey Oxford, University of North Texas, Denton

Violeta Padrón, Wake Forest University

James Parr, University of California, Riverside

Anne M. Pasero, Marquette University

Genaro J. Pérez, Texas Tech University

Janet Pérez, Texas Tech University

Oralia Preble-Niemi, University of Tennessee-Chatanooga

Kay Pritchett, University of Arkansas

Alicia Ramos, Barnard College

Elizabeth Rhodes, Boston College

Carmen S. Rivera, Wingate University

Yolanda Rosas, California State, Northridge

Leyla Rouhi, Williams College

Ana Rueda, University of Missouri, Columbia

Pilar Sáenz, emeritus, George Washington University

María A. Salgado, University of North Carolina, Chapel Hill

Ruth Sánchez Imizcoz, University of the South

Nereida Segura-Rico, College of New Rochelle

Sylvia R. Sherno, University of California, Los Angeles

Jeanne J. Smoot, North Carolina State University

María Elena Soliño, University of Houston

Elizabeth Starcevic, City College, CUNY

Anita K. Stoll, Cleveland State University

Shannon W. Sudderth, University of North Carolina, Chapel Hill

Robert Taylor, Roseburg, Oregon

Kathleen Thompson-Casado, University of Toledo

Lynn Thompson Scott, University of Florida, Gainesville

Sally Webb Thornton, Indiana University of Pennsylvania

Joan Torres-Pou, Florida International University

Carmen de Urioste, Arizona State University

Linda M. Willem, Butler University

María Alejandra Zanetta, University of Akron

Phyllis Zatlin, Rutgers University

About the Editors

JANET PÉREZ is Associate Dean of the Graduate School and Paul Whitfield Horn Professor of Spanish at Texas Tech University. She is the author, editor, or coeditor of numerous books, including the *Dictionary of Literature of the Iberian Peninsula* (Greenwood, 1993), and her articles have appeared in such journals as *Romance Notes, Studies in Short Fiction,* and *Kentucky Romance Quarterly.*

MAUREEN IHRIE is Professor of Spanish at Elon College. Her publications have appeared in numerous journals, and she is the coeditor of *Dictionary of Literature of the Iberian Peninsula* (Greenwood, 1993).